BARRON'S

SAT*SUBJECT TEST

U.S. HISTORY

4TH EDITION

Kenneth R. Senter, M.S.

Oak Ridge High School
Oak Ridge, Tennessee

Eugene V. Resnick, B.A., M.A.

Midwood High School
Brooklyn, New York

BARRON'S

*SAT is a registered trademark of the College Board, which was not involved in the production of, and does not endorse, this product.

ABOUT THE AUTHOR

Kenneth Senter has been a high school teacher for over twenty years and presently teaches AP U.S. history and AP world history courses to sophomores and juniors at Oak Ridge High School in Oak Ridge, Tennessee.

ACKNOWLEDGMENTS

The author wishes to thank Peter Mavrikis and Kristen Girardi for their patient and supportive guidance in bettering this test preparation manual, along with their team of evaluators, copy editors, artists, and marketing staff. Also, the history students in my classes never cease to challenge me to learn more and to teach more. Finally, I would like to thank my wife, Sarah, and my three children who have endured much and have encouraged me the most.

Now Available!

Go to *barronsbooks.com/TP/sat/ushistory/* to access two online practice tests or scan the QR code below.

Have your copy of *SAT U.S. History*, 4th edition handy to complete the registration process.

All inquiries should be addressed to:
Barron's Educational Series, Inc.
250 Wireless Boulevard
Hauppauge, New York 11788
www.barronseduc.com

ISBN: 978-1-4380-1074-8

Library of Congress Control Number: 2017958040

PRINTED IN THE UNITED STATES OF AMERICA

9 8 7 6 5 4 3 2

**10%
POST-CONSUMER
WASTE**
Paper contains a minimum of 10% post-consumer waste (PCW). Paper used in this book was derived from certified, sustainable forestlands.

Contents

Preface

Congratulations! You have purchased this book because you want to achieve the best possible score you can on the SAT Subject Test in U.S. History. This book presents you with the top twenty items you need to know from each era of history in order to do well on this exam, plus four new items in each chapter for deeper insight. Barron's has done the work for you in selecting the most important material to review and presenting it to you in easily digestible, bite-sized chunks.

Whether you have only a couple of weeks to study for the exam or a couple of months, this book will provide you with a study plan that is best for you. The contents of this book have been carefully selected and organized in order to provide you with the most comprehensive and effective study guide currently available.

This book has everything you need to score higher on the SAT Subject Test in U.S. History! Read the Introduction and familiarize yourself with the test format, content, and question types so there are no surprises on test day. A Diagnostic Test is provided so you can pinpoint your weaknesses, further maximizing the efficiency of your study time. Reinforce what you have learned by taking the mini quizzes that appear after every five content chapters. Three additional practice tests are included to give you more test-taking practice and provide you with further insight into what you still need to review. You also have access to two additional online practice tests. To access these tests visit *barronsbooks.com/TP/sat/ushistory/*.

You will find that when you use this book to its fullest potential, you will have discovered the most fine-tuned study materials available to maximize your score on the SAT Subject Test in U.S. History.

Welcome to the SAT Subject Test in U.S. History

1

Do what you can, with what you have, where you are.
—Theodore Roosevelt

President Roosevelt offered good advice for your situation as you face taking the SAT Subject Test in U.S. History. You've picked up this book because you face a momentous challenge. You must show college entrance and scholarship officials how much U.S. history you know in only one hour by taking a difficult multiple-choice test with ninety to ninety-five questions. The timed nature of this exam means you will have to answer each question in an average time of as little as thirty-eight seconds! Plus, you might not have taken a U.S. history course in over a year. This book is the solution to help you succeed on this difficult exam.

TEST REGISTRATION

The key to doing "what you can, with what you have" in this challenge is time. The test is offered monthly from October to January and once in both May and June. Visit the College Board website to see the dates when the exam is administered. You will need to determine how long you have to study before your scheduled exam. Whether you have six months or only two weeks to prepare for the test, this book is designed to make the most of your review efforts. Be honest with yourself about how much time you will devote to studying for this exam, and then pick the test date that will allow you that amount of time.

WHERE TO REGISTER FOR THE SAT SUBJECT TESTS

- Visit *www.collegeboard.com*
- Call toll-free domestic: 1-866-756-7346; foreign: 212-713-7789
- See your guidance counselor
- Write to: The College Board SAT Program
  P.O. Box 025505
  Miami, FL 33102

To register, visit the College Board's website, call their toll-free number, or see your guidance counselor. You can also write to the College Board SAT program for information on how to register.

HOW TO USE THIS BOOK

Within this book you'll find several tools that will help you review the history of the United States. You will also find valuable information on the format of the test so that you will be prepared and confident on test day. The time you have available to prepare for the exam will determine how you use these tools. Following this chapter you will find a Diagnostic Test to help you determine where you are now. If you have limited time before the actual test, focus your study by taking this diagnostic test and reading the answer explanation for each question, even the ones you answered correctly. The Diagnostic Test will reveal the aspects of U.S. history that you will need to review the most. The simplest and quickest way to locate this material is to look up key words from the questions you missed in the book's index. After reviewing this material, take another practice exam to see how much you have improved and to determine what areas you might still need to review. Last, read "The Big Pictures" that are located at the end of each chapter. This approach is recommended if you have come across this book with only a week or two to prepare before taking the test.

If you have a few weeks or a month to prepare for the exam, start by taking the Diagnostic Test and reading the answer explanations for each question. Next, note that each chapter in this book contains a timeline, "Overview," and a section entitled "The Top 20 Things to Know." These items have been carefully selected to represent the mainstream people, events, and ideas that are the most significant in U.S. history. Along with the "Top 20" items in each chapter, some additional items have been added in sidebars that are also important details that might come up on the SAT subject test. This second-tier glossary builds on the "Top 20" by highlighting key historical terms or by giving more specific details. Take the time to read and study these items from each chapter to give you a basic review of the critical content covered on the SAT subject test. Drill yourself by taking the mini quizzes that appear between every five chapters. Take the remaining practice exams, each time reading the answer explanations for every question. You will see your score climb with each practice test you take, and, by then, you will have done nearly all you can with what time you have before the actual exam. Just before you take the actual test, read "The Big Picture" from each chapter to provide the analytical overview you will need to work quickly and efficiently in the one hour you will have to prove yourself.

If you are fortunate enough to have several months to prepare for the exam, and especially if you haven't taken a good survey course in U.S. history recently or at all, you are encouraged to read this book alongside a reliable college-level U.S. history textbook. The Diagnostic Test might even prove discouraging in this case, so you can save it for use as a regular practice exam later. Take several practice exams after reading as much of this book as possible in the time you have to prepare. Use the answer explanations to understand why you missed each question you got wrong. Look up items you missed in your history textbook and continue to review them in greater depth. Your history textbook will contain a narrative account of U.S. history that is beyond the scope of a review text, and it will be your best bet for understanding any particular information that continues to elude you after exhausting this book. An error journal can also be of use after taking each practice exam. Find out why you got each wrong answer, and then write down in a notebook the key fact, or facts, you need to remember. Of course, you may find that many of your wrong answers occurred because you misread a question while hurrying to answer it in thirty-eight seconds! This problem is normal on a timed exam and will diminish as you continue reviewing and practicing.

You can, of course, combine these approaches using the tools provided in this book to tailor a review strategy that is best for you. You are strongly encouraged to actively combine the content review in this book with the taking of and reflection on at least two practice tests.

THREE APPROACHES FOR THREE REVIEW PACES

One or Two Weeks to Prepare

✔ Take the Diagnostic Test.
✔ Read all the answer explanations.
✔ Use the results of the Diagnostic Test to pinpoint the material you most need to review.
✔ Find the material you need to review by looking up the key topics in the index.
✔ Review this material.
✔ Take one of the practice tests at the end of the book to see how much you improved and what areas you may still need to review.
✔ Last, read "The Big Picture" located at the end of each chapter.

One Month to Prepare

✔ Take the Diagnostic Test.
✔ Read all the answer explanations.
✔ Read and study all Timelines, "Overview," and "The Top 20 Things to Know."
✔ Take each Mini Quiz.
✔ Take the remaining practice exams in the book and online, and read all the answer explanations.
✔ Before taking the actual test, brush up by reading "The Big Picture" at the end of each chapter.

Several Months to Prepare

✔ Read this book along with a reliable college-level U.S. history textbook.
✔ Save the Diagnostic Test to be used as one of your regular practice exams.
✔ After reading as much of this book as possible, take the practice exams in the book and online.
✔ Use the answer explanations to understand why you missed each question you answered incorrectly.
✔ Look up the items you missed in your history textbook and continue to review them in greater depth.
✔ Keep an error journal of your results of each practice exam. Include in the journal key facts you need to remember.

INTRODUCTION TO THE TEST

Colleges that require or recommend that you take SAT subject tests use the scores to make admissions and placement decisions. You are often asked to take three tests, and the U.S. history test is a good indicator of your mastery of material in a typical humanities course. You may take the SAT subject test in U.S. History more than once to improve your score, but this book is designed to give you a strong possibility of success on the first try. If you do very well, your score on this test could make a difference in your admission process or allow you to skip an introductory survey course in U.S. history.

Two key points about the SAT Subject Test in U.S. History are that the questions increase in difficulty as the test progresses from beginning to end, and the test is designed to discourage random guessing. Both of these points have strategy implications that are discussed later in this chapter, but you should be aware of them from the beginning. Not all questions are as difficult as they might seem, and many in the beginning deserve only a fraction of the thirty-eight seconds you have per question. As for guessing, the test is scored in such a way that random guessing is a bad idea. You are awarded one point for each correct answer but penalized a quarter point for each wrong answer. Answers left blank neither gain nor lose points.

Again, you must have a strategy for dealing with various questions under these circumstances, and that strategy is discussed below. Your goal in working with this book is to know what you will face going into the test to prepare accordingly so you will be in control of the test and achieve your maximum potential. Your goal on the test is to score as high up on the 800-point scale as possible. The College Board will convert your raw score to a traditional 800-point scale based on the difficulty level of the particular test you take. The difficulty of any given SAT subject test is determined by comparing it to previous tests and by reflecting on the performance of all students who took those tests. All of these factors and more are taken into account as the scoring scale is set. Great care is taken to make the SAT Subject Test in U.S. History a fair assessment of your mastery of the history of the United States.

Types of History on the Exam

A handy acrostic using the word *spice* will help you remember what types of history "spice up" the U.S. history covered on the exam. Social, political (including domestic and foreign policy), intellectual (including art), cultural (including religion), and economic history are covered on the test. These types of history are apportioned among the ninety to ninety-five questions on the test according to the table below. All of these topics incorporate broad social science concepts, generalizations, and approaches common to any history or social studies course.

Type of History	Approximate Percentage of Test Coverage
Social history	20–24%
Political history (with domestic and foreign policy)	44–52%
Intellectual history (with art)	6–8%
Cultural history (with religion)	6–8%
Economic history	13–17%

Types of Questions on the Exam

The questions on the SAT subject test are of several types as well as varying levels of difficulty. The simplest questions require you merely to recall basic facts and to be familiar with several terms and concepts fundamental to the study of U.S. history. You will therefore have to be familiar with many important aspects of U.S. history that are contained in the content reviews and practice tests in this book. With the more difficult questions, you will be asked to analyze and interpret lists of information; visuals like graphs, charts, paintings, political cartoons, photographs, and maps; as well as quotes from historical figures, documents, or literature. The most difficult types of questions require you to relate concepts and ideas to data supplied in the question and to evaluate that data for a particular interpretive purpose. You will have to judge what evidence supplied in the question is logically consistent with the concept being tested. You will often have to compare and contrast answer choices according to certain criteria when more than one answer seems to be correct. The only way to excel at answering questions of this type correctly is to review the content of this book thoroughly and to practice, practice, practice. The numbers in the box below correspond to questions from the Diagnostic Test that represent these styles of questioning.

Type	Description of Task	Diagnostic Test Example
1	Recall facts, terms, ideas, and generalizations	Question 9
2	Analyze or interpret information	Question 32
3	Relate concepts to given data	Question 44
4	Evaluate data for a specified purpose	Question 54
Turn to the Diagnostic Test now to review these examples.		

One other organizational component of the SAT Subject Test in U.S. History should be mentioned. Three periods of the history of the United States receive coverage on the test according to the chart below.

PERIODS COVERED

Pre-Columbian history to 1789 (the U.S. Constitution took effect)	20%
1790 to 1898 (the Spanish-American War launched imperialism)	40%
1899 to the present (updated with each new edition of this book)	40%

The SAT subject test is created by college professors and high school teachers with the goal of reflecting what is actually taught in U.S. history survey courses. There is no one textbook to which the exam is tied, and the College Board uses surveys to gather information about what college professors are actually teaching. Because the results of these surveys are confidential proprietary information, there is no way to guess what will actually be covered on any given test. The parameters above are set by the College Board, so within these guidelines your best hope of being prepared is to review all of U.S. history according to the proportions above. Trends in the emphasis of history courses change; a comprehensive review is the only way to become adequately prepared.

MULTIPLE-CHOICE STRATEGIES

Finally, before taking the Diagnostic Test, a look at strategies for successfully navigating through the topics, different difficulty levels, and different types of questions is in order. There are also general test-taking principles for taking the SAT Subject Test in U.S. History as there are for any rigorous college entrance exam. Because this exam consists only of multiple-choice questions, you will have to become proficient at answering sophisticated analytical questions as well as recalling information. You will not have an opportunity to balance your score on the multiple-choice section with your writing talent on essays.

Strategies for answering multiple-choice questions vary with the difficulty of the questions. Identification-level questions can be answered quickly and easily if you know the key data point or points, but you should still read all of the answer choices to be sure of your answer. However, most questions on the SAT Subject Test in U.S. History require more than factual recall. You will also have to demonstrate skill in recognizing categories of information, analyzing data, evaluating fine differences, understanding generalizations, and synthesizing various ideas into a larger whole. Just being aware of the use of these sophisticated social studies thinking skills on the test will make them less of a shock.

The College Board and its affiliates carefully increase the difficulty of questions by altering the options given as answer choices. They even have a special name for the wrong answers: *distracters*. Unsuspecting students will fall prey to distracters consisting of common misconceptions about U.S. history, statements that are true but irrelevant to the question at hand, statements that are either too broad or too narrow for a given question, or answers that merely sound plausible.

Furthermore, you can be rolling along answering questions rapidly and be caught by the infamous "**EXCEPT**" questions. The exam will have this word or a word like "**NOT**" in boldface print; you will have to consciously break yourself from the habit of looking for the correct answer and instead select the answer choice that is wrong. If you hurry through these questions, your instincts will simply seize on choice A, which will usually be true and correct. You have then missed the question out of habit, and it will be because you failed to read all of the answer choices.

Your fundamental strategy, therefore, is to read each question thoroughly *and* all of the answer choices knowing that each word in a question on a test of this sophistication was chosen extremely carefully and field tested. The authors of the test use words with specific, precise meanings, and the words mean exactly what the authors intend. You must unlock those meanings and pay close attention to what the question is asking. You have to choose the answer that fulfills all, not just some, of the requirements of the phrase in the question stem. Many possible answers are specifically designed to distract you by giving you that little "Aha!" feeling when your mind grabs information you recognize as being associated with the question stem. You might miss the question by not reading the rest of the distracters and therefore not finding the correct answer that will fully satisfy the logic of the question stem.

The matter of guessing deserves special attention on a test like the SAT Subject Test in U.S. History. With the scoring system described earlier in the chapter taking off a quarter of a point for every wrong answer, random guessing is dangerous. Anything but educated guesses is ill-advised. An educated guess on a multiple-choice test occurs only after you have eliminated entirely implausible options that you immediately recognized as incorrect. Because the questions on the SAT subject test give five possible answers, you will then be down to three or four. You must then intelligently consider information you do know about the era in history being discussed in the question. As you try to eliminate other wrong answers, reflect on the political, economic, and social conditions within the era to rule out one or two more distracters.

No points will be taken off for skipped questions. Just be sure that you leave those numbers blank on your answer sheet! The easiest way to ruin your hope of success is to turn in an answer sheet filled with correct answers slightly shifted from their correct spaces on the

TIP

Be on the lookout! Watch out for questions with "EXCEPT" or "NOT" in boldface. You must find the wrong answer choice to get the right answer.

TIP

Guess on a question only if you can narrow the five answer choices down to three, or preferably two, possible answers. If you cannot thus make this an educated guess, leave the question blank.

answer sheet. Also, don't skip more than five or six questions, maximum. Do not allow the fear of guessing wrong to make you leave many of the ninety to ninety-five questions blank. Besides, with thorough review and practice using this book, you should be making confident answers with the need for only a few educated guesses!

TEST-TAKING STRATEGIES

There are several principles to follow that are not specific to the SAT Subject Test in U.S. History but nonetheless apply. You have already read about the need to read the stem of each question carefully and also to read each answer choice. Having taken two or more timed practice tests you should be able to pace yourself and, as you watch the clock, know what progress you should make as the hour advances. Here are other tips to keep in mind as you take this type of test:

1. Use your test booklet for writing notes or making marks at questions you skip. Your answer sheet must be kept neat and free from stray marks.
2. Check every so often to make sure you are putting your answers in the right spot on your answer sheet in order to avoid the fatal misalignment error.
3. Watch the clock in the room or your own wristwatch (cell phones will not be allowed even for timekeeping).
4. Pace yourself steadily. Remember that the harder questions begin somewhere midway through the test and will require more time than recall questions.
5. Never worry about the sequence of the letters you bubble on your answer sheet. Tests can have several of the same letter in a row, and no pattern is ever allowed to exist in the correct answers.
6. Once you have answered the last question in your first attempt, check the time and go back to attempt to answer questions you skipped.
7. Remember to make only educated guesses.
8. When you are certain of the questions you intend to leave blank, if any, check the answers you put down for the other questions.
9. Be careful about changing answers. Unless you are certain a previous answer is wrong, leave your first answer. People often change correct answers to incorrect answers. If you do change an answer, erase the old one completely.
10. Relax and congratulate yourself when the time is up. You can be proud that you have done what you could, with what you had, where you were.

FINAL ADVICE

Regardless of how long you will study before you take the SAT Subject Test in U.S. History, the night before the exam will eventually come. You must spend the next twelve hours carefully in order to perform your best the next day. Yes, a last review is a good idea. Take one more practice test and review the answer explanations, or quickly read through all "The Big Pictures" at the end of each chapter. If you start early in the afternoon, maybe you can do both of these steps. However, you must stop this final review and be sure to sleep seven to eight hours in order to have a clear head during the test. After sleeping, the next most important step is a good breakfast. Do not try to take a test of this magnitude on an empty stomach even if you normally skip breakfast before school. Your breakfast should include protein to last the long haul as well as plenty of fluids to keep yourself hydrated.

Much of the effort you've spent reviewing U.S. history with this book can go to waste if you don't take care of your basic physical needs of rest, food, and fluids. The College Board allows you to take a snack to the testing site, and a bottle of water is also a good idea. Some hard peppermint candy can perk you up in the middle of the test as long as you unwrap the candy before testing begins. Arrive twenty to thirty minutes early at the testing site so you don't add to the stress of test day by getting lost or arriving at the last minute. There is nothing wrong with having this book with you to fill that time with a last look at history if it will help you feel like you have given this challenge all your effort. Then put this book away, relax, and listen carefully to all of the test proctor's instructions.

President Theodore Roosevelt had one more bit of advice that applies to you before you begin the Diagnostic Test and your subsequent review. He said, "Far and away the best prize that life has to offer is the chance to work hard at work worth doing." Reviewing for the SAT Subject Test in U.S. History will be hard work. Like the many other tasks you've taken on to prepare for the next stage of your education and life, this task is worth doing.

REMEMBER!
You can access two additional online practice tests at *barronsbooks.com/TP/sat/ushistory/* or by scanning the QR code below.

Have your copy of *SAT U.S. History*, 4th edition handy to complete the registration process.

ANSWER SHEET
Diagnostic Test

1. Ⓐ Ⓑ Ⓒ Ⓓ Ⓔ
2. Ⓐ Ⓑ Ⓒ Ⓓ Ⓔ
3. Ⓐ Ⓑ Ⓒ Ⓓ Ⓔ
4. Ⓐ Ⓑ Ⓒ Ⓓ Ⓔ
5. Ⓐ Ⓑ Ⓒ Ⓓ Ⓔ
6. Ⓐ Ⓑ Ⓒ Ⓓ Ⓔ
7. Ⓐ Ⓑ Ⓒ Ⓓ Ⓔ
8. Ⓐ Ⓑ Ⓒ Ⓓ Ⓔ
9. Ⓐ Ⓑ Ⓒ Ⓓ Ⓔ
10. Ⓐ Ⓑ Ⓒ Ⓓ Ⓔ
11. Ⓐ Ⓑ Ⓒ Ⓓ Ⓔ
12. Ⓐ Ⓑ Ⓒ Ⓓ Ⓔ
13. Ⓐ Ⓑ Ⓒ Ⓓ Ⓔ
14. Ⓐ Ⓑ Ⓒ Ⓓ Ⓔ
15. Ⓐ Ⓑ Ⓒ Ⓓ Ⓔ
16. Ⓐ Ⓑ Ⓒ Ⓓ Ⓔ
17. Ⓐ Ⓑ Ⓒ Ⓓ Ⓔ
18. Ⓐ Ⓑ Ⓒ Ⓓ Ⓔ
19. Ⓐ Ⓑ Ⓒ Ⓓ Ⓔ
20. Ⓐ Ⓑ Ⓒ Ⓓ Ⓔ
21. Ⓐ Ⓑ Ⓒ Ⓓ Ⓔ
22. Ⓐ Ⓑ Ⓒ Ⓓ Ⓔ
23. Ⓐ Ⓑ Ⓒ Ⓓ Ⓔ
24. Ⓐ Ⓑ Ⓒ Ⓓ Ⓔ
25. Ⓐ Ⓑ Ⓒ Ⓓ Ⓔ
26. Ⓐ Ⓑ Ⓒ Ⓓ Ⓔ
27. Ⓐ Ⓑ Ⓒ Ⓓ Ⓔ
28. Ⓐ Ⓑ Ⓒ Ⓓ Ⓔ
29. Ⓐ Ⓑ Ⓒ Ⓓ Ⓔ
30. Ⓐ Ⓑ Ⓒ Ⓓ Ⓔ

31. Ⓐ Ⓑ Ⓒ Ⓓ Ⓔ
32. Ⓐ Ⓑ Ⓒ Ⓓ Ⓔ
33. Ⓐ Ⓑ Ⓒ Ⓓ Ⓔ
34. Ⓐ Ⓑ Ⓒ Ⓓ Ⓔ
35. Ⓐ Ⓑ Ⓒ Ⓓ Ⓔ
36. Ⓐ Ⓑ Ⓒ Ⓓ Ⓔ
37. Ⓐ Ⓑ Ⓒ Ⓓ Ⓔ
38. Ⓐ Ⓑ Ⓒ Ⓓ Ⓔ
39. Ⓐ Ⓑ Ⓒ Ⓓ Ⓔ
40. Ⓐ Ⓑ Ⓒ Ⓓ Ⓔ
41. Ⓐ Ⓑ Ⓒ Ⓓ Ⓔ
42. Ⓐ Ⓑ Ⓒ Ⓓ Ⓔ
43. Ⓐ Ⓑ Ⓒ Ⓓ Ⓔ
44. Ⓐ Ⓑ Ⓒ Ⓓ Ⓔ
45. Ⓐ Ⓑ Ⓒ Ⓓ Ⓔ
46. Ⓐ Ⓑ Ⓒ Ⓓ Ⓔ
47. Ⓐ Ⓑ Ⓒ Ⓓ Ⓔ
48. Ⓐ Ⓑ Ⓒ Ⓓ Ⓔ
49. Ⓐ Ⓑ Ⓒ Ⓓ Ⓔ
50. Ⓐ Ⓑ Ⓒ Ⓓ Ⓔ
51. Ⓐ Ⓑ Ⓒ Ⓓ Ⓔ
52. Ⓐ Ⓑ Ⓒ Ⓓ Ⓔ
53. Ⓐ Ⓑ Ⓒ Ⓓ Ⓔ
54. Ⓐ Ⓑ Ⓒ Ⓓ Ⓔ
55. Ⓐ Ⓑ Ⓒ Ⓓ Ⓔ
56. Ⓐ Ⓑ Ⓒ Ⓓ Ⓔ
57. Ⓐ Ⓑ Ⓒ Ⓓ Ⓔ
58. Ⓐ Ⓑ Ⓒ Ⓓ Ⓔ
59. Ⓐ Ⓑ Ⓒ Ⓓ Ⓔ
60. Ⓐ Ⓑ Ⓒ Ⓓ Ⓔ

61. Ⓐ Ⓑ Ⓒ Ⓓ Ⓔ
62. Ⓐ Ⓑ Ⓒ Ⓓ Ⓔ
63. Ⓐ Ⓑ Ⓒ Ⓓ Ⓔ
64. Ⓐ Ⓑ Ⓒ Ⓓ Ⓔ
65. Ⓐ Ⓑ Ⓒ Ⓓ Ⓔ
66. Ⓐ Ⓑ Ⓒ Ⓓ Ⓔ
67. Ⓐ Ⓑ Ⓒ Ⓓ Ⓔ
68. Ⓐ Ⓑ Ⓒ Ⓓ Ⓔ
69. Ⓐ Ⓑ Ⓒ Ⓓ Ⓔ
70. Ⓐ Ⓑ Ⓒ Ⓓ Ⓔ
71. Ⓐ Ⓑ Ⓒ Ⓓ Ⓔ
72. Ⓐ Ⓑ Ⓒ Ⓓ Ⓔ
73. Ⓐ Ⓑ Ⓒ Ⓓ Ⓔ
74. Ⓐ Ⓑ Ⓒ Ⓓ Ⓔ
75. Ⓐ Ⓑ Ⓒ Ⓓ Ⓔ
76. Ⓐ Ⓑ Ⓒ Ⓓ Ⓔ
77. Ⓐ Ⓑ Ⓒ Ⓓ Ⓔ
78. Ⓐ Ⓑ Ⓒ Ⓓ Ⓔ
79. Ⓐ Ⓑ Ⓒ Ⓓ Ⓔ
80. Ⓐ Ⓑ Ⓒ Ⓓ Ⓔ
81. Ⓐ Ⓑ Ⓒ Ⓓ Ⓔ
82. Ⓐ Ⓑ Ⓒ Ⓓ Ⓔ
83. Ⓐ Ⓑ Ⓒ Ⓓ Ⓔ
84. Ⓐ Ⓑ Ⓒ Ⓓ Ⓔ
85. Ⓐ Ⓑ Ⓒ Ⓓ Ⓔ
86. Ⓐ Ⓑ Ⓒ Ⓓ Ⓔ
87. Ⓐ Ⓑ Ⓒ Ⓓ Ⓔ
88. Ⓐ Ⓑ Ⓒ Ⓓ Ⓔ
89. Ⓐ Ⓑ Ⓒ Ⓓ Ⓔ
90. Ⓐ Ⓑ Ⓒ Ⓓ Ⓔ

Diagnostic Test

TIME—60 MINUTES

> **Directions:** Each of the questions or incomplete statements below is followed by five suggested answers or completions. Select the one that is best in each case, and then fill in the corresponding circle on the answer sheet. You can cut the answer sheet along the dotted line to make recording your answers easier.

1. Indentured servitude in colonial America

    (A) provided African slaves a chance to earn their freedom.
    (B) contributed only small amounts of laborers to the colonial workforce.
    (C) prevented laborers from ever rising from a status of servitude.
    (D) took hold only in New England.
    (E) allowed laborers to gain freedom within four to seven years.

2. "America is not composed, as in Europe, of great lords who possess everything and of a herd of people who have nothing."

    The statement above reveals the absence in eighteenth-century America of

    (A) property rights.
    (B) an aristocracy.
    (C) social mobility.
    (D) religious freedom.
    (E) a means of taxing the rich.

3. As the first Democrat, Andrew Jackson campaigned on behalf of

    (A) women and minorities.
    (B) banks and other large corporations.
    (C) states' rights in defiance of central authority.
    (D) the common man.
    (E) New England merchants.

4. Factory workers in the late nineteenth century in the United States

    (A) had no access to labor unions to improve their working conditions.
    (B) were largely foreign-born immigrants.
    (C) were exclusively male.
    (D) received wages superior to those of any other workers.
    (E) were highly respected for their contributions.

5. The United States entered World War I for all of the following reasons **EXCEPT**

    (A) to repel German aggression in Europe.
    (B) to protect American shipments of goods to U.S. allies.
    (C) to acquire German holdings in Africa for American use.
    (D) to ward off a German-Mexican alliance.
    (E) to end German unrestricted submarine warfare.

6. "Women's fashions have always fluctuated . . . . But during and after the war the skirt disappeared altogether to be replaced by a sort of tunic barely reaching the knee. Hampering petticoats were discarded, the corset abandoned as a needless impediment to free movement."

    The statement above is most likely referring to ladies' fashion from which era?

    (A) The Early National period
    (B) Post-Civil War pioneer era
    (C) 1920s
    (D) 1950s
    (E) 1970s

7. Select the pair of twentieth-century decades when Americans most valued consumerism.

    (A) 1910s and 1920s
    (B) 1930s and 1940s
    (C) 1970s and 1980s
    (D) 1920s and 1950s
    (E) 1960s and 1990s

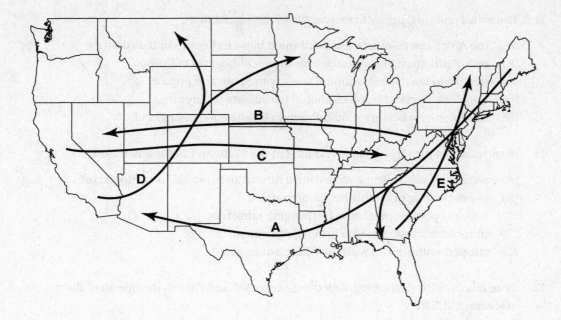

8. Which migratory arrow on the map above best illustrates the predominant internal migration path of U.S. citizens from 1950 to 1980?

    (A) A
    (B) B
    (C) C
    (D) D
    (E) E

9. Which Supreme Court decision ruled that separate but equal educational facilities for children of different races were unconstitutional?

    (A) *NAACP* v. *Alabama*
    (B) *Bartkus* v. *Board of Education of Chicago, Illinois*
    (C) *Boynton* v. *Board of Education of Richmond, Virginia*
    (D) *Brown* v. *Board of Education of Topeka, Kansas*
    (E) *Engel* v. *Vitale*

10. The stated purpose of Operation Desert Storm against Iraq in 1991 was to

    (A) drive Iraqi forces out of neighboring Kuwait.
    (B) secure access to oil from U.S. allies in the Middle East.
    (C) reach a settlement in the Arab-Israeli conflict.
    (D) enforce a no-fly zone in northern and southern Iraq.
    (E) remove the dictator Saddam Hussein from power.

11. The British colonial policy of mercantilism mandated that

   (A) the American colonists should develop basic industries in the colonies.
   (B) only Parliament, not colonial legislatures, should tax colonists.
   (C) the American colonists should trade with Spain and France.
   (D) only New England colonies should participate in shipping.
   (E) the colonial economy should function for the good of England.

12. Participants in the First Great Awakening in the 1730s and 1740s advocated a

   (A) return to Catholicism because most American colonists were Protestant.
   (B) strengthening of established churches.
   (C) ban on open-air preaching by traveling ministers.
   (D) more democratic style of church government.
   (E) strengthening of ties with the Church of England.

13. Opportunities for women expanded between 1800 and 1850 to include all of the following **EXCEPT**

   (A) access to higher education.
   (B) the right to vote.
   (C) ownership of land apart from that of fathers and husbands.
   (D) marriage choices based on affection.
   (E) access to basic manufacturing jobs.

14. Which change stated below occurred after the Civil War?

   (A) The Supreme Court became an equal branch of the federal government.
   (B) Political party rivalries calmed during the Era of Good Feelings.
   (C) Businesses in several industries consolidated into large corporations.
   (D) American Indians were pacified east of the Mississippi River.
   (E) Universal white manhood suffrage was achieved.

15. The first attempt by states to regulate large corporations was

   (A) directed toward railroad companies.
   (B) designed to bolster labor unions.
   (C) aimed at the lumber industry.
   (D) done through workers' compensation laws.
   (E) the inspection of meat-packing plants.

16. What caused the surge of nativism in the United States from 1890 to 1910?

   (A) The large number of English and Germans fleeing Europe for eastern cities
   (B) The lack of jobs resulting from the return to an agrarian economy
   (C) The difficulty most immigrants arriving during this period had in assimilating
   (D) The political instability caused by the rise of the Know-Nothing (American) Party
   (E) The passage of the Quota Act limiting access for certain immigrants

17. All of the statements below about African Americans in World War I are true **EXCEPT**

   (A) many Europeans received them warmly as liberators.
   (B) they fought in segregated units as they had in the Civil War.
   (C) one of them became the most highly decorated American soldier.
   (D) returning home to discrimination proved especially difficult.
   (E) one of them invented the mask that saved many from gas attacks.

18. Which other form of entertainment besides jazz music became popular in the 1920s?

   (A) Television
   (B) Motion pictures
   (C) Amateur soccer leagues
   (D) Professional football
   (E) Running and jogging for exercise

19. Which statement best describes the relationship between Theodore Roosevelt's Square Deal and Franklin Roosevelt's New Deal?

   (A) The New Deal was merely a continuation of the Square Deal.
   (B) The New Deal dramatically expanded from the foundation of the Square Deal.
   (C) The Roosevelts planned their policies together as a strategy for Progressivism.
   (D) The Republican Square Deal was the opposite of the Democratic New Deal.
   (E) No relationship existed between the Square Deal and the New Deal.

20. In which era did American voters participate the most in national elections?

   (A) The Era of Good Feelings (1810–1824)
   (B) The Civil War era (1854–1865)
   (C) The Gilded Age (1866–1900)
   (D) The Roaring Twenties (1920–1929)
   (E) The Stormy Sixties (1960–1969)

21. In which decade did Americans' distrust of their government reach an all-time high?

   (A) 1920s
   (B) 1940s
   (C) 1950s
   (D) 1970s
   (E) 1990s

22. What most altered the way of life for American Indians prior to 1890?

   (A) Climate change brought on by industrialization
   (B) The acquisition of firearms
   (C) Legislation offering incentives for individual assimilation
   (D) The creation of written forms of native languages
   (E) The use of horses brought to North America by Europeans

23. Why did the Articles of Confederation fail as a framework for American government?

(A) Limitations on the central government made it too weak to hold the states together.
(B) Those who designed it worked in such haste that it contained errors in judgment.
(C) The American people never trusted the process followed in its ratification.
(D) Americans did not trust its design because it originated during the crisis of a war.
(E) North/South sectionalism destroyed the "friendship" it required to work.

24. The purchase of the Louisiana Territory from France

(A) was made possible when Spain defended itself against Napoleon's attacks.
(B) resulted from Thomas Jefferson's loose interpretation of the U.S. Constitution.
(C) extended U.S. territory to the Pacific Ocean through Oregon.
(D) provided raw materials to advance Jefferson's dream of industrialization.
(E) was universally praised by the American people for doubling U.S. territory.

25. Which of the following principles is associated with Transcendentalism?

(A) All classes should share a nation's resources so all could become comfortable.
(B) People should strictly adhere to traditional Christian religious values.
(C) People should follow their own consciences tutored by observations of nature.
(D) The Creator gave all people callings in life to pursue diligently for His glory.
(E) People had to improve society because the Creator no longer heeded His creation.

26. Provisions of John Hay's Open Door Notes included all of the following **EXCEPT**

(A) every imperialist nation interested in China would receive a sphere of influence.
(B) the United States would receive a sphere of influence even though it had just arrived.
(C) no sphere nation could build a railroad in China to gain a trade advantage.
(D) China would be allowed to set its own tariff rates.
(E) China would charge all sphere nations the same tariff rates.

27. In which pair of decades in American history was the Ku Klux Klan most influential?

(A) 1850s and 1870s
(B) 1870s and 1920s
(C) 1880s and 1910s
(D) 1890s and 1950s
(E) 1930s and 1960s

28. Which of the following economic trends was an important cause of the Great Depression?

(A) The departure from the use of precious metal in American coins
(B) The rapid collapse of American productivity after the end of World War I
(C) The crippling effects on the economy of the rise of the labor movement
(D) The unchecked investment schemes of an era of unregulated banking
(E) The transition from an agrarian to an industrial economy

29. In what way did the United States support the Allies fighting World War II before direct American involvement in the war?

    (A) Guarding convoys of merchant ships with United States naval vessels
    (B) Requiring American pilots to fight disguised as airmen of the Royal Air Force
    (C) Allowing all young male immigrants to be conscripted by European armies
    (D) Repealing isolationist legislation to legalize full-scale mobilization of the economy
    (E) Drafting a large force of combatants into all branches of the American military

30. The graduated income tax was suggested by the Populists and enacted by the Progressives in order to

    (A) tax the wealthiest Americans to reduce the growing gap between rich and poor.
    (B) prevent wealthy Americans from creating an aristocracy by passing down wealth.
    (C) create more political power for the lowest classes of Americans.
    (D) provide incentives to middle-class Americans to invest in the stock market.
    (E) require major American industrialists to contribute to the war effort in Europe.

31. Which episode brought the world closest to a nuclear exchange between superpowers?

    (A) The convergence of the United States and the U.S.S.R. on Germany to end World War II
    (B) The Berlin Crisis and subsequent Berlin Airlift under President Truman
    (C) The proposal of General MacArthur to use nuclear weapons in the Korean War
    (D) The U-2 spy plane incident under President Eisenhower
    (E) The Cuban Missile Crisis under President Kennedy

32. Which American Indian culture had the most advanced civilization upon the arrival of Europeans in the New World?

    (A) The Huron of the Great Lakes region
    (B) The Navajo of the Southwest
    (C) The Iroquois of what would become New York
    (D) The Cherokee of the Appalachian region
    (E) The Aztecs of Mexico

33. Why did the Jamestown colony succeed when all previous English attempts at colonizing the New World had failed?

    (A) The arrival of second sons of the gentry due to primogeniture laws
    (B) The establishment of tobacco cultivation for export
    (C) The discovery of gold in nearby streams
    (D) The formation of the Virginia House of Burgesses for self-government
    (E) The departure of Lord de la Warr whose tyrannical rule stifled growth

34. A chief success of the Congress under the Articles of Confederation was establishing

   (A)   an effective system for taxing states for revenue to run the central government.
   (B)   a clearly defined separation of the government into three branches.
   (C)   the system to make new states out of territories given up by the original colonies.
   (D)   the power to regulate a national economic system with a currency and trade laws.
   (E)   a way to balance the power of states that satisfied both large and small states.

35. Supreme Court Chief Justice John Marshall, the last prominent Federalist, used his influence to

   (A)   expand the power of the executive branch of the federal government.
   (B)   reduce the prestige of the Supreme Court in favor of lower courts.
   (C)   establish English Common Law as the basis for all American laws.
   (D)   expand the power of the federal government at the expense of the states.
   (E)   destroy some private companies by using the new powers of taxation.

36. Which principle best summarizes the notion of Manifest Destiny?

   (A)   American Indian cultures must give way to white civilization.
   (B)   The people of each territory should decide the slavery question for themselves.
   (C)   The frontier will preserve democracy as a "safety valve" for oppressed people.
   (D)   A diversified national economy must supplant a strictly agrarian economy.
   (E)   The unique political and religious freedoms of U.S. society should expand.

37. "The words were still in the mouth of the scout, when the leader of the party, whose approaching footsteps had caught the vigilant ear of the Indian, came openly into view. A beaten path, such as those made by the periodical passage of the deer, wound through a little glen . . . and struck the river at the point where the white man and his red companions had posted themselves."

   In which American author's writings would one most likely find this passage?

   (A)   Edgar Allan Poe
   (B)   James Fenimore Cooper
   (C)   Mark Twain
   (D)   Herman Melville
   (E)   Washington Irving

38. Which statement best explains why the South failed to win its independence in the Civil War?

   (A)   The South counted on the failed effort of New York City to secede also.
   (B)   The South's invasions of the North failed to capture Washington, D. C.
   (C)   The war lasted too long for the South's population and economy to withstand.
   (D)   African Americans fought with a vengeance once they could join the Union Army.
   (E)   The North launched too many successful insurgencies in southern cities.

39.   "The contrast between the palace of the millionaire and the cottage of the laborer with us to-day measures the change which has come with civilization."

In which nineteenth-century writing would one most likely find the above quotation?

(A)   *A Century of Dishonor* by Helen Hunt Jackson
(B)   *The Impending Crisis of the South* by Hinton R. Helper
(C)   "Civil Disobedience" by Henry David Thoreau
(D)   "The Gospel of Wealth" by Andrew Carnegie
(E)   "The Significance of the Frontier in American History" by Frederick J. Turner

Percent of Women in Workforce

40.   According to the graph above, how did women's roles in the workforce after World War I compare or contrast to their roles after World War II?

(A)   A higher percentage of women stayed in the workforce after World War II.
(B)   A higher percentage of married women left the workforce after both wars.
(C)   The percentage of women in the workforce increased faster after World War I.
(D)   The rate of single women leaving the workforce after both wars was the same.
(E)   The rate of increase of women in the workforce after both wars stayed the same.

41.   Which of the following was true of the home front during World War II?

(A)   The need for workers in factories led to the repeal of Jim Crow laws.
(B)   The severity of the war required the mobilization of the entire economy.
(C)   Consumers had higher wages and could choose from a new variety of goods.
(D)   Second-generation German and Japanese immigrants were accepted into society.
(E)   New knowledge from Soviet allies boosted American math and science education.

42. How did French colonization of the New World differ from either English or Spanish colonization?

   (A) Unlike the others' Protestant colonies, French colonies were Roman Catholic.
   (B) French colonies claimed all of Canada and were thus more populous.
   (C) French colonies permitted religious dissent unlike the others' stricter colonies.
   (D) French colonies' economies were more diverse than the other colonial economies.
   (E) French colonies were based on the fur trade unlike the others' agrarian colonies.

43. Which event finally sealed the possession of Florida for the United States?

   (A) The British gave it to the United States in the Treaty of Paris that ended the Revolution.
   (B) The United States conquered it because Spain sided with the British in 1776.
   (C) Andrew Jackson defeated the Seminoles and forced them to give it to the United States.
   (D) John Quincy Adams negotiated a treaty in which Spain sold it to the United States.
   (E) Napoleon forced Spain to sell it to the United States after the Louisiana Purchase.

44. Which principle stated below best represents the view of equality embodied in the American Revolution?

   (A) Once freed from British control all Americans should share middle-class status.
   (B) All males, regardless of race, should have access to economic and political power.
   (C) All citizens should rise above unnatural restraints as far as they can through merit.
   (D) Once freed, white males should then help elevate women and African Americans.
   (E) All men are created equal, so all subservience should be abolished, even slavery.

45. In which situation did President Andrew Jackson challenge a decision of the Supreme Court?

   (A) In the Bank War over the constitutionality of the Bank of the United States
   (B) In the debate over Jackson's overuse of the veto power of the executive branch
   (C) In the Nullification Crisis over the imminent secession of South Carolina
   (D) In the aftermath of the Indian Removal Act leading to the Trail of Tears
   (E) In the controversy surrounding the first national nominating convention

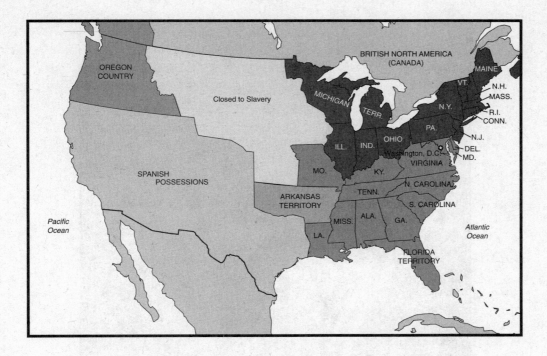

46. The map above illustrates the United States of America immediately following which event?

    (A) The Adams-Onis Treaty
    (B) The Missouri Compromise
    (C) The Mexican Cession
    (D) The Compromise of 1850
    (E) The Kansas-Nebraska Act

47. In what way was the Populist Party unprepared for lasting national success?

    (A) They barred women from leadership positions in their party.
    (B) They were largely lacking in education and political experience.
    (C) Their ideas failed to attract charismatic leaders.
    (D) They failed to recognize the significance of the national currency.
    (E) They were immigrant factory workers in an age of nativism.

48. "Combinations in industry are the result of an imperative economic law which cannot be repealed by political legislation. The effort at prohibiting all combination has substantially failed. The way out lies, not in attempting to prevent such combinations, but in completely controlling them in the interest of the public welfare."

    The quotation above is most likely a statement of which philosophy?

    (A) The ideology of William Jennings Bryan in the "Cross of Gold" speech
    (B) The antitrust policy of Woodrow Wilson's New Freedom
    (C) The good trust/bad trust stance of Theodore Roosevelt's New Nationalism
    (D) The socialist teachings of Karl Marx as supported by Eugene V. Debs
    (E) The goals of Samuel Gompers's national union, the American Federation of Labor

Courtesy of Culver Pictures

49. The political cartoon above is suggesting that

    (A) the United States needs to adjust to a new image of itself as a world power.
    (B) imperialism has caused the United States to grow too large and must be reversed.
    (C) William McKinley does not deserve to be the president of such a great nation.
    (D) Americans have grown obese and must participate in a physical fitness crusade.
    (E) the best years of the American experiment have come and gone.

50. Americans responded to the New Immigration of the first decade of the twentieth century by

    (A) embracing the new kind of European immigrants as refreshingly different.
    (B) revitalizing the centers of America's largest cities for the influx of new residents.
    (C) systematically deporting all of the illegal immigrants among this new wave.
    (D) quickly assimilating the immigrants from southern and eastern Europe into society.
    (E) passing nativist laws to restrict immigration of "undesirable" ethnicities.

51. Why did Franklin D. Roosevelt (FDR) seek a new foreign policy approach to Latin America in contrast to that of Theodore Roosevelt (TR)?

(A) FDR claimed the arrangements made by TR to be harmful to the U.S. economy.
(B) FDR believed alliances with Latin American nations essential to winning World War II.
(C) TR had admitted that his interventionist policies were only temporary.
(D) FDR wanted to end costly U.S. involvement like that of TR, Taft, and Wilson.
(E) FDR did not believe the U.S. military should be used in the Western Hemisphere.

52. Which president's administration launched the policy of containment of communism?

(A) Woodrow Wilson
(B) Franklin Roosevelt
(C) Harry Truman
(D) Dwight Eisenhower
(E) John Kennedy

53. Which principle did leaders of the American Revolution derive from the writings of John Locke?

(A) The "blank slate" of America should reject imperfect English political traditions.
(B) A revolution was permissible philosophically if the Social Contract was broken.
(C) Colonies could form a "league of friendship" against their Mother Country.
(D) Soldiers fighting for independence should be offered land in exchange for service.
(E) Only capitalism offered a fit economic system for a democratic republic.

54. "I might write to you at large about the religious liberty which is enjoyed in this province in the most extensive manner. . . . Christians of every denomination, as they choose their own ministers, so they also make provision for them. . . ."

This excerpt from a letter describes the tendency of colonial Americans to

(A) respond to the preaching of traveling evangelists in revivals.
(B) reject the notion of established churches.
(C) mistrust growing religious diversity.
(D) sympathize with Anglican ministers' complaints to the King.
(E) embrace traditional forms of church government.

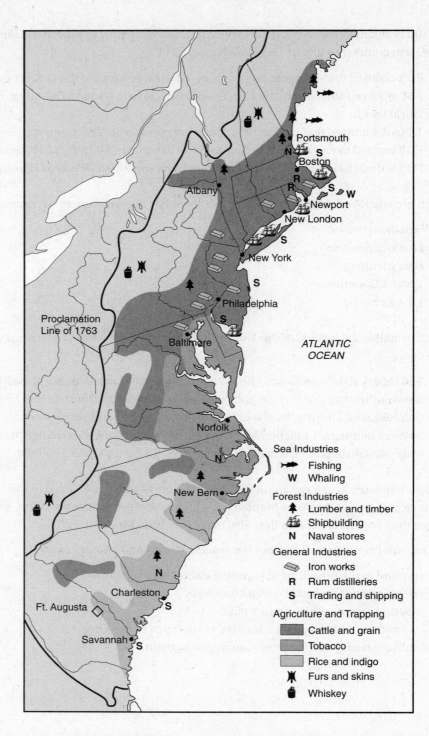

Portsmouth
N
S
Boston
R
R
S W
Newport
New London
S
New York
S
Philadelphia
S
Albany
Proclamation
Line of 1763
Baltimore
ATLANTIC
OCEAN
Norfolk
N
New Bern
N
Charleston
Ft. Augusta
S
Savannah
S

Sea Industries
🐟 Fishing
W Whaling

Forest Industries
🌲 Lumber and timber
⛵ Shipbuilding
N Naval stores

General Industries
▱ Iron works
R Rum distilleries
S Trading and shipping

Agriculture and Trapping
█ Cattle and grain
█ Tobacco
█ Rice and indigo
✳ Furs and skins
🛢 Whiskey

55. The map above illustrates which region in colonial America had the least diversified economy?

(A) New England
(B) The middle colonies
(C) The Chesapeake region
(D) The frontier
(E) The Deep South

56. What prompted President James Monroe to issue the Monroe Doctrine?

   (A)   Encroachments on American territories by England and Russia
   (B)   Resurgence of Spanish power in the New World
   (C)   Migration to America by the Chinese during the Gold Rush
   (D)   Migration to America by the Irish during the potato famine
   (E)   Growing sectionalism of the North, South, and West

57. Which initiative did Protestant Christianity most impact during the early nineteenth century?

   (A)   The move to stop imperialism known as isolationism
   (B)   The rapid development of new communication technologies
   (C)   The flourishing of the philosophical aspect of Deism
   (D)   The temperance movement
   (E)   The parochial school movement

58. Which American president sent the military into Latin America while denying European countries the right to establish spheres of influence there?

   (A)   James Monroe
   (B)   Abraham Lincoln
   (C)   William McKinley
   (D)   Theodore Roosevelt
   (E)   Harry Truman

59. Which New Deal measures did the Supreme Court consider unconstitutional?

   (A)   The Civilian Conservation Corps and the Tennessee Valley Authority
   (B)   The Federal Emergency Relief Act and the Wagner Act
   (C)   Social Security and the Federal Deposit Insurance Corporation
   (D)   Works Progress Administration and the Public Works Administration
   (E)   The Agricultural Adjustment Act and the National Recovery Administration

60. Why were Americans willing to support the Marshall Plan's expenditures of billions of dollars even after the massive expenditures for World War II?

   (A)   The American economy was so strong the amount spent was trivial.
   (B)   Few Americans realized the extent of the Marshall Plan's expenditures.
   (C)   Most Americans agreed that communism was a significant threat to world peace.
   (D)   Most Americans wanted Europe to become dependent on the United States.
   (E)   European countries paid back the funds once they restored their economies.

61. What first prompted African Americans to migrate in large numbers away from the South?

    (A) The enacting of "black codes" that led to the rule of Jim Crow
    (B) Educational opportunities offered by northern religious reformers
    (C) Passage of the Thirteenth, Fourteenth, and Fifteenth Amendments
    (D) The end of sharecropping as a viable economic arrangement after 1900
    (E) The need for workers in northern factories during the world wars

62. Which region of colonial America had the widest variety of places of origin among its white population?

    (A) New England
    (B) The middle colonies
    (C) The Chesapeake region
    (D) The frontier
    (E) The Deep South

63. Which principle was most strongly associated with Puritanism in colonial New England?

    (A) Each church member attested to God's grace through a conversion experience.
    (B) Studying the Bible was less important than following one's inner light.
    (C) Reason was superior to faith in determining what was true.
    (D) The best life was one of individualized contemplation of "higher laws."
    (E) The key to societal peace was toleration of everyone's beliefs or lack of belief.

64. What was Benjamin Franklin's most important role in the founding of the United States?

    (A) As a printer publishing all the atrocities of the British king and Parliament
    (B) As the chief author of the Declaration of Independence
    (C) As the inventor of many practical devices bettering American's lives
    (D) As the wise sage guiding the Constitutional Convention in Philadelphia
    (E) As a skillful negotiator in the diplomatic service of the Revolution

65. How did the United States end the War of 1812?

    (A) By a brilliant invasion of Canada centered on Montreal
    (B) By a stunning victory led by Andrew Jackson in the defense of New Orleans
    (C) By outlasting British resolve because England was also at war in Europe
    (D) By invading England along with its ally, Napoleon Bonaparte
    (E) By stretching the British too far by spreading the war to Europe and Asia

66. All of these reforms inspired by the Second Great Awakening were successful in the nineteenth century **EXCEPT**

   (A) the abolition of slavery.
   (B) the prohibition of the manufacture, sale, and distribution of alcohol.
   (C) the expansion of public schooling in the common school movement.
   (D) the awareness that the mentally ill should not be treated as criminals.
   (E) the recognition of the right for women to have access to higher education.

67. What accounted for the dramatic growth of the slave population of the South prior to the Civil War?

   (A) The legalization of the African slave trade again
   (B) The extensive smuggling of Africans into slavery despite laws against it
   (C) Natural reproduction through improved treatment and medical care
   (D) The ending of the regular mass deaths associated with slave rebellions
   (E) The increased demand for slaves to fill the mines and factories of the South

68. What prompted the rise of anti-Chinese sentiment leading to the Chinese Exclusion Act, the first federal law to limit immigration?

   (A) Chinese students excelled beyond native-born children in public schools.
   (B) The government suspected Chinese immigrants of espionage in World War II.
   (C) Chinese immigrants insisted on living in separate neighborhoods in large cities.
   (D) Chinese-owned businesses flourished and their neighbors became jealous.
   (E) Chinese immigrants refused to learn English and thus refused to assimilate.

69. What explains the increase in membership in labor unions despite the Great Depression of the 1930s?

   (A) Long lines of unemployed workers stood outside of all American factories.
   (B) The number of strikes in major industries tripled during the decade.
   (C) The violence associated with early labor demonstrations never returned.
   (D) The Supreme Court of the 1920s had been sympathetic to labor issues.
   (E) The Congress passed the first pro-labor legislation in over twenty years.

70. Which of the following best describes the outcome of the Korean War?

   (A) The line between North and South Korea remained where it was before the war.
   (B) With foreign aid from communist countries, North Korea won its independence.
   (C) North Korea took much territory leaving South Korea little room on the peninsula.
   (D) North Korea drove out foreigners and united the peninsula under communist rule.
   (E) United Nations forces almost ignited World War III by invading China.

71. Identify the correct era and the explanation of the largest increase of the American birthrate during the twentieth century.

    (A) The 1920s due to the sexual revolution of the Jazz Age
    (B) The 1930s due to the focus on home life during the Great Depression
    (C) The 1940s due to the high casualties of World War II
    (D) The 1950s due to restored confidence after the war
    (E) The 1960s due to the era of free love in the hippie lifestyle

72. Which ethnic group settled the Appalachian frontier during the colonial era?

    (A) The English
    (B) The Scots-Irish
    (C) The Swedish
    (D) The Dutch
    (E) The Spanish

73. Why did many Americans oppose ratification of the U.S. Constitution?

    (A) The document did not resolve the conflict between large and small states.
    (B) The document called for the founding of a central bank that was too powerful.
    (C) The document lacked protections of individual rights from government abuse.
    (D) The document allowed slave states too much power in the Congress.
    (E) The document did not make the judicial branch accountable to the people.

74. Which event reopened the sectional debate that the ratification of the U.S. Constitution had mediated?

    (A) The sudden increase in the population of California due to the gold rush
    (B) The argument over where to locate the first transcontinental railroad
    (C) The animosity of the South for the North's protective tariffs
    (D) The desire of Missouri to enter the Union as a slave state
    (E) The accusation that the Mexican War was intended to expand slavery

75. Which individual or group proposed the most punitive plan for the former Confederate states during Reconstruction?

    (A) Poor whites who resented the power of the old slaveholding class
    (B) President Abraham Lincoln
    (C) The Union Army generals in charge of the five military districts
    (D) President Andrew Johnson
    (E) The Republican majorities in charge of both houses of Congress

76. Which action of the federal government in the nineteenth century most represented the concept of *laissez-faire*?

    (A)   The issuing of land grants to encourage railroad construction
    (B)   The support of high protective tariffs
    (C)   The Homestead Act's encouragement of western settlement
    (D)   The regulation of business with antitrust legislation
    (E)   The amending of the U.S. Constitution during Reconstruction

77. Which one of the following labor organizations resorted to the most militant techniques to pursue its goals?

    (A)   The National Labor Union
    (B)   The Knights of Labor
    (C)   The Socialist Party
    (D)   The Industrial Workers of the World
    (E)   The American Federation of Labor

78. Which event below was the last major violent encounter between the U.S. military and American Indians resisting federal authority?

    (A)   The Battle of Wounded Knee
    (B)   The Nez Perce War
    (C)   The Battle of Little Big Horn
    (D)   The Sioux Rebellion
    (E)   The Blackhawk War

79. Samuel Gompers described President Woodrow Wilson's Clayton Antitrust Act as "labor's Magna Carta" because

    (A)   Wilson supported unions unlike the last Democrat, Cleveland, who opposed them.
    (B)   the law legalized collective bargaining, the bedrock principle behind labor unions.
    (C)   the law was the first federal legislation to take on big-business monopolies.
    (D)   the law gave the right for laborers to bring their grievances to the government.
    (E)   The law committed the government to end the corruptions of the Gilded Age.

80. Why was the Harlem Renaissance of the 1920s significant to the wider American society?

    (A)   It was the first inner-city revitalization movement to follow urbanization.
    (B)   It allowed African Americans and Jewish Americans to live together in peace.
    (C)   It provided the first opportunity for African Americans to open businesses.
    (D)   The work of Harlem's artists, poets, and musicians also appealed to white people.
    (E)   African Americans gained their first access to college at Columbia University.

81. What cornerstone of Jimmy Carter's administration did he also convince the United Nations to adopt as a major policy goal while he was president?

    (A) Intervening in the Arab-Israeli conflict in the Middle East
    (B) Monitoring the proliferation of nuclear weapons
    (C) Urging wealthy countries to help feed the people of developing countries
    (D) Constructing housing for homeless people around the world
    (E) Denouncing human rights violations by governments around the world

82. What event prompted President Lyndon Johnson to ask Congress to support escalation of the Vietnam War?

    (A) An invasion of South Vietnam by North Vietnam after unification talks failed
    (B) The influence of the Soviet Union in spreading communism to North Vietnam
    (C) An alleged attack by North Vietnamese forces on American naval vessels
    (D) The conspiracy of the Vietcong to mount an insurgency in South Vietnam
    (E) The assassination of the American-backed leader of South Vietnam

83. Which aspect of American government listed below was originally problematic but solved by an amendment to the U.S. Constitution?

    (A) The checks and balances system among the three branches of government
    (B) The manner in which the president and the vice president were elected
    (C) The sharing of power between the federal government and those of the states
    (D) The impact of political parties on the work of the three branches of government
    (E) The controversy between populous states and states with smaller populations

84. Alexander Hamilton was responsible for all of the following aspects of the federal government **EXCEPT**

    (A) a provision that only native-born citizens could become president of the U.S.
    (B) expansion of the power of the central government using the Elastic Clause.
    (C) creation of the Bank of the United States modeled after the Bank of England.
    (D) assumption of states' debts and funding the consequently higher national debt.
    (E) regulating the economy through expanding or contracting the national currency.

85. Which policy did the Populist Party press the federal government to adopt?

    (A) The return to the gold standard to prevent inflation of the currency
    (B) The use of federal funding to subsidize cheaper rates for shipping crude oil
    (C) The opening of the country's borders to provide cheap labor on farms
    (D) The extensive use of silver to coin money in order to create inflation
    (E) The use of the strike to achieve higher wages for migrant farmworkers

86. The style of journalism known as muckraking was best exemplified in

    (A)   war correspondent Stephen Crane's book, *The Red Badge of Courage*.
    (B)   the abolitionist novel *Uncle Tom's Cabin* by Harriet Beecher Stowe.
    (C)   the satirical writings of Samuel Clemens or Mark Twain.
    (D)   the photography of Ansel Adams and Matthew Brady.
    (E)   the photography of Jacob Riis and Lewis Hine.

87. Which statement below best describes the impact of World War I on the American economy?

    (A)   Allies' failure to pay back their loans crippled the economy for a decade.
    (B)   The war helped American farmers, but then trapped them in overproduction.
    (C)   A baby boom and suburbs led to a decade of rampant consumerism.
    (D)   The war finally compelled the American economy to industrialize.
    (E)   The need to finance the war effort led to the creation of big business trusts.

88. What was the unintended consequence of the decision made at the Atlantic Conference by Franklin Roosevelt and Winston Churchill to push for unconditional surrender of the Axis powers?

    (A)   The Axis resolved to fight to the death to avoid this humiliation.
    (B)   The Axis formalized their alliance in the face of this threat.
    (C)   The Germans attacked the Balkans in order to avoid attacking the Soviet Union.
    (D)   The Allies divided dangerously because some countries still wanted appeasement.
    (E)   Joseph Stalin left the Allies to avoid similar treatment if they turned on him.

89. Which trend began during the cultural transformation of the 1960s?

    (A)   The move of the majority of the American population into cities
    (B)   The rise of Hollywood as the capital of the motion picture industry
    (C)   The infusion of British influences into American rock 'n' roll music
    (D)   The popularity of channels on television dedicated to music videos
    (E)   The "Just Say No" campaign against rampant drug use among young people

90. What technological advance was the most responsible for the advent of the Information Age?

    (A)   The creation of vast telephone networks coast to coast in the United States
    (B)   The laying of the transatlantic cable
    (C)   The development of satellite communications
    (D)   The formation of the World Wide Web through the Internet
    (E)   The development of personal computers

1.	E	31.	E	61.	E
2.	B	32.	E	62.	B
3.	D	33.	B	63.	A
4.	B	34.	C	64.	E
5.	C	35.	D	65.	C
6.	C	36.	E	66.	B
7.	D	37.	B	67.	C
8.	A	38.	C	68.	D
9.	D	39.	D	69.	E
10.	A	40.	A	70.	A
11.	E	41.	B	71.	D
12.	D	42.	E	72.	B
13.	B	43.	D	73.	C
14.	C	44.	C	74.	D
15.	A	45.	D	75.	E
16.	C	46.	B	76.	C
17.	C	47.	B	77.	D
18.	B	48.	C	78.	A
19.	B	49.	A	79.	B
20.	C	50.	E	80.	D
21.	D	51.	D	81.	E
22.	E	52.	C	82.	C
23.	A	53.	B	83.	B
24.	B	54.	B	84.	A
25.	C	55.	C	85.	D
26.	C	56.	A	86.	E
27.	B	57.	D	87.	B
28.	D	58.	D	88.	A
29.	A	59.	E	89.	C
30.	A	60.	C	90.	D

TEST ANALYSIS

STEP 1   **Count the number of correct answers.**

      Enter the total here: _____

STEP 2   **Count the number of incorrect answers.**

      Enter the total here: _____

STEP 3   **Multiply the number of incorrect answers by .250.**

      Enter the product here: _____

STEP 4   **Subtract the results obtained in Step 3 from the total obtained in Step 1.**

      Enter the total here: _____

STEP 5   **Round the number obtained in Step 4 to the nearest whole number.**

      Raw Score = _____

Scaled Score Conversion Table

Raw Score	Scaled Score	Raw Score	Scaled Score	Raw Score	Scaled Score
90–79	800	46–45	600	8–7	400
78	790	44–43	590	6–5	390
77–76	780	42–41	580	4–3	380
75	770	40	570	2–1	370
74	760	39–38	560	0 – –1	360
73–72	750	37–36	550	–2 – –3	350
71	740	35–34	540	–4	340
70–69	730	33–32	530	–5 – –6	330
68	720	31–30	520	–7	320
67–66	710	29–28	510	–8 – –9	310
65–64	700	27	500	–10	300
63	690	26–25	490	–11 – –12	290
62–61	680	24–23	480	–13	280
60–59	670	22–21	470	–14 – –15	270
58–57	660	20–19	460	–16 – –17	260
56–55	650	18–17	450	–18 – –19	250
54–53	640	16–15	440	–20	240
52–51	630	14–13	430	–21 – –22	230
50–49	620	12–11	420		
48–47	610	10–9	410		

ANSWER EXPLATIONS

1. **(E)** Indentured servitude was widespread in the Chesapeake region and grew to be the chief source of laborers across colonial America until the African slave trade picked up, so answer (D) is incorrect. Vast numbers of indentured servants came to America, so answer (B) is wrong, and answer (A) is wrong because the opportunity to gain freedom by working for four to seven years did not apply to most African slaves. Answer (C) is incorrect because some indentured servants gained their freedom and prospered, rising into the middle and even upper classes.

2. **(B)** The phrase "great lords" in the document should be recognized as a reference to an aristocracy in the context of European colonization. All of the other answer choices did exist in colonial America to one degree or another.

3. **(D)** Andrew Jackson famously launched the age of the common man, a combination of Jefferson's yeoman farmers and the rising class of manufacturing workers, many of whom were immigrants. Like most white males of his day, including Democrats, Jackson thought little of advancing the interests mentioned in answer (A). He fought the political interests listed in answers (B) and (E) as those who preyed on the common man. Answer (C) is wrong because, even though he was a southerner, Jackson was a strong unionist as evidenced by his handling of the Nullification Crisis.

4. **(B)** All of the other answer choices were untrue in the late nineteenth century. Answer (B) relates to the fact that industrialization and free immigration coincided in a favorable relationship for the American economy.

5. **(C)** All of the other answer choices are reasons the United States entered World War I by 1917, and in doing so the United States disavowed any desire to acquire territory from the German Empire in Africa (or from any other nation or territory). This attitude stood in stark contrast with the war aims of most other combatant nations on both sides of the war.

6. **(C)** Rising hemlines came and went after World War I, but they were first higher than women's knees in the 1920s. The empowerment of the New Woman (or the "It Girl") included the dispensing with the petticoat and the corset by Flappers seeking "free movement" in the Jazz Age.

7. **(D)** Both the 1920s and the 1950s were postwar periods of affluence. The relief felt at the end of each world war was expressed in a remarkable fixation on consumer spending and on the display of wealth, or certainly the display of comfort and leisure time. Each of the other pairs had at least one decade of scarcity or as in the case of the 1960s, anti-materialism that shunned consumerism.

8. **(A)** The first arrow labeled identifies the origins in the Northeast and the general directions of the migration in this era to the Sunbelt that occurred because of the proliferation of air conditioning. Arrows (B) and (C) denote the migrations of hopeful homesteaders and pioneers going west or the return to the East of those who failed. Arrows (D) and (E) do not illustrate migrations that have occurred in U.S. history as of yet, but global warming may induce people to follow these routes.

9. **(D)** Answer (D) was the short form of the name of the famous 1954 case in which the Warren Court overturned the 1896 ruling in *Plessy* v. *Ferguson* that originated the lan-

guage, "separate but equal." The other answer choices name cases that are either fictitious or, as in the case *Engel* v. *Vitale* in answer (E), not related to segregation. *Engel* v. *Vitale* ended prayer in public schools.

10. **(A)** Answer (A) was the stated mission that prompted the first Bush administration to act militarily in Iraq. Answer (B) was the reason claimed by those who opposed the war, and answer (D) was the U.S. action set in place after repulsing Iraqi forces in one hundred hours. Answer (C), the longstanding Middle Eastern problem, had little to do with this war, and answer (E) was exactly what President George H. W. Bush said he was not going to do, although many later said it would have been better to take out Saddam Hussein at that time rather than in the Iraq War under George W. Bush.

11. **(E)** Answers (A) and (C) are contrary to British policy because according to mercantilism, the colonies were to be a source of raw materials and a market for British manufactured goods. Acts of Parliament specifically forbade trade with other countries to achieve these goals. Answer (B) is incorrect because mercantilism did not directly dictate taxation policy, and Parliament never prevented colonial legislatures from taxing colonists. Answer (D) was only partially true and the result of geography rather than policy.

12. **(D)** The First Great Awakening encouraged democratic church government and increased the number and variety of denominations of Protestant Christianity. The spirit of this revival was contrary to all of the other answers. Greater democracy, open-air preaching by ministers like George Whitefield, and the organization of mass meetings were among the societal trends that contributed to political revolution in the next generation of Americans.

13. **(B)** These societal advances for women all occurred prior to 1850 except the right to vote (suffrage), which did not come until the Nineteenth Amendment was ratified just in time for the presidential election of 1920. The women's suffrage movement did begin with the Seneca Falls Convention in 1848, but the movement sacrificially lay aside its own cause to take up abolitionism as a more pressing reform.

14. **(C)** All of these events transpired before the Civil War except the rise of big business. The Civil War was the main impetus to industrialization in the United States, and young men like Rockefeller and Carnegie got their start in business organization during the war.

15. **(A)** Because railroads were the first large corporations in the nineteenth century, it made sense for the first reform legislation to target them. States soon discovered they could not effectively regulate railroads because the business carried on across state lines. The other answers allude to circumstances more associated with federal legislation of the early twentieth century.

16. **(C)** Answer (A) refers to the type of immigrants that did not have as much difficulty assimilating into America society as those of the New Immigration that arrived during this era. These new immigrants came from southern and eastern Europe and had more trouble assimilating with the original northern and western European stock. Answer (B) is fictitious in that the United States has never returned to a strictly agrarian economy after industrializing. Answer (D) alludes to the origins of nativism much earlier and is more of an effect of nativism than a cause. The Quota Act in answer (E) was also an effect of nativism and came later in the 1920s.

17. **(C)** All of the choices are true of the experiences of African Americans in World War I except that Alvin York, a white man from Tennessee, became the most decorated American soldier.

18. **(B)** Nothing in the 1920s compared to the nearly universal appeal of the new motion picture industry that produced the first "talkie" movie in this era. The national popularity of television, soccer, professional football, and the running craze all came decades later.

19. **(B)** Answer (A) is incorrect because there was a relationship between the Square Deal and the New Deal since both were stages in the rise of Progressive Reform. In sharing progressive principles, the domestic plans of the Roosevelt administration were not opposites even though the presidents led opposite political parties as alluded to in answer (D). Answer (C) is incorrect because Franklin D. Roosevelt modeled his political career after that of Theodore Roosevelt, but they did not strategize together. The tremendous expansion of government involvement in the economy of the New Deal beyond anything Theodore Roosevelt attempted reveals that answer (B) is true, making answer (A) false.

20. **(C)** Despite the tempestuous times surrounding the correct answer (except for the era of one-party rule experienced in the Era of Good Feelings), the Gilded Age saw voter turnouts for national elections that dwarfed those of all the other eras. The two major parties remained divided geographically for decades, and political campaigns often involved dressing up in Civil War uniforms indicating that the animosities of the war lasted well into the late nineteenth century.

21. **(D)** The phenomenon of the Credibility Gap did not always exist. The origins of deep distrust in government were in the 1960s during the youth revolt and the anti-war protests associated with the Vietnam War. However, the climax of these sentiments came after the Watergate scandal of the early 1970s, when the mistrust of Nixon outpaced that of Lyndon Johnson. The present deeply divided political environment may yet produce distrust rivalling that of the 1970s, but of the answer choices given, answer (D) is the best. The other decades saw presidencies that enjoyed more widespread popularity than anything experienced by presidents Nixon, Ford, or Carter.

22. **(E)** Answers (A) and (C) had little to no impact on American Indians. There was no link between climate change and industrialization in the nineteenth century (which experienced some of the coldest winters on record) and most native peoples ignored legislation like the Dawes Severalty Act, which promised individual families homesteads if they disavowed their tribal allegiances. Answers (B) and (D) relate items borrowed from the surrounding American civilization, but neither firearms nor written languages transformed the lives of American Indians as much as the horse did. The reintroduction of the horse to North America by the Spanish affected almost all tribes to a degree and radically altered the hunting, living, and strategic activities of many tribes.

23. **(A)** The Articles of Confederation overcame all of the obstacles and perceptions described in answers (B), (C), (D), and (E) and thus saw the young United States through the crisis of the Revolutionary War. The tragic flaw of the document was that it was written in the Revolutionary Era and thus purposefully weakened the central government, so much as to make it unable to deal with peacetime foreign and domestic conflicts.

24. **(B)** Jefferson broke with his strict interpretation principles and interpreted the constitution loosely to make the purchase a treaty with France. Answer (A) is incorrect because

Napoleon's victory over Spain made it possible to acquire land that doubled the size of America. Federalists criticized the Louisiana Purchase, therefore making answer (E) incorrect. The new territory did not extend beyond Oregon to the Pacific Ocean as suggested in answer (C), and Jefferson wanted its land to prevent industrialization, not to supply it, as said in answer (D).

25. **(C)** Answer (A) is a whisper of Marxism, and even though some Transcendentalists joined communal utopian societies, they would never dream of imposing such an idea on a whole nation by force as Marx did. Answers (B) and (D) come from the traditional Christianity that Transcendentalists rejected, and answer (E) is a statement of Deistical belief. Transcendentalists evoked the idea of interaction with a Supreme Being more than Deists did. Answer (C) is a direct reference to the approach of Ralph Waldo Emerson and Henry David Thoreau in the pursuit of truth.

26. **(C)** All of the choices were a part of the Open Door Notes and the policy of Secretary of State John Hay except answer (C). Russia and Japan fought the subsequent Russo-Japanese War over railroad rights-of-way that both nations fully expected to receive.

27. **(B)** The Ku Klux Klan had its greatest influence when it formed during Reconstruction and then again in the conformist and nativist era of the Roaring Twenties.

28. **(D)** While not the only cause, answer (D) was a part of the chain of events causing the Great Depression. Answer (A) took place approximately forty years after the Great Depression began. Answer (B) is incorrect because the American economy boomed through the 1920s except in agriculture, and farmers' problems were from overproduction, not a lack of productivity. Answer (C) is incorrect because the rise of the labor movement happened back in the nineteenth century, long before the Great Depression. Answer (E) belies the fact that there were panics (depressions) before industrialization, and the American economy had had time to adjust to the industrial revolution by the 1930s.

29. **(A)** Only answer (A) was a true policy that directly supported the Allies. Franklin D. Roosevelt technically remained neutral, but took steps ever closer to war, including a peacetime draft. However, this limited buildup of American military strength did not provide any direct support. Franklin D. Roosevelt made all these preparations for war despite the Neutrality Acts that remained on the books.

30. **(A)** A graduated income tax increased the rate of taxation as individuals' income increased, a move the Populists and Progressives wanted to ease economic disparities by taking more money from wealthy Americans and redistributing the wealth in social welfare programs. The estate and capital-gains taxes hinted at in the other answers were not directly tied to the income tax, nor was the income tax directly tied to political power.

31. **(E)** Although all of these events were tense moments during the Cold War, the Cuban Missile Crisis came the closest because the exercise of brinkmanship involved the unstable Fidel Castro's being held in check by the insecure Nikita Khrushchev. Answer (C) is wrong specifically because Harry Truman rejected General MacArthur's proposal and wound up firing him.

32. **(E)** Despite the barbarity of their religious practices, the Aztecs used them to organize their large population. Their society employed sophisticated agricultural techniques,

conducted organized warfare on a large scale, and built monolithic structures. None of the other cultures matched these achievements traditionally associated with the definition of civilization although the Cherokee Indians mirrored American civilization by the early nineteenth century.

33. **(B)** Second sons of the gentry had arrived from the beginning, and the arrival of Lord de la Warr, not his departure, was a boon. He organized the colony to produce tobacco for export in 1614, five years before the House of Burgesses was required to keep order in what he had turned into a thriving colony. Virginians never discovered gold although it was one of the primary goals of the Virginia Company to find it.

34. **(C)** The government designed by the Articles of Confederation accomplished none of these tasks except resolving the states' competing land claims by taking the disputed territory and making it a source of revenue for Congress. The issues in the other answers needed to be resolved through ratification of the U.S. Constitution and served to illustrate some of the weakness of the Articles of Confederation.

35. **(D)** The Marshall Court cases generally weakened states' abilities to do things, like ignore contracts or tax businesses (like the Bank of the United States), so answer (D) is correct and answer (E) is incorrect. Marshall increased the prestige and influence of the Supreme Court while attempting to curtail executive power at times, therefore answers (A) and (B) are wrong. Answer (C) is wrong because by precedent English Common Law was the basis for American law since the colonial era.

36. **(E)** Answer (E) is the specific connotation of Manifest Destiny as a motivation for policy toward American Indians and long predated Manifest Destiny. Answer (B) evokes the idea of popular sovereignty. Answer (C) alludes to Frederick Jackson Turner's "Frontier Thesis." Answer (D) harkens back to Alexander Hamilton's vision for the economic destiny of the United States.

37. **(B)** The passage is a classic example of Cooper's writing style and subject matter taken from *The Last of the Mohicans*, one of his *Leatherstocking Tales*. Students of the history of American culture should have a passing familiarity with the style and subject matter of all these authors who each crafted a unique voice with distinctively American material and formed the foundation of American literature.

38. **(C)** Answer (A) exaggerates the importance of the secessionist impulse of New York City that had been a transportation hub for southern cotton going to England. Answer (E) is a fabrication in that nothing of the sort happened. Answers (B) and (D) were realities that hampered southern success greatly, but the fatal flaw of the Confederacy was that its economy was largely based on the cash crop of the Cotton Kingdom. With exports cut off by the Union blockade, attrition set in and the military advantages the South possessed at the beginning of the war evaporated.

39. **(D)** The only one of these famous nineteenth-century writings that dealt specifically with millionaires was Andrew Carnegie's essay, "The Gospel of Wealth." The other authors wrote, respectively, about the plight of American Indians, the economic weaknesses of slavery, the injustice of the Mexican War, and the demographics of westward migration.

40. **(A)** The exponential increase of the percentage of both married and single women in the workforce in the 1950s and 1960s makes answer (A) the best choice (World War II

ended in 1945). This exponential increase is mostly notable among married women making answer (B) incorrect. While women entered the workforce after World War I in greater numbers than before, the rate of increase after World War II was faster, so answer (C) is incorrect. Answer (D) is incorrect in that even though the graph shows that the percentage of single women took a slight downturn after World War I, which ended in 1919, there is a slight uptick in single women in the workforce after World War II before a slight downturn beginning in 1950. These ups and downs in the percentage of single women in the workforce makes answer (E) incorrect in that married women steadily increased participation in the workforce after 1920, a rate that was accelerated by World War II.

41. **(B)** World War II required a complete mobilization of the American economy to supply the resources needed by the United States and her allies to win the war. Answer (A) did not occur until the decades after the war in the Civil Rights Movement and was not directly related to war production on the part of African Americans. Wages did increase as stated in answer (C), but rationing of materials needed for the war prevented the production of a new variety of goods until the 1950s. Answer (D) is the opposite of the truth for these immigrants on the home front, and answer (E) merely hints at a phenomenon that occurred after the war during the Space Race.

42. **(E)** Answer (E) conveys the nature of an empire based largely on the fur trade; therefore, answer (D) is incorrect. Answer (A) is incorrect because the Spanish were also Roman Catholic as were many colonists in Maryland. The French did claim the vast territory of Canada, which they believed included the Ohio River Valley, but their population never reached that of either Spanish or British America. Only the British tolerated religious dissent to any degree.

43. **(D)** Florida was founded by the Spanish, taken by the English in the French and Indian War, given back to the Spanish by the United States for aid during the Revolutionary War, and finally purchased by the United States from Spain with the Adams-Onis Treaty as the Spanish Empire fell into decline. Thus, answers (A) and (C) only hint at stages of the acquisition of Florida, whereas answers (B) and (E) are fabrications.

44. **(C)** Despite revolutionary rhetoric, the only concept of equality held by the majority of Americans at the time is in answer (C). The expansion of the concept of equality in the direction of the other answers would come with time and much struggle and not exactly as stated in answers (A) and (D). The philosophical leap that slavery should be abolished by a nation seeking freedom was an ideal held by a small minority of citizens of the new country.

45. **(D)** Although all of these items relate to events directly or indirectly involving Andrew Jackson, his dispute with the Marshall Court occurred over the fate of the American Indians displaced by the Indian Removal Act of 1830 that led to the Trail of Tears, a series of evacuations of the Cherokee and other tribes from 1835 to 1838.

46. **(B)** The limit of expansion indicated on the map, as well as the shaded areas that students should recognize as demarking slave states and free states, clearly reveal the map to be of the United States right after the Missouri Compromise in 1820. Note that the border between Missouri and the Arkansas Territory is the 36° 30′ line specified in Henry Clay's first compromise.

47. **(B)** All of the other answers are exactly the opposite of the nature of the Populists and Populism. Interests like the Grange and the Farmers' Alliances led to the Populist Revolt and the Populist Party. This movement set in motion the transformation of agriculture into a business requiring highly knowledgeable and skilled workers, but its origins represented a constituency in American society largely separated from the halls of both higher education and political power back in the East.

48. **(C)** Bryan, Wilson, and Debs opposed all trusts on principle, and Gompers did not speak in terms of the government's regulating industry as much as industry and labor negotiating fair terms for mutual advance. Answer (C) is correct because Theodore Roosevelt's express purpose in regulating trusts was to separate the good from the bad, and to bust the bad for the good of the people. Those trusts he deemed to be good, he left alone, but not without "watchdog" agencies monitoring them.

49. **(A)** Whereas this political cartoon portrays McKinley as undersized, the artist treats him and the subject of imperialism positively as a step toward national greatness. The image harkens from a time in American history when being overweight was a sign of wealth, and most people lived such physically demanding lifestyles that they would view a physical fitness crusade as preposterous.

50. **(E)** Since nativists would have liked to deport virtually all people who made up the New Immigration, they certainly did not have the positive or proactive responses in answers (A), (B), or (D). Nativist attitudes of Progressives and others led to the quota system for immigration of the 1920s that limited immigration from southern and eastern Europe.

51. **(D)** After Theodore Roosevelt followed the "Big Stick" policies of his Corollary to the Monroe Doctrine, Taft developed Dollar Diplomacy and Wilson tried to teach Mexicans to elect better leaders. Franklin Roosevelt sought a less interventionist approach through his Good Neighbor Policy. None of the answers besides (D) is true. Latin America did not play a strategic role in World War II except for the U.S. Navy's ability to switch oceans quickly at the Panama Canal.

52. **(C)** Although all subsequent twentieth-century presidents had to respond in some way to the policy, containment originated with Harry Truman's administration.

53. **(B)** Locke's theories about the Social Contract indicated that a monarch acting tyrannically would break it and forfeit his subjects' obedience. Locke applied the "blank slate" mentioned in answer (A) to individuals, not states. The other answers stem from the ideas of others with the exception of answer (D), which is only loosely based on Locke's ideas about incentives to colonization expressed in the Fundamental Orders of Carolina, a type of constitution he penned for the proprietors of that colony only.

54. **(B)** Although answer (A) was true of the American religious experience, it does not touch ideas directly expressed in the quotation that more expresses sentiments contrary to established churches. The Awakenings in American history led to growing religious diversity and more democratic church government than existed in Europe. American Christians largely ignored the complaints of Anglican ministers in, for example, the Parson's Cause, that caused Patrick Henry to first label King George III a tyrant.

55. **(C)** Even the people on the frontier, who were primarily subsistence-level farmers, traded whiskey and furs back east, whereas the plantation economy of the Chesapeake

Region focused entirely on the production of cash crops. Even though the Deep South cultivated cash crops, they diversified to a degree by shipping timber and naval stores.

56. **(A)** Russia colonized Alaska and even the coast of California, and England was poised to take advantage of Spanish holdings as Spain's empire weakened, not strengthened. All the other answers allude to events that followed President Monroe's time in office.

57. **(D)** The temperance movement was a direct reform initiative inspired by new interpretations of scripture associated with the Second Great Awakening. Answer (A) is incorrect because Christians largely supported imperialism as an opportunity for missions, and the imperialism debate came in the late nineteenth century. Evangelical Christians had little to do with either answer (B) or (C). Parochial schools in the early nineteenth century originated because the Common School Movement installed a Protestant worldview in the curriculum. Therefore, Roman Catholics launched their own parallel system to maintain their own theological training for children.

58. **(D)** The policy described is the direct application of the Roosevelt Corollary to the Monroe Doctrine, and Theodore Roosevelt employed his Big Stick policy of military intervention to enforce it.

59. **(E)** Although nearly all of these New Deal agencies or policies caused conservatives pause, the Agricultural Adjustment Act and the National Recovery Administration were directly challenged in Supreme Court cases before a conservative bench left over from the Republican administrations of the 1920s. When the court struck down the laws, FDR's frustration with what he viewed as judicial overreach led to his scheme to "pack" the court.

60. **(C)** The Marshall Plan was Truman's initiative (named after his Secretary of State, George C. Marshall) to rebuild the economies of countries in Europe in order to aid former allies but also to contain the spread of communism. Most Americans came to understand the global goals of the Soviets and other communists and supported containment despite the cost. The cost of the Marshall Plan was by no means trivial, and none of the other answers is true.

61. **(E)** Even though the other answers describe true conditions for African Americans in the South or allude to truths, as in answer (D) which mentions the long, slow death of sharecropping, none of these experiences led African Americans to leave their homes in the South. They did not leave in large numbers until the "great migration" occurred to seek work in northern factories for the war effort in the Great War, a move that only accelerated after World War II began in Europe.

62. **(B)** New York and New Jersey were particularly diverse religiously and ethnically with regard to their northern and western European birthplaces. Even Pennsylvania absorbed the immigration of non-English colonists such as Germans and Scandinavians. The other regions of colonial America were more homogenous in that, for example, New Englanders were predominantly English and frontiersmen were predominantly Scots-Irish and English. The diversity of ethnicities and places of origin among African slaves in the Deep South rivaled that of colonists from Europe, but the question specifies a study of white demographics.

63. **(A)** Only answer (A) expresses Puritan doctrinal beliefs, and even that principle eroded over time with the Halfway Covenant. Answer (B) refers to a belief held by Quakers. Answer (C) stemmed from the Enlightenment and appealed to Deists and even to some Enlightened Christians. Answer (D) is more associated with Transcendentalism. Answer (E) is a more modern understanding of religious toleration held by the followers of Roger Williams in Rhode Island but by few other American colonists.

64. **(E)** All of the answers represent truths or half-truths about Franklin's incredible life, but during the founding of the nation his singular contribution was his skillful manipulation of the French that led to their invaluable contributions to the Revolutionary War. Although Franklin had made himself rich as a printer, he did so by printing royal publications earlier in life as well as other projects like his famous almanac. By the time of the American Revolution, he had sold his printing business. He was on the Declaration Committee of the Second Continental Congress, but Thomas Jefferson was the principal author of that committee's draft document. Answer (D) sets up the question whether Franklin, Madison, or Washington was the most important influence at the Constitutional Convention, but one can avoid that unhappy decision since the question asks about the founding of the United States that happened earlier.

65. **(C)** Although all of the other events would have been helpful, they were beyond the capacity of the fledgling United States except Jackson's victory at New Orleans that occurred after the Treaty of Ghent had already ended the war. The treaty negotiated a draw without the exchange of territory, but still marked a ringing accomplishment for the young country in what some call the Second War for Independence. Napoleon was a more serious threat to the United Kingdom and required the Mother Country to concentrate on him the most.

66. **(B)** The temperance movement attempted to advance this reform along with the others that were successful in the nineteenth century. Whereas some "Blue Laws" limited the sale and distribution of alcohol locally, prohibition did not succeed until the twentieth century, and then only temporarily.

67. **(C)** The United States never legalized the African slave trade again after Congress banned it in 1808. Smuggling continued, but not enough to have significant impact on the population. Choices (D) and (E) never had significant impact because both were minimal in the ante-bellum South.

68. **(D)** All of the answers portray part of the reality or mythology of Chinese immigrants' experiences except for answer (B), which happened to Japanese immigrants. The Chinese Exclusion Act occurred after the gold rush, and the construction of the first transcontinental railroad secured a place for Chinese workers in California when they had developed control of other local industries with the intention of staying permanently. Their living in separate neighborhoods was a common practice among all immigrant groups in American cities, but their economic success surprised and frightened their nativist neighbors.

69. **(E)** Only (E) is completely true, and the legislative milestones for labor referenced are the Wagner Act coming over twenty years after the Clayton Antitrust Act. Answers (B) and (C) are fictitious, and answer (D) is the opposite of the truth since the Supreme Court under Chief Justice William Howard Taft was pro-business, not pro-labor. Answer (A) was

the reality during the Great Depression that made labor unions less effective and thus less likely to attract new members.

70. **(A)** Answer (A) is the best answer because the border between North and South Korea remained where it was, roughly along the 38th parallel of latitude. All of the other answers were potential outcomes, except answer (B) since the two Koreas were already separate protectorates that the superpowers treated as independent nations after World War II.

71. **(D)** Answer (D) is the best single decade constituting the baby boom beginning in 1946 and continuing to around 1964. Answers (A), (B), and (C) are incorrect because birthrates dropped precipitously during the 1920s and remained low through the 1930s and much of the 1940s. By the time some of the baby boomers became grandparents, the birthrate dropped precipitously again in the 1990s.

72. **(B)** During the colonial era, a few Spaniards and an occasional Englishman made forays into Appalachia, but the Scots-Irish were the first group actively settling there as pioneers. They based the design of the log cabins they built, interestingly, on Swedish construction techniques.

73. **(C)** The fear of the loss of individual rights prompted some states to insist on the addition of what became the Bill of Rights before they would ratify the U.S. Constitution. The Constitution did resolve the large state/small state controversy of answer (A), and answers (D) and (E), while true, did not cause widespread resistance to ratification, partly because the interpretation in answer (D) was a much later view on the Three-fifths Compromise regarding representation in the House of Representatives. Answer (B) is incorrect in that, even though the later Bank of the United States was controversial, Alexander Hamilton used the Elastic Clause to justify it, not a specific provision calling for its founding.

74. **(D)** Missouri requested to enter the Union as a slave state in 1819 prior to all the other events. Even though Henry Clay's Missouri Compromise calmed the sectional debate for a time, the United States remained polarized because of Missouri's decision. Each of the other events deepened this divide later in the ante-bellum period.

75. **(E)** The Radical Republicans in Congress earned this name partly because they blamed Democrats of the South for the Civil War and sought to punish former Confederates by radically altering the social, political, and economic relationships between whites and African Americans. Some Radical Republicans sincerely wanted to elevate the condition of freedmen in the South, but others operated purely for political gain while "waving the bloody shirt." The two presidents listed both proposed more lenient plans for Reconstruction, and the generals enforced policy, not formed it. Poor whites were even poorer after the war and lacked the political power to shape policy; many of them became sharecroppers alongside former slaves.

76. **(C)** All of these acts of government were the commonly cited violations of a strict hands-off policy implied by the concept of laissez-faire, causing some historians to suggest laissez-faire never really existed. The Homestead Act, however, was the only one with no strings attached. The government did actually give out free land in order to settle the West, and it left homesteaders entirely to their own devices. Two-thirds of homesteaders failed and moved back east with no aid from the government to cover their losses.

77. **(D)** Although violence occurred in association with, or coincidentally alongside, the efforts of several labor organizations, the Industrial Workers of the World was the most radical and purposefully resorted to murder and sabotage to pursue its ends.

78. **(A)** The Battle of Wounded Knee was more of a massacre than a battle, but it was the result of the last American Indian uprising in American history. The year was 1890, the same year of the closing of the frontier, and these two events signified that the troubled period of settlement of the West was done.

79. **(B)** Samuel Gompers made his famous assessment for the reason stated in answer (B). The other answers hint at pieces of legislation or misleading contextual clues. Answer (A) is irrelevant to the association with the Magna Carta but does point out a difference in the first two Democrats to be president after the Civil War. Grover Cleveland used the U.S. Army to stop the Pullman Strike in 1894. Answer (C) refers instead to the Interstate Commerce Act of 1887, and answer (D) refers to rights long established under the Bill of Rights and the U.S. Constitution. No law committed the government to end the corruption of the Gilded Age as referenced in answer (E).

80. **(D)** The Harlem Renaissance was a milestone, not just because of the new vibrancy of celebrating African-American culture, but because white urban audiences enjoyed jazz music, Langston Hughes's poetry, and other cultural flourishes that went mainstream because of their wider appeal. As with other concentrations of artists and thinkers, one community's interplay influenced all of American culture. All of the other answers are false. Answer B is incorrect because, for example, Harlem was an old Jewish neighborhood that African Americans moved into as Jews moved out, and there had already been business and educational opportunities for African Americans elsewhere.

81. **(E)** The advocacy of President Carter with the United Nations marked a turning point in diplomatic history as the United Nations took on the difficult task of bringing those guilty of crimes against humanity to heel. The process is seldom successful, but this role is a positive opportunity for the United Nations to change the world. Answers (C) and (D) refer to programs Carter pursued after the presidency and answer (A) refers to Carter's unilateral diplomatic achievement without aid from the United Nations. Answer (B) was a United Nations goal before President Carter took office.

82. **(C)** Answer (A) is a misleading reference to the Korean War, but all of the other incorrect answers refer directly to events that did happen in the conflict between North and South Vietnam that was reminiscent of the earlier conflict on the Korean Peninsula. What provoked an American military response was the Gulf of Tonkin Incident described in answer (C). Johnson's misrepresentation of the incident prompted Congress to pass the Gulf of Tonkin Resolution that authorized the rest of American involvement in the Vietnam War. Only later did it come out that American espionage conducted during military maneuvers off the coast of North Vietnam provoked the attack.

83. **(B)** The Twelfth Amendment solved problems encountered in some early presidential elections. Answer (A) refers not to a problem but to a solution to several problems. Answer (C) also refers to an aspect of constitutional government in the United States that was a solution to the balance between states' rights and the central government. When problems arose later because of sectionalism, the Civil War solved them, not an amendment. Answer (D) can be problematic even today, so the Founding Fathers, who never

mentioned political parties in any provisions of the U.S. Constitution, did not come up with a solution. They did solve the problem in Answer (E) over representation in the Congress, but with the Great Compromise, not an amendment.

84. **(A)** All of the other answers were Hamiltonian schemes, but answer (A) was not because it could have prevented Hamilton from being president, as he was born on one of the islands of the British West Indies.

85. **(D)** The other answers refer to issues that were the opposite of the Populist agenda, whereas the free coinage of silver to create inflation was the cornerstone Populists believed would save the American farmer. Farmers were usually in debt and sought inflationary policies to make their debts easier to pay off with cheaper dollars.

86. **(E)** Jacob Riis and Lewis Hine were photographic journalists who famously chronicled the lives of the immigrant poor and of child laborers, respectively. They used muckraking techniques of investigatory reporting to target these key social issues. Crane's book is a classic of American realism, while Stowe's melodramatic novel was a reform classic before the age of the Progressive Reform Movement associated with muckraking. Twain's style of reform writing was more subtle than that of muckrakers. Ansel Adams was famous for landscape photography and Matthew Brady for photographs of the aftermath of Civil War battles.

87. **(B)** Answers (D) and (E) refer to the impact of the Civil War on the United States, and answer (C) stems from World War II. Answer (A) belies the fact that the American economy boomed after World War I despite the failure of almost all of America's allies to repay their loans. The economy boomed through the 1920s except for farmers who were no longer feeding American allies in Europe and suddenly experienced a drop in prices that put them in the Great Depression a decade ahead of their fellow citizens.

88. **(A)** Unconditional surrender was set as a goal in this first meeting between FDR and Churchill and then reiterated in almost every subsequent conference. An unintended result was that the Axis powers fought all the harder realizing they were in a fight to the death. The Axis powers had already formalized the Rome/Berlin/Tokyo alliance, and Hitler invaded the Balkans to secure access to more oil on his way to invading the Soviet Union. By the time of the Atlantic Conference, the Allies already understood the policy of appeasement to be foolish and dangerous. Finally, whatever Stalin might have been thinking about the future, he supported the Allied cause as an act of self-preservation under the onslaught of the German military.

89. **(C)** Answers (A) and (B) both occurred before the 1960s and (D) and (E) began in the 1980s. The year 1964 marked the arrival of the Beatles on an American tour. The "British Invasion" by the Fab Four and other artists left an impact on American rock music for much longer.

90. **(D)** Although all of these events were instrumental in launching the Information Age to one degree or another, the impact of the availability of information on the World Wide Web through the Internet is an order of magnitude higher than that of any other previous medium except for the invention of writing. Some debate exists as to what the Information Age is, and the phenomenal access to instant information via the Internet relies on all the other items mentioned except that satellites have largely replaced the transatlantic cable.

Motives and Methods of European Exploration

2

Following the light of the sun, we left the Old World.
—Christopher Columbus, 1492

TIMELINE	
8,000 B.C.	North America becomes accessible by land
c. 700	Cahokia is occupied
c. 980	Vikings explore North America
1095	Crusades begin
1271–1295	Marco Polo journeys along the Silk Road
1350	Iroquois settle in fortified villages
1394–1460	Prince Henry the Navigator lives
1440	Renaissance begins to spread
1454–1512	Amerigo Vespucci lives
1492	Christopher Columbus sails to the western hemisphere
1494	Treaty of Tordesillas is signed
1498	Vasco da Gama returns from his voyage to India
1506	Christopher Columbus dies
1509	John and Sebastian Cabot claim the fishing beds off of Canada for England
1519	Hernando Cortés lands in Mexico
1523	Giovanni de Verrazano lands in North America
1528	Cabeza de Vaca lands in North America
1530	Francisco Pizarro lands in South America
1539	Hernando de Soto lands in North America

OVERVIEW

From the late 1400s to the early 1600s, a remarkable series of events led to a broad transformation of much of the world. The meeting of three peoples—American Indians, Europeans, and West Africans—on land held by American Indians on the North American continent created a "New World."

A wide variety of social, political, and economic structures had developed among the native peoples in North America in the period before the arrival of Europeans. As native peoples migrated across North America, over time they developed a great diversity of complex social structures. These peoples both adapted to the environment and transformed it. In the Southwest, the cultivation of maize (corn) fostered economic development and social diversification among American Indians. The peoples of the Great Basin and the western Great Plains tended to develop more mobile lifestyles in response to the lack of natural resources. Along the Atlantic seaboard, many native societies developed a mix of agricultural and hunter-gatherer economies. The development of agriculture fostered the development of permanent settlements. Societies in the Northwest and in areas of present-day California experienced economic development and social diversification, developing a mix of foraging and hunting. In some areas, the peoples of the Northwest supported themselves with the vast resources of the Pacific Ocean and the rivers.

In the late 1400s and 1500s, Europeans began to embark on overseas exploration and settlement. A variety of factors help to explain why the age of exploration and conquest took place when it did. The series of religious wars in the twelfth and thirteenth centuries known as the Crusades shook the stability of European feudal society and whetted the appetites of Europeans for foreign trade goods. The Black Death, which reduced the European population by 30 to 60 percent, also played a role in weakening the feudal system. The relatively self-sufficient world of feudal Europe began its long demise during this period, as trade routes and increased economic activity shifted power and priorities. Europeans engaged in trade with the Middle East, India, and China and became interested in circumventing Mediterranean trade routes that were dominated by Italian city-states and finding new routes with the East.

The spirit of Renaissance humanism, which developed in Europe in the fourteenth to sixteenth centuries, generated curiosity about the world and inspired people to explore and map new areas. Universities and scholarly books spread knowledge of these new discoveries. Johannes Gutenberg's printing press (developed in the 1440s) helped disseminate information and stimulated interest in new discoveries. Religious movements in the sixteenth century renewed many people's religious zeal and their desire to spread their gospels. The most important religious movement was the Protestant Reformation, spearheaded by theologians Martin Luther and John Calvin. The Catholic Church itself underwent a reform in the sixteenth century. This Counter-Reformation focused on a renewed sense of spirituality within the Catholic Church. Out of this movement came the Jesuits, a Catholic order devoted to spreading their gospel throughout the world.

A series of developments in maritime technology encouraged exploration. The compass, the astrolabe, the quadrant, and the hourglass all aided navigation by helping sailors plot direction, determine speed, and assess latitude. Detailed maps called *portulanos* also helped navigators find their way. The development of the sturdy and maneuverable caravel ship also facilitated long-range ocean travel.

The age of exploration and colonization brought people together from far-flung corners of the globe. The local and regional systems of an earlier era gave way to a global system. The encounters of peoples from the Americas, Europe, and Africa led to a reordering of the world and created great wealth for some and utter destruction for others. Out of these encounters, new settlements and colonies emerged in the New World. People from all three regions had to adapt to one another as they developed new cultural patterns.

1 NORTH AMERICA

The United States is the centerpiece of a vast continent containing nearly every type of biome. When the American Indians arrived North America contained seemingly endless forests and the Great Plains. The oldest mountains, the Appalachians, are in the east. The younger and much larger Rocky Mountains in the west are part of a chain that runs from Canada all the way down the length of South America. The Great Lakes and the Grand Canyon are scars telling of the impact of tremendous geological forces over time. Two large rivers, the Missouri in the west and the Ohio in the east, join with many other lesser tributaries to form the Mississippi River that drains into the Gulf of Mexico at New Orleans. Severe climates of North America range from the arctic stretches of unbroken ice to the arid southwest deserts that contain Death Valley, the hottest, lowest, and driest place on the continent. Conveniently poised to cradle early colonial settlements on the Atlantic Ocean is a large coastal plain that permitted river transportation 100 miles inland before reaching the first impassable waterfalls. The American Indians adapted well to almost every geographical region after crossing a land bridge that existed at the Bering Strait as recently as ten thousand years ago.

2 BERING STRAIT

This stretch of ocean separating North America from Asia was, during the Ice Age, the location of a land bridge as wide as Alaska. Glaciers and other forms of ice were of such large extent that ocean levels were lowered. As recently as ten thousand years ago human migration was possible over the land bridge from Siberia, and human beings came across likely in pursuit of game. Even after the Bering Sea submerged the land bridge as the Ice Age ended, Eskimos and Aleuts made the crossing in boats. From this point of origin, American Indians dispersed down across the entire Western Hemisphere. Recent archeological evidence indicates that some American Indians may have migrated by sea directly to South America. The Hawaiian Islands, another target of migration that became U.S. soil, were not populated until around 300 A.D.

3 IROQUOIS

This word is not the name of a tribe but of a confederacy of six separate tribes centered in what would become New York. The Mohawk, Seneca, Cayuga, Onondaga, Oneida, and Tuscarora tribes united in a military alliance against the Huron tribe located in the Great Lakes region. The Iroquois called themselves a name meaning "people of the long house." A matriarchal society, the Iroquois women ran their government except in matters of trade and war, which were delegated to male chiefs. This organization of many tribes over a single region was the most developed societal structure of any in what would become U.S. territory at the time of the arrival of European colonists. Emerging victorious over the Huron in their ancestral struggle, the Iroquois proved to be useful allies to the British in the colonial wars of the eighteenth century.

THREE-SISTER FARMING

American Indians across the continent boosted their population by growing maize, beans, and squash together. The crops benefited from being grown in proximity, and the nutrition they provided improved American Indians' diet.

4 VIKINGS

Vikings were the traveling warriors of Scandinavian peoples whose cultures originated in what are now Denmark, southern Sweden, and Norway. Most of these Norsemen were farmers, but their Germanic religion predisposed them to seek adventure and to engage in violent acts with impunity. By the year 700 A.D., Viking craftsmen had perfected their most important weapon, their ships. Made entirely of oak, the Viking ships were expertly designed vessels with which to raid coastlines even across the Atlantic Ocean. The ships were constructed in such a way as to be seaworthy in the open ocean in all weathers but also with shallow enough drafts to permit following rivers far upstream. Greenland was settled by Erik the Red in the late tenth century. Documents called *The Icelandic Sagas* recount that Erik's son, Leif Eriksson, explored lands even farther west that in their descriptions are similar to the east coast of Canada. This reported discovery of the Americas five hundred years before Columbus was held in doubt until archeological evidence found in the 1960s proved that Vikings had in fact been the first Europeans to set foot in North America in what is today Newfoundland. These settlements were not permanent, however, and retreated from pressure from tribes that lived inland that the Vikings called Skraelings. Columbus called them Indians.

5 CAHOKIA

Cahokia is today merely an archeological site and a series of 120 sacred mounds. Beginning around 700 A.D., however, it housed a thriving culture based on the cultivation of maize (corn) in fertile river bottoms in what is today Illinois. Cahokians built the largest city north of Mexico before European colonization. The 30,000–40,000 inhabitants disappeared without a trace and without a linguistic or traceable ethnic legacy. A part of the Mississippian culture, Cahokia was a trade center with connections over nearly all of North America until the civilization growing there collapsed around 1300 A.D. due to disease, deforestation, dispersal, or all three. All was not peaceful in Cahokia as evidenced by a two-mile-long stockade that encircled the main city. The mounds were sometimes made in the shape of living creatures, and to this feat the inhabitants of Cahokia added the construction of large earthen pyramids that were likely the tombs of important leaders. The historical significance of Cahokia is that it provided tantalizing evidence of the potential of the original settlers of North America to produce a lasting civilization, but just as important is that they failed (or chose not to keep trying). No other North American Indians approached the level of advancement exhibited at Cahokia prior to the arrival of European colonizers.

6 RECIPROCITY

The key to all of the good and bad interactions between Europeans and American Indians as well as those among various American Indian tribes was reciprocity. The common value system shared by North American Indian tribes was based on reciprocity of gifts and favors but also of sleights and injuries. Chiefs often obtained their position by giving superior gifts to others within their tribes. Attacks or other injuries between individuals, though, could also bring about repayment by families, clans, and even whole tribes. Far from the noble savage ideal established by Rousseau and by James Fenimore Cooper, American Indians routinely made war on each other. Most of what is today the state of Kentucky was uninhabited because it served as a hunting ground and as a site for intertribal wars. When Europeans arrived they exploited the reciprocity system by trading goods and trinkets unusual to American Indians for property rights, when no such concept existed in native cultures. The worst misfortune of the reciprocity system after the arrival of Europeans occurred when ruthless individuals from both sides drew their larger cultures into inevitable wars based on a never-ending series of reprisals for atrocities.

7 CRUSADES

With the cry, "Deus volt" (God wills it!), Pope Urban II in 1095 launched the first military campaigns to take back Palestine from whom medieval Europeans considered infidels: the Muslims. The eight or more campaigns were called Crusades, and the crusaders met with some success. As the eleventh, twelfth, and thirteenth centuries unfolded, though, it became clear they would not achieve lasting control of what they considered the Holy Land. The bearing the Crusades have on the history of the United States is that these excursions stimulated the first travel and trade Europeans experienced since the collapse of the Roman Empire. Crusaders encountered silks, spices, perfumes, glass, jewels, and other goods long absent from European trade. These luxury items were sought after in earnest by royalty, aristocrats, and newly rich townsmen alike. The rebirth of world trade originated from this clash over access to the scenes of the life of Christ and his apostles. Renewed trade laid the foundation for the Renaissance that in turn provided the means and the motives for early exploration. Europeans sought a water route to India and China to skirt the dominance of Muslims in the Middle East.

8 MARCO POLO

Born into a prominent Venetian merchant family, Marco Polo at seventeen accompanied his father on the most famous journey of any European along the Silk Road through Mongolia to China. Motivated by the tales and trade items of returning Crusaders, Polo left in 1271 and did not return until twenty-four years later in 1295. Kublai Khan, a great Mongol ruler, received Marco Polo into his court. Upon his return to Venice, Polo dictated a book, *Discourse Concerning Various Experiences*. This book became a bestseller and, whether fact or fiction, a basis for maps and travel guides as overland trade with China was restored. Europe became a market hungry for Asian goods and vice versa. The curiosity inspired by Marco Polo propelled several European city-states and nations to scramble for access to the Far East along various routes.

9 RENAISSANCE

The invention of the printing press by 1440 and the rise of international commerce created both a keen interest in learning and the means to spread ideas more readily. Italian scholars rediscovered many ancient Roman works of law and literature, as well as art. The flowering of scholarship and individualistic and humanistic endeavor became known as the Renaissance, or the "rebirth." The Renaissance, along with the rise of nations, effectively ended the medieval period of European history. Renewed trade and curiosity like that earlier exhibited by Marco Polo became commonplace. Individuals, city-states, and nations vied for prominence in wealth and in artistic achievement, and ultimately in feats of navigation and exploration. As the ideas of the Renaissance spread north, the desire for reform of the Catholic Church would eventually lead to the Protestant Reformation. These two intellectual and cultural movements led to a transformation of Western civilization and to the founding of colonies in the New World by several European countries.

10 PROTESTANT REFORMATION

Several centuries of dissatisfaction with the doctrine and practice of the Roman Catholic Church climaxed in the early sixteenth century with the writings of the priest and scholar Martin Luther. Luther's emphasis on the biblical doctrines of grace transformed European, and thus American, Christianity either directly or by inspiring the Catholic Counter-Reformation. Catholics launched the Inquisition and the Society of Jesus, or Jesuits, to protect Catholic doctrine and territory. Protestantism spread to other parts of Europe and established churches independent from Rome. Continued church reform launched careers of men like John Calvin and John Knox and movements like Puritanism in England. Many colonists went to America seeking freedom to pursue doctrine and practices more in keeping with their interpretation of the Bible. Protestants held the key doctrine of each person's having an individual calling and the Christian duty to work diligently at that calling for the glory of God. The ideas of Protestantism, including this work ethic, became seminal attributes of American society through the influence of Dutch, English, Swedish, German, and French Huguenot colonists.

11 MARTIN LUTHER

Luther was a German priest and scholar who defied Rome and launched the Protestant Reformation by contesting certain teachings of the Roman Catholic Church beginning in 1517. He was a Renaissance scholar who translated the Bible into German and thus with his own actions embodied the connection between the Renaissance and the Reformation, both of which were critical to the upheaval in Europe that led to not only the exploration and colonization of the New World but also the peopling of what would become the United States. As a result of these two transforming movements in European history, the people of the United States originated through the sometimes contradictory impulses of reform and liberty of conscience.

12 JOHN CALVIN

This Frenchman began as a priest but joined the Protestant cause as a legal scholar and minister in Geneva, Switzerland. His *Institutes of the Christian Religion* became the most thorough and systematic statement of Protestant doctrine. His emphasis on the sovereignty of God in salvation and over all of life influenced the formation of the Presbyterian and Congregational churches through the English Reformation. Calvin's student, John Knox, formed the Scottish Presbyterian Church brought to the shores of America by Scots-Irish immigrants. The Puritans were also Calvinist in doctrine and were the founders of what would become Congregational churches in New England.

13 HENRY VIII OF ENGLAND

This Tudor king of England cited scriptural and national security reasons to justify his divorce from Catherine of Aragon, the daughter of Ferdinand and Isabella of Spain, and his marriage to Anne Boleyn. Since the Roman Catholic Church opposed his actions, Henry launched the English Reformation. Although other Protestant reformers would come later in English history with more sincerely spiritual motives, Henry did sever ties with Rome and permit the Bible to be printed in English legally for the first time. His next important action was to die and guide succession to the English throne with his last will and testament. His sickly son, Edward, came first, but upon his death Henry's daughters Mary and then Elizabeth held the throne. These two English monarchs were responsible for lasting war between Spain and England that led to the great clash in 1588 at which the Spanish Armada was defeated.

14 AMERIGO VESPUCCI

Born in 1454 in Florence, Vespucci was an embodiment of the Renaissance. In the employ of the powerful Medici family of Florence, Vespucci traveled to Spain, then Portugal, and on to what he was the first to realize was a New World, not the coast of Asia. In a total of three voyages he explored the coast of South America including the mouth of the Amazon River. While doing so, he was the first modern person to conceive of a way to calculate longitude and was thus able to fairly accurately determine how far west he had sailed. While sailing as a navigator for Spain, Portugal, and the Medicis, Vespucci produced many descriptive letters regarding both physical and human geography. These letters were a popular tool to acquaint Europeans with the wonders of the New World. Vespucci contracted malaria on his third voyage and died in Spain in 1512, but a German scholar familiar with his letters drew up a famous map using Vespucci's Christian name as the basis for the word *America*. Soon maps were using the word to describe both North and South America, and the names stuck.

> **CAPITALISM**
>
> The origins of this economic system lay in the commercial revolution set in motion by Renaissance bankers. With the coming infusion of bullion from the New World, money for investment was coined and "put to work" in a new international market. Capitalism became a chief motivation for the acquisition of private property and a component of freedom in American society.

15 PRINCE HENRY THE NAVIGATOR

Born the third son of the king of Portugal in 1394, the life of Prince Henry was timed to take full advantage of the Renaissance as it reached his country. While never sailing himself, Henry founded a school to advance knowledge of navigation, cartography (map making), and shipbuilding. His shipbuilders developed a new, faster craft known as a caravel that made long voyages beyond the Mediterranean practicable. He sponsored over forty separate voyages sent to explore the coast of Africa with two goals in mind, to break the superstitious ignorance that caused sea captains to fear falling off the earth and to dominate the spice trade with India. Before his death in 1460, Portuguese captains were out front and well on their way to accomplishing this mission.

> **PORTUGUESE EXPLORERS**
>
> Several Portuguese explorers followed in Prince Henry the Navigator's footsteps after his death. Bartholomeu Dias rounded the Cape of Good Hope in Africa in 1486 and Vasco da Gama proceeded all the way to India in 1497–1498. Pedro Cabral, also bound for India, was blown off course and landed on the coast of Brazil in 1500.

16 CHRISTOPHER COLUMBUS

Few men in history are as praised and hated as Christopher Columbus. The dark interpretation of his career places blame for disease, war, famine, and enslavement of the first settlers of the Western Hemisphere on his shoulders. On the other hand, no one has had more places in the United States named after him with the possible exception of George Washington. Genoese by birth, he applied to the king of Portugal for sponsorship of a voyage west to reach the Far East. Rebuffed there, Columbus found patrons in the new sovereigns of Spain: Ferdinand and Isabella. Columbus had conceived his idea of a westward voyage from extensive reading, and through determination finished successfully not one but four voyages to the Western Hemisphere. Part of the knowledge recovered by this Renaissance hero was that many ancients knew the earth was round. While Columbus did not prove this fact to the skeptical and superstitious, those who did circumnavigate the globe certainly followed in his wake. A better promoter and explorer than administrator, Columbus fell out of favor with the Spanish Crown over reported mismanagement of Hispaniola, the seat of his government. His explorations opened up the Caribbean Sea and Central America to colonization by the Spanish, thus launching the Spanish Empire. He died in 1506 in Spain still trying to recover his prestige and privileges.

17 TREATY OF TORDESILLAS

After Europe had time to digest what Columbus had done in 1492, a dispute quickly arose between Portugal and Spain. The notoriously corrupt Pope, Alexander VI, was born in Spain, and he issued two bulls (decrees) that allowed Spain to possess any new lands discovered that did not already belong to a Christian nation. A line was drawn, or imagined, that circled the globe and thus divided land targeted for imperial acquisition between the two disputing Christian nations. When more became known of just how much land these decrees gave to Spain, the king of Portugal negotiated a treaty with Ferdinand and Isabella. In 1494, the Treaty of Tordesillas was signed with the Pope's sanction to extend the boundary line west, thus giving Portugal access to what is today Brazil. The questionable nature of the pre-Reformation sway the Pope held over international affairs was heightened by the fact that nations like England, France, and the Netherlands were banned from the New World. Such actions added to the jealousy among the nations of Christendom and spurred their rivalry to include even piracy against fellow Christians.

18 HERNANDO CORTÉS

The archetype of all conquistadors, Cortés led the expedition to explore Mexico for Spain. In 1519, he landed and quickly subdued two American Indian tribes unable to withstand the attack by armored infantry and cavalrymen with long lances and firearms, including cannon. The Spanish and their American Indian allies reduced the influence of a growing Aztec Empire. Cortés held cordial talks with Montezuma at the Aztec capital city of Tenochtitlán. Over time, however, relations broke down. Montezuma was killed by his own people, and the Spanish crushed a general revolt after hard fighting. The actions of Cortés and his soldiers destroyed the Aztec Empire and ended their brutal rituals of human sacrifice and cannibalism opening the way for Spanish settlement and the transfer of mounds of gold and silver treasures. Francisco Pizarro repeated the process with the Inca civilization of Peru beginning in 1530.

19 FRANCISCO PIZARRO

Although Cortés could be just as ruthless, Francisco Pizarro retains the legacy of the most brutal acts against the civilized American Indians of South America. He arrived in 1530, fortuitously just after a civil war between two brothers fighting to become the Inca, the ruler of the natives of Peru. Pizarro's small force surrounded the winner of this struggle while he was still recovering from wounds received during the war. Pizarro took Atahualpa captive and held him for an immense ransom in gold and silver. When the Incas supplied the precious metals, Atahualpa was killed anyway. Pizarro quickly conquered the rest of Peru and ruled it with an iron fist until he was assassinated by his own men in 1541.

SPANISH EXPLORERS

Several Spaniards were inspired by the stunning successes of Cortés and Pizarro but failed to find comparable wealth in North America. Cabeza de Vaca led a harrowing expedition (1528–1537) to Florida, across the Gulf of Mexico by raft, and then into the Southwest. Hernando de Soto explored the Southeast and was the first European to cross the Mississippi River (1539–1541).

20 GIOVANNI DE VERRAZANO

In the same way other European monarchs indulged in the hiring of Italian explorers, Francis I sent the Florentine Verrazano to claim land for France. Verrazano steered his ship in 1523 toward the modern-day Carolinas, then up the coast to as far north as Nova Scotia. French interest in further exploration and colonization as well as claim to Canada were spurred by Verrazano's report back to the king. Verrazano has the distinction of being the only North American explorer known to have been killed and eaten by American Indians. His demise came in 1528. For his troubles, a modern suspension bridge was named after him in New York Harbor.

THE BIG PICTURE

1. The stage set for U.S. history on the continent of North America was a sparsely populated scene of great variety, vast distances, and virtually untapped natural resources.

2. The first settlers of North America came from Asia via the land bridge and dispersed after the Ice Age over the entire Western Hemisphere establishing varied cultures but no lasting civilizations save those in Central and South America.

3. The combined impact of the rise of nations, the return of trade, and the rebirth of learning in the Renaissance made Europeans curious, courageous, and competitive enough to launch voyages of discovery and to found colonies to exploit the New World's riches.

4. The Protestant Reformation stimulated great change in European society far beyond its religious roots and motivated religious dissenters to seek opportunities in the New World for freedom of worship according to the dictates of their consciences.

5. Beginning with the voyage of Christopher Columbus, Spanish explorers and colonizers established the largest European empire since the Roman Empire by pursuing service to God, personal glory, and wealth in the form of shiploads of silver and gold.

Spanish, French, and Dutch Colonization

3

Thereupon the gold on the shields and on all the devices was taken . . .
and the Spaniards made the gold into bricks.

—Bernardino de Sahagún in the Florentine Codex, 1547

TIMELINE	
1479	Ferdinand and Isabella unite Spain
1492	Columbian Exchange begins
1493	Missions are founded in the Americas
1517	Martin Luther contests teachings of the Roman Catholic Church; Protestant Reformation begins with Luther's *95 Theses*
1524	Council of the Indies begins management of Spain's American colonies
1534	Jacques Cartier claims land in North America for France; Henry VIII of England begins the English Reformation
1535	The Spanish king establishes viceroys as his chief colonial administrators
1536	John Calvin publishes *Institutes of the Christian Religion*
1540	The Pope approves the order known as the Jesuits
1552	Bartolome de las Casas criticizes the treatment of American Indians
1608	Samuel de Champlain founds Quebec
1624	The Dutch establish their first permanent settlement at New Amsterdam
1647	Peter Stuyvesant begins his governorship of the New Netherlands colony
1680	Pope's Rebellion begins in Spanish colonies
1682	Rene-Robert de la Salle reaches the mouth of the Mississippi River for France
1749	Junipero Serra arrives in North America

OVERVIEW

In the 1500s and 1600s, Portugal, Spain, Holland, France, and England all established colonies in the New World. The approach to colonization of each of these European powers was markedly different. This chapter will look at Spanish, French, and Dutch colonization efforts. Chapter 4 will focus on English efforts.

The first explorers and settlers in the New World were sponsored by Spain and Portugal. Spain was able to secure a dominant role in the New World following the Treaty of Tordesillas (1494) between Spain and Portugal. The treaty settled the competing claims of the two countries to the newly explored lands outside of Europe (see page 54). Within a generation of Columbus's first journey to the New World (1492), Spanish forces wrested control of much of Central and South America from the native inhabitants, transforming the economic and social structures of the region and devastating the native population. Spaniards first turned to the forced labor of native Indians in a system known as the *encomienda*. Over time, native labor was replaced by enslaved Africans.

An important result of European settlement in the New World was an exchange of animals, plants, and organisms between the Old World and the New World. One of the most significant aspects of the Columbian Exchange was germs, as the Europeans' presence in the New World led to deadly epidemics that decimated native populations. By 1650, approximately 350,000 Spaniards had migrated to the New World. This population was supplemented by more than a quarter million Africans. Indians were still the majority in Spanish America, but by 1570 their population had been reduced by approximately 90 percent from what it was in 1492. Over time, a racially mixed population developed in the Americas, characterized by caste distinctions that grew out of the intermixture of Spanish settlers, African slaves, and American Indians.

The responses of American Indians to the catastrophe of conquest were varied. Some fled from the invading Spaniards, abandoning their ancestral homelands. These migrations led to population pressures and conflicts elsewhere in the Americas. Native people engaged in violent resistance, including Pope's Rebellion, as well as more passive cultural resistance.

Following the lead of Spain, both France and the Netherlands established colonies in North America, but they differed markedly from the Spanish model. Few French or Dutch people actually settled in the New World. Rather, the French and Dutch colonies served as trading outposts. France's North American colonies were vast on paper but thinly populated when it came to French colonists. New France stretched from the mouth of the St. Lawrence River in Quebec, encompassed the Great Lakes region and the Ohio River Valley, and included the vast Great Basin of what would later become the United States and the port of New Orleans. Because the French had relatively few actual colonists in the New World, they had to rely on diplomacy with American Indian groups more than did the Spanish or the British.

The Dutch presence in the New World dates from the 1590s. The Dutch established forts and small settlements in Guyana in 1590, followed by a string of island settlements in the Caribbean. In the early 1600s, the Dutch set their sights on North America. The Dutch Republic commissioned an expedition to North America by English explorer Henry Hudson. The project was funded by the Dutch East India Company, which instructed Hudson to search for a Northwest Passage to Asia. Hudson sailed into the river that would later bear his name, past Manhattan Island, part of present-day New York City. In 1624, a fort was built at the tip of Manhattan, and the settlement of New Amsterdam began.

Spain dominated the New World in the sixteenth century and continued to have a presence in the New World until the nineteenth century. France and Holland attempted to duplicate the Spanish model but did not have the sustained level of success that Spain did. In the following century, English colonization will have as transformative effect on North America as Spain did on South and Central America. These colonial ventures transformed the New World, destabilizing native cultures and paving the way for new societies to develop.

TOP 20 THINGS TO KNOW

1 FERDINAND AND ISABELLA OF SPAIN

Ferdinand of Aragon and Isabella of Castille united the Spanish nation when their marriage ended the rivalry of their kingdoms. They also united the forces of Spain to drive out the Moors, Muslims who had taken over the Iberian Peninsula centuries before. They became the patrons of Christopher Columbus and launched the Spanish Empire upon hearing of his discoveries of a supposed water route to Asia. They established management precedents that capitalized on the treasures discovered in the New World but also served as a model for other European nations to attempt similar exploits.

2 MISSIONS

Missions were the chief method of Spanish colonization through peaceful interaction with American Indians. A friar or priest founded each mission as a self-sufficient farming village and converted the locals, or at least convinced them to work peacefully and to attend the Catholic mass. A church was erected as a town center, as well as a place of worship. This structure was surrounded by a wall behind which cooperative natives could seek shelter when hostile tribes like the Apache and Comanche marauded through. Many clergymen, especially Jesuits, sought to educate the American Indians who thereby were more easily assimilated into the combined culture that made up the bulk of the population.

3 JESUITS

Representing the highest ideals of scholarly Roman Catholicism, this religious order was founded by Ignatius Loyola and became the chief instrument of the Catholic Counter-Reformation. The Counter-Reformation sought to win back ground lost to the Protestant Reformation in Europe. Jesuits also made up a strong contingent of missionaries to the people of Central and South America. As their efforts expanded, Jesuit priests entered into North America, especially the Southwest. As their de facto control of areas of the Spanish Empire rose because of their superior education and zeal, the Spanish Crown recalled all Jesuits from the New World to prevent them from gaining too much independence. The Jesuits still left a legacy of commitment to education in the universities founded in honor of Loyola or Francis Xavier, another noted Jesuit missionary.

4 ENCOMIENDA

The *encomienda* system was the method created by the Spanish Crown for organizing American Indian labor. In the *encomienda* system, the initial Spanish settlers were given a grant that included a tract of land and a salary. More importantly, the *encomenderos* (grant holders) were given the right to extract labor from local inhabitants. American Indians were used in mining operations as well in ranching and farming. In many ways, this system of New World colonization resembled Old World feudalism. Acting as feudal lords, the *encomenderos* had a free hand to manage their holdings, as long as a percentage of gold and silver was sent back to the monarchy. The *encomienda* system led to brutal exploitation; natives were forced to do relentless labor and were subjected to extreme punishment, even death, if they resisted. The system led to Spain becoming the wealthiest country in Europe with the influx of New World gold and silver, but it also led to criticism from reformers such as the friar, Bartolomé de las Casas.

5 BARTOLOMÉ DE LAS CASAS

This Dominican friar, priest, and scholar worked tirelessly through the sixteenth century traveling back and forth between Spain and the New World decrying the plight of the American Indians. He actively lobbied the Spanish Crown for reforms of the treatment of American Indians in the military campaigns of Spanish conquest and in the *encomienda* system of Spanish colonization. He went so far as to attempt what might have been the first utopian community in the Western Hemisphere based on principles of fairer treatment of and cooperation with willing American Indians. His efforts at reform largely failed, as did his utopian dream, but his writings revealed that some Europeans questioned the policies of empire. Unfortunately, as African slavery began in the New World, some of its advocates used the writings of las Casas to justify subjugation of Africans as a means of helping American Indians.

6 REPARTIMIENTO

Spurred by critics, such as Dominican friar Bartolomé de las Casas, the Spanish Crown issued a series of reforms to the governance of Spain's New World colonies, known as the *repartimiento*. The *encomienda* system was seen as being needlessly brutal and a hindrance to one of the stated goals of Spanish colonization—conversion of the Indians to Christianity. The reforms, which were completed by 1549, led to the Crown having direct control over the governance of Spanish America rather than allowing it to be farmed out to Spanish *encomenderos* (grant holders). The Crown had grown concerned over the degree of autonomy that the *encomenderos* were exercising in the New World. Treatment of native peoples did not improve appreciably. The *repartimiento* asserted that American Indians were entitled to wages and were legally free—they could not be bought or sold. The new system still allowed Spanish authorities to require that Indians perform work, but limited it to 45 days per year. By the end of the sixteenth century, the labor of American Indians was largely supplemented by African slavery.

7 THE CASTA SYSTEM

A rigid racial hierarchy developed in New Spain called the *casta* system. Despite traditional notions about the purity of Spanish blood, a good deal of intermixing occurred in the Spanish New World colonies. Spaniards were always greatly outnumbered by native peoples. Further, Spanish men greatly outnumbered Spanish women. In these circumstances, intermarriage was common. The Spanish used the term *casta* to describe the variety of mixed race people in the New World. The *casta* system included *peninsulares* (born in Spain) and *creoles* (born in the New World of Spanish parents) at the top of the social structure. These groups usually consisted of only one or two percent of the population. Just below them in social status were *mestizos*, the children of Spanish men and Indian women. *Mestizos* comprised four to five percent of the population of Spain's New World Empire. Below them were *mulattos* (children of Spanish men and African women), followed by American Indians and Africans at the bottom of the social pyramid. The Spaniards developed even finer gradations, based on the specific percentage of each background an individual possessed.

8 POPE'S REBELLION

A Pueblo medicine man named Pope (po-pay) organized resistance to Spanish rule after being whipped at the Santa Fe mission. Pope crafted an alliance between the Zuni and Hopi tribes of the Pueblo who were persecuted by the Spanish for continuing native religious practices after their supposed conversion to Catholicism. In 1680 a widespread, coordinated attack by over 17,000 Pueblo Indians swept across the Rio Grande River Valley killing most of the friars and hundreds of Spanish men, women, and children. The Pueblo Revolt was a clear sign of continued animosity toward the Spanish invaders and for a time achieved independence for the American Indians of New Mexico. Spanish military forces returned, however, and again subjugated them.

> ### SLAVE REVOLT
> At least two early eighteenth-century slave revolts also occurred in the English colonies—one in New York in 1712 and the other on the Stono River in South Carolina in 1739. Significant revolts did not occur again in the United States until a century later.

9 COUNCIL OF THE INDIES

This advisory body in the Spanish government answered only to the Crown in shaping policies for every aspect of religious and secular life in the Spanish Empire in the New World. This agency collected meticulous records, dispensed information, dispatched imperial civil and military employees, and oversaw even the activities of the Roman Catholic clergy in the Americas. No other European imperial power could match the efficiency of the Council of the Indies, although all tried; despite corruption and the great distance involved, the agency maintained firm control of the empire for around three hundred years. When revolutions removed the Council in the nineteenth century, however, the new societies suffered from having never experienced the autonomy enjoyed by other European colonists.

10 VICEROY

Just beneath the Crown in the power structure of the Spanish Empire sat this representative position sent to govern first two divisions in the New World and then four as the empire grew in size and population. Handpicked, loyal men were placed in these positions and were periodically rotated or removed to prevent allegiances being formed that would rival the honor due the Crown. Each viceroy served as the head of the civil government but also as the commander in chief of Spanish military forces in his region. The Spanish position of viceroy served as a model for other European nations that sought stricter control over their colonies.

11 COLUMBIAN EXCHANGE

When the voyages of Columbus launched the Spanish Empire into the New World, they encountered the indigenous peoples who had developed their societies in complete isolation from the Old World. The first contact between Europeans and the peoples Columbus erroneously named "Indians" gave rise to an extensive exchange of Old and New World animals, plants, and diseases. Europeans brought with them meat and draft animals, fruit trees, grains, olives, grapes, sugarcane, honeybees, new types of vegetables, and the coffee bean. In exchange they sent back to Europe potatoes, tomatoes, squash, peppers, maize (corn), peanuts, vanilla and cocoa beans, pineapples, and new types of tobacco. This exchange of commodities, along with the precious metals the Spanish discovered in the New World, positively impacted the world economy. However, diseases to which Europeans and Africans had developed immunities caused devastation among New World peoples, who had never been exposed to smallpox, influenza, diphtheria, and typhus.

12 JUNIPERO SERRA

This Franciscan friar, priest, and scholar lived in the latter part of the Spanish Empire during the eighteenth century and followed the mainstream Spanish and Roman Catholic policies of expansion of both civil and religious authority using the mission system. Serra was personally responsible for the founding of nine missions in what would become California, including San Diego, and is thus responsible for spreading civilization to this important region. His methods, however, showed that the Spanish maintained a policy of harsh treatment of resistant American Indians that could then be considered part of the reason for the collapse of the Spanish Empire.

DENOMINATIONS

As the principle of interpreting the Bible for oneself spread through the Protestant Reformation, so did new sects of Christianity that differed over points of the doctrine. Through these splits, dozens of new denominations of Christianity were born.

13 BLACK LEGEND

The term "Black Legend" describes exaggerated anti-Spanish accounts of the treatment of American Indians written by English, Italian, Dutch, and other European writers. While American Indians certainly suffered at the hands of the Spanish, Black Legend accounts portray an almost sadistic, deliberate cruelty on the part of the Spanish. Some Black Legend accounts cite the writings of Bartolomé de las Casas, who criticized Spanish treatment of American Indians. The Black Legend provided a powerful ideological justification for English involvement in the New World. The English portrayed themselves as altruistic, bringing God and civilization to the inhabitants of the New World, in contrast to the Spanish, who were portrayed as greedy and cruel. Of course, the historical record demonstrates that the English committed their share of atrocities in the New World, probably comparable to those committed in New Spain. Black Legend accounts often reflect an anti-Catholic perspective. The biased view of Spanish-speaking peoples was deployed later in the United States to justify acquisition of Mexican territory following the Mexican War (1846–1848).

14 JACQUES CARTIER

This first French explorer of Canada worked with and learned from Giovanni de Verrazano, the Italian first hired by France to explore the New World. Cartier made a total of three voyages and is responsible for naming Canada. In 1534 he sailed as far as 1,000 miles into the interior up the St. Lawrence River and brought back rumors of an immensely rich region similar to the fabled cities of gold that motivated so much of Spanish exploration. The rumors had the same effect on the French until they realized the gold of New France wasn't precious metal but fur. Samuel de Champlain followed in Cartier's wake and founded Quebec in 1608.

15 NORTHWEST PASSAGE

With war between Spain and England as well as the dangers of the lengthy route around the southern tip of South America, all European nations that founded colonies in North America sought this nonexistent route to Asia. Believing that a water route around what would become Canada lay somewhere just around the next bend, explorers were dispatched from up and down the Atlantic seaboard in the quest for it. The desperation to find the Northwest Passage revealed the zeal the competitive nations possessed to claim a shorter route to trade with China and India that had stimulated exploration and led to the discovery of the Western Hemisphere in the first place.

16 SAMUEL DE CHAMPLAIN

One of the searchers for the fabled Northwest Passage was this ship captain and cartographer from France. Champlain explored as far south as Cape Cod, but he concentrated his search up the St. Lawrence River and as far west as the shore of two of the Great Lakes. He therefore shaped the birth of New France as he founded the settlements that would become both Quebec and Montreal. After solidifying a French alliance with the Huron Indians against their foe, the Iroquois, he lived out his days as the governor of Montreal.

17 RENE-ROBERT DE LA SALLE

This French explorer followed up on Champlain's journeys to discover more of the extent of the Great Lakes, and he followed up on the journey of Marquette and Joliet to prove their theory that the Mississippi River did indeed flow into the Gulf of Mexico. After claiming the mouth of the Mississippi River for France and naming the delta region Louisiana for the French king, la Salle returned to France and was granted power to found a colony there. Upon his return trip, however, he was unable to find the mouth of the Mississippi from the Gulf and was killed in a mutiny by his crew. The combined efforts of Champlain, la Salle, and thousands of French fur trappers, however, laid claim to the largest territory in North America for any European nation. The problem came in keeping it.

> **COUREURS DE BOIS**
>
> The French term for "runners of the woods" referred to fur-trapping settlers in the New World who used the extensive river system of the trans-Appalachian region to establish a thriving fur trade with various American Indian tribes.

18 FUR TRADE

The French established trading posts along the St. Lawrence River and in the Great Lakes region in the 1600s to obtain furs from native groups in exchange for a variety of goods. Because the French had relatively few actual colonists in the New World, they had to rely on diplomacy with American Indian groups more than did the Spanish or the British. French traders and military officers in the New World aligned themselves with Algonquian speaking tribes and learned native languages. They became well versed in American Indian diplomatic protocols, including smoking the long-stemmed calumet ("peace pipe") and giving and receiving gifts, including wampum belts. French agents often married Indian women, which promoted their efforts at maintaining good relations with native people. Despite these efforts, American Indians maintained actual control of the heart of the North American continent. In these areas, French agents had to adjust to Indian ways to maintain France's colonial presence. This French accommodation of and adaptation to American Indian ways was extremely rare among British colonists (see Chapter 4).

19 NEW AMSTERDAM

This Dutch colony in North America began on Manhattan Island by 1624 when Peter Minuit purchased the best harbor on the Atlantic seaboard from local American Indians with a few trading goods. The Dutch also proved to be competent fur traders and excellent merchants who created a fleet of ships to rival that of England, the main maritime power. As Dutch colonists settled farther onto the coastal plain up various rivers, the wider Dutch holdings became the colony of New Netherland. The Dutch were responsible for founding the most ethnically diverse colony in the settlement of New Amsterdam that, fittingly, became the site of the trade and cultural capital of the world, New York City.

20 PETER STUYVESANT

This governor of New Netherland was the last hope of Holland and the Dutch East India Company to hold on to their investments. While competent as both a civil and military leader, the challenges of being surrounded by New France, rising English colonies, and hostile American Indians proved too great. His efforts to defend Dutch interests and territory served to keep the French at bay long enough for England to establish viable colonies that could protect themselves. For his trouble the English ultimately assailed and absorbed the colony in 1664 after the Dutch were weakened by a year of war with American Indians. The English renamed New Amsterdam the city of New York, and the colony of New York became one of the original thirteen English North American colonies. Most of the Dutch colonists and their diverse neighbors within their colony were allowed to remain and to retain their property, thus further enriching the diverse colonial population of what would become the United States.

THE BIG PICTURE

1. The Spanish shifted their emphasis from conquering to colonizing and established an efficient bureaucracy to manage their far-flung New World empire by subjugating both American Indians and African slaves.

2. Spanish colonization focused on the mission system of spreading Roman Catholicism along with political and economic control, and the resulting exchange of culture and goods enriched both the Old and New Worlds but also spread deadly diseases among American Indians.

3. The nations of England, France, and the Netherlands were jealous of the immediately lucrative nature of Spain's achievements and embarked on exploration and colonization efforts in the New World.

4. France established a vast New World empire based on fur trading that stretched from the St. Lawrence River in Canada, around the Great Lakes, and down the Mississippi River to the Gulf of Mexico, and became the main competitor with England for control of North America.

5. The Dutch were the other great strain of Europeans to establish a colony in North America at New Amsterdam, and the ethnic and linguistic diversity for which New York City is known today was already evident in this colonial forerunner before it was absorbed by the English.

English Colonization

4

We . . . for the glory of God, and advancement of the Christian faith, and honor of our King and country . . . in the presence of God and one another, covenant and combine ourselves together into a civil body politic. . . .
—The Mayflower Compact, 1620

TIMELINE	
1558	Elizabeth I becomes Queen of England
1577–1580	Francis Drake circumnavigates the globe
1578	The Crown grants Sir Walter Raleigh the right to found colonies in North America
1588	The English defeat the Spanish Armada
1602	The English government first charters a joint-stock company
1607	Virginia becomes the first permanent English settlement
1610	Lord De la Warr begins as governor of Jamestown
1619	Chattel slavery begins in Virginia; Colonists form the Virginia House of Burgesses
1620	Pilgrims found the Plymouth Colony at Cape Cod and write the Mayflower Compact
1629	Puritans settle the Massachusetts Bay Colony
1632	Lord Baltimore obtains a charter for Maryland as a refuge for Roman Catholics
1638	The government of Massachusetts Bay banishes Anne Hutchinson
1643	Roger Williams obtains charter to form the colony of Rhode Island
1670	John Locke writes the Fundamental Constitution for Carolina
1677	William Penn starts the first colony in West Jersey
1681	William Penn obtains a separate charter for Pennsylvania

OVERVIEW

For most of the century following Christopher Columbus's journeys to the New World in the 1490s, England was not active in exploring and colonizing the Americas. England sponsored journeys by the Italian navigators, John Cabot and his son Sebastian, to the New World between 1497 and early 1500s, but abandoned efforts in the coming decades. For much of the 1500s, England was a second-rate power to Spain as it dealt with a great deal of internal conflict. In the second half of the 1400s, the Wars of the Roses, fought between competing factions vying for the throne, kept England in disunity. Then, in the 1500s, Henry VIII ushered in a period of religious conflict by rejecting the authority of the Roman Catholic Church and bringing the Protestant Reformation to England (see pages 52–53). Conflicts ensued between Protestants and Catholics; one monarch, Queen Mary, even moved to restore Catholicism in England. Another reason for England's late start in exploration was that it devoted significant resources and attention toward subduing Ireland in the 1500s, rather than looking across the Atlantic.

By the end of the 1500s, however, England was eager to duplicate the stunning success of the Spanish in the New World. Queen Elizabeth I assumed the throne in 1558 and ushered in a period of greater unity and military strength. Under her leadership, England set its sights on the Americas. Francis Drake's circumnavigation of the globe and plundering of Spanish ports along the way inspired other overseas adventures. The government authorized both Sir Humphrey Gilbert (1582) and Sir Walter Raleigh (1585) to establish colonies in North America; both of these initiatives failed. Soon, however, England emerged as the most powerful nation on the global stage after defeating Spain and the powerful Spanish Armada in 1588 and was finally positioned to establish its presence in the New World.

British attempts at colonization of the New World differed from the Spanish model. The early Spanish ventures were primarily funded directly by the Crown. The early English colonies, however, were privately funded by joint-stock companies. The plan was that the profits from the venture would ultimately enrich Britain. Later, the British Crown granted charters to proprietors; royal authorities expected these proprietors to be more loyal and beholden to the Crown than the joint-stock companies were. Ultimately, almost all the colonies—charter colonies and proprietary colonies—were taken over directly by the Crown and became royal colonies.

The first permanent English colony was established at Jamestown, Virginia, in 1607. The Jamestown colony nearly collapsed during its first few years of existence. The early settlers hoped to find gold and silver and to quickly duplicate the Spanish successes in Central and South America. They were not prepared to establish a community, grow crops, and sustain themselves. Over the coming decades, however, the colonies of the Chesapeake region began to thrive. Colonists began to grow tobacco for export to Europe. This model of growing staple crops for export was duplicated throughout the southern colonies of British North America.

Colonization efforts continued with the founding of the New England colonies between 1620 and 1640. The first New England settlers were devout Puritans, driven more by religious reasons than economic gain. This religious motivation helps explain the unique pattern of development in the New England colonies, which tended to draw more families and to develop more diverse economies. English colonization slowed down in the middle of the century due to the English Civil War (1642–1651) and the Commonwealth/Protectorate period (when England did not have a monarch) (1649–1660). After the monarchy was restored in 1660, several more colonies were formed. In 1663, a charter was granted for the colony of

Carolina. The following year, Dutch New Amsterdam came under English control as New York and New Jersey (see page 64). In 1681, William Penn, an English Quaker, was granted a charter to establish Pennsylvania. The last charter was granted for the colony of Georgia in 1732.

The colonies established by England in the 1600s and 1700s shared a common heritage, but developed along different lines in terms of their political structure, social make-up, and economic direction.

TOP 20 THINGS TO KNOW

1 ELIZABETH I

The daughter of Henry VIII and Anne Boleyn, this monarch of England was more responsible than any other for positioning her country to take advantage of New World discoveries. When she became queen in 1558, England was reeling from battles between Anglican Church leaders and those wanting more church reform like the Puritans. Elizabeth ended strife over religion long enough to unify the country and strengthen the military, especially the navy. Her refusal to marry kept a foreign monarch from meddling in English affairs, but the rebuffed Philip II of Spain initiated a war as a result. Elizabeth lived to see England win the war and died in 1603 only a few years from seeing a permanent English settlement in the New World.

JOHN CABOT

There were precedents for England's interest in overseas exploration before Elizabeth I. John Cabot, an Italian navigator, was commissioned by the British Crown for an exploratory mission. He landed on the North American continent in 1497. Later, his son, Sebastian, led journeys to Canada. The Cabots are therefore responsible for the first English toeholds in the New World.

2 FRANCIS DRAKE

A pirate who wound up the most celebrated sea captain of his day, Drake sought revenge for damages done by the Spanish to his merchant fleet. In a daring voyage beginning in 1577, Drake sailed his *Golden Hind* down the Atlantic coast of the Spanish Empire and plundered every port he could. When he arrived at the southern tip of the Western Hemisphere, he decided to sail on into the Pacific Ocean. He kept plundering Spanish ports up the Pacific coast and then boldly circumnavigated the globe. He arrived in 1580 with a ship laden with Spanish gold and spices acquired in the actual West Indies that Columbus had been looking for in the first place. His voyage inspired other profit-seeking ventures, and he was knighted by Elizabeth I for his troubles. He proved instrumental in the ensuing naval war by defeating the Spanish Armada in 1588.

3 SIR WALTER RALEIGH

A true Renaissance man, Raleigh won the favor of Elizabeth I by fighting the Irish and Spanish and by establishing colonies in Virginia that he named for the Virgin Queen. Although his colonizing efforts ultimately failed, he and Sir Humphrey Gilbert and others published *Discourse Concerning Western Planting*, the book that explained the rationale for English colonization. While Elizabeth lived, Raleigh defended the realm from the Spanish and was rewarded for it. After Elizabeth died, Raleigh kept on attacking the Spanish and was beheaded for it by James I, the first of the Stuart kings of England.

4 PRIMOGENITURE

This caveat of English common law stated that all the property of an English nobleman had to be passed down to the firstborn son, and only to that son. While the measure stabilized land holdings and thus the politics of England, second and third (or more) sons of the gentry were left with little to do and no land with which to build their own estates. If a career in the church or the military did not appeal to them, these landless aristocrats were all dressed up and educated but bored. The answer for thousands came in making a go of life in colonial America where land was ultimately available aplenty. A life of ease made the rigors of carving civilization out of a wilderness beyond the capacity of some, and their refusal to do manual labor was almost the ruination of Jamestown.

> ## CHARTER
>
> English colonies received this document from the British government that both permitted settlement and specified the conditions of settlement.
> The most important principle established in colonial charters was that colonists were Englishmen with the same rights as Englishmen in England.

5 JOINT-STOCK COMPANIES

These economic arrangements were the forerunners of modern corporations. Drake's voyage around the globe and eleven English colonies were backed by advertising a share in the profits if citizens of England purchased stock in the companies. A broad spectrum of English society thus took interest in the New World and minimized the risk to any one planter or group of planters. The incredible profits of Drake's voyage inspired wider investment. English colonies were private ventures that governed themselves and made several risky decisions based more on the search for profit than for the well-being of colonists. The autonomy of the original companies, however, established key political and economic precedents.

6 SPANISH ARMADA

The ill-fated invasion fleet of Spain set out for England in 1588. As the more than one hundred Spanish ships crowded into the English Channel, Sir Francis Drake attacked from behind. Several decrepit English ships were set afire and driven by the wind into the mass of Spanish ships that could only escape by sailing up and around Scotland. When they entered the North Sea, a storm destroyed even more ships. With this tremendous victory, believed to have been assisted by God, the English began their longtime supremacy of the seas. Greater capacity to extend and defend its shipping led to great zeal in England's colonization.

7 VIRGINIA

The first colony of the original thirteen began abysmally at an ill-chosen site and with ill-chosen goals. After the deaths of several thousand colonists due to disease, starvation, and American Indian attacks, the first permanent settlement of Jamestown had grown from a small settlement and a fort to a colony with towns. Key colonial precedents occurred in 1619 when John Rolfe cultivated a viable strain of hybrid tobacco and established a firm foundation for a colonial economy in cash-crop agriculture and when property owners demanded more secure justice and protection by forming a colonial government, the House of Burgesses. Although Virginia would go on to be the birthplace of presidents and famous generals, it also was the birthplace of African slavery in English America. The Virginia Company eventually went bankrupt, and the colony was salvaged by becoming a royal colony with a royal governor, William Berkeley, in 1642.

8 LORD DE LA WARR

This new governor and captain of Virginia arrived with three ships filled with new colonists and supplies at Jamestown in 1610 just as the colony was on the brink of collapse. His energetic and militaristic rule galvanized the colony and set it back on the road to viability. Lord De la Warr used his own fortune to buttress Virginia and established the key turning point in giving Virginia Company land to Virginians as their own private property. Thus the lack of incentive to follow company orders was transformed into the seeds of the American dream and of the economic system of capitalism. On a return trip to England, Lord De la Warr's ship was blown off course into the mouth of a river that was subsequently named the Delaware.

9 POWHATAN WARS

During the early years of the Jamestown colony, relations between English colonists and local American Indians deteriorated rapidly. The local Algonquian people, led by their chief Powhatan, traded corn with the settlers at first, but when the American Indians could not supply a sufficient amount of corn for their English neighbors, the English initiated raids on Powhatan's people. Hostilities grew more intense after John Smith, who had urged peaceful relations with the Indians, returned to England in 1610. Tensions lessened in 1614, with the marriage of John Rolfe and Pocahontas, Powhatan's daughter. In the following years, both Pocahontas and Powhatan died. In 1622, Powhatan's bother and successor, Opechancanough, organized a major assault on Jamestown. The raid did not destroy the Jamestown settlement, but it worsened relations between the settlers and the native people. Two years later, the Virginia Company was forced to give up its charter and Virginia became the first royal colony. A final clash between the Virginians and the Powhatan Confederacy occurred in 1644, as Opechancanough again tried to dislodge the colonists. This failed raid was the last resistance by the Powhatan people to the Virginia colony. In many ways, the incidents in Virginia foretell the history of relations between the American Indians of North America and the white settlers from Europe. Whites consistently encroached on American Indian lands and consistently defeated them in the violent encounters that resulted.

10 HOUSE OF BURGESSES

The first representative assembly in the Western Hemisphere was established in 1619 in Virginia to protect the property and other rights of Englishmen that the colonists of Jamestown and its environs had come to expect. Villages in Virginia were known as burgs, and the representatives elected from each burg were called burgesses. The establishment of the House of Burgesses proved an assertion later made by Thomas Jefferson in the Declaration of Independence that the powers of legislation are incapable of annihilation. Without firm guidance or protection from England, Virginians had no one else to turn to besides themselves. Even when England did send a royal governor, William Berkeley wisely agreed to share power with an existing colonial legislature. These steps were crucial precedents for the American Revolution.

11 PURITANISM

The founders of the colonies in New England were part of the Puritan religious movement. The roots of Puritanism can be found in the Protestant Reformation of the first half of the sixteenth century. Martin Luther and John Calvin both broke with the Catholic Church for theological reasons (see page 52). However, when King Henry VIII of England initiated his own break with the Catholic Church, his reasons were more political than theological (see pages 52–53). Because Henry's break with Rome was not theological in nature, he did not question the traditional Roman Catholic practices in the newly-formed Church of England. He retained the "High Church" style of worship, with its emphasis on hierarchy, formality, and rituals. This "halfway reformation" upset many true Protestants in England. Those who sought a full reformation in England, who wanted the Church of England to be "purified" of Catholic practices, came to be known as Puritans. The Puritans took their inspiration from Calvinism, with its emphasis on predestination (individual salvation was subject to a divine plan), strict piety, prayer, righteous living, and hard work. Calvinism held that everyone had a "calling"—work on earth that God intended the individual to do. Being diligent at one's calling, therefore, was central to Puritanism. The Puritans also valued community. They believed it was God's will that members of the community take care of one another and watch that members did not go astray. Finally, the Puritan approach to humanity and to God was markedly dour, even dark. The Puritans put a great deal of emphasis on "original sin" and saw humanity as tainted with this inheritance.

12 PLYMOUTH COLONY

The first permanent New England colony was established over a decade after Jamestown was established to the south. In 1620, Plymouth Colony was established by Separatists who later became known as the Pilgrims. Separatists shared many views with the broader Puritan movement, but they went further in wanting to separate from the Church of England, which they thought was corrupt and unredeemable, rather than reform it. William Bradford and the leadership of the Separatist community got permission from the English king to settle in the land granted to the Virginia Company. Blown off course, the one hundred survivors of the ocean passage drafted the Mayflower Compact to provide a sense of legitimacy. In a few paragraphs, the forty-one signers of the document pledged before God and those present to form a government, a "civil body politic" with just laws. The document, which is considered the first written constitution in the English-speaking world, bound the signers to obedience and mutual support. By 1630, it achieved a degree of success, but it failed to attract large numbers of mainline Puritans from England; in 1691, it was incorporated into Massachusetts Colony.

13 MASSACHUSETTS BAY COLONY

After some preliminary settlements were made in 1624, the Massachusetts Bay Company founded a Puritan colony in 1629. After that point more and more Puritans came to America until their passage became known as the Great Migration. Fleeing persecution for their religious beliefs, whole communities of Puritans came to settle Boston, Salem, and other towns and villages. Families and church congregations arrived intact and soon acquired a level of development and a lifespan significantly beyond that of the English colonists to the south.

Harvard University was founded by Puritans seeking more educated ministers in 1636. Puritan colonies, which included the expansions of Massachusetts Bay named Connecticut and New Hampshire, adopted a colonial legislature like Virginia's House of Burgesses but called it a General Court.

14 ANNE HUTCHINSON

This Bostonian began to teach doctrines the Puritans believed to be heretical in her home with several men, even ministers, in attendance. This practice incurred the ire of the Puritan authorities who put her on trial for heresy. Hutchinson held an antinomian view of Christianity more similar to Quakerism than to the Christianity of her Puritan neighbors. She stressed the importance of God's grace as all Protestants did, but departed from the need to manifest that grace through obedience to God's law. She taught that each person could receive divine revelation. In a Puritan colony these heretical doctrines took on the flavor of sedition and contempt, especially when she refused to stop teaching them. She was thus banished from Massachusetts Bay and lived in Rhode Island, then New York. Hutchinson was a pioneer in American religious liberty among colonists who had sacrificed everything to acquire it for themselves with no thought of extending it to others.

15 ROGER WILLIAMS

Another pioneer of religious liberty, Williams was a Puritan minister whose dispute with the Puritan authorities was more about civil government being in the hands of church authorities than about doctrinal issues. He is thus also among the first in centuries of European practice to advocate the separation of church and state. The Anglican Church was the established church in Virginia, and the Congregational Church was established in Massachusetts Bay, but Williams was banished because he did not think church and civil government should be one and the same or even closely related. He lived among American Indians outside of Massachusetts and ultimately founded a new colony, Rhode Island, in 1636. Here complete religious liberty became a part of the legacy of colonial American society, and Roger Williams became the father of what would be called Baptist churches in America.

16 KING PHILIP'S WAR

Relations between American Indians and English colonists grew increasingly violent in New England, just as they had in Virginia. The Puritan project of building an ideal community did not preclude them from forcing American Indian populations off land the Puritans intended to settle. The most violent episode in the first years of settlement was the Pequot War of 1634–1638. Relations between New England colonists and American Indians were relatively peaceful after the Pequot War. However, brutal conflict occurred again in the 1670s. New Englanders had steadily been pushing into the interior of New England, onto Wampanoag lands. The catalyst for combat was the 1675 execution of three Wampanoag who had been tried in a Plymouth court for killing a Christianized Wampanoag. The chief of the Wampanoag, Metacomet, also known to whites as King Philip, launched an attack on a string of Massachusetts towns. Several towns were destroyed and over a thousand colonists were killed. The counterattack by the New Englanders was fierce. Metacomet was killed by a group of Mohawks allied with the colonists, and several Wampanoag villages were destroyed by the colonists. By spring 1676, over 40 percent of the Wampanoag were killed. The war was catastrophic for both sides—the deadliest of the wars of European settlement in North America in regard to the percentage of the populations of each side killed. Those American Indians who survived were forced to move farther into the interior of the region.

17 MARYLAND

George Calvert, Lord Baltimore, sought to found a colony along the Potomac River north of Virginia as a refuge for Roman Catholics also facing persecution from the Anglican Church. Maryland became the chief outpost of Catholicism in the English colonies, but later Lord Baltimore had to step down from being the proprietor because of the influx of Protestants from Virginia. An Act of Toleration was passed in 1649, however, that permitted all Trinitarian Christians freedom of worship. The port city bearing the original proprietor's name eventually turned Maryland into a thriving shipping center.

18 JOHN LOCKE

The central figure of English political philosophy at the time of the founding of the American colonies was John Locke. Building on the ideas of Thomas Hobbes about the Social Contract, Locke theorized that governments were instituted among men for the preservation of life, liberty, and property and that they should employ a balance of powers. Beyond the fact that nearly all of the Founding Fathers were students of Locke's writings, Locke's contribution to U.S. history included the constitution he wrote for the Carolina Colony as secretary to one of its eight proprietors. This document, called the Fundamental Constitution for Carolina, set new standards for utopian planning when it was drafted in 1669. Locke tried to codify distribution of land and easy citizenship standards to encourage settlement of the colony but also wrote in firm religious freedom.

BLUE LAWS

Even in the more diverse and freewheeling colony of Pennsylvania there were restrictions against vice. Blue laws began a class of American laws against theater performances, gambling, and revelry. Later, blue laws enforced Sabbath observances, prohibition, and forbade obscenity.

19 WILLIAM PENN

Perhaps the only man to take part in the founding of three of the original thirteen colonies, William Penn was instrumental in the formation of East and West Jersey as well as his own Pennsylvania, from which Delaware sprang. Having been converted to Quakerism, or the Society of Friends, Penn lobbied the English government for this sect of antinomian Christianity. The king owed Penn's family money, and the debt was discharged by the grant of Pennsylvania, or "Penn's woods." William Penn proved to be an enlightened lawgiver who drafted several versions of a constitution for Pennsylvania as circumstances changed over his lifetime. He sowed humanitarian, even libertarian, principles into the society of his colony and made peaceful relations with the American Indians. He was such a visionary as to be the first person to propose the British colonies be placed under one government, but although that idea was ahead of its time, his ideas of government for the people were not. Because of a thriving economy Penn's colony thrived and embodied nearly all of the other "American" legacies.

20 PENNSYLVANIA

The most "American" colony of all the thirteen colonies, Pennsylvania had a diverse society and what would be the largest colonial city, Philadelphia. As one of the Middle Colonies, Pennsylvania was perfectly located to also possess a diversified economy consisting of grain farming, basic manufacturing, and shipping. The border between the Penn family holdings and the colony of Maryland was surveyed and became known as the Mason-Dixon Line, the symbolic border between North and South. As the Quaker refuge, peace lasted with American Indians in Pennsylvania the longest time of any English colony, but western expansion eventually led to armed clashes. When settlers sought aid, the pacifist Quaker government refused. In the Glorious Revolution, the Quakers again refused to support an armed conflict, this time with the very king who had granted their charter, James II. For these breaches of the social contract the Penn family lost control of its own colony, but vast tracts of land remained their private property.

THE BIG PICTURE

1. Even though English colonization began with disorganization and failure, English society had several distinct qualities that ultimately formed colonies with greater societal vitality than those of the Spanish, Dutch, or French.

2. Every English colony followed roughly the pattern experienced in the founding of Jamestown, including a point of near disaster followed by a long climb toward a feasible economy and stable self-government.

3. Each English colony contributed significant legacies to what would become the society of the United States, and some colonies, like Pennsylvania, early on experienced a culture fashioned of all of the positive colonial legacies.

4. As English settlers established colonies on lands occupied by American Indians, conflicts frequently ensued between the two groups, resulting in several wars over territory and Indians being pushed inland from coastal settlements.

5. After the defeat of the Spanish Armada in 1588 and the establishment of viable colonies in the New World starting in 1607, England began to eclipse Spain as the nation with the potential to launch a world empire.

Colonial "American" Society

5

*He is an American who, leaving behind him all his ancient prejudices
and manners, receives new ones from the new mode of life he has
embraced, the new government he obeys, and the new rank he holds.*

—Jean de Crèvecoeur, c. 1770

TIMELINE	
1614	Southern colonies commit to a cash-crop economy
1625	Social mobility sends social classes into constant flux
1632	Licenses to transport African slaves begin the triangular trade
1649	Maryland passes an Act of Toleration
1662	Puritans establish the Half-way Covenant compromising the doctrine of their churches
1689	The English government passes an Act of Toleration for England
1700	New England colonies commit to a diversified economy
1717	Scots-Irish immigrants arrive in the American colonies for the first time
1730–1750	First Great Awakening spreads throughout the colonies
1737	Jonathan Edwards publishes a book about revival during the First Great Awakening
1738	George Whitefield arrives in America to preach

OVERVIEW

Once established, the thirteen British colonies developed along different paths. We see distinct patterns of development in the three regions of colonial America—the southern colonies, New England colonies, and the middle colonies. However, there were many shared experiences that shaped colonial society and created a uniquely American society—distinct from that of Great Britain.

The southern colonies all moved toward an economy dominated by the institution of slavery. Slavery existed in all the British colonies of North America, but grew most dramatically in the five southern colonies of Virginia, Maryland, South Carolina, North Carolina, and Georgia in the 1700s. The New England colonies of Massachusetts, Rhode Island, Connecticut, and

New Hampshire could be considered successful failures. They were successful in that the economy of New England thrived during the colonial period. New England towns developed a diversified economy that generated a great deal of wealth. However, Puritan leaders expressed concern over the decline of piety in New England. By the 1700s, it seemed as if the fire that animated the first generation of Puritan settlers had been greatly diminished. The Congregational Church (as the Puritan church was called) saw a decline in membership as time went on. The establishment of the Half-Way Covenant and the First Great Awakening can be seen as responses to the decline of Puritanism. The middle colonies of New York, New Jersey, Pennsylvania, and Delaware saw the development of economic and ethnic diversity as immigrants from Europe, especially Germans and Scots-Irish, began to fill up these colonies.

Despite regional differences, the thirteen colonies were united by shared experiences. Most colonists practiced some form of Protestantism and had some relationship to the Anglican Church. The Anglican Church had grown out of the English Reformation, led by Henry VIII in the 1530s (see pages 52–53). Colonists were either sworn to be loyal Anglicans, as in Virginia, or were intent on the church becoming more reformed, as in Massachusetts. The Church of England was thus an established church run by the government that could not be ignored.

Another important facet of colonial society was an unprecedented degree of social and geographical mobility. The social ladder in America was far more fluid than the rigid social structure of Great Britain. Shrewdness, pluck, diligence, and the availability of land permitted individuals to advance their station in life usually beyond that of their parents. America was indeed a land of opportunity compared to eighteenth century Europe.

The growing economy and the high degree of social mobility resulted in dramatic demographic shifts in colonial America. The population of British North America doubled every twenty-five years, easily outstripping French and Spanish growth in the New World. In the 1700s, English immigration into the American colonies declined as the economy of Great Britain improved. However, immigration among other groups increased, including Irish, French Huguenots (Protestants), Scandinavians, and Swiss. The two biggest groups to immigrate to British North America were Germans and Scots-Irish. The southern colonies, however, became the most populous region of the thirteen colonies—far surpassing both the New England colonies and the middle colonies. The main factor in this dramatic increase was the increase in the number of slaves in the South. By 1770, approximately 20 percent of the non-Indian population of the thirteen colonies was made up of Africans and their descendants.

We begin to see, in the eighteenth century, a pattern of development in North America distinct from Great Britain. The colonists of the thirteen colonies all lived under the supervision of the Crown, but they also had some sort of colonial legislature; they all maneuvered within mercantilist trade rules; they all pushed back and fought with American Indians; and they all were exposed to new philosophical and religious ideas. These distinctions began to lay the groundwork for the political break that followed the intellectual break from the British.

1 PROPRIETORS

These dignitaries were fortunate people indeed! Most consisted of friends of the king of England or those who had done exceptional service to their monarch. All of them were granted large tracts of land in colonial America for their trouble. Families like the Penns and the Calverts were given personal possession of Pennsylvania and Maryland, respectively, and looked upon themselves as social reformers creating sanctuaries for religious minorities like Quakers and Roman Catholics. The eight proprietors of the Carolina Colony had assisted the king in the Restoration and were given land consisting of modern North and South Carolina and Tennessee. Proprietors established governments for their colonies and tried to attract colonists. They collectively represented a powerful tradition of private property rights in America, and simultaneously, how little the British monarchy valued the wilderness the British Empire had acquired in North America.

2 COASTAL PLAIN

This important geographical feature contributed profoundly to the success of the original thirteen colonies. Extending from the fall line in the foothills of the Appalachian Mountains out to the Atlantic Ocean, the Coastal Plain contained fertile soil and was crisscrossed with rivers that served as highways. Settlement went upriver as far as boats could travel and then widened out from there.

3 PIEDMONT

The Piedmont is the region between the coastal plain and the Appalachian Mountains, stretching from Alabama to New Jersey. The Piedmont, which is the French word for foothills, and the coastal plain are separated by the fall line, where elevation falls noticeably. Large-scale agriculture in this inland region was difficult because the land is hilly and removed from navigable rivers. The existence of the Piedmont allowed a freedom of movement for the colonists unimaginable in Great Britain. Indentured servants who completed the terms of service frequently obtained land in this region where they could establish subsistence-level farms. This geographic mobility contributed to the high degree of social mobility in colonial America. The movement into the interior had two other consequences. First, the movement of colonists into the Piedmont region led to clashes with American Indians, who had earlier been pushed away from the coastal plain region. Conflict on the frontier between settlers and American Indians continued well into the nineteenth century. Second, tensions frequently developed between the struggling farmers of the Piedmont region and the powerful plantation owners of the coastal plain. These tensions often manifested themselves in rebellions, most famously Bacon's Rebellion (1676) in Virginia (see page 86).

4 CAPITAL

As crucial for the growth of American society as were new colonists, sources of investment funds were necessary to support everyone from proprietors (who were often already wealthy) to new entrepreneurs to craftsmen (of which there were few) to freed indentured servants.

Banks in London and joint-stock companies provided the necessary capital to establish American economic networks until the banking industry could begin in the few American cities that existed.

5 DIVERSIFIED ECONOMY

This economy existed in the Middle Colonies and in New England, more out of necessity than by choice. Geographical constraints prevented the establishment of a cash-crop economy that was the easy route to riches. While northerners did raise food crops and livestock, most were involved with harvesting furs, lumber, and other resources. On the coast sailors sought fish and whales or became merchant shippers (Yankee traders). Although little manufacturing was begun in colonial America, a diversified economy existed that permitted flexibility in responding to market trends like the fashion of wearing beaver hats (until the beaver were gone, and then New Englanders produced rum).

> **MIDDLE PASSAGE**
>
> Considered necessary to the expansion of the colonial American economy, the growing market in African slaves created regular traffic across the Atlantic Ocean, as slave ships crammed with captured Africans experienced horrific conditions and a death rate of at least one in five.

6 CASH-CROP ECONOMY

This type of economy existed to a degree in the Middle Colonies with grain production, but the Southern Colonies were largely dedicated to it. Climate and soil as well as the long growing season permitted the cultivation of tobacco, sugar, indigo, and even rice. Since profits were impressive at first, landowners used up the soil and expanded chattel slavery. The weakness of the cash-crop economy came when the climate did not cooperate as in periods of drought, hurricanes, or other storms that destroyed whole crops. Little flexibility existed, and planters were at the mercy of market prices for their goods. All in all, the northern economy produced more capital over time and laid the foundation for the Industrial Revolution there but also for the victory of the Union over the Confederacy in the Civil War, a conflict stemming largely from the inability of the South to diversify.

7 INDENTURED SERVITUDE

Impoverished Londoners and other English men and women displaced by the population boom and failed wool market also looked for opportunity in America like their aristocratic counterparts fleeing primogeniture. These colonists, however, were too poor to afford the trip to Virginia and thus answered advertisements in London newspapers to take ship on a free voyage in return for four to seven years of service to whoever had paid their passage. The terms of the agreement were written in a contract that was subsequently torn in such a fashion as to leave a pattern of indentations in the two halves, hence the term *indentured*. When the halves were put back together they were proof of the identity of the servant and the obligation of the master to provide the means for the new freeman to establish himself as a yeoman farmer. Indentured servants often did not survive the period of their service, and even when they did, stingy masters sometimes refused to supply the land, tools, mules, seeds, and so on, needed.

8 TRIANGULAR TRADE

The shrewd merchants of New England discovered a way to capitalize on the ready supply of lumber in their forests by building ships with which they plied the seas for profit. Goods were shipped up and down the Atlantic seaboard, but more importantly across the Atlantic. Raw materials filled the hulls of ships leaving Boston, New York, and Baltimore that were sold either in England or bartered for slaves in Africa. Africans were brought back to the British colonies of the Caribbean where molasses was picked up and taken back to Boston to be made into rum. Favorable trade winds facilitated the transit both toward England and away from Africa. Profits from shipping built northern cities. Southerners were at the mercy of their northern brethren not only for charges to ship goods to Europe but also for the prices on their manufactured and luxury items ordered for return.

9 MIDDLE PASSAGE

Slave trafficking in sub-Saharan Africa became a thriving business in the eighteenth century. European traders set up operations in African coastal towns and encouraged men to venture into the interior to kidnap members of other tribal groups. These Africans—mostly young and male, with men outnumbering women, two to one—were brought to coastal ports where they were sold to European slave traders. They were then transported to the New World in horrid conditions. This grueling, and often deadly, part of the journey was known as the "middle passage" because it was the second, or middle, leg of the triangular trade. Men, women, and children were crammed into slave ships to maximize the profits of the owner of the ship. People were usually chained together in the hold of the ship. Due to disease, about one in five Africans died during the middle passage. The most famous account of the middle passage by an African is contained in the best-selling autobiography, *The Interesting Narrative of the Life of Olaudah Equiano* (1789). Equiano, who was born in present-day Nigeria, was forced into slavery as a youth but later was able to purchase his freedom.

10 CHATTEL SLAVERY

Although the original African slaves brought to Virginia were treated more like indentured servants, the legal status of African Americans soon became that of chattels. The word in English law came out of the medieval period, meaning "property," and was closely akin to cattle. Chattel slavery placed African slaves on a par with buildings or livestock and removed all human rights except those granted by the mercy or whim of masters. Abject cruelty toward slaves was later made illegal by the House of Burgesses, but chattel slaves and their descendants were reduced to this status with few exceptions until after the Civil War.

11 SOIL DEPLETION

Crops like tobacco and corn stripped nitrogen from the soil and did nothing to replace it. As soil lost its fertility, planters and small farmers had to clear more land to the west. This process pushed settlement upriver across the Coastal Plain and caused recurrent problems with American Indian tribes in almost every colony. Soil depletion remained a crucial agricultural problem until crops like alfalfa were sown for hay and clover was sown in pastures. Alfalfa and clover are legumes, like beans and peas, which fix nitrogen in the soil and thus increase and preserve soil fertility. Modern fertilizers also expanded agricultural production of nonlegume crops but with other costs.

12 FRANCHISE

A critical trend in colonial American history was the extension of the franchise, or the right to vote. While primogeniture and enclosure laws served to limit land ownership, which was the prerequisite to voting rights in England, land ownership became the norm in America. Access to property came simply by moving west with a little capital or through land grants given to former indentured servants. Therefore, a larger percentage of males became voters in American society compared to English society. Both the literal and figurative definitions of democracy were thus expanded as the first steps in a long series of stages until all adults would possess the right to vote.

13 SCOTS-IRISH

Less a crossbreed (although intermarriage did happen), this important ethnic distinction speaks of a journey. Before the Acts of Toleration, Presbyterian Scots fled persecution to Ireland and took up residence there. When persecution followed them to Ireland, many migrated to the American colonies where they found welcome in especially Carolina, New Jersey, and Pennsylvania. Fiercely independent minded and with no love of their Anglican persecutors, Scots-Irish Presbyterians were among the first white settlers of the Appalachian Mountains and beyond. They proved to be ardent revolutionaries and the ethnic origin of men like Patrick Henry and Andrew Jackson.

14 PENNSYLVANIA "DUTCH"

The other large ethnic transfer into American society was from Germany. As German kings sat on the English throne (the Hanoverian Georges), and because English was a Germanic language, German immigrants had little trouble assimilating into American colonies. Western Pennsylvania became a center of German settlement where the colonists were known as the Pennsylvania Dutch, a distortion of *Deutsch*.

15 ACTS OF TOLERATION

As time went on in the wake of the English Reformation and the English Civil War, Acts of Toleration were passed in both England and in colonies like Maryland where Protestants moved to take up residence and grew in numbers beyond the Roman Catholics who founded the colony. Certain minimum shared doctrinal positions, like that of the Trinity, were established as cultural norms. Thus, religious toleration broadened the diversity in other doctrinal matters and church practices, and served to lessen religious strife. The toleration of diversity, however, undermined the support for established churches. American society thus began the journey for complete religious liberty that was known in the colonial period in only a minority of the colonies like Rhode Island and Pennsylvania.

16 HALF-WAY COVENANT

This compromise in the doctrine of the Congregational, or Puritan, churches ultimately led to the downfall of the Puritan movement in America. As fewer people devoted themselves to religion in prosperous New England, fewer could claim an actual conversion experience. Church membership, so important in Puritan colonial societies, was a prerequisite for holding political office and even for voting. The Half-way Covenant allowed people who desired church membership but lacked credible professions of faith in Christ for salvation to join the church anyway. Over time, the churches became populated with and even led by unbelievers. Unitarianism, a religious movement that rejected the doctrine of the Trinity and thus the deity of Christ, arose out of the resulting doctrinal confusion.

17 FIRST GREAT AWAKENING

Certain ministers noticed the declining devotion to God and to the church among their parishioners who were, after all, required to come to church by law. These ministers prayed for and preached about a revival of the Christian religion as an act of God through the Holy Spirit. Beginning in Massachusetts, widespread conversions, first among church members, gathered force until revival fervor spread throughout the colonies. Missionary activity also increased among American Indians, and a greater attention toward spiritual matters and church attendance became pervasive through the decades of the 1730s and 1740s, after which the revival died down. Public morals were lastingly impacted, however, and the shared experience of the First Great Awakening was the first unifying event in the history of colonial America. Americans for the first time contemplated themselves as Americans rather than Virginians, Marylanders, New Yorkers, and so on. This newfound unity and identity was instrumental as a forerunner of the movement toward independence.

> ## ARMINIANISM
> This doctrinal counterpoint to Calvinism held that man's free will was the key to salvation, as opposed to divine decree. The first ministers of the Great Awakening were Calvinists, but more and more denominations switched to this other view.

18 JONATHAN EDWARDS

This preacher from Northampton, Massachusetts, was one of the most scholarly men ever produced in America. His book on his unusual experiences at the beginning of the First Great Awakening spread the movement both in America and in England where it was published. His famous sermon, "Sinners in the Hands of an Angry God," dramatically impacted his congregation and fostered ardent repentance. Despite the emotional response to his preaching, Edwards stressed the rationality of faith but also reconciled philosophy and mysticism as true expressions of religion along with doctrinal purity. After a doctrinal dispute led to his dismissal from his Northampton church, he turned to missionary work among American Indians and to writing. He ended his life as president of what would become Princeton University.

19 GEORGE WHITEFIELD

Whitefield was the other famous preacher of the First Great Awakening. An evangelical and Calvinist Anglican, he traveled from England to preach throughout the American colonies and was widely known because of his booming, eloquent voice. What Jonathan Edwards helped begin, George Whitefield spread both in America's most urban setting, Philadelphia, and in remote, open-air settings. Less interested in the role of the church in preserving sound doctrine, Whitefield remained a popular itinerant preacher well into the latter part of the eighteenth century.

20 THE ZENGER TRIAL

The trial of John Peter Zenger helped the precedent of freedom of the press in the thirteen colonies. In the eighteenth century, residents of the colonies had a high degree of literacy, which created a demand for printed materials. By the middle of the century, Boston had eight printers, and New York and Philadelphia each had two. By the 1730s, newspapers existed in most colonial cities, including Charleston, South Carolina, and Williamsburg, Virginia. John Peter Zenger created the *New York Weekly Journal* in 1733. In 1735, Zenger was arrested and charged with seditious libel for printing articles critical of the royal governor of New York. In Great Britain at the time, any printed criticisms of public officials could be considered libelous. In the colonies, however, courts ruled that critical items could not be considered libelous if they were truthful. Zenger's lawyer successfully argued that he had the right to print such articles because they were truthful. The jury acquitted Zenger. In the wake of the case, more newspaper publishers and editors were willing to write articles critical of royal authorities.

THE BIG PICTURE

1. A tremendous store of natural resources, vast geographical space, and advantageous climatic conditions were unlocked during the colonial period, generating prosperity and great access to social, economic, and political opportunity in America.

2. A chronic labor shortage in the colonies led to two extremes to secure enough manpower; indentured servitude allowed poor English men and women to come to America and work their way to freedom, whereas chattel slavery permitted the purchase of African slaves to be personal property for life.

3. Two distinct types of economies developed in the North and the South with the more diversified northern economy both benefiting from and surpassing the potential of the southern agrarian economy.

4. Overall the combined capacities of the two colonial economies slowly became an integral component of the wider economy of the British Empire, a fact that would eventually lead to two wars between the colonies and their mother country, then lasting peace.

5. Colonial American society was a religious society with growing religious diversity and rising and falling doctrinal purity, thus becoming a testing ground for pioneering experiments in religious liberty.

Mercantilism and Colonial Wars

6

Half the continent had changed hands at the scratch of a pen.

—Francis Parkman, historian, 1884

TIMELINE	
1660	Charles II ascends to the throne in the Restoration of the British monarchy; Parliament passes the first Navigation Act to impact American colonists
1660–1763	The British government holds a policy of salutary neglect toward the American colonies
1676	Bacon's Rebellion begins
1686	James II forms the Dominion of New England
1688–1689	Glorious Revolution takes place in England
1733	Parliament enacts the Molasses Act; Georgia becomes the last of the thirteen colonies founded
1754	Benjamin Franklin proposes the Albany Plan of Union
1754–1763	French and Indian War
1756	William Pitt becomes secretary of state of the British Empire
1758	Fort Duquesne falls to the British
1759	Quebec falls to the British
1760	George III ascends to throne of England
1763	Patrick Henry calls King George III a tyrant, and the king forbids settlers to cross the Appalachian Mountains in the Proclamation of 1763
1770	Green Mountain Boys are formed in Vermont
1775	Daniel Boone leads settlers west

OVERVIEW

England's ambitions in the new world grew out of mercantilism—a set of economic and political ideas that shaped colonial policy for the major powers in the early modern world. Mercantilism holds that nations increase their power by increasing their share of the world's wealth. One way of acquiring wealth is by maintaining a favorable balance of trade, with the value of exports exceeding the value of imports. Mercantilist theory suggests that governments should advance these goals by maintaining colonies so as to have a steady and inexpensive source for raw materials. The theory also holds that the colonies should not develop manufacturing but should purchase manufactured goods from the ruling country.

From the 1650s until the American Revolution, England passed a number of Navigation Acts. The goal of the acts, in conformity to mercantilist principles, was to define the colonies as suppliers of raw materials to England and as markets for English manufactured items. The acts proved to be a double-edged sword; the colonies could not always get the highest price for their goods, but they did have a consistent market for them. Several of the acts—such as the Wool Act (1699), the Hat Act (1732), and the Iron Act (1750)—prohibited the colonies from manufacturing these items. In this way, England gave an advantage to manufacturers in England itself.

The Navigation Acts existed on paper, but were difficult to enforce. The lax enforcement of parliamentary laws in regard to the North American colonies is often referred to as "salutary neglect." This policy was partly the result of circumstances and partly the result of intention. The policy is often attributed to Prime Minister Robert Walpole (1721–1742), who urged the Crown to not excessively interfere with the profitable trade generated by the North American colonies. However, the sheer size of the British Empire made enforcement of the Navigation Acts difficult.

One reason the policy of salutary neglect worked for the British was that the colonies themselves were profitable. The health of economic life in colonial America and the high degree of social mobility in the colonies, continued to draw immigrants from Europe. In the 1700s, English immigration dropped, but immigration among other groups increased dramatically, notably among Scots-Irish and Germans (see Chapter 5). As immigrants flowed into America and as the soil in many older farming areas became depleted, colonists ventured farther into the interior of the country—toward and even beyond the Appalachian Mountains. The movement into the backcountry of colonial North America led to tensions between settlers on the frontier and the established colonial elites along the eastern seacoast. These tensions often resulted in violent clashes, from Bacon's Rebellion in the seventeenth century to the Paxton Boys' uprising and the War of the Regulation in the eighteenth century.

The salutary neglect approach of the British government changed in the aftermath of the French and Indian War (1754–1763), which proved to be a turning point in the relations between Great Britain and the thirteen colonies. The war had its origins in the long-term rivalry between Great Britain and France as well as in tensions over control of the interior of North America. After the war, the British government enacted a series of measures that many colonists found objectionable. The British government attempted to confront an ongoing problem—the large debt that had accumulated during almost half a century of constant warfare. The British believed their victory in the French and Indian War had been especially beneficial to the colonists. In return, the British reasoned, it was fair for the colonists to assume some of the costs of the war and of continued protection. This tightening of the bonds of the empire had the effect of lessening social tensions within the thirteen colonies—backcountry farmers, southern plantation owners, and New England merchants could now find common cause in their shared dislike of Britain's new approach to governing its empire. As tensions within colonial America abated, tensions between the colonies and Great Britain increased in the 1760s and 1770s, setting the stage for protest and rebellion in the coming decade.

1 MERCANTILISM

This economic philosophy asserted that nations were in competition for a fixed amount of wealth in the world. Economic rivals were thus natural enemies competing for limited resources like access to raw materials and precious metals. Imperial governments thus carefully guarded economic secrets and monitored the shipping of goods. The British Crown and Parliament were assumed to be running the British economy for the good of all Englishmen, and they sought a favorable balance of trade not only with rival nations but also with their own American colonies. The colonists were to provide raw materials and to purchase their manufactured goods only from British merchants. Over time, the colonists in British America found these restraints stifling to their economic development.

2 NAVIGATION ACTS

The Navigation Acts were passed soon after Charles II sought a new colonial policy of control. Certain goods called enumerated commodities were to be shipped only by British merchants so that no other European powers would profit from their sale. The goal of this mercantilist policy was to raise revenue for the Crown and to keep British gold in British hands. Even such a prosperous traffic as the triangular trade operated as a virtual smuggling ring by leaving England out of the triangle. American colonists realized the laws were unenforceable over the vast stretches of the Atlantic Ocean and developed sophisticated techniques to avoid compliance.

3 RESTORATION

After the successful Puritan Revolution that prompted the English Civil War, the Protectorate was established under the rule of Oliver Cromwell, the lord protector of England. This former general of the New Model "Roundhead" army moved toward dictatorship, as a viable parliamentary government proved unworkable among religious and political strife. After Cromwell's death, the remaining members of Parliament asked the exiled son of the executed Charles I to ascend to the throne as Charles II. This event occurred in 1660, and the Restoration of the monarchy had profound implications for colonial America. For the duration of his reign and that of his successor, James II, the British Crown sought more stringent control over its New World holdings.

4 BEAVER WARS

The Beaver Wars were an especially brutal series of events in the mid and late seventeenth century. Between 1640 and 1701 a series of wars involving competing European powers, a variety of American Indian tribes, and control of the lucrative fur trade took place. Rivalries had existed among American Indian groups before 1492, but they took on new dimensions in the age of European colonization. The introduction of European firearms, often obtained in the fur trade, intensified the impact of armed conflicts. Both the Dutch and the French had established trading posts to obtain furs from native groups in exchange for a variety of goods, including firearms. French traders established a series of trading posts along the St. Lawrence

River in the early 1600s, aligning themselves with Algonquian-speaking tribes. The Dutch had established a trading post at present-day Albany in 1614 and had developed an alliance and profitable trade with the Iroquois Confederacy. The Iroquois hoped to expand their trading network, but the Huron Indians of the Great Lake region stood in their way. By 1645, long-simmering tensions between the Dutch-allied Iroquois and the French-allied Algonquian-speaking Huron exploded into open warfare. After the British took over Dutch territory in 1664, military conflicts over control of the fur trade continued for the next half century. The wars, the pressures of the fur trade, and the introduction of European firearms all contributed to a realignment of American Indian alliances and a reorganization of their societies.

5 DOMINION OF NEW ENGLAND

This scheme was the most overt effort on the part of Britain to run its colonies as the Spanish had theirs, with tight bureaucratic control. Concocted by the unpopular and domineering James II, this measure erased existing colonial boundaries and governments to establish Edmund Andros as a viceroy over New England. Having cherished their freedoms enjoyed through the period of salutary neglect, Puritans and other American colonists chafed under this insult until it was ended by the Glorious Revolution.

6 GLORIOUS REVOLUTION

Knowing that the Puritans had removed the wily Charles I by force, the British people rejected the authoritarian and nearly absolutist rule of James II in favor of his daughter, Mary, and her husband, William of Orange. Mary had the royal lineage, and William had an army. This overthrow did not include the execution of the king as did the Puritan Revolution, but both occasions served as precursors to the American Revolution.

7 GEORGIA

The last of the thirteen colonies that would become the United States, Georgia was founded in 1733 by James Oglethorpe as a reform of British debtor prisons. Georgia's particular type of colonist, bound for what amounted to a penal colony, was considered expendable. Georgia served, therefore, as a buffer colony between the southern extremity of British America and Spanish Florida. The colony was also meant to serve the British Empire as an alternate source of silk, but the unfortunate choice of the wrong type of mulberry tree ruined the enterprise.

> **LEISLER'S REBELLION**
>
> Jacob Leisler led the merchants in New York in 1689 against the acting aristocracy. This armed insurrection and others revealed American colonists' distaste for European-style political structures.

8 BACON'S REBELLION

Nathaniel Bacon was a Virginia planter and member of the colonial government who became frustrated in 1676 by Governor Berkeley's refusal to help colonists on the frontier who faced atrocities from American Indians. Bacon gathered a force of former indentured servants who attacked both the American Indians and eventually Jamestown itself. The first capital of the colony of Virginia was thus burned as Governor Berkeley fled. Bacon's Rebellion fell apart after Nathaniel Bacon died suddenly of disease. This early example of frustration with British mismanagement foreshadowed an American willingness to resort to violence during extreme conflict with British authority.

9 MOLASSES ACT

This act of Parliament proved to be only one of the measures motivated by mercantilism that grew odious to American colonists. Just as American shippers began to amass capital in the sugar trade, Great Britain insisted that American colonial merchants sell their sugar supply only to Britain. This step hampered the colonists' desire to sell to the highest bidder and inspired intense smuggling efforts.

10 FORT DUQUESNE

Fort Duquesne was a French outpost that became a flashpoint in the French and Indian War (1754–1763). In the 1740s and 1750s, more and more British colonists began to venture westward. Colonists were eager to acquire new lands for farming. Immigration among a variety of European groups—notably Germans and Scots-Irish—put pressure on the existing land in the thirteen colonies. In addition, indentured servants sought land as they completed their terms of service. Finally, the soil itself in many areas was becoming depleted after several generations of farming. Many land-hungry colonists from Virginia began to eye lands beyond the Appalachian Mountains, in the Ohio River valley—an area claimed by France. In 1747, the two older half-brothers of George Washington, Lawrence and Augustine Washington, formed the Ohio Company and obtained a land grant from the British monarch at the intersection of Ohio and Allegheny Rivers (site of present-day Pittsburgh). In 1754, George Washington was sent to the region with a small military contingent to challenge the French presence. In response, France built Fort Duquesne to defend their claim to the area. A skirmish broke out as Washington's men approached a French detachment. These were the first shots of the French and Indian War.

11 FRENCH AND INDIAN WAR

This war was the climax of several eighteenth-century military conflicts among the mercantilist nations of Great Britain, France, and Spain. Begun in 1754 by George Washington during exploration of the no-man's land between colonial France and Britain, the war soon spread to Europe where it was known as the Seven Years' War. The British government eventually fielded a superior army and with its Iroquois allies defeated France and her Huron allies. In the Treaty of Paris of 1763 France was thus largely deprived of its New World empire, and Canada and the Ohio River Valley became British soil. Parliament made an attempt to pass the costs of the war onto the American colonists who were granted peace on their frontiers. The enforcement of new taxation laws was a primary cause of the American Revolution.

12 ALBANY PLAN OF UNION

Fearing American Indian attacks and a French invasion of New England or New York, Benjamin Franklin proposed this first attempt at a central government for the colonies in order to better coordinate defense. Representatives met and listened to Franklin's proposal of a unified government for all of the British colonies except Georgia and Nova Scotia. A strong aversion to executive authority in America and a mistrust of the motives of the plan in England made it unpopular with both the colonies and the Crown. The idea was more easily resurrected in the American Revolution, however, when Franklin could even reuse his promotional political cartoon depicting a severed snake with the caption, "Join, or die."

13 WILLIAM PITT

The British Secretary of State William Pitt, who would later become prime minister, was instrumental in turning around British fortunes in the French and Indian War (1754-1763). For the war's first two years, the war was a local affair—a continuation of the skirmishes between British colonists and French forces. In 1756, Pitt focused the attention of the British government on the conflict in North America and took full charge of the war, forcing colonists into the army and seizing supplies from them. Pitt alienated many colonists with his heavy-handed tactics. The colonists resisted these moves, putting the entire British effort at risk. Finally, in 1758, Pitt began to work with colonial assemblies and also reinforced the war effort with more British troops. These steps proved to be successful. The climax of the war was a stunning victory by British forces in the Battle of Quebec in 1759. British general James Wolfe found a ravine to ascend the supposedly impenetrable fortress at Quebec. French troops and British troops fought on the Plains of Abraham. Both commanders were mortally wounded, as were the hopes of the French government to continue the war. Pitt's orchestration of the war effort proved to be successful. The war ended in 1763, with France losing its holdings in North America and Great Britain incurring a staggering war debt. Pitt himself resigned his position; he wanted to continue the fighting against France, but the new king, George III, wanted an end to hostilities.

14 GEORGE III

This third Hanoverian king of England came to power at the climax of the French and Indian War in 1760, one hundred years after the Restoration. He, like Charles II, supported efforts to exert firmer control over the colonies in America. His manner was more autocratic than even most Englishmen in Great Britain preferred, but to American colonists he became the symbol of arbitrary and abusive power. His bouts of mental illness did not help the situation, and George III was the king from whom Americans rebelled.

15 PONTIAC'S REBELLION

With the defeat of the French in the French and Indian War (1754-1763), American Indian groups that had been allied with the French found themselves in a difficult situation. The Ottawa tribe, for instance, in the northern Ohio region found itself without allies as the British colonists set their sights on traditional Ottawa lands. After the war, British troops had occupied the French-built forts. The Ottawa chief, Pontiac, and other Indian leaders organized resistance to British troops stationed around the Great Lakes and southward along several rivers. In the months after the 1763 signing of the Treaty of Paris, Indian warriors attacked British-held Fort Detroit. This attack was followed by strikes on six other forts and on colonial settlements along a swath of land from upstate New York to the area south of Lake Michigan, and along the Appalachian frontier, where settlers were entering Indian country. The attacks were initially successful; Pontiac and his allies captured several forts west of Detroit, with more than 400 British soldiers and 2,000 colonists killed or captured. British General Jeffrey Amherst was replaced by the more capable General Thomas Gage in August 1763. Bloodshed continued into 1764 when Pontiac's Rebellion was finally broken by Gage. Smaller skirmishes continued until the American Revolution.

16 PROCLAMATION OF 1763

Despite the fact that Great Britain left a standing army in America, George III declared he did not intend to use it to protect colonists from American Indian attacks west of the Appalachian Mountains. Pontiac's Rebellion made this gesture appear negligent especially because the American colonists who fought in the French and Indian War had done so largely to secure access to the lush soil of the Ohio River Valley. The king now said they could not have their prize. In fact, settlers who had already moved west of the crest of the Appalachians were supposed to return. As most of these were Scots-Irish Presbyterians, they were not about to return into the bosom of their Anglican mother country. Defiance of the Proclamation of 1763 stirred an attitude of defiance of British authority as well as expanded the horizons of colonists hungry for land.

> **PAXTON BOYS**
>
> A march led by Scots-Irish frontiersmen against the Quakers in power in Pennsylvania reached Philadelphia in 1764. Those on the frontier deposed the pacifist Quakers who did nothing to quell attacks by American Indians.

17 THE PAXTON BOYS

The Paxton Boys is the name given to frontier vigilantes in the 1760s. As early as the 1720s, farmers were settling beyond the crest of the Appalachian Mountains, in the backcountry of Pennsylvania, Virginia (in the area that would later become West Virginia), and North Carolina. Small-scale farmers in Pennsylvania specialized in growing wheat and experienced a higher standard of living than their counterparts in Europe. The Scotch-Irish farmers carried with them from Europe resentments toward British rule. In the aftermath of the French and Indian War and Pontiac's Rebellion, an armed group of these Scotch-Irish immigrants, named the Paxton Boys, organized raids against American Indians on the Pennsylvania frontier. In 1763, these raids included an attack on peaceful Conestoga Indians (many of them Christians) that resulted in 21 deaths. After the attacks on the Conestoga, in January 1764, about 250 Paxton Boys marched to Philadelphia to present their grievances to the Pennsylvania legislature. They presented a pamphlet of grievances to the legislature that reflected their bitterness toward the American Indians on the frontier of Pennsylvania, as well as their resentment of the Quaker elite of the colony for maintaining a lenient policy toward American Indians.

18 REGULATOR MOVEMENT

The War of the Regulation (1765–1771) again highlighted tensions between backcountry settlers and colonial elites. The Carolina Regulator Movement, composed of backcountry farmers in North and South Carolina, challenged the policies and practices of merchants, bankers, local officials, and the colonial government. The tensions came to a head between 1765 and 1771, when the movement took up arms against colonial authorities. A catalyst for the uprising was the collection of debts in these backcountry areas. After several years of drought and poor harvests, many farmers suffered income loss as well as shortages of basic supplies. They were forced to rely on local merchants and bankers to extend them credit and loans. The collection of debts was, the farmers contended, rife with corruption. The system of local court officials and sheriffs was perceived as an oppressive outside force. The actions of the Regulator Movement did not change the power structure in the Carolinas,

> **DANIEL BOONE**
>
> Daniel Boone, a veteran of the French and Indian War (1754–1763), came to personify the westward movement of colonists beyond the settled communities of the original thirteen colonies. He rose from obscurity to organize explorations into Kentucky in 1769, led a militia, and held positions in colonial government.

but it did establish patterns of thought and action that became evident in the coming years in the rebellion against British rule.

19 GREEN MOUNTAIN BOYS

This militia group was a classic example of frontiersmen and land speculators dissatisfied with eastern authority as they sought freedom and property in the west. In this case, Ethan Allen and others organized a resistance to the authority of New York in what would become the state of Vermont. Although considered outlaws by the British government in Albany, the Green Mountain Boys proved to be an effective militia force in the American Revolution, after which Vermont became a state.

ZENGER TRIAL

This seminal case solidified the principle of freedom of the press in New York. John Peter Zenger escaped prosecution for slander (1735) when a jury decided Zenger's criticism of the royal governor was true and thus could be put into print.

20 PATRICK HENRY

Another hero of frontier elements, this time in Virginia, was Patrick Henry. Henry started out as an innkeeper but became a lawyer and a fiery orator in the Virginia House of Burgesses. He first spoke against the king of England publicly in the Parson's Cause, a measure attempting to buttress an increasingly unpopular established church. As a Presbyterian, Henry viewed the king's unfair support of Anglican ministers as a violation of his compact binding him to look out for the interests of his subjects. He would later go on to deliver the famous, "Give me liberty, or give me death!" speech that ignited revolutionary support in Virginia and other colonies. Although an unswerving American patriot, he did not fancy the excessive centralization of power he perceived in the Constitutional Convention of 1787. He died within a decade of the ratification of the U.S. Constitution.

THE BIG PICTURE

1. As British political and economic philosophies continued to evolve, each change had lasting impact on the relationship between the mother country and her American colonies.

2. Strife arose when the British government twice attempted to exert stronger control over colonial America after many decades of inattention and lax enforcement.

3. After participating in three colonial wars on the side of the British, American colonists began to form a more independent identity and the beginnings of American societal and national unity.

4. Acts of Parliament and the attitude of several monarchs alienated Englishmen in the colonies who felt their rights were being abused or at least neglected as mercantilism and latent absolutism festered.

5. Several actual rebellions erupted that conveyed American colonists' willingness to resort to violence to seek redress of grievances, usually led by those on the frontier dissatisfied with the more conservative, loyalist eastern powers.

Mini Quiz

1. The largest organization of North American Indians in existence upon the arrival of European explorers and colonizers was the

    (A) Huron tribe located around the Great Lakes.
    (B) settlement of Cahokia in what would become Illinois.
    (C) Anasazi cultures in the Southwest.
    (D) Iroquois Nation in what would become New York.
    (E) Powhatan Confederacy of the Chesapeake region.

2. The most severe military conflict among European powers as colonization commenced existed between which two European countries?

    (A) England and France
    (B) England and Spain
    (C) Spain and Portugal
    (D) Spain and France
    (E) The Netherlands and France

3. What quality made New Spain unique among European colonies in the New World?

    (A) The presence of Roman Catholicism
    (B) The existence of a representative assembly
    (C) The monarch's strict bureaucratic control
    (D) Strong military presence
    (E) Peaceful relations with American Indians

4. The Europeans who first explored the length of the Mississippi River claimed it for which country?

    (A) England
    (B) France
    (C) The Netherlands
    (D) Portugal
    (E) Spain

5. The strength of joint-stock companies lay in which fact?

   (A) Large amounts of capital could be invested in risky enterprises with less individual risk.
   (B) Citizens of many European nations could pool their resources to fund joint ventures.
   (C) The genetic strengths of many strains of livestock could make stronger offspring.
   (D) Colonists did not have to worry about making a profit from their activities.
   (E) The English government was the chief source of funding for colonial companies.

6. Which document represented the first attempt at a written constitution in English history?

   (A) The Fundamental Constitution of Carolina
   (B) *Leviathan* by Thomas Hobbes
   (C) John Locke's Social Contract
   (D) The Magna Carta
   (E) The Mayflower Compact

7. The primary goal of the Massachusetts Bay Colony was to establish what?

   (A) A refuge for all the victims of religious persecution in England
   (B) A thriving colony based on shipping and harvesting fish and whales
   (C) A commonwealth with laws derived from Puritan doctrine
   (D) An agrarian society producing cash crops for market in Europe
   (E) A manufacturing center with basic industries and small farms

8. Most colonists to England's New World colonies arrived in America as

   (A) religious dissenters.
   (B) criminals and debtors released from prison.
   (C) second sons of the aristocracy fleeing primogeniture laws.
   (D) military conscripts.
   (E) indentured servants.

9. The English colony possessing the societal components most resembling modern American society was which colony?

   (A) Virginia
   (B) Pennsylvania
   (C) Plymouth
   (D) Georgia
   (E) Maryland

10. Most leaders in English colonies in America by 1750 came to be defined by which characteristics?

    (A) Wealth as a result of the American Dream
    (B) Distaste for organized religion
    (C) Aristocratic birth traced back to England
    (D) Competency and shrewdness proven in new challenges
    (E) Disregard for English cultural tastes

11. Religion in eighteenth-century colonial America more and more followed which trend?

    (A) The expansion of established churches to every colony
    (B) The complete religious toleration of all levels of belief or unbelief
    (C) A growing measure of democracy in church government
    (D) The increased respect for traditional doctrines of the Protestant Reformation
    (E) The insistence on having educated ministers who favored the Enlightenment

12. Mercantilism as an economic philosophy dictated that the

    (A) English government, rather than market forces, control the economy.
    (B) American colonists implement a balanced industrial and agrarian economy.
    (C) American colonists maintain a favorable balance of trade with the English people.
    (D) American colonists expand trade relations with all other European powers.
    (E) English economy focus mainly on providing resources to expand colonial holdings.

13. The French and Indian War

    (A) began in America but became a predominantly European conflict.
    (B) saw the English and the French ally against a coalition of American Indian tribes.
    (C) inspired the first successful central government for the American colonies.
    (D) was fought mostly by a professional English army shipped to America for the war.
    (E) settled the question as to which European power would control the Ohio River Valley.

14. After the French and Indian War, relations between colonists and American Indians

    (A)   generally improved.
    (B)   settled into an uneasy truce.
    (C)   escalated because of expansion of settlement west.
    (D)   experienced peaceful cultural exchanges for the first time.
    (E)   were ignored by the British government.

15. The conflicts that arose between the American colonies and the mother country occurred because of what new factor after 1760?
    (A)   The ascendancy to the throne of England by a weak monarch
    (B)   The crippling war debt resulting from England's ongoing resolve to beat the French
    (C)   The invasion of England for the first time by a French army that demanded terms
    (D)   The growing disunity among the thirteen American colonies because of English manipulation
    (E)   The growing desire on the part of most American colonists to return to English traditions

ANSWER EXPLANATIONS

1. **(D)** Both the Cahokia and Anasazi civilizations had disappeared before European arrival, and of the three other choices, the Iroquois Nation was the largest.

2. **(B)** All of these European nations were in conflict through the era of exploration and colonization, but the conflict between England and Spain prior to the defeat of the Spanish Armada in 1588 was a protracted war conducted over vast distances.

3. **(C)** Although both Spain and France were Catholic nations, only England had a colonial representative assembly. No colonies enjoyed entirely peaceful relations with American Indians and thus all had strong military presence throughout their colonial experience. Of all the colonies Spain achieved the most direct control by exerting the monarch's will through the Council of the Indies and the position of viceroys.

4. **(B)** Although Spanish explorer Hernando de Soto first discovered the Mississippi River, several French explorers eventually traversed its length and claimed the Mississippi Valley for France.

5. **(A)** Joint-stock companies were created by England and not open to broad European investment. They had nothing to do with livestock but did collect money from numerous investors and thereby kept any one investor from facing complete ruin. Colonists most assuredly were urged to make profits for these private, not government, ventures.

6. **(E)** Although the Magna Carta and other documents codified various rights of Englishmen, no attempt to form a government by writing down principles existed until the Mayflower Compact.

7. **(C)** Massachusetts Bay Colony was formed by Puritans for Puritans and predominantly for religious, not economic, reasons.

8. **(E)** Although all of these types of individuals settled in the New World, the chronic labor shortage and surplus population of England dictated that most American colonists arrived by 1700 as indentured servants.

9. **(B)** All colonies sowed key legacies into the American tradition, but early on Pennsylvania possessed all the attributes of the other colonies in one colony that closely resembled modern American society.

10. **(D)** Not all leaders in America were wealthy or high born, but most all were respected and thus elected because they exhibited competence. Most maintained some type of Christian profession in organized churches and most sought to be more, not less, like Englishmen back in England.

11. **(C)** The vagaries of the First Great Awakening undermined established churches and traditional doctrines and opened American Christianity to more democratic and less educated leadership. The heightened fervor of religious sentiment did not translate into widespread religious toleration.

12. **(A)** All other choices are either directly or indirectly the opposite of mercantilist doctrine.

13. **(E)** The French and Indian War began in and was largely fought in America by an army consisting of equal portions of colonists and regulars. England and her American Indian allies fought against France and the Huron Indians. Although the Albany Plan of Union was an attempt at a central government, it was unsuccessful.

14. **(C)** As a result of the winning of the Ohio River Valley from France, English colonists pushed westward and Pontiac's Rebellion resulted.

15. **(B)** William Pitt's resolve to pay for a victory led to the alienation through legislation enacted by Parliament and to taxation without representation for the American colonists.

The American Revolution and the War for Independence

7

*I know not what course others may take, but as for me,
give me liberty or give me death!*

—Patrick Henry's speech before the Virginia Assembly, 1775

TIMELINE	
1763	American colonists first boycott British goods
1764	Sugar Act
1765	Stamp Act
1765	Quartering Act
1766	American colonists form the Sons of Liberty; Declaratory Act
1767	Townshend Duties imposed
1770	Boston Massacre
1772	American colonists form Committees of Correspondence
1773	Boston Tea Party
1774	Coercive Acts; Quebec Act
1774	American colonies form first Continental Congress
1775	American colonies form second Continental Congress; Battles of Lexington and Concord
1776	*Common Sense* published; The Continental Congress adopts the Declaration of Independence
1777	Battle of Saratoga
1780	Battle of King's Mountain
1781	British General Cornwallis surrenders at Yorktown
1783	Treaty of Paris

OVERVIEW

The American Revolution was a monumental event in the history of the United States, as well as in world history. The American Revolution brought to the surface tensions that existed between the thirteen American colonies and the government of Great Britain. It also brought into existence a democratic republic. The democratic spirit that had animated the founding of the United States inspired movements for change—both within the United States and abroad. The governing structure that the American Revolution produced was not a perfect democracy. Americans have struggled with the meaning and extent of democracy for the intervening 240 years.

The decision to declare independence was not a foregone conclusion. Even in the decade before independence, most colonists considered themselves to be loyal subjects of the British monarch. It was only through a wrenching process that many colonists began to resist British authority and finally to break with Great Britain altogether. The Second Continental Congress formalized the break from Great Britain with the ratification of the Declaration of Independence. The eloquent preamble contains key elements of Enlightenment thinker John Locke's natural rights theory. It boldly states that "all men are created equal" and "endowed by their Creator with certain unalienable rights." If a government violates these rights, the people have the right "to alter or abolish it." These ideas have shaped democratic practices in the United States and beyond.

Even after fighting had begun between the colonists and the British, Americans were divided about their identity and their allegiance. Some colonists, known as "patriots," wanted independence, while others, known as "loyalists," wanted to retain ties to Great Britain. Of course, many colonists did not choose either side in the conflict. Both sides had good reasons for their stance—economic as well as emotional. Many colonists were convinced by the arguments put forth in Thomas Paine's pamphlet, *Common Sense* (January 1776) and by the Enlightenment ideas in the Declaration of Independence (July 1776), but loyalist sentiment remained through the end of the war.

Although the primary goal of the American Revolution was independence from Great Britain for the thirteen North American colonies, the rhetoric that was employed to justify the revolution inspired others to demand fundamental changes in society. Many called for the abolition of slavery and for greater political democracy in the new governing structures. The importance of women in the revolutionary struggle and Enlightenment ideas around equality set the stage for the evolution of ideas about gender. The ideal of "republican motherhood" emerged in the decades after the American Revolution (see Chapter 8).

The ideas of the American Revolution struck a chord among many different peoples struggling against oppressive regimes. In 1789, a little over a decade after the thirteen colonies declared independence, a revolution began in France. The French revolutionaries were inspired by some of the same Enlightenment ideas that had resonated with revolutionaries in America and by the American model itself. Two years after the French Revolution began, in 1791, a revolution occurred in Saint-Domingue (present-day Haiti), the western part of the Caribbean island of Hispaniola. This French colony was primarily a sugar-producing slave society, made up of half a million African slaves and 60,000 free people. The Haitian Revolution was the largest successful slave rebellion in human history. Of all the revolutions that occurred in the period after 1776, those in Latin America are most similar to the American Revolution. After all, in both situations, colonists decided to break long-held ties with European powers. Also, both the North American and the South American struggles for independence involved deep divisions within the respective colonial societies; rebels and loyalists clashed on both continents. Finally, both revolutionary struggles occurred in societies that included slavery.

1 SUGAR ACT

As early as 1764 Parliament set about trying to wring money from the colonies, and the Sugar Act was the first attempt to pass a law with the sole purpose of raising revenue. Although still a mercantilist, indirect tax on an enumerated commodity, sugar was the most lucrative commodity. Cleverly, the Sugar Act lowered the duties (taxes) on sugar in hopes that merchants would find it easier to go ahead and pay the tax rather than go to the trouble of smuggling, with the hopes that more revenue would actually reach the king's coffers. Certain other commodities were also regulated more stringently, making it clear to Americans that their economy was under the control of the British government whether that control was to their benefit or not.

2 STAMP ACT

This 1765 measure was Parliament's first attempt at a direct tax, a tax charged with no mercantilist justification of regulating trade. Colonists were supposed to purchase stamps to affix to all manner of legal documents, certificates, and licenses and to even humbler paper goods like playing cards and newspapers. The novelty of a direct tax and the pervasive extent of the proposed taxation met with universal opposition in America and prompted the cry, "No taxation without representation!" Resistance to the Stamp Act led to violent protests but also to the Stamp Act Congress, the first attempt since the Albany Plan of Union to gather colonial representatives and to air grievances. As a result of the opposition, Parliament did the worst possible thing if it intended to keep order—it backed down. No stamps were ever actually sold. Parliament did pass the Declaratory Act, though, which stated that it had the right to tax the colonists however it saw fit. Such a statement sounded like a petulant whimper to the colonists who soon sensed a chance for freedom.

3 SONS OF LIBERTY

This secret society was just one example of the revolutionary organizations that spontaneously formed to rally colonists to resist British authority. The Sons of Liberty led the resistance to the Stamp Act by committing acts of arson and vandalism in Boston, but chapters of the organization existed in almost every town. Prominent citizens led the meetings and planned the protests that were carried out by a cross-section of American society. In Boston, the Sons of Liberty also perpetrated the most infamous act of vandalism, the Boston Tea Party.

4 COMMITTEES OF CORRESPONDENCE

Originating in Boston under the auspices of Samuel Adams of the Sons of Liberty, this revolutionary network collected evidence of British abuses and circulated them widely over all of Massachusetts. Boycotts and other forms of resistance were coordinated through this type of communication including the publication of newspaper accounts and editorials. Newspapers became daily publications and more and more regularly used words like *independence* as a result of Adams's spreading the ideas of James Otis and other revolutionary thinkers. Ultimately, Committees of Correspondence were established across the thirteen colonies as the American Revolution reached its climax in the War for Independence.

5 BOYCOTTS

An important tactic of resistance to British policies included campaigns to halt the consumption of British-made goods. These boycotts, encouraged by the Committees of Correspondence through nonimportation and non-consumption agreements, occurred at different points in the 1760s and 1770s. Any American could contribute to the struggle by going without luxuries and even some items considered necessities. This method of protest highlighted the importance of the American colonies to the British economy as well as delineated loyalists from patriots. Boycotting of British goods first appeared during the protests against the Stamp Act in 1765. Many colonial leaders renewed their calls for boycotts of British goods after Great Britain imposed the Townshend Duties in 1767. The boycott movement gained strength throughout the thirteen colonies. One of the items boycotted was textiles, and American patriots were clearly discernable by their wearing of rougher, simpler clothes made at home, or homespun. Artisans benefitted from the boycott as Americans sought locally produced goods. These simple goods were seen as virtuous substitutes for extravagant British goods. The boycott movement opened additional avenues for women to participate in the movement to resist British policies. For example, many patriotic women engaged in producing homespun clothing.

6 DECLARATORY ACT

More of a whimper than a roar from the British lion, the Declaratory Act was passed by Parliament after it repealed the Stamp Act. The law boldly proclaimed that Parliament retained the right to tax the colonies, "in all cases whatsoever," but this pronouncement merely stirred the debate of actual versus virtual representation for the colonies in Parliament. Plus, coming after the stiff resistance in the Stamp Act Crisis, the Declaratory Act strongly resembled an exasperated parent lashing out verbally at a child who was no longer listening, and whatever respect for the British government that remained after the Stamp Act dissipated among those beginning the push for independence.

7 TOWNSHEND DUTIES

Charles Townshend was the latest in a series of ministers King George III went through trying to find a solution to the alienation created by legislation. Townshend's answer was to raise revenue by taxing particular commodities that colonists would have to buy from Britain because they couldn't produce them for themselves. He picked glass, lead, paper, paint, and tea. Nonimportation agreements, or boycotts, were so successful in shutting down the consumption of these goods among the colonies that most of the taxes were repealed. The lack of consumption was costing the British economy more than the taxes were bringing in for the government. Still, Parliament kept one tax in place as another reminder of their authority. The commodity chosen was tea, and Americans' love affair with coffee dates back to their decision to sidestep this token of direct taxation without actual representation.

8 QUARTERING ACT

Speaking of direct taxation, the Quartering Act was the most creative example hatched in Parliament's schemes both to raise money and to exert colonial control. Colonists were saddled with the duty to house and feed soldiers, the clearest manifestation of British desire to pass on the costs of protecting the American colonies with a standing army to those being protected. The installing of military personnel in private homes, however, was also a means of surveillance as the British government attempted to ferret out revolutionary leaders or to observe their movements and the schedule of their meetings.

9 BOSTON MASSACRE

The tension created by British actions and American reactions had to break out in serious violence somewhere, and Boston was the most likely spot. A handful of soldiers were assailed there by a mob hurling projectiles at them; scared for their lives, the soldiers fired into the crowd. Thus began the auspicious decade of the 1770s. Five people received mortal wounds, and the army averted a larger massacre only by withdrawing from the city, another fateful concession. While John Adams sought to prove American fairness by getting the soldiers acquitted, his cousin Sam Adams and silversmith Paul Revere turned the event into a propaganda bonanza. Revere's engraving of the incident did not reveal the mob's provocation but portrayed British regimentation of cold-blooded killing.

10 BOSTON TEA PARTY

In 1773, the first of many planned shipments of tea by the East India Company arrived in Boston. The company had recently been given a monopoly on the trade through the Tea Act. Colonists refused to pay the import tax left by the Townshend Duties, and the ship captain refused to leave until it was paid. Samuel Adams led a meeting where it was determined that the tea should be destroyed, and men disguised as Mohawk Indians worked all night to dump the £10,000 worth of tea in the harbor. This act of vandalism prompted Parliament to punish Boston with the Coercive Acts.

11 COERCIVE ACTS

The Coercive Acts, known in America as the Intolerable Acts, were a series of laws passed in 1774 designed to shut down revolutionary actions in Boston as a result of the 1773 Boston Tea Party. The port was closed and martial law was enacted giving Thomas Gage control. General Gage used his power to take over public buildings and to otherwise enforce the Quartering Act and the punitive measures of the Coercive Acts. As news of these events spread, other colonies sent supplies for the relief of Boston, a step that further united the colonies in opposition to British oppression.

12 QUEBEC ACT

Despite the severity of the more well-known acts of Parliament like the two that follow, some historians believe the 1774 Quebec Act was the most odious to American colonists. The measure certainly found its way into the Declaration of Independence, on the heels of the First

Great Awakening. The concessions made to the Roman Catholic French colonists still living in Canada were disturbing to the largely Protestant Americans. Parliament granted toleration to the Catholics in return for which the French gave up the right of local self-rule in exchange for a centralized local council answerable directly to the British government, something akin to the Council of the Indies in the Spanish Empire. Trial by a jury was also abolished in civil cases. Apart from these political and religious scruples, the dramatic enlarging of Canada down to the Ohio River again arbitrarily kept Americans from the luscious land they had fought for in the French and Indian War. The Second Continental Congress made the charge in the Declaration of Independence that the Quebec Act was merely a trial run for what England had in mind for her British subjects in America.

13 LEXINGTON AND CONCORD

Such a tense situation could not last long without the outbreak of serious violence. American militiamen gathered weapons and prepared to defend their rights. By 1775, Gage determined to confiscate the weapons rumored to be at Concord, Massachusetts. Warned by Paul Revere and others that the British were coming, groups of minutemen gathered to await developments. After skirmishes in Concord, around four thousand American militiamen gathered at various points to assail the British troops marching back to Lexington. Of the seven hundred British soldiers making the expedition, 273 were killed, wounded, or missing at the day's end. When compared to the ninety-three American casualties, these running skirmishes encouraged the colonists and convinced the British that more repressive measures were necessary.

> **OLIVE BRANCH PETITION**
>
> The Continental Congress formally professed loyalty to the British Crown in this document but asked George III to part with corrupt government ministers and seek reconciliation and end bloodshed. The king of England instead declared his colonies in America to be in open rebellion.

14 CONTINENTAL CONGRESS

After a largely unsuccessful first attempt at organizing a central government in 1774, a Second Continental Congress convened in Philadelphia in 1775 in the wake of the first armed conflicts. Those known as the Founding Fathers gathered as representatives of their respective colonies. John Hancock ultimately rose as the president of the congress, and George Washington, a representative from Virginia, was asked to take command of a Continental Army. The Second Continental Congress was the legislative body that, after some prompting, eventually issued the Declaration of Independence, the Articles of Confederation, the dollar as a currency, and otherwise led the colonies through the Revolutionary War.

15 *COMMON SENSE*

The Second Continental Congress was prompted to action by the popularity of this eloquent propaganda pamphlet written by Thomas Paine. Rather than writing a scholarly treatise of political philosophy as John Adams and others had done, Paine appealed to the common masses quoting only the Bible as a source (although Paine himself rejected Christianity). The compelling themes of the piece were that kings by their nature were evil and that an island like Britain should not rule over a continent like North America. The essay went through many printings and served to drum up support for the eventual move toward independence by the Congress.

16 DECLARATION OF INDEPENDENCE

This document placed in writing the values derived from the American colonial experience and the Enlightenment theories emanating from Europe in contradistinction to the arbitrary and oppressive acts of King George III and Parliament. Drafted by a committee consisting of Thomas Jefferson, John Adams, Benjamin Franklin, and others, it was adopted by the Second Continental Congress in the summer of 1776 after the Revolutionary War was under way with the Battle of Bunker Hill. As a sophisticated form of propaganda, the Declaration moved enough of the colonial population to support the war to make independence a reality. As a statement of the American ideals of equality and freedom that included, "life, liberty, and the pursuit of happiness," this birth certificate of the United States of America established goals that have stimulated the pursuit of human rights around the globe.

17 ABIGAIL ADAMS

As many colonists were more openly embracing a formal break with Great Britain, groups and individuals within America were rethinking other relationships regarding social class, race, and gender. This rethinking was evident in a private letter that Abigail Adams sent to her husband, John. Adams's letter expressed hope that John and other leaders of the patriot cause formulate a new legal framework that includes women on an equal footing with men. "I desire you would remember the ladies and be more generous and favorable to them than your ancestors." She requested that the new legal system "not put such unlimited power into the hands of the husbands." Some historians have dismissed the letter, and John's response, as a humorous exchange between intimates. However, in the context of other writings by Abigail Adams, it is clear that gender equality was an issue she took seriously. The letter is especially significant in the context of the American Revolution. The experience of women participating in the struggle for independence, from organizing boycotts to aiding men on the battlefield, engendered a sense of egalitarianism among many women and men. In addition, the rhetoric of the revolutionary era railed against tyrannical rule. Many found analogies between the tyranny of king over subject and the tyranny of husband over wife.

> ## VALLEY FORGE
>
> This base for Washington's army was where they spent the winter of 1777–1778 in Pennsylvania. The deprivations the soldiers experienced caused hundreds to die and over one thousand to desert.

18 BATTLE OF SARATOGA

The Battle of Saratoga in 1777 is considered an important turning point in the American Revolution. British general John Burgoyne attempted a convergence of three British armies in upstate New York. The British hoped to cut off rebellious New England from the rest of the colonies by gaining control of the Hudson River Valley. This planned assembling of an overwhelming force was thwarted, however, by assaults on the British columns from the north and west by Continental forces. British reinforcements from the south never materialized; British General William Howe diverted 5,000 troops to launch an assault on Philadelphia rather than march northward from New York City. Thus, Burgoyne met superior numbers at Saratoga under the command of Horatio Gates and wound up surrendering his whole force. The news of the battle was eagerly received by Patriot-minded Americans. The battle made it evident that the British

> ## BATTLE OF KING'S MOUNTAIN
>
> The Battle of King's Mountain proved to be the most significant battle on the frontier. Elements of the British Army under General Cornwallis were surprised by a contingent of sharpshooting frontiersmen who had crossed the Appalachian Mountains. The surrender of British forces in the battle led Cornwallis to abandon his southern campaign.

might be able to control urban centers, like New York City, but it would be very difficult for the British to control the vast wilderness of the North American interior. The battle was a setback for some leaders within the Iroquois Confederacy who had hoped a strong British presence in upstate New York would limit encroachments by colonists onto their lands. Most importantly, the battle also showed France that the colonists were a formidable force.

YORKTOWN

The final military conflict of the war occurred at Yorktown, Virginia in 1781. General Cornwallis's troops were trapped as they attempted an evacuation by sea. Peace negotiations began after a few smaller operations bottled up the remaining British forces.

19 ALLIANCE WITH FRANCE

One of the most important factors in the victory of the Continental Army over British forces was the direct support of the French military. Great Britain was initially in a strong position to end the American Revolution and destroy the Continental Army in the mid-Atlantic colonies between 1776 and 1778. The fact that the Continental Army was able to survive during this period, coupled with its stunning victory at Saratoga in 1777, convinced several European powers that the Washington's army was a force to be reckoned with. As early as 1776, the Continental Congress had dispatched diplomats to Europe to win formal recognition from potential allies. In 1778, these new developments, coupled with the diplomatic overtures of Benjamin Franklin, led powerful France to formally recognize the United States and to assist the Continental Army in the war effort. French naval and expeditionary forces, along with able military leaders such as the Marquis de Lafayette forces and competent leadership, were instrumental in bringing about the surrender of British forces.

20 TREATY OF PARIS

To the astonishment of the world the United States had held on through eight years of battles against the superior British military. Negotiations in Paris ended the war in 1783 and recognized American independence. The boundaries of the new country were set from the Atlantic Ocean to the Mississippi River and from Canada to Florida. This territory was larger than the Americans had even dreamed and finally secured for them access to westward expansion in the Ohio River Valley and beyond.

THE BIG PICTURE

1. The British government changed its administrative policies for a second time in a way that was perceived by American colonists to be unfairly restraining their prosperity without granting representation in Parliament.

2. A gradual increase in American resistance to British authority was organized by revolutionary leaders in response to repeated increases in taxes and restrictions on the American economy and on the personal liberty of colonists.

3. As tensions mounted, so did preparations on both sides for armed conflict resulting in outbreaks of both mob violence and actual military clashes.

4. The American Revolution consisted of numerous ideas regarding justice and political philosophy that resulted from a history of societal change throughout the colonial period.

5. The War for Independence was the military climax to the American Revolution and proved to be a protracted struggle among several nations resulting from ongoing mercantilist competition and latent animosity from earlier wars of empire.

The Critical Period and the Formation of American Values

8

All sober inquiries after truth, ancient and modern,
pagan and Christian, have declared that the happiness
of man, as well as his dignity, consists in virtue.

—John Adams, *Thoughts on Government . . .* , 1776

TIMELINE	
1776	American women take on new role of republican motherhood
1781	The new United States ratifies the Articles of Confederation
1783	Revolutionary War veterans found the Order of the Cincinnati
1783–1789	The United States endures the Critical Period between the Articles of Confederation and the U.S. Constitution
1785	The Continental Congress passes the Land Ordinance
1786–1787	Shays's Rebellion erupts
1787	The Continental Congress passes the Northwest Ordinance; Constitutional Convention takes place in Philadelphia; Delegates form the Great Compromise giving equal representation of states in Congress; Delegates form the Three-fifths Compromise over slavery and representation
1788	The United States ratifies the U.S. Constitution
1789	The United States government begins under the U.S. Constitution; James Madison enters the House of Representatives

OVERVIEW

The optimistic spirit of the American Revolution was evident in the culture and institutions that developed in the United States in the 1780s. Americans perceived their fellow citizens as civic minded and politically thoughtful. Many political-minded Americans looked back to the Roman Republic as inspiration for creating a modern republic. The optimism of many Americans was also a reflection of the material reality of living in the new country. The degree of social mobility was much higher in the United States than in Europe at the time. People in the new country could expect to rise above the station in life to which they were born. Individuals, through diligence and shrewdness, could rise from obscurity and poverty to greatness. Though the term "American dream" has been the subject of much debate and contention in recent decades, a basic element of it has been this high degree of social mobility. At the same time, the nation was faced with a series of threats from within and from abroad that threatened its very existence. Historians described the 1780s as America's critical period, both because it was important in terms of America's future and because the nation was seen as being in critical condition—it's very future was in doubt. By the end of the decade, the nation had shifted directions in regard to governing structure.

The decade began with the ratification of the Articles of Confederation (1781), which created a "firm league of friendship" among the states rather than a strong, centralized nation. Before 1776, colonists had lived under a powerful, distant authority and they did not want to repeat that experience. Also, many of these early leaders were fiercely loyal to their states and did not want to see state power taken away. Under the Articles, the United States faced serious economic problems. The Confederation government and the states printed millions of dollars worth of paper money, driving up inflation. In addition, the government borrowed millions of dollars during the war. After the war, the government had trouble paying off these debts and was structurally prohibited from directly levying taxes. The Confederation Congress also faced several foreign policy challenges during the Critical Period. The United States did not, for the most part, resolve these problems in a satisfactory way. To some degree the Articles of Confederation failed to unify the thirteen states and failed to allow the United States to speak with a strong, united voice.

The Confederation Congress was not without success. It made important progress in incorporating the country's western lands, persuading various states to abandon claims to lands between the Appalachian Mountains and the Mississippi River. Once the western lands came under the control of the national government, Congress set about passing a series of acts to clarify the status of these lands.

Despite some shining moments, by 1786 many Americans, especially elite property owners, began to raise concerns about the competency of such a weak central government and the stature of the United States on the world stage. With these concerns in mind, a group of reformers got approval from Congress to meet in Annapolis, Maryland, in 1786 to discuss possible changes to the Articles of Confederation. A follow-up meeting was scheduled to be held in Philadelphia for the following May (1787). In between these meetings, Shays' Rebellion erupted among farmers in Massachusetts (August 1786–February 1787). It was eventually put down, but it added fuel to the impetus to reform the governing structure. By the time of the Philadelphia meeting, the delegates were ready to scrap the entire Articles of Confederation and write something new. For four months, delegates met, argued, and wrote. These deliberations resulted in a series of compromises that formed the basis of the Constitution.

1 REPUBLIC

The form of government chosen by the founders of the United States was that of a republic. Most of the men prominent in the formation of the country were scholars familiar with republican precedents from the classical world and saw the United States as the new manifestation of political wisdom and self-government, hence the return to classical architectural styles for public buildings. The United States was technically not a democracy but a democratic republic. Power was vested in the people who were supposed to vote for representatives who then made and enforced laws. The "ruler" of a republic was designed to be the law that represented the will of the people and to which all the people, including the representatives, were subject as a part of a social contract. These provisions were thought to make a republic the least likely form of government to degenerate into either mob rule or tyranny. The Founding Fathers understood such a system to have hope of success only when the citizenry was moral and responsible.

CIVIC VIRTUE

With the formation of the American republic came the idea that democracy depended on the commitment of all citizens to work for the common good. Civic virtue asked of all Americans that they work for and even sacrifice for general societal well-being.

---

2 YEOMAN FARMERS

This class of people made up the bulk of the population for at least the first one hundred years of U.S. history once the Declaration of Independence and the Treaty of Paris established the country. Cheap, or free, land led native-born Americans and immigrants alike to push west to secure enough property to subsist as farmers with hopes of making small profits from cash crops in the future. The combination of land fever and the notion of the American Dream were powerful forces that set off large-scale migration and enough confidence in the opportunity for many farmers to go into debt to establish their holdings. The enterprising nature of the venture along with all the hard work necessary for the clearing of land and the establishment of agriculture led Thomas Jefferson to venerate this simple stock of rural Americans as the key citizens of the new republic.

3 STATE CONSTITUTIONS

As the Revolution was taking place, states decided to write down governing constitutions. This, in and of itself, represented a break with the English tradition of having an unwritten constitution. Most of the framers of state constitutions initially limited the power of the executive, perhaps recalling the arbitrary nature of governance under the British monarchy. Some state constitutions were quite radical in their embrace of democracy. The Pennsylvania constitution eliminated property qualifications for voting and abolished the office of governor altogether. Virginia, along with Pennsylvania, abolished the upper house of the legislature. The upper house of a legislative body was seen as an instrument of the elite, like the House of Lords in Great Britain. Many other states strengthened the lower house and made it more responsive to the will of the people through more frequent elections. Most state constitutions contained a bill of rights to limit governmental intrusions upon basic liberties. By the end of the decade, however, most states revised their constitutions to strengthen the executive office and limit democratic participation. For example, most constitutions called for a set yearly salary for the governor so that his compensation wouldn't be subject to the whims of elected legislatures.

4 CRITICAL PERIOD

From the ratification of the Articles of Confederation to the ratification of the U.S. Constitution was a time of great peril for the fledgling country. The vagaries of the Revolutionary War were such as to make the formation of a viable central government impossible. When the war ended in 1783, the government found itself unequal to the task of keeping the newly united states working together for the good of all. Enough time transpired without an internal or external disaster, however, for leaders to go back to the drawing board and come up with a more lasting form of government that has been the basis of American stability and prosperity ever since.

5 ARTICLES OF CONFEDERATION

Written by the same committee that wrote the Declaration of Independence, this document called into being a "league of friendship" among the thirteen states. Because of certain weaknesses in this first draft of a government, the centralized government and national unity were unraveling by the war's end. A lack of a system of taxation, poor interstate economic controls, and the absence of a sound national currency or even an executive branch in the government all doomed the Articles of Confederation to failure. Certain successes, however, allowed the country to survive the critical period. The Congress got all the states to give their western land claims to the central government as a source of income from land sales. The view that the articles needed revision led to the Annapolis Convention; the realization that a total revision was necessary led to the Constitutional Convention.

6 ORDER OF THE CINCINNATI

Named after an ancient Roman hero, Cincinnatus, this attempt at a secret society of Revolutionary War officers ran counter to the societal and political trends that set the American Revolution in motion. Some within the Order flirted with the notion of establishing themselves as a landed aristocracy for their service in the war. They even contemplated making George Washington King George I of America. George Washington himself squashed this idea, although the Order remained. His deterrence of this movement staved off the formation of a noble class and allowed America to live up to its revolutionary and republican rhetoric.

7 LAND AND NORTHWEST ORDINANCES

These measures for organization of western lands were the most successful outcomes of the government under the Articles of Confederation. Congress appropriated the lands of the Ohio River Valley extending up to the Great Lakes, the territory known as the Old Northwest, and called for it to be surveyed and sold. To this day the orderly survey lines on this flat topography are visible from the air in the forms of a grid of crisscrossed roads dividing the land into sections called townships. The ordinances also established two crucial precedents in American life. One square of each township's land was sold with the proceeds going to support education, a mainstay of republican life. The other precedent was that Congress under the Articles of Confederation banned slavery from the entire territory. Abraham Lincoln would later point to this step as a turning point in the slavery question for the whole nation.

8 PENITENTIARY

As the word implies, these prisons were established as places for criminals to be penitent. The system of solitary confinement with only the Bible as reading material bespoke the optimism inherent in American society as a result of the successful American Revolution. Republics, it was thought, had the power and the duty to improve the lives of all citizens, even criminals. Although solitary confinement is considered a more stringent form of punishment today, in the eighteenth century it was merciful and hopeful. The European propensity for capital punishment lampooned in *A Tale of Two Cities* by Charles Dickens as late as the nineteenth century was largely done away with in the United States. Fewer and fewer crimes were eligible for executions, and a higher percentage of the American population resided in penitentiaries. The reform of the criminal justice system was just the beginning of a long series of reform movements that tried, and try, to work out the principles of the American Revolution and the First and Second Great Awakenings in American life.

9 REPUBLICAN MOTHERHOOD

Societal reform started at home. Whereas American women would wrestle with second-class citizen status well into the twentieth century, a new perspective on the role of women was a result of revolutionary principles. Since a republic would only survive with a moral, responsible citizenry actively placing the common good over individual desires, American mothers were looked upon as sacred instruments in nurturing the future. This status also implied greater importance of children than had ever been contemplated by the masses. The outworking of the American Dream implied that any mother could be raising a great statesman, inventor, general, or artist.

10 TARIFFS

A long history of taxing imported goods has seen the rising and falling of tariffs, or customs duties, throughout U.S. history. The need for tariffs arose from the history of the American colonies as sources of raw materials and agricultural products. When the United States sought to increase its domestic manufacturing, tariffs leveled the playing field by making imported manufactured goods more expensive, thus allowing domestic manufacturers to compete. Tariffs became most popular with northerners whose diversified economies permitted the first widespread pursuit of manufacturing. Under the Articles of Confederation, states in the United States charged tariffs on other states. As time passed, the tariff became a disputed issue between the North, which wanted a strong protective tariff, and the South, which disliked tariffs because they offended their customers and made their own manufactured goods more expensive even if purchased from the northern manufacturers on their side of the Atlantic.

11 SHAYS'S REBELLION

In 1786 the state legislature of Massachusetts refused to issue a paper currency or to provide other relief for farmers struggling under mounting debts. Mob violence erupted that eventually coalesced into an armed rebellion under former Revolutionary War captain Daniel Shays. Shays's men numbered over 1,200, and their campaign lasted into 1787 when they nearly captured the federal arsenal at Springfield, Massachusetts. State militia forces put down the rebellion and captured Shays who was ultimately pardoned. The state legislature made it easier for farmers to seek relief in the courts, lowered taxes, and enacted policies that prevented destitution of farmers in debt trouble. The episode coincided with the onset of the Constitutional Convention and served as an impetus for strengthening the central government.

12 CONSTITUTIONAL CONVENTION

This meeting in Philadelphia in 1787 is the direct or indirect basis for the rest of American history. A fortunate collection of brilliant minds like those of James Madison, Benjamin Franklin, and Alexander Hamilton were assembled under the leadership of George Washington. These men knit together the strands of political philosophy spun by the Enlightenment and by the practical experience most of the representatives had in their home states. Noble and ignoble compromises were reached to maintain unity. A system of checks and balances was put in place to distribute power in the federal government over three branches—executive, legislative, and judiciary. Debates lasted from May to December when the process of ratification began. By June of 1788 the ninth state ratified the U.S. Constitution making it the supreme law of the land.

13 JAMES MADISON

A young understudy of Thomas Jefferson was writing drafts for the Virginia state constitution while Jefferson was writing the draft of the Declaration of Independence. From there, Madison had a hand in nearly all of the processes discussed above for Virginia as the new state made its transition from the first colony to one of the most populous of the United States. He is considered the Father of the U.S. Constitution because he drafted the Virginia Plan, the winning side in most matters, as well as the Bill of Rights. He contributed to the influential Federalist Papers discussed in Chapter 9, but later split with the Federalist Party over policy issues. He served as both secretary of state (under Jefferson) and president through some of the most important formative years, including those of the War of 1812. Madison, then, could be said to have seen Virginia and the United States through two wars for independence and through the critical period. Madison's notes on the proceedings of the Constitutional Convention are the largest portion of history's knowledge of that gathering because the Convention's deliberations were kept secret.

14 U.S. CONSTITUTION

Whereas other documents could claim status as the birth certificate of the United States, this document ranked as the crowning achievement of the American Revolution. The Preamble bespoke the very nature of a republic with its opening words, "We the People. . . ." Few other documents have altered world history more than this one, which established a stable government and pulled the new country back from the abyss of dissolution. Debates raged as to its actual motives, but the governmental instructions therein have served to guide the American people through numerous crises and through the vagaries of changing societal values. The U.S. Constitution contains within it the method whereby it can be amended, a process resorted to relatively few times in history. That fact alone attests to the powerful insights into human nature and political science with which the United States was blessed at this crucial juncture.

15 NEW JERSEY PLAN

Espoused by William Patterson of New Jersey, this plan is otherwise known as the small-state plan in that it represented the interests of the less populous states. Patterson believed the Articles of Confederation could be revised by fixing the more glaring errors of a lack of power vested in Congress to tax or to regulate commerce. He proposed an executive be elected, but would not have provided the president with a veto. In short, the small states were suspicious of their larger sister states and of a strong central government. In all matters of representation, the New Jersey Plan called for equal representation for each state as had been done through the Articles of Confederation that gave each state one vote in Congress regardless of size.

16 VIRGINIA PLAN

Drafted by James Madison but presented by another, this proposal favored an entirely new government over a revised Articles of Confederation. The outline of what would eventually become the U.S. Constitution was clearly recognizable in this plan although several provisions would be revised. All in all, however, the small states recognized that the policies proposed in the Virginia Plan would benefit large states like Virginia and New York the most.

17 ENUMERATED POWERS

Each article of the U.S. Constitution dealing with a branch of the government lists, or enumerates, several key powers or duties for the specific branches. Sometimes these powers overlap with those of other branches and with state law; others are reserved just to a particular branch or to the federal government as a whole. For example, the U.S. Constitution took away any ability of a state to have a separate foreign policy and directly assigned the administration of foreign policy to the executive branch with the consent of the Senate, which had to ratify all treaties that might be negotiated by a president or his appointees. The extent to which the Constitution limits these powers to those expressly stated in the document, or expands them to those implied by the document, is one of the problematic aspects of constitutional law and thus part of the origin of America's two-party political system.

18 CHECKS AND BALANCES

All three branches of the federal government were given by the U.S. Constitution the power to hold other branches in check as each branch sought to fulfill its duties listed in its enumerated powers. The balance would be created by both support and opposition among the branches. For example, the Supreme Court is staffed through nominations of the executive branch that must be accepted by the legislative branch before becoming legitimate. The Supreme Court can, in turn, advise the other branches on the legality of their activities. The clearest mechanisms to balance the branches are the president's veto power over laws passed by the legislative branch and the ability of Congress to override presidential vetoes. As James Madison explained in Federalist No. 51, "If men were angels, no government would be necessary. If angels were to govern men, neither external nor internal controls on government

> **ELASTIC CLAUSE**
>
> Within Article I, Section VIII of the proposed constitution is an opening for the expansion of federal power. The "necessary and proper" clause said the Congress could make laws to carry out its enumerated powers, thus granting the federal government implied powers.

would be necessary." The checks and balances inherent in the U.S. Constitution, although sometimes ignored, have always proven to be necessary in the end.

19 THE GREAT COMPROMISE

Championed at the Constitutional Convention by Roger Sherman of Connecticut, this agreement was the crucial compromise that saved the union. The argument was over proportional versus equal representation in the Congress. Sherman suggested that the U.S. Senate consist of two senators from each state, thereby ensuring equal representation in this body responsible for war and peace. The House of Representatives would comprise representatives from the states based on the population within each state, and all were assured at least one congressman regardless of size. With this hurdle out of the way, the Convention could move toward final drafting and ratification.

RATIFICATION

This process by which states were asked by the federal Congress to approve the new constitution employed special state conventions. When New Hampshire, in June 1788, became the required ninth state to ratify the U.S. Constitution, it became the "supreme law of the land."

20 THREE-FIFTHS COMPROMISE

Most of the southern slaveholding states were plagued by a handicap in smaller populations due to the rural nature of their society created by their cash-crop economy. When the Great Compromise was adopted these states proposed the counting of their slaves for representation in the House of Representatives. The North reduced the impact of this hypocritical provision by allowing only the counting of three-fifths of the southern states' slaves. Although this agreement permitted unity, it also indirectly sanctioned slavery.

THE BIG PICTURE

1. Once the American people won independence from Great Britain, the cultural trends of the colonial period were manifested in a new, optimistic outlook and the formation of an entirely unique society.

2. Every aspect of American life, from social class mobility to romantic love, was tinged with this new optimism, and every American expected his or her life to be better than that of the previous generation.

3. The difficulty to maintain national unity under the Articles of Confederation led to a revision of the American government that increased the power of the federal government while allowing the states to retain some autonomy.

4. The U.S. Constitution was the result of the development of both theoretical and practical political philosophy over many centuries of history in Western civilization.

5. The government under the new constitution divided power into three branches and provided ways for the three branches, the large and small states, and the northern and southern states to compromise in order to pull the country through the critical period.

The Federalist Age

9

*Real liberty is neither found in despotism or the extremes
of democracy, but in moderate governments.*

—Alexander Hamilton, 1787

TIMELINE	
1787–1788	*The Federalist Papers* are published in newspapers
1789	George Washington is elected as the first president; Strict versus Loose Construction debates begin
1790	Alexander Hamilton becomes secretary of the Treasury
1791	The U.S. Congress charters the Bank of the United States; The states ratify the Bill of Rights
1794	Whiskey Rebellion
1795	The United States and Great Britain sign Jay's Treaty
1796	The United States and American Indian chiefs sign the Treaty of Greenville; The United States and Spain sign Pinckney's Treaty; Newspapers publish Washington's Farewell Address; John Adams is elected president
1798	XYZ Affair with France; Federalists pass the Alien and Sedition Acts
1798–1799	Anti-Federalists (Jeffersonian Republicans) pass the Kentucky and Virginia Resolutions

OVERVIEW

The 1790s was an important period in the shaping of the U.S. political system. The Constitution had just been completed (1787), ratified (1788), and put into effect (1789). Debates over the Constitution led to the adoption of the Bill of Rights (1791) as Americans continued to debate the proper balance between liberty and order. The government was reconstituted to conform with the Constitution—three branches of government and a system of checks and balances. Very quickly, President Washington established the authority of the new federal government by emphatically putting down a rebellion of farmers in western Pennsylvania; he was determined to avoid a replay of Shays's Rebellion, which dragged on for several months (1786–1787).

It was during this period that many of the American political system's traditions and precedents—collectively known as the "unwritten Constitution"—were established. We see the development of political parties during this period. The Federalist Party and the Democratic-Republican Party constituted the first of several two-party systems in American history. The Federalist Party, which developed around the ideas of President Washington's Secretary of the Treasury, Alexander Hamilton, was more influential in the 1790s than the Democratic-Republicans. The rival Democratic-Republicans, commonly called the Republicans, developed around the ideas of Washington's Secretary of State, Thomas Jefferson. The relationship between the parties became more acrimonious as the decade progressed.

Alexander Hamilton proposed a series of economic measures meant to put the United States on sound economic footing. These measures included paying off outstanding government debt and encouraging manufacturing. To raise revenue for these expenditures, Hamilton proposed a controversial excise tax on whiskey and other distilled spirits. One of Hamilton's proposals, for the Bank of the United States, led to intense debates around the powers of the federal government under the new Constitution.

Tensions between the U.S. government and American Indians intensified in the 1790s. Following the American Revolution, thousands of settlers pushed beyond the Appalachian Mountains into the Ohio River valley. After 1790, they were pushing north into territory that was fully claimed by its American Indian inhabitants. A series of military conflicts in the Ohio territory in the 1790s ensued, leading to the Treaty of Greenville, which provided a temporary respite from the fighting.

Despite America's intention to be independent of European affairs, events in Europe greatly impacted the newly formed United States. Just as Americans were ratifying the Constitution in 1789, the French Revolution was beginning. Americans were divided over France's revolution. Divisions over the French Revolution were one of the causes of the formation of rival political parties. The debates took on greater significance after France and Great Britain went to war in 1793. A bitter debate occurred in America about its role in European conflicts. Ultimately, President Washington chose to remain neutral, signing the 1793 Neutrality Act and urging the United States to avoid permanent alliances with foreign powers in his Farewell Address. The United States resolved conflicts with Great Britain (Jay's Treaty) and Spain (Pinckney's Treaty). However, later in the decade, the United States became entangled with France, as disputes over shipping and diplomatic tensions led to the brief Quasi-War between the two nations. In the context of this conflict, Congress, dominated by the Federalist Party, passed the Alien and Sedition Acts (1798), raising the perennial question of the degree to which the government may limit civil liberties during times of crisis. Outraged Republicans, in turn, asserted that certain actions by the federal government could be nullified by state legislatures. The issue of states' rights in the face of federal authority would not be resolved until the following century.

1 FEDERALIST PARTY

The leaders who formed this first political party in American history were originally merely nationalists, or those who wanted a stronger central government to keep the United States united. Through the process of ratification of the U.S. Constitution it became apparent that they had banking and commercial interests and the desire to establish the credit of the government on a sound footing. Alexander Hamilton and John Adams masterminded the formation of their party, but even James Madison helped long enough to see the Constitution ratified. George Washington aligned himself in almost all matters with the Federalist Party, but his status as the Indispensible Man kept him somewhat above political party wrangling, which he despised. The Federalists were pro-British in foreign policy and fought to establish the Bank of the United States. Their stance on interpretation of the Constitution was loose construction, and they sought to increase the power of the federal government.

2 ANTI-FEDERALIST PARTY

The first reactionary political coalition as evidenced by its name, the Anti-Federalists formed around the genius of Thomas Jefferson. His beloved yeoman farmers, or the bulk of the population of the South and the West, rallied to him in an eventual government takeover by 1800. Until then they grumbled under the Federalist yoke, that is, they endured policies that were strict on the paying of debts and the establishment of a sound currency. Anti-Federalists wanted to hold the central government in check by using strict construction, the interpretation of the U.S. Constitution denying there were many implied powers and focusing mainly on the enumerated powers. To Hamilton's philosophy that if it doesn't say we can't, we can, the Anti-Federalists replied that if it doesn't say we can, we can't do it. The debate over the Bank of the United States was the first major testing ground for these principles, and for a time the Anti-Federalists (otherwise known by then as the Jeffersonian Republicans) gave ground. In foreign policy, they were pro-French, especially after the French Revolution. As to the economic future of the United States, Jefferson and his party hoped the country would remain agrarian and rural.

3 GEORGE WASHINGTON

The Indispensible Man was called such because of his status as the heroic champion of freedom coupled with the civility and wisdom cultivated in him as the son of one of the first families of Virginia. Less a brilliant military or political strategist than a fine judge of the capacities of other men, Washington promoted the career of Alexander Hamilton as well as those of Thomas Jefferson and James Madison. His presence on the battlefield or in the Constitutional Convention created confidence and clarity. As president he despised party politics but endured them as necessary evils. He established isolationism as the foreign policy stance of the young nation, and he knew that everything he did as the first president, especially because he was elected unanimously by the Electoral College, would set crucial precedents. For example, his choosing to retire from politics after two terms as president was followed by all presidents facing that question until Franklin Roosevelt. Then the Constitution was amended to codify Washington's wisdom. He was the perfect example of a selfless leader of a republic who sacrificed his own desires for the good of the country, but he was also human and a product of his times. He owned slaves and even spirited them away in the bottom of the presidential residence in Philadelphia, but he did release all his slaves upon his death.

4 ALEXANDER HAMILTON

A chief adviser to Washington during the Revolutionary War and as secretary of the Treasury in the first presidential administration, Hamilton had more brains but fewer endearing qualities. He was of the elitist wing of the Federalist Party he masterminded and held little faith in the goodness of yeoman farmers or any other sort of common men. Therefore, he envisioned a strong federal government that would harness the energies of the republic with both incentives and harsh punishment for rebellion. His long-term vision for the United States actually came to pass. He did everything in his power to lay the foundation for commercial and industrial strength to match the agricultural potential of the new country. He would also eventually reveal state secrets to the British, and he is the first noted American politician to openly commit adultery. This mixed persona of financial genius and unscrupulous morals met a fitting end. Provisions were specifically added to the U.S. Constitution to allow him to become president even though he was not a native-born citizen, but he died in a foolish duel over party politics. He has forever remained a historical figure both honored and despised.

5 FEDERALIST PAPERS

First written as anonymous editorials in New York newspapers, these expository essays became a crucial insight into the two great minds that both drafted the Constitution and put it into effect. James Madison and Alexander Hamilton, then, were the principal authors along with future Chief Justice of the Supreme Court John Jay. The editorials were designed to persuade New Yorkers to support ratification of the U.S. Constitution, but their lasting importance comes from the political science principles they examined. Madison's lament that government would not be necessary if all men were angels comes from Federalist No. 51, and his justification for the choice of a republic as the form of government is in Federalist No. 10. The editorials achieved their purpose but now help constitutional scholars and lawyers understand the words as well as the intentions of the Founding Fathers.

6 BILL OF RIGHTS

The greatest early contribution of the Anti-Federalist Party to the formation of the American government was their hesitancy to support the ratification of the U.S. Constitution without first demanding protections of individual and states' rights. This push took the form by 1791 of ten amendments to the Constitution, nine of which specifically protected American citizens from being abused by their government in the ways Britain abused the American colonists. The Tenth Amendment reserves to the states those powers not given to the central government, thereby forming a federal government. The Bill of Rights became a cherished American heritage and the proving ground for individual and societal liberties through many varied events and interpretations, and they remain so today.

7 NATIONAL DEBT

The American government found itself in deep debt after surviving the War for Independence. Direct loans from foreign governments like France as well as the sale of war bonds to

Americans and to people abroad were critical to the war effort. Recognizing that similar, if not worse, crises could arise in the future, Alexander Hamilton set about funding the debt as secretary of the Treasury. He realized that if the United States defaulted on these loans, no other credit would ever be extended to the government. Hamilton also proposed that bearing this burden together would make the states pull together. While this phenomenon may have been true in the early national period, the existence of a national debt henceforth was a divisive issue, especially as the national debt increased. Thomas Jefferson, in particular, abhorred the idea of passing one generation's expenses onto the next, or the next several.

> **TARIFF**
> Tariffs are taxes on imported goods. Hamilton expected these taxes to be a key source of income for the federal government, but he was also trying to give domestic manufacturers a boost over foreign competitors and earn their political support.

8 ASSUMPTION

In keeping with his notion that the national debt would be a "cement of union," Hamilton wanted to assume, or take on, the debts of states that any might have acquired in paying for the war. This figure was substantial at $25 million. Critics of the idea either said this was too much to add or came from states, like Virginia, that had already paid off their war debts and considered federal assistance unfair. Assumption revealed to just what extent Hamilton was willing to go to forge national unity.

9 FUNDING AT PAR

Even more controversial than assumption was the notion of funding at par. This Hamiltonian brainchild sought not only states to be loyal supporters of the federal government but also rich citizens who had speculated in war bonds. Through the ups and downs of the Revolutionary War, individual citizens who had purchased bonds feared they would amount to nothing. Those uncertain of ever receiving money back from their investment in independence willingly sold the bonds to wealthy buyers offering at least some cash. With independence secure, the popular notion was that the speculators had taken advantage of citizens of the new republic. Hamilton, however, wanted to reward them for their loyalty (and shrewdness) and to make them likely to buy bonds again if the government needed funding. Only through compromise could such seeming favoritism be permitted in a democratic republic, and this component of Hamilton's Financial Program (along with the Bank of the United States) was what the Federalists received for agreeing to let the South have the national capital at Washington, D.C.

10 BANK OF THE UNITED STATES

Hamilton used implied powers granted to Congress by the "elastic clause" to propose the Bank of the United States (BUS). The U.S. Constitution said Congress could have powers besides those stated if they were "necessary and proper" in carrying out duties that were stated. Hamilton wanted a BUS in order to negotiate financial arrangements and to issue a currency, both of which were stated powers. He designed the bank to allow private investment in it as well as government funding to attach the prosperity of the country to the prosperity of individuals. When the Anti-Federalists compromised regarding the location of the national capital, Hamilton's loose construction of the elastic clause allowed him, with assumption and funding at par, to establish the economic underpinnings of a sound government and a national currency. Political wrangling over Hamilton's Financial Program gave rise to the two-party system, and the first BUS and its successors were controversial until another model was selected in the twentieth century.

11 STRICT VERSUS LOOSE CONSTRUCTION

The two views of government derived from two methods of interpreting the U.S. Constitution were at the crux of the two-party system. Federalists favored loose construction because it used the elastic clause to increase the powers of the central government. Anti-Federalists favored a more limited government and used strict construction to claim that the central government should not cast about for more powers to add to those stated directly. Most presidents, Congresses, and even justices on the Supreme Court, found it difficult to adhere to either principle completely in the workings of government, but the balance between the two interpretations maintained moderation until the balance was removed. Most office holders since the twentieth century have been loose constructionists.

12 WHISKEY REBELLION

Another component of Hamilton's financial program was an excise tax on whiskey. Whiskey was in prevalent use as a derivative of corn that could be more easily transported to market than grain. Whiskey was used as a currency in the West, a fact that sidestepped Hamilton's new national currency. In 1794, blustering Pennsylvanian farmers were warned by Washington to desist or be considered an insurrection. Nearly 15,000 militia soldiers, accompanied by Washington and Hamilton, convinced the rebels to disperse without firing a shot. Only two of the leaders were tried for treason, and Washington pardoned them. The central government proved that it was going to defend the U.S. Constitution and enforce the laws, thereby establishing stability and securing another source of revenue to help fund the national debt and the government.

EXCISE TAX

These taxes were imposed on specific goods, as were tariffs, but excise taxes targeted domestic goods. They were particularly controversial not because of the tax on whiskey but because they were reminiscent of Parliament's mercantilist taxes from before the Revolution.

13 TREATY OF GREENVILLE

Where two army expeditions had failed, General Anthony Wayne and 2,500 troops sent by Washington to the Great Lakes Region finally delivered a decisive defeat to American Indians harassing pioneers on the frontier. The battle in 1795 was called the Battle of Fallen Timbers because it was fought in Ohio over ground where a tornado had passed previously. Twelve American Indian tribes signed the peace treaty that ceded much of the territory that would become the State of Ohio as well as the cities of Detroit and Chicago. The fact that the American Indians had been supplied liquor and guns by the British highlighted the tense relationship between the United States and Canada before Jay's Treaty was signed.

NEUTRALITY PROCLAMATION

George Washington issued this announcement in 1793 to avoid being drawn into the escalating war between Great Britain and France. Pro-French Americans criticized Washington for abandoning France in her time of need, but Washington knew the fledgling country could not survive any war.

14 JAY'S TREATY

Although all three of the major treaties of Washington's administration evidenced the new ability of the United States to control its own territory, Jay's Treaty, negotiated by John Jay in 1794, was the most significant. The British defied the Treaty of Paris of 1783 by keeping garrisons of soldiers on American soil. From these locations the British kept up a trade with

American Indians that disturbed the peace on the frontier. The treaty compelled the British to abandon their forts but also garnered trade concessions for the rising maritime interests of the United States to have room to grow. In return, the American government pledged to see to it that British banks were compensated for the nearly $2.5 million in prewar debts American colonists still owed but refused to pay.

15 PINCKNEY'S TREATY

The hesitancy of Spain to let the United States have free access to New Orleans with right of deposit for the storage of goods before shipping backfired. Thomas Pinckney discovered in 1795 that Spanish Florida was weakening and exacted from the Spanish not only access to New Orleans, which was so critical to the settlement of the Mississippi River Valley, but also the river itself. Rather than being merely the border between Spanish territory and the United States, the river was open to free navigation along its entire length. Thus in relations with American Indians and with foreign nations with interests in North America, the Washington administration asserted the rights of the new nation in its own neighborhood.

16 WASHINGTON'S FAREWELL ADDRESS

As he departed into private life at last, Washington published in newspapers an editorial that went down in history as his Farewell Address. While never delivered as a speech in his lifetime, his last important precedents were codified in this document. He explained why he was not pursuing a third term, warned against the factionalism of the party system and the sectionalism it would breed, urged the continuation of sound financial policy, and intoned isolationist foreign policy views with the admonition to avoid permanent alliances. None of this advice has been permanently followed by the country, but when not followed bad consequences have arisen that steer the nation back toward the wisdom of the father of his country who was "first in war, first in peace, and first in the hearts of his countrymen."

17 JOHN ADAMS

Nearly any man would have difficulty standing next to George Washington and being remembered, but Adams always lived in the shadow of Washington, Franklin, and even Jefferson. Although he was instrumental in guiding the principles of independence to fruition, his presidency marked the decline of the Federalist Party despite the firm stance for both war and peace Adams took to save the country. The Alien and Sedition Acts sullied his reputation. When faced with the possibility of war with France or Great Britain or both, Adams oversaw the construction of the first Navy frigates while at the same time negotiating a peace with both nations that saved America from being destroyed in its infancy. He preserved some Federalist voice in government for years to come by placing John Marshall on the Supreme Court.

> ### QUASI-WAR WITH FRANCE
> Fearful that Jay's Treaty marked a U.K./U.S. alliance against France, French warships seized around three hundred American merchant ships by 1797. John Adams realized, like Washington, that the United States could ill afford a war.

18 XYZ AFFAIR

Most Americans wanted a war with France after hearing of the diplomatic debacle known as the XYZ Affair. When three American diplomats approached the French foreign minister, Talleyrand, to negotiate a settlement of the Quasi-War with France, Talleyrand asked not only for a loan from America to help France in the war with Britain but also for a personal bribe of almost a quarter of a million dollars. The name of the incident stemmed from the agents making the proposal who were referred to secretly as X, Y, and Z. News of this offer enraged the American public and made it more difficult for Adams to stop the raiding of American shipping from becoming all-out war that he feared the country could not survive. The public outcry declared, "Millions for defense, but not a penny for tribute!"

19 ALIEN AND SEDITION ACTS

During the 1798 dangerous episodes of the Adams presidency, Congress acted to change the naturalization laws to favor the Federalist party. The Alien Act changed the residency requirement for citizenship from five to fourteen years, thus delaying the time when immigrants would become voters who, as farmers, voted with the Jeffersonian Republicans. The Sedition Act curbed the freedom of the press by making punishable by prison and a fine, "any false, scandalous, and malicious writing," directed at the federal government. Both these measures were passed to maintain a political advantage, but they were also enforced with partiality.

20 KENTUCKY AND VIRGINIA RESOLUTIONS

Jeffersonian Republican reaction to the Alien and Sedition Acts was voiced by these two states through their state legislatures. Because Madison and Jefferson helped pen the bills, the Resolutions represented a serious challenge to constitutional government by declaring null and void within the borders of these states the provisions they deemed unconstitutional. Southern states would resort to nullification to preserve slavery, and the northern states did so to protest a stringent fugitive slave law enacted just prior to the Civil War. One can only imagine the chaos that would ensue if every state could pick and choose which federal laws it would obey, but the Republicans found the Federalist laws so odious they were glad to test the constitutionality of their idea. The Alien and Sedition Acts were eventually agreed to be unjustified and erroneous, but in trying to solve a small crisis the Kentucky and Virginia Resolutions would set in motion a big one called the Nullification Crisis, one step before the Civil War.

THE BIG PICTURE

1. Despite the degree of unity evidenced by the ratification of the U.S. Constitution, debates about the interpretation of the document and about the workings of government gave rise to the two-party system in American politics.

2. With the leadership of men like Washington, Adams, and Hamilton the Federalist Party established stability for the new nation but at the cost of its own popularity.

3. Economic stability was provided through Hamilton's Financial Program, the provisions of which followed loose construction of the U.S. Constitution to the consternation of Thomas Jefferson and the Anti-Federalists.

4. Domestic and national security were provided for by Washington's insistence on neutrality, assertion of territorial sovereignty in treaties, and use of the military to put down rebellion and to quell frontier attacks by American Indians.

5. John Adams maintained peace when war would have been popular but disastrous, but Federalist policies sparked such ire that the Anti-Federalists defied federal law, foreshadowing the North/South conflict over sovereignty that would lead toward the Civil War.

Jeffersonian Republicans in Power

10

Still one thing more, fellow citizens—a wise and frugal Government, which shall restrain men from injuring one another, shall leave them otherwise free to regulate their own pursuits of industry and improvement, and shall not take from the mouth of labor the bread it has earned.

—Thomas Jefferson's first inaugural address, 1801

TIMELINE

1776	Adam Smith publishes *The Wealth of Nations*
1800	Election of 1800 (Jeffersonian Revolution)
1801	John Adams issues his Midnight Appointments; Thomas Jefferson begins his presidency
1801–1835	John Marshall serves as Chief Justice of the U.S. Supreme Court
1803	*Marbury* v. *Madison;* Jefferson acquires the Louisiana Purchase
1804	Aaron Burr kills Alexander Hamilton in a duel
1804–1806	Lewis and Clark expedition
1805	Sacagawea joins the Corps of Discovery
1811	Tecumseh mounts a military campaign to halt American expansion; Battle of Tippecanoe
1814–1824	Era of Good Feelings
1819	*McCulloch* v. *Maryland; Dartmouth Col.* v. *Woodward*
1824	*Gibbons* v. *Ogden*

OVERVIEW

Despite fears of turmoil, power peacefully changed hands in 1800 from the Federalist Party to the Democratic-Republicans. President Thomas Jefferson made clear in his inaugural address that he sought to break with the Federalist approach to governing. He had grown alarmed at the expansion of the size of the federal government. The Federalist use of government power to guide the economy and also to silence political opposition ran counter to Jefferson's ideals of republican simplicity. Jefferson later referred to his election as the "revolution of 1800," signifying a break with the monarchial tendencies of the Federalists. Republican rule continued with the next two presidents, continuing the domination of the White House by the so-called Virginia Dynasty (four of the first five presidents were Virginians). James Madison, the architect of the Constitution and the Bill of Rights and Jefferson's secretary of state, served from 1809 to 1817. He was succeeded by his secretary of state, James Monroe, who served from 1817 to 1825.

Several important developments occurred during the administrations of Jefferson and Madison. The United States acquired the massive Louisiana Territory (1803) from France, doubling the size of the country. As America expanded its territory, thousands of American settlers began pushing farther beyond the Appalachian Mountains, settling in lands adjacent to the Ohio and Mississippi Rivers. In the early 1800s, resistance by American Indians to the encroachment of their lands provoked bitterness not just at American Indians, but also at the British, who many Americans believed were arming American Indian groups. At the same time, tensions were rising between the United States and Great Britain over trade issues and shipping rights. These tensions with Great Britain, in the West over the American Indian question and on the Atlantic over trade issues, resulted in the War of 1812.

Though neither the United States nor Great Britain could claim a decisive victory in the War of 1812, the war had several important repercussions for the United States. First, the war fueled a growing sense of nationalism. Americans took pride in the fact that they held their own against one of the world's preeminent powers. It was during the war that Frances Scott Key wrote the poem that later was renamed the "Star Spangled Banner" and was set to music as the United States' national anthem. Politically, the war further damaged the reputation of the Federalist Party. In the aftermath of the war, the party was seen as unpatriotic for its vocal opposition to a popular war.

The decline of the Federalists as a viable party and the strong showing by the United States in the War of 1812 led to the "Era of Good Feelings"—a period free, for the most part, of partisan strife and international turmoil. America's newfound confidence on the international stage during this period was evident in President James Monroe's foreign policy pronouncement, the Monroe Doctrine, in which the United States warned European nations not to interfere in the Western Hemisphere. However, the era was not free of disagreements and sectional competition. The issue of slavery, which most politicians sought to avoid, emerged in 1820. Controversy arose between the slave-holding states and the free states in 1820 when Missouri applied for statehood as a slave state.

Although the Federalist Party declined and, by the 1820s, effectively ceased to exist, the agenda of the Federalists was largely implemented. The nation began to adopt manufacturing, just as Alexander Hamilton had hoped. Henry Clay's "American System" enacted much of Hamilton's program. In addition, the Supreme Court under John Marshall established important precedents that furthered the Federalist agenda, including judicial review, the sanctity of contractual obligations, and the supremacy of federal authority over state laws. However, debates over these questions of power and authority continued to divide Americans and later contributed to the Civil War.

1 THOMAS JEFFERSON

There are few aspects of the revolutionary and early national periods that were not fashioned in some measure by Thomas Jefferson's pen. A lawyer from Virginia, Jefferson rose through state and national offices forever putting his mark on the legacies of both his home state and the country. A short list of his accomplishments staggers the mind and includes the Declaration of Independence, the idea of public schools, the Virginia Statute on Religious Freedom (ending the establishment of the Episcopal Church), the Virginia and Kentucky Resolutions, the Louisiana Purchase, the Lewis and Clark expedition, the Embargo Act, and a revival of classical architecture. He also is directly responsible for the origins of the two-party system by leading the opposition to the Federalist Party, especially once he resigned his post as the secretary of state under Washington. Because of the original constitutional manner of electing the president, he wound up as the vice president to John Adams. His background made him influential enough to enforce his desire to weaken the central government while he was president while still being able to forge policy effectively. A true picture of the phenomenon of his achievements must include his lifelong attachment to and derision for slavery in which he personified America's entire dilemma regarding the peculiar institution. Jefferson died deep in debt on the same day as John Adams, exactly fifty years after the adoption of the Declaration of Independence. The two crucial advocates of independence had, before their deaths, reconciled as friends after a long political rivalry.

2 ELECTION OF 1800

Otherwise known as the Jeffersonian Revolution, the Election of 1800 was the first major transfer of ideological power in American history and, since it was peaceful, the first such in world history. The failure of John Adams to rally his party to peace with France and thus his failure to win a second term as president marked the decline of the Federalist Party from which it never recovered. The revolutionary aspect of Jefferson's election was a rejection of the elite leadership core that had seen the U.S. Constitution through ratification and implementation but had estranged the country with the Alien and Sedition Acts. The vote in the Electoral College ended in a tie that was resolved in the House of Representatives when Alexander Hamilton urged Federalists to choose Jefferson over Aaron Burr. This episode led to a revision in the electoral process through the Twelfth Amendment to the Constitution.

3 AARON BURR

Coming up through the officer corps in the Revolutionary War, Aaron Burr had as much ambition as his fellow New Yorker, Alexander Hamilton, but no redeeming genius. After his tie with Jefferson he became the vice president, but was later defeated in a bid for governor of New York by the direct, public intervention of Hamilton. The two fought a duel over their differences in which Hamilton was killed. Eager to be president of something, Burr later attempted to carve out territory for a new country amid the vague borders of Spain and the Louisiana Territory in the West. The Burr Conspiracy fell through when a general in the U.S. Army who had conspired with Burr turned him in. He was acquitted of treason charges, however, and died in obscurity in New York City. His exploits revealed, in part, just how hard it was going to be for the U.S. government to manage westward expansion.

4 LOUISIANA PURCHASE

When the Haitian Revolution thwarted Napoleon's New World aspirations, he shrewdly backed out of having to build a more extensive navy, cut his losses, and sold out to the United States. He did so with the intention of raising America to one day humble the British whom he despised. Jefferson eagerly accepted the deal to double the size of the country for only $15 million even though to do so required him to use loose construction. He pushed the purchase through Congress as a treaty in 1803, and then hoped the massive addition of cheap land would allow his cherished yeoman farmers all the territory they would need for over a century of expansion. Nothing he did destabilized the relationship between North and South more, however. Federalists rallied against the purchase, but their irrelevance was evident in that no one listened.

5 LEWIS AND CLARK EXPEDITION

The amazing journey of Meriwether Lewis and William Clark was only the most famous of the several expeditions dispatched to the new Louisiana Territory and beyond. For three years the Corps of Discovery set about following Jefferson's admonition to make friendly relations with the American Indians of the West while looking for economic opportunities. Although these goals eventually proved incompatible, Lewis and Clark succeeded in proving a river and land route existed that could get settlers all the way to the Pacific Ocean. Along the way they made several important scientific and geographical discoveries and returned alive. Their journal and other reports aroused great interest in western migration.

6 BARBARY WARS

President Thomas Jefferson's first foreign policy crisis involved American trade with the Middle East. At the time, trade in the Mediterranean was controlled by four seafaring North African states—Morocco, Algiers, Tunis, and Tripoli—whose domain was known as the Barbary Coast. These states demanded large payments from trading nations as tribute. Nations that did not pay tribute found their shipping subject to seizure and plundering by Barbary Coast pirates. American merchants during the colonial era had enjoyed the protection of Great Britain. When the United States became independent, Presidents George Washington and John Adams agreed to the terms set by the Barbary states. In 1801, Tripoli demanded a steep increase in payment from the United States. When Jefferson refused, Tripoli declared war on the United States. Jefferson sent warships to the region to engage in fighting and to protect American shipping. The move proved popular. The slogan "Millions for defense, but not a cent for tribute" became widespread in America. In the end, the United States did not achieve a decisive victory, but the Navy ultimately ended the immediate threat to American shipping, thanks to the daring of men like Stephen Decatur. The action boosted America's profile on the world stage.

7 SACAGAWEA

This young Shoshone woman is a poignant symbol of the rivalry among American Indian tribes as well as of the difficulties and opportunities of European/American encroachment into their territory. Having been sold to or captured by another tribe, Sacagawea wound up becoming one of the wives of a Frenchman. The two of them became a part of the Corps of Discovery, and Sacagawea provided crucial assistance as a guide, interpreter, and peaceful ambassador. Her brother was a Shoshone chief who provided Lewis and Clark and their men horses with which to cross the Rocky Mountains. The bond was such among the erstwhile band of explorers that when Sacagawea died prematurely in 1812, William Clark raised her two children.

> ### ZEBULON PIKE
> While the Corps of Discovery was exploring the northern Louisiana Purchase territory, Pike explored the west. His circuitous route went through Colorado, where a mountain still bears his name, and then he explored deep into Spanish territory that later belonged to Mexico before being won by the United States in the Mexican War.

8 JOHN MARSHALL

Another prominent Virginian, John Marshall served in the military under George Washington during the Revolutionary War and then held posts in government up to and including service as secretary of state under John Adams. Marshall was appointed to the Supreme Court as its chief justice during the fallout from the Election of 1800 and remained on the bench for over thirty years. As the last prominent Federalist who outlived his own party, Marshall placed his stamp on the workings of the Supreme Court and on the American economy. His cases were landmark decisions in the assertion of federal authority over individuals and states and in the establishment of judicial review, the concept that the Supreme Court was the final determiner of what was and was not constitutional.

9 MARBURY V. MADISON

The most important decision of the Supreme Court under Chief Justice John Marshall was in the case of *Marbury* v. *Madison* (1803). The important outcome of the case was that the principle of judicial review was established. The details of the decision have to do with the seating of judges that had been appointed in the last days of the John Adams administration. William Marbury was one of Adams's "midnight appointments" in 1801. Marbury had campaigned for Adams for president and Adams appointed him to be the justice of the peace of Washington, D.C. The new secretary of state of the Jefferson administration, James Madison, however, declined to forward Marbury's commission. When Marbury sued Madison, the case went before the Supreme Court. The Court asserted that Marbury did not have a right to bring suit under the Judiciary Act of 1789 because the act itself was inconsistent with the constitution. Marshall posited that the Judiciary Act incorrectly granted powers to the Supreme Court that are not contained in the Constitution. In the short term, the case shocked many observers because a Federalist judge sided with a Republican administration in denying the claim of a fellow Federalist. In the long term, the case established the Supreme Court's power to review laws and determine if they are consistent with the Constitution. Laws declared unconstitutional by the Court are immediately struck down. This power of judicial review contributed to the continuing centralization of power in Washington, D.C., even though it occurred during an administration that was leery of this trend.

10 EMBARGO ACT

Jefferson's solution to avoiding war was to get Congress to cut off trade in 1807. He did not want the United States involved in a conflict between England and France in fear that raids by both countries on American shipping would draw the young country to its doom. Only a southern president before the rise of the cotton kingdom could have thought so. New England Federalists and Yankee traders despised the law that threatened to ruin their economy. The Embargo Act cut off trade with all foreign countries, not just the combatant nations.

11 MACON'S BILL NO. 2

In a compromise position, this bill proposed the resumption of trade with either Britain or France, whichever nation first agreed to stop raiding American shipping. Although the Federalists still did not like any restrictions on their trade, the bill became law. Napoleon saw a chance to move the United States toward war with Great Britain and vowed to stop French predation of American merchant vessels. President Madison trusted Napoleon and reopened commerce with France, an act the British regarded as tantamount to war.

12 WAR HAWKS

Young Congressmen from the western states made it clear that they favored war with Great Britain. While not seafaring people themselves, they claimed the British practice of impressment, or forcible drafting of even American seamen into the British navy, was a violation of the dignity of the nation. The War Hawks, led by Henry Clay of Kentucky, said they would rather fight for American rights on the high seas than cower behind shady agreements with nations that viewed America as a pawn. When James Madison blamed the British for all of the affronts to American shipping (rather than the French who were also guilty), the War Hawks led Congress to declare war.

13 IMPRESSMENT

Service in the British navy occurred under such harsh conditions that men had to be drafted in order to fill crews. Press gangs came ashore in England and in other countries and essentially kidnapped men, especially those lying drunk on wharves in harbors. Because it was hard to determine whether any given seaman was of English or American origin, confusion abounded. Mistaken identities regarding those who might have escaped from British ships did not erase the fact that some men were simply shanghaied, or stolen outright. The harsh discipline aboard ship was capable of keeping involuntary recruits at work, usually. Impressment was considered an odious violation of national sovereignty by the War Hawks and by most Americans.

14 BATTLE OF TIPPECANOE

In the early 1800s, as westward settlers continued to push into the interior of the continent, American Indians began to organize resistance. Tecumseh, a Shawnee chief, and his brother, Tenskwatawa, known as the Prophet, conceived a plan to unite the various American Indians of the West into a confederacy to challenge expansion by white settlers. When Tecumseh was away on a recruiting trip, the Prophet prematurely initiated an attack on American forces near the Tippecanoe River. In the ensuing Battle of Tippecanoe (1811), forces under the command of the territorial governor of Indiana, William Henry Harrison, ousted members of Tecumseh's confederacy from their headquarters at Prophetstown, despite sustaining heavy losses. Western congressmen, who became known as the War Hawks, were convinced that Great Britain was encouraging and funding Tecumseh's confederacy. Just as relations with Britain were deteriorating over the trade issue, War Hawks led by Henry Clay of Kentucky and John C. Calhoun from South Carolina, were pushing for military action against the British. Such action, it was thought, would allow the United States to eliminate the American Indian threat and, perhaps, even allow the United States to invade Canada. This pro-war sentiment in the West and South was an important cause of the War of 1812.

15 WAR OF 1812

This second war against the mother country occurred because neither Great Britain nor the United States respected each other or could do without each other economically. Napoleon provoked animosity between the British and the Americans in order to humble the British. When James Madison got the Congress to declare war, the British attacked in three major campaigns on American soil that were all eventually repulsed. In the second campaign, major public buildings in Washington, D.C., were destroyed. The war ended in a draw with neither nation taking land from the other. All Indian resistance east of the Mississippi River was ended with the death of Tecumseh at the Battle of the Thames. The Treaty of Ghent ended the war and propelled Americans into a brief time of nationalism before sectionalism returned.

16 THE HARTFORD CONVENTION

The War of 1812 was unpopular with some Americans, especially among New England merchants, who saw their trade with Great Britain disappear. New England Federalists opposed the war with Great Britain and called for a convention to discuss their grievances. Five states sent delegates, who met prior to the Battle of New Orleans. In late 1814, as diplomats were negotiating the Treaty of Ghent to end the war, Federalists from New England convened in Hartford, Connecticut, to express their displeasure with the war. Some of the more radical delegates suggested that New England secede from the union, but this proposal was rejected by the convention. The Hartford Convention did pass a resolution calling for a two-thirds vote in Congress for future declarations of war, as well as for votes restricting trade. When their envoys reached the capital, they found it burned by the enemy and heard the news of Andrew Jackson's victory in the Battle of New Orleans. The humiliation of opposing a war that had already ended was an additional nail in the coffin of the Federalist Party.

17 ERA OF GOOD FEELINGS

The rest of the era of the Virginia dynasty saw Jefferson, Madison, and Monroe all enjoy two-term presidencies. With the demise of the Federalist Party, the Era of Good Feelings was the period when the notion of political parties gave way to the dream of national unity.

PATRONAGE

The practice of rewarding political supporters with jobs, contracts, and other favors was not practiced by Jefferson as much as by Madison and Monroe, who over time replaced civil servants originally chosen by the Federalists.

Although factions did exist, the country experienced four presidencies, including that of John Quincy Adams, when the secretary of state from the previous administration became the next president. Such a predictable harmony was not destined to last long with the rise of Andrew Jackson or the events surrounding the War of 1812.

18 MISSOURI COMPROMISE

This legislative compromise was the first engineered by Henry Clay of Kentucky. When Missouri wanted to enter the Union as a slave state, Clay's idea was to keep the balance of slave and free states in the Senate by bringing in Maine, a part of Massachusetts, as a free state. To stave off further disunion, no state other than Missouri carved out of the Louisiana Purchase north of the 36°30' line of latitude would ever be a slave state. New states below the line would be slave states. Thus Clay began his career as the Great Compromiser by avoiding further North/South conflict for a time. The debates over the compromise frightened the South into adamant defense of slavery.

19 MONROE DOCTRINE

This landmark in American foreign policy was another brainchild of John Q. Adams who served as James Monroe's secretary of state. With a crumbling Spanish Empire and encroachments in the Western Hemisphere by the British, French, and Russians, President Monroe agreed to make a stand. The Monroe Doctrine stated that the United States desired no participation in the affairs of Europe and that Europeans should no longer consider the Western Hemisphere open to colonization or any European involvement. The United States considered any violation of this policy a threat to America's national security. The Monroe Doctrine extended Washington's isolationism, and in the years to come Monroe's claim would be tested by various nations that all felt varying degrees of American ire as a result.

20 JOHN QUINCY ADAMS

This eldest son of one of the Founding Fathers was also the most traveled American of his day having been raised on international relations. He served in several diplomatic posts and in the Senate until becoming Monroe's secretary of state and the mastermind behind the Monroe Doctrine. While president he tried to remain above political wrangling and to accomplish great goals for domestic development, but he failed to acquire the latter without the former. He was elected to the House of Representatives after leaving the presidency and remained all his life an indefatigable opponent of slavery and its expansion. He later stood against Texas annexation and the Gag Rule and personally argued the case in the Supreme Court of the slaves aboard the *Amistad* who had taken over their slave ship in transit from Africa. The slaves were freed. As proof that he dedicated his life to his country he died at his desk as the only ex-president to go into the House of Representatives.

THE BIG PICTURE

1. The viability of the American republic was proven in the smooth transition between the Federalists and the Jeffersonian Republicans after the Election of 1800.

2. While the Era of Good Feelings experienced a period of one-party rule, events during the presidencies of the Jeffersonian Republicans revealed that factionalism and political parties were natural and would become a permanent part of American society.

3. Westward expansion, exploration, and settlement were established as the great national themes of the nineteenth century by the excitement generated by the Louisiana Purchase and the Lewis and Clark expedition.

4. Controversies over trade and encroachments on the citizens and property of the United States led to a second war of American independence known as the War of 1812.

5. John Marshall was a stabilizing influence for American law and the American economy as he presided over a nationalist Supreme Court and asserted the power of the judicial branch through the concept of judicial review.

The Market Revolution

11

The progress of the United States under our free and happy institutions has surpassed the most sanguine hopes of the founders of the Republic.

—Andrew Jackson, farewell address, 1837

TIMELINE	
1790	Samuel Slater opens the first American textile mill
1793	Eli Whitney invents the cotton gin
1797	USS *Constitution* is launched
1807	Embargo Act
1810	Macon's Bill No. 2; New York City has a population of almost 120,000
1811	John Jacob Astor establishes the Astoria trading post
1812–1814	The War of 1812
1813	Tecumseh is killed at the Battle of the Thames; Battle of Plattsburgh
1814	Francis Scott Key composes the National Anthem
1815	Battle of New Orleans
1825	Erie Canal opens triggering Canal Mania
1828	Andrew Jackson is elected president
1830	Baltimore and Ohio Railroad begins service; Congress passes the Indian Removal Act
1835	Samuel F. B. Morse invents the telegraph
1845	Irish Potato Famine begins

OVERVIEW

In the decades between the War of 1812 and the Civil War, the U.S. economy saw rapid growth and expansion. The subsistence economy was giving way to a market economy with a national and even international reach. The expanding money supply fueled new investments and enterprises. This market revolution looked different in the North and South. The northern states saw the birth of Industrialization, while in the South, slavery grew dramatically alongside the cultivation of cotton (see Chapter 14). Even as the regions of the United States became more interlinked, as local economies became national markets, the issue of free-versus-slave-labor pushed the country further apart.

There were several important factors that contributed to the market revolution. Improvements in transportation allowed production to reach faraway markets. By 1850, the eastern half of the United States was crisscrossed by a series of roads, canals, and railroads that, along with navigable rivers, moved goods from city to city and from the interior to the coast. The development of the steamship and trans-Atlantic cargo lines facilitated trade with Europe and beyond. Advances in communications contributed to the growing scale of economic activity. Samuel Morse developed and patented the telegraph and sent the first message—"What hath God Wrought?"—in 1844. Previously, it could take weeks to send information across the sea, and days to send it across the country. Banking and credit began to play an increasingly important role in economic expansion, especially after the War of 1812. The increased level of credit and speculative activity in the economy also created instability. The United States experienced economic downturns after the Panics of 1819 and 1837. The federal and state governments aided economic growth in the nineteenth century in a number of ways, such as funding internal improvements, issuing patents, chartering banks, and loosening incorporation laws.

Finally, the antebellum period (the period before the Civil War) experienced the first steps toward the industrial, mass production of goods. This trend continued with even greater energy after the Civil War. Mass production of goods for distant markets developed slowly and often existed side-by-side with older methods of production. An early step toward mass production was the "putting-out system" in which men and women would perform a task at their home (arranged by an agent) and would be paid by the piece produced. The development of manufacturing products with interchangeable parts was another important step toward mass production. By the 1820s, entrepreneurs brought all the operations of manufacturing under one roof in the factory system using unskilled or semi-skilled workers, including women and immigrants.

The impact of the market revolution was primarily on the economy, but it also reverberated in the social and political realms. Many Americans were drawn to the more optimistic outlook of the Second Great Awakening religious revival to help them make sense of the dramatic changes occurring in the United States. One of the centers of the Second Great Awakening, the so called "burned-over district" of upstate New York, is a case in point. New towns along the Erie Canal, such as Utica, Schenectady, Syracuse, and especially Rochester, were centers of entrepreneurial activity as well as intense religious revival. In addition, the wage laborers who found work in manufacturing gravitated toward the democratic message of Andrew Jackson. As states eliminated property requirements for voting in the antebellum period, working-class men helped propel Jackson to the presidency (see page 149).

1 ADAM SMITH

This British economist's book, *The Wealth of Nations*, was published the same year as the Declaration of Independence and proved equally revolutionary. Smith attacked mercantilism by arguing the law of supply and demand, rather than government, should determine the priorities of a country's economy. He reasoned that people knew instinctively what would work to produce wealth and were best suited to make the adjustments in their practices according to market forces. His phrase, "the invisible hand," achieved lasting fame as the underpinnings for laissez-faire, the American political philosophy of the nineteenth century that advocated government support for economic growth with a minimum of interference. Smith's theories were based on observations of the economic dynamic that would become known as capitalism and served to popularize this economic philosophy that supplanted mercantilism.

2 SAMUEL SLATER

In 1793, Samuel Slater built the first factory in the United States. He had secretly left Great Britain in 1789 at age 21, smuggling machinery plans out of the country. He had learned about textile machinery working as an apprentice to an early pioneer in the British textile industry. He worked with a local Rhode Island entrepreneur, Moses Brown. Slater's mill spun cotton and wool into yarn or thread. The weaving of fabric was still done by hand looms in people's homes; later mills brought all the textile operations under one roof. The spinning machines in Slater's mill were powered by the fast-flowing Blackstone River. After developing this mill, Slater instituted principles of management which he had learned from his time working in English mills. Slater built thirteen spinning mills and soon amassed a fortune. He built towns adjacent to his mills to house workers, including Slatersville, Rhode Island. Slater's mill in Pawtucket represents the first step the United States took toward becoming a more industrialized and urban society.

> **NON-INTERCOURSE ACT**
>
> Upon repeal of the Embargo Act, the Congress passed this law in 1809 opening foreign trade again but not with the best customers of the U.S. economy: Great Britain and France.

3 ELI WHITNEY

Whitney was the other great founder of American industry. A mechanical genius with a degree from Yale, he seized on the problem of processing raw cotton while traveling in the South. In 1793 he invented the cotton engine, or gin, to separate the cotton fibers from the seeds ten times faster than could be done by hand. With improvements to the machine and a patent in hand, he set about revolutionizing the production of cotton for market. Along the way he sought to expand his manufacturing business by earning a contract with the federal government to make muskets rapidly. To speed the process and to make the finished muskets uniform and easily repaired, Whitney used machines to manufacture interchangeable parts. His manufacturing process for both the cotton gin and muskets was the basis for modern mass production once Henry Ford put the process in motion on a continuously moving assembly line.

4 THE AMERICAN SYSTEM

Henry Clay was the first statesman to articulate a plan that tied the strengths and weaknesses of the three sections of the nation together in a viable national economy. His principles of a high protective tariff, a high demand for land in the West, the stabilizing influence of the BUS, and the use of public money to build roads and canals were all designed to improve the economy on a national scale. A weakness of his plan was that few others could understand the concept of national markets when he first used the term *American System* in 1824. Clay wanted the West to feed grain to the East and the South to feed cotton to northern mills. He wanted transportation improvements to facilitate this commerce in order to boost the role of America in the world economy. His vision came true but not in his lifetime.

5 CANAL MANIA

A crucial step in the transportation revolution that opened the West for settlement was the era of canal building known as Canal Mania. Beginning with the Erie Canal, which was constructed from 1817 to 1825, states and private companies sought to dig canals wherever they appeared to be feasible. Although canal boats traveled no faster than the horses or people pulling them along, they could more easily transfer large cargoes than wagons over land. Canals facilitated the migration of people west and the shipping of grain back east. Canals also bred an endearing folk hero in flatboat men like Mike Fink, who were said to embody the great enterprising spirit and wildness of the frontier that so captivated the imaginations of Americans and stimulated westward migration.

6 NEW YORK CITY

Because of the Erie Canal's connecting of Buffalo on the Great Lakes with the Hudson River, New York City became the transit point for oceangoing goods and people coming into the country, while goods, especially grain, were funneled in from the West. Even cotton was brought up from the South to New York in order to be shipped from there to Europe. The natural advantages of the harbor discerned by the first Dutch settlers of New Amsterdam worked to the advantage of this city, the first in America to have one million inhabitants. Because of its early diversity, wealth, and population, New York City became and remains a driving force in American and world culture.

7 RAILROADS

Although the original steam engines and steam locomotives were made practical in Great Britain, only the sweeping geography of North America (or later Russia) would unlock the potential of railroads to shrink space. As roads, bridges, canals, and steamboats advanced transportation, railroads revolutionized it by allowing travel faster than ever before. Railroads could go up and down hill much faster than the lock systems of canals and could carry heavier loads. If mountains were too high to cross, tunnels allowed railroads to pass through. Because railroads were foundational to the expansion of commerce, travel, and thus industry, they became the first big business. Therefore, managers and lawyers working for railroads invented business practices that all other industries and corporations copied. Walt Whitman selected the steam locomotive for one of his poems as the symbol of American energy, innovation, and potential for greatness.

8 SAMUEL F. B. MORSE

Another in a growing series of inventors who transformed life on Earth, Morse contributed to a communications revolution with his development of the telegraph and the code that bears his name. The communication revolution literally paralleled the transportation revolution as telegraph wires were strung on poles alongside railroad tracks. These two inventions together made time zones necessary because rapid travel and almost instantaneous communication required a relative concept of time. Morse was an artist who became fascinated with the concepts of electromagnetism and proved that messages could be sent over vast distances along a continuous wire.

9 JOHN JACOB ASTOR

Astor deserves mention as the first of many rags-to-riches stories that are associated with the American Dream. He is also an example of how German immigrants had a smoother transition to success in American society than other groups like the Irish. Born at the end of the French and Indian War in 1763, by the end of the Revolutionary War in 1783 Astor had worked and saved enough money for passage to New York City. He and his wife embodied the typical path to wealth followed by so many who came after. They lived frugally, worked diligently in their business, and watched for good investments. His original business was the organization of the fur trade taking some of the most independent-minded men in America, fur trappers, and creating a system of regular trafficking that benefited all. Astor traveled extensively and was the first to set up a trading post at the mouth of the Columbia River on the Pacific coast at what would become Astoria. When the fur trade declined he sold out and shrewdly managed his profits. At his death he was the richest man in America.

10 BANKING

Banking and credit began to play an increasingly important role in the economic expansion that characterized the market revolution. The number of state-chartered banks grew dramatically immediately following the War of 1812 and fueled unprecedented economic growth. The number of banks continued to grow in the antebellum period. At this time, the federal government did not issue paper money; it only issued hard currency (gold or silver, or certificates that could be traded in for gold or silver). Banks filled this gap in the economy by issuing paper money—banknotes that could be used as currency. Banks put these banknotes into circulation by lending money to entrepreneurs to enable them to start new businesses or expand existing ones. Banks therefore served two functions that were important to the market revolution—increasing the supply of currency to facilitate economic activity and extending credit to facilitate economic expansion. The system of banknotes as currency was imperfect. Notes from one state might have less value in another state. The system not only created economic growth, but it also created economic volatility. The rapid economic expansion of 1815–1818 was followed by the Panic of 1819.

11 PANICS OF 1819 AND 1837

The Panics of 1819 and 1837 were the nation's first of several economic downturns that grew successively more severe until the Great Depression of the 1930s. The panics reflected the growing interconnectedness of the economy as the scope of the market revolution increased. The Panic of 1819 brought the economic boom of the previous few years to a crashing halt. As banks extended credit and put more and more banknotes into circulation, speculation abounded and inflation occurred. Many benefited from investments, but inflation made it difficult for many Americans to afford products. During this expansion, the Second Bank of the United States did not attempt to rein in the practices of state banks. Finally, the Second Bank changed course in an attempt to cool down the overheated economy by suspending loans and calling in outstanding loans. This led to a contraction of the money supply at the same time that an economic crisis in Europe dampened demand for American products. The Panic of 1837 stemmed largely from the manipulations of the financial industry by the Jackson and Van Buren administrations. Jackson's war on the Second Bank of the United States led to a flow of money into state banks, and the resulting speculation led to a boom followed by a bust. These two panics clearly illustrated the volatile nature of economic activity in the age of the market revolution and the central role that government policies can play, for better or for worse.

12 MCCULLOCH v. MARYLAND

Many years later in 1819 the Marshall Court struck a blow maintaining a powerful central government when Maryland attempted to tax a branch of the Bank of the United States in order to check its influence. After the wrangling over Hamilton's Financial Plan in the Congress, this case was the first opportunity for the Supreme Court to weigh the concept of implied powers. Saying that "The power to tax involves the power to destroy," Marshall voiced the majority opinion on the Court that the federal government's institutions were impervious to state control just as federal law was superior to state law. He forever established the use of the elastic clause with the assertion, "Let the end be legitimate, let it be within the scope of the Constitution, and all means which are appropriate, which are plainly adapted to that end, which are not prohibited, but consist with the letter and spirit of the Constitution, are constitutional." Of course, this phrase also forever established the power of the Supreme Court to decide what was "appropriate," "plainly adapted," and so forth.

13 DARTMOUTH COLLEGE v. WOODWARD

Also in 1819, this case clearly established the superiority of federal law over state law. Dartmouth College had existed since before the American Revolution and was chartered by King George III. When New Hampshire became a state the state legislature eventually sought to change the original charter, something the college resisted. The most distinguished graduate of Dartmouth, Daniel Webster, came to the defense of his alma mater and argued the case before the Supreme Court. Marshall merely pronounced that the original charter had been a contract and that New Hampshire had no power to break a contract. The college survived, but more importantly the states were humbled. The long-term result was to aid businesses of all types by protecting the sanctity of all contracts before the law.

14 GIBBONS v. OGDEN

Known as the "steamboat case," this 1824 suit symbolized both the continuing strength of the federal government and also the rising importance of interstate transportation and commerce. Alexander Hamilton's state of New York attempted to grant a monopoly on water transportation between New York and New Jersey to one company operated by Aaron Ogden but with the backing of Robert Fulton, the inventor of the first practical steamboat. Although the Constitution protected contracts and inventors' patents, Marshall said it did not grant to states the power to control interstate commerce. That arena was the sole prerogative of the federal government, and another giant precedent was set just as the nation was moving toward national markets for products.

15 TEXTILE MILLS

Following Samuel Slater's lead, textile mill towns were established throughout the Northeast between the 1810s and 1840s. Francis Cabot Lowell was an important early innovator and entrepreneur in the textile industry, bringing weaving and spinning together under one roof at mills in Massachusetts—Waltham in 1813 and Lowell in 1821. One reason the United States did not industrialize even more rapidly was a limited labor supply. The vast majority of Americans worked on farms at the beginning of the nineteenth century and many urban workers were skilled artisans. By the 1820s, however, changes in agriculture helped solve the labor problem. New agricultural technology allowed for fewer farmers to tend larger farms. Improvements in transportation allowed Midwest farms to help meet the food needs of eastern cities and towns. Industrialists, therefore, were able to induce more Americans to become machine operators. The emerging water-powered factories used one of two strategies for recruiting workers. In larger urban centers, such as New York City, it was common practice to draw entire families to the location of the factory and employ all the members of the family, including children. In rural New England, factory owners recruited the daughters of New England farm families to move to mill towns. This system was first employed at the Lowell mills along the Merrimack River. By the 1840s, immigrants from Ireland and elsewhere in Europe began replacing native-born factory hands in many factories.

16 LOWELL GIRLS

The Lowell textile mills in Massachusetts solved their labor supply problems by recruiting the daughters of New England farm families. The first mills in Lowell opened in 1821; by 1830, eight Lowell mills employed more than 6,000 women. The young women who worked in the mills were known as "Lowell Girls." It was thought that these women could be paid less and would only be temporary factory hands. It was assumed that they would eventually get married and be replaced by new women, who would be recruited to replace them. The fathers of these young women were assured by factory recruiters that their daughters would be working in a "factory in the garden"—a clean, bucolic setting, unlike the dirty and dangerous factory cities of Great Britain. The women tended to live in closely supervised boarding houses, and the work was also strictly monitored. Despite this scrutiny, both on the job and even at the boarding houses, the Lowell Girls experienced a degree of freedom and autonomy unheard of for young women at the time. Many participated in producing a periodical called the *Lowell Offering*. They demonstrated their sense of solidarity and assertiveness by going on strike in

1834 and again in 1836, following announced wage cuts. The 1836 strike restored their original wages, but by the 1840s the young farm women were being replaced by Irish immigrants who were in dire straits and ready to work for lower wages.

17 IRISH IMMIGRATION

A sudden blight caused by a fungus in September 1845 destroyed the potato crop in Ireland. The disease lingered, and tariff laws protecting the wealthy classes prevented the importation of grain to stave off the hunger stalking the land, as the lower classes of Ireland subsisted almost entirely on potatoes. Estimates range from four hundred thousand to one million Irish succumbed to starvation while much of what food was produced continued to be shipped to England according to existing contracts. Under conditions like these, almost two million Irish migrated to the United States in the middle of the nineteenth century. The Irish arrived impoverished and had little hope at first of anything beyond meager factory wages to keep them alive in eastern cities. In time, however, the Irish made a lasting cultural contribution to America and became important in the power structures of New York, Boston, and Chicago among other cities.

18 GERMAN IMMIGRATION

After the Irish, the second largest immigrant group during the first half of the nineteenth century was German. German immigrants, who had been arriving to the United States from the colonial period (see page 80), tended to be better off than their Irish counterparts. Many were skilled craftsmen and entrepreneurs who emigrated to the United States to escape political repression following the failed Revolution of 1848 in the German states. German immigrants were more likely to have the resources to continue their journeys beyond their initial city of disembarkation (usually New York City). Many settled in the "German triangle" of western cities, such as Cincinnati, St. Louis, and Milwaukee, where they became artisans or small business owners. The beer brewing industry of the Midwest came to be dominated by Germans. The availability of affordable farmland along the Ohio and Mississippi Rivers also attracted Germans to this region. By 1860, there were approximately one million German-born people in the United States.

19 NATIVISM

The first half of the nineteenth century witnessed a dramatic increase in immigration from Europe, with thousands of Irish and German immigrants entering the country. A strong nativist, or anti-immigrant, movement resulted. The movement focused especially, but not exclusively, on Irish immigrants. The main goal of this movement was to limit the power and influence of newly arrived immigrants. Nativism was both an emotional impulse as well as an organized movement. Many Americans thought that the Irish Catholic immigrants lacked the self-control of "proper" middle-class Protestant Americans. For nativists, this lack of self-control was evident in the drinking habits of immigrants. Nativists tried to regulate and weaken the drinking culture of immigrant communities, which manifested itself in Irish pubs and German beer halls. In addition, many working-class people feared that immigrants would drive down wages. Many Irish immigrants were desperate to find any work and accepted wages that were below the going rate for native-born workers. In the 1840s and 1850s, the newly-formed American Party (or Know-Nothing Party) gave this nativist impulse a political platform (see page 187).

20 "CULT OF DOMESTICITY"

The market revolution had a profound impact on gender and family roles. Antebellum society underwent a redefinition of women's "proper" role in society. During the antebellum period, many Americans came to see separate spheres in society—a male-dominated public sphere and a female-oriented private sphere. In an increasingly market-oriented society, women were seen as belonging outside of this rough-and-tumble world of money and politics. A set of domestic ideals, that came to be derisively called the "cult of domesticity," developed in the first decades of the nineteenth century. The ideas of "republican motherhood," which shaped gender roles in the decades after the American Revolution, gave way to a less public-minded conception of a middle-class woman's "place." Commentators in the first half of the nineteenth century tended to see women as intellectually inferior and insisted that their proper role was maintaining the house and caring for children. This "cult of domesticity" insisted that women keep a proper Christian home, separate from the male sphere of politics, business, and competition.

THE BIG PICTURE

1. Changes in the financial system and a series of Supreme Court decisions that prioritized contractual obligations paved the way for the development of a market economy that transformed the economy of the United States.

2. Entrepreneurs and innovators developed the factory system in the United States, changing patterns of work, bringing many operations under one roof, and ushering in the mass production techniques.

3. Immigration picked up in the middle of the nineteenth century with Irish and Germans helping to swell eastern cities just in time for the beginnings of the Industrial Revolution.

4. Transportation and communication were both revolutionized and contributed dramatically to the transformation of the American economy.

5. Economic growth and the development of regional and national markets provided a higher standard of living for most Americans, created vast fortunes for some, and powerfully impacted the less fortunate like immigrant factory workers.

Mini Quiz

1. The reason the Stamp Act caused such alarm among Americans in 1765 was that the new tax

   (A) showed that George III and Parliament intended to control the colonial economy.
   (B) highlighted colonial dependence on England for manufactured goods like paper.
   (C) was intended to control colonial court proceedings by the stamp requirement.
   (D) was the first direct tax merely for revenue rather than mercantilist control.
   (E) made it impossible for Americans to advance in professional careers.

2. The colonial representative assembly to issue the Declaration of Independence was the

   (A) Albany Congress.
   (B) First Continental Congress.
   (C) Second Continental Congress.
   (D) Stamp Act Congress.
   (E) Philadelphia Convention.

3. Among which of the following factors was the chief reason the United States won its independence?

   (A) The Continental Army and the French Navy together amounted to a superior military force.
   (B) George Washington was a brilliant military strategist.
   (C) Large portions of the British military deserted to join the American forces.
   (D) The growing free market economy of America outpaced that of mercantilist England.
   (E) British resolve was insufficient to surmount the tremendous physical challenges of the war.

4. The foundation of the American republic depended on all of the following principles **EXCEPT**

    (A) the national government would be divided into three branches.

    (B) the power in the country was exercised by the voting citizens.

    (C) the government operated through representatives rather than through direct democracy.

    (D) legislators expressed the will of the people by making laws.

    (E) all citizens, even the rulers, were subject to the country's laws.

5. The leader of the American Revolution NOT present at the Constitutional Convention was

    (A) Benjamin Franklin.

    (B) George Washington.

    (C) Thomas Jefferson.

    (D) Roger Sherman.

    (E) Alexander Hamilton.

6. What attitude toward state governments existed after the ratification of the U.S. Constitution and the Bill of Rights?

    (A) State governments would lose all importance once the central government got on its feet.

    (B) State governments would share some powers with the central government and lose others.

    (C) State governments would continue just as they were from the founding of the country.

    (D) State governments would gain new powers to hold the new central government in check.

    (E) State governments would forfeit all access to military power.

7. George Washington's chief political and administrative adviser in his new government was

    (A) Secretary of State Thomas Jefferson.

    (B) Secretary of War Henry Knox.

    (C) Chief Justice of the Supreme Court John Jay.

    (D) Secretary of Treasury Alexander Hamilton.

    (E) Attorney General Edmund Randolph.

8. The first compromise hammered out in the U.S. Congress that could be said to be a North/South compromise was over what issue(s)?

    (A) The slave trade in the national capital

    (B) The excise tax on whiskey

    (C) The national debt and payment of war bonds at par

    (D) The Bank of the United States and the location of the national capital

    (E) The representation of slaveholding states in the House of Representatives

9. George Washington's foreign policy position is best expressed how?

(A) Foreign powers should not interfere in America nor fear American interference.
(B) The United States needed to test its military prowess against some European power.
(C) The United States should acquire territories at sea to facilitate foreign trade.
(D) France could count on the United States for a long-term military alliance against England.
(E) The United States should join in an association of nations dedicated to world peace.

10. Thomas Jefferson's political views could be summed up with what phrase?

(A) A strong central government was the best assurance of national unity.
(B) The U.S. Constitution should be viewed as a general guide for shaping policy.
(C) The American economy needed to diversify in the quest for world power status.
(D) An educated elite made up the natural rulers of any society.
(E) Whatever was good for simple rural citizens was good for America.

11. Which two men were most responsible for the Louisiana Purchase?

(A) Thomas Jefferson and French Foreign Minister Talleyrand
(B) Aaron Burr and Robert Livingston
(C) Napoleon Bonaparte and Toussaint L'Ouverture
(D) Meriwether Lewis and William Clark
(E) John Quincy Adams and James Madison

12. Which position in the government usually produced the next president during the Virginia dynasty?

(A) Vice president
(B) Secretary of state
(C) Secretary of war
(D) Secretary of treasury
(E) General in the U.S. Army

13. Which previous treaty was most responsible for the breakdown in relations that led to the War of 1812?

(A) The 1763 Treaty of Paris
(B) Pinckney's Treaty
(C) The Treaty of Greenville
(D) Jay's Treaty
(E) The Treaty of Washington

14. In which region did the United States experience its greatest success against the British military in the fighting associated with the War of 1812?

   (A) The Chesapeake region
   (B) The region nearest the border with Canada
   (C) The Great Lakes region
   (D) The region around New York
   (E) The region around New Orleans

15. Which technological advance did NOT occur prior to 1850?

   (A) Interchangeable parts as the basis for mass production
   (B) The cotton gin
   (C) Textile manufacturing mills
   (D) The steam locomotive
   (E) The assembly line

ANSWER EXPLANATIONS

1. **(D)** The Stamp Act's primary offense in the eyes of Americans was its departure from indirect taxation designed to control the economy to direct taxation designed merely to raise money to pay the war debt.

2. **(C)** The famous gathering of the Founding Fathers that declared American independence was the Second Continental Congress.

3. **(E)** Choice (E) is the only answer that was true of the Revolutionary War.

4. **(A)** This principle was not a part of the Articles of Confederation but came later with the U.S. Constitution.

5. **(C)** Thomas Jefferson, although often assumed to have written the U.S. Constitution, was away from the country as an ambassador to France during the Constitutional Convention.

6. **(B)** A major part of the revision of the government in the Critical Period was the removal of certain powers from the states, like issuing currency and charging tariffs, but the definition of a federal government is also that states would share power with the central government.

7. **(D)** Although George Washington selected and respected all of these men for their roles in the new government, Alexander Hamilton organized the finances of the new government, the beginnings of the Federalist Party, and the practical workings of government through several precedents supported by President Washington.

8. **(D)** The Bank of the United States and the moving of the national capital was the direct swap between Federalists in the North and Anti-Federalists from the South. No compromise was reached on answer (A) until 1850, whereas answers (B) and (C) were a part of the general financial program proposed by Hamilton that antagonized others than just southerners. Answer (E) occurred during the Constitutional Convention in Philadelphia.

9. **(A)** Washington's policy was isolationist and was either directly or indirectly opposed to all the other choices.

10. **(E)** Thomas Jefferson was opposed to all the rest of the ideas even though he was an elite aristocrat. He was a strict constructionist and believed America should retain an agrarian economy. He valued yeoman farmers above all other citizens and acted as their chief advocate.

11. **(C)** All these men played a role directly or indirectly in the Louisiana Purchase or in the Louisiana Territory, but Napoleon's plans set all the rest in motion until thwarted by L'Ouverture's Haitian Revolution, which caused Napoleon to choose to sell the land to Jefferson through Livingston's negotiations with Talleyrand.

12. **(B)** All of the Virginia dynasty presidents were first secretaries of state except for Washington.

13. **(D)** Of these only Jay's Treaty had any relevant bearing on the British during the era of the War of 1812, and the failure of the treaty strained Anglo-American relations to the breaking point.

14. **(E)** Most of these regions saw mostly American failures, some that were atrocious. One small victory on the Great Lakes and a significant turning point at Lake Champlain could not compare with the glory of the lopsided victory at New Orleans.

15. **(E)** All of these advances occurred before 1850 except for Henry Ford's assembly line that was not perfected until the 1920s.

The Age of Jackson

12

Get up on all occasions, and sometimes on no occasion at all, and make long-winded speeches, though composed of nothing else than wind.

—Davy Crockett's advice to politicians, 1836

TIMELINE	
1810	Henry Clay begins his influence in the Senate
1816	Clay proposes his American System to stabilize the economy
1819	Panic of 1819 begins
1820	Missouri Compromise
1824	Andrew Jackson accuses John Quincy Adams and Henry Clay of making a Corrupt Bargain; Election of 1824 is contested in the House of Representatives
1825	John Quincy Adams becomes president
1828	John C. Calhoun writes "South Carolina Exposition and Protest"; Andrew Jackson wins the presidency in the Election of 1828; Daniel Webster begins his influence in the Senate
1829	Kitchen Cabinet meetings begin in the Jackson administration; Jackson employs the Spoils System of rotation in office for civil servants
1829–1836	Bank War develops between the Senate and the Jackson administration
1830	Webster-Hayne Debates take place in the Senate
1832	Whigs and Democrats restore the two-party system to American politics; Nullification Crisis begins
1833	Jackson secures the Force Bill from Congress
1836	Martin Van Buren is elected president
1836–1844	Congress imposes the Gag Rule
1837	Panic of 1837 begins

OVERVIEW

President Andrew Jackson was a towering, controversial figure in American history. The years of his presidency (1829–1837), as well as the immediate aftermath, bear the name the Age of Jackson, or the Age of Jacksonian Democracy. Jackson expanded presidential power in several ways. After South Carolina asserted its intent to nullify the Tariff Act of 1828, Jackson challenged and prevented the move. Later, in the case of *Worcester* v. *Georgia* (1832), when the Supreme Court ruled that the Cherokee people were not subject to removal under the 1830 Indian Removal Act, Jackson and the state of Georgia began moving them to the West anyway. Finally, Jackson took actions that led to the destruction of the Second Bank of the United States in the 1830s. His critics labeled him King Andrew in response to these heavy-handed measures.

Jackson was elected to the presidency in 1828. As he was running that year, he and his supporters held onto accusations that President John Quincy Adams had made a "corrupt bargain" four years earlier to block Jackson from the presidency. In the election of 1828, Jackson's supporters painted Adams as out of touch and elitist, while Adams's supporters portrayed Jackson as ill-tempered. Jackson's backwoods, populist appeal helped him win the election.

The election of 1828 is considered by many historians to be the first modern election. First, the electorate was much broader than in previous elections. In the 1820s, most states reduced or removed property qualifications for voting and office holding so that most free males had the right to vote. During the difficult economic times following the Panic of 1819, many people began to demand an end to property restrictions on voting, as property ownership seemed out of reach to many. In 1800, just three states, Kentucky, New Hampshire, and Vermont, had universal white manhood suffrage. By 1830, ten states permitted white manhood suffrage without qualification. Consequently, candidates had to campaign more aggressively and tailor their appeal to reach a broader audience. An increased focus on character and personality accompanied the democratization of the voting process.

Jackson's policies aroused a great deal of controversy. His war on the Second Bank of the United States became a lightning rod for criticism. In response to this increased political rancor, a new political alignment emerged. The tense unity of the one-party "Era of Good Feelings" broke apart as the Jacksonian branch of the Democratic-Republicans became known simply as the Democratic Party and Jackson's opponents organized themselves as the Whig Party (1833). These two parties formed the second two-party system in the nation's history, following the rivalry between the Democratic-Republicans and the Federalists (1790s–1810s).

The fortunes of the historical memory of Andrew Jackson have risen and fallen repeatedly throughout the nearly two centuries since his presidency. In the latter part of the nineteenth century, he was scoffed at in historical literature. New England historians portrayed him as boorish, arrogant, ignorant, and authoritarian. By the early twentieth century, Progressive Era historians took a more favorable view of Jackson. He was seen as a champion of the common man who brought a democratic, pioneer spirit with him to the White House. More recently, historians and the public have looked more critically at Jackson. Many Americans have become more attuned to the historical suffering of American Indians. In this context, the Indian Removal Act and the "Trail of Tears" began to loom large in the historical memory of Jackson. During the Obama administration, the Treasury Department took steps to remove Jackson from the $20 bill. That move has met resistance from the Trump administration.

1 ANDREW JACKSON

The epitome of a self-made man, Andrew Jackson was orphaned by the Revolutionary War but then pulled himself up from poverty, taught himself enough law to practice on the frontier, and wound up a planter aristocrat of the South. He got into politics but proved too hot-headed and combative. These qualities served him well on a military campaign against the Creek Indians, however, which brought him in close proximity to New Orleans, the defense of which he took on himself. The Battle of New Orleans catapulted him to national fame and eventually the presidency. His forceful style of leadership manifested itself in prolific use of the veto, American Indian removal, the Bank War, and other episodes of a career that led historians to name the period from 1820 to 1840 the Age of Jackson.

2 ELECTIONS OF 1824 AND 1828

These presidential elections were the first modern elections with strategies and procedures recognizable today. John Quincy Adams won in 1824 over Andrew Jackson in the House of Representatives because no clear majority existed in the Electoral College. The result infuriated Jackson because he had won the popular vote in the election and believed that Henry Clay and Adams had conspired to steal the election. Jackson won outright in 1828, however, and brought his common man democratic values to bear on the nation's problems. These two elections ended the Era of Good Feelings, and Americans have embraced the two-party system ever since.

3 CORRUPT BARGAIN

Jackson's (and his supporters') belief that the Election of 1824 was stolen stemmed from his accusation that Henry Clay dropped out of the election in order to be president later. Clay did throw his support behind John Quincy Adams thereby securing the vote in the House of Representatives for Adams, but Jackson accused the two of conspiring to bring Clay into the cabinet as secretary of state. Most presidents to that point had been the secretary of state of the previous president, so when Clay was chosen for the slot Jackson cried foul. No evidence exists to prove that Adams and Clay actually made a deal, but Jackson was Clay's sworn enemy for the rest of their lives.

4 SPOILS SYSTEM

This name for patronage is associated with Andrew Jackson's presidency because he quoted the phrase from the classical world, "To the victor belong the spoils." All presidents before his time and since selected many of their supporters as advisers and to hold positions in government. Jackson was simply the first to do so after the Era of Good Feelings when one-party rule had left a class of civil servants in power for almost three decades. Jackson said rotation in office was necessary to prevent these individuals from becoming parasites or from acquiring too much influence even though they were not elected

> **RUSH-BAGOT AGREEMENT**
>
> After the War of 1812, the United States and Britain decided in 1817 that the Great Lakes should be demilitarized. Naval armaments were limited, and a lasting peace between the United States and Canada was begun.

to office. In the context of his campaign and subsequent political struggles Jackson's supporters viewed the measures as "cleaning house," whereas his enemies accused him of giving away the government to his friends. Of course, most presidents of the nineteenth century gave the government away to their friends.

5 KITCHEN CABINET

Speaking of the friends and associates of Andrew Jackson, he liked to meet with them in the kitchen after state dinners to discuss policy where they could feel free to spit tobacco on the floor. Jackson's informal advisers were usually more important in his decision-making process than was his actual cabinet. His enemies therefore used this pejorative phrase to portray these closed-door sessions with cronies as giving them undue influence. All presidents, however, have trusted private advisers to help them accomplish the monumental task of running the executive branch.

6 NATIONAL NOMINATING CONVENTION

Another lasting legacy to arise from the Age of Jackson was the national nominating convention. In an age of growing democracy, the shady caucus system of the party leadership's selecting the candidates for president and vice president in secret was replaced with a more open system. By 1832, the modern Democratic Party was born and selected Jackson as their candidate. The conventions also served to let delegates debate and hammer out a party platform that their chosen candidate was supposed to go out and stump for on the campaign trail and implement if and when he took office.

> **ANTI-MASONIC PARTY**
>
> The first third party in U.S. history formed in New York in 1828 to oppose the perceived conspiracy of freemasons to take over the republic. This one-issue party was the first to hold a national nominating convention.

7 NULLIFICATION CRISIS

The 1828 tariff was a protective tariff so high as to earn the title the Tariff of Abominations in the South. Tariffs helped northern manufacturers compete with cheaper imported goods, therefore, making manufactured products more expensive while alienating foreign customers of exports like cotton. Although the 1832 tariff was slightly lower, it was still protective, and South Carolina nullified it. This step threatened national unity with secession. Andrew Jackson firmly supported the Union and threatened to invade South Carolina if she seceded. Again, Henry Clay calmed the crisis with a compromise tariff reduced annually over nine years.

8 JOHN C. CALHOUN

Another constellation of the antebellum political sky was John C. Calhoun of South Carolina. He also held cabinet positions and desired the presidency but rose to prominence only in the Senate. Despite his stint as vice president under Jackson, Calhoun took South Carolina's side in the Nullification Crisis and anonymously published editorials against Jackson's policies. Calhoun was an ardent believer in states' rights, slavery, and thus nullification and eventually secession. He abandoned the Calvinist doctrines of his Scots-Irish heritage but kept all of the stubbornness. He was the southern star in the powerful triumvirate of senators who opposed Andrew Jackson but compromised in order to keep the peace.

9 FORCE BILL

The Force Bill was a sign of the severity of the conflict between South Carolina and President Andrew Jackson during the Nullification Crisis. If the customs agents in South Carolina refused to collect the protective tariff, Jackson vowed to prosecute them as traitors. The Force Bill said that the president could use the military to enforce the law. Jackson said, "If you secede, we will invade." South Carolina nullified the Force Bill, which implied that if the president led the U.S. Army into South Carolina that the Force Bill would not be in effect the moment they entered the state. Jackson refrained when he realized it was an election year and he needed the southern planter aristocratic class to win. Instead of pressing the Force Bill, Jackson made a peaceful gesture of stopping the mail service of the abolitionist press. South Carolina accepted the offered gesture and cooperated with Henry Clay's compromise tariff plan.

10 GAG RULE

This resolution in the House of Representatives is as responsible for the onset of the Civil War as any of the other more famous causes. The Gag Rule was adopted in 1836 and remained in effect until 1844 during the very time the constitutional process of debate and majority rule could have helped both sides toward gradual emancipation of slaves and compensation for their owners. Instead, where the debates were most intense because of the South's handicap in representation due to its lower population, the capacity for peaceful debate was silenced. The rules stated that any abolitionist resolution or bill brought before the House would be immediately tabled, or postponed indefinitely. While this kept arguments from arising in the Congress, they arose later anyway when tempers were hotter, the compromising Senate leaders were dead, and the conflict between North and South inevitably ended in a terrible war.

11 BANK WAR

Jackson's other big confrontation with his rivals in the Senate was the conflict over the Bank of the United States (BUS). Jackson had publicly called the bank and its national currency a conspiracy against the rights of the people. In trying to diminish Jackson's popularity, Henry Clay and Daniel Webster sought to recharter the BUS early during a presidential election year. While the Whig Party and business interests of the country had come to think of the bank as a necessary part of the economy, Jackson saw it as an enemy of the common man. The showdown came when Jackson vetoed the recharter bill and began the transfer of federal funds into his supporter's private banks in various states. Drained of funds, the BUS was bankrupted and Jackson was more popular than ever. The machinations of Nicholas Biddle, the bank's director, contributed to the coming Panic of 1837, however, as did Jackson's "pet banks" by encouraging rampant speculation in a burgeoning economy.

12 SPECIE CIRCULAR

In 1836, in an effort to stabilize the currency and thus the economy, Jackson issued an executive order called the Specie Circular (1836). In the immediate aftermath of Jackson's destruction of the Second Bank of the United States, the economy heated up. Freed up from federal regulation, banks began to print and issue more and more bank notes. In addition, a large amount of silver from Mexican mines made its way into U.S. banks. Entrepreneurs freely borrowed money to invest in business ventures. In this economic environment, inflation occurred, with basic commodities rising in price by 50 percent or more. In addition, speculation in western land increased. In 1834, over four million acres of public land were sold; in 1836, five times that amount of land was sold. Jackson moved to slow down the speculation in western land. He feared that western land was being bought by eastern capitalists rather than by small-scale farmers. He issued the Specie Circular mandating that land could only be purchased with gold or silver coin. The move slowed land speculation in the West and resulted in a shortage of government funds. Both the destruction of the Second Bank of the United States and the Specie Circular contributed to the economic downturn known as the Panic of 1837.

13 HENRY CLAY

As influential a senator and failed presidential candidate as there has ever been, Henry Clay was a slave-owning attorney from Kentucky who represented his young state from his old War Hawk days until his death in 1852. He was responsible for the Missouri Compromise,

> **TARIFF OF 1816**
>
> As a part of Clay's American System, the Tariff of 1816 was the first protective tariff. A protective tariff is one designed more to protect domestic manufacturers than to raise revenue.

the compromise tariff, and the Compromise of 1850, partly due to his ability to cooperate with John C. Calhoun as a planter aristocrat and with Daniel Webster as a Whig, the opposition party Clay helped to found. He was the first major statesman of the Age of Jackson to follow through with Alexander Hamilton's vision of a national economy. Clay's American System attempted to use the influence of the federal government to stimulate the economy and to stabilize it at the same time. He supported the Second Bank of the United States, a high protective tariff, and internal transportation improvements using federal dollars.

14 DANIEL WEBSTER

Considered the greatest political orator of his day, this Massachusetts senator embodied New England principles of education and commerce. Famous for his defense of his alma mater, Dartmouth, before the Supreme Court, he applied his oratory to larger issues as the Age of Jackson unfolded. As a Whig leader he cooperated with Henry Clay in defending the BUS and promoting the American System, but his singular contribution was enunciating the North's view that secession was unconstitutional. In a debate with Senator Hayne from South Carolina, Webster agreed with Jackson in one regard: that secession would never occur peacefully. His ringing line was, "Liberty and Union, now and forever, one and inseparable." Before the days of the Pledge of Allegiance, Webster voiced the principles that would carry the country toward actual nationhood through the trials of the Civil War.

15 WHIGS VERSUS DEMOCRATS

These were the two significant parties that restored the two-party system to American politics. The Democrats coalesced around the heroic stature of Andrew Jackson as a champion of the common man, an instigator of westward expansion, and a member of the aristocratic planter class. The Whigs derived their party name from the traditional name for an opposition party in English politics. Henry Clay, Daniel Webster, and even Abraham Lincoln were Whigs. The first split of the Jeffersonian Republican Party that ended the Era of Good Feelings was that of the National Republicans and the Democratic Republicans. The National Republicans became the Whigs and the Democratic Republicans became the Democrats. While the Democrats remain a party today, northern Whigs were later absorbed with other smaller parties into the modern Republican Party in 1854. As to policy, the Democratic Party originally adopted the notion that common people deserved a voice in government just as did the Jeffersonian Republicans, but after Andrew Jackson was president they adopted the desire to have a strong central government from the Federalists. The main plank of the Whig Party was to block whatever Andrew Jackson wanted to do.

16 WEBSTER-HAYNE DEBATES

These 1830 debates in the Senate began over a Connecticut senator's desire to slow down the sale of western lands. What they became was a showdown between those who interpreted the Constitution as creating a nation and those who still viewed it as continuing a league of friendship among states. Northerners feared that open access to land in the West would drain the new factories of their laborers. The nationalism born of the War of 1812 was clearly dissipated when Robert Hayne of South Carolina created an alliance of the South and the West against the North by insisting that the lands remain open for sale as a source of new slave territories. Daniel Webster exploded in oratory about all the issues then dividing the nation including the sale of lands, the tariff, the spread of slavery, and especially states' rights. Webster made it clear that he was a unionist and that all talk of one state or section going its own way was detrimental to the core understanding of the American republic, a nation created by the will of the people, not the will of states. The rancor over these and other issues revealed that, while the Founding Fathers were astute in forming the U.S. Constitution, certain intentional and inadvertent ambiguities dangerously threatened the Union when men from every section differed over the very nature of the republic.

17 INDIAN REMOVAL ACT

In the first decades of the nineteenth century, Americans hungered for more land as the population grew and the economy expanded. As the profitability of cotton production rose in the first half of the nineteenth century, the value of land in the interior of the South increased dramatically. These pressures led to passage of the Indian Removal Act (1830), which was controversial even in its day. It called for the removal of the Cherokee, Creek, Chickasaw, Choctaw, and Seminole tribes from their traditional lands in the South. These so-called "Five Civilized Tribes" would then be given land in what would become the state of Oklahoma. As far back as the Jefferson administration, federal policy had been to respect the rights of American Indians to inhabit this land. However, President Andrew Jackson abandoned this policy and, in deference to market and land pressures, adopted a policy of Indian removal. This policy applied to the American Indians of the South as well as the Old Northwest and, to a lesser degree, New England and New York. Jackson asserted that it was necessary for these peoples to be removed to the areas of the United States beyond the Mississippi River. He said, perhaps disingenuously, that this was in the best interests of the Indians themselves, who were being forced off their traditional lands by the encroachment of white settlers.

18 WORCESTER v. GEORGIA

In 1831, the state of Georgia moved to seize the land of the Cherokee under the auspices of the Indian Removal Act (1830), but the Cherokee were given a temporary reprieve from the Supreme Court in *Worcester* v. *Georgia* (1832). The Cherokee used a variety of means, including the legal system, to challenge their removal to the West. The Worcester case grew out of a different issue involving the Cherokee. Missionaries were working closely with the Cherokee to help them resist removal. The state of Georgia, therefore, passed a law prohibiting non-American Indians from being present on American Indian lands without a license from the state. A missionary named Samuel Worcester was arrested for violating this statute. The Court invalidated this statute; it ruled that the states had no authority in American Indian affairs. The decision also had the effect of also invalidating Georgia's order to seize the Cherokee's land because it was the federal government—not the state governments—that has the sole authority to deal with American Indian tribes. The Cherokee were "a distinct community, occupying its own territory," the Court asserted; "the laws of Georgia can have no force." The decision was largely ignored by the U.S. government as it pursued its Indian removal policy, but it clarified the relationship between American Indian tribes and the federal government.

19 TRAIL OF TEARS

By the late 1830s, the Cherokee had exhausted their attempts to challenge the Indian Removal Act of 1830 and remain on their traditional lands. The state of Georgia, with the support of President Andrew Jackson and then Jackson's successor, President Martin Van Buren, initiated the process of moving American Indians to the West. The state, with Jackson's blessing, side-stepped the Supreme Court decision in *Worcester* v. *Georgia* (1832), which had ruled that American Indian tribes were subject to federal treaties, not to the actions of states. Some Cherokee cooperated with removal and ceded their land. However, the majority, led by the Cherokee "principal chief" John Ross, adopted a policy of passive resistance to remain on their land. Federal troops were dispatched to enforce Georgia's removal policy. During the resulting expulsion, labeled the "Trail of Tears," the Cherokee marchers were subjected to extortion and violence along the route. The removal of 18,000 American Indians, during a brutal winter, resulted in the deaths of approximately a quarter of the people on the journey.

20 MARTIN VAN BUREN

Affectionately known as "Old Kinderhook" because of his birthplace in New York, his campaigns may be the origin of the Americanism, "OK." He transformed a keen legal mind into a keen political one that rose from obscurity to become the intellect behind the bluster and force of Andrew Jackson as one of Old Hickory's top advisers. In doing so, Van Buren was the organizing force behind the first political party to survive into the modern day, the Democratic Party. Unlike his fierce friend from Tennessee, however, Van Buren opposed the extension of slavery and thus blocked the annexation of Texas. As president, he stuck to Jackson's policy of allowing public land to be bought only with gold or silver and was thus partly responsible for the Panic of 1837, the worst depression the country had ever seen to that point. When the blow fell, Van Buren attempted to stop speculation by taking federal money out of state banks and keeping it in independent treasuries where it was unable to do anybody any good. The panic deepened, and Van Buren was rejected even by his own party in favor of James K. Polk in 1844.

THE BIG PICTURE

1. The Age of Jackson was a time of tremendous energy and volatile sentiments much like the man for whom it was named.

2. Slavery and the spread of slavery were contentious issues throughout the period and were not far below the surface of every other political and economic issue discussed.

3. As more Americans began moving into the interior of the United States in search of land for settlement and agriculture, the government took actions to remove American Indians, which led to displacement and mistreatment.

4. Andrew Jackson restored the executive branch to its prominent position in the federal government through several presidential legacies including the spoils system, actual use of the veto, and the national nominating convention.

5. Through the ups and downs of antebellum economic and political changes, the two-party system was restored to American political life and has endured ever since.

The Second Great Awakening and the Reform Impulse

13

Gentlemen, I commit to you this sacred cause. Your action upon this subject will affect the present and future condition of hundreds and of thousands.

—Dorothea Dix, report to the Massachusetts legislature, 1843

TIMELINE	
1819	Franz Joseph Gall publishes research on phrenology
1826	Temperance movement begins; Joseph Smith reports seeing a vision that begins Mormonism
1830	Joseph Smith publishes the *Book of Mormon*
1830–1850	Second Great Awakening
1832	Lyman Beecher becomes the president of Lane Theological Seminary
1833	Oberlin College is founded
1834	Lyceum movement inspires its 3,000th chapter
1835	Charles G. Finney becomes a professor at Oberlin College
1836	McGuffey Readers are first published
1837	Horace Mann becomes secretary of the Massachusetts Board of Education; Common School movement begins in Massachusetts
1840	Shakers attain their peak membership
1841	Brook Farm is founded; Ralph Waldo Emerson publishes his first essays
1843	Dorothea Dix reports to the Massachusetts legislature
1845	Henry David Thoreau moves to Walden Pond
1847	Brigham Young begins leadership of Mormon church; Brook Farm closes
1848	Seneca Falls Convention launches the women's suffrage movement

OVERVIEW

Although reform movements and voluntary organizations have existed throughout most of American history, the first half of the nineteenth century saw a dramatic upswing in reform activity. Reform movements in the antebellum period (before the Civil War) worked on a variety of issues, including temperance, women's rights, public education, abolitionism, and fair treatment for prisoners and the mentally ill, and had varying degrees of success.

The reform movements of the period are often linked to the Second Great Awakening (the First Great Awakening was a century earlier in the 1730s and 1740s). Beginning as early as the first decade of the nineteenth century, Christian camp meeting revivals appeared in Virginia, Kentucky, and Tennessee. By the 1830s and 1840s, the revivals had spread across the country including to eastern cities; they were especially prevalent in upstate New York and western Pennsylvania. The growing towns adjacent to the Erie Canal came to be known as the "burned-over district" because of the intensity of the religious revival there. Many ministers encouraged this Second Great Awakening because they became worried that Americans seemed more captivated by politics—forming and building a new nation—than by God and salvation. In addition, many ordinary Americans also felt a yearning to get in touch with a more immediate religious experience.

The Second Great Awakening told the individual that salvation was in his or her hands. Righteous living, self-control, and a strong moral compass would lead to salvation. This idea that one could determine his or her eternal life was very different from the old Puritan notion of predestination, which held that one's eternal life was planned out by God. The Second Great Awakening not only encouraged individual redemption, but also societal reformation. Not only could one become perfect in the eyes of God, but one could work to perfect society as well. In this respect, the Second Great Awakening acted as a springboard for a variety of reform movements.

The temperance movement was the largest reform movement of the first half of the nineteenth century. Many temperance activists focused on individual self-control, they encouraged people to voluntarily take an oath of abstinence from alcohol. Others sought to use the power of government to limit or eliminate the consumption of alcoholic beverages. Another powerful movement was the abolitionist movement (discussed in Chapter 14). Many abolitionists saw slavery as a profoundly immoral practice. In addition, they noted that masters exhibited a lack of restraint in subjecting their slaves to rape and wanton violence. A women's rights movement also developed in the antebellum period, seeking to address gender inequalities and to improve opportunities for women. The movement expressed its ideals at the 1848 Seneca Falls Convention in Western New York. Reformers tackled a whole host of other issues during this period, pushing society in new directions and altering the parameters of democracy.

1 CHARLES G. FINNEY

This Presbyterian minister was singularly responsible for departing from the Calvinist doctrines of traditional Presbyterianism and for ushering in new methods of seeking converts. Finney organized camp meetings during the Second Great Awakening where fervent, less polished preaching was combined with techniques designed to soften the hearts of those in attendance. Camp meetings were gatherings in the open air where one or more revival preachers exhorted frontier families to change their own lives in response to the message of the Christian Gospel. Modern evangelicalism received its emotionalism and persuasive tendencies from Finney's New Light methods. Conservative, or Old Light, Christian leaders criticized Finney for abandoning orthodoxy and for using empty spiritual enthusiasm to make superficial converts. Finney became the president of Oberlin College after leaving the frontier for a time to test his methods in the urban East.

2 CIRCUIT-RIDING PREACHERS

These men were about as popular a frontier folk hero stereotype as that of riverboat men or long hunters. Since there were too few ministers to fill the need for preaching in churches founded during the Second Great Awakening, missionary preachers would ride on a circuit like circuit judges and preach in a different church each Sunday. Their temporal news was as readily devoured as their eternal news, and their appearances became popular community events because marriages, baptisms, and funerals were conducted while they were present. The difficulty for frontier Christianity, however, was that in their absence lay leaders would conduct services and minister to the church members, a process that over time served to decrease adherence to orthodoxy, or sound doctrine. Some frontier lay preachers preached without actually being able to read the scriptures, but such was the nature of American culture during the new era of the common man that men like Charles G. Finney appealed to the democratic and enterprising spirit of the age just as Andrew Jackson did.

3 TEMPERANCE MOVEMENT

At the bottom of many of societies' evils, according to many of the preachers of the Second Great Awakening, was the excessive consumption of alcohol. Domestic abuse and other crimes were blamed on "demon rum." Of course societies were formed to attack this vice behind the vices, including the Women's Christian Temperance Union and the Anti-Saloon League. The original purpose of these reformers was to encourage moderate use of alcohol, but the temperance movement eventually turned into the Prohibition movement that ultimately amended the Constitution to outlaw even the production and sale of alcoholic beverages. Those opposed to the legislation inspired by the temperance movements said that the reform violated their freedom both to sell alcohol and consume it. Slaveholders later used the same argument against abolition with much less success.

> **MAINE LAW**
>
> Neal S. Dow of Maine secured this law from his state legislature in 1851 after intense lobbying. The Maine Law prohibited the manufacture and sale of intoxicating beverages. A dozen states followed this model for the later Prohibition movement.

4 DOROTHEA DIX

The headmistress at a Boston school for girls, Dorothea Dix dedicated her life to reforming prisons, almshouses, and asylums. She gathered data on the conditions in these institutions in Massachusetts and other states and presented her findings in 1843 to the Massachusetts legislature. Her efforts led to the improvement of conditions for the mentally ill in at least fifteen states, and she was placed in charge of all female nurses during the Civil War. One can hardly imagine a more ardent pioneer in any field, and she established the techniques of investigation and reform that applied to many later humanitarian efforts.

5 INDIAN RESERVATIONS

Some reformers set their sights on the American Indian population within the United States. These reformers were troubled by the approach of the U.S. government toward American Indians— the removal or extermination to make way for white settlement. The idea of establishing reservations grew, in part, out of a desire to protect the American Indians from the growing encroachment of whites moving westward. Of course, the idea of establishing reservations in the West—the first ones were established in Oklahoma—neatly complemented the removal policy established earlier by the government. In 1851, the Indian Appropriations Act established reservations that were to be enclosed and protected by the federal government. Reformers also believed that American Indians could be transformed in this new setting—that they could learn the ways of civilization and be uplifted and regenerated (to use the rhetoric of the reformers). The impulse to create humane penitentiaries where prisoners could reflect and reform also animated the movement to create Indian reservations.

6 SENECA FALLS CONVENTION

Lucretia Mott and Elizabeth Cady Stanton launched the women's suffrage movement at this meeting of around three hundred women and men in New York in 1848. Beyond demanding the vote, the document listing their grievances, "The Declaration of Sentiments," called for the ending of discriminatory practices and lay the groundwork for the modern feminist movement. From there, Mott and Stanton worked with Susan B. Anthony and other activists to secure women's suffrage, although the movement paused its efforts at the climax of the abolitionist crusade.

7 LYMAN BEECHER

This Connecticut minister was not only the father of Harriet Beecher Stowe (the author of *Uncle Tom's Cabin*) and abolitionist preacher Henry Ward Beecher but also the father of the reform association. Beecher did not believe government even in a democratic republic was sufficient to guide morals and protect liberty. He insisted that American citizens needed education and Christian teachings to properly reform themselves and society. His widely circulated sermons and pamphlets inspired the formation of numerous associations, or societies, dedicated to reforming all manner of social ills. He was a perfect example of the twofold nature of most reformers as educators and as religious leaders because he was both.

8 COMMON SCHOOL MOVEMENT

Like so many other reforms, the common school movement originated up out of the Massachusetts Puritan tradition that sought both to convert people to Christianity but also to educate them so as to prepare them for callings. Although Thomas Jefferson espoused public education, tax-supported schools did not spread across the country as the basis for modern public schools until the efforts of Horace Mann and others picked up after Jefferson's death. With the influx of large immigrant populations, common schools provided a shared educational experience to assimilate Americans from differing backgrounds into a common culture. In the nineteenth century, this culture was Protestant, hence the formation of Catholic school systems. Educational reform was seen by nearly all reformers as a key investment in the long-term preservation of American civilization. Education was made available for free but was not compulsory at first.

9 HORACE MANN

An attorney and humanitarian reformer, Horace Mann became a legislator and educational advocate on the Massachusetts State Board of Education. He was responsible for implementing almost all of the aspects of public schooling as a pioneer of modern school systems. Common schools were open for a minimum of six months of the year. Mann secured increased funding for the schools and for teacher salaries and revised curriculums and methods of instruction. He also founded the first state-operated teacher-training school in the country. The Massachusetts common school movement was picked up as a model in western states first, then back East in Virginia, and then became universal as the twentieth century opened.

10 MCGUFFEY READERS

William McGuffey was another minister/educator who was asked by a publishing company to produce a series of readers for children to use as textbooks. He began publishing the series in the 1830s so its use coincided nicely with the rise of common schools. The books were designed to progressively improve the students' reading ability, literary taste, and morals, and espoused a set of values descended from the Puritans. Widely criticized for emphasizing white, Anglo-Saxon Protestant values as superior to others, the books still were instrumental in educating generations of Americans even on the frontier.

11 OBERLIN COLLEGE

Oberlin College was founded by missionaries in 1833 when northeastern Ohio was still a frontier. The express mission of the school was to educate teachers and other leaders to help develop the frontier both morally and intellectually. In keeping with the atmosphere of reform, Oberlin allowed women and minorities to enroll and graduated the first women with college degrees from an American university. The school early on became associated with Presbyterian minister Charles G. Finney and the style of revivalism prevalent on the frontier during the Second Great Awakening.

12 LYCEUM MOVEMENT

The secular answer to the Second Great Awakening was the Lyceum movement. The aura of self-improvement inspired even non-Christians and nontraditional Christians to desire societal reform. The original Lyceum was Aristotle's school, and the movement in America in the Age of Jackson was also an educational institution. Lyceums were public lecture halls dedicated to adult education and public debate. These halls were favorite venues for Transcendentalists to discuss their philosophy and for scientists to astound audiences with experiments and with new machines. Some of the presenters and lecturers in Lyceums were charlatans, but the fact that people actually came to hear information just to better themselves speaks to the ongoing prevalence of optimism in American society.

13 PHRENOLOGY

Originated by Franz Joseph Gall, this pseudoscience became popular during the reform era as a means of explaining human behavior and personality. Phrenologists posited maps of the human brain that placed various aspects of temperament, talent, and proclivities in various regions that could be assessed by measuring the skull. Lyceums gave phrenologists the opportunity to perform public demonstrations and schedule private screenings. The new confidence in science as a method of investigating and explaining all natural phenomena contributed to the popularity of such a system, and for a time phrenology was given by some serious consideration in screening individuals for employment and other purposes as another method of self-improvement.

14 BROOK FARM

This utopian community was the most interesting of its type largely due to the luminaries who attempted to join in creating a perfect alternate society there. A Unitarian minister named George Ripley purchased a farm outside Boston, and from 1841 until 1847 the likes of Ralph Waldo Emerson, Henry David Thoreau, Margaret Fuller, and Nathaniel Hawthorne made varying degrees of physical and financial commitments to creating a model society. Thus the community was based on Unitarian and Transcendentalist principles, although the intense individualism of the latter undermined the communal impulse. Brook Farm practiced radical forms of equality and universal education that made the society certainly different than typical American society, but most of the better-educated members chafed under the rigors of farm life. Those who found the atmosphere too stifling left, and Ripley's mismanagement led the community toward bankruptcy.

15 SHAKERS

Celibate neighbors to the free-love Oneida community, the Shakers were founded even before the United States in 1774 by a woman named Mother Ann Lee. They were a monastic sect of Christianity that devoted themselves to work and worship. Shaker villages were organized into families, although males and females led segregated lives. The Shakers founded villages in New York but then spread out to New England and beyond until they reached a peak membership in 1830. Shaker villages declined over the next century because celibacy left no other way to propagate their faith except through conversions. Shaker missionaries were less and less successful as the reform era passed and their doctrine of pacifism estranged them from other Americans who fought the first modern wars. The Shaker lifestyle was simple as was their elegant furniture. Shakers represented not only the reform impulse but also a millennial view of Christianity that taught humanitarian reforms as utopian communities were trying to perfect society so that Christ would return.

> ### ONEIDA COMMUNITY
> Oneida was a utopian society founded by John Humphrey Noyes in 1848 in New York. The community shared all property in common and a form of free love called "complex marriage." This organization lasted until the 1870s when such members as were left adopted traditional marriage and became a silverware company.

16 RALPH WALDO EMERSON

This star of the Lyceum circuit was a scholar and minister who found Unitarianism too constraining and thus founded Transcendentalism, a romantic philosophy that combined idealism and Eastern mysticism. With Margaret Fuller and others he published *The Dial* in the 1840s to spread transcendental ideas. Emerson became an abolitionist and published many of his lectures, like "Self-Reliance." He captured the individualism and optimism of American society as a chief proponent of these ideas for a wide audience.

17 HENRY DAVID THOREAU

Thoreau was accused of being a Harvard graduate with no ambition, but he taught school and made pencils, as well as wrote poems, essays, and philosophical works like *Walden*. A close associate of Emerson, Thoreau experimented with a simple life by living alone on Walden Pond outside Concord, Massachusetts, for over two years. While observing minute details in nature he wrote of higher laws available for guidance beyond the established institutions of human society. His opposition to the Mexican War and to slavery led him to write the essay "Civil Disobedience" that codified a pattern of passive resistance popular in the civil rights movement and in Gandhi's movement for Indian independence from the British Empire.

18 JOSEPH SMITH

Joseph Smith published the *Book of Mormon* in the 1830s that became the foundation of a new religion calling itself the Church of Jesus Christ of Latter-Day Saints. Smith claimed to have translated the book with the help of an angel from golden tablets he had discovered. In the Burned-Over District of New York, called such because of the fervent revivals of the Second Great Awakening in the area, Smith garnered some followers. The Mormons, as they were called, founded settlements and thus were a new type of utopian communalists that sought to reform society. Smith instituted the practice of polygamy, as well as militaristic tendencies, as the Mormons experienced persecution. While jailed for destruction of property and for treason, a mob murdered Smith and his brother who then became martyrs inspiring their roughly eighteen thousand followers to move west to escape persecution.

19 BRIGHAM YOUNG

A laborer and farmer in his youth, Brigham Young was an early convert to Mormonism. After the death of Joseph Smith he became the head of the religion and moved Mormons west. His leadership held the Mormons together and guided their settlement of Deseret, their colony or new country in the Valley of the Great Salt Lake. The government recognized their settlement as the Utah Territory in 1850, but after claiming to have seceded from the United States Brigham Young was removed as the territorial governor. Young still led the Mormon community, however, and put in place an administrative structure that far outlived his own impact. Brigham Young had twenty-three wives and fathered fifty-six children.

20 MORMONISM

The *Book of Mormon* gave rise to Mormonism, the first religion born in the United States. Converts came from as far away as Europe, for while the Mormons were moving west they were also sending out missionaries. Their settlements in the West forged trails to Utah and to California that eventually opened up the path of the first transcontinental railroad. Mormons worked diligently to irrigate the soil in arid climates and otherwise proved to be hard workers living in close-knit communities. With their legal, and nearly military, clash with the federal government they were the prime example of the extent to which reformers and utopian communalists could exist in the United States without so alienating their fellow citizens as to spark expulsion or destruction. Intense persecution displaced the Mormons, but it did not intimidate or silence them. Therefore, they were also a prime example of the ability of a tradition of religious freedom to keep the peace in a pluralist society.

THE BIG PICTURE

1. The Age of Jackson was an era of humanitarian reforms as well as political advancement for the common man.

2. Religious revivals stimulated associations of reformers to assault numerous societal evils including drunkenness, abuse of the mentally ill, discrimination against women, and slavery.

3. Religion and education worked together as ministers of the Second Great Awakening either directly or indirectly supported the common school movement and the development of universities on the frontier.

4. Secular and nontraditional religious reforms included Transcendentalism, Unitarianism, and the Lyceum movement that mutually elevated their ideas before a listening and reading public.

5. Numerous communal societies sprang up as groups formed radical alternative programs for the pursuit of utopia, but none were so successful and lasting as Mormonism.

The Ramifications of Slavery

14

Our fancies with regard to the condition of the slaves proceed from our northern repugnance to slavery, stimulated by many things that we read.

—Nehemiah Adams, *A South-Side View of Slavery*, 1854

TIMELINE

1793	Cotton gin increases the demand for African slaves
1800	Gabriel Prosser plans a slave rebellion
1800–1865	"Cotton Kingdom" describes the era of the Southern plantation economy
1816	American Colonization Society is founded
1822	Denmark Vesey leads a slave rebellion in Charleston, South Carolina
1831	William Lloyd Garrison founds *The Liberator* newspaper; Nat Turner leads a slave rebellion in Virginia
1833	Southern states toughen their Slave Codes
1845	Frederick Douglass publishes his autobiography
1848	Illinois passes the most stringent Black Codes
1849	Harriet Tubman escapes slavery
1850	The Underground Railroad frees its 100,000th slave
1854	George Fitzhugh publishes *Sociology for the South*
1857	Hinton R. Helper publishes *Impending Crisis in the South*

OVERVIEW

The market revolution affected different parts of the country differently. The economies of the North and the South were moving in separate directions in the period leading up to the Civil War. The economy of the North was increasingly focused on a free-labor model, with manufacturing industries at its base; the economy of the South was increasingly dependent on a slave-labor, agricultural economy. In some ways, the regions of the United States became more interlinked as local economies were drawn into national markets, but at the same time, the issue of free versus slave labor pushed the country farther apart.

Cotton became central to the U.S. economy in the first half of the nineteenth century (see page 167). The raw material of the newly-built mills of New England, cotton became the agricultural basis of the Southern economy. The invention of the cotton gin by Eli Whitney (1793) allowed for the rapid processing of cotton. The demand for cotton in the North, as well as in Great Britain, led to more and more acres being put under cultivation. By 1860, 58 percent of American exports consisted of cotton. With an increase in cotton production came an increase in slavery.

Slavery had existed in colonial North America from nearly the beginning of European settlement. The first enslaved Africans were brought to Virginia in 1619. Slavery developed gradually in the 1600s and more rapidly in the 1700s. It was strongest in the Southern colonies, but on the eve of the American Revolution, it existed throughout colonial North America. However, by the first decades of the nineteenth century, all the Northern states had voted to abolish slavery either outright or gradually. In 1807, Great Britain outlawed the international slave trade. The following year, the United States took the same step (the international slave trade had been protected by the Constitution until 1808). Just as slavery was dying out in the North and was becoming unpopular in the eyes of the world, it was becoming further entrenched in the South. In 1790, there were approximately 700,000 slaves in the United States; that figure climbed to two million by 1830 and four million by 1860.

For white Southerners, slavery was part of their way of life. Even whites who did not own slaves (the majority of white households) defended the institution. In the late 1700s, there was a degree of ambivalence about slavery. Some Southerners referred to it as a necessary evil. From the 1830s onward, when abolitionist activism became more vocal, Southerners defended slavery more vigorously. They argued that it was a "positive good"—beneficial to the country and to slaves themselves. In the nineteenth century, slavery was often referred to as the South's "peculiar institution" by John Calhoun and other Southerners, who were either proud of the unique nature of American slavery or ashamed of it and wanted to avoid directly naming it.

For the slaves themselves, slavery was a brutal daily reality. Slaves had to endure long hours, whippings and beatings, forced separations from loved ones, and daily humiliations. There was no end in sight for these cruelties except for death. Slaves were not passive as they endured their harsh lives. Certainly, they learned that outright rebellion would almost definitely end in failure and death. Many tried running away, but most were quickly apprehended and returned to their owners. A few made it to the North or Canada with the assistance of the Underground Railroad. Slaves also developed cultural practices that constituted subtler forms of resistance—practices that sustained families and communities, and that attempted to carve out some degree of autonomy in the face of near total control. Slaves passed on fanciful stories from generation to generation that often had a pointed message, for example, in the Br'er Rabbit stories, the weak often got the better of the strong. Music that combined African traditions with the traditions of the South provided some relief from the unremitting drudgery of slavery.

Despite its contribution to the American economy, slavery contributed to pointed political and ideological differences from the 1830s onward. These differences would come to overshadow commonalities and would lead to the Civil War.

1 COTTON KINGDOM

This title glorified the importance of cotton to the American and world economies. The Deep South and parts of Texas were ideally suited in climate, soil, and length of the growing season for the production of cotton. Once inventions like the cotton gin and the screw press made the production of cotton lucrative, more and more Southerners planted this cash crop. Cotton was the raw material needed by British and American textile factories. Cotton made up the bulk of what Americans exported to the world as well as what the British imported from America. The zeal of the planter aristocrats of the South to make wealth from such a sure thing inexorably led them to seek independence from the United States even though their society could not long support their participation in a drawn-out war with modern weapons.

> **MASON-DIXON LINE**
>
> This line surveyed by two men after whom it was named was the border between Maryland and Pennsylvania. Along with the Ohio River it became the symbolic divider between the North and the South, between slave states and free states.

2 COTTON GIN

Eli Whitney's invention was manufactured in various sizes from those that could be hand cranked to those operated by steam engines. Because the machine made the separation of cotton fibers from the seed and other base material easier, more cotton could be produced for market rather than just for the clothing needs of a plantation. Even small yeoman farmers could raise enough to make a little cash after renting a plantation's cotton gin to process the year's harvest. The device worked by pulling the fibers through a wire comb thereby stripping off the unwanted material, and even the hand-cranked version of the device could "gin" fifty times more cotton than by hand. With the increased production of cotton came a higher demand for cotton cloth and thus for more slaves to pick more cotton to feed the Industrial Revolution in the North and abroad.

3 SLAVE CODES

These laws controlled not only slaves but also slave owners. A general understanding of slavery was that if masters were allowed to be too harsh with their own slaves, fugitive slaves would incite uprisings. Therefore, egregious abuse was forbidden, but harsh punishments and even murder of slaves was tolerated in many cases. In regard to the slaves themselves, Slave Codes enforced the white supremacy of the South by considering slaves to be clever subhumans capable of crimes but not capable of testifying against criminals as witnesses. Slaves could not own property or travel freely without written permission from their masters. Slaves could work for money, but the use of the pay was at the discretion of the master.

4 MANUMISSION

Manumission was the legal term for formal freeing of slaves by their masters. Some of the Founding Fathers, like George Washington, freed their slaves especially in their wills. Other slaves could be freed or were permitted to buy their way out of bondage if they had the means to make and keep money. The earliest slaves in colonial Virginia were manumitted just as indentured servants were, but as the Age of Jackson became identifiably the antebellum period, laws on manumission were tightened to prevent increase in the free African-American population of the South. By and large, few planter aristocrats condoned or practiced manumission because so few could imagine either how the plantations could be run any other way or how free African Americans could support themselves.

5 CHRISTIAN PATERNALISM

Although the Second Great Awakening stimulated Northerners to begin the abolitionist crusade, the revivals in the South were often shared by slave owners and slaves alike. Christian masters in the wake of revivals treated their slaves better and saw themselves as having the responsibility to see to the salvation of their own slaves. Some churches in the South admitted African Americans to full membership and even to church office, but even paternalistic masters were often against manumission. When slaves were treated better with more favorable living conditions and medical care, production on the plantations improved, a fact not lost on Christian and non-Christian masters alike.

6 GABRIEL PROSSER

The first leader of a significant slave insurrection since the formation of the United States was Gabriel Prosser of Virginia. In 1800, Prosser and other leaders plotted and amassed weapons and ammunition and were said to have hundreds if not thousands of slaves ready to rise up. The original attack was thwarted by a heavy rain, but word of the conspiracy was leaked to the governor of Virginia who mobilized militia forces immediately. Prosser and over thirty other conspirators were hanged. The quick response was indicative of the unity of the people of Virginia, and soon of other states, to prepare for the possibility of a slave revolt.

7 DENMARK VESEY

Vesey was a Charleston, South Carolina, slave who acquired an education as well as his freedom by purchasing it from his master with six hundred dollars of lottery winnings. He established himself as a carpenter in Charleston but grew increasingly dissatisfied with the condition of slaves by reading abolitionist literature. By 1822, Denmark Vesey had amassed nine thousand Charleston slaves ready to rise up, storm arsenals in order to commandeer weapons, and slaughter all whites in the city. A servant divulged the plot and Vesey and over thirty other leaders were hanged. Vesey wanted to model his insurrection after the revolution in Haiti, and it is said that John Brown's later plot was so similar as to likely have been inspired by Vesey's plan.

8 NAT TURNER

The most successful slave uprising in the history of the United States was another plot in Virginia, this one led by an African-American slave preacher named Nat Turner. In 1831, Turner and his followers killed almost sixty white men, women, and children. In the move to put down the revolt, over one hundred African Americans were killed, and Turner and nineteen other leaders were captured and hanged. This crescendo of slave rebellions caused the South to become more militantly supportive of slavery in political battles, and the Nat Turner rebellion served to silence all abolitionist sentiment in the slaveholding states.

9 DAVID WALKER

An important early figure in the anti-slavery movement was David Walker. Walker, an African American, was born in 1796 and inherited his mother's status as a free person even though his father, who died before he was born, was a slave. As he grew up in North Carolina, he grew increasingly resentful of the oppression of enslaved African Americans. He moved to Boston in 1825 and started a used clothing business. He became increasingly involved in religious and civic organizations and frequently spoke against slavery. In 1829, he issued a pamphlet entitled "David Walker's Appeal to the Coloured Citizens of the World." He called for unity and self-help among African Americans. This radical tract also called on people of African descent to resist slavery by any and every means. His praise of self-defense made Southerners furious. Several Southern legislatures declared the pamphlet seditious and enacted penalties against anyone caught distributing it. Walker's approach to ending slavery and his embrace of violent resistance situated him on the radical wing of the abolitionist movement. Walker's influence can be seen in Frederick Douglass as well, as in other twentieth century African-American leaders such as W. E. B. Du Bois and Malcolm X.

10 FREDERICK DOUGLASS

Douglass began as the son of a slave and a white man and rose to become the nation's noted African-American abolitionist, author, and orator. He was educated in secret as a house servant in Baltimore, and he acquired a trade as a ship's caulker. He escaped from Baltimore and moved to New York and Massachusetts where he supported a wife by working at his trade. He began giving abolitionist speeches in 1841 and wrote his famous *Narrative of the Life of Frederick Douglass* in 1845. He traveled abroad and returned to the United States with enough in donations to purchase his freedom. His stirring oratory moved audiences across the North, and he edited an abolitionist newspaper called the *North Star*. He was an adviser to John Brown before the Civil War and to Abraham Lincoln during the war in which he was responsible for raising African-American regiments for the Union Army. His efforts inspired white abolitionists as well as Sojourner Truth, a woman who had also escaped slavery and toured as an abolitionist orator.

11 NEGRO SPIRITUALS

Like the other forms of unique culture created by American slaves, "negro spirituals" were a combination of African and American influences, in this case rhythms and lyrics. Slaves often converted to Christianity in the South prior to the Civil War, and after the normal worship services they sometimes held singings where illiterate worshippers could learn and enjoy the hymns of slavery. Negro spirituals were also used to pass the time in the fields or to coordinate hauling and other especially difficult labor. A slave song leader often sang out calls to the rest of the slave teams, who answered in unison. In conjunction with the Underground Railroad, several "negro spirituals" were later shown to be coded messages regarding places and times of departure for escaping slaves.

12 SLAVE SOCIETY

Slave societies existed throughout the world and far back into ancient times. The American South under the cotton kingdom was such a society where the laws and customs elevated to power those who held property and acquired wealth through the labor of slaves. The planter aristocrats of the South held political and economic power with roughly three thousand families in the top class with large plantations holding two to four hundred slaves. These families maintained the apparatus of slavery such as cotton gins and screw presses to make bales easily, as well as the horses, dogs, and weapons necessary to form slave posses. Slave posses were dispatched to round up escaped slaves, and in the case of slave revolts they formed the nucleus of state militias. Although most white people of the South owned few or no slaves, the entire society was based on not only an acceptance of the peculiar institution but also an aspiration on the part of yeoman farmers to one day acquire enough slaves to join the leisure class.

13 FREE BLACKS IN THE SLAVE SOUTH

In 1860, approximately a half million free Blacks lived in the United States, with the vast majority living in the South (the slave population was around four million). Many of these free Blacks were descended from slaves who had been freed by their masters in the aftermath of the American Revolution. Others were able to purchase their own freedom or were freed by their masters. The lives of free Blacks in the South were defined, in many ways, by the existence of slavery. Southern society generally equated "Black" with "slave." To live outside of this equation was problematic in the eyes of Southern white society. Many of the restrictions that applied to slaves also applied to free Blacks in the South. For instance, free Blacks could not testify in court or serve on juries, nor could they own a gun or a dog. Free Blacks had to carry their "freedom papers" on them. Most free Blacks in the South worked in agriculture, either hiring themselves out or owning small plots. Some were artisans and a few prospered. Frequently, there were ties—social, romantic, and familial—between the free Black community and the slave community. Most Southern free Blacks lived in the Upper South. On the eve of the Civil War, half of the Black population of Maryland was free.

14 HINTON R. HELPER

Helper was a southerner and a failed gold prospector returned from California who took up printing and writing while living in the North. He published the book *The Impending Crisis of the South* that used statistics from the 1850 census to examine the economic weaknesses of the slaveholding states. The book was popular in the North not only because of its abolitionist message but because of how Helper praised the society and economy of the free states. His book also lambasted the leaders of the slave society for unfairly keeping not only African Americans but also lower-class whites from rising up. His analysis was used before the war to mobilize the abolitionist cause but after the war, coupled with his later writings, dismissed as violent racism against African Americans whom he wanted deported to Africa.

15 POSITIVE GOOD THEORY

Although men like Thomas Jefferson referred to slavery as a "necessary evil," the next generations of Southern leaders developed the notion that slavery was a "positive good," to borrow a phrase from John C. Calhoun. When slavery came under renewed scrutiny in the Missouri Compromise and the Nullification Crisis, the South developed defenses of slavery against the rising abolitionist crusade. Among other defenses, supporters of slavery said that slaves had lives that were better than Africans in Africa and even better lives than Northern factory workers who were essentially wage slaves. Christian paternalism sanctioned slavery as perhaps the only opportunity Africans would have to hear the Christian message. Because of racist views of "negro inferiority," supporters of slavery maintained that African Americans needed the guidance and provision of their white masters to organize their lives.

16 GEORGE FITZHUGH

One of the most outspoken proponents of the positive good theory was the Virginian lawyer and author George Fitzhugh. He originated the argument that African slaves in the South were better off than wage slaves in the North who never saw the sun because they worked from before dawn to after dark in factories. His views were not only racist but bordered on evoking the ideas of class warfare. Because he viewed the slave society of the South as the ideal society, he advocated the expansion of slavery virtually globally as he recognized the free labor and slave labor systems were incompatible. Fitzhugh predicted that if African Americans were ever freed and sent North, they would be unable to function in the free labor system.

> **ELIJAH P. LOVEJOY**
>
> The editor and publisher of an abolitionist newspaper in Illinois, Lovejoy was killed by a mob in 1837. He was considered to be the first white man to die in the slavery controversy.

17 WILLIAM LLOYD GARRISON

A background in the newspaper business and a talent for virulent writing propelled William Lloyd Garrison to prominence as the editor of *The Liberator*, the leading abolitionist newspaper. While his inflammatory editorials bordered on libel and led him to actually burn a copy of the U.S. Constitution, he organized abolitionist societies and published his newspaper for thirty-five years. Garrison espoused Northern secession in order to cut off ties with the compromises that had kept peace with the South. He also preached the breaking of the Fugitive Slave Law. Once Abraham Lincoln issued the Emancipation Proclamation his rhetoric toned down to full support for the war effort. After the war, Garrison continued agitating for reform in the fight to ban alcohol and in the women's suffrage movement. As an advocate for women's rights, Garrison was at least partly responsible for delaying votes for women until after slavery was abolished.

18 HARRIET TUBMAN

As an escaped slave, Harriet Tubman became a leading "conductor" on the Underground Railroad. In other words, she was a guide who helped other slaves escape and make their way north to Canada by way of a series of safe houses supported by northerners. Tubman is thought to have personally guided as many as three hundred slaves from Maryland to Canada despite chronic headaches resulting from an injury to the head received from her master. For her efforts before the Civil War she was known as "Moses," and she even served as a guide for African-American soldiers during the war.

19 UNDERGROUND RAILROAD

By 1840 a secret series of houses and people supportive of the emancipation of individual slaves had formed in defiance of federal laws regarding the return of fugitive slaves to the South. The Underground Railroad assisted and transported escaped slaves to safety in sympathetic communities in the North or to complete freedom from recapture in Canada. From 1830 to 1860 as many as 3,200 African-American and white workers helped as many as fifty thousand slaves escape. Sung about in "negro spirituals," the Underground Railroad was a network of Quakers and other abolitionists, including Senator William H. Seward of New York, who actively pursued their principles rather than just reading and writing about them. Certain Northern states passed personal liberty laws to protect escaped slaves as a result of widespread support for the activities of the Underground Railroad "conductors."

20 AMERICAN COLONIZATION SOCIETY

Founded in 1817 and headed by presidents Monroe and Madison and by other such luminaries as John Marshall and Henry Clay, the American Colonization Society (ACS) advocated the transportation of free African Americans back to Africa. At first Sierra Leone was a transfer point, but eventually the Republic of Liberia was founded when land was purchased by the ACS in Africa to establish a permanent location. Over fifteen thousand African Americans left the United States to join the colony by 1860, but most such emigration from the South was shut down after the Nat Turner rebellion in 1831. While the mission of the ACS was popular for a time, the motives of the society were more to rid the United States of what was considered to be an unsolvable problem rather than to elevate African Americans or to encourage African development.

THE BIG PICTURE

1. Slavery and cotton shaped the economic, societal, and political dynamics of the South into a culture in dramatic contrast with that of the North.

2. Although the reform impulse based on humanitarian and religious principles in the North created the abolitionist crusade, Southerners were bent on reforming the institution of African slavery as a positive good.

3. African-American slaves developed a unique culture of their own that saw varying degrees of cooperation with and resistance toward their white masters, up to and including violent rebellion.

4. Northern abolitionists used powerful oral and written rhetoric to gradually develop animosity toward the institution of African slavery, but the quest for an end to slavery did not immediately equate to a quest for African-American equality.

5. As their peculiar institution came under attack, Southerners developed pro-slavery arguments and political tactics that nearly thwarted the abolitionist crusade largely because of the demand in the North for Southern cotton.

Westward Expansion and Manifest Destiny

15

I consider the annexation of Texas . . . as a measure compromising the national character, involving us certainly in war with Mexico . . . [and] dangerous to the integrity of the Union.

—Henry Clay, "Raleigh Letter," 1844

TIMELINE	
1819	Adams-Onís Treaty is signed with Spain
1822	Florida is organized as a U.S. territory
1823	The Monroe administration introduces the Monroe Doctrine; Stephen Austin begins colonizing Texas
1825	First three hundred American families arrive in Texas
1833	Santa Anna is elected president of Mexico
1835	Sam Houston forms an army for Texas
1835–1836	Texas War for Independence
1836	Alamo falls to Mexican forces
1840	John Tyler is elected president
1844	James K. Polk is elected president
1845	Polk authorizes Slidell's Mission; John O'Sullivan coins the phrase "Manifest Destiny"
1846	John C. Fremont foments the Bear Flag Revolt
1847	Congress hears the Spot Resolutions
1848	Oregon becomes an organized U.S. territory; Treaty of Guadalupe Hidalgo ends the Mexican War
1853	Gadsden Purchase

OVERVIEW

As the American economy grew in the decades between the War of 1812 and the Civil War, many Americans continued the push farther and farther into the continent. The movement west included several notable developments: Texas's independence from Mexico (1836), the opening of the Oregon Trail (1841), the Mexican War (1846–48), the Mormon exodus to Utah (1847), and the California Gold Rush (1849). This westward movement had ominous implications for neighboring nations as well as for American-Indian nations within the borders of the growing United States.

Many Americans came to believe that it was the "manifest destiny" of the United States to expand westward and extend its power in the Western Hemisphere. Manifest Destiny refers to the movement of individuals to the West, but it also alludes to the political extension of U.S. territory. The term *Manifest Destiny* was coined in an 1845 newspaper article by John O'Sullivan. It captured the fervor of the westward expansion movement, implying that it was God's plan that the United States take over and settle the entire continent.

Initially the idea of Manifest Destiny was popular with many Northerners in the wake of the Second Great Awakening. It captured the spirit of reform and transformation. Protestants would be able to free people in newly-acquired territory from political and religious oppression. However, as large numbers of Southerners made their way to the West and brought the practice of slavery with them, many Northerners came to resist further expansion.

The spirit of Manifest Destiny grew out of several fundamental beliefs that were held by many Americans in the antebellum (pre-Civil War) period. In many ways, the ideology of Manifest Destiny reinforced contemporary notions of race. Americans had come to believe that the variety of peoples who inhabited the North American continent—Mexicans, American Indians, and African Americans—were incapable of establishing or participating in democratic, efficient governance. This racial justification for westward expansion, which developed in the decades after 1810, drew on several sources. European Romanticism, which became increasingly influential in these decades, put more emphasis on uniqueness and individual difference. Earlier, the Enlightenment thinking, which animated many of the founding generation of Americans, embodied a more benevolent outlook, stressing universal principles and a common humanity. In addition, there was a rise in scientific racialism in the early 1800s, which held that races were fundamentally different from one another and that the Anglo-Saxon race was superior to non-whites. The zoologist Louis Agassiz was an important proponent of this view (see page 215). The movement westward was seen as proof of the superiority of the so-called Anglo-Saxon race over the "savage tribes" of the West.

In addition to using racial theories, many Americans justified Manifest Destiny by asserting the superiority of American institutions and practices. These Americans cited the strong tradition of democratic practices in the United States. The conquest of Mexico was seen as a victory by liberty-loving Protestants over tyrannical and anti-republican Catholics. Ultimately, the acquisition of additional territory enflamed sectional tensions and undermined democratic practice, as the bitter debates over the expansion of slavery led to civil war.

1 ANGLOPHOBIA

Whether it was personal, as with Andrew Jackson, or philosophical, as with Thomas Jefferson, American presidents from Washington to James K. Polk operated under the assumption that America's mother country was out to get them. The War of 1812 was clear evidence that the fear was grounded in fact, but at some point in the early nineteenth century the excuse that America should annex territory or else the British would take it began to wear thin. Dependence on the British for trade contributed to anxiety when markets became strained or tariff wars erupted, and Great Britain was moving into its heyday as an expansionist world empire. The refusal of Canada to join the American republic also caused suspicion. The "natural enemy" status between the two powers would last until after the American Civil War.

2 FLORIDA

This peninsula had changed hands through the colonial wars but wound up with Spain after the American Revolution. Like France, Spain had backed American independence as a way to humble Great Britain. But the Spanish Empire was in decline by the opening of the nineteenth century. The Spanish colonial administration was growing weaker and claimed it was unable to stop African-American slaves from escaping into Florida and American Indians from raiding American settlements. Andrew Jackson had pursued Creek and Seminole Indians into Florida as a result. While there, Jackson confirmed fears that Great Britain had designs for a new colony in Florida by capturing two British agents supplying the American Indians with weapons. Jackson promptly hanged the men as spies. The events surrounding Jackson's invasion of Spanish Florida led to conflicts known as the Seminole War that saw around three thousand American soldiers fighting against Seminole Indians and escaped slaves. The issues were not resolved until the British backed off and the Spanish caved in. The war against the Seminole Indians proved to be the fiercest conflict in the history of warfare between the United States and indigenous peoples.

> **BLACK HAWK WAR**
>
> Chief Black Hawk of the Sauk and Fox tribes tried in 1832 to recover lands lost under the Indian Removal Act. The resulting clashes in Illinois and Wisconsin were a foreshadowing of the Great Plains War to come.

3 ADAMS-ONÍS TREATY

John Quincy Adams skillfully capitalized on Andrew Jackson's aggression in Florida even though he privately complained to the hero of the Battle of New Orleans that he had no authorization to invade a foreign country. Of all the Spanish holdings in the New World, however, foreign minister Luis de Onís recognized that Florida was the most tenuous. In order to clarify the borders of the Louisiana Purchase, Spain agreed to sell Florida to the United States in this treaty ratified by both countries in 1821. The United States gave up claim to Texas, and Spain gave up claim to the Oregon Territory in the Northwest. Florida entered the United States as a slave state in 1845.

4 MOUNTAIN MEN

Various intrepid individualistic men, and at least one woman, departed from civilized society and forged paths into the wilderness in pursuit of furs and, presumably, freedom from constraints. Men from Daniel Boone to Jim Bridger conducted extensive forays into the unchartered wilderness of unsettled American territory. Mountain men negotiated with various American Indian tribes for permission to trap, hunt, and trade on tribal lands and were thus often the first white men known intimately on the frontier. The great service these lone explorers performed was to open up trails for western settlement and to send back rumors of, say, the fertile soil of the Oregon Territory. Like the cowboy, mountain men were an iconic American stereotype whose image lasted far longer than the actual era when such a lifestyle was possible.

5 STEPHEN AUSTIN

Austin was the founder of Texas in the northern province of Mexico by virtue of a grant from the Mexican government as it became free from Spain. Despite the abolition of slavery by the Mexican government, Austin negotiated permission for American slaves to enter Texas as indentured servants, but the Southern Americans who came believed they were merely expanding the cotton kingdom and the plantation lifestyle. As war broke out between Texans and Mexico, Austin became the chief liaison between Texas and the United States.

6 TEXAS

The Mexican government encouraged settlement of their northern provinces by Americans because of the ferocity of the Apache and Comanche Indians. Neither the Spanish nor the Mexicans made successful incursions into the region, but men like Stephen Austin and Jim Bowie did. Santa Anna, the president of Mexico, attempted to ban the further importation of slaves as well as any further settlement by American immigrants. He also chose to operate as an authoritarian dictator rather than a constitutional executive. As Texans experienced success in the production of cotton and in cattle ranching, they chafed under the confines of a system worse than that of British colonies prior to the American Revolution. Texans likewise decided to declare independence, and the Texas War for Independence was the result.

7 SANTA ANNA

His full name was Antonio López de Santa Anna, and he rose up through the ranks of the officer corps of the Spanish military to eventually lead in the Mexican Revolution. He liberated his birthplace, Vera Cruz, and declared Mexico to be a free republic. When independence from Spain was secure, he put down insurrections for the new Mexican government and rose to the top of the rival factions struggling for power by 1834. To quell further internal strife, Santa Anna was granted dictatorial powers backed up by an army of men famous for their ability to endure the hot climate and infamous for the atrocities they committed on Santa Anna's opponents.

8 TEXAS WAR FOR INDEPENDENCE

Texans declared their independence from Mexico in 1836 and appointed Sam Houston as the commander of the military. Volunteers from Tennessee, including Davy Crockett, joined the militia. Houston ordered William Travis and other volunteers to hold the mission church called the Alamo in San Antonio while he set about organizing and training the rest of the army. After massacres at the Alamo and at Goliad, Houston drew Santa Anna's remaining army into a chase across Texas that ended at the Battle of San Jacinto. Texans cried, "Remember the Alamo!" as they assaulted the Mexican positions, defeated the remnants of the Mexican army, and captured Santa Anna. The war ended when Santa Anna was forced at gunpoint to sign a treaty declaring Texas independent with a border along the Rio Grande River.

9 ALAMO

One of the many Spanish mission sites in San Antonio, the Alamo became the hallowed ground of the Texas Republic. Santa Anna's three thousand troops attacked the Alamo's garrison of 187 men for thirteen days. When the walls were finally breached all of the defenders of the Alamo were killed and their bodies burned. Their sacrifice, however, took many times their number of Mexican lives and allowed Sam Houston to mount an effective strategic retreat all the way to San Jacinto and victory. A larger massacre of over three hundred men at Goliad was perpetrated by Santa Anna even after the defenders surrendered, which William Travis had refused to do at the Alamo. Perhaps the refusal to surrender earned for Travis, Crockett, Bowie, and the other defenders of the Alamo the immortal love of Texans.

10 SAM HOUSTON

Houston fought in Andrew Jackson's militia army from Tennessee in the war against the Creeks and other American Indians marauding in the Southeast during the War of 1812. He lived for three years among the Cherokee Indians who had been his allies in the Creek War, and he was eventually adopted into the Creek nation. Between the War of 1812 and the Texas War for Independence, he studied law, served as a congressman, and became the governor of Tennessee. After a failed marriage, Houston was sent to Texas by President Jackson to negotiate with American Indians. He moved to Texas and became the commander of its army fighting Santa Anna. He was elected president of the Republic of Texas and negotiated with the United States for recognition and then annexation of Texas at which point he became a senator. He was elected governor of Texas just prior to the Civil War, but opposed secession and was deposed, dying in 1861 just as war commenced.

11 JOHN TYLER

Tyler was a lawyer from Virginia and rose from being governor there to being vice president under William Henry Harrison, the hero of the Battle of Tippecanoe. Thus was born the slogan, "Tippecanoe and Tyler, too" in the "Log Cabin and Hard Cider" campaign for the Election of 1840 (although Harrison was a wealthy planter, he had been born in a log cabin). As a result of Harrison's premature death, Tyler became the first "accidental" president, or the first vice president to succeed a fallen president. Harrison had been a Whig and had placed Whigs in his cabinet, but when Tyler took office his policies clashed with the Whigs who resigned en masse. To the horror of Northern Whigs and the consternation of Henry Clay and John Quincy Adams, Tyler backed the annexation of Texas by a joint resolution of Congress, and the Republic of Texas became a giant slave state.

12 JAMES K. POLK

Another Tennessee lawyer-turned-statesman was James K. Polk who made a conscious point to follow in Andrew Jackson's footsteps. Polk was thus a Democrat who favored expansion of the country and expansion of slavery. As the winner of the presidential election of 1844, he accomplished everything he promised in his campaign including the acquisition of the Oregon Territory, overseeing Texas statehood, reestablishing Van Buren's independent treasury system, and settling the border dispute and debt issues with Mexico by starting and winning the Mexican War. Polk thus brought in every territory of the American West beyond the Louisiana Purchase except that of the Gadsden Purchase and therefore is responsible for enlarging the country more than any other president. For all his acquiring of land at the expense of Mexico, he did stop forces within his own party from annexing "all of Mexico." He accomplished his final pledge made during his campaign of holding only one term as president by refusing to seek reelection.

13 OREGON TERRITORY

The far Northwest was desired for settlement by the United States, Great Britain, and even Russia. John Jacob Astor had founded an American trading post at the mouth of the Columbia River as early as 1811, and mountain men regularly harvested furs from the region throughout the early nineteenth century. Missionaries Marcus and Narcissa Whitman established contacts with American Indians and a permanent settlement before being killed by those they were trying to convert. Stories from mountain men and the missionaries, however, ignited a land fever causing settlers to take the Oregon Trail to claim land. Because more Americans moved to Oregon than did Canadians or Russians, President Polk seized the initiative to annex the territory to the United States. Despite some Americans' desire to take all of the territory with the slogan, "54°40' or fight," Polk negotiated a settlement with Great Britain establishing the border with Canada along the 49th parallel of latitude, the longest unfortified border in the world. The North was relieved that while slavery was expanding west, the nation also acquired territory where slavery would never be feasible.

14 BEAR FLAG REVOLT

When hostilities broke out between Mexico and the United States, Polk had not only provoked the clash but positioned American military forces in California in anticipation of war. John C. Fremont led the expedition across the Rocky Mountains, and the Bear Flag Revolt was the result. With Fremont's assistance, Californians of Spanish descent as well as American settlers rose up against the Mexican government to secure California's independence. Fremont's campaign was joined by that of Stephen Kearney who traveled from Kansas to California as the Mexican War commenced, and thus the Bear Flag Revolt became a theater of that war. The name comes from the flag created for the original indigenous rebellion, which remains the flag of the state of California. California was eventually brought into the United States as a part of the Mexican Cession.

15 SLIDELL'S MISSION

Revealing of Polk's willingness to start the Mexican War, John Slidell was sent to Santa Anna to first offer to purchase the northern provinces of Mexico for up to $40 million. The Mexican government originally agreed to negotiate, but when the nature of Slidell's offer became known, the people of Mexico raised such complaints that negotiations were called off. Part of the negotiations were to include the erasing of the debts Mexico owed to the United States, but when the Slidell Mission ended in failure, Polk was willing to start the war just to force the Mexicans to pay the debt he had offered to pay for them. Before protests from Whigs could gain ground, provocations from military maneuvers on the Rio Grande River had ignited an exchange of fire. Polk used the clash to get Congress to declare war against Mexico in 1846.

16 SPOT RESOLUTIONS

Abraham Lincoln and other Whigs in Congress attempted to stop the expansionist policies motivated by Manifest Destiny that were dragging the nation to war against Mexico by offering the Spot Resolutions in Congress. In his war message, President Polk had said, "American blood has been spilled on American soil." The Spot Resolutions drew into question who had shot whom first by asking the president to show the Congress where the blood was spilled on American soil on a map of the region. Although the Spot Resolutions failed to stop the war, they did give voice to the coming sectional debate between expansionist southern Democrats interested in spreading and protecting slavery and those northerners from many political parties who would eventually form the modern Republican Party and run John C. Fremont as their first presidential candidate in 1856.

> ## CONSCIENCE WHIGS
>
> This faction within the Whig Party foreshadowed the coming North/South split in the only opposition party able to keep the balance against the expansionist policies of Polk's Democratic Party. Conscience Whigs opposed the Mexican War and were from the North.

17 CIVIL DISOBEDIENCE

In 1846, as President James K. Polk was calling for war between the United States and Mexico, a vocal antiwar movement developed in the United States. Congressional Whigs feared that the possible acquisition of territory could reignite the slavery question. The transcendentalist writer Henry David Thoreau also came out publicly against the war, but his reasons went beyond the Whigs' arguments. In the famous 1849 essay, *Resistance to Civil Government* (more commonly known as *Civil Disobedience*), Thoreau expressed his moral opposition to the existence of slavery. He urged individuals not to cooperate with policies that would further slavery. He argued that it was not enough to simply speak out against unjust policies; people had to act. They had an obligation not to give injustice their practical support, he argued. Toward this, he refused to pay a poll tax and was briefly imprisoned. Thoreau saw a government that aided and abetted slavery as illegitimate and not worthy of obedience: "I cannot for an instant recognize as my government [that] which is the slave's government also." Thoreau's essay inspired Mahatma Gandhi and Martin Luther King Jr.; however, Thoreau did not specifically advocate nonviolence. The "civil" in the title of his essay refers to the relationship between citizens and the state, as in "civil rights." It does not, in this case, refer to being orderly or polite. In the following decade, Thoreau supported John Brown's armed raid on the arsenal at Harper's Ferry, Virginia.

18 TREATY OF GUADALUPE HIDALGO

Nicolas Trist negotiated this treaty as Polk's envoy to the Mexican government. After systematically invading Mexico and Mexico City and beating armies larger than their own, U.S. Army generals like Winfield Scott and Zachary Taylor humbled Santa Anna who consented to surrender in 1848. The Treaty of Guadalupe Hidalgo provided that the United States would pay $15 million for the territory known as the Mexican Cession and for the confirmation that the Rio Grande River was the border between Texas and Mexico. Trist even agreed for the United States to write off the over $3 million in debt the Mexican government had earlier refused to pay. This generous settlement with a beaten foe revealed that the level of resistance toward the expansion of slave territories required a magnanimous gesture to Mexico or else the Senate would never ratify the treaty. A deep division was revealed within the United States by the Mexican War just as many of the men who would lead the opposing armies in the Civil War were gaining military experience as comrades against the Mexicans.

19 GOLD RUSH

Gold was discovered in the American River near Sacramento, California, in 1848 by a crew working to build a sawmill for John Sutter. News of the discovery spread, and the influx of gold seekers in 1849 from across the United States and overseas was called the gold rush. Prospectors came from as far away as Australia and China. By the next year, one hundred thousand "Forty-niners" had swelled California's population, putting it on the fast track to statehood. Miners kept coming for over two years to strike it rich. A few prospectors did find significant amounts of gold. However, very soon, the easily accessible gold was panned from riverbeds. To get access to gold beneath the surface, capital-intensive methods were required. The expensive machinery necessary for such an operation was beyond the reach of ordinary prospectors. Still, discoveries of mineral resources in the West were a powerful draw on westward migration. The various discoveries of gold and silver from 1848 until the 1880s led to a repeated pattern of rushes, boomtowns, and economic consolidation, as lone prospectors and crowds of fortune seekers gave way to industrial-mining operations.

20 GADSDEN PURCHASE

A final adjustment to the border between the United States and Mexico was gained at the expense of another $10 million in 1853. James Gadsden was sent to negotiate by Franklin Pierce. The small piece of land was desirable as the best route for a southern transcontinental railroad across the mountains and to the Pacific Ocean. Although construction of the railroad was delayed by the Civil War, the addition of the Gadsden Purchase marked the end of the addition of contiguous territory to the United States.

THE BIG PICTURE

1. The era from 1803 to 1853 saw the major expansion of the contiguous territory of the United States, and the driving force behind it was the notion of Manifest Destiny.

2. The region of Texas was settled by Americans and became the cause of two wars with Santa Anna, the dictator of Mexico.

3. The Whigs and the Democrats were national parties compelled by the events surrounding the Mexican War to operate along sectional lines.

4. Although many Americans sought new opportunities by migrating west, Southerners went west first in greater numbers, and their desire to expand slavery antagonized Northerners motivated by humanitarian reforms to abolish slavery.

5. The annexation of Florida, Texas, and Oregon Territory along with the Mexican Cession unlocked great potential for Americans to pursue national greatness and world power status but not without unleashing a deadly Civil War.

The Last Attempts at Compromise

16

*The constitutional compact has been deliberately broken
and disregarded by the nonslaveholding states; and . . .
South Carolina is released from her obligation.*

—South Carolina Declaration, 1860

TIMELINE	
1846	Congress fails to pass the Wilmot Proviso; Stephen A. Douglas enters the Senate
1849	Gold Rush
1850	Compromise of 1850; Fugitive Slave Law
1852	Harriet Beecher Stowe publishes *Uncle Tom's Cabin* in book form
1854	Kansas-Nebraska Act; Republican Party is founded
1854–1856	Know-Nothing Party exerts its greatest influence
1854–1858	Bleeding Kansas
1856	Brooks-Sumner Affair
1857	Lecompton Constitution; *Dred Scott* case
1858	Lincoln-Douglas debates
1859	John Brown raids the arsenal at Harper's Ferry, Virginia
1860	Election of 1860; Crittenden Compromise fails in the Congress
1860–1861	Eleven Southern states secede

OVERVIEW

The acquisition and settlement of new territories in the western half of the North American continent opened up a question that many politicians had sought to avoid: should these new territories allow slavery? Most Northern politicians were not abolitionists. Indeed, abolition-ism was a minority position in the North in 1850. However, the issue of the expansion of slavery became increasingly divisive in the 1850s. Some Northerners adopted the "free soil" approach, the idea that lands out West should be open to small-scale farming, without com-petition from large-scale plantation agriculture using slave labor. By the end of the decade, more Northerners were grappling with the moral issues around slavery. Positions became decidedly more entrenched on the eve of the Civil War.

The issue of slavery in the territories came to the forefront in the aftermath of the Mexican War (1846–1848). In quick succession, the United States was granted a huge por-tion of Mexico for a mere $15 million, gold was discovered in California, and the residents of California applied for statehood. The Compromise of 1850, which allowed for California to enter the Union as a free state and provided for a stronger Fugitive Slave Law, seemed to lessen sectional tensions, but appearances were deceiving. First, the compromise itself was not exactly a compromise. The different elements of the bill were unbundled so that each item was voted on separately. Each of the items passed as moderate senators voted with one or the other faction. Second, a series of other developments in the decade kept the issue of slavery front and center. Contention over the enforcement of the Fugitive Slave Law continued agitation by abolitionists, and publication of the novel *Uncle Tom's Cabin* all contributed to an increase in sectional tensions in the early 1850s. However, the most serious rupture occurred as a result of the Kansas-Nebraska Act (1854), which opened the territories of Kansas and Nebraska to slavery under the principle of popular sovereignty, after they had been closed to slavery by the 1820 Missouri Compromise. The act led to violence in Bleeding Kansas and to the realignment of the major political parties. Violence even occurred on the floor of the Senate in the aftermath of the act. Later in the decade, a raid on a federal armory in Harper's Ferry, Virginia, led by the abolitionist John Brown and the Supreme Court's deci-sion in the case of Dred Scott further enflamed sectional tensions and made the possibility of compromise seem remote.

The election of 1860 was the final straw. The Republican candidate Abraham Lincoln, an opponent of slavery, indicated that if elected president he would not nor could not tamper with slavery where it already existed. Even if Lincoln kept his promise not to interfere with slavery in the slave states, many Southern slaveholders still would not have been satisfied. In many ways, slavery needed to grow in order to remain economically viable. Even before Lincoln was inaugurated, the states of the Deep South began seceding. The process set the stage for the Civil War.

1 WILMOT PROVISO

During the Mexican War, Pennsylvania representative David Wilmot proposed that any land acquired from Mexico would be closed to slavery. Wilmot entered the bill in the House, and Northern congressmen passed the bill over the objections of their Southern colleagues. The bill was defeated in the Senate. The debate over the Wilmot Proviso revealed the tenuous party unity of both the Democratic and Whig parties because members of both parties voted for sectional loyalties rather than party lines.

2 POPULAR SOVEREIGNTY

Lewis Cass, a Northern senator, developed the notion of a democratic solution to the nation's debate over the spread of slavery into the territories. Senator Stephen Douglas of Illinois coined the ringing phrase that promised to let the people decide the issue. Cass suggested that a vote be taken by the settlers of a territory to determine whether it would be open to slavery or not. In the major bills of the 1850s the idea took root. Abraham Lincoln eventually dismissed the idea as amoral and opposed to the precedents of the central government's banning slavery in the Old Northwest Territory. The Supreme Court also disapproved of the practice in the *Dred Scott* case because the pro-slavery justices feared slaveholders would have their property taken away from them if they took slaves West and then their neighbors voted for freedom.

> **WEBSTER-ASHBURTON TREATY**
>
> While borders with Mexico were in question, this treaty in 1842 specified the border between Canada and the United States from Maine to the Rocky Mountains. The two countries agreed to share use of the Great Lakes and to exist on either side of the 49th parallel of latitude, a line that was extended to the Pacific Ocean after the dispute over Oregon was settled.

3 COMPROMISE OF 1850

The gold rush set in motion the disruptive news that California wanted to join the Union as a free state. This proposition would not only cut off the Pacific coast from slaveholding states but also upset the balance of power in the Senate that had been maintained since the Missouri Compromise in 1820. The furor was temporarily settled by the last great compromise from Henry Clay who entered resolutions that were eventually passed as five separate laws collectively known as the Compromise of 1850. The North was pleased that California did come in as a free state, but the South demanded that popular sovereignty decide the question in the rest of the territories acquired from Mexico. Texas was reduced in size to make more potential slave states but was compensated with $10 million. Northerners seized the opportunity to ban the slave trade in Washington, D.C., while Southerners demanded a more stringent Fugitive Slave Law. The Compromise of 1850 did keep the peace, but its measures were poorly enforced. As the great senators began to die off, the country lacked confidence that the Congress could withstand another such shock without coming apart.

> **FREE SOIL PARTY**
>
> This party formed in 1848 and opposed the spread of slavery into the territories on the grounds that slaves would compete with free laborers. The party's platform was adopted by the Republican Party in 1854.

4 STEPHEN DOUGLAS

Douglas himself revealed the wisdom in going west as a young man. He was born in Vermont but moved to Illinois where he taught school and became a lawyer. He rose steadily through the ranks of state politics and by the years of crisis was a U.S. senator. He came to power as the chairman of the Committee on Territories and, as the champion of popular sovereignty, seemed to want to make peace in the slavery controversy. His actions were also directed toward his ambition to become president, however, and his Kansas-Nebraska Bill created nothing but strife. He sparred with Abraham Lincoln for the Senate seat in 1858 and then again in the Election of 1860 for the presidency. Known as the "Little Giant" for his powerful oratory despite his small stature, he eventually supported Lincoln's measures once the Civil War began.

5 FUGITIVE SLAVE LAW

This component of the Compromise of 1850 was especially odious to Northerners. As the Underground Railroad continued its work and as abolition gained more and more supporters, the South accused the North of violating the provisions in the Constitution for the return of escaped slaves. When the Southerners in Congress discovered how objectionable the slave trade in Washington, D.C., was to Northern congressmen, they saw their chance to stiffen the laws for the return of escaped slaves. Furthermore, as the law was implemented in the North, judges were paid $10 per case if they determined an African American was an escaped slave and only $5 if they freed him or her. Under these circumstances, even African Americans born free in the North were sent South into slavery. Among the other causes of the demise of the capacity to compromise was the passive and active resistance to the Fugitive Slave Law by the increasingly determined humanitarian reformers of the North. Even Walt Whitman wrote in a poem about helping an escaped slave on to Canada and freedom.

6 *UNCLE TOM'S CABIN*

Harriet Beecher Stowe had grown up in reformer Lyman Beecher's home. Her husband was a professor at Lane Theological Seminary, her father's seminary that turned out many ardent abolitionists. She saw in the controversy over the Fugitive Slave Law a chance to produce a work that would not only stir hearts to end slavery but also sell well. *Uncle Tom's Cabin* was the melodramatic story of the ruination of a slave's family and life after he was sold to pay off his master's gambling debts. Uncle Tom faced fiercer oppression the farther South he went as the whites involved in slavery became more and more degenerate. The book, and the play derived from it, received heated criticism in the South and just as emotional a reception in the North and around the world.

7 OSTEND MANIFESTO

The growing tensions between Northern and Southern politicians were evident in the fallout from the Ostend Manifesto. Southern politicians had long eyed the island of Cuba, a mere ninety miles off the shore of Florida, with its profitable sugar plantations. For these expansionists, the manifest destiny of the United States did not stop at the Pacific. In 1848 President James K. Polk offered to purchase the island from Spain. When Spain balked, some American adventurers, including John L. Sullivan (who popularized the term *manifest destiny*), unsuccessfully tried to organize a group of "filibusters" (irregular soldiers) to take Cuba by force. After that, American presidents shied away from the Cuba question. In 1853, President Franklin Pierce (Democrat) put the question of the annexation of Cuba back on the agenda. He sent pro-southern diplomats to Belgium to secretly negotiate the purchase of Cuba. They wrote up their goals as the Ostend Manifesto (1854), which implied that the United States should declare war if Spain refused. When news of the manifesto was made public, it was quickly and angrily denounced by Northern members of Congress. The incident shows how the issue of manifest destiny became increasingly sectionalized in the 1850s.

8 KANSAS-NEBRASKA ACT

This law was the brainchild of Senator Stephen Douglas who wanted to facilitate the construction of the first transcontinental railroad and his own path to the presidency. In order to make the railroad worth the investment, the Indian Territory from which Kansas, Nebraska, and other states were carved needed to be organized and civilized. Deeply committed to his ideal of popular sovereignty, Douglas and other backers in the North garnered support by promising Southerners the chance to vote on extending slavery far north of the Missouri Compromise line. The Missouri Compromise had to be repealed. The sudden possibility of slavery's spread into the northern reaches of the Louisiana Purchase galvanized several parties to join forces and form the modern Republican Party in 1854, the year the Kansas-Nebraska Act passed.

9 DEMISE OF THE WHIG PARTY

The 1850s witnessed the decline of the Whig Party over the issue of the expansion of slavery into the territories. By 1854, the Whig Party dissolved as a functioning party. For much of its history, the Whigs tried to keep discussion of slavery on the back burner. The party stressed issues that united different strands of the party: economic growth, development of Henry Clay's American System, and internal improvements. However, as the issue of the expansion of slavery came to dominate politics in the 1850s, the Whigs could not paper over major differences within the party. The party split into pro-slavery and anti-slavery factions during the debates surrounding the Compromise of 1850. The schism was evident in the party's nominating convention for president in 1852. Northern Whigs were able to block the nomination of President Millard Fillmore and nominate Winfield Scott instead; the party lost badly in the general election. Further, the two towering figures of the party, Daniel Webster and Henry Clay, both died in 1852. As the second two-party system of the Whigs and Democrats was torn asunder by the question of the expansion of slavery, it became clear after the election of 1856 that a new two-party system was emerging, the Democrats and the Republicans. For the time being, the dissolution of the Whigs represented an end of nationally-oriented political parties and the rise of sectional parties. With political parties only attempting to appeal to a particular section, there was far less incentive for compromise on fundamental issues.

10 KNOW-NOTHING PARTY

Stemming from violent clashes in Philadelphia between Protestants and Catholics that killed twenty and injured one hundred people in 1844, a nativist party arose in the 1850s. Calling itself the American Party, the members tried to maintain secrecy by responding, "I know nothing," if questioned. Opponents then called the American Party the Know-Nothing Party. The real nucleus of the political movement was the clandestine fraternal order called the Order of the Star Spangled Banner. The Know-Nothings were anti-Catholic and anti-immigration and proposed barring both groups from holding public office and for immigrants to have to wait twenty-one years for citizenship. The American Party sidestepped the slavery issue and thus made itself irrelevant by the Election of 1856.

11 REPUBLICAN PARTY

Numerous parties in the North and West realigned in response to the Kansas-Nebraska Act. The shock that slavery could jump the 36°30' line awakened fears that it would gain ground in the West and enough political momentum to restart the slave trade from Africa. The Republican Party thus began as a coalition among the Free Soil and Liberty Parties, as well as northern Whigs and even northern anti-slavery Democrats. The new party originally called for the repeal of the Kansas-Nebraska Act and the Fugitive Slave Law, and the abolition of slavery in Washington, D.C. Because many of those who joined were abolitionists, the Republican Party began with a curious mix of radical social ideas and conservative economic ideas. John C. Fremont of Bear Flag Revolt fame was the party's first presidential candidate in the Election of 1856.

12 JOHN BROWN

A divisive figure, John Brown was beloved by some, demonized by others, and lamented by the rest. From a family that participated in the Underground Railroad, Brown was a failed businessman who became obsessed with the idea of a slave insurrection. He led a local militia in Kansas in the midst of the events known as Bleeding Kansas and began terrorist attacks with the Pottawatomie Massacre. After murdering five pro-slavery Kansans there, Brown came to the attention of ardent abolitionists in New England who funded his mission into the South known as the Harpers Ferry Raid. When captured after the mission failed, Brown was executed in Virginia and became a martyr for the abolitionist cause. Historians agree that Brown's actions were the major cause of the formation of militias in the South by an aggrieved people who said those who condemned Brown in the North did so only because his raid failed.

13 BLEEDING KANSAS

During the period from 1854 to 1858 much blood was shed in the violence ignited by popular sovereignty at the organization of a territorial government of Kansas. Two governments were formed, a pro-slavery one at Lecompton and an anti-slavery one in Topeka. By 1856 clashes between the rival factions led to the destruction of the free-soil settlement of Lawrence and to Brown's Pottawatomie slayings. Brown's militia defended another free-soil town from an attack, and a murderous civil war ensued. The violence stemmed from the fraudulent nature of the vote to organize a government due to the presence in Kansas of Missourians and others who voted illegally just to spread slavery. Between two and three hundred people died in the fighting prior to the Civil War during which Kansas entered the Union as a free state in 1861.

14 BROOKS-SUMNER AFFAIR

After lambasting the slavery interests in the Senate in a speech about the rape of Kansas, Charles Sumner sat down at his desk in the Senate chamber. Preston Brooks, a senator from South Carolina, then beat Sumner with a cane so badly that Sumner could not return to his seat in the Senate for three years. Brooks resigned amid horrified Northern criticism but widespread praise in the South. He was reelected to his seat unanimously. Meanwhile, Sumner's seat was left vacant for symbolic effect. Tempers flared around the country when it became known that the violence in Kansas had reached the floor of the nation's highest deliberative body.

15 LECOMPTON CONSTITUTION

In the midst of the strife in Kansas, four separate constitutions were submitted to organize the government. The Lecompton Constitution was a pro-slavery foundation for statehood that was supported by President James Buchanan who agreed with popular sovereignty so much that he would later do nothing to stop secession of the Southern states. He also proposed an amendment to the U.S. Constitution that would directly legalize slavery once and for all. While the Congress accepted the Lecompton Constitution, its opponents demanded another vote in Kansas to ratify it before it could take effect. The second vote on the Lecompton Constitution was ten to one against it. The rejection of the pro-slavery government of Kansas ensured entry as a free state, but also served to enrage the forces in Kansas and in Congress who wanted the peculiar institution not only to survive but to grow.

16 *DRED SCOTT* CASE

Dred Scott was a household slave of an army surgeon whose master had taken him to both a free state and a free territory. Therefore, Scott had lived as a slave for around four years where slavery was illegal. With the help of abolitionists, Scott sued his master for his liberty at first in 1846. A Missouri court agreed with Scott, but that decision was overturned in 1852 by the state supreme court. When the case came to the U.S. Supreme Court in 1856, a majority of the justices determined that neither Dred Scott nor any slave or descendant of slaves was a citizen of the country and were not able to sue in the federal court system. In the process, the Supreme Court declared the Missouri Compromise to have been unconstitutional since it deprived citizens of their Fifth Amendment rights to property, their slaves. This case, then, was only the second time the Supreme Court had declared an act of Congress unconstitutional, the first being in the *Marbury* v. *Madison* case that had established judicial review back in 1803. In short, the South was jubilant and the North was aghast. The grip of the Democratic Party on the presidency for the bulk of the Age of Jackson, with only two Whigs holding the presidency and both of them dying in office, had established a solidly pro-slavery, pro-expansionist court by the eve of the Civil War.

17 LINCOLN-DOUGLAS DEBATES

Lincoln challenged his opponent for the Senate seat of Illinois to a series of debates in 1858. Seven debates between Abraham Lincoln and Stephen A. Douglas, then, were held in a state-wide campaign. At Freeport, Lincoln pointed out the inconsistency of Douglas's position of popular sovereignty with the heavily Democratic Supreme Court's decision in the *Dred Scott* case. Douglas's response became known as the Freeport Doctrine. Douglas said the vote for or against slavery would occur before a state was in the Union and that slavery would only exist if the people were willing to use force to maintain it. Douglas therefore was caught in a position as a Northern Democrat of sidestepping the Supreme Court ruling that the South cherished, so a fatal split in the Democratic Party was opened. Lincoln came out and said he regarded slavery as "a moral, a social, and a political wrong" although he backed away from supporting the equality of all races. The debates in Illinois did not win Lincoln the Senate seat but did win him national fame. His reputation for homegrown wit and sagacity was captured in his famous line, "You can fool all of the people some of the time, and some of the people all of the time, but you cannot fool all of the people all of the time."

18 ELECTION OF 1860

Two years after the famous Lincoln-Douglas debates for the Senate seat in Illinois, Lincoln and Douglas squared off again, but this time for the presidency. In addition, the southern Democrats had split off in a bid to support states' rights and slavery with John C. Breckinridge as their candidate. John Bell of Tennessee also headed a ticket for what was known as the Constitutional Union Party. The Republican Party seized the opportunity of a divided opposition to put forward a platform of national advancement that garnered support not only in the North but also in the West. Lincoln campaigned for a transcontinental railroad, the Homestead Act, and a protective tariff and against reopening the African slave trade and the spread of slavery into any territories. Lincoln won even though he was not on the ballot in ten Southern states. Lincoln's election was the last straw for South Carolina and six other Southern states that then seceded from the Union.

> **STATES' RIGHTS**
>
> This principle was the constitutional interpretation upon which the Confederate States of America was founded. Extending back to Jefferson's belief in a weak central government, states' rights were championed by the likes of John C. Calhoun and assailed by the tariff and slavery controversies. Calhoun expressed the ideal of states' rights in his famous toast, "To the Union, next to our liberties most dear."

19 CRITTENDEN COMPROMISE

With secession looming, Senator John Crittenden of Kentucky attempted a last effort at peace in the spirit of his predecessor, Henry Clay. With the lame duck president James Buchanan doing nothing to stop secession, Crittenden proposed the reestablishment of the 36°30' line and its extension to the Pacific Ocean. Crittenden hoped that if such a definitive boundary could be drawn between slavery and freedom that the seceding states would return and war could be averted. Abraham Lincoln made it clear, however, that the Republican Party meant what it said in the campaign, that slavery should not expand into any territories, not even those from the Mexican Cession that were below the proposed compromise line. The fact that this compromise was rejected and that nothing came from a peace convention held in Washington, D.C., revealed that the era of compromise over the issues of slavery and federal authority were over.

20 SECESSION

Aside from the firing on Fort Sumter, secession was the last cause in the unfortunate series of events that led the nation to the Civil War. Southern secessionists reasoned that they had the constitutional right to back out of the Union that they had only joined as a league of friendship in opposition to the British in the American Revolution. The U.S. Constitution had replaced the Articles of Confederation but had not codified that status of states in subordination to the federal government clearly enough to avoid differing interpretations. South Carolina led the way out of the United States in February of 1861. Abraham Lincoln said the states had no right to leave the Union or to take the mouth of the Mississippi River with them. The six states that followed South Carolina met in Montgomery, Alabama, to write a new constitution for a new country, the Confederate States of America. Lincoln called for seventy-five thousand volunteers to form an army to put down the rebellion in the South.

THE BIG PICTURE

1. The capacity of the Congress to compromise over the spread of slavery into the territories was slowly eroded by the accelerating events of the 1850s.

2. The crusade to abolish slavery escalated as a result of popular works of literature, continued agitation for humanitarian reforms, and dramatic events.

3. The South was more and more determined to defend slavery once the Congress opened territories to its spread through popular sovereignty, and the Supreme Court determined that slaves were property protected by the Bill of Rights.

4. Violence between anti-slavery and pro-slavery forces erupted in the territories, at a federal arsenal, and even in the U.S. Senate.

5. A crescendo of divisive events culminated with the election of Abraham Lincoln in 1860 and the rapid secession of seven southern states that formed the Confederate States of America.

Mini Quiz

1. In the Election of 1824, John Quincy Adams

    (A) became the last of the Virginia dynasty presidents.
    (B) won with more electoral votes even though Andrew Jackson won the popular vote.
    (C) won when the election was decided in the House of Representatives.
    (D) lost to Andrew Jackson in the first election with only two political parties represented.
    (E) won because he exchanged the vice presidency for Henry Clay's support.

2. The Nullification Crisis was resolved in 1833 when

    (A) Andrew Jackson invaded South Carolina to stop secession.
    (B) the Congress voted to end the use of high protective tariffs.
    (C) John C. Calhoun proved nullification was constitutional.
    (D) the Gag Rule was passed to end the discussion.
    (E) Henry Clay negotiated the reduction of the tariff over nine years.

3. Andrew Jackson's presidency possessed all of the following legacies **EXCEPT**

    (A) the president's reliance upon a team of trusted advisers other than his cabinet.
    (B) a shift in power west as the population moved in that direction.
    (C) frequent use of the veto to increase the executive branch's power and influence.
    (D) a growing focus on the interests of merchants and bankers in government policy.
    (E) the placing of political supporters in government jobs, or rotation in office.

4. Which reformer in the antebellum period established common, or public, schools?

    (A) Dorothea Dix
    (B) Horace Mann
    (C) William Lloyd Garrison
    (D) Bronson Alcott
    (E) Ralph Waldo Emerson

5. Which of the experiences below would likely **NOT** occur at a Lyceum meeting?

    (A) A scientist demonstrates a laboratory experiment
    (B) A transcendentalist delivers a lecture on self-reliance
    (C) A Methodist revival preacher delivers a sermon
    (D) A phrenologist demonstrates analysis of the brain and then offers private screenings
    (E) A local orchestra performs a new composition from Europe

6. The clash between the Mormon settlers of Utah and the federal government ended when

    (A) the Mormons burned Salt Lake City before federal troops arrived.
    (B) Joseph Smith was captured and killed by a mob.
    (C) federal troops soundly defeated the Mormon militia.
    (D) federal troops arrived to find Salt Lake City deserted and then left.
    (E) neighboring settlers drove the Mormons from their homes and burned Salt Lake City.

7. What was the impact of Eli Whitney's cotton gin on the South?

    (A) The cotton gin convinced the South to begin the cultivation of cotton.
    (B) The cotton gin dramatically eased the labor involved in the harvesting of cotton.
    (C) The cotton gin had little to no impact on the demand for slaves.
    (D) The cotton gin reduced the demand for slaves by saving on manual labor.
    (E) The cotton gin made cotton lucrative and thus increased the demand for slaves.

8. Which activity below was forbidden in connection with slavery by federal law prior to the Civil War?

    (A) Buying Africans directly from Africa
    (B) Manumission, or freeing of slaves by choice
    (C) Separating slave families and marriages by selling them as individuals
    (D) Allowing slaves to work for money for self-purchase
    (E) Teaching slaves to read

9. The experience of African Americans in slavery

    (A) was uniformly harsh because slavery was an institution based on violence.
    (B) varied widely depending on their particular role and their masters' temperaments.
    (C) was so harsh as to lead to constant slave rebellions.
    (D) grew harsher the closer they lived to the North.
    (E) erased the opportunity for expressions of human culture because slaves were property.

10. Which answer below best summarizes America's relationship with Great Britain before the Civil War?

(A) The United States and England were allies against the Spanish as Spain's Empire crumbled.

(B) Britain feared the rise of the United States as a world power and thus actively thwarted it.

(C) The United States feared British encroachment on any territory in the New World.

(D) The two nations saw each other as economic equals and thus experienced competition.

(E) The United States leaned toward annexation of Canada regardless of British protests.

11. Which two men made unlikely allies in stopping Texas annexation immediately following the Lone Star Republic's independence from Mexico?

(A) Andrew Jackson and John Quincy Adams

(B) Andrew Jackson and John C. Calhoun

(C) Andrew Jackson and Henry Clay

(D) Henry Clay and James K. Polk

(E) Sam Houston and Daniel Webster

12. What made the Gadsden Purchase so valuable as the last addition of contiguous territory to the continental United States?

(A) More gold deposits had been discovered there.

(B) The territory supplied a seaport on the Gulf of California.

(C) The territory contained the best pass through the Rockies for a railroad.

(D) The Apache and Comanche Indians refused to go there for religious reasons.

(E) The border with Mexico became more defensible because of natural boundaries.

13. The Wilmot Proviso suggested that

(A) the Gadsden Purchase be extended to the sea.

(B) the United States annex all of Mexico.

(C) popular sovereignty be used to determine the status of slavery in the Mexican Cession.

(D) no territory acquired from Mexico would become open to slavery.

(E) a canal in Central America be exclusively the property of the United States.

14. During the slavery debates, the South interpreted the U.S. Constitution to mean that

    (A) the federal government had the right to block the spread of slavery in the territories.
    (B) states that disagreed with the trends of federal power could constitutionally leave the union.
    (C) state law must always defer to federal law in times of disagreement.
    (D) slavery's extent was governed by natural geographic and climatic boundaries.
    (E) the reference in the Bill of Rights to due process did not extend to slaves as property.

15. Abraham Lincoln's stated position on slavery was that slavery

    (A) should be abolished because it was immoral despite federal laws protecting it.
    (B) should be decided in the territories by the will of the people, or popular sovereignty.
    (C) violated the natural equality of all men that was established by God.
    (D) should end by allowing each new African American born into slavery to be freed.
    (E) would end naturally as long as the federal government banned its spread.

ANSWER EXPLANATIONS

1. **(C)** Adams was from Massachusetts and received fewer popular and electoral votes than Jackson, who still did not gain enough electoral votes to win among four challengers. Adams thus won in the House of Representatives, and the "corrupt bargain" hinted at in answer (E) involved Clay's becoming the secretary of state.

2. **(E)** Henry Clay negotiated the compromise tariff as stated, whereas the rest of the items were related to the Nullification Crisis; none of them are true as stated.

3. **(D)** All of the items listed were major legacies of Andrew Jackson's presidency except answer (D) because Jackson was the president who advanced the interests of the common man, not commercial interests.

4. **(B)** Horace Mann was the secretary of the Massachusetts Board of Education who advanced the common school movement, the origin of modern public schools.

5. **(C)** A sermon would not likely happen at a Lyceum because the types of reform embodied in the Lyceum movement were secular, not religious.

6. **(D)** When Albert Sydney Johnston's troops arrived in Salt Lake City the Mormons had evacuated to avoid a violent clash, although all but answer (A) either happened or were possibilities in the history of the Church of Jesus Christ of Latter Day Saints.

7. **(E)** Because the cotton gin dramatically cut the labor required not to harvest but to process cotton by removing the seeds and other material from the cotton fiber, many more slaves were needed to perform all the other tasks of cotton cultivation that was turned into a lucrative cash crop.

8. **(A)** The U.S. Congress banned the African slave trade in 1808. All of the other activities were either legal or banned only by state laws.

9. **(B)** Slaves who were field hands, especially those of the Deep South, had much harsher lives than household slaves or those living in the border states. Such slave rebellions that occurred were by no means constant, and although oppressed, slaves developed their own unique cultures and maintained family ties as proof of their participation in human culture.

10. **(C)** Only this choice is true and is the background for the Monroe Doctrine as well as the expansion associated with Manifest Destiny. All hopes of annexing Canada were given up after the War of 1812.

11. **(A)** Although all of these pairings would have made unlikely alliances in the 1830s and 1840s, Jackson and Adams were by no means fond of each other but agreed that Texas annexation would be too hazardous for the nation right after it broke free from Mexico. Both men thwarted annexation if for different reasons.

12. **(C)** Only this choice was in the minds of those who purchased this afterthought on the Mexican Cession.

13. **(D)** Although all of these ideas were expressed in this era at one time or another, David Wilmot was most concerned to prevent slavery being restored by the United States where

the dictator Santa Anna had abolished it. Yet the Wilmot Proviso passed the House of Representatives on a sectional vote but failed to pass in the Senate.

14. **(B)** This choice was the whole basis for secession and the formation of the Confederacy, whereas few Southerners, if any, would have believed or openly acknowledged the others.

15. **(E)** This choice was not only Lincoln's position but part of the official platform of the Republican Party. Lincoln actively opposed or disagreed with the other ideas that were indeed held by others of his day.

The Civil War

17

> *. . . and the war came.*
>
> —Abraham Lincoln's second inaugural address, 1865

TIMELINE	
1860 November	Abraham Lincoln is elected president
1861 February	Jefferson Davis is elected president of the CSA
April	Fort Sumter
April–June	Lincoln retains four border states and loses four to secession after Sumter
July	First Battle of Bull Run
August	Greenbacks are first issued as Federal currency
1862	Conscription begins for the Confederacy
March	*Monitor* v. *Merrimac*
April	Battle of Shiloh
June	Robert E. Lee becomes commander of the Army of Northern Virginia
September	Battle of Antietam
December	Battle of Fredericksburg
1863 January	Emancipation Proclamation becomes effective
May	Thomas J. "Stonewall" Jackson dies
July	Battle of Gettysburg
July	Siege of Vicksburg ends
November	Ulysses S. Grant becomes commander of all Union forces; Conscription begins for the Union
1864 Nov.–Dec.	Sherman's March to the Sea
November	Election of 1864
1865 April	Lee surrenders at Appomattox Courthouse

OVERVIEW

As the United States expanded its borders, its economy, and its population, regional tensions, most notably over slavery, led to a civil war. The acquisition and settlement of new territories in the western half of the North American continent opened up a question that politicians had sought to avoid—should these new territories allow slavery? The issue of the expansion of slavery became increasingly divisive in the 1850s. Some Northerners adopted the *free-soil* ethos, the idea that lands out West should be open to small-scale farming, without competition from large-scale plantation agriculture using slave labor. By the end of the decade, more Northerners were grappling with the moral issues around slavery. Positions became decidedly more entrenched on the eve of the Civil War. The collapse of the two-party system in the 1850s and the tendency toward sectional, rather than national political, parties made compromise difficult. The election of the Republican Abraham Lincoln initiated the process of secession for the Southern states. Once inaugurated, Lincoln made clear that he would not allow the Union to be broken apart. Neither side had wanted war, Lincoln said in his Second Inaugural Address (1865), "but one of them [the seceding South] would make war rather than let the nation survive, and the other [the Union] would accept war rather than let it perish. And the war came."

Both sides had advantages as the war began. The Union had a far greater population than that of the rebellious Southern states (22 million to 6 million). It also had a far greater military capacity than the South, a more diverse economy, and an extensive network of railroad tracks. All of these advantages would become especially significant in a lengthy war. The Union had the capability to resupply its troops and to recruit reinforcements for fallen soldiers. The main advantage of the Confederacy was that it simply had to fight a defensive war. It did not have to invade and conquer the North in order to declare victory. The Union, on the other hand, had to fight an offensive war in Southern territory. Another advantage of the Confederacy was the rich military tradition of the South. It had able generals and a cohort of military men to draw from.

The Civil War and its aftermath dramatically transformed American society. The war spurred rapid industrialization of the North. During the Civil War, the Union government required an enormous amount of war materials, from guns and bullets to boots and uniforms. Manufacturers rose to the occasion by rapidly modernizing production. These changes in production sped up the process of industrialization that was in its beginning stages before the war. Industrialization stimulated a long period of economic growth, turning the United States into a world economic power.

Perhaps the most important outcome of the war was the abolition of slavery. The issuing of the Emancipation Proclamation expanded the focus of the Civil War from preserving the union to emancipating the slaves. This move proved to be decisive to Northern victory; it opened up the possibility of large-scale enlistment of African Americans, and it contributed to the Confederacy remaining isolated diplomatically on the international scene. The Thirteenth Amendment, abolishing slavery forever in the United States, was ratified as the war was ending.

The outcome of the Civil War, especially in light of Lincoln's understanding of the conflict, played an important role in the growth of the United States as a modern nation. First, the war made it clear that the states did not have the autonomy to secede and that the nation was indivisible, larger than the sum of its parts. From the time of the Civil War, the United States was increasingly referred to as a nation, rather than a union of states. Lincoln was the first major leader in American history to refer to the United States as a singular noun, and he made it one. Historians, such as Eric Foner, see this transition in the context of nation-building processes in different parts of the world in the nineteenth century (such as the Meiji Restoration in Japan in 1868 or the Risorgimento that resulted in the formation of Italy, completed in 1871). The unification that occurred in the United States, however, was built around a set of democratic principles rather than around a particular ethnicity.

TOP 20 THINGS TO KNOW

1 ABRAHAM LINCOLN

Abraham Lincoln grew up in a strict Separate Baptist household; his family was morally opposed to alcohol, dancing, and slavery. Lincoln rose from a storekeeper and militia captain in Illinois to a postmaster and a successful lawyer in Springfield, Illinois. He belonged to the Whig Party and served one term in the House of Representatives (1847–1849). In 1856, he joined the new Republican Party, which had been founded two years earlier in opposition to the Kansas-Nebraska Act. Lincoln ran in 1858 against the incumbent Senator Stephen A. Douglas. Lincoln read extensively from the Bible, from which he used the line, "A house divided against itself cannot stand," and from Shakespeare. These sources helped Lincoln craft the original rhetorical style that became famous in the Lincoln-Douglas debates, in his first and second inaugural addresses, and in the Gettysburg Address. His victory in the 1860 presidential election, with no Southern electoral votes, proved to be the last straw for many Southerners. Despite his assurances that he was prohibited by the Constitution from abolishing slavery where it already existed, Southern states began to secede—seven states in the South seceded before the hostilities began at Fort Sumter, and four more states in the upper South seceded afterward. Lincoln used a trial and error approach to choosing effective military leadership before choosing General Ulysses S. Grant. In 1863, he issued the Emancipation Proclamation, changing the nature of the war. In 1864, in a gesture of conciliation to the South, he chose a Southern unionist, Andrew Johnson, to be his running-mate as he ran for a second term. Having guided the Union to victory and having advocated a quick restoration of the seceded states, Lincoln was assassinated by John Wilkes Booth in April 1865. When he died, Secretary of War Edwin Stanton said, "Now he belongs to the ages." No other president, with the possible exception of Franklin D. Roosevelt, has had to carry such a burden or face such dangers for the country.

2 JEFFERSON DAVIS

Davis was a West Point graduate who served in the Black Hawk War (as did Lincoln) and the Mexican War in which he was wounded. Between the wars he opened a plantation in Mississippi that he called "Brierfield." He served as a Democratic U.S. congressman, senator, and secretary of war for Franklin Pierce. These experiences made him a clear choice to lead the Confederate States of America (CSA) once Mississippi seceded, but after he was elected president his authoritarian demeanor and military opinions did not endear him to other Confederate leaders, military or civilian. His heavy hand partly undid the Confederacy, but in his defense he was constantly hampered in leading the central government by the very principle upon which the CSA was founded—states' rights. Warned by Robert E. Lee to flee Richmond, President Davis was captured, charged with treason, and imprisoned from 1865 through 1867 when the charges were dropped.

3 FORT SUMTER

Fort Sumter was a federal installation located at the opening of Charleston harbor off the coast of South Carolina. Although it was not the first fort fired upon (that was in Pensacola, Florida), South Carolinians were the first to secede and considered by the North to be the culprits who started the war. Intolerable to Southern pride and impossible to ignore because Charleston was one of the largest cities in the South, the fort was fired upon by Confederate batteries at 4:30 A.M. on April 12, 1861. The fort returned fire, but after thirty-four hours of sustained bombardment the commander inside Ft. Sumter, Major Robert Anderson, surrendered. Neither the Confederate nor the Union forces sustained any casualties, but four additional states seceded to make eleven, and Lincoln decided to respond militarily instead of diplomatically. Lincoln is said to have engineered the whole episode by sending a supply ship that he calculated would provoke the South to attack but also not be considered by objective observers to have been an act of aggression. Lincoln and others claimed, therefore, that the Confederacy started the Civil War.

> **FORTS HENRY AND DONELSON**
>
> The capture of these two forts on the Tennessee and Cumberland rivers was the first step toward Ulysses S. Grant's rise to command of all Union armies. Grant kept Kentucky from seceding and opened the way for Union victory in the western theater.

4 BORDER STATES

Missouri, Kentucky, Maryland, and Delaware were slave states that remained loyal to the Union (later to include West Virginia). The Republican Party platform mandated that slavery be left alone where it existed, and Lincoln strove to convince these four states not to secede. He reasoned that if these states left, the Union would be dissolved. In convincing the citizens of especially Missouri, Kentucky, and Maryland he did not hesitate to use military force and the police powers of the federal government in ways that were later deemed to be unconstitutional.

5 ROBERT E. LEE

A descendant of one of the first families of Virginia, he declined President Lincoln's offer to command the Union Army in 1861. Although opposed to both slavery and secession, he joined the Confederate cause and was given command of the Army of Northern Virginia. Lee's iron will and unimpeachable character provided much of the Confederacy's resolve. After his army was whittled down to thirty thousand troops, he surrendered to General U.S. Grant at Appomattox in 1865. Lee is credited with using his influence over his countrymen to urge a peaceful resolution to the war by resisting all efforts to continue armed conflict that might have prolonged the war.

6 ULYSSES S. GRANT

A West Point graduate from Ohio, Grant was decorated for gallantry in the Mexican War and was said to be an excellent horseman. While pulling off some astounding tactical victories during the Civil War in the West, including the reduction of Vicksburg and the freeing of the Mississippi River, as Grant rose in responsibility he relied on attrition. Therefore, this other memorable top general of the Civil War is also not considered a tactical genius, and he is often remembered as a butcher of his own men. The numbers were all in Grant's favor, however, and the brutal wearing down of the Confederate army prevailed. As a war hero,

Grant was elected president in 1868 and served two terms. His was the first scandal-ridden presidency of the Gilded Age.

7 FIRST BATTLE OF BULL RUN

The Battle of Bull Run, or Manassas, was the first major conflict (1861) of what many politicians said would be a short war. Thomas J. Jackson's refusal to retreat rallied flee-ing Confederate forces and earned him the nickname "Stonewall." Confederate reinforcements were brought by train for the first time in warfare and allowed the South to turn the tide. The Confederate rout of the Union Army and the five thousand casualties caused many U.S. leaders to realize the Civil War could be long and bloody.

> ### TRENT AFFAIR
> When a British ship, the *Trent*, was boarded by a Union vessel and two Confederate diplomats arrested, the British almost entered the Civil War on the side of the Confederacy. Lincoln released the prisoners instead.

8 MONITOR V. MERRIMAC

This clash of ironclad ships marked a turning point in world naval conflicts and is part of the reason the Civil War was the first modern war. The Confederate ship *Virginia* (the refitted *Merrimac*) was wreaking havoc with wooden Union ships until the newly designed *Monitor* arrived. The two ironclad ships pounded each other for five hours before calling it a draw. The Confederates later scuttled the *Virginia* rather than allowing it to be captured. The Confederacy foreshadowed modern naval warfare even more with the first successful combatant submarine, the *Hunley*.

9 CONFISCATION ACTS

President Abraham Lincoln had been an opponent of slavery throughout his adult life. However, before the Civil War, Lincoln was not an abolitionist. Starting in the 1840s, Lincoln came to support the ideas of gradual emancipation and voluntary colonization. As president, Lincoln did not believe that he had the constitutional right to touch slavery in the states where it already existed. Even after the Civil War started, Lincoln was reluctant to take action against slavery, both for constitutional reasons and for fear of pushing the Border States toward secession and joining the Confederacy. However, many Republicans in Congress were eager to move against slavery. Some of these Republicans used the context of the war to frame the question of slavery as a military matter. Since some slaves were pressed into service by the Confederate Army, they could be considered "contraband of war." Republicans, therefore, introduced the first Confiscation Act in 1861, declaring that any slaves pressed into working for the Confederacy could be taken as "confiscated property." It was generally recognized that a nation at war could seize enemy property if that property aided the enemy's war effort. The Confiscation Act, however, broke new ground in applying this principle to slaves and to the unusual circumstances of a civil war. The second act, passed in 1862, allowed for the seizure of the slaves owned by Confederate officials. Despite Lincoln's reservations about these acts, he signed them both. His tacit support of the confiscation approach indicated his evolving position on slavery. It was only months after signing the Second Confiscation Act that Lincoln issued the Emancipation Proclamation (see next page).

> ### ALABAMA
> The *Alabama* was the most notoriously successful Confederate raider during the war. The fact that she was built for the Confederacy in a British shipyard, along with many other ships, became a source of the last major diplomatic crisis between the United States and the United Kingdom.

10 ANTIETAM

Antietam was the bloodiest one-day battle of the war with twenty-three thousand casualties from both sides and the one time George McClellan thwarted Robert E. Lee's plans. The retreat of Lee into Virginia was the first significant good news for the Union forces and spurred Lincoln to issue the Emancipation Proclamation. Foreign recognition of the Confederacy was also stymied, a fact that severely crippled Confederate hopes for European aid or intervention.

11 EMANCIPATION PROCLAMATION

Lincoln's issuance of this document was his single most important act in saving the Union by providing a moral justification for continuing the war. It provided that after January 1, 1863, all slaves in states still in rebellion would be "then, thenceforward, and forever free." Black soldiers were also permitted to fight for the freedom of their race after this document met with popular approval. While no states still in rebellion would honor Lincoln's executive order, every subsequently conquered state had to. Thus Lincoln made the war about "a new birth of freedom" and boosted the nation's morale.

12 BATTLE OF GETTYSBURG

This battle was the largest ever fought in the Western Hemisphere and the most crucial of the Civil War. It marked the Confederate Army's last invasion of the North and started when the forces unexpectedly ran into one another in a small Pennsylvania town in July of 1863. Lee unsuccessfully attacked the Union forces several times including the disastrous Pickett's Charge. The Confederates retreated into Virginia, but the new Union commander, George Meade, refused Lincoln's orders to give chase. Over fifty thousand men were killed or wounded. Lee's offer to resign after the battle was ignored by the Confederate government that struggled on, but most people even in the South realized that Gettysburg spelled the doom of the Confederacy.

13 SIEGE OF VICKSBURG

This last Confederate stronghold on the Mississippi River fell on July 4, 1863, after a six-week siege by General Grant's army. The Union victory came the same day General Lee's army retreated from Gettysburg. This double blow demoralized Southerners for the first time. The fall of the city of Vicksburg meant the Union controlled the Mississippi River, a key aim in its original war strategy to split the Confederacy geographically.

14 THE GETTYSBURG ADDRESS

The Battle of Gettysburg (1863) was a major turning point in the Civil War (see above). Several months after the battle, President Lincoln went to Gettysburg to dedicate a military cemetery at the site. His address at the ceremony succinctly framed the Civil War in the larger context of fulfilling the democratic goals that were implicit in the founding documents of the United States. He invoked the Declaration of Independence, which had been ratified "four score and seven years" before his "Gettysburg Address." He stated that the United States was "conceived in Liberty," and that an important founding principle was that "all men are created equal." The Civil War was, in Lincoln's thinking, a test of whether a nation conceived around the principles of liberty and equality can last. The men who died trying to make these principles a reality had made the battlefield a sacred site. It was up to the living, Lincoln asserted, to bring those principles to fruition, to ensure that there shall be "a new birth of freedom."

15 SUSPENSION OF HABEAS CORPUS

President Abraham Lincoln suspended the writ of habeas corpus in 1863, authorizing the arrest, without due process, of rebels and traitors. A writ of habeas corpus is an order forcing the government to release a person who has been improperly imprisoned. This privilege was included in the Constitution to curtail the age-old practice of tyrannical rulers throwing people in jail without formal procedures or even just cause. Under the Constitution, a person can only be sentenced to prison after being formally charged, tried, and found guilty. However, the Constitution does state that this privilege can be suspended during times of national emergency. This clause illustrates an important concept in American democracy—civil liberties are not absolute. Lincoln was responding to riots and threats of militia action in the border state of Maryland. After the war, the Supreme Court, in *Ex Parte Milligan* (1866), ruled that the suspension of habeas corpus did not empower the president to try and convict citizens before military tribunals; civilians can be tried in military courts only if civilian courts are not operating.

16 GREENBACKS

This war-time emergency remedy that persisted after the Civil War was not the first but the most extensive issuing of paper currency. Both the North and the South eventually circulated paper currencies backed with no precious metals and touched off intense inflation. The Union currency was printed with green ink, hence its "colorful" name.

17 NEW YORK CITY DRAFT RIOTS

By 1863, both sides in the Civil War had instituted drafts to maintain troop strength in their respective armies. All men, ages 20–45 were eligible for the draft. Neither draft law was greeted enthusiastically by the public. One element of the Union draft was especially galling to many working-class Northerners—men of means could pay a $300 commutation fee to hire a substitute to serve. In 1863, $300 was a sizable sum—equivalent to over $9,000 in 2017 dollars. (The Confederate draft law had a similar stipulation.) When news of the names being drafted appeared in newspapers alongside a list of casualties from Gettysburg, a series of protests erupted in New York City. In the subsequent days, the protests turned violent, and the target became the city's African-American population. The outpouring of violence against the city's African-American community revealed long-standing bitterness among many Irish immigrants toward their African-American neighbors. The two communities often lived cheek-by-jowl in the impoverished Sixth Ward of the city (home of the Five Points neighborhood). At least 120 people were killed in the riots. Four days of rampaging were finally put down by exhausted troops returning from Gettysburg. The New York City draft riots were one of the most significant episodes of resistance to Union policies. Over the course of the war, Lincoln had to respond to a great deal of resistance to the war within the borders of the loyal states.

18 COPPERHEADS

As the Civil war progressed, a faction of the Democratic Party in the Northern states who opposed the American Civil War became increasingly vocal. They insisted on an immediate peace settlement with the Confederates. Republicans called these anti-war Democrats "Copperheads," after the poisonous snake. Copperheadism was especially strong in the Midwest states above the Ohio River, as well as among Irish Catholic immigrants in eastern cities. Many of the Copperheads in the Midwest had migrated from the South; some had retained economic ties with the South and were alarmed that these ties had been severed. These Midwestern Copperheads, historians note, were attached to a more traditional, rural vision of the United States and rejected the economic revolution that the industrializing North represented. In this, they could be considered the successors of Jacksonian agrarians. By 1863, Copperheads openly lambasted Lincoln and his evolving total war policies. Copperheads went so far as to support General George McClellan's grudge against Lincoln to unseat him and end the Civil War with a divided America.

19 LINCOLN'S SECOND INAUGURAL ADDRESS

President Abraham Lincoln delivered his Second Inaugural Address in March 1865, with the end of the war and of slavery in sight. In it, Lincoln displayed a lenient and forgiving attitude toward the secessionist South. The phrase "with malice toward none; with charity for all" seemed to indicate Lincoln's desire to quickly bring the nation together, without excessively harsh treatment of the South. Lincoln's charitable attitude is evident in several actions he took. Earlier, in 1863, he announced his "ten percent" plan. For each Southern state, if ten percent of the voters from the 1860 election took an oath of allegiance to the United States and promised to abide by emancipation, then that state could establish a new government and send representatives to Congress. In 1864, he vetoed the Wade-Davis Bill, which would have established much stricter standards for the Southern states to meet. Lincoln was assassinated less than a month after his second inauguration, so it is difficult to surmise how he would have negotiated the difficulties of the Reconstruction era. If the address reflected a somewhat lenient attitude toward the South, it spoke of the evils of slavery in unflinching terms. He spoke of the entire war as a divine punishment inflicted on *both* sides for benefitting from the cruel institution of slavery. The war may continue, he said, "until every drop of blood drawn with the lash shall be paid by another drawn with the sword."

20 APPOMATTOX COURTHOUSE

With Union armies encircling the Army of Northern Virginia, General Lee surrendered to General Grant in April 1865. Lee received rations for his men and permission for officers to keep their swords and all soldiers to keep their own horses and mules. Lee's urging of his men to surrender and return to civilian life was his greatest contribution to peace.

THE BIG PICTURE

1. The Civil War was a tragic clash of forces holding opposing interpretations of the powers of the federal government, and the Union victory established the United States as a more unified nation with new perspectives on both the U.S. Constitution and the Declaration of Independence.

2. Both sides in the Civil War originally employed military tactics unsuited to their modern weaponry and infrastructure, but the North adopted techniques of total warfare that foreshadowed the terrible nature of twentieth-century conflicts in which civilian populations and resources were attacked and destroyed.

3. Abraham Lincoln's skillful management of the war earned him the top rank among presidents, status as a model for all subsequent presidents, and the legacy of being a martyr for American freedom.

4. By surviving this harrowing national ordeal, the federal government emerged from the Civil War with greater powers and authority not only over states but also over individuals.

5. Major consequences of the war included defining the ever-changing relationships between the races and economic transformations that launched the settlement of the West and the rise of industrialized big business.

Reconstruction

18

*This is the most important subject which now engages the attention of
the American people, for on it depends the future welfare of the nation,
and the destinies of a race but partially redeemed from bondage.*

—Philip A. Bell, editorial in the *Elevator*, 1865

TIMELINE	
1863	Lincoln proposes his Ten Percent Plan
1865	Ku Klux Klan is founded; Congress establishes a Committee on Reconstruction; Lincoln is assassinated and Andrew Johnson becomes president; Thirteenth Amendment is ratified
1865–1871	Freedmen's Bureau operates for six years
1865–1877	Reconstruction spans twelve years
1866	Thaddeus Stevens leads the Radical Republican takeover of Congress
1867	Congress passes the Military Reconstruction Act; Congress passes the Tenure of Office Act
1868	Impeachment of President Johnson; Fourteenth Amendment is ratified
1870	Fifteenth Amendment is ratified
1877	Compromise of 1877
1882	Congress passes the Chinese Exclusion Act

OVERVIEW

As the Civil War was coming to an end, President Abraham Lincoln and the Republican Party began to address several questions regarding the post-war world. These questions included: What accommodations would be made for the freed men and women of the South? How would the secessionist South be reintegrated into the United States? What punishments, if any, would be meted out to those who rebelled against the United States? Finally, who held responsibility for reuniting and reconstructing the country—the president or Congress? Did, as the president argued, the secessionist states still exist as political entities, simply awaiting new governing personnel, or had they committed "suicide"? Many Congressional Republicans argued that the states had ceased to exist, and therefore needed to be readmitted by Congress. The answers to these questions formed the basis of competing visions of what Reconstruction would entail.

A primary goal of President Abraham Lincoln's post-Civil War policy was restoring the Union as quickly as possible. In 1863, he announced his "ten percent" plan, establishing a low bar for the secessionist states to comply with in order to reestablish state governments. In 1864, he vetoed the Wade-Davis Bill, which would have established much stricter standards for the Southern states to meet. After Lincoln's assassination, his vice president, Andrew Johnson, assumed power. Johnson continued with the lenient and rapid approach to Reconstruction that Lincoln had mapped out. Johnson, a native of Tennessee, quickly recognized the new Southern state governments as legitimate after they repudiated secession and ratified the Thirteenth Amendment banning slavery. In the South, many members of the old slave owning class were now back in power. These men tried to replicate the conditions of the old South, including passing a series of restrictive laws known as the Black Codes. Post-war conditions were so similar to pre-war conditions that many Northerners wondered if they had "won the war, but lost the peace."

It was in this context that Republicans in Congress won a resounding victory in the 1866 elections and embarked on more sweeping measures. This phase of Reconstruction, known alternatively as "Radical Reconstruction" or "Congressional Reconstruction," showed the potential of a biracial democracy in the United States, while also showing the limits of federal resolve and the strength of white Southern opposition. Republicans were able to push through the Reconstruction Acts of 1867, which withdrew recognition of the former Confederacy as states, and divided the South (except for Tennessee) into five military districts. These areas could only rejoin the United States if they guaranteed basic rights to African Americans. Republicans in Congress also passed the Civil Rights Act of 1867, guaranteeing equal treatment for African Americans in public accommodations.

As President Johnson tried to block these measures, tensions between the president and Congress intensified. The clash degenerated to such an extent by 1868 that the Republicans voted to impeach Johnson. The Senate narrowly found Johnson not guilty, but the whole procedure rendered Johnson powerless to stop Congress's Reconstruction plans.

Congressional Reconstruction, although short lived, brought sweeping changes to the South. New state governments were formed as the southern states rejoined the United States. African-American families were reunited. Laws were passed guaranteeing equality and new economic patterns emerged. African Americans were elected to local, state, and federal offices. Two African Americans were elected to the U.S. Senate, Hiram Revels and Blanche K. Bruce, and more than a dozen representatives were elected to the House of Representatives. Reconstruction lasted only a decade; its accomplishments were limited and short-lived. However, in many respects, the failures of Reconstruction in the nineteenth century set the stage for a "second reconstruction" in the twentieth century. The democratic spirit of the Reconstruction period inspired civil rights activists throughout the twentieth century. Furthermore, the principles established in the Fourteenth Amendment were invoked in several important Supreme Court decisions in the twentieth century—most notably, *Brown* v. *Board of Education* (1954).

1 TEN PERCENT PLAN

Based on his belief that the seceded states had never left the country because they had lost their war for independence, Abraham Lincoln sought to ease the country back to peace with a lenient plan for Reconstruction. His plan first gave amnesty to almost all Confederates, and then he called for states to emancipate their slaves and swear loyalty to the Union. Once ten percent of a state's population took the oath, Lincoln planned to recognize the state's government as legitimate. Most Northerners thought this arrangement was too lenient, but Lincoln could have perhaps guided his proposals through to a benevolent peace if it were not for his assassination by John Wilkes Booth.

2 BLACK CODES

Immediately after the Civil War, in 1865 and 1866, Southern states passed Black Codes. These statutes regulated the activities of African Americans and in many ways recreated the conditions of slavery. Certain Black Codes forbade African Americans from owning land or owning a business. A central feature of the Black Codes was a broad and harsh set of vagrancy laws, which allowed the arrest of freed people for minor infractions. Such laws could include criminalizing being on a public road without having a certain amount of money. Punishments for violations of Black Codes frequently included forcing African Americans to labor on a plantation for a period of time. Mississippi was the first state to pass Black Codes in 1865—all the other ten states of the former Confederacy soon followed its model. Post-war conditions were so similar to pre-war conditions that many Northerners wondered if they had "won the war, but lost the peace." In this atmosphere, a group of Republicans in Congress initiated a more sweeping Reconstruction program, implementing much of it by overriding President Johnson's vetoes.

> **WADE-DAVIS BILL**
>
> The Radical Republicans in Congress passed this law to retaliate against Lincoln's leniency. They increased the threshold for citizens taking the loyalty oath to 50 percent and pressed for emancipation. Lincoln did not sign the bill before his assassination.

3 ANDREW JOHNSON

A self-educated tailor, Johnson had risen to become the governor of Tennessee and then a U.S. senator just prior to the Civil War. Because he did not approve of secession and did not leave the Senate when Tennessee seceded, Lincoln made him vice president in 1864. He became president after Lincoln's assassination but proved to be inadequate to the task of carrying out Lincoln's policies. Even his more stringent plan for Reconstruction met with resistance from the Radical Republicans in Congress who eventually tried to get rid of Johnson through an impeachment trial. Johnson was not removed from office, but his presidency still ended in failure. He, like President Grant, was plagued by accusations of alcoholism. His attempts as a southerner to end Reconstruction served only to isolate him from his political party.

4 THIRTEENTH AMENDMENT

This amendment to the Constitution that abolished slavery was foreshadowed by the Emancipation Proclamation and was a penalty for the secession of the slaveholding states and the Civil War. Once Lincoln issued his proclamation, the Union fought on to secure emancipation as its new unifying impulse. This step, completed with ratification late in 1865, was the one measure that Lincoln, Johnson, and the Radical Republicans all agreed should occur before Reconstruction could be considered a success. The Thirteenth Amendment was considered by some to be the end of the abolitionist movement and its crowning achievement. The events of Reconstruction, however, left the freedmen in a general condition not much different from their status before the war.

5 RADICAL REPUBLICANS

This wing of the Republican Party in Congress sought to punish the South for having caused the Civil War and to elevate the freedmen. Some viewed the latter issue as another attempt to humiliate the South, whereas others were sincerely interested in advancing African Americans to a position of equality. All the Radicals were said to "wave the bloody shirt," or to continually gain political advantage by blaming the Democratic Party for the war. The Radicals used their numerical advantage in the Congress to vie for control of Reconstruction with President Johnson, and they represented the only opportunity to secure the Thirteenth, Fourteenth, and Fifteenth Amendments to the Constitution for nearly a century because they held complete control while most southern whites could not vote.

CIVIL RIGHTS BILL

The Radical Republicans also balked at Johnson's plan for reconstruction by passing this law. They wanted to make freedmen official citizens and undermine Black Codes that were returning in southern states. Johnson vetoed the bill, and the Congress set its sights on removing Johnson from office.

6 FREEDMEN'S BUREAU

In response to the Southern states' laws known as the Black Codes, the federal government expanded this agency originally formed to transfer abandoned land to former slaves. Under the leadership of Oliver O. Howard, the Bureau sought to provide freedmen with basic necessities until they could either own land or secure jobs. Bureau agents were supposed to monitor the working conditions to which African Americans were subjected, but the land for distribution and the staff were never enough. The Freedmen's Bureau's greatest success was the establishment of the first serious efforts to educate African Americans in the South. President Johnson vetoed the legislation and said that the U.S. Constitution did not call for the federal government to set up welfare agencies looking out for individual citizens' needs. The attempt to elevate African Americans for their sakes and to humiliate the South saw this first welfare agency established when the Radical Republicans overrode the president's veto.

7 THADDEUS STEVENS

This Pennsylvania lawyer and politician practiced, ironically, in Gettysburg before the Civil War. With the rise of the Republican Party, Stevens rose to national prominence as the leader of the Radical Republicans in the House of Representatives. He and his counterpart in the Senate, the caned Senator Charles Sumner, formulated Reconstruction policies meant to force a punitive peace upon the South. He chaired the Committee on Reconstruction and organized the impeachment of President Johnson. Whether he believed in complete equality of the races is impossible to tell, but at death he did have himself buried in an African-American cemetery.

8 FOURTEENTH AMENDMENT

When the Congress tried to confer citizenship rights on freedmen with the Civil Rights Act of 1866, the law was considered such a usurpation of the rights of states to determine citizenship that the Committee on Reconstruction resolved to amend the Constitution. Once it was ratified in the North, the Committee demanded that each Southern state do so as a condition of Reconstruction. The amendment clarified the citizenship status of African Americans and of all people born on American soil. Furthermore, the federal government was put in charge of monitoring whether or not states abused the civil rights of their citizens. Provisions of the amendment were also designed to punish high-ranking Confederate leaders by barring them from holding public office. The Committee on Reconstruction designed the policies to further punish the South, and the Fourteenth Amendment was the basis for federal action during the civil rights movement.

> ### *EX PARTE* MILLIGAN
>
> This case before the Supreme Court in 1866 strained the federal government as it wrestled with Reconstruction. The court ruled that military tribunals could not try civilians if civilian courts were open, even if the country was at war. Congress ignored the ruling during military Reconstruction, and the Supreme Court acquiesced.

9 MILITARY RECONSTRUCTION ACT

After issuing his own Reconstruction program, Andrew Johnson had to bow to the will of Congress who rejected the governments and representatives thus assembled. With the Military Reconstruction Act of 1867, Congress added the indignity of combining the seceded states, except for Tennessee, into five military districts each headed by a general with regular army and African-American militia troops to impose order and to protect African-American voters once the Fifteenth Amendment was passed. During military Reconstruction those Southerners who cooperated with the process were known as scalawags, whereas the Northerners who came to the South to participate were known as carpetbaggers.

10 TENURE OF OFFICE ACT

In a quest to rid themselves of Andrew Johnson in order to freely reshape the South in Reconstruction, the Radical Republicans passed the Tenure of Office Act. This innocuous-sounding name hid the fact that the law was a trap. Reasoning from the constitutional power of the Congress to review appointments of the executive branch, they sought to require Congressional consent for any firings as well. In his ongoing animosity for the legislative assertion of one-party power, Johnson tested the law by firing Secretary of War Edwin Stanton. He had first asked permission from the Congress, but they said no. Johnson's going ahead with the firing was the grounds whereby the Radical Republicans impeached him for "high crimes and misdemeanors."

11 IMPEACHMENT

Although a constitutional process, impeachment was used during Reconstruction as a political weapon. The House of Representatives reviewed the case against Andrew Johnson for his violation of the Tenure of Office Act and determined that there was enough evidence to send him to the Senate for trial. At that point the president was impeached. In his trial in the Senate, however, the senators came one vote short of the two-thirds majority necessary for removal from office.

12 FIFTEENTH AMENDMENT

The Radical Republicans' final constitutional blow against the former Confederate states was the Fifteenth Amendment. African-American males were given the right to vote in local and national elections before many white southern men and before all white women. Ratified in 1870, the Fifteenth Amendment was used to legalize African-American male suffrage even in the North where only a small minority of states permitted blacks to vote. The Radical Republicans further humiliated the South by finally providing full citizenship rights to former slaves. Women suffragists rallied against both the Fourteenth and the Fifteenth Amendments because they were the first uses of the word *male* in the U.S. Constitution and were another hurdle women would have to leap before they could claim full citizenship.

13 HIRAM REVELS

Hiram Revels was one of sixteen African Americans who were elected to the U.S. Congress during the Reconstruction period. Revels was the first African American to serve in the U.S. Senate, serving just one year (1870–1871). Revels was born free to free parents. He was ordained as a minister in the African Methodist Episcopal Church and served as a minister in several churches in the Midwest in the 1850s. In 1857, he moved to Baltimore and became the principal of an African-American high school. He helped recruit African-American soldiers during the Civil War and participated in the battle of Vicksburg. He later took a ministerial position in Mississippi before being elected to the Senate from that state. The Fifteenth Amendment and the presence of federal troops in the South assured that African Americans could exercise the right to vote. For the first time, African Americans were elected to local office and state legislatures in addition to the two senators and fourteen representatives elected to Congress. In South Carolina, a state with a majority African-American population, African Americans briefly comprised a majority in the legislature. Critics of Reconstruction, both contemporary and subsequent, have exaggerated the power of African Americans during the period and highlighted incidents of corruption. They have argued that the experiences of the Reconstruction period justify the exclusion of African Americans from the political process. However, Reconstruction governments, under the Republican banner, passed laws ending discrimination, built an infrastructure, and created an extensive educational system.

14 SHARECROPPING

This form of tenant farming permitted workers, black and white, to live on a former plantation's land while working the cotton or tobacco crops for the landowner. When the crop was harvested, a portion of the proceeds would be given to the workers as income, share by share. Most former slaves and many poor whites displaced by the Civil War accepted this arrangement as their only viable option to make a living. Sharecropping generally provided a meager existence, however, due to manipulation by the landowner or by merchants who supplied the sharecroppers with tools and seed on credit. Furthermore, natural agricultural problems like drought or hailstorms could ruin crops and leave sharecropping families in debt for generations. Families falling prey to the system lived little better than the serfs of the medieval period in Europe, and the existence for former slaves was almost exactly reminiscent of slavery. As the only plausible labor arrangement for the ruined cotton kingdom, however, sharecropping existed in the South through the Great Depression and World War II.

15 THE SLAUGHTER-HOUSE CASES

The Supreme Court consolidated three similar cases in 1873 under the collective name *Slaughter-House Cases.* The three cases had nothing to do with Reconstruction or the rights of African Americans, but the decisions in the cases did a great deal to undermine the Fourteenth Amendment and paved the way for the passage of Jim Crow laws in the South after Reconstruction ended. Advocates of civil rights for African Americans had hoped that the Fourteenth Amendment, ratified five years earlier (in 1868) would prevent the implementation of segregation laws. The amendment asserts that "No State shall make or enforce any law which shall abridge the privileges or immunities of citizens of the United States." This clause was intended to prevent states from passing laws limiting people's rights. In the *Slaughter-House Cases*, several slaughter-houses in and around New Orleans sued the government of Louisiana. The state, in an attempt to remove the smelly and disease-ridden businesses from populated areas, granted a corporation a charter to run a centralized facility that other smaller slaughter-houses would have to rent space in. Citing the Fourteenth Amendment, the smaller slaughter-houses argued that their privileges and immunities were being denied by this forced removal. The Court denied their motion and ruled that the Fourteenth Amendment applied only to national citizenship rights, such as the right to vote in national elections and the right to travel between states. The Court said that the amendment did not apply to rights that derived from "state citizenship." Southern states used this decision to assert that the Fourteenth Amendment would not be of use in prohibiting *state* Jim Crow laws.

16 LOUIS AGASSIZ

A Swiss-born scientist with an emphasis in zoology, Louis Agassiz came to the United States in 1846 to give a series of lectures. The advantages of American life and the opportunities for research, especially on fishes of the Western Hemisphere, impelled him to stay. He is noted as the first scientist to propose the idea, derived from studying the boulder-strewn reaches of upper North America, that an ice age had once gripped the earth and carved the landscape with glaciers. With his fame as a preeminent scientist, Agassiz's statements on race were used as justification for the racist policies of the South during and after Reconstruction. Although he defied the theory of evolution in his studies of animals until his death in 1873, he considered African Americans inferior and believed in natural selection insofar as it applied to them. Agassiz predicted that African Americans would die off because of an inability to organize, a condition that if true anecdotally, could easily be explained by their recent escape from bondage. The acceptance of Agassiz's views and the theories about race derived from Darwinism were continuing evidence of the latent racism and white supremacy of both the North and the South.

17 KU KLUX KLAN

At the close of the Civil War the Ku Klux Klan was founded in Pulaski, Tennessee, as a social and commemorative club lamenting the Lost Cause. Nathan Bedford Forrest, the Confederate cavalry genius, became its first Grand Wizard. As Reconstruction progressed the Klan became more a force for intimidation and terrorism. The use of violence included the burning of African-American churches and schools, forcible displacement from homes, lynching, and outright murder. Lynching was the process of violently executing a supposed criminal without a trial. Both African Americans and whites fell prey to the Klan's intimidation and murder because the Klansmen targeted anyone who supported congressional and military Reconstruction. The early goal of the Klan was Home Rule, that is, the return of state governments under the control of the Democratic Party with the ability to enact Black Codes to "keep the negro in his place." As this goal was achieved, the Klan's violent intimidation tapered off, but not entirely, and the main focus became political organization to maintain southern autonomy. Whole states were led by members of the Ku Klux Klan, and as rising nativism spread up through the 1920s, some of the states controlled by the Klan were in the North.

18 COMPROMISE OF 1877

Because the returns from the three states still unreconstructed by the Election of 1876 sent in disputed election returns, the country experienced a constitutional crisis. Florida, South Carolina, and Louisiana had failed to jump through all the hoops set out for them by the Radical Republicans, and these states were still under military occupation. A congressional committee was formed to review the election returns, but the committee was skewed with eight Republicans and only seven Democrats. The Republicans said they believed Rutherford B. Hayes had won the three states, whereas the Democrats looked at the same evidence and determined that Samuel B. Tilden, the Democratic challenger, had won. The South was outraged that the election might be stolen by stacking the deck, and trouble was brewing until a compromise was reached. In an unspecified process, what became known as the Compromise of 1877 saw the South trade the presidency for receiving the three states back under Home Rule. The military was withdrawn from the states in question and Reconstruction was considered to be over. Because of the fatigue resulting from decades of wrangling over slavery and its consequences, Northern and Southern racism, and constitutional limitations on federal power, African Americans were left at the mercy of their former masters who were quickly restored across the South as a political ruling class.

19 DISENFRANCHISEMENT

Despite the ratification of the Fifteenth Amendment, when states received self-government again they instituted policies that systematically limited or removed African Americans' voting rights. The discrimination was originally hidden in that the regulations applied to all voters, but the regulations were not equally enforced. Literacy tests hampered the right to vote of freedmen for obvious reasons, but even literate, articulate African Americans could not interpret sections of state constitutions to "the satisfaction of the registrar." In other words, the voting officials could in almost all cases tell if a person was of African descent and simply disallow any attempt on the part of that person to pass the test. Poll taxes, even if low, barred sharecropping African Americans from voting because they existed in a nearly cashless economy near to the life of serfs. Remarkably, tacit restrictions on voting for African Americans were not entirely eliminated in the South until nearly one hundred years after the ratification of the Fifteenth Amendment.

20 JIM CROW

Jim Crow was the name of a comic Vaudeville character of a white comedian whose act mocked African-American stereotypes. During Reconstruction the character's name came to symbolize the institutionalized racism of the Solid South. As each southern state was restored to self-government, the Democratic Party enacted restrictions on the personal freedom and on the new constitutional rights of the freedmen. These laws included poll taxes and literacy tests that disenfranchised African-American voters. In addition to losing their right to vote, segregation laws deeply divided southern society by banning African Americans from public facilities like schools, restaurants, transportation, and even restrooms and water fountains. As the grip of these laws returned freedmen almost to the impotence of their life as slaves, Jim Crow was a descriptor for all of Southern society after Home Rule was reestablished and the North ended efforts at Reconstruction.

THE BIG PICTURE

1. The period known as Reconstruction proved to be a difficult era of social, political, and economic strife as the country tried to heal the wounds of the Civil War.

2. The main political battles occurred between the restored national political parties but also between the executive and legislative branches of the federal government.

3. Radical Republicans were intent on punishing the South for starting the Civil War and enacted reform laws, policies, and even constitutional amendments while they held a powerful majority in the U.S. Congress.

4. The capacity for change in southern society regarding the status of African Americans was severely hampered by racism and the difficulty in rebuilding the southern economy without the institution of slavery.

5. Crippling laws and poor economic conditions reduced the freedmen of the South to a status not far removed from that of slaves, and African Americans found themselves working on plantations without voting or other civil rights and with little to no opportunities to advance.

The Settlement of the West

19

Hear me, my Chiefs! I am tired; my heart is sick and sad.
From where the sun now stands I will fight no more forever.

—Chief Joseph of the Nez Perce Tribe, surrender speech, 1877

	TIMELINE
1861	Telegraph line reaches San Francisco
1862	Congress passes the Homestead Act; Sioux Rebellion
1862–1869	Transcontinental Railroad is constructed
1864	Chivington Massacre
1865	First meat-packing plant processing Texas Longhorns opens in Chicago
1867	Archduke Maximilian is executed; The United States purchases Alaska
1869	Indian Bureau appoints first American Indian as commissioner
1871	Fire engulfs Chicago; The United States signs the Treaty of Washington with Great Britain
1873	George Armstrong Custer is sent to the Dakota Territory
1876	Battle of Little Big Horn; Alexander Graham Bell invents the telephone
1877	Crazy Horse surrenders
1881	Sitting Bull surrenders; Helen Hunt Jackson publishes *A Century of Dishonor*
1884	The buffalo is nearly extinct
1887	Congress passes the Dawes Severalty Act
1893	Frederick Jackson Turner publishes his frontier thesis

OVERVIEW

During and after the Civil War, government policies and economic opportunity encouraged waves of settlers to make their way West. The Midwest became a major agricultural region and the center of a politicized and determined farmers' movement. As settlers ventured farther West, clashes ensued with American Indian groups that lived on lands coveted by others. These clashes led to the demise of autonomous American Indian groups within the U.S. borders.

A variety of factors brought hundreds of thousands of settlers to the West in the period after the Civil War. Railroad companies were anxious to sell the land they had been granted in order to build rail lines. They relentlessly promoted land sales in the overcrowded cities of the East. In addition, the Homestead Act of 1862 drew large numbers of settlers to the West. The populations of Minnesota, the Dakotas, Kansas, and Nebraska all grew dramatically between the end of the Civil War and 1900, from less than half a million to over five million. Immigrants from Scandinavia, Germany, Canada, and Great Britain mingled with native-born whites and African-American migrants from the South in this multicultural West. By the late 1800s, a system of agricultural production and distribution developed, drawing western farmers into national and international markets. Chicago became the transportation and financial nexus of these markets; grain and cattle came through Chicago before being traded, processed, and shipped to the population centers of the East and beyond.

As more and more white settlers made their way to the West, American Indians felt their world narrowing. The period between the end of the Civil War and the turn of the twentieth century saw the last large scale military conflicts between the United States and American Indian groups. From the earliest encounters between white people and American Indians, white settlers have encroached upon American Indian lands and, using superior firepower, pushed Indians farther into the interior of the continent. American attitudes and policies toward American Indians sometimes emphasized assimilation, sometimes removal, and sometimes extermination. All these approaches saw American Indians as a problem that needed to be rectified. By the 1880s, the "Indian wars" resulted in defeat for American Indians, as the last autonomous Indian groups came under the control of the U.S. government.

1 ALASKA

Americans had first turned their attention to Alaska back when Russians had made colonies there and the Oregon dispute with Britain threatened military conflict with Britain and Mexico at the same time. President Polk restrained the idea of expansion to Alaska then, but Russia's continued presence was technically a violation of the Monroe Doctrine even though relations with Russia were positive. After the Civil War, Secretary of State William H. Seward took advantage of Russia's need for cash in her imperial problems in Europe by purchasing this last giant acquisition of territory for only $7.2 million. While most Americans could not conceive of what could come from a frozen wilderness one fifth the size of the rest of the country, Seward's Folly, as the purchase was known, not only prevented instability in Russia from opening up a new foothold for other European powers in North America, but opened up vast mineral wealth. Alaska's natural resources are still largely untapped even after the Klondike gold rush and an oil boom.

2 INDIAN BUREAU

Created by John C. Calhoun in the War Department back in 1824, the Indian Bureau was the agency managing the interaction of the United States with over five hundred American Indian tribes. In 1849, the Bureau was transferred to the Department of the Interior, and after the Civil War its agenda was to assimilate American Indians into American life by working to end tribal governments and communal ownership of land. Bureau agents were supposed to Christianize and civilize those in their charge, but during the Gilded Age most agents skimmed off the top of the supplies they were given for their wards. The Indian Bureau did not have a commissioner who understood and appreciated tribal cultures until 1869, and even then it was not until 1934 that the Indian Reorganization Act sought to restore tribal governments. Through the long history of territorial and cultural conflict between American Indians and the United States, tribes were considered foreign powers operating under the sanctions of the original treaties negotiated as civilization advanced. The 1924 Indian Citizenship Act, however, transferred to all American Indians the same citizenship rights protected in the Fourteenth Amendment.

> ### RESERVATION SYSTEM
> Beginning in the 1850s, land was set aside by the federal government for American Indian tribes to live communally. The legal arrangements were conducted on the basis of making treaties with foreign entities living on American soil. When American Indians wanted to be treated on a tribal level they had to stay on their allotted lands.

3 SIOUX REBELLION

The Dakota Sioux recognized that their Indian Bureau agents on their Minnesota reservation were unscrupulous. All game on the reservation was hunted to extinction, and the Sioux were near starvation, yet the agents would not release warehouses filled with food. The agents had designed to sell the food to white pioneers. In 1862, young Sioux warriors left the reservation and killed a family on a neighboring farm. Minor victories over responding American forces encouraged wider resistance and sporadic fighting on the part of the Sioux. When the Sioux were once again defeated, thirty-eight of those responsible were hanged in what remains the largest mass execution in American history. The rest of the Sioux were split up and distributed to various new reservations. The whole episode illustrated the unfortunate circumstances of Gilded Age corruption exacerbating already tense relations between American Indians, who were considered savages, and the increasing numbers of white settlers.

4 CHIVINGTON MASSACRE

This event, otherwise known as the Sand Creek Massacre, was an unfortunate clash based on conflict, misunderstanding, and superior force. In the Colorado Territory in 1864 young Cheyenne and Arapaho warriors raided traffic traveling to and from Denver. The isolated citizens of Denver asked for rescue. The Cheyenne chief Black Kettle declared that he could not control his young warriors, and other chiefs negotiated a settlement requiring the Cheyenne to come to forts in the territory to register as a peaceful tribe. Black Kettle merely put an American flag and a white flag up over his tepee at a settlement of around five hundred warriors and their families at Sand Creek. Colonel John Chivington and seven hundred or more troopers descended on the technically unauthorized camp and killed around two hundred American Indians, two-thirds of whom were women and children. In the review of his actions Chivington was found to have gone beyond his orders although he acted on a sentiment that was prevalent in the territory after the raids by the infamous Cheyenne Dog Soldiers. Although Chivington retired from the army before receiving any formal punishment, he faced divided opinions about his actions for the rest of his life. As for the Cheyenne, their power structure was undone by the massacre because of the loss of so many chiefs.

GERONIMO

This Apache chief resisted control of both the Mexican and American governments and surrendered only after leading a U.S. army cavalry troop on a torturous pursuit in Arizona. Geronimo led many raids and evaded capture for almost thirty years. He surrendered in 1886.

5 CRAZY HORSE

This Lakota Sioux chief was a fierce warrior even as a young man, and he led the resistance against the United States after 1876 when all Cheyenne and Sioux were ordered to go to reservations provided by the government from public lands. He was adamant about maintaining traditional Sioux ways even to the point of never allowing himself to be photographed. During the events leading up to the slaughter of Custer's force at Little Big Horn, Crazy Horse not only solidified the alliance between the Sioux and the Cheyenne, he personally led the war party that stopped the unification of Custer's forces. He then took his force to help Sitting Bull annihilate Custer and his Seventh Cavalry. After the campaign to subdue the Plains Indians was successful, however, Crazy Horse left the reservation without permission, was captured, and bayoneted to death in a struggle. The image of Crazy Horse is being captured in stone in a Mount Rushmore-size memorial to all American Indians, so his legacy will be the poignant reminder of the war on the Great Plains long into the future.

6 GEORGE ARMSTRONG CUSTER

Little could match the tale of Custer's bravado and gallantry during the Civil War. He was the youngest general officer of the Union Army, a rank he achieved through repeated acts of daring that some called reckless. In total he had eleven horses shot from beneath him in his fourteen years of nearly constant warfare, plus one he accidentally shot from under himself. After the Civil War Custer headed the Seventh Cavalry in the war against the Sioux in which he planned an attack in the region of the Little Big Horn River and the Black Hills in South Dakota. Without knowing the strength of the united Sioux tribes, Custer divided his forces for a three-pronged attack on Sioux and Cheyenne settlements off their reservations. The villages together contained nine thousand Indians, approximately four thousand of whom were warriors. Custer, with 1,100 troopers, had calculated his odds were far better based on fraudulent Indian Bureau statistics submitted by crooked agents lining their own pockets. He and a third of his divided cavalry force numbering some 270 men were isolated and killed by the combined forces of Crazy Horse and Sitting Bull. The Battle of Little Big Horn was the most significant defeat inflicted by Indians in American history.

7 BATTLE OF LITTLE BIG HORN

This battle, otherwise known as Custer's Last Stand, has been blamed on George Armstrong Custer's hot-headedness, but with false statistics from the Indian Bureau Custer assumed he would be facing a smaller enemy force than he found in 1876 in what would become Montana. He did divide his forces in the face of an enemy of unknown number and attacked without properly scouting in fear that the elusive Dog Warriors of Crazy Horse's renegade Sioux would escape. The pyrrhic nature of this victory in which Custer and his force of 267 men were killed was evident in that it confirmed in the American public's mind that the Plains Indians were savages who refused to cooperate with federal policy designed to keep the peace. Forgetting that the sudden influx of fifteen thousand miners into the sacred territory of the Black Hills had provoked the Sioux in the first place, the U.S. Army continued to hound them until both Sitting Bull and Crazy Horse were defeated. The Great Plains War continued with little public dissent until the Battle of Wounded Knee when another Sioux uprising ended in a massacre in 1890.

8 THE GHOST DANCE MOVEMENT

In the midst of the devastating losses suffered by American Indians in the 1870s and 1880s, some tribes adopted a spiritual practice known as the Ghost Dance. The Ghost Dance movement was developed by a Northern Paiute prophet named Wovoka. He drew on traditional American Indian rituals and emphasized cooperation among tribes and clean living and honesty. Wovoka had visions of an apocalyptic battle which would end in victory over the whites. After the battle, he told his followers that Indian soldiers who had been killed would return to life and the buffalo would return to the land. Ghost Dancers came to believe that wearing a white ghost shirt made them impervious to soldiers' bullets. The movement, which gathered adherents across the Great Plains among a diversity of tribes, struck fear among white authorities. Fearing an uprising among Ghost Dancers in the Sioux community, President Benjamin Harrison sent thousands of troops to South Dakota in 1889. Ultimately, the movement was not successful in stopping white incursions, but it led to a spiritual revival that had a profound effect on Indian tribes into the twentieth century.

9 SITTING BULL

Sitting Bull was a Dakota Sioux medicine man and chief whose reservation in the Black Hills of South Dakota became the location of intense strife after the discovery of gold there. His vision, in which he foresaw that all of the white soldiers would be killed, partly inspired

American Indian resistance and the Battle of Little Big Horn. Escaping into Canada for a time, Sitting Bull held out until his tribe's resources were entirely expended by the demise of the buffalo. He surrendered to federal authority in 1881 and was kept in federal custody until 1883. In 1884, he met the sharpshooter and performer Annie Oakley. The following year, Sitting Bull performed as a novelty in Buffalo Bill's Wild West show. Buffalo Bill Cody created extremely popular shows that mythologized the "Wild West" even as the last battles of American Indian resistance were taking place in the actual West. After 1885, he returned to Standing Rock Reservation. By 1890, the Ghost Dance movement had come to Standing Rock. Sitting Bull allowed the participants in the movement to enter his camp and may, himself, have participated in the dance. At this time, with the U.S. officials fearing a general uprising among American Indians, government agents began putting Indian chiefs in custody. In late 1890, an official with the United States Indian Agency ordered the arrest of Sitting Bull. While carrying out his arrest, agents shot and killed Sitting Bull.

10 BATTLE OF WOUNDED KNEE

After the death of Sitting Bull in 1890, many of his followers fled the Standing Rock Reservation and joined with Chief Spotted Elk of the Miniconjou Sioux. Spotted Elk and many of Sitting Bull's followers, fearing reprisals, traveled to the Pine Ridge Reservation near Wounded Knee, South Dakota. This group of over 250 people was apprehended by the Seventh Cavalry, the old regiment of George Armstrong Custer. The troops ordered the Indians to put down their weapons. The troops grew impatient with a deaf Indian named Black Coyote, who did not put down his rifle when ordered to do so. As U.S. troops seized him, a shot was fired. At this point, the cavalry opened fire with rapid-fire Hotchkiss mountain guns. More than 200 Lakota men, women, and children were killed, as were 29 U.S. Army soldiers. The massacre at Wounded Knee represented an end to the "Indian wars" of the West. After this, there were no more large-scaled incidents of armed resistance among American Indians to U.S. authorities.

11 BUFFALO

Properly called bison, these animals ranged across the Great Prairie of North America and were the source of sustenance for American Indians, especially when Europeans reintroduced the horse. Upwards of two hundred million buffalo are thought to have existed before this time. American Indians became proficient buffalo killers, but their cultural values mandated the killing of just what was needed and the use of nearly every part of each buffalo carcass. White hunters began actively killing buffalo for their hides in the nineteenth century. In the winter of 1872 alone 1.5 million buffalo were killed and their carcasses shipped east. Buffalo Bill earned his name by killing four thousand in just two years by order of the federal government that determined the solution to the American Indian problem was the elimination of the buffalo. The herds that used to range as far as the eye could see were reduced by 1880 to just a few thousand animals. The Great Plains Indians lost their way of life with the near extinction of this iconic American creature.

NEZ PERCE WAR

Chief Joseph of the Nez Perce tribe in Idaho tried to escape the reservation system by leading around seven hundred of his people on a circuitous flight to Canada. After three months of battles, Joseph surrendered. He lobbied the U.S. Congress until his people were removed from reservations in Kansas and the survivors returned to Idaho.

12 A CENTURY OF DISHONOR

Helen Hunt Jackson was a Massachusetts novelist and friend of poet Emily Dickinson. However, with her 1881 nonfiction exposé, *A Century of Dishonor*, she became nearly the lone voice of protest against the treatment of American Indians during the nineteenth century. Her work catalogs the violations of treaties and other repressions that she was among the first to call a violation of American Indians' human rights. She traveled personally to collect data, presented her book to the Indian Bureau, and then sent a copy to every member of Congress. In the style of the antebellum humanitarian reformers, she lectured continually and advocated for better treatment for American Indians for the last four years of her life.

13 DAWES SEVERALTY ACT

In keeping with its policy to assimilate American Indians into American culture and to reduce the authority of tribal governments, the federal government abandoned the policy of giving land to tribes to be owned communally. The Dawes Act of 1887 granted 160 acres of land to heads of American Indian families as the Homestead Act had done for white settlers. American Indians were encouraged to farm their private land and to abandon their tribal affiliations and traditional religion. Just as with the Freedmen's Bureau and the Indian Bureau, however, government ineptitude and corruption hampered the implementation of the Dawes Act that was abandoned. The attempt to turn Plains Indians into American citizens and farmers failed and for a time merely increased American Indian resistance.

14 HOMESTEAD ACT

The federal government enacted this plank of the Republican Party's 1860 campaign platform by 1862. In an effort to encourage settlement of the West, the government surveyed 160-acre tracts of land for any twenty-one-year-old head of household, citizen or immigrant, who would work the land and reside there for five years. The only cost to the settler was a small registration fee. After six months, the land could be purchased outright for $1.25 per acre. The invention of barbed wire by Joseph Glidden in 1874 and the pacification of the Plains Indians helped settlers protect their lands from trespass. The era of long cattle drives over public lands ended as a result. Two-thirds of the homesteaders, however, failed to establish viable agriculture in the dry west, and much of the land given to private individuals was eventually sold to large companies and real estate speculators.

15 FRONTIER THESIS

Frederick Jackson Turner delivered a paper called "The Significance of the Frontier in American History" at a conference for historians in Chicago in 1893. His thesis for the paper stated that the frontier experiences had transformed American society and democracy into more robust institutions and Americans into rugged individualists. The essay was an expression of nationalism maintaining that Americans were to be distinguished from their European ancestors as more enterprising, dynamic, and innovative. The failure of many homesteaders, however, belied Turner's assertion that the frontier was a "pressure valve" that eased societal tension by giving any American with pluck the opportunity for a new life in the West.

16 TELEGRAPH

Samuel F. B. Morse invented the telegraph in 1844, and he first successfully transmitted a message from Baltimore to Washington, D.C., about the nomination of James K. Polk for the presidency. By 1860, 50,000 miles of telegraph wire were strewn across America connecting most parts of the country to the communication revolution. A direct line almost 3,600 miles long connected New York to San Francisco in time to relay news about the Civil War to the West. The Western Union Telegraph Company monopolized the telegraph from that point on. Never had people been able to communicate virtually instantly over such vast distances before, and because the dots and dashes of Morse code could be perceived over greater distances on radio waves than could the human voice, the influence of Samuel Morse outlasted the telegraph itself. A transatlantic cable laid between the United States and Great Britain in 1866 opened instantaneous communication with Europe. Subsequent cables were a chief source of information until they were replaced by satellite communication beginning in the 1960s.

17 TELEPHONE

The invention of a teacher of the deaf, Alexander Graham Bell, the first practical telephone service connecting American cities was in place by 1877. There were nearly as many miles of telephone wires as telegraph wires by 1890, and by 1895 New York and Chicago were connected. Many smaller companies were consolidated into the American Telephone and Telegraph Company. The awareness of the need for time zones occurred because of the communication revolution and began as early as 1883. The boost to the American economy of the inventions of the telegraph and the telephone is impossible to calculate, but the ease with which business could be conducted granted America an advantage in achieving national and international markets.

18 TRANSCONTINENTAL RAILROAD

The first railroad line to span the continent was begun in 1862 by two companies and was completed in 1869 with a ceremony at Promontory Point, Utah, near Salt Lake City. The Central Pacific began in Sacramento, California, and had the daunting task of crossing the Sierra Nevada Mountains. The Union Pacific railroad was built from Omaha, Nebraska. The Union Pacific was built largely by Irish immigrants and the Central Pacific was built with the help of Chinese immigrants who came to California during the gold rush. Both crews built the many miles of track and all the trestles and bridges virtually by hand and often under the threat of American Indian attack. The transcontinental railroad when finished was considered the greatest civil engineering feat in American history to that time, and it reduced the time of travel across the continent from two months to ten days. National markets for all American products were achieved by 1874 as a result. Five transcontinental railroads existed by 1900. These railroads took homesteaders west and their products back east and contributed to the decimation of buffalo herds with shooting excursion trains. The Plains Indians resisted the construction of the railroad across their lands but held grudging admiration for a society that could bring such a machine into the wilds.

19 CHINESE EXCLUSION ACT

Chinese immigrants had flocked to California during the gold rush and were still around when construction of the transcontinental railroad began in 1862. The Chinese workers were instrumental in the success of the Central Pacific Railroad in crossing the Sierra Nevada Mountains from Sacramento all the way to Promontory Point, Utah. Tensions arose in San Francisco and other California cities when it became apparent that not only were the Chinese not going back to China but also they were taking over segments of the economy and establishing themselves permanently. The first expression of nativist immigration law was passed in 1882 and barred any further Chinese immigration for ten years.

20 TEXAS LONGHORNS

These cattle were free-ranging by the time the West was being settled because the Spanish had left them, and the cattle's horns provided ample protection from predators. The wild cattle fed on the grasses of the Trans-Mississippi West until cowboys rounded them up on long drives to railheads for shipment to meat-packing plants in Chicago. Few such bonanzas of wealth in livestock have ever occurred, and the process continued until barbed wire closed off most of the land. The era of the cowboy was thus short but remains the most lasting iconographic image of the Wild West and of the capacity of America to tame the land but not all of its young men.

THE BIG PICTURE

1. After enduring the threat of the Civil War, the United States finally got down to the business of settling the vast lands acquired in the antebellum period, a process that lasted from 1862 to 1890.

2. White encroachment on tribal lands and territorial reserves of the Great Plains Indians touched off violent conflict that escalated from sporadic fighting to an intensive effort to eliminate the Plains Indian culture.

3. The availability of and increasing access to free land in the West set in motion one of history's vast human migrations as immigrants and citizens moved to take advantage of vast natural resources.

4. A communication and a transportation revolution accompanied westward migration and transformed the way in which Americans, and indeed all the people of the world, viewed space and time and lived their lives.

5. Because of the largely untapped resources of the West, the spanning of the continent with a railroad set in motion an incredible economic boom that built huge cities and distributed all American products to national markets by 1874.

The New American Economy

20

This, then, is held to be the duty of the man of wealth: . . . to consider all surplus revenues which come to him simply as trust funds . . . to administer in the manner which, in his judgment, is best calculated to produce the most beneficial results for the community. . . .

—Andrew Carnegie, "The Gospel of Wealth," 1889

TIMELINE	
1855	Bessemer process receives a patent
1870	John D. Rockefeller forms Standard Oil of Ohio
1877	The term "Social Darwinism" is coined
1879	Henry George publishes *Progress and Poverty*
1883	Brooklyn Bridge is completed
1885	The first skyscraper is completed
1887	Congress passes the Interstate Commerce Act; The Whiskey Pool is formed
1888	Edward Bellamy publishes *Looking Backward*
1889	Andrew Carnegie publishes "The Gospel of Wealth"
1890	Congress passes the Sherman Antitrust Act
1893	James J. Hill finishes his Great Northern Railroad
1894	Henry Demarest Lloyd publishes *Wealth Against Commonwealth*
1895	J. P. Morgan begins his own investment firm; The Stock Market begins to issue annual reports
1901	Andrew Carnegie sells his steel company

OVERVIEW

The U.S. economy expanded rapidly in the late 1800s as the country experienced an industrial revolution. This expansion was facilitated by government support for innovation as well as transformative technological developments. The era of industrial expansion after the Reconstruction period is known as the *Gilded Age*. During the Gilded Age of the late 1800s, the era of small, local-oriented businesses began to give way to large corporations and trusts that came to dominate entire industries. The three most important industries of the era were the railroad industry, the steel industry, and the oil industry.

Although the nation as a whole enjoyed an increase in its wealth, that wealth was not equally distributed. The owners of big businesses, labeled "robber barons" by their critics, enjoyed unparalleled wealth, whereas many of the workers lived in poverty in working class slums. The contrast between the mansions of Andrew Carnegie and Henry Frick along New York City's Fifth Avenue and the tenements depicted in Jacob Riis's *How the Other Half Lives* (1890) startled many Americans.

The rise of giant corporations ran counter to traditional American notions about the economy and society. Before the Civil War, the "free labor" ideology put forth the idea that working for another man was a temporary condition; eventually each employee would accumulate enough money to start his own farm or shop. However, with the army of unskilled workers flooding into the massive companies of the Gilded Age, it became increasingly clear that these men, and their offspring, were not going to rise to become independent businessmen. These men will come to comprise a permanent working class.

As older ideas about the nature of the American economy, such as the "free labor" ideology, became outdated, new ones gained traction. Social Darwinism, popularized in the United States by social scientist William Graham Sumner in the 1880s, appealed to owners of large corporations because it both justified their great wealth and power and warned against any type of regulation or reform. This "hands-off" approach to economic activities is known by the French phrase, *laissez-faire*.

Critics of the laissez-faire approach believed that it was important for the government to act as a referee in the modern economy. They pushed the government to take steps to rein in these massive corporations. The Sherman Antitrust Act, for instance, was one such attempt to rein in corporate power. However, these efforts at regulation were often hampered by the courts and by lax enforcement. Some critics of corporate power went further than calling for reform and advocated alternatives to capitalism. Henry George's call for a "single tax" amounted to making land the common property of all, while Edward Bellamy argued for a socialist future. Many of the proposals for greater government involvement in the economy came to fruition in the Progressive era of the 1900s and 1910s, and the New Deal of the 1930s.

1 PATENTS

Originally a British idea, patents were instrumental in the expansion of the new American economy of the nineteenth century. The Founding Fathers sewed this incentive into the Constitution in 1790 along with copyright laws. Writers and inventors were thus assured the ability to benefit from their intellectual property and to defend their products from imitators. A total reorganization of patent law, along with the construction of a Patent Office, occurred in 1836 just in time for the spate of inventions and innovations that began to transform American industry and society. Both inventions and significant alterations of existing technology earned patents, and by the end of the nineteenth century thousands of patents were being issued annually.

> ### *WABASH* CASE
>
> In 1886, the Supreme Court ruled in this case that the railroads were immune to regulations by state governments because they were engaged in interstate commerce.

2 INCORPORATION

The Gilded Age saw the growth of business entities whose reach was regional, national, and even international. The proliferation of these large-scale companies was facilitated by changes in laws around incorporation. In the late 1700s and early 1800s, corporate charters were granted to groups of individuals, but mainly on a temporary basis, and mainly for a public-oriented purpose, such as building a bridge or a road. However, by the middle of the nineteenth century, states began rewriting corporate laws allowing for the chartering of businesses. These laws allowed for the establishment of an entity—a corporation—in which members of the public could invest their money. Incorporation laws provided investors with "limited liability." Investors could only lose the amount they had invested; they were not liable for any debts beyond their investments, nor could they be held liable in any civil suits. States generally removed restrictions on corporations; no longer would the state oversee governance rules of corporations, nor would they require corporations to comply with the purposes expressed in their charters. In the following decades, the number of corporations and investors grew dramatically.

3 STOCK MARKET

Bond trading in American history goes back at least to the American Revolution, and a market in such commodities has existed ever since. Private banks also raised capital by issuing stocks following the colonial model of a joint-stock company. Several merchants in New York City began trading these commodities in 1792 in the open air on Wall Street, and thus the New York Stock Exchange was born. The rapid growth of the American economy after the Civil War found companies hungry for sources of capital to expand their business. The chief source of this capital by 1900 was the sale of stocks on Wall Street, still conducted in the open air until 1921. By then investors realized that the stocks themselves could be bought and sold depending on the public perception of a company's soundness or potential for expansion. With some obvious setbacks, the stock market expanded throughout the twentieth century as a wealth builder for the rich and an overall reliable investment for the masses.

4 JAMES J. HILL

Rising from birth in a log cabin in Canada to fame and fortune in the United States, James J. Hill had a singular rags-to-riches story. His Great Northern Railroad was the only transcontinental line built without government assistance. He built the railroad in increments across the unchartered wilderness of the Rocky and Cascade Mountains in the United States and Canada. From 1878 until he reached Seattle in 1893, Hill built segments of the railway and then attracted settlers until each segment was prospering. Hill also innovated by building trunk lines off from his mainline to access specific mines, logging operations, and ranches. His mansion completed in 1891 was a far cry from the log cabin of his origins and at the time of completion the largest and most expensive home in all of Minnesota.

CORNELIUS VANDERBILT

Having made himself wealthy in steamboat lines, Vanderbilt consolidated railroads in the East until he had formed an empire for his son, William. He pioneered the use of steel rails set at a uniform width, or gauge, and thus vastly improved service.

5 JOHN D. ROCKEFELLER

Rockefeller was a pioneer of the oil industry and of business combination. His company, Standard Oil of Ohio, became the model for all subsequent large corporations. Rockefeller capitalized on the new petroleum industry by building his first oil refinery with his own funds in 1863 in Cleveland. Standard Oil was a prime example of efficiency and technical innovation. By 1882 Rockefeller monopolized the oil industry through horizontal combination, and his success attracted attacks by individuals and regulation by the U.S. government. This notoriety culminated in the 1911 breakup of Standard Oil under the Sherman Antitrust Act. By 1897, however, Rockefeller had dedicated his life to philanthropy and before his death given more than $500 million to various foundations and charities.

6 BESSEMER PROCESS

American William Kelly invented a process whereby air was forced up through molten iron, raising the temperature and burning off more carbon to make steel. At the same time, Henry Bessemer had been making similar strides in Great Britain. After a bankruptcy, Kelly sold his patent to Bessemer who developed the process that was the height of steel-making technology in the nineteenth century. The Bessemer process allowed the cheaper manufacture of better steel, and readily available sources of steel were instrumental in the construction of railroads, bridges, and skyscrapers that formed the crucial infrastructure of the new American economy.

7 ANDREW CARNEGIE

As a young Scottish immigrant to the United States, Carnegie mastered the telegraph with such skill that he became the personal secretary sending the messages of the manager of the Pennsylvania Railroad. Thus Carnegie learned business sense directly, and he saved money and made wise investments. He foresaw an opportunity in the iron bridges being built across the United States and entered the steel industry by use of the Bessemer process. His company by 1900 produced more steel than all of Great Britain, and through vertical combination employed 170,000 workers. After selling his steel company, Carnegie turned to philanthropy. He believed his funding of 2,500 public libraries across the country far more beneficial than merely giving money to poor individuals. He had gained much of his own education and personal growth by visiting a small library for working class youths. By the end of his life he had donated $350 million to various foundations and causes and is famous for his "Gospel of Wealth," an essay explaining his economic and societal views.

8 THE GOSPEL OF WEALTH

Andrew Carnegie's manifesto expressed his firm belief that "The man who dies rich dies disgraced." Published in 1889, the essay explained his view that the amassing of large fortunes by capable entrepreneurs was a natural process with which the government should not interfere. The wealthy held their accumulated resources in trust and were by their accomplishments proven to be wise judges of how the wealth should be used for the benefit of the entire community that produced it. Considered inspirational at the time, the essay is now usually interpreted to be an egregious example of Social Darwinism.

9 SOCIAL DARWINISM

A contemporary biologist with Charles Darwin, British philosopher Herbert Spencer coined the phrase "survival of the fittest." When he applied this notion to ethics and sociology, the theory of Social Darwinism was born. Spencer claimed that the rich deserved to be rich because of their superior capacity for adaptation, but most interpreters of his ideas could not help but see him as an elitist who associated being rich with being good. Critics of his philosophy said he was too quick to believe that whatever he observed in the natural world justified the abuse of the weak by the strong in human society. At best, the theories of Social Darwinism could be said to have both inspired the philanthropy of the great industrialists but also channeled the donations toward long-term productive ends rather than merely passing charity toward individuals. At worst, Social Darwinism was a justification for social engineering (including eugenics) and policies that unfairly favored the wealthy.

10 ROBBER BARONS VERSUS LIONS OF CAPITALISM

A difficult yet crucial distinction to make is whether men like Rockefeller and Carnegie were heroes or villains. The great industrialists argued that the consolidation of their businesses was necessary to survive competition. They also parried envious attacks against their success by pointing to the fact that they were the only Americans who could accomplish the growth of the industrial strength of America that proved to be so crucial to the country's victories in the coming global conflicts. Their wealth, however, staggered the imagination in an era when there were no income taxes and no inheritance taxes; hence the phrase "Robber Baron" stemmed from the fact that inherited wealth was not earned and could establish an impregnable aristocracy threatening American democracy. The growing gap between the rich and the poor in nineteenth-century America made the majority of Americans suspicious of the industrialists despite their philanthropic endeavors. The political views of the major parties in the twentieth century were largely shaped by the nineteenth-century debate over the wealth created by the rise of big business, the use of that wealth for gaining political influence, and the attempts to check the economic and political power of the trusts.

11 WHISKEY POOL

Distilleries in the late 1800s sought to reduce competition in an effort to maintain a strong demand for whiskey and thus a higher price. A pool was an informal alliance of producers in any industry, even railroads, who agreed to share markets at specified rates, and among whiskey distillers the pool agreed to reduce output in order to create an artificial shortage. Because the agreement was entirely based on the integrity of industry leaders willing to cheat the public, during economic downturns the members of the pool were also willing to cheat each other. In the Whiskey Pool this fact meant that some distillers secretly increased their production beyond what they agreed in order to garner more profits for themselves. The failure of some pool members to keep their word led many business leaders to seek a more binding form of business combination.

TRUST

A financial arrangement whereby one company gains control of another company by purchasing a majority of stock. Large corporations used trusts to control smaller companies within the same industry, and thus reduced competition within each industry.

---

12 HORIZONTAL COMBINATION

This form of trust was maintained by industries that cooperated in business combinations consisting of many companies involved in the production of a given commodity. A single company, like Standard Oil of Ohio, would organize the trust based on its complete control over one step in the production process. In using horizontal combination, John D. Rockefeller invited the owners of other companies to sit on the Board of Directors of Standard Oil and thus to share in decisions and inside information regarding the entire oil industry. These interlocking directorates agreed on rates their companies would charge each other and the prices at which the commodity would be sold to the public. If any company stepped out of line, the trust could punish it by cutting it out of the system and replacing it with a competitor that would stick to the plan.

13 VERTICAL COMBINATION

A much simpler form of business monopoly occurred when a company owned facilities in every stage of the production process as did Andrew Carnegie in the steel industry and Gustavus Swift in the meat-packing industry. From ore mines to marketing of finished steel products, Carnegie employed experts and maintained state-of-the-art technology in each type of facility required to gather natural resources, transport them, and turn them into marketable shapes. The total control of a corporation by one man and his hand-picked managers permitted a maximum level of efficiency in an industry and thus both cheaper prices for consumers and higher profits for the company.

14 J. P. MORGAN

One of the giant tycoons who was not a rags-to-riches self-made man, John Pierpont Morgan was a New England banker's son who was educated both in the United States and abroad. Morgan returned home and opened up a branch bank for his father in New York City just before the Civil War. By 1871 he had expanded his banking business with branches in London and Paris to become one of the leading banks in the world. He acquired companies and railroads as other men acquired farms or fine horses. Morgan's influence and wealth stabilized the entire American economy, especially during the Panics of 1893 and 1907 when he personally bailed out the U.S. Treasury. He purchased Carnegie's steel company and turned it into U.S. Steel. Always a target of envy and scrutiny, Morgan was the dark face of the Robber Baron class to those who believed such wealth and influence should not be under the control of one man.

15 LESTER FRANK WARD

During an era when the ideas of Social Darwinism and laissez-faire economic policies dominated public discourse, Lester Frank Ward encouraged a different reading of Charles Darwin's ideas. Ward, a

> **NEW SOUTH**
>
> Men like Henry W. Grady attempted to popularize an economic revival for the South through the construction of railroads and cotton mills. The idea of a New South still included agricultural productivity (and racism) but infusions of northern capital developed textile and other industries and began the growth of large cities like Atlanta.

sociologist with a background in botany and paleontology, supported the idea of Darwinian evolution but believed that in regard to society, human intelligence—the power of mind—was capable of influencing and shaping that evolution. He supported an active government guiding the evolution of human society toward conscious progress, rather than allowing evolution to take its own fitful and unpredictable course as proposed by Social Darwinists such as William Graham Sumner and Herbert Spencer. Ward was a constant critic of Social Darwinism and the conservative approach to the economy it entailed. In his monumental work, *Dynamic Sociology* (1883), he argued that humanity wasn't helpless before the impersonal forces of nature and evolution.

16 HENRY GEORGE

After a varied background as a seaman, typesetter, and prospector, Henry George settled down as a journalist and economic reformer. He originated the idea of a single tax in 1871, and by 1879 had published his theories in the book *Progress and Poverty*. The single-tax idea stemmed from George's belief that all people share the earth in common and thus the wealth derived from owning land should be the only source of tax revenue. He was thus opposed to taxation on the incomes of wage-earning laborers or any other form of tax other than property taxes on land. He believed that such a tax would raise sufficient revenue to operate the government while not burdening the classes of people who could least afford to pay. His ideas were never seriously applied in the United States but formed some of the incentive for Americans to move toward a graduated income tax.

17 EDWARD BELLAMY

In an age where questions of wealth and class were experiencing dramatic debate, Bellamy promoted a utopian philosophy that he expressed in his 1888 novel, *Looking Backward*. In the bestselling book he posited that within one century the United States would have nationalized its economy, removed all class consciousness and strife, and equalized the distribution of wealth. Although his predictions proved false, in his day they inspired a new spate of utopian communities filled with intellectuals who once again proved that perfect societies could not exist on earth. Not revolutionary enough for actual Socialists like Eugene V. Debs, and not practical enough for the masses of Americans alienated by the elitist tendencies in Bellamy's vision, his ideas faded from popularity even before the nineteenth century ended.

18 HENRY DEMAREST LLOYD

This minister's son was a graduate of law school who saw it as his calling to wield his pen against the societal injustices he observed around him in New York City and Chicago. Lloyd was thus a forerunner of the muckraking journalists associated with Progressivism. He scooped Ida Tarbell by writing about the practices of Standard Oil of Ohio through the 1870s and 1880s while he was on the staff of the *Chicago Tribune*. He used these exposé articles as the background for his most famous book, *Wealth Against Commonwealth*, published in 1894. In this regard Lloyd could have been merely an investigative journalist, but his work championing the cause of laborers inspired the likes of Samuel Gompers, the leader of the American Federation of Labor. His defense of the accused in the Haymarket Square Riots cost him his job at the *Tribune* even though his father-in-law was the one doing the firing. His journalism turned into activism, which led to his being a Populist candidate for president, but never quite a Socialist. Upon his death, however, his son helped found the Communist Labor Party of America. Just as H. L. Mencken would later inspire the Lost Generation of the 1920s, Lloyd's work inspired Progressive journalists and politicians alike.

19 INTERSTATE COMMERCE ACT

As the centrality of railroad companies to the success of the American economy became evident in the 1870s, the practices of railroads came under close scrutiny. States attempted to regulate railroad rates and other policies within their borders, but railroads defied these regulations saying that their business was interstate, not intrastate, and they should not be subject to state laws. The Supreme Court decided in *Munn* v. *Illinois* in 1877 that state laws and regulations did apply, but the Congress went further with the Interstate Commerce Act. If a railroad went beyond a single state's border, the law said the rates charged had to be just and that pools were illegal. To monitor such behavior the law called into being the first federal regulatory agency in American history, the Interstate Commerce Commission. By the end of the nineteenth century, however, corporate lawyers working for railroads had devised ways to circumvent the actions of the Commission, which was reduced to a bureau collecting statistics as a result.

20 SHERMAN ANTITRUST ACT

As a sign of the response to large business combinations, Senator John Sherman of Ohio was able to garner widespread support for this law in 1890. It stated that "Every contract, or conspiracy, in restraint of trade or commerce among the several states, or with foreign nations, is hereby declared illegal." The law authorized the federal court system to prosecute trusts thought to be guilty of monopolistic conspiracies. With a legacy of federal judges placed by Gilded Age Republican presidents, however, the ambiguity of terms like *trust* and *restraint* led to few trusts being prosecuted before 1901. Only eighteen suits were pursued, and four of those were against labor unions. Once trustbuster Theodore Roosevelt arrived on the scene, however, this law became (and remains) the chief legal grounds for enforcing federal regulatory policy.

THE BIG PICTURE

1. Profound developments in technology and infrastructure engineering led to a dramatic expansion of the American economy after the Civil War.

2. Individuals who organized large business enterprises formed giant corporations that allowed them to amass immense personal fortunes.

3. In the face of competition in major industries, industrialists combined markets and resources to stabilize the business cycle, maintain efficiency, and support long-term economic growth.

4. The growing gap between the rich and the poor as a result of the rise of big business led to the search for the means to regulate business practices and to limit the economic and political power of individual business tycoons and their trusts.

5. The U.S. Congress passed legislation that clarified the power of the federal government to control corporations by monitoring business practices and by prosecuting monopolistic conspiracies in the federal courts.

Society and Politics in the Gilded Age

21

*Everybody is talkin' these days about Tammany men growin'
rich on graft, but nobody thinks of drawin' the distinction
between honest graft and dishonest graft.*

—George Washington Plunkitt, in the *New York Evening Post*, 1905

TIMELINE	
1857	*Harper's Weekly* begins publication
1860–1901	The Gilded Age spans forty-one years
1860	William Marcy "Boss" Tweed begins leadership of Tammany Hall
1867	Thomas Nast first lampoons Boss Tweed; Roscoe Conkling is elected to the Senate
1869–1877	Grant administration spans two terms of the presidency
1872	The Irish take control of Tammany Hall; Credit Mobilier scandal
1875	Whiskey Ring scandal
1876	"Bloody shirt" is last used to elect a president
1878	Stalwarts back Grant for a third term
1880	Civil Service Reform association is formed
1880	Mugwumps back civil service reform
1881	James A. Garfield is assassinated
1883	Congress passes the Pendleton Act
1884	Mulligan letters are used to attack James G. Blaine; Mark Twain publishes *Adventures of Huckleberry Finn*; Grover Cleveland is elected president
1888	Benjamin Harrison is elected president
1892	Grover Cleveland is elected president again

OVERVIEW

The era of rapid industrial and economic expansion in the late nineteenth century saw the dramatic transformation in American society and politics. Americans experienced new cultural products, new patterns of work and leisure, and new class and ethnic divisions. In many ways, the political parties bent to the will of the new industrial order as ideology took a backseat to the prerogatives of economic growth.

These new aspects of American life were most evident in America's growing cities. The pre-Civil War city of densely-packed, low-lying, wood and brick buildings was virtually unrecognizable by the end of the nineteenth century. Cities became centers of industrial production and magnets for the large number of immigrants coming into the United States. These immigrants settled into and reshaped American cities. New technologies also reshaped American cities, as steel-framed skyscrapers, electric lighting, suspension bridges, and rail lines propelled cities upward and outward. At the same time, agriculture was becoming more mechanized, requiring fewer people in rural areas. New York retained its stature as the largest American city, with Chicago, Cleveland, Detroit, and other cities of the Midwest and the Northeast also growing rapidly. Rapid urbanization was accompanied by the availability of mass produced goods, new opportunities for leisure-time activities, and innovations in art and culture.

In terms of politics, the Gilded Age saw the two main political parties, the Democrats and the Republicans, become increasingly removed from the concerns of ordinary Americans. Both parties seemed more responsive to the priorities of the newly formed trusts and industrial giants than to needs of farmers, workers, or the urban poor. Issues like child labor, the consolidation of industries, workplace safety, and abuses by railroad companies, were either avoided or dealt with in a superficial fashion. Neither party did much to protect the rights of African Americans or American Indians, nor did they address the call of many women for the right to vote. The two issues that animated party debates in the Gilded Age were tariff rates and civil service reform.

The Republicans controlled the White House for most of the period from 1869 to the turn of the century (the exceptions were the two non-consecutive terms of Grover Cleveland). However, the elections were extremely close, with no presidential candidate receiving a clear majority of the popular vote in any election between 1872 and 1896. In addition, control of Congress was split. The Republicans controlled the Senate for most of the period, and the Democrats controlled the House. Only briefly, for three different two-year periods, did one of the parties control the White House and both houses of Congress. Corruption permeated political life during the Gilded Age, from the backrooms of local political clubhouses to the corridors of power in Washington, D.C. Owners of major companies openly curried favor with congressmen with contributions, gifts, and outright bribery. Political leaders, even the presidents of the age, seemed to shrink in importance when compared with the towering industrial figures of the day. John D. Rockefeller and Andrew Carnegie are far more clearly imprinted on the national collective memory than the "forgotten presidents" of the day.

1 THE GILDED AGE

This phrase, taken from the title of a book by Mark Twain, reflected the nature of the era from 1865 to 1900 so well that historians seized on it as the basis for their own interpretations. The postwar time period was one of rapid, unprecedented economic growth, hence the golden exterior. The undue influence of business tycoons in politics as well as the corrupt actions of politicians from both major parties formed the dark inner core of American power. Although the standard of living rose considerably for most Americans, the cost of living rose also. A wide gap developed between the upper and lower classes, and local, state, and federal government agencies and leaders were often steeped in scandals involving expanding the privileges and profits of the wealthy at the expense of the working class.

> ### CIVIL RIGHTS ACT OF 1875
>
> One of the unrealized ideas of the Gilded Age came with this last piece of federal legislation aimed to elevate African Americans until the Civil Rights movement of the twentieth century. The law sought to end segregation in public places, but was not enforced and later declared unconstitutional.

2 MARK TWAIN

The Gilded Age was also Mark Twain's era, a time when this southern writer could say, "I am not just an American; I am *the* American." Mark Twain was a pen name, taken from steamboat parlance on the Mississippi River, for Samuel Langhorne Clemens. Twain was a humorist and novelist who began as a newspaperman and steamboat pilot who gathered material for his books through traveling widely in the West and abroad. His famous works include *Huckleberry Finn* (a book Ernest Hemingway said was the first American novel), *Roughing It, Innocents Abroad,* and *Life on the Mississippi.* Twain's characters spoke in dialect to add local color to his writings that collectively captured the humor and pathos of southern and frontier life.

3 TAMMANY HALL

The name for the headquarters of the Democratic Party in New York City was likely taken from that of an American Indian chief. Tammany Hall was the epicenter of the Tweed Ring's exploits. The Tweed Ring consisted of William Tweed, George Washington Plunkitt, and other corrupt managers who not only selected who would run for which office, but used unscrupulous practices to fix who would win. The Tweed Ring stole between $75 million and $200 million from taxpayers for overcharged bills, false vouchers, fake contracts, and kickbacks from real contracts.

4 WILLIAM MARCY "BOSS" TWEED

The epitome of corrupt Gilded Age politics was the career of William Tweed, the leader of the New York City Democratic headquarters, Tammany Hall. Holding office no higher than a state senator, Tweed controlled state and local political offices and allotted state and municipal contracts from the 1850s to the 1870s to his cronies. Tweed pocketed money from all sorts of graft and bought companies that then received state and local contracts for business. A favorite victim of Thomas Nast's political cartooning, Tweed was arrested after some of his inner circle told their story to *The New York Times*, and he died in a federal prison in 1878 after being convicted for 204 of the 220 charges against him.

5 NEW IMMIGRATION

As prosperity returned to Germany, fewer and fewer Germans migrated to the United States. As migration from northern and western Europe decreased, southern and eastern European migration grew. From 1885 to 1917, almost 70 percent of immigrants were from these new regions. Major migrations from Russia, Poland, Austria-Hungary, Italy, and the Balkans brought many Slavic peoples into America. This new group of immigrants either found it difficult to assimilate into American culture or chose not to do so. Most of the New Immigrants settled in eastern cities or in Chicago and found work in factories, mills, construction, or the meat-packing industry. Nativism that had been directed toward the Irish was now directed with greater severity toward the New Immigrants. This nativism continued into the twentieth century and intensified during and after World War I, resulting in legislative initiatives to restrict immigration.

> **PANIC OF 1873**
>
> Like all depressions until the Great Depression, this Panic was the worst the country had yet seen. A large bank failure set in motion not only the Depression but also the quest for wider use of paper money and silver coins to inflate the currency and give relief to debtors.

6 LOWER EAST SIDE

The rapid industrial growth of the Gilded Age brought with it rapid urbanization. The densest urban area in the world in the late 1800s was the Lower East Side of New York. Conditions on the Lower East Side, which was only a few miles from the mansions of Andrew Carnegie and Henry Clay Frick on Fifth Avenue, were typical of many similar districts in other cities. Many people were packed into small apartments in substandard tenement buildings, ventilation and light were lacking, streets were thick with horse dung, and there was a lack of basic municipal services, such as sewer lines, running water, and garbage removal. These conditions were chronicled in photojournalist Jacob Riis's *How the Other Half Lives*. His grim photographs of tenement life drew many people's attention to the plight of the poor. The neighborhood became a center for various ethnicities, especially Eastern European Jews. The Lower East Side was home to the Yiddish-language *Jewish Daily Forward*. In the Lower East Side and other immigrant enclaves, ethnic groups established savings institutions, insurance programs, choruses, political organizations, and summer camps. The various ethnic enclaves of the Gilded Age city provided grocery stores so that immigrants could purchase foods reminiscent of their countries of origin.

7 BROOKLYN BRIDGE

John Roebling was a manufacturer of steel cable who proposed the idea of spanning the East River in New York City with a suspension bridge, and he convinced city leaders that bridges were the key to growth. He died as a result of an injury, but his son, Washington Roebling, continued the work as chief engineer. The Brooklyn Bridge was begun in 1870 and dedicated in 1883 and ranked as the greatest civil engineering feat of its kind for decades.

8 CHICAGO

Begun as a village in 1833 and achieving a population of over a million by 1890, Chicago overcame the Great Fire of 1871 that destroyed a third of its buildings to build the world's first skyscraper in 1885. Few other cities in history experienced such rapid growth. Because of its location near the origins of the first continental railroad and on Lake Michigan, Chicago became the next great transportation hub after New York City and New Orleans. Chicago became a transfer point and processing center for the agricultural commodities of the Midwest and the West before they were shipped to the population centers of the East. Chicago's great grain elevators made transferring wheat and corn an efficient enterprise and helped the city compete successfully with St. Louis, where grain was still loaded in sacks, by hand. Chicago meat-packing plants were the end of the line for Texas longhorns and for swine and livestock. The invention of the refrigerated railroad car helped the United States become the first country to have an economy that provided meat in the daily diet of ordinary families. The meat packing industry was the setting for *The Jungle*, by Upton Sinclair, a book that rivals *Uncle Tom's Cabin* in terms of its impact on inspiring change in the United States. Chicago's industrial growth in the Gilded Age made it an attractive destination for immigrants who had the means to travel beyond the East Coast.

9 WORLD'S COLUMBIAN EXHIBITION

If cities such as New York and Chicago seemed ridden with disease, poverty, violence, and crime, the 1893 World's Columbian Exhibition, more commonly referred to as the Chicago's World's Fair, put forth an alternative vision of what a city could be. The fair was organized by Daniel Burnham, an architect and urban planner who later created a comprehensive plan for Chicago (1909)—the first such plan for the controlled growth of an American city. He hired the landscape architect Frederick Law Olmstead to design the grounds; Olmstead had gained fame earlier for his plan for Central Park (1858). The white, colonnaded neoclassical buildings, the plazas, and the formal design of the fair's main concourse, known as the "White City," influenced urban planning and architecture for the next several decades. The fair was extremely popular, drawing 27 million visitors in the six months it was open, despite the fact that the Panic of 1893 began just a few weeks after the gates initially opened. The fair occurred as mass production and commercialization were chang-

> **JIM FISK AND JAY GOULD**
>
> These business partners manipulated President Grant while attempting to gain control of the market for gold and enrich themselves as the price rose. Grant released gold for sale from the U.S. Treasury, but this step only destabilized the market and ruined scores of innocent investors.

ing the daily lives of Americans. Several new commercial products were available at the fair for the first time, including Aunt Jemima pancake mix and Shredded Wheat cereal. The vision of an orderly, pristine, harmonious city, free of the strife and squalor of actual cities, proved to be an elusive dream. The elegant buildings of the White City were made of cheap gypsum plaster. The following winter, the entire fairgrounds burned to the ground.

10 SKYSCRAPERS

These innovative buildings capitalized on the new capacity of the United States to produce steel, the strength of which allowed for maximum use of interior space and ever-climbing heights. The first skyscraper was only ten stories high, built in Chicago in 1874. Louis Sullivan unlocked the potential of this new style of construction that made the most of the limited real estate available in the old city centers of the East. With the construction of the Woolworth Building and the Empire State Building in the 1920s, skyscrapers became status symbols of a new civilization able to build structures taller than anything created in the ancient world.

11 CENTRAL PARK

The most important urban park project of the nineteenth century was New York's Central Park (1858). As cities became denser and more disease-ridden in the nineteenth century, reformers sought to provide more opportunities for working-class men, women, and children to enjoy outdoor recreation. Doctors and municipal reformers came to embrace the idea that our environment played a significant role in our health; disease was no longer seen as divine punishment for sinful behavior (later in the century, doctors adopted the germ theory of disease causation, put forth by Robert Koch). Public parks were part of a strategy to provide alternative recreation options to dirty streets and alleyways, as well as saloons. New York City opened a design competition in 1857, which was won by Frederick Law Olmsted and Calvert Vaux. Park construction began in 1858 and was largely completed by the early 1870s. The park embodies some of the contradictions of the parks movement. On the one hand, Olmsted sought to create a democratic meeting place where the city's different classes could congregate and enjoy the benefits of nature. He argued, for example, against ornate European-style entrances to the park; he thought simple unadorned gates would be more welcoming to all classes of people. On the other hand, working-class advocates wondered aloud why the park was built so far from the working-class districts of the city. Also, the rules and regulations of the park made the park seem, to some people, more about control than enjoyment.

12 CONEY ISLAND

From the 1880s until the middle of the twentieth century, Coney Island was the largest amusement area in the United States, attracting several million visitors per year. The amusements of Coney Island were a welcome refuge for New York City's growing working-class population. As class divisions became more pronounced in the United States during the Gilded Age, residential patterns and leisure-time activities reflected this growing divide. Substandard tenements and unsanitary conditions came to characterize working-class neighborhoods. Apart from these enclaves were the more orderly and manicured middle and upper-class neighborhoods. Cheap amusements, such as dance halls, saloons, music houses, ball parks, and amusement parks, provided an escape for the working-class. Leisure-time activities became more commercialized in this era. Even factory workers had more spending money in the Gilded Age. Coney Island was initially a middle-class resort area, with lavish oceanside hotels. By the 1890s, the area was transformed into a destination for some of the most elaborate amusement parks in the United States. The three largest were Steeplechase Park (1897), Luna Park (1903), and Dreamland (1904). Coney Island also included a boardwalk, vaudeville theaters, and other assorted attractions.

13 PLESSY v. FERGUSON

In 1896, the Supreme Court upheld a Louisiana law that segregated passenger trains and railroad facilities. The Court determined that as long as the facilities were "separate but equal" then such separation did not violate the civil rights of African Americans as constituted in the

Fourteenth Amendment. *Plessy* v. *Ferguson*, therefore, justified and extended the Jim Crow policies of the South and denied African Americans not only equal protection under the law but also access to equal facilities. In practice, segregation usually led to the facilities reserved for African Americans receiving poor maintenance and funding and their generally falling into disrepair. The findings in the case were applied not only to railroads but to schools across the South, and not until the Supreme Court picked up the issue again in the 1950s did it acknowledge that the whole premise behind "separate but equal" was flawed.

14 *HARPER'S WEEKLY*

A prime example of an early news magazine, *Harper's Weekly* was published by four brothers (the Harpers) and had a circulation of over two hundred thousand by the outbreak of the Civil War. Along with political commentary, the magazine launched the career of the cartoonist Thomas Nast. The magazine was so influential in spreading Republican Party ideas that it was said to be responsible for the elections of Ulysses S. Grant and Rutherford B. Hayes. Perhaps it was more the influence of Thomas Nast's cartoons, for when Nast switched his support to Grover Cleveland, Cleveland became the only Democrat elected to the presidency in the entire Gilded Age.

15 THOMAS NAST

Illustrator and cartoonist Thomas Nast was a German immigrant intent on making his adopted country free from the evils of political corruption and other societal ills. He worked for *Harper's Weekly* for twenty years and established such lasting icons as the Democratic donkey, the Republican elephant, the image of Santa Claus, and that of Uncle Sam himself. Nast distorted the features of those he wanted to attack and thus created the genre of caricature. He was instrumental in the downfall of Boss Tweed even after Tweed offered him a $200,000 bribe to stop making the unflattering pictures.

16 THE GRANT ADMINISTRATION

Having led the Union Army to victory in the Civil War, Republican Ulysses S. Grant won the presidency in 1868 and again in 1872, the second time with the help of the newly enfranchised African-American voters of the South. His judgment of men's character, however, was less well developed than his military prowess. Grant's advisors, cabinet members, and staff saw their positions of power as opportunities to enrich themselves. Although remaining above suspicion, Grant presided over the first scandal-ridden administration in American history. The Credit Mobilier scandal involved the Union Pacific Railroad and a bank established by railroad shareholders, the Credit Mobilier. Bribes were made, through the bank, of government officials so that these officials would extend generous subsidies for construction of the transcontinental railroad. The scandal occurred before Grant's term in office, but when it broke (as he was running for reelection in 1872) officials in his administration, including his vice president, were implicated. The Whiskey Ring scandal involved one of Grant's appointees, his personal secretary, Orville E. Babcock. Babcock was part of a ring of political appointees, tax agents, whiskey distillers, and distributors. Their scheme involved distillers bribing government officials, and those officials, in turn, helping the distillers to evade federal taxes on the whiskey they produced and sold. In total, 238 people were indicted for their involvement in the ring, but Babcock avoided prosecution because President Grant testified on his behalf. The scandals tarnished the moral standing of the party that, in the previous decade, had issued the Emancipation Proclamation. The Republican Party was moving away from the commitment to racial justice that shaped Civil War and Reconstruction era policies. The corruption of the Grant administration was emblematic of politics in the Gilded Age.

17 CIVIL SERVICE REFORM

Corruption, nepotism, graft, and bribery became endemic in American politics in the post-Civil War world. A Civil Service Commission was established in 1871, but to little avail. Corrupt schemes became front page news during the Republican administration of President Ulysses S. Grant. Members of the president's party were divided around the issue of corruption. Some did not see corruption as a problem. This wing, labelled the Stalwarts, accepted Andrew Jackson's notion that "To the victor belong the spoils." They saw appointments, contracts, and other privileges as the bread and butter of patronage within a political party. This faction was led by Roscoe Conklin, a chief advisor to Grant. He came to fill the role for the Republican Party that "Boss" Tweed filled for the Democratic Party, the quintessential grafter. A rival faction of the party, the Half-Breeds, favored a degree of civil service reform and a merit system for political appointments. The Half-Breeds, led by James Blaine of Maine, were considered moderate Republicans. A third faction, the Mugwumps, consisted of reform-minded politicians from New York and Massachusetts. Mugwumps became so disgusted by Republican corruption that they abandoned the party altogether in 1884 and supported the Democratic candidate for president, Grover Cleveland. The issue of civil service reform came to a head in 1881 when a deranged campaign worker, Charles Guiteau, assassinated President James Garfield. Guiteau had been passed over for a political appointment, so Garfield became a martyr for civil service reform.

18 PENDLETON ACT

Garfield's assassination made even many Stalwarts favor reform in the face of Democratic advances and public outcry. Senator George Pendleton sponsored this bill that called for a new Civil Service Commission. The commission was to have three administrators to guard against patronage by, among other things, issuing competency tests for prospective civil servants. By the time the bill made it through the Congress, the Pendleton Act issued exams for only one-tenth of federal jobs. With this start, however, future presidents were able to expand this amount and create a civil service hiring process based more on merit than on patronage. Chester Arthur signed the Pendleton Act into law but set about dispensing patronage in the form of jobs just as if he were back at the New York Customs House.

BILLION-DOLLAR CONGRESS

By 1890 patronage and the actual expenses of the federal government had grown to reach this level of spending. Congress passed the McKinley Tariff, the highest ever peacetime tax on imported goods at almost 50 percent, in an effort to cover the costs of the Gilded Age.

19 "BLOODY SHIRT"

In an age when political oratory was more eloquent but also more melodramatic, "waving the bloody shirt" was a rhetorical device that reminded listeners that the Southerners who started the Civil War were Democrats. This device preserved the grip of the Republican Party on power in the federal government throughout the Gilded Age. The phrase is thought to have been developed when a Massachusetts member of the House of Representatives was given a blood-stained shirt from a carpetbagger in the South who had been attacked by the Ku Klux Klan.

20 CUSTODIAL PRESIDENCY

The term "custodial" is often used to describe the presidents of the Gilded Age. The presidents of the late 1800s failed to make an impression on the country. Presidents Rutherford B. Hayes, James Garfield, Chester Arthur, Grover Cleveland, and Benjamin Harrison are often labeled the "forgotten presidents." Hayes (1877–1881) assumed the presidency after an agreement settled the disputed election of 1876 and officially ended the Reconstruction period. Garfield (1881) served less than six months and is remembered primarily for being assassinated; his assassination was a catalyst for passage of the Pendleton Act. He was replaced by his vice president, Arthur (1881–1885). Cleveland (1885–1889 and 1893–1897) holds the distinction of being the only man to serve two non-consecutive terms as president. Cleveland lost the support of reform-minded Republicans by supporting a lowering of tariff rates. He lost the 1888 election to Benjamin Harrison (1889–1893), the grandson of President William Henry Harrison. Harrison supported civil service reform, placing Theodore Roosevelt as head of the Civil Service Commission. He also signed into law the Sherman Antitrust Act (1890). He was pro-tariff, pro-imperialism, and pro-silver; all positions that marked him in opposition to Cleveland, who defeated him for the presidency in 1892. When Cleveland regained the presidency, he walked right into the Panic of 1893, the worst economic depression the country had seen up to that point. He rejected the annexation of Hawaii and returned the country closer to a gold standard by leading efforts to repeal the Sherman Silver Purchase Act. Most presidential tickets presented much the same policies for governing as did their opponents. The executive branch waned in power while the power of Congress waxed, and behind Congress stood the industrialists and their wealth.

THE BIG PICTURE

1. The Gilded Age was an era of unprecedented economic growth, but nearly one-party rule on the federal level and the duplicity of individual politicians led to an atmosphere of rampant corruption.

2. A wave of southern and eastern European immigrants, drawn to the United States by economic opportunities in the expanding industrial cities, transformed demographic patterns in American cities.

3. American cities grew during the Gilded Age as new technology, industry, and expanding tenement housing, drew more people to cities, while urban reformers and planners put forth alternative visions of the city.

4. The attempt to reform government and purge it from corruption did not gain ground until after the assassination of a president by a frustrated job seeker, and even then those involved in graft were slow to relinquish their abuses of power.

5. If the control of the federal government by Democrats in the early nineteenth century led to the Civil War, the control by the Republicans in the Gilded Age proved that prolonged periods of unchecked power in the hands of either party were detrimental to the nation.

Mini Quiz

1. Abraham Lincoln did not consider the abolition of slavery as an option at the beginning of the Civil War because he

    (A) wanted abolition but had no plan for what to do with the freed slaves.
    (B) knew there was no serious support for abolition in the North.
    (C) feared that the slave states still in the Union would also secede.
    (D) knew slavery was necessary to supply cotton to the textile mills of the North.
    (E) did not think the country could afford to pay compensation to slave owners.

2. The Union strategy to conquer the South in the Civil War was called the
    (A) Ten Percent Plan.
    (B) Border State Plan.
    (C) McClellan Plan.
    (D) Anaconda Plan.
    (E) Elephant Plan.

3. The most devastating turning point for the Confederacy came

    (A) at Shiloh in Tennessee where more Americans fell than in all previous wars.
    (B) with Sherman's devastating March to the Sea from Atlanta to Savannah.
    (C) at Gettysburg and Vicksburg ending Southern offenses and control of the Mississippi.
    (D) at Antietam, the bloodiest single day of the war.
    (E) at First Bull Run, when Stonewall Jackson was accidentally killed.

4. The Freedmen's Bureau's main success came with which one of its initiatives?

    (A) Creating the first systematic effort to educate African Americans in Southern history
    (B) Confiscating plantation land and redistributing it to former slaves
    (C) Overseeing work relations between former slaves and their new employers
    (D) Providing basic necessities for former slaves and war refugees
    (E) Initiating African Americans' entry into the political process

5. All of the following realities were limitations on the rise of freedmen out of slavery toward a new social standing **EXCEPT**

   (A) southern society in general maintained a belief in white supremacy.
   (B) southern racism had a repressive militant wing in the Ku Klux Klan.
   (C) the theories of American followers of Charles Darwin encouraged even Northern racism.
   (D) the readily viable economic arrangement of sharecropping strongly resembled slavery.
   (E) the Radical Republicans in Congress did nothing to elevate the status of former slaves.

6. President Andrew Johnson was impeached because he

   (A) held strong views against Reconstruction's goals.
   (B) believed the South had never successfully seceded and blocked the return of the states.
   (C) was guilty of a high crime and misdemeanor and the U.S. Constitution had to be followed.
   (D) wrestled with the Congress for control of the Reconstruction process.
   (E) exceeded the powers of the executive branch according to the Supreme Court.

7. The most severe blow to the American Indians in the Great Plains War was the

   (A) completion of the transcontinental railroad.
   (B) Dawes Severalty Act's enticing of American Indians away from tribal loyalties.
   (C) Sand Creek, or Chivington, Massacre.
   (D) near extinction of the American bison through deliberate slaughter.
   (E) execution of thirty-eight chiefs after the Sioux Rebellion was crushed.

8. Where were most of the cattle rounded up by cowboys in Texas taken for slaughter in the years following the Civil War?

   (A) Abilene
   (B) Baltimore
   (C) Chicago
   (D) Denver
   (E) New York City

9. Which treaty brought lasting peace between Great Britain and the United States?

    (A)   The Treaty of Paris, 1783
    (B)   Jay's Treaty
    (C)   The Treaty of Ghent
    (D)   The Webster-Ashburton Treaty
    (E)   The Treaty of Washington

10. The "Gospel of Wealth" by Andrew Carnegie was an argument for what principle?

    (A)   Government regulation of business through redistribution of wealth
    (B)   Leaving the decision of the use of wealth to philanthropic capitalists
    (C)   Consolidation of all corporations through vertical integration
    (D)   The amassing of vast fortunes by families over generations
    (E)   The role of providence in determining which individuals would become wealthy

11. Which individual was the strongest and most influential financier through the Gilded Age?

    (A)   Andrew Carnegie
    (B)   John D. Rockefeller
    (C)   J. P. Morgan
    (D)   Samuel C. T. Dodd
    (E)   Cornelius Vanderbilt

12. Which law eventually became the most successful in checking the power of big business?

    (A)   The Sherman Antitrust Act
    (B)   The Sherman Silver Purchase Act
    (C)   The Interstate Commerce Act
    (D)   The Clayton Antitrust Act
    (E)   The Morrill Land Grant Act

13. The coverup of the Credit Mobilier Scandal occurred when the

    (A)   Central Pacific Railroad lied about who was constructing their railroad.
    (B)   former Union military officer building the Union Pacific was cleared by President Grant.
    (C)   owners of the railroad company gave stock in their company to Vice President Colfax.
    (D)   Credit Mobilier board of directors turned on the owners of the Union Pacific Railroad.
    (E)   attorney general received kickbacks from both transcontinental railroad companies.

14. Which Gilded Age president was assassinated by a frustrated office seeker as a result of the graft of the spoils system?

    (A) Ulysses S. Grant
    (B) Rutherford B. Hayes
    (C) Chester A. Arthur
    (D) James A. Garfield
    (E) William McKinley

15. How did the Pendleton Act seek to reform the civil service?

    (A) By preventing labor unions from contributing to the campaigns of political candidates
    (B) By preventing corporations from contributing to the campaigns of political candidates
    (C) By forcing presidential administrations to honor the appointments of previous administrations
    (D) By preventing office holders from appointing friends and relatives to civil service jobs
    (E) By requiring those working in the civil service to pass tests proving their competence

ANSWER EXPLANATIONS

1. **(C)** Lincoln guessed that the slave-owning border states would secede if he pressed for abolition and feared it because the South would likely win its independence if they did.

2. **(D)** The name of the Anaconda Plan referred to the process of blockading the South with the Union navy while dividing the Confederacy into thirds by taking the Mississippi River and the Shenandoah Valley to squeeze each third into submission.

3. **(C)** All of the choices occurred except Stonewall Jackson did not die at First Bull Run. Gettysburg and Vicksburg, however, were the dual blows suffered by the Confederacy from which even Southerners realized they could not recover.

4. **(A)** Although answers (B), (C), and (D) were goals of the Freedmen's Bureau, the success of these initiatives was limited. The Bureau did produce the first successful effort to educate large numbers of African Americans in the South. Selection (E) was only indirectly a result of the Bureau's work.

5. **(E)** All of the other conditions were true, and although the Radical Republicans had other goals for the Thirteenth, Fourteenth, and Fifteenth Amendments and military occupation than just helping former slaves, their basic goal was to advance the social, economic, and political standing of African Americans.

6. **(D)** Some of the selections have shades of truth in them, but the bottom line was that the Congress wanted Johnson out of the way so they could conduct a punitive Reconstruction plan without interference from the executive branch.

7. **(D)** Although all of the choices were part of the destruction of the Plains Indian cultures, the systematic destruction of the vast herds of bison accomplished its intended goal of breaking the capacity of the Plains Indians to resist federal authority.

8. **(C)** Although some of these other cities were a part of the long drives or destinations for the processed beef, Chicago became the meat-packing capital of America because the railroads running west converged there on the way to the large markets of the East.

9. **(E)** Serious conflicts between Great Britain and the United States erupted after each of these treaties except the Treaty of Washington that forged a peace that lasted until the present day.

10. **(B)** Andrew Carnegie would have disagreed all or in part with all the rest of the principles, and his essay made the case that successful businessmen were the citizens with the most wisdom about how the nation's surplus wealth should be used for the good of all.

11. **(C)** J. P. Morgan was the only individual in the list that could be strictly classified as a financier, and he was even the strongest and most influential of all those in America who could be classified as financiers.

12. **(A)** Although the Interstate Commerce Act and the Clayton Antitrust Act both tried to regulate businesses to prevent monopolistic behavior, only the Sherman Antitrust Act proved to be a workable piece of legislation despite its rocky start.

13. **(C)** All of the other scenarios are merely plausible fabrications, whereas Schuyler Colfax did accept gifts of stocks in order to thwart the investigations into the allegations of corruption.

14. **(D)** William McKinley was the only other assassinated president in the list, and he was killed by an anarchist, whereas Garfield was killed by a job seeker whom he had denied a position.

15. **(E)** Although nearly all of these ideas have occurred to various reformers, only the civil service exam system became a reality and grew into a successful tool for warding off rampant corruption.

The Revolt of the Common Man

22

. . . the union of the labor forces of the United States this day consummated shall be permanent and perpetual; may its spirit enter all hearts for the salvation of the republic and the uplifting of mankind!

—Populist Party Platform, July 4, 1892

TIMELINE	
1866	National Labor Union is founded
1867	Patrons of Husbandry is founded
1869	Knights of Labor (KOL) is founded
1877	Six Molly Maguires are hanged; National Railroad Strike
1879	Terence V. Powderly takes control of the KOL
1881	Samuel Gompers founds the precursor to the AFL
1886	American Federation of Labor (AFL) is founded; Haymarket Square Riot
1890	Mary Lease becomes populist orator
1891	Populist Party is founded
1892	Homestead Strike
1894	Pullman Strike; Jacob Coxey leads march on Washington
1896	William Jennings Bryan delivers his "Cross of Gold" speech; Election of 1896; William McKinley is elected president
1904–1920	Eugene V. Debs's tenure as the Socialist Party presidential candidate

OVERVIEW

The Gilded Age brought dramatic changes to many aspects of society. Industrialization, urbanization, mass immigration, changing patterns of ownership, transformations of the agricultural sector, and dramatic swings in economic activity all characterized the last three decades of the nineteenth century. While the era brought remarkable economic growth, many Americans were troubled by the changes afoot and took actions to resist certain changes and maintain their position in a changing world.

The Gilded Age saw some of the fiercest workplace conflicts in American history. Workers saw their position and status erode during this period, as cutthroat competition and mechanization of the work process pushed down wages and worsened working conditions. The wealth generated by the rapid expansion of industry in the post-Civil War period was certainly not evenly distributed. Wages for workers did rise incrementally in the decades after the Civil War, but were well below levels that economists consider necessary for a minimum degree of comfort. Further, wages could be cut during economic downturns, as is evident in the years following the Panics of 1873 and 1893.

Workers' grievances during the Gilded Age went beyond low wages. Workers were alarmed at how the changing workplace eroded their sense of autonomy and control on the work process. Mass-production techniques entailed the breakdown of processes so that workers could perform a specific task that did not require a great deal of training or skill. The age of the autonomous craftsman, who determined the conditions and pace of work, went by the wayside in the age of industrial capitalism. This "de-skilling" of the work process led to a loss of any sense of pride in one's work, but also to an increase in unsafe and unsanitary conditions. The loss of control of the work process was often a root cause of worker grievances of the Gilded Age. Many workers responded by forming and joining labor organizations, or unions, to advance their cause through collective bargaining and, if all else failed, through striking. The fierce labor battles were almost exclusively won by management, with its near-monopoly on fire power, the support of the government and the courts, and vast numbers of poor, working-class men willing to serve as strike-breakers.

A similar process occurred in the agricultural sector. The position of the small-scale, independent family farmer declined during the Gilded Age. Large-scale, mechanized farming operations created economies of scale that smaller operations could not match. The rate of farm foreclosures increased dramatically in the last decades of the nineteenth century. Those small and medium sized farms that survived increasingly felt they were being squeezed from all sides. Railroad companies overcharged farmers for carrying their produce to Chicago and other destinations. Also, the tight supply of currency in the United States was making it difficult for farmers to pay off their debts and was driving down the commodity prices they received for their crops. These problems led farmers to seek solutions through political action. Some of their political agitation was carried out within the two-party system, but, significantly, they decided to also work outside of mainstream politics, most notably through the Populist Party.

Many Americans began to question the basic assumptions of capitalism and embraced alternative ideologies, such as anarchism and socialism. These radical ideas never gained the number of adherents in the United States that they did in Europe. Still, these movements had followers in the United States. For example, after the utter failure of the Pullman strike, Eugene V. Debs moved away from the labor movement and toward socialism. He was one of the founders the Socialist Party of America in 1901. As collective bargaining became more accepted in the twentieth century, the lure of radical movements began to fade for America's working class.

1 NATIONAL LABOR UNION

Organized by the Boston machinist Ira Stewart, the National Labor Union was the first attempt to build a labor movement on a national scale. The National Labor Union met first in Baltimore in 1866 and declared their goal to be an eight-hour work day. Later labor movements would pursue this goal with the slogan, "Eight hours for work, eight hours for sleep, and eight hours for what we will." While the National Labor Union unraveled during the Panic of 1873, the federal government did begin a federal eight-hour work day for laborers and mechanics working on behalf of the United States.

2 KNIGHTS OF LABOR

Uriah Stephens began the Knights of Labor (KOL) in Philadelphia in 1871. Under Terence Powderly in 1879 the KOL included all industrial laborers, including skilled and unskilled workers, regardless of sex or race. Powderly preferred boycotts over strikes, and this tactic succeeded in forcing negotiations between the KOL and the Union Pacific Railroad in 1884. While more and more of the seven hundred thousand or so members of the KOL wanted to use strikes, Powderly urged them instead to educate themselves and stand together in brotherhood. The Haymarket Square Riot precipitated the decline of the KOL, and the American Federation of Labor rose to prominence as a result.

> ### MOTHER JONES
> Mary Harris Jones acquired this nickname as she became a labor organizer for the Knights of Labor among coal miners in Illinois.

3 TERENCE V. POWDERLY

President of the Knights of Labor (KOL) from 1879 to 1893, Powderly was a machinist by trade who joined the KOL in 1872. More of a reformer than an agitator, he stressed the formation of cooperatives, regulation of trusts, currency reform, and the abolition of child labor instead of pushing for immediate goals regarding wages, working conditions, or shorter hours. As the KOL organization declined, Powderly turned more to politics as a candidate of the Greenback Labor Party and as a civil servant working with immigration issues under Republican administrations.

4 EUGENE V. DEBS

A railroad worker and socialist labor organizer, Debs organized the American Railway Union in 1893. He organized the Pullman Strike and was sentenced to jail for contempt of court for defying Cleveland's injunction to start the trains moving again. After his release he worked to establish the Social Democratic Party by 1897. Debs ran five times for the presidency as a Socialist and was sentenced to ten years in jail for violating the World War I Sedition and Espionage Acts. While there Debs received almost one million votes in the Election of 1920. Warren G. Harding had Debs released from jail after serving only three years but did not restore his citizenship. Debs edited Socialist periodicals until his death in 1926.

5 MOLLY MAGUIRES

The Molly Maguires were a secret organization of miners imported from Ireland who began promoting labor violence in Pennsylvania as early as 1862. The Ancient Order of the Hibernians had been organized in Ireland to combat the encroachments of landlords, and when members of the Order migrated to the United States they employed intimidation tactics and murdered managers. The Philadelphia and Reading Railroad employed the Pinkerton Detective Agency to infiltrate the Molly Maguires. As a result, twenty-four of the organization's leaders were prosecuted. Fourteen spent from two to seven years in jail, and ten were hanged for murder. The reputation of all other labor movements suffered in the public eye because of the actions of subversive and violent individuals and groups like the Molly Maguires.

6 PINKERTON DETECTIVES

Allan Pinkerton was a Scottish immigrant who stumbled on the hideout of a counterfeiting gang outside Chicago and thus began a career as a private detective. His successes led him to become the head of spying on the Confederacy during the Civil War after which he returned to his detective agency. The Pinkertons continued after the death of their founder and were often hired by large corporations to protect property and scabs, or workers hired to replace workers on strike. The use of armed Pinkerton detectives alienated corporate leaders like Andrew Carnegie even further from those sympathetic to labor interests.

7 NATIONAL RAILROAD STRIKE

Just as railroads had many "firsts" as they formed the first giant corporations in American history, the first major strike also occurred in this industry. As a result of the Panic of 1873, railroads sought to cut costs by reducing workers' wages. The National Railroad Strike began in 1877 when the workers of the Baltimore and Ohio Railroad went on strike after receiving their second pay cut. The strike spread across the nation, and violence erupted. President Hayes even sent the U.S. military into West Virginia at the request of the governor, the first time a president intervened in a strike in this way. Hayes said he was protecting the U.S. Mail, but workers blamed him for merely protecting the railroad's private property. The strikers backed down, but an era of labor violence had begun.

8 HAYMARKET SQUARE RIOT

In Chicago in 1886, workers at the McCormick Harvesting Machine Company organized a strike trying to reduce their twelve-hour work days to the eight-hour Knights of Labor (KOL) goal. The first day of the strike demonstrators struggled with the police and a worker was killed. A second day of demonstrations was planned in protest of the killing, and around two thousand people assembled in Haymarket Square. When police advanced to clear the square, anarchists in the crowd threw a bomb that killed seven police officers and injured sixty people. The two hundred policemen then fired into the crowd killing four and injuring dozens. Eight anarchists were put on trial and seven were sentenced to be executed. The KOL reputation was tarnished by the riot, and Americans assumed that anarchists and socialists filled the unions.

9 SAMUEL GOMPERS

Gompers's was the tale of millions of immigrants in that he arrived in New York City, a Dutch Jew from London, and lived in a tenement apartment. He picked up the trade of making cigars as a boy and by 1875 rose to be the local president of the international union for such workers. Gompers recognized the limitations of the Knights of Labor after the Haymarket Square Riot and in 1886 organized the American Federation of Labor (AFL), which became the most successful national labor organization in American history. Except for one year, Gompers was the president of the AFL from its founding until his death in 1924. Gompers stressed practical measures to achieve practical ends and distanced himself from the radical elements in the American labor movement.

10 AMERICAN FEDERATION OF LABOR

Under Gompers's leadership the American Federation of Labor (AFL) gained 150,000 members its first year. Much of the membership of the Knights of Labor (KOL) joined the AFL, and by his death Gompers led three million skilled workers in America's largest union. The AFL was a craft or trade union made up of unions of skilled workers who had organized together locally. Gompers said that skilled and unskilled workers had nothing in common. Furthermore, although Powderly and the KOL were not supposed to advocate strikes, the AFL readily used strikes and other forms of demonstrations to achieve shorter hours, higher wages, and safer working conditions. Before these victories, however, the AFL had to achieve recognition of their right to collective bargaining in the first place. The practical nature of the AFL approach and the leadership of Gompers went a long way in overcoming the negative reputation of labor unions.

11 CLOSED VERSUS OPEN SHOP

A goal of many unions was to acquire complete compliance with all workers in a factory, mine, railroad, or other industrial facility working together as members of the same union. If every worker in the "shop" belonged, and if the union had negotiated with management the exclusion of all nonunion workers, the union was said to have achieved a "closed shop." Closed shops could conceivably demand higher wages, shorter hours, and better working conditions than the open shops where nonunion workers could still find work. Employers sought to prevent closed shops by issuing what unions called "yellow-dog contracts," or documents signed by prospective employees saying they would never join a union.

12 HOMESTEAD STRIKE

Although Andrew Carnegie had negotiated with unions among his workers, when he left his Homestead steel plant in the care of Henry Clay Frick, Frick took measures to break them. A workers' demonstration turned violent, and Frick closed down the plant in a "lockout." To protect the plant's property, Frick hired three hundred Pinkerton detectives who landed a barge at the plant's dock on the Monongahela River. The workers attacked, and three Pinkertons and seven workers were killed. The governor of Pennsylvania then called out the National Guard and after five months the workers gave in. Some Homestead workers were hired again, whereas many were "blacklisted" or placed on a list shared with other plants to prevent their ever securing jobs in the steel industry again. The Homestead plant was without a viable union for the next forty years as a result.

13 PULLMAN STRIKE

Eugene V. Debs called a strike against the Pullman Palace Car Company by the American Railway Union in 1894. In less than two weeks, every railroad in the Midwest was incapacitated. The attorney general sent in 3,400 men to move the trains and restart mail service, but violence broke out between these federal "scabs" and the striking workers. Grover Cleveland sent in federal troops to restore order, move the U.S. Mail, and to reestablish general commerce. A federal court backed the president's actions with an injunction, or court order, forbidding the interference with transit. When Debs resisted he was found guilty of contempt of court and jailed, and the strikers gave up. Nearly three hundred injunctions followed this method of ending strikes by 1928.

14 JACOB COXEY

Coxey was a Pennsylvania mill worker who opened a quarry in Ohio and became a successful businessman, reformer, and Populist political candidate. He ran for the House of Representatives, the Senate, the governorship, and the presidency, and lost every time. In the depths of the Panic of 1893, Coxey supported the idea of public works providing jobs for the poor by leading a march on Washington, D.C. He wanted the federal government to fund a road-building campaign to employ men who had lost jobs in the Depression. While his technique of a demonstration march would be picked up by dozens of causes, his own collection of around five hundred marchers were referred to as "Coxey's Army" and dispersed by the police immediately upon arriving in the national capital. Coxey and other leaders were arrested for trespassing in 1894. His actions generated national publicity but his proposals were ignored, that is, until the Great Depression when they were applied on a massive scale in the New Deal. Coxey did win one public office, the mayor of a small town.

15 PATRONS OF HUSBANDRY

Otherwise known as the Grange, the Patrons of Husbandry was a secret fraternal organization designed to advance the interests of agriculture beginning in 1867. Farmers who joined the Grange sought to reduce the influence of corporate monopolies, especially railroads whose rates the Grangers wanted fixed with no rebates to large corporate shippers. Positive aims were the establishment of agricultural and mechanical universities and the cooperation of farmers in purchasing supplies and in marketing their products. Small merchants and other businessmen were also their allies in that they supported laws that made it illegal for a railroad to charge more for shipment of loads short distances than for long-distance loads. Such regulations were collectively known as Granger Laws. Although the Patrons of Husbandry was not a political organization, the Populist Party sprang up from the collective action of farmers through their Grange chapters across the South and the West.

16 POPULIST PARTY

As the Patrons of Husbandry, or the Grange, developed political will they formed Farmers' Alliances and other national organizations to lobby for laws attacking eastern moneyed interests. By 1891 these efforts coalesced into the People's Party, otherwise known as the Populist Party. The Populist Party sought to unite industrial laborers and agricultural laborers in a movement to stand against the capitalists for the advancement of the common man. The first national convention of the new third party met in Omaha, Nebraska, in 1892 and selected James B. Weaver as its presidential candidate. The Populists wanted a long list of reforms that included a new national currency, the free coinage of silver, government ownership of all transportation and communication components, a graduated income tax, direct election of senators, shorter working hours for industrial laborers, and restrictions on immigration. While the new party lost the presidential election, they gained ground in the farming states, and even though their party did not live to see their ideas implemented, nearly every one of the Populist Party's issues from the 1892 platform became a part of American political and economic life.

17 MARY LEASE

An early example of the new generation of politically active women, Mary Lease was a lawyer, orator, and founding member of the Populist Party leadership. Her potent quotes included "Raise less corn and more hell!" and "The country belongs to Wall Street." She gave over 160 speeches in the campaign to elect James B. Weaver whose nomination she had seconded at the national convention in Omaha. She resisted the Populist Party's self-destructive support for William Jennings Bryan in the Election of 1896, but she continued to fight for progressive causes including women's suffrage and prohibition.

18 WILLIAM JENNINGS BRYAN

An Illinois lawyer who backed the Democratic Party and the free coinage of silver, Bryan was elected to the Congress just as the Populist Party was getting started in his adopted state of Nebraska. His powers of oratory kept him in demand as a public speaker even after losing a bid for the Senate in 1894. At the Democratic National Convention in Chicago in 1896 he delivered his most famous "Cross of Gold" speech against the gold standard and for inflation as a means of easing the plight of farmers. He was awarded the nomination for the Democratic presidential candidate and launched a national speaking tour. His message gained the support of the Populists who were dismayed that their crusading hero went on to lose the election. He strove to obtain the presidency but rose only to be the secretary of state under Woodrow Wilson whom he served until Wilson went against the original position of U.S. neutrality in World War I. Bryan opposed the teaching of the theory of evolution in schools and appeared on the public stage one last time in the Scopes Trial in 1925, dying two weeks after winning the case for the prosecution but losing the war of ideas.

> **GOLD STANDARD**
>
> This principle of currency regulation established the value of "promissory notes" issued by the government based on the amount of gold in possession of the U.S. Treasury. Under the Gold Standard paper currency could be exchanged, or "redeemed," for gold at banks. The limited supply of gold as the basis for a currency made some forces in the American economy clamor to abandon the Gold Standard to expand the supply of currency.

19 WILLIAM MCKINLEY

Civil War officer William McKinley became a lawyer in Ohio and ultimately served in the Congress and as the state's governor. He was a typical Republican Party political machine candidate for the presidency in 1896 after gaining attention supporting the protective tariff that bore his name in 1890. Marcus A. Hanna, the Ohio Republican boss, backed McKinley's candidacy on a platform of a high tariff and the gold standard for a sound currency. As president he signed the Dingley Tariff, the highest tariff rate in American history. He led the country through the Spanish-American War and won a second term to the presidency but was assassinated in 1901 by an anarchist.

20 ELECTION OF 1896

The next presidential election marking a turning point in American history, the Election of 1896 surpasses even the elections of 1800 and 1860 in the impact on the nation's direction. After William Jennings Bryan said at the Democratic convention, "You shall not press down upon the brow of labor this crown of thorns, you shall not crucify mankind upon a cross of gold!" the campaign became a battle between the silver interests, including farmers, and the urban capitalists in favor of the gold standard. Bryan traveled 13,000 miles through twenty-nine states and trumpeted about the debtor and the farmer while William McKinley sat in Ohio and campaigned for the creditor and sound money. The election results put yet another Gilded Age Republican in the presidency, but its real significance lay in who would be McKinley's vice president in his bid for a second term. Mark Hanna had fought the choice of Theodore Roosevelt by asking, "Don't you realize there's only one heartbeat between that madman and the presidency?" The Republicans wanted to capitalize on Roosevelt's tremendous popularity earned in the Spanish-American War, however, and when McKinley was assassinated Roosevelt was catapulted into power.

THE BIG PICTURE

1. An awareness arose among American laborers after the Civil War that collective action on their part could alleviate their grievances regarding their wages, hours, and working conditions.

2. Labor demonstrations and strikes resulted in violence so often that labor unions were stigmatized as subversive elements in American society.

3. After many trials a national labor organization finally shunned radicalism in favor of practical goals reached through practical means, and the path toward acceptance of collective bargaining was opened.

4. American farmers also sought collective action to address their economic grievances in the first grassroots movement resulting in the most successful third party in American political history.

5. The end of the Gilded Age was in sight after the Election of 1896 since the Republican winner chose Theodore Roosevelt for his vice presidential running mate in a bid for a second term.

The Progressive Reform Movement

23

We have in America a fast-growing number of cultivated young people who have no recognized outlet for the active faculties . . . [who] feel nervously the need for putting theory into action, and respond quickly to the Settlement form of activity.

—Jane Addams, *The Subjective Necessity for Social Settlements*, 1892

TIMELINE	
1889	Jane Addams founds Hull House
1890	Jacob Riis publishes *How the Other Half Lives*; William James publishes *Principles of Psychology*
1892	John Muir founds the Sierra Club
1895	Jane Addams publishes *Hull House Maps and Papers*
1901	Robert La Follette is elected governor of Wisconsin; William McKinley is assassinated and Theodore Roosevelt becomes president
1902	Lincoln Steffens publishes *Shame of the Cities*
1903	Ida Tarbell begins publishing *The History of Standard Oil*
1904	Theodore Roosevelt coins his Square Deal campaign slogan; Upton Sinclair publishes *The Jungle*; Congress passes the Meat Packing Act
1906	Congress passes the Pure Food and Drug Act
1908	Lewis Hine begins photographing child laborers
1916	John Dewey publishes *Democracy and Education*

OVERVIEW

The Progressive movement was a response to the excesses of rapid industrialization, political corruption, and unplanned urbanization. Progressivism existed at the grass-roots level, on the state level, and on the national level. This chapter will focus on the sources and origins of the movement and its manifestations on the local and state level. Chapter 24 will focus on the reforms on the national level.

After the collapse of the Populist movement in the 1890s, Progressivism took up the mantle of reform, reshaping many aspects of the relationship between the American government and the American people. Progressive reformers put forth a set of political principles that grew to be the dominant political ethos in the early twentieth century. They challenged traditional notions about the role of government in society. Throughout early American history, the political consensus favored limiting the power of the government. Progressives, on the other hand, sought to expand government power by including more citizen input and by encouraging greater government oversight and intervention in a variety of areas. The Progressive movement was more successful than the Populist movement because it tended to have more middle class, college-educated, and articulate activists and leaders. The Progressive movement effectively challenged the rampant political corruption and the unregulated economic activity of the Gilded Age.

The Progressive movement was more an amalgam of interests, ideas, groups, and individuals, rather than a tight-knit cohort of activists with a cohesive ideology and a clearly articulated vision of the future. The movement was a bundle of contradictions. It championed reforms to benefit the working class, but looked at the actual working class with a mix of paternalism and suspicion. The movement challenged women's exclusion from the political process but largely accepted the prevailing social views of African Americans. To some degree, progressivism challenged the abuses of unbridled capitalism, but, at the same time, many industrialists embraced progressive legislation in order to rationalize the freewheeling nature of the capitalist system.

Progressive reformers were of two minds when it came to challenging the power of corrupt political machines. While many progressive reformers looked to experts and managers to counteract governmental corruption, a large segment of the movement pushed for Democratic empowerment of the citizenry. This push for greater democracy did not address the most obvious impediment to democratic participation—laws and practices preventing the majority of African Americans from voting. Many African-American activists challenged Jim Crow segregation and developed strategies for challenging white supremacy, but most mainstream white Progressives were silent on this issue. Despite the limitations of the movement, a host of reforms were adopted to make local, state, and national government more responsive to the popular will.

1 SOCIAL GOSPEL

The Social Gospel was a reform movement within American Christianity that sought to deemphasize doctrinal purity and traditional worship in favor of social activism. In working out the implications of the antebellum Second Great Awakening, Social Gospelites attempted to continue the ardor created by the humanitarian reform movements in order to boost church attendance. In the classical balance between faith and works, then, the Social Gospel became more interested in works. Largely an urban phenomenon, Social Gospel advocates reached out to the poor, especially immigrants, in an effort to help the needy but also to make religion more practical and inspiring. Critics of the Social Gospel claimed that the movement sacrificed spiritual solutions for merely pragmatic solutions that addressed only physical needs. Young, college-educated women were often the chief activists of the Social Gospel, and they were thus transformed into soldiers on the front lines of the Progressive movement.

2 JANE ADDAMS

The chief female social reformer and Progressive activist was Jane Addams from Illinois. She founded Hull House in Chicago in 1889 as the first of many centers of the settlement house movement. Her actions virtually created the field of social work as she attempted to improve the lives of the immigrant poor. Addams was a leading advocate for other Progressive causes like women's suffrage and prohibition as well as a world-renowned pacifist who eventually received the Nobel Peace Prize in 1931 for her efforts. Her books based on her experiences during forty years of settlement house work became models for scientific inquiry into social problems because they were the first systematic compilation of statistics and observation techniques that became the mainstay of several social sciences.

3 HULL HOUSE

The settlement house founded by Jane Addams was the first dedicated to community intervention and improvement of civic life in a slum, the Nineteenth Ward of Chicago. Beginning in 1889, Addams sought to provide cultural instruction for immigrant children. Hull House programs shifted to practical assimilation instruction in personal hygiene and the English language. The settlement house movement spread to other cities where immigrant families were separated as both parents worked long hours in factories. Settlement houses provided day care, educational materials and periodicals in reading rooms, and medical care. The movement was a training ground for Social Gospel workers and anti-child labor activists who awakened American women to political activity.

4 HAZEN PINGREE

Pingree ran a shoe factory in Detroit and became a Progressive from inside the Republican Party. He became Detroit's mayor in 1890 and enacted several Progressive reforms. His goal was to break up the system of graft associated with city contracts and to create municipal utility companies to compete with the privately owned utilities in order to lower rates through competition. In the Panic of 1893 Pingree created relief programs through public works projects that built schools, parks, and bathhouses. He gained notoriety by turning vacant lots into gardens for the growing of potatoes to feed the city's poor. Pingree was eventually elected as governor of Michigan and exemplified the type of Republican Progressivism that became the driving force of the political career of Theodore Roosevelt.

5 TOM JOHNSON

In contrast to Pingree, Tom Johnson was a Progressive Democrat who became the mayor of Cleveland, Ohio. He was also a Confederate veteran, whereas Pingree had fought in the Union Army. After a business apprenticeship working for others, Johnson opened his own streetcar company in Indianapolis, Indiana, that soon expanded to other major cities. Johnson sparred with the Ohio Republican boss Marcus Hanna in both business and political struggles. He became a congressman and then ran for the mayor of Cleveland in order to pursue all of the Progressive goals for which Pingree was famous. He was elected in 1901 and succeeded in a nearly identical career to Pingree's proving that Progressivism emanated from both major parties. He ran for governor of Ohio but lost even though the famous muckraking journalist, Lincoln Steffens, had described him as the best mayor in the United States.

6 WILLIAM JAMES

A Harvard-educated medical doctor, William James pioneered in the fields of psychology and physiology but gravitated toward a professorship in philosophy. As an empiricist, James originated the indigenous American philosophy of pragmatism, or the testing of truth based on the practical consequences of ideas. He praised American cultural values like individuality, initiative, drive, spontaneity, and a love of novelty. He opposed the excesses of Transcendentalism, and by saying truth must come down to reform reality both described and inspired the Progressive Reform movement.

7 JOHN DEWEY

A philosopher and professor, John Dewey's career led him to Columbia University, which became a fount of Progressive ideas. Dewey applied the pragmatism of William James to his own field of education and developed the notion of functional reality. He advocated a new approach to education where children would be freer to explore knowledge and come to their own conclusions about truth. He wrote widely and in his books and classes advocated the relativism that increasingly pervaded American culture as the country developed a pluralist society.

MUCKRAKERS

Named such by Theodore Roosevelt after a character in *Pilgrim's Progress*, these journalists dredged up dirt about American society. Their exposés, however, were instrumental in motivating individuals and governments to root out corruption and to reform American life.

8 LEWIS HINE

Hine was an educator who developed an interest in photography more as a tool than a hobby. He went on to study sociology at Columbia University and became the official photographer of an organization trying to end child labor. In this pursuit he photographed child workers in mines, factories, canneries, textile mills, and farms. His photographs implied that child labor led to widespread deprivation and cultural desolation and were instrumental in the advance of anti-child labor laws. Hine worked for the Red Cross in Europe during World War I and returned to the United States to take a famous series of photographs documenting the construction of the Empire State Building. During the Great Depression he was the head photographer for the New Deal Works Progress Administration.

9 JACOB RIIS

The most famous muckraking photographer was Jacob Riis. His life exemplified the struggle of immigrants as he came to America from Denmark in 1870 and did not find employment until 1877. As a reporter for a New York newspaper he developed an interest in photography. His book, *How the Other Half Lives* (1890), was a classic work of muckraking journalism that brought him to the attention of Theodore Roosevelt. Riis cataloged the various types of poor who lived in the Lower East Side of New York City and documented their plight with photographs and rather prejudiced ethnic stereotypes. He portrayed women and children in need of assistance but men as less deserving if they were poor. His book contributed to Progressive Reform, but he did not proscribe an active welfare state because he portrayed many of the immigrant poor's problems as being self-inflicted.

10 LINCOLN STEFFENS

Steffens settled in New York City by 1892. He eventually rose to be the editor of *McClure's* magazine, a major muckraking periodical that advanced the careers of Jack London, Ida Tarbell, Upton Sinclair, Willa Cather, and Ray Stannard Baker. That list alone is enough to seal Steffens a place in American letters, but his own articles were collected by 1904 in a book titled *The Shame of the Cities*. His style of journalism became the model for future investigative journalists. His articles attacked machine politics for election tampering, police corruption, and graft, as well as questionable business practices. Steffens became enamored of Lenin and communism on a trip to Bolshevik Russia and advocated Progressive, or liberal, political reforms the rest of his life. Having lived in Mussolini's Italy, however, he recognized that both fascism and communism denied the freedoms of speech, press, and assembly but also freedom of thought. He ultimately denounced communism in his 1931 autobiography.

11 IDA TARBELL

Reared in the oil fields of Pennsylvania, Ida Tarbell went on to be the only woman in her college graduating class and a muckraking journalist for *McClure's*. She became the magazine's most popular writer with serialized biographies of Lincoln and Napoleon, but her most influential work was called *The History of the Standard Oil Company*. This investigative report appeared in nineteen separate articles from 1902 to 1904 and was written as an exposé of the type of business practices that Rockefeller had used to absorb independent oilmen like her father. The articles did not condemn capitalism and actually acknowledged Rockefeller's genius and efficiency, but they ended in a personal attack that revealed her deep animosity and obsession with her target. Rockefeller never responded to her attacks and referred to Ida Tarbell only as a "misguided woman." Interestingly, Tarbell disagreed with woman's suffrage despite her being recognized as one of the most important women in America. She said the suffrage movement had gone too far in belittling the contributions of women who chose traditional roles.

12 ROBERT LA FOLLETTE

A Wisconsin lawyer and three-term congressman, La Follette was a typical Republican until his constituents fired him for supporting the McKinley Tariff. By the 1890s he was a pariah among Republicans until he bolted the party, barnstormed around the state, and became a three-term independent Progressive governor. What Roosevelt would go on to do for the nation, La Follette did in Wisconsin by pushing a broad spectrum of reforms. La Follette moved into the Senate and became a presidential contender. Shoved aside by Roosevelt in 1912, La Follette did run as the Progressive Party candidate in 1924. He received almost five million votes but took them mostly from Democrats giving Republican Calvin Coolidge a solid victory. His use of independent regulatory commissions filled with experts as sources of policy ideas became known as the Wisconsin Idea and was the basis of much of Progressive Reform.

13 WISCONSIN IDEA

As the governor of Wisconsin, Robert La Follette hit upon the strategy of gaining advice from university professors and other "leading experts" to help him shape Reform policies. Just as in the independent regulatory commissions established in Progressive cities, La Follette invited his experts to sit on regulatory agencies but now at the state level. Professors and their universities received prestige, and La Follette received ideas that "Back to the people Bob" could take back to the people and popularize through his passionate oratory. When expanded to the national level, the Wisconsin Idea became the mechanism whereby a more and more populous middle class consented to be ruled by the educated elite of the country. In the process the American people grew accustomed to turning to government for solutions to problems, and hence the Wisconsin Idea was part of the end of "rugged individualism."

14 REFORM OF CITY GOVERNMENT

City governance at the turn of the twentieth century was notoriously inefficient and corrupt. Many cities were run by corrupt political machines similar to New York City's Tammany Hall run by "Boss" William Marcy Tweed from the 1850s to the 1870s. Inefficiency and incompetence also plagued many city governments. Important tasks, like those involving planning, sanitation, or providing water, were carried out by political machines unanswerable to the public. The issues of municipal inefficiency and corruption came to the fore in the aftermath of a devastating hurricane and flood that struck Galveston, Texas, in 1900. Upwards of 8,000 people died in the disaster. Given the ineffective response by the city government, local leaders were convinced to create commissions to spearhead the cleanup and rebuilding of the city. This commission form of government soon spread from Galveston to other cities. Elected commissioners ran the city and headed various departments, such as public works, fire, and sanitation. The idea of the commission form of government was that city officials would not be under the sway of powerful political bosses. Other cities hired managers, with professional training, to administer municipal affairs.

> **ELKINS ACT**
>
> In 1903, Congress passed this law to fine railroads and their customers who used rebates. Rebates were discounts offered to large-volume shippers that made small farmers and other individuals decry the practice when they had to pay more than did corporations for rail service.

15 REFERENDUM, RECALL, AND INITIATIVE

Progressive reformers hoped that by expanding democracy, the power of political machines would be lessened. In states across the United States, progressives proposed, and often implemented, reforms to expand democracy. Three important innovations were the referendum, the recall, and the initiative. The referendum is a reform that allowed people to vote directly on proposed legislation. A proposed referendum item would appear on the ballot on election day, and voters would either vote "yes" or "no." Several states and municipalities still have the referendum. The recall empowered the people of a city or state to remove an elected official before his or her term ended. Citizens would not have to wait until the next scheduled election to challenge an official perceived as incompetent, corrupt, or unpopular. Several states still have the recall. In 2003, Californians recalled Governor Gray Davis and replaced him with Arnold Schwarzenegger. The initiative allowed citizens to introduce a bill to the local or state legislature by petition. Once a certain number of citizens signed the initiative, the legislature had to address the item.

> **HEPBURN ACT**
>
> In 1906, Congress outlawed the issuing of free passes by railroads as favors to individuals and businessmen who had helped railroads avoid regulations.

16 BRANDEIS BRIEF

The Harvard legal and economic scholar, Louis Brandeis, shaped legal practice in the Progressive era by crafting legal briefs (or arguments) citing copious scientific, psychological, and sociological studies to bolster the case at hand (traditionally, legal briefs had relied on legal precedents as the basis for an argument). This type of legal argument has come to be known as a "Brandeis Brief." Brandies crafted such a brief in the case of *Muller* v. *Oregon* (1908). The case revolved around an Oregon law that limited the number of hours women could work in a day. The decision in the *Muller* case was a double-edged sword for many Progressives. Some were critical of the decision because it set a precedent for sex-based discrimination in the future, allowing for laws that treated women differently because of their supposed physical limitations. Other Progressives applauded the decision because it upheld the right of the government to regulate workplace rules and conditions. Previously, in the case of *Lochner* v. *New York* (1905), the Court had ruled that the conditions and hours of work were a private, contractual matter between the employer and employee. Just three years later, in the *Muller* case, the Court opened the door for additional Progressive legislation designed to protect workers. In the coming years, Brandeis became an advisor to President Woodrow Wilson, bringing "Wisconsin Idea" advice to issues of trust legislation, currency, and labor problems (see above). He was later appointed by Wilson as the first Jewish member of the Supreme Court in 1916. The use of non-legal information in legal matters would become increasingly common in the twentieth century, including in the *Brown* v. *Board of Education of Topeka* case (1954).

17 THE TRIANGLE FACTORY FIRE

A tragic fire that swept through the Triangle Shirtwaist Factory in 1911 and killed 146 workers became a catalyst for Progressive reform. The factory, which produced women's blouses (then known as "shirtwaists"), was located on the upper floors of a factory building in the

Greenwich Village section of New York City. The employees were mostly young women, many of whom were recent Italian or Jewish immigrants. A fire began in one of the scrap bins and soon spread. The workers discovered that one of the entrances was blocked by the flames and another was locked (perhaps to keep the workers in, or to keep union organizers out). Some escaped by elevator and others by a fire escape before it collapsed. The workers who could not escape (123 women and 23 men) perished either in the fire or by jumping to their deaths. The tragedy led to more intense organizing by the Women's Trade Union League, but also to a breathtaking wave of Progressive legislation. A Factory Investigating Commission was established and toured factories around New York State. It ended up recommending sixty-four laws; sixty of them passed. The state passed laws mandating better building access and exits, fireproofing requirements, the availability of fire extinguishers, the installation of alarm systems and automatic sprinklers, and better eating and toilet facilities for workers. Laws also limited the number of hours that women and children could work. Many of these laws served as models for legislation in other states.

18 BOOKER T. WASHINGTON

Like Frederick Douglass, Booker T. Washington was the son of an African-American slave and white man. He worked his way through school after being freed from slavery. As a distinguished educator in Virginia, he was chosen by the Alabama legislature to start a vocational school for African Americans in Tuskegee, Alabama. Tuskegee Institute became a normal and industrial school for African-American students, that is, it trained teachers and workers in the trades. As the foremost educator of his race in his day he was a sought-after speaker on race relations, and he clashed with W. E. B. Du Bois over strategy. Washington stressed the importance of giving African Americans in the South skills that would get them off the plantations and give them an opportunity to pursue the American Dream, which for him meant a gradual march toward self-respect and the respect of white Americans. He rejected the ideas that political and civil rights were the first priority for African Americans and that they should be demanded.

19 TUSKEGEE INSTITUTE

Claiming that the opportunity to earn a dollar was more important than the opportunity to spend a dollar in an opera house, Booker T. Washington established Tuskegee Institute in 1881. Starting with only thirty students and no buildings, Washington developed a program that turned out African-American teachers, prepared others for work in trades and modern agriculture, and wove into all instruction the cultivation of dignity through cleanliness, orderliness, and thrift. As a result of Washington's extensive speaking tours, donations came in from North and South, and Tuskegee Institute became a major recipient of philanthropy from great industrialists. By 1915 the campus came to consist of almost 300 acres and over five thousand faculty and students. Among its most famous benefactors was George Washington Carver, who headed the Department of Agriculture at Tuskegee Institute for almost fifty years, all the while making great strides in the development of uses for southern agricultural products.

20 W. E. B. DU BOIS

Born in Massachusetts, Du Bois (pronounced "duh boyz") was the first African-American graduate of Harvard University and became a professor at Atlanta University in history and economics from 1896 to 1910. He studied and wrote about the sociology of the African-American experience and became a more militant advocate for civil rights than Booker T. Washington. His famous 1903 book, *The Souls of Black Folk*, traced case studies of the lives of African Americans after he conducted research similar to that done by Jane Addams with immigrants in Chicago. Du Bois helped lead the National Association for the Advancement of Colored People (NAACP) and many other organizations and conferences dealing with race relations. As opposed to Washington, Du Bois demanded that American society grant immediate equality to African Americans, including the removal of all restrictions on the right to vote that had thwarted the Fifteenth Amendment in the Jim Crow South. Frustrated with the slow pace of change, Du Bois expatriated to Ghana where he developed Marxist leanings and died in 1963.

THE BIG PICTURE

1. The backlash to the corruption and scandals of the Gilded Age came in the form of a widening series of ideas called the Progressive Reform movement.

2. Progressives originally came from the ranks of social workers trying to aid in the assimilation of immigrants into American urban life.

3. Professionals from all walks of life quickly picked up the ideas of Progressive Reform and expanded their application until states like Wisconsin implemented a wide series of political reforms.

4. Investigative studies done by historians, writers, social workers, and photographers exposed the problems of American society and compelled widespread support for Progressive reforms.

5. The mainstream Progressive movement did not, for the most part, address the Jim Crow system of racial discrimination; however, African-American activists organized opposition to racism and debated the most effective strategies for creating a more just democracy.

Progressivism on the National Level

24

In a very few years, with our free and compulsory schools, our free libraries, and the economic opportunities which this country has to offer, these people were transformed into ambitious, self-respecting, public-spirited citizens.

—Harvard professor A. Piatt Andrew, *North American Review*, 1914

TIMELINE	
1881	Booker T. Washington founds the Tuskegee Institute
1885–1917	The New Immigration spans thirty-two years
1895	Booker T. Washington delivers his "Atlanta Compromise" speech
1896	*Plessy* v. *Ferguson*
1902	Oliver Wendell Holmes, Jr. is appointed to the Supreme Court
1903	W. E. B. Du Bois publishes *The Souls of Black Folk*
1908	William Howard Taft is elected president; The play, *The Melting Pot*, is first staged
1909	Ballinger-Pinchot Affair begins
1910	New Nationalism is announced by Theodore Roosevelt
1912	Woodrow Wilson announces his New Freedom campaign; "Bull Moose" Progressive Party is founded; Election of 1912; Wilson is elected president
1913	Congress passes the Underwood Tariff; Congress passes the Federal Reserve Act
1914	Congress passes the Clayton Antitrust Act
1916	Louis Brandeis is appointed to the Supreme Court
1920	Nineteenth Amendment is ratified

OVERVIEW

Progressive reformers had a great deal of influence on national politics in the United States in the first decades of the twentieth century. Chapter 23 discussed the origins of the movement and its impact on the local and state level. This chapter focuses on the national level, as progressive ideas and approaches entered the discourse of the national political parties.

The first decades of the twentieth century demonstrate the interconnectedness between grassroots activism and policy choices on the national level. Developments in the media, including mass circulation magazines with photography, and effective organizing by Progressive activists put reform on the national agenda. Theodore Roosevelt enthusiastically took up the reform mantle. He assumed the presidency following the assassination of William McKinley (1901) and quickly began to move the Republican Party and the nation itself in a progressive direction on a variety of issues, including the environment, corporate power, and consumer protection. Roosevelt, a Republican, embraced many progressive reforms, but his handpicked successor, President William H. Taft, proved to be a disappointment to the Progressive movement. On many issues, Taft worked with the "Old Guard" of the Republican Party, which was eager to put the brakes on Progressive reform. The "Old Guard," led in the Senate by Henry Cabot Lodge, wanted to return the Republican Party to its Gilded Age conservative stance. Roosevelt challenged Taft for the Republican nomination in 1912, was unsuccessful in his bid, and then ran for the presidency as a third-party candidate.

The divisions within the Republican Party led to the electoral victory in 1912 of the Democrat Woodrow Wilson. The pervasiveness of the progressive ideology crossed party lines, and Wilson implemented many important progressive reforms. He pushed for a strengthening of antitrust legislation, regulation of the banking industry, and greater consumer protection. With Congress controlled by the Democrats, Wilson was able to implement much of his agenda. During his tenure, amendments to the Constitution were ratified to create an income tax and to mandate the direct election of senators. Wilson entered office at the height of the women's suffrage movement. Initially he was lukewarm toward the idea, but by 1918 he embraced the cause and played an important role in Congress approving the amendment (1919) and sending it to the states for ratification (see Chapter 27).

The movement claimed many legislative victories, and ultimately influenced politics in the twentieth century. The push for a more activist and engaged federal government found voice in President Franklin D. Roosevelt's New Deal, in the environmental and consumer protection movements of the 1960s, in President Lyndon B. Johnson's Great Society agenda, in the Occupational Safety and Health Act of 1971, and in the Affordable Care Act of 2010. Progressives built on the precedents of the Indian Bureau and the Freedmen's Bureau to create the modern welfare state and shape twentieth-century liberalism.

1 THEODORE ROOSEVELT

Theodore Roosevelt, or TR, both wrote about and lived what he called "the strenuous life." Born in the family of a New York banker, TR rejected any notion that he continue in the family business or even take up the legal profession for which he began studies after graduating from Harvard. Instead, he dove into New York City and state politics and other jungles. He spent his entire adult life following his motto of "Get action; do things!" TR served as a sort of police chief for New York City, a state legislator, a civil service reform commissioner, an assistant secretary of the Navy, a soldier in the Spanish-American War, governor of New York, vice president, and eventually president upon William McKinley's assassination. Throughout his many experiences he wrote articles and books that earned him as much as $750,000 per year in modern dollars. As president, Roosevelt launched Progressive Reform on the national level. After his presidency he went on safari in Africa and toured Europe, becoming the most famous American of his day. His fame and ambition drew him back into politics in the Election of 1912 when he and his supporters split the Republican Party by forming the "Bull Moose" Progressive Party. The split ensured the victory of Woodrow Wilson in 1912. In regard to foreign policy, TR was aggressively nationalistic and even imperialistic. He claimed to be single-handedly responsible for the construction of the Panama Canal by the United States. TR's presidency and personal style ended the Gilded Age string of forgotten presidents in an unforgettable way, and every subsequent American president inherited from him the capacity to act as the most powerful individual on the planet. For good and for ill, TR's political talents entirely altered the American political landscape. For this reason he is the only twentieth-century president to alter the landscape of Mt. Rushmore with his visage.

2 SQUARE DEAL

Theodore Roosevelt's (TR's) coined phrase for his Progressive agenda was the Square Deal. Among his reform principles the three most important were controlling corporations, consumer protection, and conservation of natural resources. TR wielded the Sherman Antitrust Act effectively for the first time and earned the title, the "Great Trustbuster," by bringing antitrust suits against corporations he deemed to be "bad trusts." He backed the Pure Food and Drug and the Meat Packing Acts as a result of reading *The Jungle* (1906) by Upton Sinclair. As a result of his love of the outdoors and his friendship with John Muir, TR was also known as the "Great Conservationist" for the reserving of land for national parks and national forests as well as coal reserves. Together these initiatives created a government with an entirely new orientation as a "watchdog," protecting its citizens and its resources in unprecedented ways. In some sense TR's Square Deal was continued by future presidents as the New Freedom, the New Deal, the Fair Deal, the New Frontier, the Great Society, the Bridge to the Twenty-first Century, and even Hope and Change.

3 PUBLICATION OF *THE JUNGLE*

The most sensational muckraking novel of the Progressive Era was *The Jungle* (1906) by Upton Sinclair. The book contained actual scenes of muckraking on the floors of Chicago's hog and cattle meat-packing slaughterhouses, and the tales of what went into the nation's sausage turned many stomachs including that of President Roosevelt. Sinclair had gone undercover into the meat-packing industry in a classic example of investigative journalism to reveal the plight of the workers, not the animals or the customers. The novel traces the struggle of Jurgis, a Lithuanian immigrant, and his family to survive in the slipshod housing and brutal conditions associated with the workers of the meat-packing plants. As many in the family perish, Jurgis grows increasingly embittered. As his character moved toward socialism, so Sinclair wanted to move the nation, but as he said, "I aimed at the public's heart, and by accident I hit it in the stomach." The novel was a main impetus toward the Progressive initiative of consumer protection through increased regulation of the food and drug industries. Because it contributed to Roosevelt's support for Progressivism, *The Jungle* proved to be one of the most influential books in all American literature in bringing about societal change.

4 PURE FOOD AND DRUG ACT

This 1906 law was a direct assault on the quackery associated with nineteenth-century remedies that were peddled about the country as well as the use of fillers and otherwise tainted food products. The Pure Food and Drug Act forbade the manufacture, sale, or shipping of impure or fraudulently labeled foodstuffs or drugs involved in interstate commerce. The law served as a forerunner of the later Food and Drug Administration (FDA), and its language was ultimately applied to alcoholic beverages by the Volstead Act during prohibition.

5 MEAT PACKING ACT

Otherwise known as the Meat Inspection Act, this law was also passed in 1906 on the heels of the publication of *The Jungle* in that year. Although it did have provisions to address the dangers to meat packers, the law also addressed the disreputable practices in the industry as cited in Sinclair's exposé novel. Sanitary regulations were enforced by making all meat-packing plants selling their products in interstate commerce susceptible to surprise inspections by federal regulators. The price of meat went up as a result of the new federal regulations, and many smaller packers were forced into bankruptcy.

HETCH HETCHY VALLEY

Despite the appeals of John Muir and his Sierra Club, the city of San Francisco was allowed to place a dam in this California valley in 1913. Muir decried the destruction of a unique natural environment for the practical need of providing water to a city.

6 CONSERVATION VERSUS PRESERVATION

President Theodore Roosevelt embraced the cause of environmental conservation. He endorsed the view that the nation's natural resources should be used in a responsible way so they will continue to exist for future generations. In keeping with the progressive reliance on expertise, he appointed the scientifically trained Gifford Pinchot to head the U.S. Forest Service and to lead the government's conservation efforts. President Roosevelt expanded the National Parks system, creating five additional national parks. He also established 150 national forests, including Shoshone National Forest, the nation's first national forest. Ultimately, Roosevelt put over 200 million acres under public protection. Conservationism can be contrasted with the views of environmental preservationists. Preservationists want society to have a hands off approach to the remaining relatively untouched natural areas. Conservationism, by contrast, with its emphasis on regulation and responsible economic utilization of resources, tapped into major strands of progressive thinking—efficiency, expertise, scientific management, and government intervention. An early preservationist was John Muir, one of the founders of the Sierra Club (1892), an organization dedicated to preserving wilderness. Muir was born in Scotland and immigrated to the United States in 1849. He traveled extensively as a wandering naturalist in the spirit of Henry David Thoreau. He wrote extensively about his struggle to preserve natural wonders. Though he and Roosevelt became friends, they embodied different approaches to the environment.

7 WILLIAM HOWARD TAFT

This Ohio attorney and judge was appointed by William McKinley as the first governor of the Philippines after the islands became U.S. territory. He performed so well in this task that Theodore Roosevelt (TR) made him secretary of war and then suggested the American people elect him president, which they did upon TR's departure in 1908. Taft busted trusts like Standard Oil and American Tobacco, but he favored the highly protective Payne-Aldrich Tariff and lost the confidence of TR and other Progressives. TR tried to win the Republican nomination for the presidency in 1912 to reclaim ground from the Republican Old Guard, but was rejected by his old party. Taft went on to lose the election when TR helped launch the Progressive Party and ran against his protégé. The split between TR and Taft was a bitter personal feud, but Taft eventually received the slot he most desired. Warren G. Harding placed him on the Supreme Court as chief justice. He formed a solidly conservative bench in the 1920s with pro-business and anti-labor decisions.

8 BALLINGER-PINCHOT AFFAIR

Reminiscent of the Gilded Age was this scandal erupting during the Taft administration. In 1910, Secretary of the Interior Richard Ballinger reversed a decision made by the Theodore Roosevelt (TR) administration concerning some land in Wyoming, Montana, and Alaska. Gifford Pinchot of the U.S. Forest Service accused Ballinger publicly of allowing corporations to abuse the land. Taft backed Ballinger, and as the controversy heated up he sacked Pinchot. A congressional committee investigated and agreed that Ballinger had acted properly in questioning the legality of some of TR's conservation policies, a fact that irrevocably deepened the split between TR and Taft. Ballinger, although exonerated, resigned in an effort to spare Taft's presidency from any further public outcry.

> ### ATLANTA COMPROMISE
> Booker T. Washington was criticized for accommodation to racism when he expressed his views in Atlanta in 1895. In New Orleans that same year he said, "In all things that are purely social, we can be as separated as the fingers, yet one as the hand in all things essential to mutual progress."

9 "BULL MOOSE" PROGRESSIVE PARTY

When the Republican nominating convention in Chicago refused to nominate Theodore Roosevelt (TR) in 1912, TR and other Progressives bolted the party and formed the Progressive Party on the spot. The Progressive platform was called "A Contract with the People," and TR launched a bitter campaign through which he accused the Republicans of using unscrupulous practices to steal the nomination from him in the first place. The Progressive Party trumpeted its characteristic reforms including the direct election of senators and a push for nationwide primaries for choosing presidential candidates. The initiative, referendum, and recall were planks in the platform as were women's suffrage and even minimum wage laws for women workers. Together Taft and TR received over 7.5 million popular votes in the Election of 1912 compared to Wilson's 6.2 million. TR had named the party by another inspired quip when asked about his fitness to run again for the presidency, but after his defeat he retreated from public life. The Progressive Party went through many iterations but disappeared from American political life by 1952.

10 ELECTION OF 1912

This presidential election was a major turning point in modern American politics. Three of the four candidates were Progressive or ultra-Progressive (the socialist Eugene V. Debs) and Progressivism gained three-quarters of the popular vote. Theodore Roosevelt (TR) and Taft split the Republican vote giving Woodrow Wilson the presidency as the first Southerner since the Civil War to attain the office. Debs gained nearly one million votes, or 6 percent of those cast. Woodrow Wilson interpreted the election as a mandate to take the country in a new direction, which he did. TR's assertiveness might have been well received by the nation if he had won, but in losing he departed from public life except as a writer and explorer.

11 NEW NATIONALISM

Theodore Roosevelt (TR) had campaigned on the notion that he could go on busting the bad trusts as he had during his presidency. He announced this decision and dubbed his principles New Nationalism at Osawatomie, Kansas, after returning from Africa and Europe to find Taft failing to continue his energetic leadership style. Other aspects of New Nationalism alarmed many including the removal of judges from federal courts who struck down Progressive policies and a theory of regulation that assailed private property rights. The Progressive Party also endorsed women's suffrage. Even some Progressives feared where TR's ambition and fame would have taken the country had he won the presidency again. Republicans returned to their original assessment of him as a radical and madman.

12 WOODROW WILSON

Wilson was born in Virginia and rose in fame as a lawyer, professor, and expert on political economics and constitutional law. He became the president of his alma mater, Princeton University, and eventually the governor of New Jersey just before being elected to the presidency in the Election of 1912. The reform governor proved to be a reform president, and the Wilson administration oversaw a lowered tariff, the creation of the Federal Reserve and the Federal Trade Commission, and passage of the Clayton Antitrust Act. As war erupted in Europe in 1914, Wilson maintained neutrality and was elected in 1916 on a platform of staying out of the war. Events after his election pushed him toward war, however, and he wound up bringing the United States into World War I as the war to "make the world safe for democracy." He shaped much of the future of international relations with his proposal of a League of Nations but could not bring the Senate to support his ideas. In attempting to persuade the people to force the Senate to accept membership in the League, Wilson had a stroke and never fully recovered his faculties but lived out his second term while communicating with his cabinet through his wife.

13 NEW FREEDOM

Taking a cue from his rival, Theodore Roosevelt (TR), Wilson coined a phrase to sell his domestic agenda to the American people. New Freedom was a response to TR's desire within New Nationalism to discern between "good trusts" and "bad trusts." Wilson said all trusts were bad and that a powerful president needed to end all monopolistic business combinations intended to reduce competition so the American people could be free from corporate control. As president, however, Wilson could only practically pursue a limited number of the most egregious violators of the Clayton Antitrust Act. Thus, Wilson's idealism gravitated toward TR's policy of regulation and limited use of antitrust suits.

14 OLIVER WENDELL HOLMES, JR.

Famous son of a famous father, Oliver Wendell Holmes, Jr. graduated from Harvard and fought with distinction in the Civil War. After Holmes advanced in American law as a lawyer, professor, and judge, Theodore Roosevelt nominated him in 1902 to the Supreme Court where he stayed until his death at the age of ninety. Although most of the Court was held over from the Gilded Age, Holmes dissented regularly from the majority opinions and ultimately led the way in increasing the federal government's power to regulate commerce. He stood against child labor, intellectual oppression, and wiretapping and gave American law the phrase, "clear and present danger."

15 KEATING-OWEN CHILD LABOR ACT

Progressive activists took up the issue of child labor, challenging a common practice in industrial America. In 1900, the U.S. Census estimated that roughly 1.75 million children were in the workforce. Historians estimate that children 10 to 15 years old made up as much as eighteen percent of the nation's total labor force. In 1904 the National Child Labor Committee, an organization dedicated to abolishing child labor, was formed to better protect children. The campaign to end child labor was aided by troubling photographs of children in workplace settings by photographers such as Lewis Hine, which brought the issue of child labor to public attention. In 1916, the movement had a short lived success, when Congress passed the Keating-Owen Child Labor Act. Realizing that local factory rules were under the domain of state law, Congress addressed the issue of child labor by prohibiting the sale, across state lines, of goods produced by factories that employed children under fourteen. Congress used its power to regulate interstate commerce. Less than a year later, in the case of *Hammer* v. *Dagenhart* (1917), the Supreme Court shot down the act. The Court asserted that the goods being regulated were not inherently immoral, as prostitution or liquor might be. Therefore, what was being addressed by the law was manufacturing practices and manufacturing practices were subject to state law, not federal law. Child labor was not effectively addressed until federal fair labor standards were established during the New Deal era of the 1930s.

16 SIXTEENTH AMENDMENT

The Sixteenth Amendment, ratified in 1913, allows for a federal income tax. Many Progressive reformers supported the creation of a national income tax so that those with higher incomes would pay more than the poor. A graduated income tax had been a major plank in the Populist

Platform of 1892 and was a demand of the Socialist Party. It was seen both as a means to create a more equitable society and as a way of funding government initiatives. An income tax had been created to raise revenue for the Civil War. The wartime income tax expired in 1872, but a new income tax law was enacted in 1894 with the support of William Jennings Bryan and the Democratic Party. That law was soon declared unconstitutional; In *Pollock* v. *Farmers' Loan & Trust Co.* (1896), the Court ruled that income taxes were unapportioned direct taxes and were therefore in violation of the Constitution. The Court cited the Constitutional clause that "Representatives and direct taxes shall be *apportioned* among the several States." That is, direct taxes on individuals could only be based on the population of a particular state, just as representatives are. A state with a large population, like New York, would be responsible for paying more taxes to the federal government than a state with a small population, like Wyoming, regardless of the incomes of individuals in those states. Under this interpretation of the Constitution, a federal income tax on individuals' income would be unworkable. The Sixteenth Amendment specifically exempts income taxes from the allotment restriction on direct taxes in the Constitution. Congress enacted an income tax later in 1913.

17 SEVENTEENTH AMENDMENT

The Seventeenth Amendment (1913) calls for the direct election of senators. Until the ratification of the amendment, the senators for each state were selected by that state's legislature. The framers of the Constitution saw the Senate as a more deliberative body; the longer terms (six years) and avoidance of popular election were intended to make the Senate a body that could temper the Populism of the House. Senators would be able to make more long term and detached decisions. In addition, the fact that state legislatures retained the right, in theory at least, to instruct their senators on how to vote on particular issues, gave the states indirect representation in the federal government. Calls for the direct election of senators were made as early as the 1820s, but they grew louder with the Populist Party putting the direct election of senators in their 1892 platform. The Populists saw it as an important means of making officials more accountable to the public. Reformers pushed the issue on two fronts. On the national level, they called for a constitutional amendment. On the state level, they encouraged the adoption of state-wide, non-binding votes for Senate candidates, effectively serving as advisory straw polls for state legislatures on how to vote. By 1908, ten states had adopted such a measure; that number rose to thirty-three in 1912. Congress approved a measure to amend the Constitution in 1912 and it was ratified by the states in 1913.

> ### WORKINGMEN'S COMPENSATION ACT
>
> President Wilson extended financial assistance to federal employees who became disabled. This law established a major precedent for labor relations for the twentieth century and beyond.

18 UNDERWOOD TARIFF

The origins of the income tax lay in the effort of Woodrow Wilson, as the first southern president since the Civil War, to reduce the tariff further than any Republican administration since Lincoln was elected. Wilson went personally to Congress to ask for a reduced tariff, the first time a president directly addressed a Congress since Thomas Jefferson stopped the practice. The Underwood Tariff of 1913 lowered customs duties to 30 percent, and duties were removed entirely from iron, steel, raw wool, and sugar. The income tax was enacted, after the Sixteenth Amendment legalized it, to make up for the lost revenue from tariffs. Together the lowering of the tariff and the first income tax were blows against the wealthy industrialists long desired by Progressives and therefore major successes of Wilson's domestic agenda.

19 CLAYTON ANTITRUST ACT

The Wilson administration pushed the Clayton Antitrust Act of 1914. This new trustbuster law was designed to close some of the loopholes in the Sherman Antitrust Act that corporate America had exploited since 1890. The legislation established labor unions as legitimate institutions in American society, and Samuel Gompers called the law the "Magna Carta of labor" because it legalized collective bargaining and protected labor unions from attacks using antitrust legislation. The Clayton Antitrust Act was to be enforced by the Federal Trade Commission. Wilson's antitrust legislation specifically targeted the interlocking directorates and the exclusion of individual business leaders from prosecution that had so strengthened Standard Oil and other trusts. Due to the need for American industry to produce for World War I and to the interpretations by the Taft Court, the Clayton Antitrust Act proved unworkable.

> **HOLDING COMPANIES**
>
> These companies were a new kind of trust. They invested in stocks and achieved control of industries as trusts did, but the holding companies had no actual operations in the industries they controlled. The Clayton Antitrust Act attempted to regulate holding companies as mere monopolies on capital.

20 FEDERAL RESERVE ACT

The establishment of the Federal Reserve by this law in 1913 was the first major reform of the national banking system since the Civil War. Twelve regions contained a Federal Reserve Bank to which private banks could belong. The system was overseen by up to eight members of the Federal Reserve Board who set the rate at which banks could borrow money from the national system, and thus determined the basic rate at which private banks could loan money to individuals and businesses. Both the interest rates and the amount of the new national currency, the Federal Reserve Notes, could fluctuate according to the rising and falling of the business cycle in an effort to stabilize the American economy.

> **ADAMSON ACT**
>
> Wilson established another societal precedent with this law that limited railroad workers to an eight-hour work day and mandated extra pay for working overtime.

THE BIG PICTURE

1. The ideas and proposals of grassroots Progressive activists and reformers went from the municipal and state level to the national level, as politicians in both political parties embraced the cause of Progressive reform and shifted the national debate.

2. The Gilded Age came to a close with the rise to the presidency of Theodore Roosevelt whose Square Deal policies revolutionized American government and made many Progressive policies permanent fixtures in American life.

3. The Election of 1912 was a major turning point in American politics in that most voters after the Gilded Age voted for some type of Progressive Reform candidate.

4. Progressive Reform was established in all three branches of the federal government, which enacted legislation and interpreted the Constitution to permit greater involvement of government in actively regulating business and shepherding the lives of American citizens.

5. The Wilson administration revised the federal government's involvement in the American economy in ways that have had lasting impact by establishing the taxation, regulation, and banking systems still in place today.

The Spanish-American War and the Imperialism Debate

25

The obligations of humanity demanded that we take possession of the Philippine Islands in order to prevent the anarchy which would certainly have followed had we taken any other course than that which we did.

—Joseph Henry Crooker decrying a popular argument for imperialism, 1900

TIMELINE	
1890	Alfred Thayer Mahan publishes *The Influence of Sea Power Upon History*
1895	Joseph Pulitzer purchases the *New York Journal* newspaper; Cuban Revolution
1898	USS *Maine* explodes; Spanish-American War; Congress enacts the Teller Amendment; Rough Riders make their famous charge; The United States annexes Hawaii
1899	John Hay initiates the Open Door Policy
1901	Congress enacts the Platt Amendment; Insular cases begin in the Supreme Court; Coalition forces put down the Boxer Rebellion in China
1902	The United States puts down the Filipino Insurrection
1904	TR announces the Roosevelt Corollary to the Monroe Doctrine
1907	The Great White Fleet circumnavigates the globe
1909	Dollar Diplomacy sees its first significant use
1914	Panama Canal is completed
1916	Pancho Villa raids territory belonging to the United States

OVERVIEW

The late nineteenth century and early twentieth century proved to be a turning point in terms of America's relationship with the world. In many ways, it moved away from the neutrality and isolationism that President George Washington advocated in his Farewell Address (see page 119). Within a few short years in the 1890s and 1900s, the United States annexed the islands of Hawaii, defeated Spain in the Spanish-American War, acquired many of Spain's oversees holdings, fought a long and brutal war in the Philippines, and forcefully acquired land to build the Panama Canal. By the early twentieth century, the United States had established two important guiding principles in regard to its expansionist foreign policy. It announced the Open Door Policy in regard to securing access to trade in China and beyond, and it established the Western Hemisphere as its sphere of influence with the Roosevelt Corollary to the Monroe Doctrine.

The United States entered the overseas imperialism scramble a little after the major European powers began carving up Africa and Asia. The powerful nations of Europe—Great Britain, France, Germany, Belgium—had been expanding their empires rapidly as the world was shrinking due to new transportation and communication technologies. The push toward imperialism created a major debate within the United States.

Many Americans resisted the idea of the United States embarking on overseas expansion; after all, the United States was born in a war against a major imperial power. Others believed such a step would violate the core principles that caused the American colonies to seek independence in the first place. Pacifists and humanitarian reformers argued that to participate in imperialism would be the ultimate hypocrisy. Some anti-imperialists feared that if the United States acquired additional lands, non-white residents of these lands would then make their way to the United States. This concern dovetailed with nativist views that certain people were incapable of assimilating into American culture.

However, several factors led United States political leaders to engage in overseas expansion. Some policy makers came to see the establishment of overseas possessions and the maintenance of a strong navy as key components to being a world power. Contributing to the push for imperialism was the unprecedented growth of American industry. After the growth of the American economy through the Gilded Age, manufacturers sought new markets and new sources for raw materials. Some policy makers thought that imperialism would become necessary if the United States were to become the world's predominant industrial power. Many imperialists believed that America was uniquely situated to spread the blessings of civilization to foreign peoples.

1 SPHERES OF INFLUENCE

When nations in the nineteenth century expanded economic or military control into specific regions, the territories in question were called spheres of influence. The essence of imperialism involved a nation's acquiring control or ownership of territory beyond its national boundaries. Spheres of influence were different from colonies in that an imperialistic nation's control came by privileges that had been granted by sovereign nations or tribal regions. These privileges might be the exclusive right to secure raw materials and/or sell products in a region or the right to use the territory as a base of operations in the event of military conflict. Regions of the world that were undeveloped, like Africa, or falling into decline, like China, became ripe pickings for the acquisition of spheres of influence by the United Kingdom, France, Germany, Japan, and eventually the United States.

2 ALFRED THAYER MAHAN

Mahan lectured on naval history and tactics at the Newport War College. In 1890, he published *The Influence of Sea Power Upon History* in which he examined the impact of naval power, strategy, and technology during the time period from 1660 to 1783. He later illustrated how British sea power held Napoleon in check despite his land victories. Mahan's ideas led to a buildup of the U.S. Navy and made imperialists desire naval bases around the world. The United Kingdom acknowledged his praise for the accomplishments of the British Navy by building the largest empire in world history, and both the United States and Germany tried to catch up.

3 "THE WHITE MAN'S BURDEN"

The United States' push toward an imperialist policy was motivated in part, by a particular set of cultural ideas that put forth the existence of a racial hierarchy. Mainstream thinking in the United States in the late 1800s posited the superiority of the descendants of the Anglo-Saxon people and the inferiority of the non-white peoples of the world. This racist notion was widely held, but it led to divergent impulses. Some white Americans felt it was the duty of the civilized peoples of the world to uplift the less fortunate; others felt that the inferior races would simply disappear in a struggle for the survival of the fittest. The push to uplift the peoples of the world was made clear in Rudyard Kipling's famous poem, "The White Man's Burden" (1899). Josiah Strong, a Protestant clergyman, echoed Kipling's sentiment. He argued that the Anglo-Saxon race had a responsibility to civilize and Christianize the world. Many imperialists echoed these sentiments in justifying overseas ventures.

4 JOSEPH PULITZER AND "YELLOW JOURNALISM"

Joseph Pulitzer's career after coming to the United States in 1864 foreshadowed that of Theodore Roosevelt's in that Pulitzer rose from being a soldier and a politician to a major shaper of public opinion. Pulitzer's "bully pulpit," however, was his newspaper empire culminating in publication of the *Evening World* beginning in 1887. Pulitzer employed the technique of "yellow journalism," or the sensationalizing of the news through large headlines and sleazy crime stories, in order to boost his circulation. This sensationalizing reached its peak in Pulitzer's competition with William Randolph Hearst's *Evening Journal* as the two publishers outdid each other in promoting war against Spain with their readers. Later Pulitzer's *World* developed higher standards and gained increasing credibility. In his will, Pulitzer left millions to start a School of Journalism at Columbia University and the prize that bears his name, which rewards singular achievements in many varied fields of publishing, public service, and the arts.

5 CUBAN REVOLUTION

Spain held onto Cuba the longest of all of its New World Empire because of the lucrative nature of its sugar, tobacco, and coffee plantations. Early revolts in the 1860s led to two hundred thousand deaths, but Spain held on despite the animosity of world opinion against the continuation of African slavery. Exiled Cubans in the United States raised funding and public awareness of the plight of the Cuban people who were suffering far worse repression than Americans had prior to 1776. The United States responded with economic sanctions against Spain, but some Cuban slaves responded by launching another revolt in 1895. This revolt was also crushed by the Spanish military, but a firmer resistance was established with modern weapons supplied to Cuban revolutionaries by the Cuban Revolutionary Party and the exiles in America. As the revolutionary forces burned plantations and attacked Cuban cities, Spain sent General Valeriano "Butcher" Weyler who began a policy of placing peasants who supported the rebels into concentration camps. Tortures and murders committed by the Spanish were reported in American newspapers, and many Americans came to believe intervention was a duty.

6 THE SINKING OF THE USS *MAINE*

After riots in early 1898 in Havana, Cuba, the battleship *Maine* was ordered to protect American life and property there. On February 15 the battleship was destroyed and sunk in an explosion that killed 260 of its officers and crew. Yellow journalists pounced on the story as another Spanish atrocity and made "Remember the *Maine*!" the slogan of the campaign demanding American intervention in the Cuban Revolution. The U.S. Congress voted unanimously to spend $50 million on building up defenses. A naval court of inquiry confirmed what had been alleged in the newspapers, that the battleship had been destroyed by a submersible mine, but could not prove that Spain was the culprit. William McKinley tried to refrain from asking the Congress to declare war, but the sinking of the *Maine* was the last straw. Congress declared war on Spain by April. The mast of the USS *Maine* was recovered and placed as a memorial flagpole in Arlington National Cemetery.

7 SPANISH-AMERICAN WAR

Because of numerous atrocities reported from Cuba in the American press, the public clamored for President McKinley to declare war against Spain. The Cuban Revolution had reached a crisis point by 1898, and Americans were evacuated from Cuba. With the sinking of the USS *Maine* and other provocations, McKinley and the Congress authorized an invasion of Cuba and the Philippines. American fleets beat the Spanish fleets in the Atlantic and the Pacific Oceans, and the invasion of Cuba secured victory in just four months. The Spanish-American

War was the background for the heroic rise of Theodore Roosevelt who had volunteered to lead the Rough Riders. The war also left the United States to decide what to do with Cuba, the Philippine Islands, Guam, and Puerto Rico, all of which were liberated from Spain. Spain's world power status, long on the wane, was shattered.

8 TELLER AND PLATT AMENDMENTS

The Teller Amendment to the war resolution against Spain declared the United States had no desire to make Cuba anything more than a sphere of influence. The government of Cuba would be left to Cubans after they were freed from Spain. At the end of the war Cuba was occupied militarily, and the American government decided not to withdraw immediately in fear that instability would threaten the Cuban people. A public health and sanitation campaign was launched and stamped out yellow fever. The U.S. military commander, General Leonard Wood, oversaw the establishment of a Cuban constitutional government. The Platt Amendment said that the United States would not withdraw until Cuba agreed not to sign a treaty with any foreign power threatening Cuban independence and not to acquire too much debt. Furthermore, Cuba had to agree that the United States could intervene if law and order or Cuban independence were ever threatened and had to allow a U.S. naval base at Guantanamo Bay. The Platt Amendment rendered Cuba a protectorate of the United States.

9 HAWAII

The Spanish-American War drew attention to the convenience of Hawaii as a naval installation. Grover Cleveland had forestalled annexation of Hawaii after the 1893 overthrow of the autocratic government of Queen Liliuokalani by a committee of safety assembled by Americans who were sugar and fruit planters on the islands. While Sanford B. Dole was proclaimed president of Hawaii with the protection of U.S. marines, the Hawaii question languished until William McKinley was elected and the war with Spain was won. McKinley was pro-annexation, and when the Japanese complained about American interests in Hawaii, McKinley was all the more resolved to take them. A joint resolution of Congress annexed the Hawaiian Islands even before another Treaty of Paris officially ended the Spanish-American War. Hawaii was the only territory acquired in the era of American imperialism to eventually earn statehood, which it did right after Alaska in 1959.

10 COALING STATIONS

As the era of the great clipper ships gave way to the power of the steam engine, coal became the indispensable material fueling national security and the merchant marine. The Pacific Ocean is the largest on earth, and American interests required that American ships conquer its vastness for military and economic reasons. The islands acquired from Spain in the Spanish-American War, as well as others picked up along the way, became the solution. Instead of filling a ship's hold with coal and a small amount of cargo, ships could be filled with cargo and pick up coal (and other supplies) along the way at the islands. When islands were stocked with coal for this purpose they were known as coaling stations, and the United States acquired enough of these by the turn of the twentieth century to help turn that era into what it became, the American Century.

11 ANTI-IMPERIALIST LEAGUE

In 1898, as the Treaty of Paris was debated in the Senate, critics of American imperialism formed the American Anti-Imperialist League. The league was a coalition of conservative Democrats (known at the time as "Bourbon Democrats") as well as more progressive elements. The league included the American author Mark Twain, who wrote some of the league's more scathing condemnations of imperialism. Anti-imperialists were weary of the United States gaining control of lands beyond America's existing borders. These acquisitions, they argued, were markedly different from earlier acquisitions; these new islands were densely populated and were far away from the settled parts of the United States, unlike the Louisiana Purchase (1803) or the Mexican Cession (1848). They argued that the earlier territorial gains of the United States were intended to absorb American citizens and to eventually achieve statehood and equal footing with the existing states. There was no expectation, however, that newer acquisitions, such as the Philippines, would absorb large numbers of American citizens. The United States would, indefinitely, rule over a foreign population, much as Great Britain had ruled over the Thirteen Colonies.

12 INSULAR CASES

As the United States entered the debate over imperialism and actually acquired what amounted to colonies, thorny questions about the U.S. Constitution kept presenting themselves. Islands like the Philippines, Puerto Rico, and Guam were in a state of constitutional limbo in which they were not even considered territories, let alone states. Puerto Ricans, for example, were granted citizenship in the United States in 1917, but not granted self-government nor the ability to send voting representatives to the U.S. Congress. The question became whether U.S. law would apply equally to these islands, or as it was asked then, "Does the Constitution follow the flag?" The Supreme Court decided, in a series of cases called the Insular cases, that although the islanders in question were ruled by the United States, they would not receive full rights as American citizens.

13 FILIPINO INSURRECTION

During the Spanish-American War the United States helped the revolutionary leader, Emilio Aguinaldo, to throw off Spanish authority. Germany, however, had aspirations to take over the Philippine Islands, and the United States did not believe the Filipino people were ready for self-government or that they could mount a defense against German or British acquisition. McKinley decided it was the Manifest Destiny of the United States to help the Filipinos by governing them. After an incident in which three Filipinos were shot by American soldiers, fighting erupted that became the Filipino Insurrection. In two years of fighting, 4,200 Americans and 16,000 Filipinos were killed. During the transition to peaceful government over 200,000 civilians died from disease and deprivation. Emilio Aguinaldo directed the insurgency, which employed guerrilla warfare tactics in daunting jungle conditions. Aguinaldo was captured, however, in 1901 and called for an end to hostilities, but fighting continued another year.

14 OPEN DOOR POLICY

With the urgings of Mahan and other imperialists, Secretary of State John Hay sent a diplomatic note to the nations carving up China at the turn of the century. Hay wanted these nations to keep China intact as a sovereign nation and to keep their encroachments from leading to a general conflict. In other words, Hay did not want other imperial powers to divide China and exclude the United States from trading there. Neither the United Kingdom, France, Germany, Russia, nor Japan assented to the proposal, but Hay announced to the world that the Open Door Policy was in effect. As feared, competition for spheres of influence did touch off the 1904 Russo-Japanese War, which was ultimately mediated by Theodore Roosevelt with the Portsmouth Treaty in 1905 (a feat for which he received the Nobel Peace Prize). The implications of the Open Door Policy would not be settled until after World War II.

15 BOXER REBELLION

As Hay distributed his Open Door Note, Chinese nationalists were forming a secret society called the Righteous and Harmonious Fists. Westerners referred to the group as the Boxers because of their public displays of martial arts. The Boxer Rebellion occurred because the nationalists wanted to overthrow the Qing Dynasty for their complicity with foreigners in allowing the type of incursions that prompted the Open Door Note. The Empress Dowager then backed the Boxers who set about trying to rid China of all foreigners by massacre. Missionaries and Chinese Christians were killed across China, but by 1900 the Boxers had moved into Peking and attacked foreigners there, even killing the German ambassador. Open Door nations including the United States sent troops to crush the Boxers, and the combined forces of the imperial armies recaptured Peking. By 1911, the Qing Dynasty was overthrown by a revolution that established a republic, but the subsequent instabilities prompted a civil war that paved the way for communism to control China after World War II.

16 ROOSEVELT COROLLARY

When the Dominican Republic collapsed in 1904, Theodore Roosevelt (TR) reiterated the principles of the Monroe Doctrine in a speech before Congress. His main concern was that a European power would do just what James K. Polk had done in regard to Mexico, that is, use military force for the stated purpose of collecting debts but with the real purpose of acquiring new territory. TR said that the United States wanted no new land, but he and the government of the United States did want stability, order, and prosperity across the Western Hemisphere. What TR did not want was a nation or nations guilty of "chronic wrongdoing" to ruin peace for the rest of the Americas. Therefore, he suggested that the United States act as an international police force since European nations had to stay away. Directly this meant that the United States intervened in short order in the Dominican Republic, Cuba, Nicaragua, Mexico, and Haiti. Indirectly, the Roosevelt Corollary led to the rise to world power status of the United States that exercised police powers across the world for the rest of the twentieth century and beyond. The difficulty faced by each president became where America should intervene when so much of the world routinely experienced conflict, instability, and even massacres.

17 PANAMA CANAL

Picking up from failed French attempts at producing a canal in Central America that would join the Atlantic and Pacific Oceans, the United States pursued at first a route in Nicaragua but moved the project to Panama. Since Panama belonged to Colombia and Colombia appeared unwilling to negotiate with the United States, Theodore Roosevelt (TR) moved the U.S. Navy to Panama, landed a few U.S. marines, and otherwise encouraged Panama to revolt from Colombia. The 1903 Panamanian Revolution was nearly bloodless, and from its inception the new country allowed a 10-mile-wide canal zone to be leased by the United States as specified in the Hay-Bunau-Varilla Treaty of 1904. After herculean effort the Panama Canal was open for business by 1914. Therefore, TR set in motion what even the original Spanish explorers recognized would revolutionize world trade, a canal at the isthmus. The Panama Canal dramatically increased the speed with which American naval forces could switch oceans in times of crisis.

18 GREAT WHITE FLEET

When Theodore Roosevelt (TR) said, "Speak softly and carry a big stick" as a principle of foreign policy, the stick was the U.S. Navy. If the world did not get the message about the ability to project power in the Panamanian Revolution, TR sent sixteen battleships painted white to circumnavigate the globe. The trip lasted from 1907 to 1909 and put into harbor at all major points along the way to display American might. Battleships were named after states, so their voyage inspired nationalism for the states thus represented and were an expression of collective militarism aided by the coaling stations acquired with imperialism. The future friends and enemies of the United States had to take into account that the Melting Pot was forging giant steel platforms for rifled cannons capable of firing many miles inland or at other ships in the open seas.

19 DOLLAR DIPLOMACY

William Howard Taft's twist on the Monroe Doctrine revealed Taft agreed with Theodore Roosevelt that America should intervene in the affairs of nations in the Western Hemisphere but not that the intervention should use the military. As a representative of the business community, Taft wanted stability in Latin America, too, in order for American investors to feel confident in helping develop commercial opportunities. In Nicaragua, for example, Taft allowed American dollars to support a revolution and guaranteed the new government loans. If nations in Latin America cooperated with the interests of the United States, Taft allowed more investment dollars to flow into those countries. If a country resisted American interests, it could find itself with a ban on such investment. This policy was extended on a global scale during and after the twentieth-century world wars and by no means precluded the use of military intervention, not even in Nicaragua where Taft began the policy. Ever since the Taft administration presidents have faced the accusation that the United States was bribing other nations and manipulating events for oil or other forms of wealth. A struggle within every presidential administration was whether or not this accusation was true.

20 PANCHO VILLA

Son of a sharecropper, Pancho Villa became a bandit leader who resisted the oppression by the upper classes of Mexico. As the Mexican revolution of 1911 unfolded, Villa became a guerrilla fighter joining Francisco Madero's forces. In the revolving loyalties and alliances of the crumbling revolution, Villa found himself in prison. He switched sides, then switched sides again and before 1914 had served under three separate aspirants to the presidency of Mexico. When the United States backed Venustiano Carranza, Villa led the first invasion on American soil since the War of 1812. His raid on Columbus, New Mexico, and other actions killed a total of thirty-seven Americans. Woodrow Wilson ordered American military forces to hunt down Villa in Mexico but after over a year of searching they failed to catch him. When Mexico stabilized in 1920, Villa retired but was murdered by 1923.

THE BIG PICTURE

1. The Spanish-American War came as a result of Spanish actions and policies in Cuba and the sensationalizing of events by pro-war journalistic giants.

2. The United States found itself in the awkward position of mulling over what to do with colonial holdings acquired from Spain after winning the Spanish-American War.

3. Imperialists convinced the American government to hold on to useful territories in the Pacific Ocean as European nations and Japan jockeyed for position in seeking spheres of influence in China.

4. In the interests of increasing American sea power, Theodore Roosevelt began the process of constructing a canal in the newly formed nation of Panama and dispatched the Great White Fleet of battleships to sail around the world.

5. With America's new position as a rising world power, American presidents innovated new ways to protect interests and to exert influence on events on a global scale.

American Involvement in the Great War

26

*We are disloyal to our ideals if we refuse
to let our country enlist in this cause.*

—Senator James D. Phelan, in support
of the League of Nations, 1919

TIMELINE	
1914	Archduke Franz Ferdinand of Austria-Hungary is assassinated
1914–1919	The Great War spans five years
1915	The *Lusitania* is torpedoed and sinks; Germany issues the *Arabic* Pledge
1916	Germany issues the *Sussex* Pledge; Election of 1916
1917	John J. Pershing begins command of American forces in Europe; George Creel heads Committee on Public Information; Congress passes the Espionage Act; Zimmermann Telegram is exposed
1918	Meuse-Argonne Offensive; Congress passes the Sedition Act; President Wilson delivers the Fourteen Point Address to Congress
1919	Treaty of Versailles; Henry Cabot Lodge attempts compromise treaty; Irreconcilables lead opposition to the Treaty of Versailles in Congress
1920	The League of Nations holds its first general assembly

OVERVIEW

President Woodrow Wilson was eager to embark on a program of domestic reforms upon winning the presidency in 1912. However, events in Europe would soon occupy much of his presidency. Several factors set the stage for the Great War, including the growth of nationalism among different peoples, longstanding tensions in Europe over imperial claims, the stockpiling of military equipment, and a complicated alliance system. The conflict would last over four years and result in the deaths of an astounding 8.5 million soldiers. When the Great War, later known as World War I, began in August 1914, most Americans were not eager to join the conflict. The United States initially proclaimed neutrality when World War I began. The war seemed to be a continuation of the age-old rivalries among the European nations, beyond America's immediate interests.

As the conflict dragged on, a number of factors pushed America toward intervention. Public opinion began to shift toward Great Britain and France. Wartime news coverage tended to present Germany as aggressive, and even barbaric, in its execution of the war. After Russia left the war, the Allied Powers seemed to be more clearly the democratic side of the war. In pushing for intervention, President Wilson called on America to make the world "safe for democracy." He also emphasized the principle of "freedom of the seas." Wilson indicated that the United States would trade and sell weaponry to either side in the conflict, but Great Britain had effectively blockaded Germany. Between the start of the war in 1914 and 1917, U.S. trade with Britain tripled, while trade with Germany shrank to almost nothing. As American ships were increasingly targeted by German U-boats, the push toward intervention grew louder. In April 1917, Wilson asked Congress for a declaration of war, and within days, Congress complied.

The United States played an important role during the final year of World War I. American troops, organized as the American Expeditionary Forces, were effectively commanded by Major General John Pershing. The Americans fought in units independent of the other allied powers. The infusion of fresh American troops helped tip the balance of World War I in favor of the Allies.

The domestic impact of the war was profound. The war resulted in a massive propaganda campaign by the government to support the war effort. Those who actively dissented from the war effort might have found themselves subject to the Espionage and Sedition Acts. Culturally, the country became more fervently nationalistic and conservative over the course of the war. The war served as a transition from the progressivism of the pre-war period to the conservatism of the late 1910s and early 1920s. The reform impulse that led to the Pure Food and Drug Act and laws regulating conditions and child labor was replaced by the Red Scare and rigid quotas on immigration. In addition, the war expanded the role of the federal government as a variety of federal agencies were created to coordinate mobilization for the war. Finally, the war contributed to the Great Migration of African Americans from the rural South to the urban North (see pages 313–314).

Following World War I, President Woodrow Wilson was active in the negotiations for a peace treaty. His idealistic vision for a just peace and a new world order, embodied in his Fourteen Points document, were largely rejected by the European victors in the war. His proposal to create the League of Nations—an institution to maintain world peace—was adopted in the Treaty of Versailles. However, American participation in the League caused strenuous debates in the United States. Ultimately, the U.S. Senate refused to ratify the Treaty of Versailles and rejected American involvement in the League of Nations. The rejection of the treaty, and of membership in the League of Nations, signaled a withdrawal from global engagement and a return to a more isolationist foreign policy in the 1920s and 1930s.

1 ARCHDUKE FRANZ FERDINAND

As the heir apparent to the dual throne of the empire of Austria-Hungary, Franz Ferdinand was sent to inspect the army at Sarajevo in Bosnia in June 1914. Despite the fact that the Archduke had been searching for ways to reform imperial policy to satisfy Serbian and Slavic discontent, he was selected for assassination by a terrorist organization called the Black Hand. The Black Hand stood for Serbian nationalism and independence, and a push among Slavic peoples to create a Slavic country in the Balkans (Yugoslavia) perceived Germanic treatment of Serbia as a flashpoint for their ancestral ethnic conflict. The Archduke's motorcade had been attacked and the Archduke and his wife had escaped harm, but having taken a wrong turn the motorcade ironically brought the royal couple right by Gavrilo Princip, a conspirator in the Black Hand plot. Princip shot both Franz Ferdinand and his wife, Sophie, and the assassination was used as justification for the actions of Austria-Hungary and her ally Germany in starting World War I.

2 THE GREAT WAR

Austria-Hungary gave Serbia a list of several demands after the assassination of their Archduke Franz Ferdinand that were impossible to meet. Backed by Germany, Austria-Hungary declared war on Serbia for revenge. These actions ignited the powder keg that was the European continent. Steeped in competitive nationalism, militarism, and imperialism, Europe soon divided into the Central Powers of Germany, Austria-Hungary, and their allies, and the Allied Powers of France, England, Russia, and their allies. Germany recognized that both Russia and France would attack, so Kaiser Wilhelm's forces struck first through Belgium into France. This assault was stopped outside Paris where the two sides entrenched to survive the murderous new weapons of the machine gun, poison gas, and long-range artillery. The trenches extended north and south across Europe but moved very little east or west for the remainder of the war. The Great War was named World War I only in hindsight after World War II had begun.

3 CENTRAL POWERS

Named such because of their location in central Europe, the Central Powers were Germany, Austria-Hungary, and their empires; the Ottoman Empire (Turkey); and Bulgaria. A previous alliance called the Triple Alliance was the basis for this grouping since the 1880s, but when war came Italy backed out of the Triple Alliance and sided with the Allied Powers. Because of legal questions surrounding the war, the Central Powers were considered to have started the war, although all combatant nations participated in imperialism and militarism as expressions of ardent nationalism before the Great War commenced. Since the Central Powers were defeated, they bore the brunt of the blame, lost their empires, and were ordered to pay damages.

4 ALLIED POWERS

In a counterpoint to the Triple Alliance, England, France, and Russia had formed the Triple Entente. Again, when imperial powers went to war so did their empires, so numerous other principalities supported the Allied war effort either directly or indirectly. Other significant combatant nations that joined the Allied Powers, however, included Italy, Japan, and the United States. Russia sought to fend off Germanic imperialism and to support its fellow Slavs against German aggression. France was allied with Russia against the German threat, and the United Kingdom joined the Allied Powers, as did Belgium, when Germany invaded France through neutral Belgium. The United States eventually joined the Allied Powers after, among other causes, the hostile provocations from German submarines.

5 U-BOATS

The German U-boats, or submarines, were the hope of the Central Powers in breaking the blockade of its shores by the British navy. The United States traded with both sides of the war prior to 1917, although the Allied blockade considerably reduced the supplies reaching the Central Powers. Germany possessed twenty-nine submarines at the start of World War I but by war's end had constructed 360. German U-boats attacked enemy naval vessels but also merchant ships, troop transport ships, and even passenger liners. Submarines could surface unexpectedly and capture enemy ships as prizes or simply sink the ships without warning by firing torpedoes from beneath the surface. After several warnings to stop what was then considered to be dishonorable attacks, Germany's unrestricted submarine warfare brought the United States into the war. U-boats sank passenger vessels with Americans on board and then American merchant vessels. These last were considered to be the final straw and the main justification for a reluctant president to seek a declaration of war.

6 *LUSITANIA*

The German embassy warned Americans not to board the *Lusitania*, a British passenger steamship that was sunk by a submarine in May of 1915. The attack killed 1,198 people including 128 Americans. Germany had accused the British of running small arms from America to Europe hidden aboard passenger ships. That this accusation was true did not keep Germany's enemies, and public opinion in the United States, from assuming the German people to be barbarous. The United States issued a demand that Germany stop unrestricted submarine warfare. Germany justified the sinking because of the weapons on board, but Wilson ordered his secretary of state, William Jennings Bryan, to issue another demand. Bryan, a pacifist and isolationist, refused on the grounds that the note would provoke a war with Germany, and Wilson accepted his resignation.

7 *ARABIC* PLEDGE

Another British passenger steamer was sunk in August 1915. Two American lives were lost when the *Arabic* went down. The German Ambassador himself issued the *Arabic* Pledge saying, "Liners will not be sunk by our submarines without warning and without safety of the lives of non-combatants, provided that the liners do not try to escape or offer resistance." These words were not comforting, especially to people facing a plunge into the icy waters of the North Atlantic, but Germany did for a time focus attacks only on cargo ships. The United States claimed a diplomatic victory in this regard. Subsequent violations of the *Arabic* Pledge were all the more shocking as a result.

8 SUSSEX PLEDGE

The next year a German submarine sank the French passenger steamer, the *Sussex*. A secret order had gone out to German U-boat captains to sink all ships in the English Channel as possible troop transports. While no Americans were killed in the attack on the *Sussex*, some were injured. Wilson called the attack a violation of the *Arabic* Pledge. His advisers suggested an immediate break in diplomatic relations was necessary, but Wilson insisted on giving the Germans one more chance. In what amounted to the *Sussex* Pledge, Wilson said that unless Germany abandoned its method of submarine warfare that the United States would break off diplomatic ties, a classic step toward war. Wilson's unwillingness to respond after an incident he himself said violated the *Arabic* Pledge and his subsequent election to a second term on a neutrality platform only encouraged the Germans to think the United States was weak.

9 ZIMMERMANN TELEGRAM

The German attitude toward the United States was revealed in an intercepted telegram from Germany's foreign secretary, Arthur Zimmermann, to the German ambassador to Mexico. Believing that tensions between Mexico and the United States could serve the Central Powers, Zimmermann authorized the ambassador, in the event of war between Germany and the United States, to say, "That we shall make war together and together make peace. We shall give generous financial support, and it is understood that Mexico is to reconquer the lost territory in New Mexico, Texas, and Arizona." When this message was decoded, the state department released it to the press, and Woodrow Wilson, who had vacillated in his policy toward Mexico, was in exactly the same position as William McKinley after the release of the Depuy de Lome letter prior to the Spanish-American War. Wilson did not want a war, but if he failed to act he would appear weak. Before he could decide what to do, events exploded in the shape of four American merchant vessels sunk by submarines in less than two weeks, all within the same month the Zimmermann Telegram was released to the press. Just over a week later Wilson went to the Congress and secured a declaration of war against Germany because, as he said, Germany was making "warfare against mankind."

10 ELECTION OF 1916

The slogan "He kept us out of war" put Wilson back in the White House after campaigning against Supreme Court Justice Charles Evans Hughes who said the United States should enter the Great War and end it. Women were already getting the vote in some states, and Wilson's promise not to send their sons to war in Europe had dramatic appeal. Still, the election was so close that no decision could be rendered until California had voted. Wilson won California by fewer than four thousand votes, but his election was interpreted by Germany to mean the United States did not want to enter the war in Europe and would not do so even under continued provocation. Within just a few months of the election Wilson was preparing for war through funding measures and the Selective Service Act requiring all men between the ages of twenty-one and thirty to register for the draft. As the severity of a war that had been allowed to drift on became apparent, the draft age was expanded to the ages of eighteen to forty-five in 1918.

11 UNCLE SAM

The name came from a Samuel Wilson who in the War of 1812 supplied beef in barrels to American soldiers. Wilson stamped the barrels with the initials "U.S." for United States, but soldiers began to say the meat came from Uncle Sam. Before long "Uncle Sam" became a euphemism for the federal government. Thomas Nast picked up on the metaphor and personified the United States in the striped pants and top hat familiar today. James Flagg used the image in the most successful recruiting poster of World War I, or of any American war. The simple message, "I want you for the U.S. Army," was emblazoned across an image of Uncle Sam pointing at passersby. The eyes and the finger of the poster were designed to follow people and remain fixed upon them because of the use of foreshortening and an optical illusion in the eyes. Of the four million men and women who were in uniform during World War I, 2.5 million volunteered to serve their country.

BATTLE OF CHÂTEAU THIERRY

This 1918 battle marked the end of one part of the Monroe Doctrine that Americans would not engage in European conflicts. France and others of the Allied Powers were relieved to have direct American military support at last.

12 JOHN J. PERSHING

Pershing was a cavalry officer who had fought American Indians and served in the Spanish-American War. He then served in the Philippines and was caught up in the Russo-Japanese War as an observer of the Japanese military. Pershing then returned to the United States in time to be dispatched by Wilson into Mexico to lead the hunt for Pancho Villa. As America's most seasoned cavalry commander, Pershing was promoted to major general at the outbreak of World War I and commander of the American Expeditionary Force, or AEF, when the United States entered the war. In leading the four million American personnel, Pershing insisted that Americans fight as separate units rather than be placed piecemeal into the trenches as reinforcements of the exhausted Allied Powers. For his efforts Pershing was promoted to full general and given the title "General of the Armies of the United States," a rank reminiscent of that of Napoleon. He served after the war in the more traditional role of army chief of staff and retired in 1924. Medium-range nuclear missiles later bore his name during the Cold War.

NATIONAL WAR LABOR BOARD

Former president Taft led this organization, formed in 1918, which was designed to prevent labor disputes during World War I. Taft listened to laborers' grievances, urged employers to pay higher wages and reduce hours, and strove to keep American production from interruption.

13 MEUSE-ARGONNE OFFENSIVE

The Meuse-Argonne Offensive was the largest commitment of American fighting units of the war. As part of an overall offensive designed by the French commander, all available American forces were put into combat in September 1918 along a sector between the Meuse River and the Argonne Forest. The American force amounted to 1.2 million men whose objective was to cut the main German supply line to the Western Front. The Germans were worn down slowly through the autumn, but by the first of November they were in full retreat. On November 11, 1918, an armistice was called that ended the fighting and allowed the combatants to negotiate the Treaty of Versailles. In the Meuse-Argonne Offensive, America lost 120,000 wounded, dead, or missing casualties, or 10 percent of the force.

14 GEORGE CREEL

Back home in the United States, Woodrow Wilson chose Madison Avenue advertising executive George Creel to head the Committee on Public Information. After his narrow victory in 1916, Wilson realized as war loomed that he now needed some system to sell the war to the American people. Creel had been steeped in the use of propaganda as a muckraking journalist, and he said his goal for the campaign was to create "a passionate belief in the justice of America's cause" and to turn that passion into recruits for the military and dollars for the war effort. The Committee on Public Information sponsored "Four Minute Men" who gave patriotic, pro-war speeches in movie theaters, produced films showcasing America's commitment, and published millions of posters that were distributed to increase the sale of war bonds and enlistment in the military. The activities of the Committee on Public Information were criticized even in their day as maudlin political propaganda, but a similar campaign was mounted again on a larger scale for World War II.

> ### BERNARD BARUCH
> Wall Street speculator Bernard Baruch was tapped by President Wilson to head the War Industrial Board in 1918. The new government agency set a precedent for the federal government's planning of the economy in times of crisis. Baruch was later a delegate to the United Nations and proposed an agency be established to regulate the use of atomic energy (and thus atomic weapons).

15 ESPIONAGE AND SEDITION ACTS

Revealing even more insecurity about war aims, Wilson and a Democratic Congress passed the Espionage and Sedition Acts in a similar vein to the Alien and Sedition Acts passed by John Adams and the Federalists. The Espionage Act of 1917 imposed severe fines and up to twenty years' imprisonment for persons found guilty of aiding the enemy, obstructing recruiting, causing insubordination, stirring up disloyalty, or inspiring the refusal of duty in the military. Such a law served to touch off a wave of anti-German sentiments regarding German immigrants who had long been in the United States as citizens. In 1918, the Sedition Act was an amendment to the Espionage Act that applied the penalties to those proven to lie about the government or to use "disloyal, profane, scurrilous, or abusive language" about America, its government, its patriotic symbols, or its armed forces. The law was aimed mainly at socialists and pacifists because the Soviet Union had backed out of the Allied Powers just as the United States had joined the war effort. Breaking this law landed Eugene V. Debs in jail from where he ran for president in 1920.

16 FOURTEEN POINT ADDRESS

After the Bolsheviks succeeded in the communist revolution that began the Soviet Union, Lenin pulled the new communist state out of the war and revealed documents that portrayed the alliance system agreed on by the czar as shamelessly imperialistic. In response, Woodrow Wilson addressed the U.S. Congress in January 1918 and delivered his Fourteen Point Address denying any desire on the part of the United States for acquisition of territory. Instead, the Fourteen Points were a series of principles that Wilson and his advisers thought were the only hope of a lasting peace. The first several points directly attacked the nationalism, imperialism, militarism, and alliances that had brought on the war and proposed measures to keep these forces in check in international relations. The rest of the points, except the last one, dealt with establishing self-government for various oppressed peoples in the empires of the Central Powers or struggling nationalities that lacked actual nations. The fourteenth point sought the formation of the League of Nations, a body where member nations would commit to collective security but also the arbitration of international disputes. Many of the provisions were adopted in the peace after World War I, but many were so idealistic as to require another world war before gaining wide support.

17 TREATY OF VERSAILLES

After heated discussion in Europe by the Big Four—the United States, the United Kingdom, France, and Italy—Wilson was unable to persuade the other leaders to grant the Central Powers a benevolent peace. The 1919 Treaty of Versailles, therefore, was a punitive peace. Germany, in particular, had to accept the blame for starting the war, give up all her colonies, give land back to France taken in a previous war, pay ultimately $56 billion in reparations, and relinquish any offensive military forces. The peace also ended the Austro-Hungarian Empire and the Ottoman Empire. The Treaty of Versailles also laid the groundwork for the League of Nations and excluded the Central Powers from membership. Wilson brought the treaty back to Washington for ratification by the Senate even though he was deeply dissatisfied. Adolph Hitler later pointed to the Treaty of Versailles as an injustice and used animosity toward the punitive peace as a key to unifying the German people behind the rule of the Nazi Party. Thus, the peace of World War I actually was a major cause of World War II. Even the Germans who signed the Treaty of Versailles said at the ceremony, "We will see you again in twenty years." Their prediction was nearly perfectly accurate because the official start of World War II came with Germany's invasion of Poland in 1939.

18 LEAGUE OF NATIONS

This provision of the Fourteen Points and the Treaty of Versailles was built on the nineteenth-century belief in arbitration as the miracle cure for international strife. The League had two great handicaps, however, as the member nations sought to keep the peace between World War I and World War II. First, Woodrow Wilson could not convince his own country to support the notion and to join the League, so his moral high ground as the "Savior of Europe" was lost. Whatever success American involvement might have accomplished will never be known, but the second handicap was simply that the League of Nations did not do what it said it would do. A few minor problems between small nations were solved without war, but when Japan and Italy began aggressively pursuing nationalistic, militaristic, and imperialistic goals in the 1920s and 1930s, the League did not respond. Hitler and the Germans learned that the League could be ignored, and Germany withdrew from membership in the League that had been granted as appeasement for the punitive nature of the Treaty of Versailles. The principles of the League of Nations were resurrected in the form of the United Nations after the League itself was destroyed by the horrible catastrophe that was World War II.

19 HENRY CABOT LODGE

Woodrow Wilson's nemesis in the Senate was Massachusetts senator Henry Cabot Lodge. Lodge had received the first political science Ph.D. degree ever given by Harvard University in 1876. He went on to lecture there in American history. As a member of the House of

Representatives he was a civil service reformer and personal friend of Theodore Roosevelt (TR) who helped draft much of the legislation behind the Square Deal, but the two men had a falling out over TR's bid for the presidency in 1912. By then Lodge was a prominent senator, imperialist, and leader of the Old Guard. He led the "Irreconcilables" in the battle against Woodrow Wilson's desire to draw the United States into the League of Nations.

20 IRRECONCILABLES

Henry Cabot Lodge and other conservative Republicans in the Senate had supported the involvement of the United States in World War I but could not bring themselves to support the League of Nations. Much of the nation desired to "return to normalcy," a phrase that in part meant the restoring of isolationism as the mainstay of American foreign policy. The Irreconcilables opposed Wilson's collective security idea on the grounds that the United States had not had a military alliance in times of peace with any nation but France immediately after the War for Independence, and under the wise leadership of George Washington had dispensed with the alliance as soon as possible. Even during World War I the United States never formally joined the Allied Powers but merely declared war independently on the enemies of the Allied Powers. Lodge and the Irreconcilables said an alliance pledging the United States would go to war if other members of the League of Nations were attacked violated the constitutional power of the Congress to both make war and to declare peace. Many senators were, of course, skeptical of Wilson's notion that World War I had been the war to end all wars. The difficulty with this stance after World War I, however, was that the United States had become a creditor nation for the first time. On top of the food, oil, and men America had contributed to the war effort were loans granted to the Allied Powers that only one, Finland, ever actually paid off. Dollar diplomacy and the possession of spheres of influence around the globe created a situation where the isolationist policies of the Irreconcilables proved impossible to maintain.

THE BIG PICTURE

1. The United States was drawn into the worst war the world had ever seen by a series of events that made it impossible to remain neutral in World War I.

2. Once the decision to enter World War I was made, the United States mobilized the tremendous manpower and natural resources of the nation to make a significant contribution toward the victory of the Allied Powers.

3. Although the most significant contribution made by the United States was the economic support provided by American food, oil, and money, the American Expeditionary Force distinguished itself on the battlefield and contributed to forcing the Central Powers to surrender.

4. Woodrow Wilson conceived of a plan for world peace that proved impossible to implement successfully in his lifetime, but the visionary ideals of the Fourteen Point Address became the model for a more lasting peace after World War II.

5. The American system of constitutional checks and balances served to avoid the extremes of one-man rule or those of ceaseless parliamentary debate in order to allow the United States to become a more balanced world power.

Mini Quiz

1. The first organization that could be termed a national labor union was the

    (A) Molly Maguires.
    (B) American Federation of Labor.
    (C) American Railway Union.
    (D) National Labor Union.
    (E) The Knights of Labor.

2. The Granger Laws included a regulation that

    (A) limited the number of attorneys a corporation could employ in its defense in a federal lawsuit.
    (B) granted a ten-year period of use before an inventor could earn profits on agricultural patents.
    (C) kept railroads from charging higher prices for carrying loads shorter distances than for long.
    (D) set aside some western land in each state for agricultural and mechanical universities.
    (E) increased the number of silos in the West where farmers could store their grain.

3. William Jennings Bryan delivered his famous "Cross of Gold" speech while he was

    (A) campaigning as the Democratic candidate for the Election of 1896.
    (B) preaching to his congregation and contemplating a bid for the presidency.
    (C) speaking about currency issues at the World's Fair in Chicago.
    (D) addressing a crowd of Populists trying to persuade them to join the Democrats.
    (E) attempting to secure the nomination for the presidency for the Democratic Party.

4. Jane Addams was considered a pioneer in

    (A) social work among urban dwellers.
    (B) international relations with countries sending immigrants to the United States.
    (C) municipal government reforms.
    (D) modern library management.
    (E) activism on behalf of farmers in the Populist movement.

5. Which of the following is an example of how Theodore Roosevelt used the Wisconsin Idea?

   (A) Development of more modern dairy facilities to produce cleaner products for consumers
   (B) The collection of large game animals as specimens for museums around the world
   (C) Singling out some bad trusts to be prosecuted by federal law while advancing other trusts
   (D) Personally intervening in the coal miners' strike as a matter of national security
   (E) Consulting with John Muir about natural resource management in national forests and parks

6. Muckraking journalist Ida Tarbell wrote exposés about the

   (A) insurance industry.
   (B) oil industry.
   (C) meat-packing industry.
   (D) steel industry.
   (E) transportation industry.

7. William Howard Taft most disagreed with Theodore Roosevelt over

   (A) intervention in Central America with American money and military power.
   (B) American control of the Panama Canal.
   (C) conservation of natural resources like timber and coal.
   (D) intervention in World War I in Europe.
   (E) domestic regulatory and tariff policies.

8. The first federal income tax legalized by the Sixteenth Amendment to the U.S. Constitution was intended to raise funds as a result of

   (A) American involvement in World War I.
   (B) a recession that lasted from 1910 to 1911.
   (C) a push to expand telephone wires to connect all American towns and cities.
   (D) a lowered tariff's reducing of federal revenues.
   (E) the formation of the federal reserve system.

9. Besides being from a different part of Europe, most immigrants to America from 1885 to 1917 were also different in that they

   (A) were war refugees.
   (B) came fleeing famines.
   (C) were not Protestant Christians.
   (D) established businesses in urban centers upon their arrival.
   (E) were already accustomed to factory work.

10. All of the following arguments were used to attack support for imperialism **EXCEPT**

   (A) the U.S. Constitution made no provision for creating spheres of influence abroad.
   (B) subjecting others to American rule violated the principles of the Declaration of Independence.
   (C) the United States did not need to add more nonwhite people to its concerns.
   (D) America's military was already stretched beyond its capacity to protect American interests.
   (E) the rhetoric about spreading a better way of life was just a cover for greed for more profits.

11. The annexation of Hawaii was reminiscent of that of Texas because

   (A) the president of the United States made a treaty to acquire the territory.
   (B) a joint resolution of Congress approved the annexation.
   (C) the land was purchased from a foreign power.
   (D) the annexation occurred without the approval of the people living in the annexed territory.
   (E) a monarch was toppled in order for the land to be available for annexation.

12. Which of the following statements is most accurate in regard to the role of the United States in the building of the Panama Canal?

   (A) After taking over the isthmus from Colombia, the United States built the canal from scratch.
   (B) The United States took over a construction project in Panama that had been abandoned by the French.
   (C) After helping the Panamanians acquire freedom, the United States then bought the Canal Zone.
   (D) The United States built a naval base on the tip of the Yucatan Peninsula to protect the Panama Canal.
   (E) An American's plan to control malaria made construction of the canal feasible.

13. The most significant factor in bringing the United States into World War I was the

   (A) use of propaganda by the British in imploring the United States to uphold a shared heritage.
   (B) domestic propaganda created by the Committee on Public Information.
   (C) diplomatic crisis created by the leaking of secret German-Mexican negotiations.
   (D) desperation of Germany to break the Allied blockade by using submarine warfare.
   (E) increase in anti-German sentiment after the discovery of spies operating in the United States.

14. The most important contribution of the United States in winning World War I was the

    (A) demand by John J. Pershing that American forces fight together.
    (B) heroism and skill of individual Americans in battle.
    (C) diplomatic skill of Woodrow Wilson, the first president to go to Europe while in office.
    (D) economic boost through supplying food, fuel oil, and financial backing to allies.
    (E) American invention of the tank to combat machine guns in trench warfare.

15. A main theme of Woodrow Wilson's Fourteen Points Address besides the quest for world peace was the

    (A) diplomatic isolation of Germany, Austria, and Hungary.
    (B) right of small nations released from empires to determine their own destinies.
    (C) elimination of military power as an instrument of national policies.
    (D) recognition of the rise of Russia as a force to be contended with in the twentieth century.
    (E) reparations to be paid to the victors by the aggressor nations that started the war.

ANSWER EXPLANATIONS

1. **(D)** Neither the Molly Maguires nor the American Railway Union could be called national labor unions, and both the Knights of Labor and the American Federation of Labor followed the National Labor Union as the first successful organization to achieve a national voice.

2. **(C)** Although farmers associated with the Grange or the Populist Party might have approved of all of these measures, only answer (D) was a real action on the part of the government. Answer (C) describes the law meant to address the circumstances farmers in the West found so frustrating, that a man like John D. Rockefeller could get rebates for shipping a large volume of product that would allow him to pay less to ship oil farther than they paid to ship their grain.

3. **(E)** All of the answers evoke images of the Great Commoner in action, and answer (D) conveys the results of the "Cross of Gold" speech, but the speech was delivered at the Democratic National Convention and not only secured Bryan the nomination but swept the Populists into his ill-fated campaign against William McKinley in 1896.

4. **(A)** Although answer (C) is close to the truth in that Jane Addams criticized the municipal government of Chicago and pressured them into making changes, the reason they listened to her at all was because she had already made a name for herself as the Mother of Social Work in reaching out to the immigrant poor through the urban settlement house movement she began at Hull House.

5. **(E)** Answers (B), (C), and (D) are certainly pursuits in which Theodore Roosevelt (TR) participated and/or led, and answer (A) is a nod to Wisconsin's dairy industry. The Wisconsin Idea, however, had nothing to do with dairies directly. The Wisconsin Idea was that government leaders should consult with "experts" like John Muir in order to determine what policies to apply to problems like the conservation of natural resources. TR took Muir's advice in many cases, and although the two did not see eye to eye in all matters, they maintained a powerful working relationship when it came to preserving the American wilderness.

6. **(B)** Ida Tarbell wrote her serialized *The History of the Standard Oil Company* for *McClure's* magazine in an attempt to expose what she considered to be the nefarious business practices of John D. Rockefeller. Other muckrakers focused on each of the other industries as targets of what was coming into vogue, "investigative" journalism.

7. **(E)** Although Republican presidents Theodore Roosevelt (TR) and Taft agreed in their earlier days about the Progressive Reform movement, as President Taft began to go his own way he operated more in tune with the Old Guard Republicans. This stance led him to approve of the Payne-Aldrich Tariff that began as a bill to lower the tariff but wound up a law to raise the tariff. In regard to which trusts should be targeted for busting and in other domestic policies TR was horrified that his protégé was not following in his footsteps. TR and Taft largely agreed in the areas of policy referred to in the other answers.

8. **(D)** When Woodrow Wilson won the Election of 1912, one of his first acts was to push the Underwood Tariff through Congress in order to lower taxes on imported goods. He then backed the Sixteenth Amendment to make income taxes constitutional in order to replace the revenue lost by the lowered tariff rates. Answer (A) certainly was grounds for

raising income tax rates, but answer (B) was not true because the United States had not yet resorted to deficit spending and higher taxation to address recessions or depressions (panics). Neither the Federal Reserve mentioned in answer (E) nor internal improvements like the expansion of telephone lines in answer (C) were used as a justification to legalize an income tax.

9. **(C)** Answers (A) and (B) would not have made the immigrants of the New Immigration unique because both were causes of immigration to America before and after the time period mentioned in the question. Few of these new types of immigrant families could afford to establish businesses in their first generations, although many did in the next generation. Most stepped into factory jobs upon their arrival, although most did not have experience with this type of work back in their regions of Europe. Answer (C) is correct in that most of these immigrants were Roman Catholics, Jews, and Eastern Orthodox Christians. Even though most Irish coming to America were Catholics, most immigrants prior to 1885 were Protestant.

10. **(D)** All of the other answers were actively used by anti-imperialists to make their case. Answer (D) was not true in that anti-imperialists said the military would be stretched, not that it was already beyond its capacity. To acknowledge that the U.S. military was stretched beyond its capacity just after the Spanish-American War and after the voyage of the Great White Fleet might have been interpreted as a severe lack of patriotism in such a nationalistic era, and anti-imperialists were careful to maintain the stance that they were the true patriots guarding the cherished principles of the founding fathers recorded in the venerated founding documents.

11. **(B)** Answers (A) and (C) are references to the Louisiana Purchase and the Alaska Purchase, respectively. Answer (D) was not the case in either Texas or Hawaii because both populations earnestly sought entrance into the United States. Answer (E) refers to the deposing of Queen Liliuokalani, but Texans did not topple a monarch; they declared independence from an autocratic leader who called himself a president.

12. **(E)** All of the other answers are twists on the story of the Panama Canal in that the United States did not take over Panama but instead helped the Panamanians break free from Colombia. American engineers did start from scratch after a treaty granted the United States the right to build the canal, but they took over the project from the French who had failed in Nicaragua, partly due to the debilitating effects of malaria. The United States leased the Canal Zone instead of purchasing it. Answer (D) is a reference to the naval base at Guantanamo Bay on the tip of Cuba, not the Yucatan region of Mexico. Walter Reed confirmed the discoveries of other scientists about the transmission of malaria by mosquitoes and developed a plan to control the disease's spread. Of these choices, answer (E) best expresses how Americans achieved this monumental task.

13. **(D)** All of the answers either contributed to the decision of the U.S. Congress to enter the Great War on the side of the Allied Powers or increased support for the war once Americans were fighting. Only answer (D), however, can be said to be the most significant factor. The sinking of passenger ships with Americans on board and the sinking of unarmed American merchant vessels compelled a reluctant Woodrow Wilson to ask the Congress for a declaration of war. Wilson considered unrestricted submarine warfare a sign of German barbarism, especially after the Germans had pledged not to do it.

Resorting to such a measure, new to warfare, was a sign of how desperate the Germans were to break the Allied blockade that threatened their supplies, many of which they received from the United States prior to American involvement.

14. **(D)** Answers (A), (B), and (C) were all important contributions even though Wilson's diplomatic intervention failed to avoid a punitive peace. Answer (E) is incorrect in that the British invented the first practical tanks to combat machine gun emplacements. The invention of the airplane by the United States had little impact on the outcome of World War I, but in the deadly attrition created by trench warfare, the Allied Powers would likely not have prevailed without American food, oil, and money. World War I made the U.S. transition away from being a debtor nation to being a creditor nation.

15. **(B)** Answer (B) conveys Wilson's cherished notion of self-determination, and many nations were created out of the four collapsed empires at the end of the war partly because of Wilson's firm stand. Wilson actually opposed the punitive nature of the provisions expressed in answers (A) and (E). Answer (C) is incorrect in that, although Wilson urged disarmament, even he was not as idealistic as the authors of the Kellogg-Briand Peace Pact to which answer (C) refers. Wilson had used military power in Central America enough to know it was sometimes necessary, let alone having sent Americans into Europe. Neither Wilson nor many other observers could have looked at the chaos of the Bolshevik Revolution in Russia during World War I and predicted the role the Soviet Union would eventually play as suggested in answer (D).

The 1920s—A Decade of Contradictions

27

*With but little equipment one can call the life of the
rest of the world from the air, and this equipment can
be purchased piecemeal at the ten-cent store.*

—Robert S. Lynd and Helen Merrell Lynd, *Middletown*, 1929

TIMELINE	
1914	Henry Ford introduces the $5-per-day minimum wage
1918	Flu epidemic kills from 25 to 50 million people worldwide
1919	Congress enforces Prohibition with the Volstead Act; Red Scare begins; Palmer Raids begin
1920	Warren G. Harding is elected president; Marcus Garvey launches the Liberia Program; The first radio news show is broadcast
1921	Andrew Mellon becomes secretary of the Treasury
1922	Teapot Dome scandal breaks
1923	President Harding dies, and Calvin Coolidge becomes president
1924	H. L. Mencken founds *American Mercury* magazine
1925	Scopes monkey trial
1927	The defendants in the Sacco and Vanzetti case are executed; Henry Ford replaces the Model T car with the new Model A; Charles Lindbergh makes the first nonstop flight across the Atlantic Ocean

OVERVIEW

During the 1920s we see the development of some of the cultural divisions that have existed in American culture in the decades since then. Many historians note the resurgence of traditional values in the United States in response to the unfolding of a more modern America. This tension between tradition and modernity shaped much of the historical work on the 1920s.

In many ways, the 1920s was a conservative decade. The years during and immediately following World War I saw a backlash against the experimentation of the Progressive era and a rise in patriotism and xenophobia (anti-immigrant sentiment). Government restrictions on freedom of speech during World War I were followed by a Red Scare against suspected radicals and labor activists after the war. The conservative impulses of the immediate post-war period continued into the 1920s. Key elements of the decade include a strong fundamentalist Christian movement, anti-immigrant legislation, a large and active Ku Klux Klan, and a resurgence of rural, traditional values. Not all Americans subscribed to these conservative values, but these values greatly shaped public debates and politics in the 1920s.

The Republican Party controlled the White House for twelve years, from 1921 to 1933. The presidents of the 1920s, Warren G. Harding, Calvin Coolidge, and Herbert Hoover, all tended to pursue conservative, pro-business policies. Coolidge once said, "The man who builds a factory, builds a temple." Another element of the turn toward conservatism is the rise of isolationist sentiment in the United States. Many Americans were disillusioned about World War I, while others had grown resentful of the wave of new immigrants that had come to America.

While the 1920s saw the resurgence of conservative, traditional values in the United States, the decade also witnessed the unprecedented economic, technological, and cultural changes that ushered in the modern world. The production and consumption of consumer goods contributed to economic growth for much of the 1920s; the wealth of the country more than doubled over the course of the decade. New products, such as automobiles and radios, captured the public's imagination, and new production techniques increased industrial output. The nation became increasingly urban. For the first time in American history, census data revealed that the majority of Americans live in cities. Despite the nation's experiment with Prohibition, which began in 1920, Americans continued to consume alcohol in the 1920s. The exciting nightlife of cities such as Chicago and New York led to the decade being labeled the Roarin' Twenties or the Jazz Age. Many young people rebelled against the Victorian sensibilities of their parents' generation. While the journalist and cultural critic, H. L. Mencken, grew increasingly disillusioned with American culture in the 1920s, the decade saw the rise of two literary movements that have stood the test of time—the Harlem Renaissance and the Lost Generation. The participants of both of these movements stood somewhat outside of the mainstream of American society and critiqued what they observed.

1 FLU EPIDEMIC

From 1918 to 1919 an influenza epidemic spread from the trenches of World War I around the world and killed from twenty-five to fifty million people. The disease spread in the United States across military installations and then broke out in the general public. The proximity of military personnel and workers in cities made the death toll particularly severe among those between the ages of twenty and forty. In the United States the flu killed more Americans than had the Civil War, roughly 675,000. These deaths were also far more than those of Americans killed in Europe, and the combined effects of war and one of the worst outbreaks of disease dramatically impacted the social fabric of the United States.

2 RED SCARE

With the creation of the world's first communist state in Russia, the Soviets set about pro-pagandizing against Western nations, and this rhetoric created a panic in American society. The Communist Party in America existed as early as 1919 even before the death of Lenin. The already tenuous history of the labor movement in America made nativist and anticom-munist fears erupt in the anti-immigration laws of the 1920s, which were another decade of the repression of labor interests. Americans feared that Bolsheviks, or communists, were infiltrating labor unions, universities, and other institutions with the purpose of plotting the overthrow of the government. Enough evidence of such infiltration was discovered to raise public hysteria. During the Roaring Twenties the civil liber-ties of certain elements of society were sacrificed in the process of ferreting out radicals.

> **INDUSTRIAL WORKERS OF THE WORLD (IWW)**
>
> This labor organization, formed in 1905, proved to be the most radical in U.S. history. Bill Haywood led the IWW (otherwise known as "The Wobbies") and openly approved murder and sabotage. The rhetoric and actual crimes of the IWW inflamed the Red Scare as the organization reached its peak in 1923.

3 PALMER RAIDS

Attorney General A. Mitchell Palmer began a series of mass arrests of subversives and agitators in the country's labor unions. Those immigrants arrested who had not yet received citizenship were simply deported. Anarchists, socialists, and communists, as well as innocent bystanders were all caught in the net of the many Palmer Raids in what became the First Red Scare. In January 1920, Palmer ordered raids in thirty-three cities that took 2,700 people into custody. Palmer cited the phrase from Oliver Wendell Holmes Jr. regarding a "clear and present danger" to national security in justifying the arrests and the confiscation of labor publications with suspicious content. A. Mitchell Palmer was nearly killed by a mail bomb after which point the Palmer Raids diminished, but a fear of communist infiltration remained as a basis for the Cold War.

4 GREAT MIGRATION

One of the largest internal migrations in American history is the migration of African Americans out of the South during the period from World War I to the Great Depression (a second wave of the migration occurred during and after World War II). The main factor that drew African Americans to the North was increased employment opportunities. By the turn of the twentieth century, the Industrial Revolution was in full swing in northern cities such as New York and Chicago. Factories using new mass production techniques were able, at first, to fill the jobs with local people and European immigrants. But World War I created a labor crisis for these factories, which were producing military goods around the clock. With immigration from Europe at a standstill because of the war and with almost three million potential factory hands in the U.S. military, factories were desperate for workers. Factory agents from the North frequently made recruiting trips to the South, offering immediate employment and free passage to the North. Many African Americans did not need a great deal of enticing. Many African Americans were eager to escape the mistreatment they received in the South. Jim Crow segregation laws were a constant reminder to African Americans of their second-class citizenship. In addition, African Americans were excluded from the political system in the South. It is estimated that more than six million African Americans left the South between 1916 and 1970. Before the Great Migration, over 90 percent of the African-American population lived in the South; that figure dropped to approximately 53 percent by the end of the migration.

5 REBIRTH OF THE KU KLUX KLAN

The period following World War I witnessed a rise in racial antagonism in the United States. This racial hostility was, in part, an offshoot of the reactionary political backlash against progressivism following World War I and, in part, a reaction to the demographic changes brought about by the Great Migration. By the 1920s, the Ku Klux Klan was a genuine mass movement. The original Klan, a violent, racist group with its roots in the immediate aftermath of the Civil War, had died out by the 1870s. A new Klan was founded in 1915, and by 1925, it grew to three million members, according to its own estimates. The Klan was devoted to white supremacy and "100 percent Americanism." The white supremacist ideology of the Ku Klux Klan was evident in a number of race riots in the United States in the late 1910s and 1920s. There were at least 25 significant race riots in 1919 alone. In July 1919, a riot against African Americans occurred in Washington, D.C., and an even more violent riot in Chicago left 38 people dead and more than 500 injured. The deadliest race riot in American history occurred in Tulsa, Oklahoma, in 1921. The immediate cause of the rioting was an encounter in an elevator between a young white female elevator operator and a young African-American male shoe shiner. A wave of violence ensued as white residents, including police and National Guardsmen, rioted through the Greenwood District of Tulsa, which was the center of the African-American community. The district was destroyed by the rioting, over 10,000 people left homeless, and more than 300 African Americans were killed.

6 IMMIGRATION RESTRICTION

In the 1920s, Congress passed restrictive immigration quota acts, responding to a rise in xenophobia in America in the late 1910s and 1920s. The Emergency Quota Act (1921) and the National Origins Act (1924) set quotas for new immigrants based on nationality. The first act set the quota for each nationality at three percent of the number of people from that country who were already living in the United States in 1910. The second act reduced the percentage to two percent and moved the year back to 1890. This had the effect of setting very low quotas for many of the "New Immigrants" who arrived from eastern and southern Europe between 1880 and 1920 (see page 242). The acts were passed in response to a sharp rise in nativism, or anti-immigrant sentiment, after World War I. Some Americans were anti-European after the trauma of World War I. Some nativists associated immigrants with radical movements; the rise in nativism went hand-in-hand with the Red Scare. Some nativists focused on the fact that most of the New Immigrants were not Protestant. Poles and Italians tended to be Catholic, Russians and Greeks tended to be Eastern Orthodox, and Jews came from several countries in Eastern Europe. The cacophony of languages heard on the streets of New York or Chicago repelled many nativists. Finally, working-class people feared that low-wage immigrant laborers would take jobs from native-born American workers.

7 SACCO AND VANZETTI CASE

Nicola Sacco and Bartolomeo Vanzetti were two Italian immigrants who were arrested in 1927 for murder. They were convicted after one of America's first show trials on what many considered insufficient evidence, and a widespread belief developed that they were found guilty only because they were anarchists. The two men were sentenced to death, but when defense attorneys succeeded in throwing enough doubt on their convictions as to secure a stay of their executions, liberal and radical Americans resorted to mass demonstrations to secure their release. As a result of the protests, the governor of Massachusetts (the original murders were committed in Braintree, Massachusetts) ordered a review of the case by a special commission. The commission ruled that the men actually were guilty and that the trial had been conducted appropriately, so Sacco and Vanzetti were each executed in the electric chair. Their case was considered by some to be the result of the mass hysteria created by the civil liberties abuses of the Red Scare.

8 SCOPES MONKEY TRIAL

Sixty-six years after the debate opened with the publication of *On the Origin of Species* by Charles Darwin, the state of Tennessee banned the teaching of the theory of evolution in public schools. John T. Scopes, a biology teacher in Dayton, Tennessee, agreed to test the law when approached by the American Civil Liberties Union (ACLU). Scopes was arrested, and his trial turned into a part-circus, part-epicenter show trial that became the focus of the debate between Fundamentalist Christianity and Modernism, a movement that tried to reconcile Darwinism and the Bible. Clarence Darrow, a famous agnostic defense attorney, took up Scopes's case while William Jennings Bryan acted as the prosecutor. Darrow trapped the aging Bryan into testifying on the stand, and Darrow went on to befuddle Bryan with a series of questions about the veracity of the Bible. Scopes was eventually found guilty and fined, but the case brought derision on Tennessee in particular and the South in general. William Jennings Bryan died shortly after the trial, which became a milestone of revolutionary changes in values.

9 WARREN G. HARDING

Harding was a flashback to the Gilded Age in that he was a Republican with strong ties to the political machine created in Ohio by Marcus Hanna. He rose from editing a newspaper up through Ohio politics and into the U.S. Senate. He was nominated as a dependable and predictable Republican to run for the presidency in 1920, and his plea for America to "return to normalcy" struck a chord with American voters tired of Progressive Reform and the horrors of World War I. He achieved the largest margin of victory yet in a presidential election but proved to be an incompetent administrator who, like Ulysses S. Grant, surrounded himself with unscrupulous men. His one foreign policy coup, the Washington Naval Conference, seemed to end the dangerous arms race among the United Kingdom, the United States, France, Italy, and Japan but it did not spare him from a growing public frustration with a return to corruption instead of normalcy. After traveling to Alaska on a tour to regain the respect of the American people he died on the return trip leaving Calvin Coolidge in the White House.

10 TEAPOT DOME SCANDAL

This scandal reminiscent of the Ballinger-Pinchot Affair in the Taft administration was the most widely known case of corruption in the Harding administration. Reports of wrongdoing in the Navy, Justice, and Interior Departments were only the tip of the iceberg. Members of the executive branch were indicted for fraud, conspiracy, and bribery. Albert B. Fall was the best example of the "Ohio Gang," the group of grafters using their connections to Harding to line their own pockets. Fall was appointed by Harding in 1924 to oversee the oil reserves at Teapot Dome, Wyoming, that were supposed to be set aside for the national security needs of the U.S. Navy. Fall leased the Wyoming oil fields, and others in California, to private developers. The developers paid Fall at least $125,000 for the access. Fall, who had tried to retire, was sentenced to prison and fined $100,000. Before Warren G. Harding died nearly every member of his cabinet had fallen under suspicion. The character and reputation of Calvin Coolidge were all the more remarkable after the Harding administration in that Vice President Coolidge was never connected to any of the Harding scandals.

11 CALVIN COOLIDGE

The integrity of Calvin Coolidge had propelled him up through Massachusetts politics even as a Vermonter, and as governor of Massachusetts during the Boston police strike he gained national fame for saying "There is no right to strike against the public safety by anybody, anywhere, any time." This reputation led to his election as vice president that led to his ascension to the presidency after Harding's death. Coolidge had the good fortune to preside over a booming economy and a calm world. His hands-off policy was nearly a flashback to laissez-faire and Jeffersonian principles of limited government. In other words, whatever Theodore Roosevelt had done as a Republican president, Calvin Coolidge did not. After winning a term to the presidency in his own right, he did not seek a second term and went off as had John Adams to work his New England farm. He left Herbert Hoover to deal with the inevitable crash after a decade of wild economic growth.

FREDERICK TAYLOR

Taylor did motion studies of laborers at their work and developed the principles known as Scientific Management. He sought to eliminate wasted motion in order to boost productivity in an age of mass production and mass consumption.

12 HENRY FORD

Henry Ford's ingenious contribution to the American economy was in pioneering techniques of mass production that allowed a standardized car, the Model T, to come within the means of the average citizen (under $300). This nearly indestructible product was made using a continuously moving assembly line. Workers mastered a few tasks in the assembling of the Model T and repeated them endlessly as the product moved from worker to worker. His innovations revolutionized American industry and helped America meet the massive industrial requirements of the two world wars. He also introduced in his manufacturing plants the eight-hour workday and the $5-a-day minimum wage, which was twice that of other factory workers. Ford Motor Company therefore was able to avoid many of the problems with labor unions that plagued other industries. He and his son, Edsel, began the Ford Foundation, which would become a major American philanthropic organization. Ford also displayed anti-Semitic tendencies, publishing *The International Jew*, a four-volume set of booklets, in the early 1920s. The articles in it were culled from his personal newspaper, *The Dearborn Independent*. While Ford stubbornly continued to produce black Model T's, General Motors began introducing new models and a variety of colors, tapping into consumer demand. The automobile became a status symbol in the United States, provided greater mobility for people, contributed to the growth of the suburbs, and provided youthful couples a break from parental supervision.

13 JAZZ AGE

This nickname for the Roaring Twenties paid homage to one of America's great cultural innovations, jazz music. Called "negro music" because its origins lay in the syncopated rhythms of the legacy of African music among American slaves, jazz led the way for country, rockabilly, and rock 'n' roll as indigenous musical forms. Jazz became a major avenue for cultural exchange between African-American musicians and white youths frequenting famous dance clubs like the Cotton Club in New York City. Jazz expressed a spirit of revolt from traditional musical standards as musicians performed through improvisation, and its spontaneity became a metaphor for the youth revolt. The cultural impact of jazz was evident in that the first motion picture with sound was *The Jazz Singer* in which a white actor portrayed an African-American performer. The style of dancing that accompanied jazz music at nightclubs also expressed deliberate revolt in that couples moved in a manner rarely if ever seen in public.

> ### RADIO
>
> The entertainment and advertising industries were revolutionized by the invention of radio. By the end of the 1920s, most households had a radio. The Pittsburgh station, KDKA, became the first to air election results when Warren G. Harding was elected president in 1920. The radio was not grasped as a political tool until the so-called fireside chats of President Franklin D. Roosevelt in the 1930s.

14 HARLEM RENAISSANCE

The Harlem Renaissance was a literary, artistic, and intellectual movement centered in the primarily Black neighborhood of Harlem, in New York City. The Great Migration of African Americans from the rural South to the urban North set the stage for the Harlem Renaissance. A common goal of participants in the movement was to increase pride in Black culture by celebrating African-American life and forging a new cultural identity among African-American people. Contributions included the poetry of Langston Hughes, Claude McKay, and Countee Cullen and the jazz music of Louis Armstrong, Duke Ellington, and Bessie Smith. Langston Hughes's poems include "Harlem," "The Negro Speaks of Rivers," and "I, Too, Sing America." He wrote an essay that became a manifesto for Harlem Renaissance writers and artists, entitled "The Negro Artist and the Racial Mountain." Duke Ellington is perhaps the most important figure in twentieth-century jazz. Some of his most important compositions are "Mood Indigo," "Don't Get Around Much Anymore," and "Take the A Train."

15 MARCUS GARVEY

Garvey was born in Jamaica and rose from being a printer to being a journalist and editor of radical newspapers. After traveling widely and reading Booker T. Washington's *Up from Slavery*, Garvey became a passionate supporter of African nationalism. He formed the Universal Negro Improvement Association, or UNIA, "to work for the general uplift of the Negro peoples of the world." Garvey brought his message to America in 1916 and resurrected the idea that the descendants of American slaves should go back to Africa to develop an independent civilization of their own. Until that goal could be reached, Garvey dressed flamboyantly in flashy military-style uniforms and spread the word that "black is beautiful." He supported segregated African-American churches and maintained that Jesus and Mary were of African descent, and Garvey went so far as to say African-American children should play with black dolls. Garvey suggested African Americans should become businessmen and achieve economic independence. Through scandals in the financing of a shipping company, Garvey was convicted of squandering investors' money and served two years in prison. He was then deported back to Jamaica as his land grants and early attempts at colonizing in Liberia also fell through. His movement at its peak consisted of eight million readers and followers, and he laid the groundwork for much of the modern emphasis on African-American history and African heritage.

FUNDAMENTALISM

This Protestant Christian movement emphasized five tenets in the face of liberalism growing in U.S. churches. These doctrines included belief in the inerrancy of the Bible, the virgin birth of Christ, the atonement provided by Christ's death, the resurrection of Christ, and the miracles of Christ that would culminate with his second coming.

---

16 LOST GENERATION

This phrase was a reference to the generation of European youth whose lives were literally or figuratively blasted into smithereens by World War I, but it was applied in the 1920s in America to certain literary figures who expatriated. Gertrude Stein famously used the phrase in reference to Ernest Hemingway, and the writings of many of the American authors who lived abroad reflected the fact that American youth had lost a moral compass. The Lost Generation is evidence that Western Civilization was alienated from its traditional values by the collapse into the chaos of World War I. Many of these poets and novelists lived in Paris or London and from that distance portrayed American society as materialistic and devoid of substantive values. Among them were Hemingway, F. Scott Fitzgerald, and T. S. Eliot. Their portrayal of society both reflected and encouraged the esoteric, the eccentric, and the amoral values of the urban youth revolt as it searched for meaning in gin and jazz music.

17 THE NINETEENTH AMENDMENT AND THE "NEW WOMAN"

Ideas around gender and proper behavior for women were challenged and altered in the 1920s. The term "new woman" was used in the 1920s to describe women who were more engaged in public issues. Although women were involved in reform movements for most of American history, a key shift occurred when women achieved the right to vote in 1920 with the ratification of the Nineteenth Amendment. This had been a demand of suffragists from at least as far back as the Seneca Falls Convention of 1848. The movement gained new urgency during the Progressive era. In 1919, President Woodrow Wilson finally endorsed the idea and soon Congress sent the amendment to the states for ratification. In addition to participating in political life, women were working in occupations that were previously closed to them. The most common occupation for women in the mid-nineteenth century was in the field of domestic service. In the late nineteenth century, more women were working in factories and, by the first decades of the twentieth century, office work became their primary occupation. New opportunities for women were not confined to the workplace. With more women in the paid workforce, women were able to participate more fully in the new consumer culture of the 1920s. The new image of women during the 1920s was symbolized by the popularity of the "flappers" and their style of dress. Flappers were independent-minded young women of the 1920s who openly defied Victorian moral codes about "proper" lady-like behavior. They were more likely than their mothers to use tobacco and alcohol, even though the latter was illegal in the 1920s. The "new woman" was also more likely to use birth control and to choose when, if at all, to become a mother.

18 PROHIBITION

The term Prohibition applies to the period following the ratification of the Eighteenth Amendment, when the manufacture, sale, and transportation of alcoholic beverages were illegal. Prohibition went into effect in 1920 and ended when the Twenty-First Amendment (1933) repealed the Eighteenth Amendment. The movement to limit or prohibit the drinking of alcoholic beverages stretches back to the Second Great Awakening (see Chapter 13). It became the largest reform movement throughout the nineteenth century, with the Women's Christian Temperance Union leading the charge at the end of the century. The 1919 Volstead Act defines alcoholic beverages as any that were more than 0.5 percent alcohol by volume. Americans still found ways to drink during Prohibition. Illegal bars, called speakeasies, opened throughout America, especially in large cities. It is estimated that 20,000 to 100,000 operated in New York City alone. Al Capone and other gangsters developed a network of bootleggers to distribute liquor illegally. Bribing of law enforcement agents was common. The existence of sophisticated smuggling rings and subversive hideouts made the youth revolt all the more exciting and the lack of respect for the law all the more pervasive. America's experiment with Prohibition led to the only repeal of a constitutional amendment and a general loosening of morals resulting from a deliberate revolt against a federal law.

19 H. L. MENCKEN

Nietzsche spoke, and there was H. L. Mencken. Mencken was a journalist from Baltimore whose talents lay in the clever use of language to criticize virtually everything and everyone around him. His cynicism proved addictive to many other writers and thinkers who followed Mencken's biting wit through the pages of his *The American Mercury* magazine. He referred to his fellow Americans as of the species, "Boobus Americanus," and he wrote disparagingly of American democracy. He personally covered the Scopes Monkey Trial for his magazine and wrote that Dayton, Tennessee, was a medieval town that would soon burn John T. Scopes at the stake. His style of muckraking journalism channeled the disillusion with Western Civilization and traditional values that was the spirit of the age. Later, when Americans were depressed enough by the Great Depression, his readers grew weary of Mencken's continued scorn and sought authors who were more constructive than destructive in their criticism.

20 CHARLES LINDBERGH

As evidence of the frivolous nature of American culture, the public idolized sports heroes like Babe Ruth, people who sat atop flagpoles for days on end, and pioneer aviator Charles Lindbergh. Lindbergh was an airmail pilot and plane mechanic who pursued a $25,000 prize for the first person to fly a nonstop flight from New York to Paris. With backing from investors in St. Louis, Missouri, Lindbergh designed a plane he dubbed "The Spirit of St. Louis" and flew the distance to Paris in 33.5 hours. Bemedaled and promoted, Lindbergh returned a national hero. He married, but his first child was kidnapped and murdered, the news of which was a sensationalized national crime story. Having toured Germany between the world wars, Lindbergh returned to America saying Hitler was a "great man" and headed the America First Committee, an isolationist organization that opposed American involvement in World War II. When war came, however, Lindbergh again moved up the ranks of the American military as a test pilot and eventually as a combat pilot. His fame was evidence of the new American fascination with aeronautical technology, travel, and celebrities that became hallmarks of the postwar world.

THE BIG PICTURE

1. The post-World War I period saw bitter debates as some Americans put forth a more conservative vision, harkening back to an earlier era, while many Americans embraced the rapid technological, economic, cultural, and demographic shifts that were occurring in the 1920s.

2. Ideas about gender were debated in the 1920s, as women gained the right to vote, challenged traditional expectations, entered employment in new fields, and participated in a moral and sexual revolution.

3. The 1920s witnessed a rise in intolerance as anti-immigrant sentiment, racism, and the "Red Scare" became more widespread and led to a narrow definition of "one hundred percent Americanism."

4. A lack of forceful leadership contributed to cultural drift that resulted in the rejection of American society by many intellectuals and artists as well as a general decline of belief in traditional Christianity.

5. The era of Prohibition was a climax of the temperance movement but proved to undermine respect for lawmaking and for authority in general.

The Great Depression and the New Deal

28

The selling pressure was wholly without precedent. It was coming from everywhere. When the closing bell rang, the great bull market was dead and buried. Not only the little speculators, but the lordly, experienced big traders had been wiped out by the violence of the crash, and the whole financial structure of the nation had been shaken to its foundations.

—Jonathan Norton Leonard, journalist, 1929

TIMELINE	
1929	Stock Market Crash; Herbert Hoover begins his presidency
1929–1941	The Great Depression spans twelve years
1932	The Hoover administration charters the Reconstruction Finance Corporation; The Bonus Army marches on Washington, D.C.; Election of 1932
1933	Franklin Delano Roosevelt (FDR) begins his presidency; Frances Perkins is appointed Secretary of Labor; FDR's administration passes New Deal legislation in its first hundred days; FDR announces a Bank holiday
1933–1941	The New Deal spans eleven years
1934	John Maynard Keynes meets FDR
1935	Huey P. Long is assassinated
1936	Eleanor Roosevelt begins her "My Day" newspaper column

OVERVIEW

The Great Depression was the most devastating economic downturn in American history. It was one of several downturns in American history—notable ones include the Panics of 1819, 1837, 1857, 1873, and 1893. However, in none of these panics did the country reach the depths of despair reached during the Great Depression. Citizens lost confidence in the American banking system and rushed to withdraw their savings before bank runs made their banks bankrupt. Over 5,000 banks closed, and their account holders lost whatever assets they had deposited, an amount estimated at over $3.4 billion. Unemployment rose to a high of nearly 25 percent nationally, and in some cities, as many as a third of the adult population was unemployed. Rural areas were also hard hit, especially the Dust Bowl region. The Great Depression spanned the globe as international trade diminished, causing some countries to experience crippling hyperinflation and bankruptcy.

The precise reasons for the Great Depression are still debated by historians, but the following explanations are frequently mentioned. Industrial production greatly expanded in the 1920s. New products, such as automobiles and radios, captured the public's imagination, and new production techniques, such as the assembly line and "scientific management," increased industrial output. For much of the 1920s, the public, induced by easy credit and seductive advertising, was able to absorb this increased industrial output, but by 1927 manufacturers noticed that warehouse inventories were on the rise. Consumption just couldn't keep up with production. A weak labor movement in the twenties led to stagnant wages. This contributed to a growing gap between the wealthy and the poor. By the late 1920s, manufacturers made the logical decision of beginning layoffs, worsening an already bad situation. In addition, the agricultural sector lagged behind the rest of the economy. Farmers had put more acres under cultivation during World War I to meet increased demand for agricultural goods. By the twenties, Europe was back on its feet, yet American farmers did not cut back on production. Mechanization and expansion left the farmers of the 1920s in a cycle of debt, overproduction, and falling commodity prices. Increased tariff rates and an isolationist foreign policy further reduced the international market for American agricultural goods. The stock market crash of October 1929 pushed the economy over the edge. For years, stock prices had been rising dramatically, but serious investors began to see that stock prices were reaching new heights as the actual earnings of major corporations were declining. This discrepancy between the price per share and the actual earnings of corporations led investors to begin selling stocks, which stimulated the crash of 1929.

President Herbert Hoover seemed to be the right man to deal with the problems associated with the Great Depression. He had demonstrated his organizational skills as head of the Food Administration during World War I. However, Hoover was very reluctant to harness the power of the central government to intervene in economic matters. He feared that government intervention into the Depression would stifle individual initiative. He did implement the Reconstruction Finance Corporation in 1932 and began public works projects. Despite the actions of the Hoover administration, the economy was in critical condition by the time Franklin D. Roosevelt (FDR) took the reins. Though Roosevelt was from a wealthy background, he was able to convey to the public a sense of empathy and warmth. Further, his openness to experimentation allowed for a more flexible response to the Depression than Hoover's more ideological approach. Roosevelt took the federal government in a new direction by asserting that it should take some responsibility for the welfare of the people. The Roosevelt administration developed a series of programs that are known as the New Deal. Roosevelt believed that the government needed to take action in the face of the unprecedented levels of poverty and unemployment brought on by the Great Depression.

TOP 20 THINGS TO KNOW

1 STOCK MARKET CRASH

The period from 1922 to 1929 was one of an unprecedented rise in speculation in stocks and other securities. The subsequent Stock Market Crash was the major sign that the world was facing a global Great Depression. The Crash came after thirteen million shares sold on October 24, 1929. On October 29, sixteen million shares were sold with very few buyers buying. The result was a precipitous drop in the value of stocks and the evaporation of the theoretical wealth created after nearly a decade of margin buying, pumping and dumping, and other inflationary practices.

2 MARGIN BUYING

During the years of wild speculation on the stock market, stock values climbed so high and so fast that it was possible to borrow as much as 90 percent of the purchase price of a stock from one's broker, pay the payments for a few months, sell the stock, and still make a profit after paying off the purchase loan. Most speculators then used that profit as another 10 percent down on another even larger purchase of stocks on margin. The repetition of this process contributed to the value of stocks on the stock market being widely separated from the actual value of the American economy. When the Stock Market Crash hit, brokers called in their margin loans. This step meant that the creditors demanded all the money from the purchase loans of their clients who had little to no cash to cover the expense. As stock prices fell, investors sold their stocks at a fraction of their original value and wound up defaulting on their margin loans and walking out into the street penniless.

3 PUMPING AND DUMPING

Rings of large speculators used pump-and-dump schemes to dupe the public into raising the artificial value of certain stocks even faster than the speculative boom would have done on its own. A few rich investors would sell a certain stock among themselves while bribing journalists to write glowing reports of the business's potential for growth. The volume of shares being exchanged made small investors believe it was a hot stock, and masses of unsuspecting Americans would jump on board. That open-market sale of the stock would also boost the price higher until the original conspirators sold all their shares at considerable profits. The conspirators would own so much of the stock, however, that their sell-off would catch the market by surprise and create a crash in value. Thankfully, just as most young people in the 1920s were not flappers and most Americans drank less liquor during Prohibition, most Americans thought the stock market was too risky to participate. Until laws were passed to regulate the market and make severe margin-buying and pump-and-dump schemes illegal, it was too risky.

4 HERBERT HOOVER

The man who had the unfortunate timing to become president before the Stock Market Crash was really something of an economic genius and a self-made millionaire. Herbert Hoover was a mining engineer who traveled the globe overseeing numerous projects. During World War I his organizational skills were instrumental in running the U.S. Food Administration, which was responsible for supporting the Allies with food they could not grow for themselves. Hoover served as Secretary of Commerce in the biggest decade of commerce in American history, the Roaring Twenties. Once the Great Depression began during his presidential administration, Hoover hoped natural economic forces would fix the problem. He was eventually convinced, however, to extend federal loans to banks and large corporations through his Reconstruction Finance Corporation. Defeated in the landslide victory of Franklin Roosevelt in 1932, Hoover applied his organizational skills to a review of how the executive branch of the United States government was run, otherwise known as the Hoover Commission. Herbert Hoover was another capable man who, like Martin Van Buren, assumed the presidency at a time when nothing he did would be viewed positively. He was, and likely will remain, America's last isolationist president.

5 HAWLEY-SMOOT TARIFF

In 1930, President Herbert Hoover signed into law the Hawley-Smoot Tariff Act, which increased tariffs to their second highest rate in U.S. history, exceeded only by the "Tariff of Abominations" (1828). The push toward erecting trade barriers through high tariff rates reflected the isolationist tendencies of the Republican presidents of the 1920s and early 1930s. Earlier, in 1922, President Warren Harding signed the Fordney-McCumber Act, which dramatically raised tariff rates. The logic of the Hawley-Smoot Tariff Act was to keep foreign goods out of the country in order to protect American farmers and factory jobs. Opponents of the bill urged Hoover to veto it. Over one thousand economists signed a petition arguing that higher tariffs would hurt the American economy by reducing trade. Several industrialists, including Henry Ford, also asked Hoover to reject the bill. Hoover himself had reservations about the impact of the bill, but he signed it anyway to appease Congressional Republicans. After the bill became law, other countries, including Canada, implemented retaliatory increases in tariff rates. The impact of the act on the Great Depression is open to debate by historians and economists. Some argue that its impact was minimal; some argue that it exacerbated the Great Depression.

6 CHARLES MITCHELL

Mitchell was a fast learner like Andrew Carnegie who rose by serving capable men and learning from them before starting out on his own as a New York City financier. By 1921 he was elected president of the National City Bank. He, more than other financial wizards, believed stocks would be popular investments for even the middle class, and he organized the sale of millions of dollars of stock in his own bank. Mitchell in turn used that money for investment schemes, a practice later blamed for the crash and which became either highly regulated or outright illegal after the Stock Market Crash depending on the nature and risk of the investments. When stock prices dropped on October 24, 1929, Charles Mitchell and his associates were so wealthy as to be able to turn the market around by simply putting in their personal wealth (and their banks' wealth) as buyers. When the Stock Market Crash happened, however, Mitchell and his partners were ruined. Unlike some great financiers who either committed suicide or died impoverished, Mitchell made a comeback, regained respect, and left a fortune to his children.

7 JOSEPH P. KENNEDY

The father of John, Robert, and Ted Kennedy was so well connected as an Irish banker's son in Boston that because of a shrewd maneuver to save Boston's only Irish-owned bank he was appointed president of the bank at the age of twenty-five. He dabbled in other businesses, including liquor importing (allegedly during Prohibition) and through shrewd investments became the richest man in America. He played the stock market all through the 1920s but pulled out all of his cash just before the Crash. During the Great Depression Franklin Roosevelt made him the head of the new Securities and Exchange Commission that was the New Deal agency designed to regulate the stock market. Some considered this appointment similar to letting a wolf loose among sheep, but Kennedy actually established the agency's integrity as John Marshall had done for the Supreme Court. Joseph Kennedy was later appointed as ambassador to the United Kingdom, a prestigious position from which Kennedy attempted to use his wealth to back his sons as presidential candidates.

> **MCNARY-HAUGEN BILL**
>
> In the 1920s this law attempted to aid the plight of farmers by authorizing the government to buy up surplus crops. Calvin Coolidge vetoed the measure, but the idea would resurface during the New Deal.

8 RECONSTRUCTION FINANCE CORPORATION

When Hoover relented and began to use the federal government as a tool to attempt recovery from the Great Depression, the Reconstruction Finance Corporation (RFC) used federal monies to make loans to banks and large corporations like railroads. Hoover hoped that these loans would stop deflation and maintain the financial structure that would allow consumption and employment to rebound. The Congress authorized Hoover to disperse $500 million through the RFC at first, an amount later extended to $2 billion of borrowed money to be loaned in turn to banks in emergencies. The RFC could even buy corporations and run them directly if such a measure seemed necessary. Hoover signed the RFC into law in 1932 and within six months had loaned out $1.2 billion. The first step of Franklin Roosevelt's New Deal was to continue the RFC and to expand its operations.

9 BONUS ARMY

World War I veterans called for their promised retirement bonuses to be issued early because of the severity of the Great Depression. In July 1932, about one thousand veterans marched on Washington, D.C., to make the request of Congress in person. When Congress failed to act, a total of seventeen thousand veterans and their families descended on the national capital and resolved to camp there until their demands were met. The House of Representatives passed a bill to issue $2.4 billion, but the Senate defeated it. The Congress then offered money to pay for the veterans' expenses to get home, and most took advantage of that offer and left town. About two thousand veterans refused to leave, however, and when Washington police tried to force their evacuation an altercation killed two protestors and two policemen.

Hoover then called out the U.S. Army and drove the veterans away using infantry and cavalry, including tanks. In some sense Hoover's reputation never recovered from this act, but he maintained that the situation was dangerous and merited the response.

10 ELECTION OF 1932

When nominated by the Democratic Party for the 1932 presidential campaign, Franklin D. Roosevelt (FDR) appeared in Chicago in person and delivered an acceptance speech, something only done once before at Theodore Roosevelt's (TR's) acceptance of the nomination of the Progressive Party in 1912. In the speech, the second Roosevelt said, "I pledge you, I pledge myself, to a new deal for the American people." In many other ways FDR's rise to political power mirrored that of TR, his cousin. FDR proposed sweeping government involvement in the direct operation of the American economy in order to help the "forgotten man at the bottom of the economic pyramid," but he said such measures should be "only as a last resort." When he won a landslide victory over Hoover (472 electoral votes to 59) and the Democratic Party won both branches of Congress, FDR immediately set about resorting to his last resort. The result was a reassertion of the principles of Progressive Reform on a massive scale, and to one degree or another Progressivism has been the style of government management considered normal and proper ever since.

11 FRANKLIN DELANO ROOSEVELT

Just like his cousin Theodore Roosevelt (TR), Franklin D. Roosevelt (FDR) graduated from Harvard, studied law, served in the state legislature of New York, was the assistant secretary of the Navy, and eventually governor of New York. In the course of his political career he contracted polio and suffered paralysis of his legs. He differed from TR in that his Progressivism originated up out of the Democratic Party. He defeated Herbert Hoover in a landslide victory in the Election of 1932 and told the nation, "The only thing we have to fear is fear itself." His New Deal promised relief, recovery, and reform. FDR's preferred approach to providing relief was through public works projects financed with deficit spending as advised by John Maynard Keynes, a British economist. He faced the Great Depression with a willingness to try any solution, and he inspired the American people through fireside chats on the radio to hang on through the struggle. He also exceeded the traditional restraints on executive power, not the least of which was George Washington's two-term precedent that FDR smashed by being elected four times to the presidency. Facing World War II on top of the Great Depression, however, Americans largely accepted the campaign notion of not switching horses in midstream. FDR and the leaders of Allied nations were largely responsible for fighting the Axis Powers until they submitted to unconditional surrender and for designing the international relationships of the postwar world. FDR died of a brain hemorrhage just three months after his fourth election and within a few weeks of being able to see the victory over the Axis he had worked so hard to achieve.

12 NEW DEAL

Upon being inaugurated to the presidency in 1933, Franklin D. Roosevelt (FDR) immediately set about sending proposed pieces of legislation to his "Rubber Stamp" Congress. The New Deal was a flurry of the laws that established agencies within a sweeping bureaucracy that aimed money at the problems of the Great Depression. Each agency was targeted to address relief, recovery, or reform—or all three. Through a system of trial and error, the Roosevelt administration enacted regulations, incentives, and grants to put people back to work. New Deal agencies became known by the three or four initials of their names such as CCC, TVA, FDIC, and the WPA. Although FDR was getting action and doing things in pure Rooseveltian Progressive style, the New Deal failed to organize the sometimes contradictory programs into a comprehensive plan. Some economic historians believe that the New Deal actually prolonged the Great Depression, which was declared over only after World War II required a full-scale mobilization of the economy.

13 ELEANOR ROOSEVELT

The daughter of Theodore Roosevelt's alcoholic younger brother, Elliott, Eleanor Roosevelt rose from a childhood of neglect to become the most influential First Lady to date after marrying Franklin D. Rooselevet (FDR), a distant cousin. Her activism was a powerful counterpoint to FDR's stricken physical condition. Not only did she perform the normal hospitality duties of a president's wife, Eleanor Roosevelt traveled across the country, gave lectures and radio broadcasts, and wrote a newspaper column in which she recounted her daily activities. In this capacity she informed her husband about conditions of average Americans and presented a caring face for the impersonal forces of the New Deal bureaucracy. During World War II she even visited soldiers abroad. Upon her husband's death she made what she considered her greatest contribution by leading in the formation of the United Nations Universal Declaration of Human Rights.

14 FRANCES PERKINS

A sociologist and economist, Frances Perkins possessed the best Progressive pedigree possible in that she had worked at Hull House in Chicago. She moved to New York City where she studied industrial conditions and became an advocate for hygiene and safety for workers, especially after the Triangle Shirtwaist Factory fire in 1911 that killed 146 young women. She also helped guide legislation that reduced the work week for women from fifty-four to forty-eight hours. Through her work on many other industrial boards and commissions she came to the attention of Franklin Roosevelt who made her Secretary of Labor and the first woman to hold a cabinet post. Throughout the New Deal she guided policies and laws pertaining to labor relations and working conditions that embroiled her in controversy as she advocated the fixing of wages and prices. She supported laws that limited the employment of children under the age of sixteen, pushed for unemployment compensation, and championed the Civilian Conservation Corps (CCC), which employed young men in forestry and other public works.

15 HARRY HOPKINS

Harry Hopkins was one of President Franklin D. Roosevelt's top advisers and one of the main architects of the New Deal. Hopkins had been a social worker devoted to the social gospel. After graduating from Grinnell College, he began work at Christodora House, a social settlement house in New York City's Lower East Side. He later worked with New York City's Association for Improving the Condition of the Poor and with the Red Cross. During the Great

Depression, Hopkins first came to the attention of FDR, who was then governor of New York, when he took on the role of executive director of a New York State agency, the Temporary Emergency Relief Administration. Hopkins began a friendship with Eleanor Roosevelt and soon became a confidant of FDR. His ideas influenced the creation of the Federal Emergency Relief Act, the Works Progress Administration (WPA), and, later, the Lend-Lease Act. Under his leadership, the WPA became the largest employer in the country. The brunt of much criticism from conservatives, Hopkins became the face of the more socialist tendencies in the New Deal. While accused of being pro-Soviet in World War II, Hopkins responded by saying he was anti-German.

16 BRAINS TRUST

Frances Perkins was only one of the formal and informal advisers to Franklin D. Roosevelt (FDR) known as his "Brains Trust." The New Deal required the "Wisconsin Idea" to be in operation constantly developing innovative ways to either attack the Great Depression or create activity that would assure people that the Roosevelt administration was doing everything in its power to end the crisis. In the early New Deal era, several handpicked professors provided FDR with ideas for bank regulation and other aspects of the First Hundred Days.

In the later New Deal the group widened to include lawyers, military officers, and even more academicians (usually economists). The leftward leanings of some of FDR's advisors and New Deal administrators attracted criticism, especially after some toured the Soviet Union and returned with glowing reports. By and large, however, the Brains Trust did assure the American people that the best minds in the country were contributing to the government's grip on the situation.

BEER AND WINE REVENUE ACT

An example of a New Deal measure aimed at relief and recovery was this law passed in 1933. The government took this step to jump-start the economy by relaxing prohibition for the first time. By amending the Volstead Act, the law paved the way for the formal repeal of Prohibition in the Twenty-First Amendment to the Constitution.

17 RELIEF, RECOVERY, AND REFORM

As Theodore Roosevelt's Square Deal had three Cs, Franklin D. Roosevelt (FDR) imposed at least that level of organization on the New Deal. With the history of the Freedmen's Bureau and the Indian Bureau as precedents, the federal government actively began providing for the welfare of citizens in the relief measures. While there were some direct welfare payments, FDR preferred providing public works projects that employed those who had lost their jobs in various trades including the arts. Therefore, the first goal of the New Deal was to provide for the basic needs of the unemployed. Recovery New Deal measures were designed to take care of the basic needs of the whole economy, that is, to boost consumption, restore the confidence of employers, and raise farm prices. Reform measures were aimed at preventing an economic crisis of the magnitude of the Great Depression from ever happening again. These policies involved regulation of the banking industry and the stock market as well as the general notions of deficit spending and Progressive Reform that have become the norm in American politics.

18 FIRST HUNDRED DAYS

Franklin D. Roosevelt (FDR) had promised immediate action and delivered by setting to work right after his inauguration. Within the first one hundred days the executive branch had sent an unprecedented number of prospective bills to Congress in consultation with the new Democratic majorities in both houses of the legislative branch. These first measures of the New Deal were aimed at fixing banking, bolstering industry and agriculture, managing labor issues, and giving relief to the unemployed. Eight major components of the New Deal and several more minor ones were established starting with the Emergency Banking Relief Act in March of 1933 running through the National Industrial Recovery Act in June. The special session of Congress FDR had called to deal with the economic emergency then adjourned. Critics dubbed the Seventy-third Congress the "Rubber Stamp" Congress because it did nothing to challenge the will of the executive branch. Two major pieces of New Deal legislation passed during the First Hundred Days, the Agricultural Adjustment Act and the National Industrial Recovery Act, were later judged to be unconstitutional by the Supreme Court. Still, presidents ever since FDR have felt compelled to accomplish significant strides within the first hundred days of their administrations.

19 BANK HOLIDAY

To stop bank runs the first act Franklin D. Roosevelt (FDR) did to address the emergency was to declare a four-day national bank holiday that officially ended all transactions of banks and other financial organizations. Having said "The only thing we have to fear is fear itself," FDR thus stopped panic from sending even more banks into bankruptcy. After the bank holiday, over five thousand banks reopened within the first three days. Therefore, three-quarters of all the banks that belonged to the Federal Reserve System were supported through the initial panic. Two weeks later stock prices began to rise and banks reported that people were putting currency and gold back into their bank accounts. One week after starting the Bank Holiday FDR delivered his first fireside chat, a national radio address in which he explained his actions in simple language in an effort to reassure the American people that the crisis had passed. Then because fear subsided, a worse crisis was avoided.

20 JOHN MAYNARD KEYNES

Keynes was a British economist whose revolutionary theories were so controversial as to become a whole school of thought called Keynesian economics, and his work marked a turning point in the twentieth century. Having risen to a position of prominence in the Treasury, Keynes was sent to Versailles as England's main economic adviser. He viewed the Treaty of Versailles to be economically unfeasible for the Germans to endure and resigned in protest. He published a book in 1919 that won him fame, especially after his predictions regarding Germany came true. His *Economic Consequences of the Peace* was only one of his many major works analyzing the economic problems of England, her allies, and her enemies. Keynes advocated the type of interest rate adjustments on the part of governments that were embodied in Woodrow Wilson's Federal Reserve System, but during the Great Depression he suggested that the central governments of countries should abandon balanced budgets and use deficit spending to "prime the pump" by hiring unemployed people to work on public works. Franklin Roosevelt adopted Keynesian economics and agreed that in the absence of progress from corporate America that the federal government should act in the stead of big business to mobilize the economic resources of the country.

Challenges to the New Deal

29

The issue of Government has always been whether individual men and women will have to serve some system of Government or economics, or whether a system of Government and economics exists to serve individual men and women....

—Franklin D. Roosevelt, speech before the Commonwealth Club, 1932

TIMELINE	
1931	Ida B. Wells dies
1933	Civilian Conservation Corps (CCC); Agricultural Adjustment Act (AAA); Tennessee Valley Authority (TVA); National Recovery Administration (NRA); Public Works Administration (PWA); Federal Deposit Insurance Corporation (FDIC)
1934	Securities and Exchange Commission (SEC)
1935	Congress passes the Wagner Act; The Dust Bowl hits beginning on "Black Sunday"; Works Progress Administration (WPA); Sick-Chicken case is argued before the Supreme Court; Social Security program begins
1936	Election of 1936
1937	FDR reveals his Pack-the-Court Scheme
1938	The Congress of Industrial Organizations (CIO) rivals the AFL
1941	John L. Lewis resigns as head of the CIO

OVERVIEW

President Franklin D. Roosevelt had to navigate the New Deal through the tumultuous political currents of the 1930s. A variety of social and political movements emerged, each offering different solutions to the economic crisis. To some degree, these movements hindered the New Deal and to some degree, they influenced it. The initial flurry of New Deal programs, such as the Civilian Conservation Corps, the National Recovery Administration, and the Agricultural Adjustment Act (the so called "Alphabet Soup" agencies), generated a national debate about the role of the government in the economic and social life of the country.

On the one hand, many voices from the left criticized the New Deal as being overly cautious. Upton Sinclair (author of *The Jungle*) ran for governor of California in 1934 under the banner "End Poverty in California," proposing sweeping, somewhat socialistic solutions. Francis Townsend, also from California, proposed a tax to generate enough money to give everyone over sixty a monthly stipend. The most serious threat to Roosevelt from the left came from Huey Long. His "Share the Wealth" platform, announced in 1934, proposed breaking up the fortunes of the rich and distributing them to everyone else. In addition, many civil rights activists urged FDR to do more for the African-American community. African Americans, already in a vulnerable position in U.S. society before the Great Depression, were especially hard hit by the economic difficulties of the 1930s. On the other hand, many conservatives argued that the New Deal had gone too far. Organizations such as the American Liberty League came into existence to challenge the New Deal. Many business leaders saw the New Deal as burdensome and tyrannical.

In addition, FDR had to deal with an unfriendly Supreme Court that struck down several early New Deal acts as unconstitutional. The Schechter decision (1935) ended the National Industrial Recovery Act, and, several months later, the *Butler* decision (1936) declared the Agricultural Adjustment Act unconstitutional. With mounting pressure from a variety of Populist and leftwing forces, and with a presidential election looming in 1936, Roosevelt introduced a second set of programs known as the second New Deal. This second phase of the New Deal was less about involvement with the different sectors of the economy, and more about providing assistance and support to the working class.

After FDR's landslide election victory in 1936, he again shifted direction. First, he put forth a proposal to add justices to the Supreme Court. His "court packing" scheme was roundly criticized and was not implemented. However, in its aftermath, the Court was friendlier to New Deal legislation. In late 1937 and 1938, President Roosevelt took the New Deal in a new direction that, many historians believe, hurt the economy. By 1937, the economy was showing signs of improvement. Unemployment was going down and banks and businesses were showing signs of stability. Roosevelt took the advice of some of the more conservative members of his cabinet and cut back on spending with the goal of balancing the budget. This move contributed to a further downturn in economic activity, known as the "Roosevelt Recession." Later, in 1938, Roosevelt shifted direction again and increased government spending. The economy did show signs of growth, but the real boost came in 1939 as the United States began producing armaments and supplies in the looming shadow of World War II.

The 1930s witnessed the emergence of the political and ideological alignment that has persisted, to some extent, to the present. President Hoover's generally conservative laissez-faire approach has been echoed in the policies of Republican President Ronald Reagan and both Presidents Bush, while Roosevelt's generally liberal interventionist approach inspired Democratic President Lyndon B. Johnson's "Great Society." Today, Democratic leaders debate how closely their party should be associated with New Deal liberalism, while Republicans brand their opponents "tax and spend" liberals. The debates of the 1930s are still part of political culture.

1 CIVILIAN CONSERVATION CORPS

The Civilian Conservation Corps (CCC) provided work for unemployed young men ages eighteen to twenty-five in projects ranging from planting trees to building hiking trails, roads, structures, and flood-control facilities for national parks. The young men lived in camps, wore uniforms, and were led by army officers. A portion of their $30/month salary was automatically sent to their families to provide relief. As many as five hundred thousand young men worked for the CCC at a time, and by the opening of World War II two million had been employed. CCC corpsmen were preconditioned to military life prior to the entry of the United States in the war. Reforestation had never received such a focus by any government in history.

2 AGRICULTURAL ADJUSTMENT ACT

The Agricultural Adjustment Act (AAA) addressed the prices for agricultural products that collapsed since the end of World War I. The government tried to eliminate farm surpluses by paying farmers not to produce with the goal of reducing supply in order to boost prices. The Populist Party's idea of farm subsidies had arrived as farmers were paid to cut the supply of corn, cotton, wheat, rice, hogs, and dairy products. The AAA established the Agricultural Adjustment Administration to monitor compliance as well as to tax companies that processed food in order to fund distributions to farmers. Refinancing of farm mortgages was also included to slow foreclosures. The AAA also authorized the president to create inflation with silver coinage and paper currency. The Supreme Court determined that the AAA was unconstitutional in 1936, but when Franklin D. Roosevelt was reelected he stepped around the ruling by couching the subsidies in terms of soil conservation, another Progressive goal with clear precedents in the Square Deal.

3 TENNESSEE VALLEY AUTHORITY

The Tennessee Valley Authority (TVA) arose from a World War I installation at Muscle Shoals on the Tennessee River in Alabama. A hydroelectric dam had been constructed that powered two munitions plants. Senator George Norris of Nebraska attempted to have the federal government operate the plants to produce fertilizer, but both Calvin Coolidge and Herbert Hoover opposed the idea saying the government should not compete with private industry. Franklin D. Roosevelt (FDR) was not averse to the possibility having pursued similar policies as governor of New York. After FDR visited Muscle Shoals in 1933, the TVA was begun both to provide electricity through water power but also to control flooding. Dams and power plants were constructed beginning in a model town in Tennessee that was named for Senator Norris. The goals of the TVA went beyond rural electrification to include conservation measures as well as the wider development of social programs in the region. TVA built nine dams before the end of World War II that helped provide electricity for the Manhattan Project and aluminum smelting facilities as well as the production of fertilizers and explosives. Because the TVA competed directly with private utilities it was considered by critics of the New Deal to be the most socialistic agency, but it has remained in operation as a public utility company ever since.

4 NATIONAL RECOVERY ADMINISTRATION

The National Recovery Administration (NRA) was begun by the National Industrial Recovery Act during the First Hundred Days and was designed to boost employment but also industrial and business activity. Modeled after the voluntary compliance system developed during World War I, the NRA relied on self-regulation by business owners according to a set of standards, or codes, created by the federal government. The president was also permitted to enforce the codes, and any agreements made with the president by an industry were exempt from prosecution under the Sherman or Clayton Antitrust Acts. The NRA reiterated the Clayton Antitrust Act's affirmation of collective bargaining. At its peak the NRA controlled five hundred separate industries, and its policies impacted around twenty-two million employees. The NRA was another New Deal agency determined to be unconstitutional by the Supreme Court in 1935.

5 PUBLIC WORKS ADMINISTRATION

The Public Works Administration (PWA) extended from a provision of the National Industrial Recovery Act (NIRA) and was a widespread program funding the construction of roads, post offices, and other public buildings. Over $4.2 billion was spent on over thirty-four thousand projects to provide relief for workers and recovery once the money given to construction workers was spent on consumer goods. The PWA was the last New Deal agency passed during the First Hundred Days and revealed the extent of Franklin D. Roosevelt's belief in Keynesian theories of the government's responsibility to "prime the pump" of the economy through deficit spending. The idea of public works for the pump priming came from Frances Perkins as the Roosevelt administration sought to spend "big bucks on big projects." Although the PWA did not reverse the Depression, such activity encouraged American citizens that something was happening until World War II and the need for production for the war effort made it obsolete. The PWA was discontinued in 1941 as a result.

6 WORKS PROGRESS ADMINISTRATION

The Works Progress Administration (WPA) was the significant relief agency of the second New Deal that channeled $11 billion into public works projects between 1935 and 1943. The administrators of the WPA held down the numbers of hours each worker could work in a week in order to provide an income to as many unemployed people as possible, and they spent 85 percent of all the funds on wages. When it was terminated in 1943, the WPA had provided jobs for 8.5 million people involved in over 1.4 billion projects. Most public works were focused on manual labor, but the WPA also hired writers, actors, artists, and musicians. Historians, for example, were hired to write histories of every state, and John Steinbeck was paid to write *The Grapes of Wrath*. Artists painted murals that featured New Deal accomplishments in nearly every post office in America. The WPA also built over 650,000 miles of roads, almost 125,000 bridges, over 125,000 public buildings, over 8,000 parks, and 853 landing fields for airplanes. WPA workers also managed the recreational facilities they had built. Extensive waste associated with the projects angered critics, but defenders of the New Deal said that those who were employed were now consumers again.

7 FEDERAL DEPOSIT INSURANCE CORPORATION

The Federal Deposit Insurance Corporation (FDIC) was created in 1933 by the Glass-Steagall Banking Act and guaranteed individual banking deposits up to $5,000 per account. The call for deposit insurance arose from the collapse of banks in the early part of the Great Depression. The language of the Glass-Steagall Act clearly blamed the Stock Market Crash and the subsequent Depression on the banking industry, and the law gave the Federal Reserve more power to prevent unsound banking practices in the future. The FDIC, then, was a reform measure designed to prevent a panic of the severity of the Great Depression from ever happening again, and the agency did restore confidence in the nation's banks over time. More banks were permitted to join the Federal Reserve and more branches of the Federal Reserve banks were opened. The main reforms of banking included the power to curtail speculative investments that used credit as well as the prevention of the banks' use of depositors' money in investment schemes.

8 SECURITIES AND EXCHANGE COMMISSION

The Securities and Exchange Commission (SEC) was a New Deal measure aimed at the third R, reform. The SEC became a licensing agency with the power to regulate the sale of stocks and other securities by denying licenses to those exchanges using unscrupulous practices. Begun by the Securities Exchange Act of 1934, the SEC prohibited price-manipulation schemes like the pump-and-dump conspiracies, insider trading, and excessive margin buying. All of these measures were designed to hold in check the wild speculation that had led to the Stock Market Crash, but the SEC went on to develop a system of brakes to slow the market in times of large sell-offs, and today it requires corporations trading on licensed stock exchanges to publish reports of their companies' financial information.

9 SOCIAL SECURITY

As a result of some of the radical critics of the New Deal, Franklin D. Roosevelt pursued policies of unemployment insurance, old-age insurance, and a system of social services all wrapped up in the economic safety net called Social Security. Although some states had unemployment insurance, the New Deal federalized the program and began to collect taxes from employers that would be redistributed to the unemployed. Employees as well as employers were taxed to support the Social Security measures designed to help the old, orphans, and widows. Individuals who retired at the age of sixty-five beginning in 1942 would receive what amounted to federal pensions ranging from $10 to $85 per month depending on how many years the retirees had paid taxes into the system. Other payments were authorized to states to help them provide relief for the blind, the homeless, the crippled, and for dependent and delinquent children. The Social Security Administration also provided public health care for indigents, especially mothers with dependent children, as well as vocational training and job-seeking assistance to the unemployed. Of all the New Deal measures, the Social Security Administration has had the longest-lasting impact on American society even as it became increasingly hard to fund.

10 WAGNER ACT

This law created the National Labor Relations Board (NLRB) in 1935. The NLRB was to review the elections of labor leaders and certify them as legitimate in an effort to eliminate corruption in the collective bargaining process. The NLRB also heard testimony about workers' grievances and was the official agency through which the Roosevelt administration sought to intervene in labor issues. Along with the injunctions the president or federal courts could issue, the NLRB could issue cease-and-desist orders to address abuses. The Wagner Act reiterated that even in times of depression workers could join unions and bargain collectively with their employers through their chosen representatives. Similar to William Howard Taft's labor board during World War I, the NLRB allowed direct management of labor relations and therefore prevented many strikes in a time when the American economy could least afford them.

FAIR LABOR STANDARDS ACT

This 1938 law established several New Deal workplace principles. Minimum wages and maximum hours were set, and children under age sixteen were banned from working. These measures applied only to employees of businesses involved in interstate commerce, thus leaving many American workers unprotected.

11 RUBBER STAMP CONGRESS

Because Franklin D. Roosevelt (FDR) had Democratic majorities in the House of Representatives and in the Senate upon his election in 1932, the legislation of the New Deal passed during the First Hundred Days worked its way through the Congress with unprecedented speed. The emergency banking measures were passed on the day they were presented and thus went into effect immediately to address the banking crisis. Critics of the New Deal, however, said the Congress was simply a rubber stamp for whatever ideas FDR and his advisers presented and were thereby abdicating their responsibility to use checks and balances to prevent the executive branch from wielding dictatorial powers. Since FDR attempted to alter the Supreme Court and, for example, personally set the price of gold each day, it was disturbing to people to find their president wielding such power even in a crisis. Defenders of the Roosevelt administration said that FDR was using extreme measures to attempt to preserve the existing institutions of the American economy and government in a situation that otherwise might have led to widespread civic unrest and even revolution. Other presidents with substantial majorities in both houses of Congress have faced the "Rubber Stamp" charge when the phenomenon is really a natural part of the electoral process in a republic. The pendulum of power has swung back and forth through the twentieth century and maintained an overall moderate course. This fact still does not prevent both major parties from hurling identical slurs at each other.

12 DUST BOWL

The Dust Bowl referred to the drought that struck during the 1930s during the Great Depression. Giant dust storms were created when the topsoil from tilled fields that bore no crops was simply blown away in vast clouds that traveled hundreds of miles. Dust storms occurred with increasing severity and frequency from 1932 until they reached their peak in 1935 when it was estimated that one hundred million acres of land had been stripped. Dust clouds blocked out the sun and forced dirt into every crevice in homes throughout the Great Plains and the Midwest reaching as far east as Washington, D.C., where lawmakers passed the Soil Conservation Act to require the Department of Agriculture to prevent soil erosion. The drought helped farmers who could produce grain receive higher prices for their crops, and the Dust Bowl became the symbolic background for the entire Depression in Steinbeck's classic *The Grapes of Wrath* in which ruined farmers sold out to large corporate farms and moved west to California.

13 HUEY P. LONG

Jumping on the Progressive Reform resurgence bandwagon, certain national figures and politicians claimed that Franklin D. Roosevelt (FDR) had not gone far enough in the first New Deal measures. Governor Huey P. Long of Louisiana wanted more radical change. Long had been a populist lawyer who entered politics as a commissioner for a state transportation and communication agency through which he pushed Progressive reforms. He ran for governor against the oil-industry-backed New Orleans Democratic Party machine and won in 1928. He immediately taxed the oil interests to fund state projects like highways and schools. He then co-opted the political machine and engineered his election to the U.S. Senate while retaining the governorship. Back home he built highways and hospitals and expanded Louisiana State University while pushing radical reforms in Washington, D.C. By then the state referred to Huey Long as the "Kingfish," and Long capitalized on the name saying he wanted to make every man a king. He proposed that the federal government guarantee every American family a minimum annual income of $2,500. While running Louisiana as a virtual dictator, Long announced he would run for the presidency to further his agenda. In 1935, before his campaign could gain ground, Long was assassinated at the Capitol Building in Baton Rouge. Huey Long, Dr. Francis E. Townsend, and Father Charles E. Coughlin all presented the radical fringe that allowed the later New Deal to forward the legislation that led to Social Security.

14 AMERICAN LIBERTY LEAGUE

President Franklin D. Roosevelt had to deal with criticism of the New Deal from the right. The most prominent group on the right was the American Liberty League (founded in 1934), which consisted primarily of conservative businessmen. Many conservative critics saw the New Deal as socialism in disguise. Businessmen in the league saw New Deal regulations and programs as impingements on their freedom to conduct business; The National Industrial Recovery Agency was a favorite target of the group. The New Deal, they argued, had gone too far, pushing the government too far into new realms. The group supported conservative politicians of both parties and promoted the "open shop"—a business in which the employees are not required to join a union. FDR's "court packing" scheme added fuel to their attacks on the "dictator" Franklin D. Roosevelt. Many of the criticisms of the American Liberty League were echoed by Father Charles Coughlin, who used his popular national radio show to label FDR as a communist and a dictator. Coughlin had initially supported Roosevelt in 1932, but grew increasingly critical of the New Deal, adding anti-Semitic and even fascistic elements to his broadcast. The American Liberty League was most active from 1934 to 1936. After FDR's landslide victory in 1936, the group lost energy. It disbanded in 1940.

15 AFRICAN AMERICANS AND THE NEW DEAL

Many New Deal programs ignored African Americans, such as the Agricultural Adjustment Act, which did not help tenant farmers. Like many people who came out of the Progressive reform tradition, President Franklin D. Roosevelt was generally quiet on issues of race. As president, he was wary of losing the support of the southern wing of the Democratic Party, so he did not push for civil rights legislation. One of the main frustrations of many civil rights activists was that FDR refused to endorse federal anti-lynching legislation. The issue of lynching had been the subject of a nationwide campaign led by Ida B. Wells starting in in the 1890s. Her journalism dispelled many of the myths around lynching, most importantly, that lynching was carried out in response to the crime of interracial rape. Despite FDR's reluctance to take the lead in civil-rights or anti-lynching legislation, the majority of African-Americans voters switched their allegiance from the party of Lincoln (the Republicans) to the Democratic Party in the 1936 election. The percentage of African Americans who voted for FDR went from 23 percent in 1932 to 71 percent in 1936. There are several reasons for this historic shift. First Lady Eleanor Roosevelt and Interior Secretary Harold Ickes did champion civil rights causes. Also, the president met periodically with a group of African-American advisors, called the "Black Cabinet." Finally, African Americans believed that Roosevelt, despite his shortcomings, was attempting to improve conditions for poor and working-class people.

MARIAN ANDERSON

Marian Anderson was one of the most renowned opera singers of the twentieth century. In 1939, the Daughters of the American Revolution refused permission for Anderson, who was African-American, to perform to an integrated audience at Constitution Hall. Eleanor Roosevelt organized a concert by Anderson on the steps of the Lincoln Memorial that was attended by 75,000 people and was heard by a radio audience in the millions.

THE "SCOTTSBORO BOYS"

The racial biases of the justice system in the 1930s were demonstrated in the highly publicized "Scottsboro Boys" case (1931–1935). Nine African-American youths were convicted of rape in Alabama on flimsy evidence. In 1932, the Supreme Court reversed most of the convictions. A retrial found the defendants again guilty, even after one of the alleged victims admitted fabricating her story.

16 SICK-CHICKEN CASE

This 1935 Supreme Court case was just the type of obstructionism that caused Franklin D. Roosevelt (FDR) such consternation. His National Recovery Administration (NRA) set up by the National Industrial Recovery Act was deemed unconstitutional as it applied to the operation of the Schechter Poultry Corporation. The NRA set codes for poultry workers including maximum hours of work and minimum wages. The suit against the Schechter company claimed that the poultry supplier had resisted the codes and the inspections that were meant to enforce them. The Supreme Court in its ruling first declared that the executive branch was exerting too much power over the economy. The Court said that FDR's codes against "unfair competition" were too ambiguous to actually enforce and that federal law did not apply to the Schechter Corporation because its alleged offenses occurred entirely within one state, New York.

17 ELECTION OF 1936

The Republican Party attacked the New Deal in the Election of 1936 saying that Franklin D. Roosevelt (FDR) had begun to make laws himself, many of which were unconstitutional. They decried the violation of free enterprise represented by the federal government's participation in the economy. By 1936 even some conservative Democrats supported a curtailment of New Deal policies. Even FDR had slowed the use of deficit spending prior to the election. Still, the Republicans and their Democratic allies submitted no specific plan to the people of America that they could perceive as helpful during the ongoing Depression. FDR merely stood on his record of action, and the Dust Bowl and downturn in the economy after the easing of federal spending did the rest. He said, "The true conservative seeks to protect the system of private property and free enterprise by correcting such injustices and inequalities as arise from it." In the election, FDR carried every state but Maine and Vermont, piling up a smashing 523 to 8 margin in the Electoral College. Majorities were maintained for the Democratic Party in both houses of Congress. FDR interpreted the Election of 1936 as a mandate from the American people to restart deficit spending, which he did in earnest. The false conclusion about the spending was revealed, however, in that the American economy did not rebound in the latter half of the 1930s despite larger expenditures than ever before. FDR went on to say, famously, in his inauguration that, "I see one-third of a nation ill-housed, ill-clad, ill-nourished."

> **HATCH ACT**
>
> Passed in 1939, this law forbade civil servants working in the executive branch from participating in partisan political activities. The highest executive officials like the president, vice president, and others were excluded. Public money and public service were supposed to be above being used for political ends.

18 COURT-PACKING SCHEME

After his landslide victory in the Election of 1936, Franklin D. Roosevelt (FDR) chafed under the continued resistance toward the New Deal by the Supreme Court. Early in 1937 he submitted a plan to Congress to reorganize the Court by increasing the number of judges from nine to as many as fifteen if those over the age of seventy failed to retire. He also proposed many changes to the lower federal courts that would make it more difficult for the judicial branch to impede the progress of his second New Deal. The proposal met with sharp criticism and the accusation that FDR was merely trying to "pack" the Supreme Court with his pliant appointees to overbalance the conservatives who lingered there. Opponents of the measure claimed that it would destroy the independence of the Court and effectively end the checks and balances inherent in the U.S. Constitution on an already overpowerful executive. Even Democrats in Congress broke with FDR over the proposed changes. Chief Justice Charles Evans Hughes pointed out that the Supreme Court was not behind in its caseload. FDR defended the measures in speeches and fireside chats. Meanwhile, the Supreme Court actually supported the constitutionality of the Social Security Act and the Wagner Labor Relations Act and other New Deal measures. The original proposal thus never made it out of the Senate. FDR's image was tainted by his impatience, and legislation became harder to achieve. By constitutional means FDR was later able to replace seven justices on the Supreme Court before his death in 1945.

19 JOHN L. LEWIS

Lewis was an Illinois coal miner who became a representative for the American Federation of Labor (AFL) and eventually the president of the United Mine Workers (UMW) in 1920. He called crippling strikes in bituminous coal mines that led to victories for the mine workers. Lewis rose to be the vice president of the AFL but split off in 1938 to form the Congress of Industrial Organizations or CIO. He supported Franklin D. Roosevelt (FDR) in the Election of 1936 but later withdrew his support. After World War II, Lewis called another massive strike that caused President Harry S. Truman to seize the mines just as Theodore Roosevelt had threatened to do. Lewis defied an injunction and was convicted of contempt of court, but after the strike received all the UMW demands from the mine owners. Lewis was venerated by coal miners as a result and remained president of the UMW until his death in 1960.

20 CONGRESS OF INDUSTRIAL ORGANIZATIONS

Begun by John L. Lewis as the Committee for Industrial Organizations (CIO) within the American Federation of Labor (AFL), the CIO eventually split off to become its own organization. Lewis believed that industries like coal mining, steel and rubber production, and automobile manufacturing were thwarting the goals of labor because they involved so much unskilled labor. He parted from the AFL to include skilled and unskilled workers in a successful national organization that became the AFL's chief rival. Four million laborers bolted the AFL to join the CIO when it formed in 1938, and by 1945 CIO membership rose to six million. The CIO moved next to purge its ranks of communists and expelled eleven unions with communist ties. By 1955 the old division about skilled and unskilled workers had become so ambiguous that the two major unions joined to become the AFL-CIO.

THE BIG PICTURE

1. The climax of Progressive Reform came in the New Deal policies of Franklin D. Roosevelt during the Great Depression.

2. The Roosevelt administration, backed by a Democratic Congress, experimented boldly with the power of the federal government to regulate the economy and to provide for the welfare of its citizens.

3. The extent to which the New Deal controlled the economy with social welfare programs and business regulation became controversial, especially because the funding of the programs came from deficit spending.

4. Critics of the New Deal ranged from those who thought Franklin D. Roosevelt had not gone far enough to those who believed he abused the powers of the executive branch and undermined the foundation of free-market capitalism that was the basis of the American Dream.

5. An objective assessment of the New Deal era must balance the prolonging of the Great Depression through often contradictory federal policies with the fact that Franklin D. Roosevelt was personally responsible for maintaining the unity and tenacity of the American people in the face of both the Great Depression and World War II.

World War II

30

No realistic American can expect from a dictator's peace, international generosity, or return to true independence, or world disarmament, or freedom of expression, or freedom of religion—or even good business.

—Franklin D. Roosevelt, State of the Union address, 1941

TIMELINE	
1936	The Nye Commission holds its final hearings
1939	Adolf Hitler orders invasion of Poland; George C. Marshall is promoted to full general
1941	Congress passes the Lend-Lease Act; Douglas MacArthur takes command in the Far East; The Japanese Empire attacks Pearl Harbor, Hawaii
1942	FDR's administration establishes the War Production Board; Japanese internment begins; Battle of Midway; The U.S. government launches the first Rosie the Riveter campaign; The Holocaust begins as the Nazis build six extermination camps in Poland
1943	George S. Patton takes command in North Africa
1944	Battle of Normandy (D-Day)
1945	Battle of Iwo Jima; The United Nations is founded; Atomic bombs produced by the Manhattan Project are dropped on Japan
1946	The first series of the Nuremberg Trials are completed

OVERVIEW

After World War I, public sentiment pushed the United States away from engagement in the affairs in Europe. Isolationists carried the day in 1920 in the American rejection of the Treaty of Versailles, which precluded American membership in the League of Nations. This isolationist sentiment continued into the 1930s. However, as the world degenerated in the 1930s, President Franklin D. Roosevelt guided the United States into a more engaged role on the world stage.

In the 1930s, the Nazi war machine of Germany combined forces with the fascist dictator of Italy, Benito Mussolini, and the fascist war ministers of Japan to form the Rome/Berlin/Tokyo Axis. These dictatorial governments all took aggressive actions: Japan attacked China in 1931; Germany occupied the demilitarized Rhineland in 1936, annexed Austria in 1937, and occupied Czechoslovakia in 1939; and Italy conquered Ethiopia in 1936. After Hitler attacked Poland in 1939, Great Britain and France quickly declared war on Germany, beginning World War II. Later, the Soviet Union joined the war when Hitler attacked it (1941). The United States did not initially join the war, but took steps away from neutrality and toward engagement. After the attack on Pearl Harbor (1941), neutrality was no longer an option. Americans came to see World War II as more than a conventional military conflict. As details of Japanese wartime atrocities and of the Holocaust began to emerge, many Americans came to see the war as a desperate fight for freedom and democracy against powerful militarist and fascist forces.

In many ways, World War II required the participation of the entire American public, not simply members of the military. These efforts created a sense of unity and common cause in the country. Starting in 1942, the Office of Price Administration began rationing key commodities to civilians. The War Production Board, and later the Office of War Mobilization, oversaw the conversion from civilian industry to war production. Millions of Americans were recruited to work in war-related factories, including African Americans and women, as the Great Depression quickly came to an end.

The United States assumed a leadership role in the Allied victory over the Axis powers. American leaders participated in joint political and military efforts with the other Allied countries. In addition, American industrial production and advances in technology and science played important parts in the war effort. Finally, the commitment of large sections of the American public to victory and to the advancement of democratic ideals helped the overall war effort. Through the first two years of American involvement in World War II, the United States sent more of its troops to the Pacific theater than to Europe. Even though the defeat of Hitler was a top priority for the United States, it was Japan that had directly attacked the United States. In June 1944, American and allied troops stormed the beaches of Normandy, France, and began pushing Hitler's forces back toward Germany. In order to defeat Japan, the United States began employing a strategy by the end of 1943 called "island hopping" (also known as "leapfrogging") to capture key Japanese-held islands in the Pacific. The United States used the newly-developed atomic bomb twice on Japan in August 1945. Soon after the second bomb, Japan surrendered, ending World War II.

World War II was a cataclysmic event that profoundly transformed the nations that had participated, including the United States. World War II set in motion a series of demographic, political, and social trends that would shape American history for the remainder of the twentieth century. The "baby boom," the population shift to the "Sun Belt" of the West, and the growth of suburbia are all connected to the experience of the war. Wartime participation inspired both African Americans and women, setting the stage for the civil rights movement and the women's liberation movement. The United States did not retreat into an isolationist stance after the war, as the wartime alliance of the United States and the Soviet Union would soon degenerate into a cold war.

1 FASCISM

Fascism was an economic, political, and societal system whereby intense nationalism subsumed individual citizens into a coordinated militancy. Fascist nations were run by dictators who mobilized the aggrieved sentiments of their nations through powerful rhetoric and patriotic spectacles in order to achieve totalitarian control. Fascist governments had control of the means of production and were thus a form of socialism but left industry in private hands and openly attacked Marxists, socialists, and communists. Dissenters were harassed, imprisoned, or murdered just as in other totalitarian states. Benito Mussolini fabricated fascism as a replacement for the Marxism he abandoned during World War I, and in his own words as the fascist leader of Italy he described fascism thus: "The citizen in the Fascist State is no longer a selfish individual who has the anti-social right of rebelling against any law of the Collectivity. The Fascist State with its cooperative conception puts men and their possibilities into productive work and interprets for them the duties they have to fulfill." For the fascist leaders of World War II, the work their citizens had to fulfill was the domination of their neighbors in aggressive imperialism and militant nationalism.

2 ADOLF HITLER

Hitler was born in Austria and aspired to the life of an artist, but the best he could do was peddle his postcards. He was relieved when World War I broke out and offered the opportunity for a life of discipline and heroism. Hitler served on the front lines and was highly decorated for valor even as a corporal. After the war he rose to leadership in a political organization that would eventually become the National Socialist, or Nazi, Party. His oratorical skills inspired an attempted attack on the government in 1923 that failed, but while in prison he crafted his life vision in a work entitled *Mein Kampf.* After serving nine months of a five-year prison term he was released and immediately returned to political agitation. Hitler rose to power in a legitimate appointment as chancellor but ultimately combined the offices of president and chancellor to become a fascist dictator. Hitler's railing against the Treaty of Versailles, communism, and a supposed conspiracy of Jews increased his power until he was able to silence his enemies and launch the expansion of the Third Reich that began World War II. The Nazi Party used propaganda, intimidation, and terrorism to launch both a seemingly unstoppable blitzkrieg attack on neighboring countries in Europe, and also the Holocaust. When the Nazi forces were forced back to Berlin, Hitler committed suicide in an underground bunker in 1945.

> ### QUARANTINE SPEECH
> Among FDR's first actions amid the growing world crisis was to deliver this speech in 1937. He stated that the United States would break off trade and other interactions with dictators who had aggressively taken land from their neighbors.

3 NYE COMMISSION

In 1934, the U.S. Senate had set up a commission under Senator Gerald Nye of North Dakota to investigate any connection between American munitions manufacturers and the country's involvement in World War I. The Nye Commission focused on the large profits such companies had made even before America entered the war and asserted, without conclusive evidence, that lobbying on the part of the munitions manufacturers had persuaded President Wilson and the Congress to declare war against the Central Powers. As Hitler rose to power in Germany, the Nye Committee worked until 1936 to preserve an isolationist stance in American foreign policy. The Neutrality Acts of 1935, 1936, and 1937 were a direct result and forbade American manufacturers to sell war materials to combatant nations if war erupted. Neutrality of this extent was designed to prevent American ships from being sunk by German submarines and repeating the process that dragged the United States into the Great War. A 1939 Neutrality Act eventually permitted combatant nations to buy American arms as long as they shipped the goods on their own ships in a policy called "cash and carry."

4 THE LEND-LEASE ACT

In early 1941, Franklin D. Roosevelt (FDR) signed into law the Lend-Lease Act, a measure to help primarily Great Britain receive war supplies despite having run out of credit. The law allowed the president to designate which countries were acting in the interests of the United States and, in a massive outpouring of Dollar Diplomacy, to open the faucet wide for the transfer of resources. Originally designed to keep America from having to enter World War II, the Lend-Lease Act continued until 1945 long after the United States had joined the Allied Powers. In total, $50.6 billion worth of supplies was given in this manner.

GOOD NEIGHBOR POLICY

This policy of FDR (and Hoover) departed from the interventionist attitude in Latin America established by the Roosevelt Corollary. FDR avoided the use of military force when Mexico continued its policy of nationalization of oil reserves, and U.S. relations improved across the region.

5 PEARL HARBOR

On Sunday, December 7, 1941, the naval and air forces of Japan conducted a sneak attack on the U.S. naval base at Pearl Harbor, Hawaii. The attack damaged all eight of the American battleships moored in the harbor and destroyed three. Nineteen total ships were lost along with around 150 planes. Of casualties there were over 2,400 killed and nearly 1,200 wounded. The next day the U.S. Congress declared war on Japan with only one dissenting vote. Three days later Germany and Italy declared war against the United States. Because of the nature of naval warfare in World War II, the United States was extremely fortunate that her aircraft carriers were at sea at the time of the Pearl Harbor attack.

6 WAR PRODUCTION BOARD

Franklin D. Roosevelt launched the War Production Board (WPB) in 1942 to mobilize all aspects of the American economy to fight and win the war. The WPB halted on nonessential domestic New Deal projects and redirected all major industries from making consumer products to making war material including jeeps, trucks, tanks, ships, and planes. The WPB achieved almost complete employment, especially because so many men from the ages of eighteen to forty-four were drafted for military service. Having helped America win the war and end the Great Depression, the WPB disbanded and allowed the American economy to return to civilian uses in the control of private industry.

BRACERO PROGRAM

The U.S. and Mexican governments agreed to initiate this program in 1942 to allow Mexican agricultural workers to boost the wartime labor force in U.S. fields. The program continued until 1964.

7 RATIONING AND RECYCLING

During the war, there were shortages of key items because of the needs of the military. Starting in 1941, the Office of Price Administration began rationing key commodities to civilians, such as gasoline and tires. Next, the government began rationing food—sugar, meat, coffee, lard, butter, and many other items. Families were given ration books, and would use ration stamps, along with cash, when they purchased the effected items. The system was designed not only to conserve materials for the military, but also to keep inflation down. During times of war inflation is a constant threat, due to the lack of consumer goods and the additional money that people have in their pockets from all the work available in defense-related industries. Government efforts to control inflation were moderately successful; inflation was about half as much as it was during World War I. In addition, children organized Tin Can Clubs to collect scrap metal to be melted down to produce weapons and ammunition. To promote the rationing and recycling effort, the Office of War Information put out a series of propaganda posters, urging Americans to do their part for the war effort. A famous poster encouraged carpooling by showing a driver in a car with an outline of Hitler in the passenger seat. The caption read, "When you drive alone, you drive with Hitler." The campaign asserted that wasting resources hurt the war effort and helped the enemy.

8 ROSIE THE RIVETER

Even though women had worked in war industries during World War I, the New Deal era frowned on their participation in industry when so many men were out of work. When large numbers of men were drafted into the military for World War II, however, women helped fulfill the requirements of the War Production Board. Rosie the Riveter became an iconographic example of the importance of women to the war effort as the accomplishments of an actual riveter in an airplane factory were celebrated in order to draw more women into the workforce. At the beginning of World War II, women made up only one-quarter of the workforce, but by the end they made up one-third. Proving the slogan, "We Can Do It," six million women entered the workforce during the war years, half working in war factories in traditionally male jobs.

9 JAPANESE INTERNMENT

Since the 1907 Gentlemen's Agreement made with Japan by Theodore Roosevelt, Japanese immigrants were supposed to be given better treatment in Hawaii and California where most lived. After the Pearl Harbor attack, however, anti-Japanese sentiment seethed in many Americans who assumed Japanese-Americans had somehow aided Japan in planning the surprise attack. Franklin D. Roosevelt's (FDR's) administration bowed to pressure from citizens and authorized the removal of around 110,000 Americans of Japanese descent from sensitive coastal areas where it was thought they might collaborate with the enemy. In February of 1942, FDR ordered that both *Isei* (Japanese immigrants) and *Nisei* (native-born Japanese-Americans) be interned in inland camps that were later thought to bear a frightening resemblance to concentration camps in Germany. While generally well treated within the internment camps, Japanese-Americans suffered humiliation and loss of private property and businesses. Some young men volunteered or were drafted from within the internment camps and went on to serve with great distinction in the U.S. armed forces as World

War II unfolded. Many years after the end of Japanese internment, Presidents Carter and Reagan investigated the events and signed legislation giving each surviving internee $20,000 in reparations.

10 "DOUBLE V" CAMPAIGN

The National Association for the Advancement of Colored People (NAACP) encouraged African Americans to take part in the "Double V" campaign—promoting victory against fascism abroad and victory against racism in their home country. Ultimately, 125,000 African Americans served overseas during World War II. The most famous segregated African-American units were the Tuskegee Airmen and the 761st Tank Battalion. African Americans also contributed to the war effort on the home front. African Americans joined millions of other Americans in producing materials in factories. The Great Migration that began in World War I continued, with African Americans moving to the West Coast in addition to moving to northern industrial cities. Initially, many war industries were reluctant to hire African Americans. An important African-American labor leader, A. Phillip Randolph, the president of the Brotherhood of Sleeping Car Porters, planned a public demonstration in Washington, D.C. in 1941 to protest discrimination in war-related industries. When the Roosevelt administration heard of these plans, it worked out a bargain. Roosevelt issued Executive Order 8802, banning discrimination in war-related industries and Randolph called off the march.

11 DOUGLAS MACARTHUR

Having graduated from the U.S. Military Academy in 1903, Douglas MacArthur saw service in the Philippines and Japan in peacekeeping forces and saw combat in World War I. MacArthur was wounded twice during World War I despite the fact that he was the commanding general of an infantry brigade. He spent the rest of his career in the Far East, which made him the perfect candidate to command all the American forces in the Pacific Theater of World War II. After escaping the Japanese as they took over the Philippines, MacArthur employed a strategy of "leapfrogging" around unnecessary targets in Japan's empire and led the Allied campaigns that eventually threatened the Japanese mainland. After the war was over he commanded the occupation of Japan and the United Nations forces that repelled a communist attack on South Korea in the Korean War. As a result of a disagreement about strategy, MacArthur was fired by President Harry S. Truman in 1951 and said in a famous address to Congress, "Old soldiers never die, they just fade away."

> **GEORGE C. MARSHALL**
>
> Marshall was the chief of staff of the Army through World War II. His service in the war is overshadowed by the famous generals he assigned, but it was Marshall's grand strategy that the Allies pursued to push back the Axis powers. After the war, he became secretary of state and architect of the plan to aid European nations that bears his name.

12 GEORGE S. PATTON

A Scots-Irish Californian, Patton graduated from West Point and was a veteran of Pershing's hunt for Pancho Villa as well as World War I where he first studied tank warfare. In World War II Patton commanded armored cavalry units in nearly every major campaign in North Africa and Europe. His insistence on rigorous discipline and aggressive offensive tactics belied the fact that his troops sustained fewer casualties than the units serving under other generals. General Patton vied for prominence in key actions with British general Bernard Montgomery such that one of General

Dwight Eisenhower's main accomplishments was keeping these rivals for glory fighting the Germans instead of each other. In the campaign on the European mainland Patton's forces routinely outdistanced both supply lines and other Allied forces. General Patton was a man of many faults, but his contemporaries said of him that he was, ". . . unrivalled in his ability to inspire and lead large forces of men in a desperate and ultimately victorious struggle against a determined enemy." Patton died in an automobile accident in Europe shortly after World War II ended.

13 BATTLE OF MIDWAY

This battle was the turning point in the Allied victory over Japan. For three days American carrier-based aircraft exchanged fire with the invasion force of Admiral Yamamoto. Admiral Chester W. Nimitz had guessed the Japanese plan based on intelligence reports, and through valorous service and good fortune the navy bombers destroyed four of Japan's aircraft carriers. The U.S. Navy lost only one carrier and not only saved Midway Island as a crucial military base but equalized Japanese and American naval strength from that point on.

14 D-DAY

Though Allied forces had clawed their way onto the European continent in Italy, the invasion of Normandy beginning on June 6, 1944, was the largest and most important amphibious assault in world history. While the Russians pushed Germany from the east, the D-Day invasion was the crucial "Second Front" to divide Germany's forces and bring about the end of the Nazi regime. U.S. General Dwight D. Eisenhower planned and ordered Operation Overlord that saw three divisions of American and British paratroopers dropped behind enemy lines and the main American, British, and Canadian forces land on Utah, Omaha, Gold, Juno, and Sword beaches. A beachhead was established from which more and more men and machines were unloaded that eventually allowed the Allied Powers to reclaim France and push the Nazis back to Germany and destruction.

15 IWO JIMA

This island became the most famous of the amphibious assaults that were part of Douglas MacArthur's island-hopping strategy largely because of Joe Rosenthal's famous photograph of the raising of an American flag on Mount Suribachi, the island's dormant volcano. Before surmounting that obstacle, however, American Marines suffered horrendously violent assaults from the Japanese forces that had burrowed into the volcanic rock of the island to make defenses. Sworn to fight to the end, only 212 of the twenty-two thousand Japanese defenders were taken prisoner. Almost seven thousand Marines were killed and over eighteen thousand wounded. The importance of Iwo Jima and Okinawa was that these islands were "unsinkable aircraft carriers" from which long-range bombers could attack the mainland of Japan.

16 YALTA CONFERENCE

The United States played a lead role in shaping the post-World War II world through several important peace conferences and settlements. The most important of these conferences was the Yalta Conference, held in February 1945. It was the last meeting of the "big three"— Prime Minister Winston Churchill of Great Britain; Joseph Stalin, leader of the Soviet Union; and President Franklin D. Roosevelt. At Yalta, a coastal city in Crimea, the three leaders agreed to divide Germany into four military zones of occupation (the fourth zone would be occupied by France). Stalin agreed to allow free elections in Poland in the future, with a Soviet-dominated interim government immediately following the war. Also at the meeting, secret agreements were made allowing for Soviet control of Outer Mongolia, the Kurile Islands, and part of Sakhalin Island, as well as Soviet railroad rights in Manchuria. Critics later faulted Roosevelt and Churchill for "abandoning" Poland and the rest of Eastern Europe to communist forces. However, there was little the United States and Britain could do to dislodge the Red Army from Eastern Europe, short of starting a third world war.

17 HIROSHIMA AND NAGASAKI

The dropping of atomic bombs on the Japanese cities of Hiroshima and Nagasaki on two separate days in August 1945 led to Japan's surrender within days. The development of the atomic bomb was the result of a secret race with Germany and Japan to be first to harness the destructive power of an atomic reaction. Albert Einstein had warned President Franklin D. Roosevelt that the Germans were conducting research in atomic energy for this purpose, and the United States responded by pouring incredible amounts of natural resources, manpower, and technical expertise into this effort. The project began in offices in New York City—hence named the Manhattan Project—and soon spread to facilities in different parts of the United States. J. Robert Oppenheimer was responsible for overseeing the $2 billion project. With the defeat of Japan in pitched battles in Iwo Jima and Okinawa in the spring of 1945, Japan had lost all of its possessions. As American forces were preparing for a final onslaught on the Japanese home island, President Harry S. Truman learned in July that the United States had just successfully tested an atomic bomb and that more bombs were ready for use. It was in this context that President Truman decided to drop this powerful bomb—first on Hiroshima on August 6, 1945, and then, when Japan did not immediately surrender, on Nagasaki on August 9. Over 105,000 people were killed immediately in the two cities with severe, long-term health consequences—radiation sickness, terrible burns, and cancer—for thousands of people. Some historians have been critical of Truman's decision to use the atomic bomb, asserting that Japan was ready to negotiate a surrender before the dropping of the bomb; they speculate that the bomb was more important in establishing dominance in the coming Cold War than in defeating Japan. Others contend that the decision to drop the bomb was reasonable and may have saved many hundreds of thousands of lives by bringing the war to a quick conclusion.

18 HOLOCAUST

Having claimed that the Jews of Europe were conspiring for the destruction of Germany, Hitler set about isolating and persecuting them immediately upon taking office in 1933. The nine million Jews of Europe lived largely in countries that would eventually fall under German control, and as the Nazis consolidated power over Central Europe they initiated what they called the Final Solution. The word *Holocaust* meant "sacrifice by fire," and the Final Solution would eventually kill six million Jews and hundreds of thousands of other victims the Nazis found undesirable like Gypsies, the physically and mentally handicapped, socialists, communists, Jehovah's Witnesses, and homosexuals. Jews under German occupation were first quarantined in ghettos. Killing squads followed the front-line German troops and committed mass murder, but then Jews and other victims were rounded up into concentration camps to perform slave labor for the Nazi war machine. Ultimately, many of the concentration camps became death camps as Jews were exterminated and their bodies burned with mass-production efficiency. Hitler diverted large amounts of resources to the Final Solution that did not stop until Allied forces liberated the camps by force.

19 NUREMBERG TRIALS

A body called the International Military Tribunal tried twenty-two Nazi leaders who survived the war for crimes against peace, crimes against humanity, and other war crimes. The trials lasted from late 1945 into 1946 and established a precedent of holding the instigators of aggressive war accountable as well as perpetrators of atrocities and genocides like the Holocaust. Twelve of the defendants were sentenced to death. The rest were given varying prison sentences from life down to ten years while three were acquitted. A similar trial of twenty-eight Japanese war criminals was held in Tokyo. Seven of the Japanese defendants, including Hideki Tojo, were sentenced to death. As for the fascist leader of Italy, Benito Mussolini, he was mobbed when caught trying to escape Italy in 1945 and shot by his own people.

> **DUMBARTON OAKS CONFERENCE**
>
> In 1944, representatives from the United States, the United Kingdom, the Republic of China, and the USSR met at this estate in Washington, D.C., to propose the foundation of an international organization that became the United Nations.

20 UNITED NATIONS

The phrase *United Nations* came from a term Franklin D. Roosevelt (FDR) used to refer to the Allied Powers. The idea of the United Nations arose from the International Peace Conference that established the International Court at The Hague, but was more fully elaborated by Woodrow Wilson in his Fourteen Point Address. The League of Nations was founded as a result of the Treaty of Versailles that ended World War I. FDR and Winston Churchill reiterated the need for such an organization during their Atlantic Conference even though the League of Nations had been unable or unwilling to stop the rise of fascist empires. In 1945, fifty nations met at the San Francisco Conference to establish a charter for the United Nations even before the end of World War II. When the document was ratified by the five permanent members of the Security Council (China, France, the Soviet Union, the United Kingdom, and the United States), in October of 1945 the United Nations was born. The first resolution adopted by the General Assembly of the United Nations was for the peaceful use of atomic energy and the elimination of atomic weapons.

THE BIG PICTURE

1. The menace of aggressive war was unleashed upon Europe and Asia by fascist regimes in Italy, Germany, and Japan beginning in 1937 with the Japanese invasion of China and in 1939 with the German invasion of Poland.

2. The United States tried to remain neutral as World War II erupted, but the surprise attack by the Japanese on Pearl Harbor, Hawaii, forced the nation to join the Allied Powers in the war against the Axis Powers.

3. A full-scale mobilization of the American economy was initiated to meet the demands of war production, and women swelled the ranks of the workforce as millions of American men served in the military.

4. World War II was the worst war in history because of its global scale but also because of new technical innovations that made aerial bombing, ground warfare, and sea warfare more deadly.

5. The United States helped the Allies secure victory in Europe but fought largely alone against the Japanese who were turned back at the Battle of Midway and finally surrendered after two atomic bombs were dropped on cities on the Japanese mainland.

Cold War Foreign Policy, from Truman to Kennedy

31

*The main element of any United States policy toward the
Soviet Union must be that of a long-term, patient but firm and
vigilant containment of Russian expansive tendencies.*

—George F. Kennan, "The Sources of Soviet Conflict," 1947

TIMELINE

1945	FDR dies and Harry S. Truman becomes president
1946	The policy of containment is first articulated in the Cold War
1946–1964	The Baby Boom generation's birth spans eighteen years
1947	Congress passes the National Security Act; The WW II "OSS" becomes the Central Intelligence Agency (CIA); President Truman delivers a speech announcing the Truman Doctrine
1948	Marshall Plan begins; President Truman launches his Fair Deal domestic program
1948–1949	Berlin Airlift
1949	NATO is founded
1950	Senator Joseph McCarthy launches McCarthyism
1950–1953	Korean War
1952	Dwight D. Eisenhower is elected president
1955	Warsaw Pact is founded
1956	Elvis Presley first appears on television; Congress passes the Federal Highway Act
1957	Intercontinental ballistic missiles are first deployed by the Soviet Union
1958	Congress passes the National Defense Education Act
1960	U-2 Incident

OVERVIEW

The Cold War began after World War II, when two former allies, the United States and the
Soviet Union, emerged as rival superpowers. Tensions existed between the United States
and the Soviet Union from the time of the Russian Revolution (1917) when the United States

opposed the communists. However, historians tend to date the beginning of the Cold War from the close of World War II. After the war, the United States believed the Soviets were intent upon extending their control over Europe. As the war ended, the Soviet Union left its Red Army troops occupying Eastern Europe, where the countries became Soviet satellites. The Soviets indicated they would allow free elections in Poland, but instead they installed a puppet regime. The United States worried the Soviets would try to push into Western Europe. The leader of the Soviet Union, Joseph Stalin, insisted that he only wanted to have friendly nations on his borders after numerous attacks from Western powers on Russia and the Soviet Union.

The United States adopted a policy of containment, attempting to limit the influence of the Soviet Union and communism internationally. Toward this end, the United States sought to build a system of international security as well as a stable global economy. The United States took several important steps to contain communism, including sending military aid to Greece and Turkey, initiating the Marshall Plan in Europe, helping form the North Atlantic Treaty Organization, and airlifting supplies into Berlin during the Berlin blockade.

The initial conflicts of the Cold War occurred in Europe, but, by the late 1940s, American policy makers became increasingly concerned about events in Asia. The United States Cold War policies had mixed results in Asia. The United States successfully ushered Japan toward democracy and economic self-sufficiency. The United States also granted independence to the Philippines in 1946. However, China proved to be a difficult problem for President Harry S. Truman. China had been enmeshed in an ongoing civil war. The United States had allied itself with the Nationalist side, led by Jiang Jieshi (Chiang Kai-shek). However, the opposition Communist Party, led by Mao Zedong (Mao Tse-tung), was amassing a huge following among the poor rural population of China. Mao's forces won in 1949 and the People's Republic of China was established. Republicans accused President Truman of "losing" China, although in reality there was not much that could have been done to prevent the eventual outcome. In June 1950, North Korean troops, using Soviet equipment, invaded South Korea. President Truman decided to commit troops to support South Korea and managed to secure United Nations sponsorship. The United States and allied forces successfully pushed North Korean troops out of South Korea; the war ended as it began—with North Korea and South Korea divided at the thirty-eighth parallel.

After the Korean War, the United States pursued containment in several different ways, including a robust nuclear weapons program and the Space Race with the Soviet Union. In the developing world, the United States supported certain governments and helped to topple others, based on which side they favored in the Cold War, not on their level of commitment to democratic practices. For instance, in 1960, the United States approved of, and may have played a role in, the ouster of the first democratically elected leader of the Congo, Patrice Lumumba. By the early 1960s, Cold War concerns emerged closer to home. The Cuban Revolution of 1959 led to the presence of a Communist government ninety miles from Florida. Also in the early 1960s, the United States became more involved in defending the government of South Vietnam. At first, the United States sent advisors and a limited amount of personnel; by 1965, the United States was involved in full scale war in Vietnam (see Chapter 35).

The United States changed in many ways as a result of the Cold War. The country became much more engaged in world affairs and assumed the leading role in the opposition to communism. It developed the world's most powerful military and its most potent nuclear arsenal. At home, new governmental initiatives—from loyalty oaths to civil defense programs—were initiated during the Cold War (see Chapter 32). Some of these actions helped allay people's concerns about the threat of communism, while some initiatives might have added to people's fears.

1 HARRY S. TRUMAN

Truman served in the First World War as a captain of artillery and returned to enter Missouri politics as a part of the Pendergrass machine, an association he later repudiated. He rose to be a senator and vice president for Franklin D. Roosevelt's (FDR's) last election in 1944. He became president upon FDR's death in office, and then won the Election of 1948 in his own right. Overnight Truman had to learn of the secret atomic bomb project and then decided to authorize use of the bombs to end the war with Japan. He won reelection even though he lost the Congress in the midterm elections by coming out against the antilabor Taft-Hartley Act and coming out for an extension of New Deal programs Truman called the Fair Deal. No other peacetime president had ever faced such daunting foreign policy challenges as Truman who in his second term had to deal with the Cold War Soviet aggression in Europe *and* Chinese and North Korean aggression in Asia while negotiating the peace treaties with Germany and Japan.

2 COLD WAR

After World War II the United States and the Soviet Union, former allies, began to view each other with suspicion. The two superpowers wound up controlling the East and the West, but each viewed the actions of the other as aggressively expansionist. The conflict known as the Cold War became a bizarre chess game where espionage, the space race, and the arms race caused the opponents to feed off of each other's insecurities in a global competition where the stakes were total annihilation of the human race. The bizarre aspect of the conflict was that the threat of thermonuclear war kept the conflict from escalating to that point and prevented any direct clash between the superpowers or their surrogate nations from widening into a third world war. The Cold War lasted over forty years until the collapse of the Soviet Union left the United States as the incredulous victor. Along the way the superpowers used all possible means to align the rest of the nations into the "Free World" and the "Communist Bloc." The Cold War following so closely on the heels of World War II is what kept the United States from ever being able to seriously contemplate isolationism as a viable policy again.

3 CONTAINMENT

After Winston Churchill's 1946 observation that an "Iron Curtain," had fallen across Europe, the Western nations contemplated Russian imperial tendencies, now animated by communist zeal. The idea of containment of Soviet expansion originated with diplomat George Kennan, a Russian specialist in the American Foreign Service who later served as ambassador to the Soviet Union. He explained his policy in a famous 1947 article that he signed only as "X." He said containment was a political solution to a political problem rather than a military solution to a military problem. Still, he recommended the consistent application of counterforce to any shifting Soviet geographical designs to spread communism throughout the world. Containment drove the foreign policy decisions of the United States for the next forty years even though Kennan himself thought it became obsolete upon the death of Joseph Stalin and the discovery of animosity between Soviet and Chinese communists.

4 CENTRAL INTELLIGENCE AGENCY

While spying was nothing new in American history, the high stakes of the Cold War compelled the federal government to organize intelligence gathering on a global scale. The forerunner of the Central Intelligence Agency (CIA) was the World War II agency known as the Office of Strategic Services (OSS). Harry S. Truman discovered after the OSS was disbanded after the war that the position of the United States demanded the greater coordination and sophistication provided by the National Security Act. The CIA was charged with the responsibility not only of gathering intelligence but also of coordinating with other branches of the government like the Secret Service (also begun under Truman after a nearly successful assassination attempt) and the FBI. The CIA was therefore the warehouse for all military, diplomatic, and other forms of monitoring of information for national security purposes, and the director of the CIA operated as the chairman of the National Security Council. After a second National Security Act in 1949 the budget of the CIA as well as its activities was permitted to be clandestine.

5 TRUMAN DOCTRINE

Harry S. Truman acted on behalf of Turkey and Greece when the British announced in 1947 that they no longer possessed the means to look after these countries' welfare. In an address to Congress, Truman asked for $400 million to aid the countries saying that the United States should help any European nation in order to "support free peoples who are resisting attempted subjugation by armed minorities or outside pressures." Some critics noted that this policy was the exact opposite of the Monroe Doctrine and that the United Nations should take the lead role in organizing resistance to communist aggression, but Truman noted that the Soviet Union and the Chinese were able to thwart the designs of the United Nations by using their permanent seats on the Security Council. Therefore, Truman committed the United States to leadership in keeping Europe free from communism, a burden that subsequent Cold War presidents expanded.

6 MARSHALL PLAN

In keeping with the Truman Doctrine, George C. Marshall as secretary of state proposed that European nations should cooperate in a coordinated effort to rebuild their countries and keep them free from communist influence. By 1948 he proposed that the United States should pay for it. The Marshall Plan was said to be directed "not against any country or doctrine but against hunger, poverty, desperation, and chaos." The intentions of the aid, however, were to build up strong economies in Western Europe in order to maintain political stability and to thwart communist infiltration. The Soviets interpreted the generous measure as an imperialist plot, but the original pledge of $12 billion was provided without American territorial designs. The amount of aid rose to over $22 billion in four years as Truman expanded the Marshall Plan into his European Recovery Program. Analysts concluded that the plan was imminently successful and cheaper than the maintenance of conventional military forces that would have rendered the free nations of Europe merely American proxies. The expenditures of the Marshall Plan, the Truman Doctrine, the formation of the United Nations, the formation of the nation of Israel, and many others revealed the United States to have become the most generous nation of any in history during the Truman presidency alone.

7 BERLIN AIRLIFT

After General Eisenhower allowed the Soviets the glory (and the casualties) of capturing the German capital city of Berlin, the Soviets occupied half of the city. American, British, and French forces established zones in the western half. In the period of determining what should be done with Germany, the Soviets gradually cut off access to the city by ground because it lay entirely inside the eastern portion of Germany that they controlled. By 1948 this blockade of Berlin was total. The three western powers decided to supply the more than two million residents of West Berlin food, coal, and medical supplies via round-the-clock flights known as the Berlin Airlift. When the matter was referred to the United Nations, the Soviet Union used its veto power on the Security Council to block a compromise and then boycotted any further discussions. The Soviets watched the resolve of the West to maintain the flights for 321 days. Over 270,000 flights delivered 2.3 million tons of supplies as American policy toward the Soviets hardened. When the blockade was finally lifted in 1949, Berlin became a symbol of American resolve to win the Cold War. In response to massive migration from communist Berlin to free Berlin, the Soviets built the Berlin Wall.

8 NATO

The North Atlantic Treaty Organization (NATO) was formed when President Truman sought an arrangement with Canada for mutual security and wound up attracting twelve nations to the idea. A treaty was signed in Washington, D.C., in 1949 that committed all the NATO nations to the idea that an attack on one of their number was an attack on all of them. Each NATO nation was to take "individually and in concert with the other Parties, such action as it deems necessary, including the use of armed force, to restore and maintain the security of the North Atlantic area." NATO nations were to permit new nations to join the alliance upon the unanimous vote of the existing members, and Greece and Turkey joined by 1952. General Dwight D. Eisenhower was picked to coordinate the military component of the agreement, and his skill in diplomacy evidenced through the war years made NATO all the more successful in unifying the security effort. The treaty forming NATO marked the first time since abandoning the treaty with France after the War for Independence that the United States made a peacetime alliance. By 2009, twenty-eight nations belonged to NATO, many of them having previously been Soviet Bloc satellite nations.

9 WARSAW PACT

In a classic Cold War response the Soviet Union answered the formation of NATO with an organization of their own erroneously named the Warsaw Pact. Eight nations did meet in Poland in 1955 to form the alliance based on mutual security, but it quickly appeared evident that the Soviet Union considered the Eastern European Warsaw Pact nations to be its own empire. During the Cold War the Warsaw Pact nations combined their militaries under Soviet control twice to attack their own members, Hungary and Czechoslovakia, when the nations sought to operate independently. After the collapse of the Soviet Union the Warsaw Pact was dissolved in 1991.

10 KOREAN WAR

Korea had also been divided between Soviet and American influence after World War II, and as a result two competing worldviews took up residence on the Korean Peninsula. The United Nations tried merely to divide the country at the thirty-eighth parallel of latitude, but in 1950, North Korea crossed the border and invaded South Korea with the intention of uniting all of Korea under communist rule by force. Because North Korea was backed by the Soviet Union and later by Communist China, the Korean War became another dangerous Cold War showdown. Douglas MacArthur landed United Nations forces at both the southern extremity of the peninsula and behind North Korean lines at Inchon. This maneuver forced the communist aggressors back across the thirty-eighth parallel, and MacArthur's assault drove them up against the Chinese border. When massive wave attacks indicated that Chinese forces were invading the peninsula, the United Nations forces were driven back to a cease-fire line at the thirty-eighth parallel by 1953. The Korean Peninsula remains divided at this heavily fortified border to this day without any peace treaty to enforce the cease-fire. Over one million Koreans and Chinese were killed in the war, and over fifty-four thousand Americans died in battle or of other causes. During the conflict disagreements between General MacArthur and President Truman led to MacArthur's being fired and replaced, proving America's tradition of the subordination of military leaders to civilian rulers. The Korean War heightened tensions in America during the Second Red Scare and led to the election of Dwight Eisenhower to the presidency as the first Republican since Herbert Hoover twenty years earlier.

11 DWIGHT D. EISENHOWER

Eisenhower graduated from the U.S. Military Academy in 1915 and rose to the rank of captain by the end of World War I, but only as a training officer. Eisenhower did not lead troops into combat until Operation Torch when American troops landed in North Africa to begin to push the German armies back toward Italy and Germany. Eisenhower, or Ike, exhibited crucial diplomatic skill in coordinating the efforts of the various Allied forces and rose to the rank of the supreme commander in Europe. He organized the D-Day invasion of Normandy and the broad-front strategy encircling Berlin that ended the war in Europe. After the war he served as the chief of staff of the military and eventually the commander of North Atlantic Treaty Organization (NATO) forces. He was elected to the presidency in 1952 with the largest popular vote to that time in history saying he would personally go to Korea to end the war there, which he did by 1953. He won a second term to the presidency and was the chief architect of the Cold War policies of the United States through the decade of tension and high stakes. Meanwhile he managed several domestic crises as the cultural changes of the 1950s developed. Like Coolidge, he was president during a period of widespread prosperity, but unlike any other president Eisenhower was the first to have to contemplate the implications of the existence of intercontinental ballistic missiles with nuclear warheads.

12 SPUTNIK

During the Eisenhower administration the Soviet Union started the space race and the arms race of the Cold War by launching the first artificial satellite into orbit around the Earth. *Sputnik I* was launched in 1957 almost four months before the United States responded with *Explorer I.* The space race reflected the Cold War fears of both superpowers that each other's technology would outpace the opposing side and achieve an advantage in rocket technology. *Sputnik I* precipitated large federal expenditures of money to boost math, science, and foreign language instruction in public schools through the National Defense Education Act. Over $500 million was dedicated to provide scholarships for prospective teachers and direct grants to schools. Although the *Sputnik* satellites were merely roving radio transmitters, the impression that the Soviets could be dropping atomic bombs on the United States from space spurred the creation of the National Aeronautics and Space Administration (NASA) and the development of the capacity for both nations actually to drop atomic weapons on each other from space using intercontinental ballistic missiles (ICBMs).

13 NATIONAL DEFENSE EDUCATION ACT

Along with the G.I. Bill that funded the college educations of war veterans, the National Defense Education Act represented millions of dollars of federal spending for education. After the Soviet Union placed the first artificial satellite, *Sputnik*, into orbit, the federal government in 1958 sought to boost instruction in math, the sciences, and foreign languages to help the country catch up to the Soviets. Grants were given to college students who were studying to become teachers and directly to school systems to fund facilities and curriculum development. This response to having been beaten by the Soviets into outer space was the origin of the Space Race, another area of Cold War competition between the superpowers.

14 NATIONAL AERONAUTICS AND SPACE ADMINISTRATION

One year after *Sputnik*, in 1958, President Eisenhower started the National Aeronautics and Space Administration, or NASA, to conduct scientific space exploration. NASA combined all previous research agencies under one organization with eight thousand employees and an annual budget of $100 million. America's own first satellite in orbit, *Explorer I*, symbolized the scientific emphasis of NASA by confirming the existence of radiation belts around the earth but also the military competitiveness of the superpowers. *Mercury* and *Gemini* missions tested manned space flight, and the *Apollo* missions succeeded in landing a man on the moon in 1969 six months ahead of President Kennedy's schedule. Various probes were launched into the solar system and beyond to explore the outer planets while NASA scientists developed more and more sophisticated technologies, and scientific and then communications satellites (as well as secret military satellites) were launched into orbit. NASA then placed a laboratory for astronauts called *Skylab* in space and developed the Shuttle program to create a vehicle that could launch and service satellites and return to earth only to be used again like a space truck. Through various tragedies and glorious achievements that fascinated the nation and worried the Soviets (although the Soviets launched the first satellite, the first man, and the first woman into space), NASA embodied the American spirit and spun off hundreds of technologies for civilian use to improve the American standard of living. As the Cold War waned, however, the costs involved in, for example, exploring Mars with robots in preparation for a manned mission, have come under greater and greater scrutiny.

> **DR. BENJAMIN SPOCK**
>
> Among the popular cultural influences of the 1950s was the book *The Common Sense Book of Baby and Child Care*, published by Dr. Spock in 1945. The Baby Boom generation was raised with many parents consulting the advice of this book, which some critics said created parenting that was too permissive.

15 MISSILE TECHNOLOGY

Intercontinental ballistic missiles (ICBMs) are missiles, like the ones launching astronauts into space, which are large enough to exit the Earth's atmosphere and then descend over targets on other continents to deliver atomic bombs. During the Cold War, both the United States and the Soviet Union developed the capacity to strike any part of each other's countries. Based on the research begun by American and German scientists during World War II, the United States developed the *Atlas* missile program followed by the creation of the *Titan* missiles that were even larger than the *Atlas* rockets that were used in the *Apollo* space missions. In the 1960s, the solid-fuel *Minuteman* rocket was developed that was more stable and easier to maintain, and at the peak of the Cold War one thousand *Minuteman* rockets were deployed, ready to launch on short notice by an authorization from the president. Other missiles could also be launched from submarines, and eventually multiple individually targeted reentry vehicles (MIRVs) were developed. MIRVs had the capacity to deliver multiple nuclear warheads on each ballistic missile. The aptly named *Peackeeper* missiles, otherwise known as the *MX* missiles, were the last stage of the nuclear arms race in that these missiles could be launched from mobile launchers rather than fixed missile silos. *MX* missiles were operational by 1972, but retired with the ending of the Cold War.

16 HYDROGEN BOMB

The United States wanted to regain the "lead" in the arms race after the Rosenbergs and other Americans spying for the Soviets transferred critical bomb-making secrets to allow the Russians to catch up. American scientists first tested a hydrogen bomb in 1952. Whereas the atomic bomb had the explosive power of thousands of tons of TNT, the hydrogen bombs were approximately one thousand times more destructive. The H-Bomb used a fission bomb to accomplish fusion, the power of the sun. The scientist who led the construction of the A-Bomb, Robert Oppenheimer, opposed the H-Bomb on moral grounds, but President Truman pushed for the test on November 1, 1952, on Bikini Atoll in the Marshall Islands in the Pacific Ocean. When the bomb was detonated, a radioactive cloud was shot 25 miles into the sky. The blast made a canyon in the floor of the ocean 1 mile wide and 175 feet deep. The world was frightened to learn that the Soviets had an H-Bomb by 1953, and even the British did by 1957. Dwight Eisenhower viewed the development of nuclear weapons as a way to reduce military budgets because they provided "more bang for the buck." The goal was not only to make the deployment of American military forces cheaper but also to bring down the cost of maintaining peace. As revealed at Dien Bien Phu in 1954, however, Ike was reluctant to nuke. What followed was the Vietnam War.

17 U-2 INCIDENT

As the Arms Race continued between the United States and the Soviet Union, high-flying espionage aircraft helped the American military keep tabs on the development and deployment of Soviet missile technology. In 1960, an American pilot named Francis Gary Powers had his U-2 reconnaissance aircraft shot down by a Soviet missile 1,200 miles inside the Soviet Union. Eisenhower and the National Aeronautics and Space Administration (NASA) had tried to cover up the secret surveillance flights by claiming the plane was a weather research plane that had flown off course, but Powers survived and confessed to being a Central Intelligence Agency (CIA) agent. Caught red-handed by the gloating Reds, Eisenhower made an unprecedented disclosure of international espionage by a world leader. A planned Summit Conference was boycotted by the Soviets because of this admission, and Eisenhower's reputation as a Cold War master strategist was tarnished. Powers was convicted of espionage by the righteously indignant Soviet government, but his release was secured by an exchange of a convicted Russian spy in an effort to show the world the Soviets were not innocent victims.

18 PEACE CORPS

John F. Kennedy (JFK) launched this program by executive order as a new component of the involvement of the United States in global issues. By the time Congress approved the measure and established it as a permanent volunteer organization, over thirteen thousand Americans had answered JFK's call in his inaugural address to "Ask not what your country can do for you, but what you can do for your country." Young Americans served two-year stints in developing nations as teachers, medical workers, and technical advisers in implementing economic and human resource development strategies. A similar program was launched to subsidize volunteer work at home called VISTA. Since its launch in 1961, the Peace Corps has now sent over two hundred thousand volunteers into 139 countries.

19 BAY OF PIGS

President Eisenhower had authorized the training of Cuban exiles for a mission to return to Cuba to overthrow Fidel Castro, the communist dictator who led a coup against Fulgencio Batista. Under the advice of the Central Intelligence Agency (CIA) and other national security advisers, John F. Kennedy (JFK) allowed the mission to go forward despite his own misgivings. Kennedy denied the revolutionaries any direct support from the American military, however, and when the fifteen hundred-man invasion force landed at the Bay of Pigs, they were all killed or captured in just three days. The incident drew international criticism of Kennedy, and the United States and made a permanent breech in negotiations with Castro. A meeting of the Organization of American States (OAS) condemned Castro's loyalty to Marxism-Leninism and initiated an embargo against Cuba that was first loosened by the Obama administration. President Barack Obama re-opened formal relations with Cuba and allowed some individuals to travel to Cuba in 2015.

20 CUBAN MISSILE CRISIS

The Soviet Union had been supplying Castro with the resources he used to consolidate his control of Cuba, but by 1962 this support took the form of missile installations in Cuba just 90 miles away from Florida. The Kennedy administration pronounced that the United States would deter any further expansion of communism on the part of Castro or the Soviets and would respond with force if the Soviets used Cuba as a base from which to threaten the nation's security. When photographic evidence proved that missile bases were being constructed in Cuba, Kennedy demanded their removal and blockaded the island nation. Kennedy called on the Organization of American States (OAS) and the United Nations to intervene and called on Nikita Khrushchev to personally take responsibility for the threat to peace. After the U.S. Navy began stopping Soviet ships, Khrushchev offered to remove the missiles under United Nations' supervision if Kennedy would pledge not to attack Cuba and if the United States would dismantle similar missile installations in Turkey. Kennedy ended the standoff by pledging not to attack and standing down the American missiles aimed at the Soviet Union from Turkey. Kennedy was able to save face, but Nikita Khrushchev could not and was removed from office as the leader of the Soviet Union. Just how dangerous the tense situation was became apparent later when it was revealed that the Soviets had to restrain Castro from firing missiles into the United States, a step that would have likely resulted in thermonuclear war.

THE BIG PICTURE

1. Harry S. Truman and Dwight D. Eisenhower were the first presidents of the United States to wrestle with the problems of world leadership thrust upon them by the end of World War II and the opening of the Cold War.

2. The federal government of the United States organized new agencies to manage national security issues and designed programs using deficit spending to support and stabilize nations in an effort to contain the spread of communism.

3. The Cold War competition between the superpowers of the United States and the Soviet Union involved the proliferation of nuclear weapons, a dramatic increase in the military budget, and a race to explore outer space.

4. The United States became more engaged in nations in the developing world, extending support to nations it viewed as allies in the Cold War and working to undermine regimes it viewed as hostile to its Cold War aims.

5. The Cold War continued into the 1960s and came closer to U.S. territory as Cuba became a communist country and formed an alliance with the Soviet Union, leading to an increase in Cold War tensions.

Mini Quiz

1. The Ford Motor Company transformed the automobile industry by

    (A) making the first functional automobiles with internal combustion gasoline engines.
    (B) producing new model innovations and color choices each year to increase consumer interest.
    (C) being the first major automobile manufacturer to sell cars using installment credit.
    (D) producing cars efficiently and making the price within the means of the average person.
    (E) borrowing the technologies used in racing vehicles to improve cars for the general public.

2. Attorney General A. Mitchell Palmer responded to the hysteria associated with the first Red Scare in the 1920s by

    (A) declaring the influx of radicals among immigrants to be an act of war by Soviet Russia.
    (B) requiring all rail and ship passengers to be searched for weapons before boarding.
    (C) raiding the headquarters of labor organizations looking for subversive literature.
    (D) arresting immigrants who could not produce the proper paperwork in roadblocks.
    (E) censoring the publications of radical organizations and stopping their mail service.

3. Warren G. Harding's major failure as president was his

    (A) inability to judge the character of those working for him in the executive branch.
    (B) overemphasis on foreign policy in an era of extreme domestic societal change.
    (C) misinterpreting his landslide victory as a mandate to expand the power of the government.
    (D) lack of sincere, moral leadership because of his personal character flaws.
    (E) unfamiliarity with the world of journalism during a new era of mass communication.

4. Margin buying allowed investors to

   (A) purchase stock in many companies at once.
   (B) borrow money to buy stocks with only a small cash payment.
   (C) pool capital to allow more leverage in company takeovers.
   (D) buy and sell stocks through second-party transactions by brokers.
   (E) sell stock in companies that owned no assets and produced no products.

5. Herbert Hoover's approach toward the growing depression in the wake of the Stock Market Crash was to

   (A) order the Federal Reserve to restrict access to capital to prevent wild speculation.
   (B) appeal to major banking firms for support in issuing gold bonds to stabilize the dollar.
   (C) give Americans scapegoats by arresting bankers and stock brokers guilty of insider trading.
   (D) slowly mobilize the resources of the federal government to support the financial industry.
   (E) enact a series of laws to provide for the basic needs of the people who had lost their jobs.

6. All of the following attributes linked Franklin D. Roosevelt's New Deal to the earlier goals of Progressive Reform **EXCEPT**

   (A) a focus on new regulations on the economy enforced by the federal government.
   (B) collective action of a broad spectrum of American citizens seeking reform.
   (C) isolating a segment of the population as those who selfishly ruined the economy for others.
   (D) popularizing reform measures through the skillful use of rhetorical devices.
   (E) taking an expert's advice to use deficit spending to "prime" the economic "pump."

7. The agency of the New Deal most criticized as an expression of socialism was the

   (A) National Recovery Administration.
   (B) Agricultural Adjustment Administration.
   (C) Tennessee Valley Authority.
   (D) Securities and Exchange Commission.
   (E) Works Progress Administration.

8. Franklin D. Roosevelt justified the radical nature of some New Deal programs by stating his position that

   (A) the government should take from each according to his or her ability and give to each according to his or her need.
   (B) the businesses of the United States were cooperating with the New Deal measures out of voluntary compliance because of patriotism just like back in World War I.
   (C) the people demanded the specific programs he was championing and he was merely acting as a public servant carrying out their wishes.
   (D) the New Deal was protecting private property and free enterprise by preventing a revolution based on injustices and inequalities that had arisen in the American economic system.
   (E) whatever excesses were committed by his desire to provide relief, recovery, and reform to the American people would be corrected because these emergency measures were temporary.

9. John L. Lewis broke away from the American Federation of Labor (AFL) and formed the Congress of Industrial Organizations because he believed that

   (A) the AFL had been infiltrated by too many socialists and communists from abroad.
   (B) in the crisis of the Great Depression skilled and unskilled workers needed to stick together.
   (C) the AFL was ignoring the needs of Appalachian coal miners because they were southerners.
   (D) although the AFL looked out for Jewish workers, it did not respect African Americans.
   (E) a more radical approach was necessary requiring an alliance with the Socialist Party.

10. The findings of the Nye Commission led the United States between the world wars to

   (A) institute the first peacetime draft in American history.
   (B) provide all aid short of war to the Allies standing against Nazi aggression in Europe.
   (C) mobilize the American economy for the production of weapons and armored vehicles.
   (D) ban all Americans from participating in war in Europe even as volunteers.
   (E) pass laws restricting trade with combatant nations.

11. American women could help the war effort during World War II in all of the following ways **EXCEPT**

   (A) helping comfort female prisoners when concentration camps were liberated.
   (B) enduring the hardships associated with the rationing of many staple products.
   (C) working in war industries to replace the labor of men called off to war.
   (D) serving in uniform as nurses, signal corps personnel, and clerical staff.
   (E) touring American military bases as entertainers for the United Service Organization (USO).

12. The primary goal of Douglas MacArthur's "island-hopping" strategy in the Pacific during World War II was to

   (A) conserve his dwindling number of transport ships that were falling to kamikaze attacks.
   (B) confuse the Japanese as to which of their fortified islands he would attack next.
   (C) take only necessary islands, especially those from which airplanes could attack Japan.
   (D) prevent loss of Japanese lives because their soldiers were sworn to fight to the death.
   (E) fight the least fortified Japanese-held islands first before coming back to tougher targets.

13. The general opinion of Harry S. Truman held by most Americans when he succeeded to the presidency after the death of Franklin D. Roosevelt (FDR) was that

   (A) they trusted FDR's judgment and Truman must be the best successor.
   (B) as a World War I veteran he was better able to lead the country in war than FDR.
   (C) as a former businessman he would be well equipped to restart the peacetime economy.
   (D) he was a tough leader who had fought political corruption and would fight to win the war.
   (E) he was not up to the challenges America faced in World War II and the Great Depression.

14. The first American politician to effectively use the potential of television to spread a political message was

    (A)   Harry S. Truman.

    (B)   Dwight D. Eisenhower.

    (C)   Adlai E. Stevenson.

    (D)   Joseph McCarthy.

    (E)   George C. Marshall.

15. The Soviet Union's launch of the first artificial satellite into orbit around the earth impacted the United States most by

    (A)   proving that the nation was vulnerable to nuclear attack from space.

    (B)   causing Americans to doubt the free enterprise system because communists won the space race.

    (C)   mandating a higher percentage of America's gross domestic product be spent on defense than the Soviets spent.

    (D)   increasing federal support for educational goals that would increase national security.

    (E)   causing the Congress to authorize the development of a missile defense system.

ANSWER EXPLANATIONS

1. **(D)** Answer (A) is incorrect in that European and American companies had been making gasoline-powered automobiles even before the turn of the twentieth century. Ford's genius was in making a simple, durable model on an assembly line, thus reducing overhead costs and bringing the cost of a car within the reach of the middle class. Answers (B) and (C) were innovations General Motors used to try to compete with Ford, and answer (E) was a later step in the automobile industry.

2. **(C)** The Palmer Raids of the first Red Scare were focused on subversive elements like socialists and communists in existing labor organizations. Palmer authorized the raids to seize both literature and immigrants, but he did not use roadblocks as suggested in answer (D).

3. **(A)** In the same way President Grant's administration became scandal ridden, the Harding administration suffered from the corruption of the president's subordinates. Harding tried to contract the power of government and had been a newspaper editor himself, so answers (C) and (E) are the opposite of the truth. Answers (B) and (D) could be said to be true of Harding, but the scandals erupted when men he thought were befriending him for the good of the country had other intentions.

4. **(B)** The inflation of stock prices that led to the Stock Market Crash in 1929 was largely due to the rampant speculation produced by the ability of buyers to borrow most of the money they invested. In the rapid rise of stock prices in the 1920s they could make profits for a while, but when prices fell they could not cover their debts.

5. **(D)** All of the other answers reflect the actions of other presidents under similar and different economic conditions, but answer (D) was Hoover's approach during his crisis management. He originally balked at profound intervention in the economy, but as the Depression deepened he resorted to attempts to stem the tide that actually formed a model for some of the measures of the New Deal like the Reconstruction Finance Corporation.

6. **(E)** Because Progressive Reform was begun during the upswing from a depression, Progressives did not resort to deficit spending as a purposeful policy nor see it as their duty to do so. Franklin D. Roosevelt's (FDR's) taking the advice of John Maynard Keynes to "prime the pump" was an example of the Wisconsin Idea in action, but unlike all the other answers, was not practiced extensively in peacetime until the Great Depression. All of the other answers express ideas and actions that could be said to be shared values between Theodore Roosevelt's Square Deal and FDR's New Deal.

7. **(C)** Since the Tennessee Valley Authority (TVA) "took over the means of production" by producing electrical power in such a way that private companies could not compete, critics identified it with socialism. The other agencies in the other answers were viewed this way by some, but the TVA was a government-owned utility company that transformed an area of the Southeast that had little to no industrial potential into one with great potential but no competition in providing electrical power.

8. **(D)** Answers (B), (C), and (E) are plausible explanations except that many of the New Deal measures were intended as permanent reforms and are still operating today.

Answers (B) and (C) would serve as justifications for typical government involvement in setting economic policy, but Franklin D. Roosevelt (FDR) specifically stated the position in answer (D) to explain his belief that the government had to be radicalized for a time. He believed his actions were conservative in that they were using liberal policies to guard against an overthrow of the status quo. Answer (A) is an example of Marxist rhetoric that FDR did not employ.

9. **(B)** The Congress of Industrial Organizations (CIO) allowed skilled and unskilled workers to unite in industrial unions unlike the American Federation of Labor (AFL) that had broken away from the Knights of Labor to focus on the needs only of skilled workers. Later the AFL and the CIO united to form the AFL-CIO.

10. **(E)** Answers (A), (B), and (C) described actual actions of the Roosevelt administration in preparation for American involvement in World War II prior to his overcoming of the Neutrality Acts inspired by the Nye Committee as stated in answer (E). After Pearl Harbor, Franklin D. Roosevelt did not have to convince the American people to set aside their traditional isolationism; it had been set aside for them. Answer (D) is a reference to the voluntary service of Americans in the British military and that of other nations prior to Pearl Harbor.

11. **(A)** All of the other answers were paths open to women in supporting the war effort. By its nature the liberation of Nazi concentration camps was a combat operation, and women in World War II were barred from serving in combat roles.

12. **(C)** All of the answers hint at realities of the terrible warfare faced by Americans and their allies in the Pacific Theater of World War II, and some were partially used to justify MacArthur's innovative strategy. The overall goal of the whole procedure, however, was to focus on acquiring islands like Iwo Jima and Okinawa to use as "unsinkable aircraft carriers" from which constant bombing of the Japanese mainland could help end the war as it had in Europe.

13. **(E)** Although Truman later proved to be a tough fighter who made sure "the buck stops here" at his desk, he was originally thought to be inadequate as stated in answer (E). He had fought in World War I and had run a gentleman's clothing store, but these were not foremost in the minds of the American public when Franklin D. Roosevelt (FDR) died after being elected to an unprecedented fourth term as president. No one could have taken the office at that moment with the full confidence of the American people, especially because a good portion of the people fighting the war had never known another president besides FDR.

14. **(D)** Whereas Franklin D. Roosevelt had shown all politicians the path toward mass communication with his fireside chats, Joseph McCarthy first seized on television as a political tool. His hearings, when broadcast on television, won for him and for his cause the heartfelt support of the majority of Americans until McCarthy's campaign to root out communists from the government backfired on himself. Richard Nixon, for one, never forgot how powerful a tool television could be; he saved his political career by delivering his "Checkers" speech but lost the presidency to John Kennedy who proved an even better master of the new medium.

15. **(D)** Answers (A), (B), and (C) are the opposite of the truth in that despite hysteria President Eisenhower and the government knew the Russian's launch of *Sputnik* did not immediately threaten the United States. Americans turned all the more toward private enterprise to devise new technologies, and the spending on national defense by the United States during the Cold War as a percentage of the gross domestic product (GDP) never approached the nearly 50-percent mark the Soviets had to expend to keep up. The two philosophical and economic systems were sharply contrasted by the fact that the United States never spent more than about 4 percent of its GDP on national defense during the height of the Cold War. A missile defense shield was a goal much later in the Cold War than in 1957 when *Sputnik* orbited the earth. The original strategy of the Cold War was to have a strong defense by maintaining a strong offense, one so strong it could destroy the planet several times over. The direct and most significant impact of the launch of *Sputnik* was passage of the National Defense Education Act the next year to boost instruction in math, sciences, and foreign languages. These courses were offered at the college level in high school by funding the College Board and other initiatives in an attempt to catch and to surpass the Soviets.

Post-War Domestic Issues, 1945–1963

32

We are people of this generation, bred in at least modest comfort, housed now in universities, looking uncomfortably to the world we inherit.

—Tom Hayden, "The Port Huron Statement," 1962

TIMELINE	
1953–1969	Warren Court (Earl Warren's tenure as chief justice of Supreme Court)
1954	*Brown* v. *Board of Education of Topeka*
1958	John Kenneth Galbraith publishes *The Affluent Society*
1960	John Fitzgerald Kennedy (JFK) launches his New Frontier campaign slogan
1961	JFK becomes president; JFK establishes the Peace Corps; Bay of Pigs incident
1962	Rachel Carson publishes *Silent Spring*; Cuban Missile Crisis
1963	Kennedy is assassinated; Lyndon Baines Johnson (LBJ) becomes president
1964	Barry Goldwater runs as Republican candidate for president; *Escobedo* v. *Illinois*; LBJ announces his War on Poverty program
1965	LBJ launches his "Great Society" domestic agenda; Congress establishes Medicare and Medicaid; Congress launches the Head Start program
1966	*Miranda* v. *Arizona*
1968	The Democratic Convention is held in Chicago
1971	The U.S. government creates a fiat currency

OVERVIEW

Perhaps the most remarkable development of the post-World War II years was the unprecedented growth of the economy and the rising living standard for millions of Americans. The gross domestic product of the country—the total value of goods and services produced in the United States in a year—rose dramatically between 1945 and 1960, from $200 billion to $500 billion. Such growth is unprecedented in American history.

In this period, we see a dramatic rise in the middle class, as millions of Americans from working-class backgrounds were able to achieve many of the markers of middle-class life—home and car ownership, a college education, and a comfortable income. The G.I. Bill contributed to the growth of the middle class, as did a strong labor movement that was successful in securing higher wages for industrial workers in the 1940s.

The post-war world was almost indistinguishable from the pre-war world. A more modern, more affluent society emerged in the post-war era—one unimaginable in the depths of the Great Depression. Many families moved from cities to suburbs in the late 1940s and 1950s. Inexpensive suburban housing, government assistance, and the building of highways all aided the move to the suburbs. However, the economic gains of the 1950s were not equally distributed. Pockets of intense poverty persisted in America's older urban centers. As middle-class families moved to the suburbs, they took with them their ability to pay local taxes. Cities saw their tax bases shrink dramatically. With funds scarce, cities had to cut back on basic services like policing and education. Crime became an unavoidable urban reality and city schools deteriorated.

During the 1950s, Americans became increasingly concerned about Communist "infiltration" in the United States. The "loss" of China to communists in 1949, the first Soviet detonation of a nuclear bomb (1949), and the Korean War (1950–1953) all contributed to concerns about communism. Senator Joseph McCarthy in the early 1950s heightened these concerns with bold, and often unsubstantiated, claims about the spread of domestic communism. This second Red Scare led to loyalty oaths for government employees, Congressional investigations, blacklists in the entertainment industry, and an atmosphere of fear and suspicion. The playwright Arthur Miller's 1953 play, *The Crucible*, depicted the narrow-mindedness, unfounded accusations, and general sense of paranoia surrounding the Salem witch trials in 1692. However, it was clear that the play was drawing analogies between the witch trials of the colonial period and the excesses of anti-communism in the 1950s. The second Red Scare abated somewhat with the Senate censure of McCarthy in 1954.

The 1950s are often presented as a decade of bland conformity. While there were pressures to conform to mainstream norms of proper behavior, there were also undercurrents of non-conformity and resistance to these norms. Several trends in the 1950s flew in the face of conformity—the most obvious one being the civil rights movement (see Chapter 33). The 1950s also saw the birth of the Beat Generation literary movement, the popularity of rock 'n' roll, and the stirrings of the women's liberation movement.

1 FAIR DEAL

Despite being preoccupied with the difficulties of the Cold War, Truman did propose in his campaign for the Election of 1948 a domestic agenda he called the Fair Deal. His vision of expanding the New Deal included national health insurance, federal aid to education, an increased minimum wage, expanded Social Security benefits, greater farm subsidies, expansion of federal housing programs for the poor, and even civil rights legislation. Although these promises and his prolabor stand against the Taft-Hartley Act won him a surprise victory over Thomas Dewey, the Congress after the election showed that it had moved Right during the war years. Conservatives in both parties prevented much of the Fair Deal from being implemented, although the minimum wage was almost doubled from forty cents an hour to seventy-five cents and social security benefits were expanded. Soon the Korean War distracted even President Truman from pursuing more domestic reforms.

2 G.I. BILL

Otherwise known as the Serviceman's Readjustment Act, this 1944 law provided cash payments for tuition and living expenses for veterans attending college, as well as low-interest loans for veterans to purchase homes and start businesses. The intent of the G.I. Bill was to help the veterans of World War II adjust to life during peacetime. The program was very successful. It helped millions of veterans advance economically. A college education and home ownership have been seen as key components of entrance into the middle class. By the mid-1950s, over eight million veterans had used G.I. Bill benefits for some sort of training or educational program; by 1952, over two million veterans secured mortgages with backing through the G.I. Bill. The generous benefits extended to World War II veterans stood in contrast to the sparse benefits extended to World War I veterans. World War I veterans staged a major protest in 1932, the "Bonus March," to pressure the government to pay bonuses for military service immediately rather than in the following decade, as originally promised.

3 BABY BOOM

Contributing to the cultural changes of the 1950s was the release of the pent-up urge to procreate that had plagued the dark years of World War II and the Great Depression. Suburbia was born and rampant consumerism was reborn as the baby boom, a huge increase in the number of births, expanded through the decade. At its peak, 4.3 million babies were born in two separate years during the era. From 1946 to 1964 a total of seventy-nine million babies swelled the population of the country. As baby boomers retire, however, the federal government will face a significant burden in meeting its commitments from the New Deal program of social security.

4 SUBURBANIZATION

An important trend in the United States after World War II was the growth of suburbs. New suburban communities were built just outside of major American cities to meet the housing crunch created by all the returning World War II soldiers. Huge numbers of these soldiers quickly married, had children, and looked for affordable housing. Race also played a factor in the development of suburbia. Many white families did not want to live in urban neighborhoods that had become integrated after many southern, rural African Americans had moved north to work in war industries. Developers facilitated the move to the suburbs. An innovative developer was William Levitt, who took large tracts of land outside of major cities (often farm land) and built huge developments of nearly identical, modest houses. Levitt, who had gained skill in rapid construction of housing during World War II, applied the techniques of mass production to these houses, building them rapidly and cheaply. Levittown, on Long Island, New York, became synonymous with these mass-produced communities of similarly-styled homes. These developments were not without their critics. Songwriter Malvina Reynolds skewered the monotony of life in these developments in the song "Little Boxes" (1962).

5 TELEVISION

Television became an extremely popular medium in the 1950s. By the end of the decade nearly 90 percent of American homes owned a television set. After an initial burst of creativity in the late 1940s and early 1950s, television programming settled into safe, predictable genres. The most emblematic genre of the 1950s was the suburban situation comedy (sitcom), complete with a stay-at-home mother, such as *Leave it to Beaver* and *Father Knows Best*. Westerns, such as *Bonanza* and *Gunsmoke*, and daytime dramas (labeled "soap operas" because of sponsorship by soap manufacturers) such as *The Guiding Light* and *Search for Tomorrow*, dominated the airwaves. Many of these genres were carryovers from radio. The Ed Sullivan Show, a variety show, was extremely popular, airing from 1948 to 1971.

6 FEDERAL HIGHWAY ACT

Dwight Eisenhower advanced a New Deal public works project of his own by backing the 1956 Federal Highway Act. Having seen the German autobahn system in Europe, Ike envisioned creating the Interstate Highway System to facilitate military travel during times of national emergencies. Larger than any other single public works project in American history, the law authorized the expenditure of $30 billion to construct 41,000 miles of state-of-the-art highways over thirteen years. The federal highway system employed tens of thousands of citizens and contributed to the automobile, recreational, and entertainment industries so significantly that through the 1960s one in seven Americans had their livelihood from some economic endeavor connected to this new transportation revolution. Just like the railroad before it, however, the highway system chose some areas for greatness and doomed others to obscurity. The Eisenhower Interstate System has never been used for its original purpose of fending off invading armies, although its design as emergency landing fields for airplanes has from time to time saved lives.

7 TAFT-HARTLEY ACT

The Taft-Hartley Act, passed in 1947 over President Harry S. Truman's veto, was designed to monitor and restrict the activities of organized labor. The law imposed restrictions on unions that made it more difficult to strike. It allowed states to pass "right to work" laws, banning union shops (a union shop is a workplace in which all the workers are required to join the union after a majority had voted to do so). The law also required union leaders to pledge that they were not members of the Communist Party. The law was passed by the conservative,

Republican-dominated Congress that had been elected in 1946. In many ways, the law was passed as a response to the largest strike wave in its history, as five million workers walked off their jobs in 1946. Unions, which had refrained from striking during the war, feared that the gains they had made during the war would be taken away. The strike wave was largely successful, boosting wages for factory workers and allowing them to partake in the consumer culture of the era.

8 THE HOLLYWOOD 10

The "Hollywood 10" was a group of directors and screenwriters who refused to cooperate with the anti-communist investigations of the post-World War II period. After the war, anti-communist sentiment began to grow in the context of the Cold War with the Soviet Union. The House Un-American Activities Committee (HUAC), which formed in 1938, became more active in investigating supposed Communist activity in the United States by opening an investigation of the entertainment industry in 1947. Subsequently, both Senate and House committees investigated supposed Communist infiltration in various walks of American life, but Congress especially targeted the entertainment industry, fearing that Communists would subtly get their message out through television and movies. In 1947, HUAC summoned seventy-nine individuals in the film and television industry to testify. Many refused to testify or had scheduling conflicts. Eventually, ten screenwriters and directors, including Ring Lardner Jr. and Dalton Trumbo, came before the committee. This group refused to cooperate and challenged the legitimacy of the committee to investigate individuals' political activities, citing First Amendment rights to freedom of speech and assembly. The ten were fined and sentenced to six-month jail terms for contempt of Congress. They and others who refused to cooperate with Congressional committees were "blacklisted" in the 1950s, unable to find work in Hollywood. (One of the ten, Edward Dmytryk, did agree to testify in 1951 and was able to continue directing in the 1950s; he directed *The Caine Mutiny* in 1954).

9 MCCARTHYISM

Joseph McCarthy represented a backlash against the liberal policies that had brewed in Wisconsin since the opening of the Progressive Reform movement under Robert La Follette. McCarthy served in World War II in the Marine Corps after practicing law and holding a minor political office. After the war he was elected to the U.S. Senate. In 1950, Senator McCarthy delivered a speech in Wheeling, West Virginia, in which he declared he possessed a list of "card-carrying" members of the Communist Party who worked in the State Department. Without ever having named a single State Department official who was a communist, McCarthy started the Second Red Scare by holding a series of televised hearings from 1951 to 1954. During the hearings, McCarthy charged civil servants, writers, actors, professors, labor leaders, and eventually even army officers as having membership in the Communist Party or communist leanings. Such accusations spurred the House of Representatives to open their own hearings of a body called the House Un-American Activities Committee (HUAC). As a new wave of hysteria swept the nation in the Cold War, such accusations ruined the careers of many innocent and some guilty individuals who were together blacklisted, or barred from working in their professions. Civil rights advocates attacked McCarthy as a bully and someone who did not truly believe in the freedoms enshrined in the Bill of Rights. Among the accused were even such leaders as George C. Marshall and Adlai E. Stevenson, and when McCarthy pursued more attacks against U.S. Army personnel the Senate moved to censure him for his abuses. His influence diminished rapidly and he soon died of the effects of alcoholism.

10 THE ROSENBERG CASE

When the United States learned that the Soviet Union had built and tested a nuclear bomb in 1949, many Americans were convinced that communists in the United States, loyal to the Soviet Union, had provided the Soviets with essential information about the bomb. In 1950, Clause Fuchs, a German physicist who had worked on the Manhattan Project (see page 348), admitted to delivering secrets to the Soviet Union during and after World War II. His testimony to American and British intelligence agents eventually led to the arrest of an American couple, Ethel and Julius Rosenberg. They were accused in 1951 of orchestrating a ring of spies that passed secrets of the atomic bomb to the Soviet Union. The Rosenbergs, who were members of the Communist Party, insisted on their innocence but were sent to the electric chair in 1953. Evidence has emerged since the end of the Cold War that indicates that Julius had been involved in espionage on behalf of the Soviet Union, but critics of the government's case insist that Ethel was not involved.

11 DESEGREGATING THE MILITARY

In 1948, President Truman issued Executive Order 9981 to ban segregation in the military. Before the order, African Americans were not only segregated into separate units from white members of the military, but they worked under different rules. For example, qualified African-American enlistees had to wait up to three years before they could begin combat training. This delayed their entry into combat situations. By contrast, white enlistees would begin training within months of being qualified. Opinion within the military toward African-American troops changed during World War II. White officers commanding African-American units were consistently impressed by the effectiveness of their units on the battlefield. The most famous segregated African-American units were the Tuskegee Airmen and the 761st Tank Battalion. During the war, many African-American troops pushed for civil rights within the military and beyond. The National Association for the Advancement of Colored People encouraged African Americans to take part in the "Double V" campaign—promoting victory against fascism abroad and victory against racism at home. Ultimately, 125,000 African Americans served overseas during the war. These factors led Truman to take action. However, he failed to implement the order until the Korean War, when the military needed additional personnel.

12 *BROWN v. BOARD OF EDUCATION OF TOPEKA, KANSAS*

The U.S. Supreme Court under Earl Warren voted unanimously in 1954 that segregation of African-American and white students in schools denied children the equal protection of the laws. The Warren Court directed public schools to admit African-American students to schools with white children "with all deliberate speed." That clause was interpreted to admit a wide range of speeds by states, some of which complied immediately and others of which staged protests in the form of administrative hurdles all the way to a resolution for nullification in Alabama. The activities of the National Association for the Advancement of Colored People (NAACP) to advance desegregation were met with the activities of White Citizens' Councils to hamper it. In 1956, a document called the "Southern Manifesto" was signed by over one hundred members of the U.S. Congress saying that the South would use "all lawful means" to resist the Supreme Court's decision.

13 ELVIS PRESLEY

Few kings have risen from such obscurity to change the world as did the king of rock 'n' roll. Elvis Aaron Presley picked up a guitar at the age of ten and cut his first single record in 1954. As he began touring, the young people of America were drawn to his style of singing and dancing that, according to his producer, was like having an African-American man in a white man's body. Elvis's mix of Negro spiritual roots with jazz, the blues, and country music produced rockabilly and ultimately rock 'n' roll. Presley's musical career was interrupted by a stint in the military, but upon completing his service he entered into a movie career. He personified the new youth culture that was coming out of the stresses of World War II and the ongoing Cold War seeking a freer lifestyle, and he set the pattern for dissipation and untimely death through drug addiction that so many rock 'n' roll performers would follow. His work, which included eighteen number-one hit songs, and his image became so iconographic that he remains one of the richest dead men in history, that is, his estate still makes millions of dollars for his heirs.

14 THE BEAT GENERATION

The Beat Generation literary movement represented a subversive undercurrent in the 1950s. The beats represented a rejection of mainstream social values in the 1950s—the suburban lifestyle, the consumer society, and patriotism. The most important text of the beat movement is *On the Road*, by Jack Kerouac (1957). Initially written on a scroll, a stream of consciousness screed, the book depicts a life of spontaneity and freedom. Also important is Allen Ginsberg's book of poems, *Howl* (1956), which ripped apart the foundations of Cold War, materialistic American society. The literature of the beats resonated with many young people who rejected the conformity and racism of contemporary society. The Beat Generation was in many ways a precursor to the counterculture of the 1960s (see page 397).

15 *THE FEMININE MYSTIQUE*

The 1960s and 1970s were the era of the modern women's liberation movement, or the feminist movement. In this era women made up more than half of the population of America but struggled under sexual discrimination. The momentum that began with the Nineteenth Amendment to the Constitution had dwindled, but the publication of *The Feminine Mystique* by Betty Friedan in 1963 sparked a revival of female activism. Through interviews with suburban women, Friedan exposed a general lack of enthusiasm for the postwar American Dream being lived out in row after row of houses that exactly resembled those of their neighbors. Friedan said that this new version of the cult of domesticity, for which her book's title was a synonym, said that deeply frustrated and unhappy women were being buried alive, and she called the American suburb a "comfortable concentration camp." Friedan and other feminists identified discrimination spanning from sexual harassment to the "glass ceiling," the practice of passing over competent women for promotion to the highest levels of corporate power. In response, the largest women's liberation organization was founded by Betty Friedan in 1966, the National Organization for Women, or NOW. Friedan co-founded another feminist organization with Gloria Steinem in 1971. Steinem founded *Ms.* magazine the same year and would go on to become the most famous feminist leader in the United States, if not the world.

16 THE LONELY CROWD

In their book *The Lonely Crowd* (1950), sociologists David Riesman, Nathan Glazer, and Reuel Denney, noted that in the post-World War II era, Americans were more eager to mold their ideas to societal standards than they were to think independently. They argued that many Americans seemed "other-directed" and that they lacked resources to look within themselves to discover what was necessary to live a meaningful life. Americans, they argued, looked outward and based their lives on established norms. This quality seemed to characterize many Americans who felt intimidated from appearing non-conformist in the 1950s. William H. Whyte's book *The Organization Man* (1956) echoed the theme of conformity by describing the stultifying atmosphere of the modern corporation where employees were pressured to think like the group.

17 THE AFFLUENT SOCIETY

This book by John Kenneth Galbraith sparked discussion as the United States moved into the 1960s after a large expansion of the American economy in the 1950s. Published in 1958, *The Affluent Society* criticized the consumerism and waste of a society obsessed with increasing productivity managed by private industries bent on making profits. Galbraith identified post-war America as the richest society in history, but he also criticized the advertising industry for making Americans want to consume more resources than any previous society. Because Americans, he said, had not developed an adequate system of managing unprecedented affluence, the government should moderate the excesses of consumerism by devoting more resources to the public sector, especially to public education. Galbraith's ideas rejected traditional economic views and professed that poverty could be eradicated from society, but many Americans recognized that the productivity of the United States had won World War II and were suspicious of intellectuals who told them their spending on themselves was ultimately destructive. Galbraith's ideas, however, were the natural extension of Keynesian economics and Progressive Reform and won him fame and influence among political liberals, including John F. Kennedy who made Galbraith one of his chief advisers.

> ### DÉTENTE
> From the French word for *relaxation*, this term was expressed by JFK as a goal for his policy of peaceful coexistence with the USSR during the Cold War. Because of subsequent events, the thawing of Cold War tensions more belonged at intervals to the Nixon, Ford, and Reagan administrations.

18 JOHN FITZGERALD KENNEDY

Kennedy was the son of the wealthy banker and realtor, Joseph P. Kennedy, who brought his Harvard-educated son to London while ambassador to England. John F. Kennedy (JFK) was critical of England's lack of preparedness and foresight in the face of the rise of Nazism, and when the United States entered World War II he became a decorated war hero. He entered politics upon returning to the United States and served three terms in the House of Representatives. His defeat of veteran Republican Senator Henry Cabot Lodge in the 1952 Senate race won Kennedy fame with Democrats around the nation, and his dashing good looks and attractive wife appealed to a nation becoming fixated on youthfulness. After a failed bid for the vice presidency, JFK returned to the Senate. In the Election of 1960, however, he won the presidency and became the first Roman Catholic and the youngest man elected to the executive branch (Theodore Roosevelt had been younger when he replaced McKinley but was not elected to do so). Kennedy inherited many dangerous Cold War threats from the Eisenhower administration and made strong showings against communists in Cuba and in Berlin. He was assassinated by Lee Harvey Oswald in Dallas, Texas, in November 1963, just as he was beginning to mature in the presidential office. His policies on civil rights had waivered and then become so firm as to alienate southern Democrats, hence the trip to Dallas. The president's being cut down in the apparent prime of life after beginning to make strides in both foreign and domestic issues caused shock and grief across the nation and instability in the world.

> ### AFFIRMATIVE ACTION
> JFK issued an executive order in 1961 to remove race as a factor for hiring for projects paid for with federal money. As the idea developed as a form of reparation for slavery, affirmative action led to preferential consideration for African Americans in hiring and promotions.

19 NEW FRONTIER

John F. Kennedy (JFK) called his Progressive agenda the New Frontier, and because he entered the presidency with a Democratic Congress as had Franklin D. Roosevelt, expectations were high that sweeping reforms would be passed in another First Hundred Days. The results were disappointing to liberals, however, despite Kennedy's capable advisers and popularity. Kennedy's cabinet overhauled the executive branch's operations, but Kennedy failed to install a new Department of Urban Affairs. Congress also defeated his proposed measures on housing, medical care for the elderly, and federal grants for public education. He did succeed in securing an increase in the minimum wage to $1.25 per hour, but despite stirring rhetoric could not make the plight of African Americans a viable goal of white Progressives. The phrase *New Frontier* seemed more applicable to his outreach to the world in the Peace Corps and his announcement that the United States was planning on "landing a man on the moon and returning him safely to earth" by the end of the decade.

> ### RALPH NADER
> Nader published the book *Unsafe at Any Speed* to decry the Ford Corvair's supposed safety flaws. Nader went on to make a career as a consumer advocate and encouraged a more litigious society. He entered politics and ran, among other times, in the presidential election of 2000. The over 2.7 percent of popular vote he received reduced Al Gore's chance of winning.

20 KENNEDY ASSASSINATION

Having gone to Dallas to shore up support from the Democrats of Texas, Kennedy was shot twice while traveling in an open car in a motorcade. Lee Harvey Oswald, a former Marine who had visited the Soviet Union and exhibited leftist leanings, was apprehended after killing a Dallas policeman and accused of assassinating the president. Kennedy was pronounced dead thirty minutes after the shooting. Lyndon B. Johnson was sworn in as president. While Oswald was being moved from a prison cell he was shot by nightclub owner Jack Ruby as America watched on television. Chief Justice Earl Warren headed a commission investigating the assassination that announced that Oswald had acted alone. A later report by a committee of the House of Representatives concluded that an unknown assailant had fired a shot that perhaps had delivered the mortal wound to the head. Kennedy's assassination shocked the world and devastated the grief-stricken nation, but Lyndon Johnson was able to present Kennedy as a martyr, thereby making way for many of Kennedy's (and his own) policies' passage by Congress.

The Civil Rights Movement

33

We have waited for more than three hundred and
forty years for our constitutional and God-given rights.

—Martin Luther King Jr., "Letter from Birmingham Jail," 1963

TIMELINE	
1955	Emmett Till is murdered; Rosa Parks refuses to give up her seat on a bus in Montgomery, Alabama
1956	Martin Luther King Jr. organizes the Montgomery Bus Boycott
1957	The Southern Christian Leadership Conference (SCLC) is founded; The NAACP backs the Little Rock Nine
1960	Students stage sit-ins at Woolworths in Greensboro, North Carolina, and Nashville, Tennessee
1961	The Student Nonviolent Coordinating Committee (SNCC) is founded
1963	Freedom Rides first challenge segregation; Medgar Evers is assassinated; Activists and residents of Birmingham, Alabama mount a civil rights campaign; Civil Rights activists hold a March on Washington, D.C.
1964	The Congress of Racial Equality (CORE) launches Chicago sit-ins; Malcolm X makes his pilgrimage to Mecca; Freedom schools begin in Mississippi; Martin Luther King Jr. wins the Nobel Peace Prize
1965	Congress passes the Voting Rights Act
1966	Activists hold symbolic marches in Selma, Alabama
1967	Black Panther Party is founded; Stokely Carmichael publishes *Black Power*

OVERVIEW

One of the most significant reform movements in American history occurred in the 1950s and 1960s—the civil rights movement. The movement challenged the legal basis of the segregation of African Americans in the United States, but it also challenged the pervasive racism of American society. This racism had justified the existence of slavery and the persistence of Jim Crow segregation. The movement forced America to examine its most cherished institutions and also to reevaluate its patterns of thought.

The origins of the movement are hard to pinpoint. Certainly, activism by African Americans has existed throughout American history. Precedents for the civil rights activism can be seen in the abolitionist struggles before the Civil War, in the South Carolina Colored People's Convention following the Civil War, in the Colored Farmers' National Alliance in the 1880s, in the formation of the National Association for the Advancement of Colored People in 1909, and in Marcus Garvey's Universal Negro Improvement Association, founded in 1914 (to name a few). Many historians cite World War II as a major turning point in the modern civil rights movement. Many returning soldiers felt a sense of empowerment and engagement that they had not previously felt. These veterans had taken part in the NAACP's "Double V" campaign during the war, urging victory against fascism abroad and victory against racism at home. The injustices of American life seemed especially reprehensible to men who had just risked their lives serving their country. In addition, the migration of many African-American men and women from the familiar patterns of rural southern life to the new challenges of urban, industrial America whetted their appetite for change and justice. This was the generation that would become the leaders of the civil rights movement in the decades after the war.

Civil rights activists used a variety of strategies and tactics, including legal challenges, civil disobedience, non-violent protests, and direct action, to press for an end to racial discrimination. The civil rights movement gained national attention with the Montgomery Bus Boycott of 1954–1955, following the arrest of Rosa Parks. The boycott thrust its leader, Martin Luther King Jr., into the national spotlight as well. King remained a central figure in the movement until his death in 1968; his "I Have a Dream Speech" at the 1963 March on Washington was one of the highpoints of the movement. The movement encountered significant, often violent, resistance from Southern whites. Opposition to the desegregation of Central High School in Little Rock, Arkansas (1957), led to national headlines and to intervention by the federal government. This pattern of activism, resistance, headlines, and federal intervention was repeated in other situations, including the Freedom Rides of 1963. As the 1960s began, a younger generation of activists began to play a prominent role in the movement. Over time, rifts developed between the older, church-based leadership of the movement and a younger cadre of activists.

The movement achieved some stunning successes. President Lyndon Johnson championed the cause of civil rights and successfully pushed for passage of the 1964 Civil Rights Act, banning racial discrimination in public places. The following year, the Voting Rights Act authorized the federal government to oversee voter registration in counties with low African-American registration and also outlawed literacy tests and poll taxes. However, confronting economic problems in regard to housing and employment proved to be a more difficult task. King shifted his focus at the end of his life toward these economic issues. It was in support of striking sanitation workers that King was drawn to Memphis, Tennessee, in 1968, where he was killed by an assassin. Problems of discrimination and poverty still exist in the African-American community.

1 SEGREGATION

Segregation was a key component of the Jim Crow laws that survived the Reconstruction era. Such laws mandated that African Americans and white Americans should not share schools, restaurant facilities, public bathrooms and water fountains, public transportation, playgrounds, or even jails. Although churches were segregated by the Freedmen's Bureau in some states, the long-standing segregation that occurred in churches was by choice rather than by state or federal law. Racial segregation was sanctioned by the Supreme Court in *Plessy* v. *Ferguson* in 1896, although dissenting justices claimed such laws would only fan racial hatred and mistrust. A chief strategy of the civil rights movement was to purposefully break segregation laws in acts of civil disobedience. The 1954 *Brown* v. *Board of Education of Topeka, Kansas* case called for the end of segregation in public schools after Harry S. Truman had desegregated the U.S. Armed Forces in the Korean War. The

> **LITTLE ROCK, ARKANSAS**
>
> The attention of the nation was drawn to the efforts of nine African-American students to integrate Central High School in this southern city in 1957. President Eisenhower had to send U.S. Army troops to enforce the Supreme Court's ruling before mob violence abated.

Warren Court also struck down laws barring interracial marriage in 1967, and by 1971 the Supreme Court banned all forms of segregation and approved of a wide range of tools governments could use to end practices like busing and the reapportioning of school districts.

2 EMMETT TILL

Emmett Till was a fourteen-year-old African-American from Chicago in 1955 when he went south into Mississippi to visit an uncle. On a dare from a local youth, Till approached a young white woman working at a grocery store and said, "Bye, baby," and whistled as he left the store. The woman's husband and brother-in-law later removed Till from his uncle's home by force and beat and shot the boy to death. His body was later recovered out of the Tallahatchie River by a fisherman. Despite the fact that over five hundred African Americans had been lynched with impunity in Mississippi since the end of Reconstruction, Till's murderers were brought to trial. The case drew national attention as did photographs that were published in *Ebony* magazine of Till's face before and after the murder. Predictably, the all-white jury found the two men innocent. In the tension following the *Brown* decision by the Supreme Court the previous year, outrage over Emmett Till's death prompted Rosa Parks and other African-American leaders to launch the civil rights movement.

3 ROSA PARKS

During World War II Rosa Parks joined the Montgomery, Alabama, National Association for the Advancement of Colored People (NAACP) and became the secretary to its president. She was a seamstress who commuted to her work on city buses, and in 1955, three months after the Emmett Till murder case, she was asked to move from the front of the "black section" of the bus to allow a white man to sit because the "white section" was full. This practice sometimes made African-American passengers have to exit the bus entirely if enough whites boarded to fill a bus. Rosa Parks said, "Why do you push us around?" and refused to move.

The protest of her arrest prompted the Montgomery Bus Boycott and launched the activities of Martin Luther King Jr. Parks moved north upon release and served as a secretary to a member of the House of Representatives. She remained a leader and iconic symbol of the civil rights movement for the rest of her life.

4 MONTGOMERY BUS BOYCOTT

Martin Luther King Jr. began his leadership in the civil rights movement by organizing the Montgomery Bus Boycott, a protest on the part of African Americans for the arrest and fine imposed on Rosa Parks. In Montgomery, Alabama, African Americans walked and carpooled to work, whereas before the boycott they had made up the majority of the passengers riding the buses. The boycott lasted 381 days and cost the bus company 65 percent of its normal income. The Warren Court decreed that the segregation of the buses should end.

5 MARTIN LUTHER KING JR.

For his efforts in the Montgomery Bus Boycott, the Rev. Martin Luther King's church was machine-gunned. Like his namesake, however, attacks simply hardened his resolve to fight on. As a leader of the Southern Christian Leadership Conference (SCLC), King advocated nonviolent resistance modeled after that of Henry David Thoreau and Gandhi. The SCLC prompted African Americans to rally in churches and to launch voter registration drives, boycotts, sit-ins, and freedom rides. King was arrested in 1963 after leading demonstrations in Birmingham, Alabama, and eloquently defended his actions in a document called "Letter from Birmingham Jail" written to local white ministers. The episode moved John F. Kennedy to push for stronger civil rights measures that alienated southern Democrats, leading Kennedy to Dallas and his death. As one of the leaders of a March on Washington, King addressed more than two hundred thousand people with his "I have a dream" speech. For his moral courage, eloquence, and activism King was awarded the Nobel Peace Prize in 1964. He led a march from Selma, Alabama, to Montgomery in 1965 and had begun to protest de facto segregation, the plight of the poor, and the Vietnam War when he was killed in Memphis, Tennessee, in 1968.

6 THE SOUTHERN CHRISTIAN LEADERSHIP CONFERENCE

The Southern Christian Leadership Conference (SCLC) was formed to coordinate protests around the South in the wake of the Montgomery Bus Boycott. Sixty people, mostly African-American ministers, from ten states created the organization and resolved that the civil rights of all citizens are necessary for true democracy to work. The SCLC sought to end segregation by urging African Americans to resist the practice in all its forms and to do so nonviolently. The first convention of the SCLC was held in Montgomery, Alabama, in 1957 where Dr. Martin Luther King Jr. was elected president. Other leaders in the organization included Dr. Ralph David Abernathy, whose house and church were bombed, and the Reverend C. K. Steele. The SCLC also resolved to open its membership to all regardless of race, religion, or background. The organization revealed the centrality of African-American churches to the early civil rights movement.

7 NATIONAL ASSOCIATION FOR THE ADVANCEMENT OF COLORED PEOPLE

The National Association for the Advancement of Colored People (NAACP) had been in existence since its founding by W. E. B. Du Bois, Ida B. Wells, and others in 1909 as a result of a lynching and racial riot in Springfield, Illinois, the hometown of Abraham Lincoln. Both whites and blacks joined the organization dedicated to securing the rights within the Thirteenth, Fourteenth, and Fifteenth Amendments for African Americans across the nation. Further goals were to secure the political, educational, social, and economic equality of minorities and people of color and to end racial prejudice. As the oldest civil rights organization, the NAACP hired Thurgood Marshall to argue the 1954 *Brown* case before the Supreme Court, and Marshall went on to become the first African-American justice on the Court. In the civil rights era of the 1950s and 1960s, NAACP leaders became targets of Ku Klux Klan reprisals and were sometimes murdered. The organization focused more on lobbying government to achieve legislative and judicial advances, but during the height of the activist period of civil rights protests the NAACP provided legal counsel and representation to participants across the civil rights spectrum.

8 CONGRESS OF RACIAL EQUALITY

Formed in 1942 by James Farmer, the Congress of Racial Equality (CORE) stood against racial segregation of public transportation and other public facilities in the North prior to the civil rights era. Mainly white members joined starting from the University of Chicago, but the organization spread nationally and inspired African Americans to employ direct protest tactics like sit-ins and freedom rides. When these tactics led to arrests, CORE members said they were also employing jail-ins. These same tactics were picked up by the Southern Christian Leadership Conference (SCLC) and other organizations on a wider scale through the 1960s, and CORE continued its operations as well.

9 SIT-INS

In a reenactment of the Congress of Racial Equality's (CORE's) first sit-in that took place in North Carolina in 1947, four African-American males sat down at a Woolworth's department store lunch counter in Greensboro early in 1960. The four politely asked for service but were refused according to the South's segregation policies. When asked to leave, the four young men refused. The students asserted that they were able to purchase goods from other parts of the store so they should be able to buy lunch. At the store's closing, the protestors were forced to leave. They returned the next day, however, and their sit-in touched off a six-month protest that culminated in the desegregation of Greensboro's lunch counters. Other students across the South picked up the tactic and also staged sit-ins at Woolworth's stores because the department store was a national chain. Even northern students picketed outside the stores, and sit-ins became a chief strategy of the subsequent antiwar protests of the youth revolt.

10 STUDENT NONVIOLENT COORDINATING COMMITTEE

The Student Nonviolent Coordinating Committee (SNCC or Snick) formed as a youth spin-off from the Southern Christian Leadership Conference (SCLC) in the wake of the Montgomery

Bus Boycott, and after the Greensboro sit-in, launched a sit-in at a Woolworth's in Nashville, Tennessee. Forty students of local African-American colleges initiated the sit-in, but as they were arrested, hundreds more replaced them at the lunch counter. Despite beatings, verbal abuse, and other forms of intimidation by white youths, the SNCC protestors did not strike back. After three months the city of Nashville ordered the integration of public dining facilities. SNCC widened its sit-in tactics to target public parks, swimming pools, theaters, churches, libraries, museums, and beaches. John Lewis, a seminary student and later U.S. congressman, became the chairman of SNCC in 1963 and helped organize the March on Washington, the Selma march, freedom rides, and freedom schools in cooperation with the Congress of Racial Equality (CORE) and the National Association for the Advancement of Colored People (NAACP). Stokely Carmichael became the chairman in 1966 and moved SNCC toward a more militant position of Black Power. As more extremists took up leadership in the organization, SNCC lost membership and ceased to exist in 1970.

11 FREEDOM RIDES

Northern lawyers, teachers, and students of both races organized bus rides of activists and protestors to enter the South during what became known as the long, hot summers of the civil rights era. The protestors helped challenge the segregation laws and the practices that had disenfranchised African Americans and helped establish and staff Freedom schools. As tension mounted, the voter registration drives inaugurated by Freedom Riders led to reprisals like beatings and the burning of buses. This tactic was especially designed to raise awareness in the North as the family members, neighbors, and colleagues of the protestors followed the events that resulted from the confrontations. White supremacists in the South said they were motivated by a desire to defend their way of life, but the violence aimed at the Freedom Riders served only to expose the injustices of southern society in the media, especially television, and to harden the resolve of all ranks of civil rights protestors. The murder of three Freedom Riders by Klansmen during the Johnson administration led to passage of the Civil Rights Act and the Voting Rights Act for which Lyndon B. Johnson was famous.

12 MEDGAR EVERS

Evers was an African-American World War II veteran who returned to Mississippi and resolved to end racial discrimination in his home state after defending freedom in Europe. He rose in the ranks of the National Association for the Advancement of Colored People (NAACP) to become the field secretary, an office through which he organized new chapters of the organization and voter registration drives across the state as well as African-American boycotts of white businesses. As the face of the NAACP, Evers and his family received numerous threats, and their house in the state capital of Jackson was firebombed. Medgar Evers was shot in the back by a sniper in the summer of 1963 and died. Not until after thirty-one years was the killer brought to justice.

13 BIRMINGHAM, ALABAMA

Birmingham had been the site of eighteen unsolved bombings of African-American neighborhoods in six years and was thus nicknamed "Bombingham." A mob in the city had attacked a Freedom Rider bus in 1961. Martin Luther King Jr. was invited to the city by a local African-American minister in 1963 during protests that saw commissioner of public safety, Bull Connor, use police dogs to disperse crowds. King was arrested after leading a march and wrote "Letter from Birmingham Jail" while in custody. After King's release from jail, he and other leaders organized a walkout by school children who gathered and marched downtown singing the civil rights anthem, "We Shall Overcome." Almost one thousand students were arrested, filling Birmingham's jails. When another thousand students protested the next day, Bull Connor had the fire department turn high-pressure hoses on the children as well as using dogs again. By then pictures of the confrontation had received worldwide attention and drew the ire of President Kennedy who went on television to decry the events in Birmingham with his famous "Race has no place in American life or law" speech. Birmingham business leaders agreed to open lunch counters and to hire more African-American workers as a result.

14 MARCH ON WASHINGTON

After John F. Kennedy announced his support for the end of segregation before his assassination, two hundred thousand demonstrators marched on the national capital in August 1963 demanding "jobs and freedom." John Lewis and Dr. King delivered famous speeches (King's "I have a dream" speech) during an event that marked the high point of civil rights activists' unity and nonviolent "soul force." The march was also designed to lobby leaders in Washington to support a Civil Rights Bill that passed the House early in 1964 and later the Senate. President Johnson signed the Civil Rights Act almost a year after the March on Washington, and the law banned segregation in public facilities; discrimination in employment based on race, color, religion, sex, or national origin; and the denial of registration to vote based on immaterial errors on registration forms. The law also authorized the attorney general to sue agencies, businesses, and school systems that barred desegregation.

15 VOTING RIGHTS ACT

In 1965, the Johnson administration followed the Civil Rights Act with the Voting Rights Act. The law removed all bars toward voting for African Americans in the South including literacy and other tests. The federal government was also given the task to supervise voting registration in state and local voting districts where fewer than half of potential voters were registered or had voted. At the time of the passage of the Voting Rights Act, seven states in the South still used Reconstruction era literacy tests.

> **TWENTY-FOURTH AMENDMENT**
> This amendment to the Constitution was adopted in 1964 and banned the denying or abridging of the right to vote by levying poll taxes.

16 FREEDOM SCHOOLS

One goal of the Freedom Rides of the 1960s was to instill greater pride in southern African-American communities. Freedom schools were held during the summers and taught African-American history and the nonviolent philosophies of the civil rights movement in order to prepare the next generation to continue the struggle. Proposed as early as 1963, freedom schools spread across Mississippi in 1964 and 1965 until over three thousand children were meeting in over forty organized efforts. The meeting places of the schools and the homes of the organizers were often targets of firebombing and some schools were attacked by white mobs. The founder of the freedom school movement, Charles Cobb, said the purpose of the schools was "to create an educational experience for students which will make it possible for them to challenge the myths of our society, to perceive more clearly its realities, and to find alternatives—ultimately new directions for action."

17 SELMA, ALABAMA

Selma was the scene of a climactic series of marches in which the first march of Student Nonviolent Coordinating Committee (SNCC) leaders organized as a protest turned into a televised riot. As a peaceful line of marchers approached the Edmund Pettus Bridge in the spring of 1965, the local sheriff and highway patrolmen dispersed the march using tear gas. Television cameras caught the scene of the troopers wailing away at the marchers with clubs while wearing gas masks to protect themselves from the tear gas. This coverage prompted Martin Luther King Jr. to bring support from the Southern Christian Leadership Conference (SCLC) and lead another march, this time having sought protection under the law from a federal district court. Over three thousand people, five times the number of marchers in the original attempt, began a five-day 54-mile march to Montgomery, Alabama. By the time the march arrived in Montgomery, twenty-five thousand people had joined in order to help the protestors petition their government with grievances regarding racial discrimination. Within five months the U.S. Congress passed the Voting Rights Act.

18 MALCOLM X

Malcolm X was born Malcolm Little in the home of a Baptist minister who was a follower of Marcus Garvey. After his family fled reprisals for his father's activities and moved to Michigan, the family home was burned and his father killed. Little dropped out of school and moved to New York City and to Boston where he was arrested for burglary. While in prison, Little came under the influence of the Nation of Islam, a Muslim religious organization led by Elijah Muhammad. After converting to Islam, Malcolm Little changed his last name to "X" to symbolize the loss of his African ancestors' tribal name. With Malcolm X's articulate and charismatic leadership the Nation of Islam increased its membership from five hundred to thirty thousand in just nine years. Malcom X adhered strictly to celibacy before marriage as a Muslim teaching, but discovered that Elijah Muhammad was having sexual relations with six different women. Over time, Malcolm X severed his ties to the Nation of Islam, and after making a pilgrimage to Mecca renounced his racist views that sought separation from white society. After giving a speech in New York City in 1965, Malcolm X was assassinated by three gunmen from the Nation of Islam.

19 STOKELY CARMICHAEL

Another spin on African-American civil rights came from Stokely Carmichael who became the leader of a movement called "black nationalism." Carmichael coined the phrase "Black Power," and rejected the nonviolent strategies espoused by earlier leaders. Having come through the Student Nonviolent Coordinating Committee (SNCC) organization and participated in Freedom Rides, Carmichael's break with the majority opinion caused a rift in the civil rights movement. As chairman of SNCC, in 1966 he espoused self-defense training, self-determination, the pursuit of political and economic power, and racial pride. A political organization he helped found in Alabama was the first to adopt a black panther as its symbol. Carmichael left the United States and moved to West Africa taking the name Kwame Toure.

20 BLACK PANTHER PARTY

This organization was founded in Oakland, California, in 1966 by Huey Newton and Bobby Seale. The Black Panthers formed a militant wing of the "black nationalism" movement and patrolled in African-American neighborhoods protecting residents from police brutality. The Black Panthers adopted Marxist ideology and called for all African Americans to arm themselves. The group demanded from the federal government the release of all African Americans from jails, their exemption from the draft, and reparation payments for the history of white oppression in America. After several shoot-outs with police in California, Huey Newton was arrested for murdering a policeman. The Black Panther Party's goals and tactics were shunned by most other civil rights leaders. The Black Panthers grew less militant over time and were disbanded in the 1980s.

BLACK POWER

This ideology of certain civil rights activists espoused militancy and separation and rejected pacifism. The positive expression of black power promoted the heritage of African Americans.

THE BIG PICTURE

1. After a century of repression following the Civil War, the actions of a few individuals ignited the activism on behalf of African Americans known as the civil rights movement.

2. Prominent ministers and other leaders organized national reform associations to coordinate protests and to mobilize African-American communities in the face of segregation and other forms of racial discrimination.

3. African-American protestors and those of other races gathered in the South from all over America to help advance the causes of voter registration and desegregation through sit-ins, marches, and other forms of nonviolent protest that resulted in important federal legislation promoting equality.

4. A campaign on the part of white supremacist organizations and individuals in the South harassed civil rights leaders and murdered several prominent as well as many average citizens involved in civil rights activism.

5. Several African-American activists grew impatient with the pace of change through nonviolent means and advocated a more militant approach through "black pride," "black power," and "black nationalism" to achieve a separation of the races as racist as that espoused by white supremacists.

The Rise of Liberalism and Challenges to the Status Quo in the 1960s

34

Over this war—and all Asia—is another reality: the deepening shadow of Communist China. . . . The contest in Vietnam is part of a wider pattern of aggressive purposes.

—Lyndon B. Johnson, speech at Johns Hopkins University, 1965

TIMELINE	
1949	Harry S. Truman announces the Point IV Plan
1954	Southeast Asia Treaty Organization (SEATO) is formed; Ho Chi Minh becomes president of North Vietnam
1955–1975	American involvement in Vietnam spans twenty years
1962	Students for a Democratic Society (SDS) adopts the Port Huron Statement
1964	Congress passes the Gulf of Tonkin Resolution; General William C. Westmoreland takes command in Vietnam
1965	Battle of Pleiku; Watts Riot in Los Angeles
1965–1968	Operation Rolling Thunder spans three years
1966	Women's liberation movement forms the National Organization for Women
1968	Viet Cong forces launch the Tet Offensive; Battle of Khe Sanh; My Lai Massacre
1970	Kent State shootings
1973	Congress passes the War Powers Resolution

OVERVIEW

In many ways, the 1960s marked a highpoint of American liberalism. The implementation of President Lyndon Johnson's Great Society programs, the issuing of several decisions by the Warren Court, and the successful passage of landmark civil rights legislation shaped the agenda for liberalism in the next generation.

Liberalism was the belief in the efficacy of government initiatives in addressing a series of social problems. This belief can be traced back to the Progressive agenda of the 1900s and 1910s, as well as to the New Deal of the 1930s. Liberals looked favorably upon the thinking of economist John Maynard Keynes, who encouraged government expenditures both to stimulate economic activity as well as to address broader social and economic goals. The liberal coalition that coalesced in the mid-century included moderates within the labor movement, critics of the excesses of McCarthyism, and supporters of civil rights for African Americans. The coalition also included civil-society groups, such as the American Civil Liberties Union and Americans for Democratic Action. The election of the youthful John F. Kennedy to the White House in 1960 represented a break with the conservatism of the 1950s, but the liberal agenda was more fully embraced by his successor, Lyndon B. Johnson. He was able to successfully implement a broad range of initiatives, including Medicare, immigration reform, the Head Start Program, and the Civil Rights Act.

The visibility and successes of the civil rights movement (see Chapter 33) inspired other movements for social change in the 1960s. These movements addressed a host of inequalities and injustices in American society. The women's liberation movement challenged gender expectations as well as more structural forms of gender discrimination. In the latter part of the 1960s, a vocal gay liberation movement developed in the United States in the aftermath of the Stonewall riots. In the 1960s, concerns about ecological destruction led to the first Earth Day and a growing environmental movement. In addition, a vibrant counterculture developed in the 1960s, providing an alternative to mainstream culture. The counterculture was visible from "hippie" enclaves in urban centers to rural communes.

The 1960s also saw the unraveling of the liberal agenda as the war in Vietnam (see Chapter 35) sucked valuable resources from social programs, and urban rioting highlighted the limits of the federal government's ability to address the problems of the African-American underclass. This liberal agenda came under attack from groups and individuals on the left who insisted that the steps being taken were insufficient to create a truly just and equitable world. This critique of 1960s liberalism was central to the New Left, an activist and intellectual movement that was associated with the organization, Students for a Democratic Society. Later, the gains of liberalism would also come under attack from a resurgent conservative movement that showed signs of life in the 1960s and 1970s, but did not come to fruition until the last decades of the twentieth century (see Chapter 37).

1 LYNDON BAINES JOHNSON

Another World War II naval-hero-turned-politician was the big Texan, Lyndon B. Johnson (LBJ), although Johnson was already in the House of Representatives when he joined the navy. He was elected to the Senate in 1949 and became the Democratic Majority Leader by 1955. He was elected vice president under John F. Kennedy in 1960. After becoming president because of Kennedy's assassination, LBJ won in his own right in 1964 against Barry Goldwater. Lyndon Johnson's presidency was one of tremendous advance for the welfare programs and civil rights legislation of the liberal version of Progressive Reform, but his escalation of the Vietnam War without developing a winning strategy was his undoing. Although constitutionally able to run in the Election of 1968 he declined to do so.

2 GREAT SOCIETY

Lyndon B. Johnson's (LBJ's) reform agenda outstripped any previous presidential liberal initiative save the New Deal. Whereas John F. Kennedy had been stymied in his attempts at reform, LBJ was able to turn the nation's injury in losing its youthful president into solid legislative advances. His advances included civil rights legislation, the War on Poverty, VISTA, Head Start, and even a resurrection of the Civilian Conservation Corps (CCC) called the Job Corps. After soundly beating Barry Goldwater, LBJ was able to receive passage of pollution control laws and other environmental legislation, the National Endowment for the Arts, funding to public schools, Medicare and Medicaid, the end of discriminatory immigration quotas, consumer safety regulations for products, and funding for public housing for low-income families. The Great Society began to unravel, though, as more federal dollars were diverted to the Vietnam War. Conservatives decried his spending for liberal domestic programs, and liberals decried his spending for a flawed foreign policy commitment.

> ### DIEN BIEN PHU
>
> This 1954 battle was the last effort of France to retain its colony of Indochina. Viet Minh nationalists soundly defeated the French, who gave up their claims to Vietnam, Laos, and Cambodia. The French pullout left the United Nations and the United States to pick up the pieces in the context of Cold War tensions.

3 WAR ON POVERTY

Lyndon B. Johnson (LBJ) declared in a state of the union address that the United States would fight an "unconditional war on poverty." He said in the affluent society created after World War II there should not be thirty million people living in poverty, thirteen million of whom were children. The Head Start program was aimed at reaching the disadvantaged children, the first one opening in rural Mississippi, which was the most impoverished state. Urban programs, however, were also begun to address a lack of housing and jobs. LBJ addressed the symptoms of poverty by stressing education and jobs training without acknowledging that because of the development of the welfare state a crisis lay in the fact that certain citizens chose to receive a meager existence from the government rather than to better themselves through government programs. Poverty rates in the United States dropped at the onset of the War on Poverty but have remained largely the same since the 1970s.

4 MEDICARE/MEDICAID

Lyndon B. Johnson (LBJ) backed a 1965 change in the Social Security Administration to incorporate an idea Harry S. Truman initiated in the Fair Deal, saying that the elderly in America were the most likely to live in poverty and that half of them did not have health insurance. Medicare was designed to provide medical care for the elderly attached to their social security payments and funded by social security taxes, which had to be raised. Those citizens sixty-five or older receiving social security also received hospitalization insurance, coverage of physicians' and surgeons' expenses, and home health care. Medicaid was designed to provide similar benefits for the poor and disabled. Costs for Medicaid were divided between the states and the federal government. Nineteen million elderly Americans were receiving Medicare payments by 1966, and the programs have been routinely expanded every three to five years since.

5 HEAD START PROGRAM

One of the War on Poverty programs was known as Head Start, originally a summer program for disadvantaged children overseen by the Office of Economic Opportunity. The program was designed to build the emotional and physical health of preschool children in order to help them overcome the social and economic conditions into which they were born. Children as young as three participated in the program when it started in 1965. In 1969, the Head Start program came under the oversight of the new Department of Health, Education, and Welfare. The summer program model was transformed into year-round day care and preschool instruction as early as 1967. The age at which children could enter an Early Head Start program was dropped to zero, or infancy, and was the source of critics' phrase "from the cradle to the grave" in complaining of the desire of the federal government to control citizens' lives through the extension of the welfare state.

6 WARREN COURT

Earl Warren was such a popular governor of California that both the Republican and the Democratic parties nominated him for the office in 1946. He became the chief justice of the Supreme Court under Eisenhower and served from 1953 to 1969. Apart from serving as the chairman of the Warren Commission that investigated the Kennedy assassination, Earl Warren and his colleagues guided the Court through its most activist era during another time period of great societal flux. The Warren Court fostered such sweeping changes in the application of the U.S. Constitution that some said the Supreme Court was making laws rather than interpreting them, whereas others rejoiced that aspects of the Bill of Rights were being applied to certain minorities in particular cases for the first time in history. The Warren Court promoted a radically equal society as well as one in which civil liberties were secured and preserved for all Americans regardless of race, religion, or other attributes that might have placed them outside the mainstream. The most important decision of the Warren Court was the landmark case *Brown* v. *Board of Education of Topeka, Kansas*, but other cases contributed to redefining First Amendment rights, the right to privacy, law enforcement procedures, and voting and representation issues.

7 ESCOBEDO v. ILLINOIS

Danny Escobedo was arrested, freed, and rearrested for the murder of his brother-in-law in 1960. During police questioning, Escobedo asked repeatedly to talk to his lawyer. When police said they had an eyewitness accusing Escobedo of the murder, Escobedo denied killing the man but gave information that led police to believe he had been at the scene of the killing. Escobedo was thus charged with the murder of his brother-in-law after being tripped up in the investigation, and his case was appealed ultimately to the Warren Court. The majority opinion of the Court was that Escobedo's prosecution had been based on evidence obtained while the police were denying the accused the right to have legal counsel. This case laid the groundwork for the *Miranda* case by setting the precedent of an accused criminal's right to remain silent until a lawyer could be provided. Law enforcement advocates decried the decision as one that would make convictions far more difficult to obtain, which is exactly what the civil rights advocates on the Court intended.

8 MIRANDA v. ARIZONA

In 1966, the Warren Court followed the *Escobedo* case with a more specific ruling after Ernesto Miranda was arrested and coerced into confessing to a kidnapping and rape of an eighteen-year-old woman. The Supreme Court ruled that the original evidence had been circumstantial and that the conviction could not stand because Miranda had at no time been informed of his rights to legal counsel. Miranda was retried and convicted again on more substantial evidence and went on to serve five years of a much longer sentence before he was paroled and later stabbed to death in a bar fight. His name has been turned into a verb, though, as police officers "mirandize" anyone being arrested by telling the person that he or she has the right to remain silent, that anything said could be used against him or her, that he or she has the right to consult with an attorney, and that if the person could not afford an attorney, a public defender would be appointed for him or her. The Supreme Court thereby effectively made a new law in that statements obtained before the Miranda rights were read to a suspect would be inadmissible in courts as evidence.

9 TINKER v. DES MOINES

In the case of *Tinker* v. *Des Moines* (1969), the Supreme Court ruled that a school prohibition against students wearing black armbands in protest of the war in Vietnam was unconstitutional. The case grew out of the decision by two siblings, John F. Tinker and Mary Beth Tinker, and a friend of theirs, Christopher Eckhardt, to wear black armbands to school in protest of the Vietnam War and in support of the idea of a "Christmas truce," called for by Senator Robert Kennedy. The principal of the school, along with other Des Moines principals, decided to create a policy forbidding the wearing of such armbands. When the Tinkers and Eckhardt decided not to comply with the policy, they were suspended from school. The defendants appealed and the case made its way to the Supreme Court. The Court ruled that students in school had the right to free speech, including symbolic speech, as long as their actions did not interfere with the educational process. The Court said, "Students do not shed their constitutional rights at the schoolhouse gate." Another student-related Warren Court decision upheld the separation of church and state in regard to public schools. In the case of *Engel* v. *Vitale* (1962), the Court ruled that school-sponsored prayers violated the Constitution.

10 THE PILL

Research on an oral contraceptive began as early as the 1950s. By 1960 the first pill believed to be 100 percent effective at preventing pregnancy was marketed and became immediately popular. The Pill contained a synthetic hormone (progesterone) that convinced a woman's body she was already pregnant and therefore suppressed ovulation. What the Pill did not suppress was sexual activity, which increased among unmarried women as a result of the sexual and moral revolution of the 1960s and 1970s. A convenient oral contraceptive increased promiscuity and often resulted in unwanted pregnancies if women accidentally skipped some of the daily doses of the pills. By 1968 six million American women, or nearly 20 percent of all women of child-bearing age, used the Pill.

11 WOMEN'S LIBERATION MOVEMENT

The "Second Wave" of the feminist movement occurred in the 1960s and 1970s amid the societal upheaval of the Vietnam era. Building on the success of the suffrage movement, women's liberation activities sprang from the 1963 book, *The Feminine Mystique*, by Betty Friedan. Friedan chronicled the dissatisfaction of women coming out of the materialism of the 1950s who sought to move outside the traditional women's role of housewives and mothers into a more overtly political stance that opposed all forms of sexist discrimination in American society and culture. By 1966 Friedan was elected president of a new civil rights organization called the National Organization for Women (NOW). The members of NOW and other feminists advocated greater equality of the sexes in educational and employment opportunities as well as in political office. The women's liberation movement also lobbied the government to reform family, marriage, and divorce laws and generally sought to redefine gender roles in American culture. As in the African-American civil rights movement, tactics of the women's liberation movement varied widely from nonviolent marches and bra burnings to protests against beauty pageants.

NO-FAULT DIVORCE

Divorces in which it was not necessary to prove a spouse had committed adultery or otherwise violated his or her marriage vows became legal in some states as early as 1970. By 1976, divorce rates tripled from their level in 1960. In states where no-fault divorces were available, domestic violence, murder, and suicide all went down. The resulting breakup of families, though, led some to advocate National Care Day, a proposal that was vetoed by President Nixon in 1972.

12 NATIONAL ORGANIZATION FOR WOMEN

This organization demanded better educational opportunities for women and more outlets for suburban housewives and denounced traditional marriage and family values. The National Organization for Women (NOW) called for "a fully equal partnership of the sexes, as part of the worldwide revolution of human rights," and the organization took action to "bring women into full participation in the mainstream of American society now, exercising all privileges and responsibilities thereof. . . ." Over half a million women belong to this, the largest feminist organization in America. National conferences and campaigns organized by the various chapters across the country have mobilized women in dozens of legislative and legal battles since NOW was founded. The organization particularly focuses on issues concerning access to abortions, domestic abuse, Constitutional rights for women, diversity, rights for homosexuals, and economic factors that pertain specifically to women.

13 ROE v. WADE

This Supreme Court case in 1973 struck down state antiabortion laws saying that such laws violated a woman's right to privacy. The Court said that the Fourteenth Amendment guaranteed the personal liberty of women in deciding to terminate a pregnancy. The court specified that these laws could not interfere through the first trimester, or the first three months, of a pregnancy. Second-trimester abortions could be regulated by state laws as they pertained to the mother's health, and last-trimester abortions could be banned. The decision of the Supreme Court launched an ongoing debate about the legality and morality of abortion that endures to this day. Pro-choice groups sought to expand abortion rights while antiabortion groups sought to define life as beginning at the moment of conception and to restore states' abilities to ban the practice entirely or in varying degrees of permissible abortions due to rape or a threat to the mother's life. During the 1970s and 1980s Congress limited the use of federal funds for abortions through Medicaid, and the Supreme Court upheld a state's right not to fund an abortion. Opponents of bans on abortions argued that making the practice illegal would only return women to seeking the termination of pregnancies through more dangerous means, and the number of legalized abortions increased steadily. Since the *Roe* v. *Wade* decision in 1973 there have been an estimated forty-six million abortions performed in the United States.

14 THE NEW LEFT

In the 1960s, many individuals and groups criticized the liberal initiatives of the 1960s, including President Lyndon Johnson's Great Society, for doing too little to significantly challenge the economic and racial inequalities at home and for pursuing an immoral foreign policy. The broad array of activists who shared this critique came to be known as the New Left. This movement can be contrasted with earlier left-wing or Marxist movements. The approach of the New Left broke with the worker-oriented, top-down, leftist movement that developed in the United States in the 1930s. At the center of the New Left was the organization, Students for a Democratic Society (see below), which took its name in 1960 (growing out of an earlier group). Many participants in the New Left were inspired by the tactics and commitment of the civil rights movement. The New Left emphasized participatory democracy and community-building. In addition, it was critical of the nuclear arms build-up and the excesses of anticommunism. It organized around issues of economic inequality, racial discrimination, and the power of large corporations. As the Vietnam War intensified, the New Left became almost synonymous with the antiwar movement. By the late 1960s, the idealism of the early Students for a Democratic Society gave way to doctrinal rigidity, factional infighting, and, in some cases, acts of violent direct action.

> ### AGENT ORANGE
>
> Among the other hardships suffered by American soldiers in Vietnam was exposure to this mixture of chemical herbicides used in an effort to defoliate the jungle and make finding the enemy easier. Toxins contaminating the basic formula proved to be detrimental to the health of millions of Vietnamese and thousands of American soldiers.

15 STUDENTS FOR A DEMOCRATIC SOCIETY

Beginning in 1960, the campuses of American universities experienced political and social activism on the part of the Students for a Democratic Society (SDS). SDS was associated with the New Left movement and consisted of college students who protested social injustices and the Vietnam War. In the Port Huron Statement of 1962, SDS leaders decried the materialism and discrimination of American society and advocated the take-over of university campuses as instruments of political change. The SDS claimed alliance with the National Liberation Front in Vietnam and called for the immediate withdrawal of troops from the war zone. By the late 1960s, SDS had moved even farther left toward radical Marxist revolutionary rhetoric. After prompting campus takeovers at Columbia University and New York University as well as the protests that led to the Kent State shootings in Ohio, SDS splintered into various other groups including the terrorist organization that called itself the Weathermen. As tensions deescalated in the 1970s, the fragmentation of the SDS led to its end as an organizing force.

16 FREE SPEECH MOVEMENT

The Free Speech movement (1964–1965) at the University of California at Berkeley was a key moment in the growth of the New Left, demonstrating the possibility of the mass mobilization of students to effect social and political change. The movement grew on campus after the administration banned political activity at an area adjacent to a busy entrance to the university that had been used as a free speech area by a variety of campus groups. The university had long banned most political activities—rallies, tabling, fund-raising—from the campus itself. In response to this general ban, student groups set up tables on an area of sidewalk at the corner of Bancroft Way and Telegraph Avenues. Students were under the impression that this was city property. However, in September 1964, the university asserted that the free speech area was on campus property and ordered a ban on political activity there. In October, campus police arrested Jack Weinberg, a former graduate student, who was staffing a table for the Congress of Racial Equality. A crowd of several thousand gathered around the police car in which Weinberg was held and refused to let the car leave. The standoff lasted 32 hours, with students using the police car itself as a podium from which to make speeches. The Free Speech movement grew from this initial encounter, with philosophy student Mario Savio emerging as an eloquent and effective leader of the movement. Many of the student activists had worked to register African-American voters in the South in the Freedom Summer project in the summer of 1964. The experience of participating in the Civil Rights movement had provided inspiration to these college students to examine the conditions of their own lives. In December, students gathered inside Sprague Hall to protest the ban on political activities and the singling out of four student activists for punishment. On the steps of the hall, Savio made an impassioned speech, asserting that "[t]here's a time when the operation of the machine becomes so odious—makes you so sick at heart—that you can't take part…. And you've got to put your bodies upon the gears and upon the wheels … and you've got to make it stop." The demonstrations continued throughout the 1964–1965 school year, eventually leading to the university backing down from the ban on political activities.

17 DEMOCRATIC CONVENTION IN CHICAGO

The national nominating convention for the Democratic Party in 1968 occurred during one of the most tumultuous years in American history. Both Martin Luther King Jr. and Robert Kennedy had been assassinated, and the Vietnam War had become so unpopular that Lyndon B. Johnson's (LBJ) support for it had wrecked his presidency. Johnson stepped aside and did not seek reelection. Mayor Richard Daley had turned the convention center into a fortification manned with around twelve thousand policemen and the National Guard. Antiwar protestors turned out in great numbers and clashed with the established leaders of the Democratic Party who nominated Hubert Humphrey, LBJ's vice president and a supporter of Johnson's escalation of the war. When police moved on the crowd and began using nightsticks and tear gas to disperse them, a riot ensued that was caught on television. Around one hundred protestors and one hundred policemen were injured, and many young people decided the political system of the United States was irrevocably damaged. After a long summer of riots in Los Angeles and other cities around the country, Richard Nixon's law-and-order campaign won him the Election of 1968.

18 STONEWALL REBELLION

The beginnings of the gay liberation movement are often traced to a series of riots that occurred outside the Stonewall Inn, a gay bar in New York's Greenwich Village, in 1969. The bar existed as a private "bottle club" without a liquor license. It attracted young and frequently marginal gay men, including transvestites and working class men of different races. Raids on the bar were frequent, occurring about once a month. Generally, a raid would occur, some arrests might be made, and the bar would be operating later that same evening. Usually, the owners were tipped off before the raid occurred. However, the raid on June 28, 1969 occurred later in the evening than usual, and the bar was crowded with over 200 patrons. Many tried to flee, but the police blocked the doors. The police began arresting patrons; those not arrested congregated outside the bar. Others gathered as well, seeing a crowd and a large police presence. After police used physical force to arrest a woman, people began throwing objects and resisting the police. Soon, a riot erupted—complete with garbage cans set on fire, flying debris, and broken windows. Tactical riot police were called in. Riots occurred again in the coming evenings. The event brought a series of grievances into the open. Gay men and women had suffered discrimination in many walks of life, including in government civil service jobs. Many gays attempted to avoid such discrimination by concealing their sexual identity and remaining "in the closet." The subsequent protests sparked a new level of militant activism for civil rights for homosexuals and increased awareness of issues related to the lesbian, gay, bisexual, transgender, and queer (LGBTQ) community. Every year, New York City's "Gay Pride" march commemorates that event.

19 COUNTERCULTURE

A wide-ranging counterculture developed among young people in the 1960s. As the baby-boom generation came of age in the 1960s, it grew increasingly weary of the culture of the previous generation, which seemed inauthentic, materialistic, conformist, and corporate-controlled. The counterculture became visible in the late 1960s in "hippie" neighborhoods such as San Francisco's Haight-Ashbury and New York's Lower East Side. A variety of activities came to be associated with the hippie movement, including urban and rural communal living, a "do-it-yourself" approach to the varied tasks of life, mystic spiritual experiences, drug use, experimental music, and avant-garde art. The counterculture reached its peak and showed its limits in two important events, months apart from each other, in 1969. The Woodstock Festival, in August, attracted half a million people to a farm in upstate New York and seemed to provide a glimpse of a utopian future for many participants. In December, promoters tried to duplicate the success of Woodstock with a giant music festival at the Altamont Speedway in California. However, the Altamont event was marred by incidents of violence; one concert-goer, armed and apparently crazed, was stopped and stabbed to death by a member of the Hell's Angels Motorcycle Club security detail as the Rolling Stones performed. Ultimately, the counterculture influenced a broader range of attitudes around sexuality and relationships, concern for the environment, a critique of militarism, a greater informality in everyday life, and an increased emphasis on nutrition and natural foods.

20 *SILENT SPRING* AND THE ENVIRONMENTAL MOVEMENT

Environmental issues were brought to the public's attention with the publication of scientist and naturalist Rachel Carson's 1962 book, *Silent Spring*. The book attacked the use of DDT, an insecticide used by the government to fight mosquitos during World War II, which had come into common use in the United States. After three years of research, she reported in the book that DDT built up in the food chain over time and thus poisoned top predators like the bald eagle. An attempt by chemical companies to halt publication of the book only helped its sales, and by 1963 President John F. Kennedy had set up a committee to investigate environmental issues. In 1972, DDT was banned by the government after the National Cancer Institute publishing findings linking the chemical to an increased incidence of cancer. Concerns around environmental pollution generated a large-scale movement. Many participants in the movement were veterans of the New Left and had developed a critique of corporate power and influence. Some environmental activists came out of the counterculture of the 1960s which encouraged people to rid themselves of material possessions and live a simpler life (see previous page). The movement became a national phenomenon and led to some important changes in laws and consciousness (see Environmental Protection Agency, pages 411–412).

EARTH DAY

This annual event, held on April 22, began in 1970 and became a rallying point for the environmentalist movement. Encouraging environmental activism and policy awareness among colleges, schools, and communities, Earth Day is a celebration in 192 countries.

THE BIG PICTURE

1. After the Kennedy assassination, the Johnson administration successfully passed a wide range of measures addressing domestic reforms in Johnson's Great Society program.

2. Specific advances in the liberal Democratic progam included medical insurance for the old and the indigent, environmental legistlation, and measures designed to close an achievement gap between poor students and more affluent students.

3. The Supreme Court under Chief Justice Earl Warren advanced numerous civil rights issues with such force as to give the nine members of the Court the ability to virtually make laws outside the legislative powers of states and of the U.S. Congress.

4. Throughout the decade of the 1960s, a host of social change movements, inspired by the successes of the civil rights movement, addressed inequalities involving gender, sexuality, and ethnicity.

5. The counterculture of the 1960s, culminating in the Woodstock Festival of 1969, challenged the mainstream culture of the 1950s and 1960s, which was perceived as being overly materialistic and conformist.

The War in Vietnam and the Antiwar Movement

35

I believe that this Nation should commit itself to achieving the goal, before this decade is out, of landing a man on the moon and returning him safely to earth.

—John F. Kennedy, speech before a joint session of Congress, 1961

TIMELINE	
1951	The United States develops the hydrogen bomb
1957	The Soviet Union launches *Sputnik*
1958	The Congress establishes NASA
1959	The United States first tests intercontinental ballistic missiles (ICBMs)
1968	The Nixon campaign launches the "Southern Strategy"
1969	Richard M. Nixon begins his presidency; The Nixon administration first implements Vietnamization; Henry Kissinger begins as National Security Advisor; Apollo missions result in the first moon landing
1970	The United States deploys multiple independently targeted reentry vehicles (MIRVs)
1971	The Nixon administration creates the Environmental Protection Agency; Negotiations produce the first Strategic Arms Limitation Treaty (SALT I)
1972	Daniel Ellsberg leaks the Pentagon Papers; The Nixon administration first institutes revenue sharing
1974	The Democratic National Convention nominates George McGovern; Watergate Scandal leads to the resignation of President Nixon; White House tapes are subpoenaed by the House Judiciary Committee; Newly appointed President Gerald Ford pardons Richard Nixon

OVERVIEW

Vietnam is a small country hugging the edge of the Indochina peninsula in Southeast Asia. From the mid-nineteenth century to the mid-twentieth century, it was a colony of France. It was occupied by Japan during World War II. After the war, many Vietnamese hoped to finally be free of foreign control, but France reoccupied it. A resistance movement, led by Ho Chi Minh, intensified in the 1950s. In 1954, French forces were defeated at the Vietnamese town of Dien Bien Phu, and France withdrew from the region. Vietnam was divided at the 38th parallel between a communist controlled North Vietnam, led by Ho Chi Minh, and a western-allied South Vietnam. A rebel movement, known as the Vietcong, continued to press its cause in South Vietnam.

American observers came to the conclusion that the government of South Vietnam could very likely fall to Communist rebels without outside help. United States involvement in Vietnam began in the 1950s when it sent military advisors and assistance to the government of South Vietnam. The United States became heavily involved in the Vietnam War after Congress gave President Johnson a blank check with the Tonkin Gulf Resolution (1964).

By 1968, the war in Vietnam seemed increasingly unwinnable. The war in Vietnam became a quagmire that the United States neither could win nor could successfully extricate itself from. Americans began to grow impatient with the war effort, as the number of troops and the number of casualties increased. The Vietcong and North Vietnamese forces launched the Tet Offensive in January 1968, shocking the American public. Further, extensive, uncensored media coverage of the war left many Americans questioning the morality and propriety of the war. The war generated a vocal antiwar movement and doomed Johnson's presidency. Johnson refused to run for a second full term in 1968.

The war continued to loom large in the administration of President Richard Nixon, who was elected in 1968. Although Nixon assured the American people that he had a plan to attain "peace with honor" in the Vietnam War, he widened the war to Cambodia in 1970. Starting in 1969, Nixon began the policy known as Vietnamization, replacing American troops with Vietnamese troops. However, all the measures that Nixon took would not lead to American victory. The United States pulled out of Vietnam in 1973. By 1975, the side that the United States had supported, South Vietnam, was defeated. Vietnam was then reunited as a communist country.

After the experience of the Vietnam War, some commentators believed that the United States was less willing to fully participate in military engagements abroad. In a 1980 speech, Ronald Reagan pledged to pursue a more interventionist foreign policy, saying that, "For too long, we have lived with the 'Vietnam Syndrome.'" The legacy of the war still divides historians and Americans in general, although there is less discussion of the "Vietnam Syndrome" in the post-9/11 world.

1 POINT IV PLAN

The name of this plan was taken from the section of Harry S. Truman's inaugural address in which he called for a "bold new program" of assistance to developing countries. Truman sought permission from the Congress to allow dollar diplomacy and American technical assistance in these areas, and by 1950 $35 million had been allocated. The Point IV Plan extended the Truman Doctrine to include areas of the world like Indochina that would play key roles in the Cold War.

2 DOMINO THEORY

The domino theory is closely associated with American military involvement in Vietnam. The domino theory asserts that when a nation becomes communist, its neighbors will be more likely to become communist as well. The name of the theory alludes to the game of lining up dominos in a row, so that when the first one is pushed over, the next ones in the row will each in turn be knocked over as well. The theory presumes that communism is imposed on a country from the outside—it does not develop as a result of internal conditions. The term was part of foreign policy discussions in the 1950s. In a 1954 news conference, President Dwight Eisenhower discussed the "broader considerations" of American foreign policy. He said that there was a "'falling domino' principle" that the United States must consider. Once the first one is "knocked over," there could be the "beginning of a disintegration" in a particular region. The news conference occurred as France was losing its grip on control of Vietnam. Weeks later, French forces were defeated at Dien Bien Phu (see below). After Vietnam was subsequently divided (1954), the United States began to become more involved in supporting South Vietnam. The United States became heavily involved in the Vietnam War after Congress gave President Johnson a blank check with the Tonkin Gulf Resolution (1964) (see below).

3 VIETNAM

The country of Vietnam experienced the same type of divided support after World War II that Korea did, and the result was the same. The United States, France, the United Kingdom, the Soviet Union, Communist China, and the new countries made from French Indochina met in 1954 at the Geneva Conference in order to resolve the nationalist impulses of the former colonial peoples. The agreement reached called for a cease-fire of all combatants and divided Vietnam at the seventeenth parallel of latitude as Korea was divided at the thirty-eighth. Vietnamese citizens were given the choice of country in which to live, and general elections were scheduled for 1956. Ho Chi Minh became the leader of North Vietnam while Ngo Dinh Diem became the president of South Vietnam. The Eisenhower administration committed the United States to provide South Vietnam with military, economic, and political support.

4 SOUTHEAST ASIA TREATY ORGANIZATION

As France lost control of its colony of French Indochina in 1954, new Cold War policies were being crafted for the United States by Eisenhower's secretary of state, John Foster Dulles. The "New Look" in national security policy departed from the containment policies of the

Truman administration and began to discuss "rolling back" communism and responding to any aggression on the part of the Soviet Union with "massive retaliation." As French Indochina was broken up by the United Nations and nationalist forces created North and South Vietnam, Laos, and Cambodia, Eisenhower presented the idea that if one of these nations fell to communism, then the rest would fall like dominoes. The Domino Theory prompted the formation of the Southeast Asia Treaty Organization (SEATO), a mutual defense treaty modeled after the North Atlantic Treaty Organization (NATO). Unlike NATO, however, the treaty did not create a unified military command and left the United States to defend South Vietnam alone.

5 VIETCONG

The Vietcong were the guerrilla fighters within South Vietnam who represented the National Liberation Front, a nationalist yet communist organization fighting to unite all of Vietnam under one communist government. Vietcong fighters coordinated their attacks on a national basis but could also operate as tiny insurgents assassinating South Vietnamese leaders and sabotaging American installations. Although supplied with modern weaponry by the Soviet and Chinese governments, the Vietcong also employed booby traps made from simple materials from the jungle and unexploded bombs dropped by the United States. Extensive tunnel systems helped hide the Vietcong soldiers who also used sewer drains to infiltrate cities. A major difficulty in the war in Vietnam was in distinguishing which Vietnamese were peaceful and which were the enemy.

6 GULF OF TONKIN RESOLUTION

Under the Kennedy administration the United States looked the other way while a military coup deposed and assassinated Ngo Dinh Diem, the president of South Vietnam. The Vietcong increased their activities in South Vietnam, and under Lyndon B. Johnson (LBJ) the surveillance of North Vietnam using clandestine military operations began. In the summer of 1964 North Vietnamese forces attacked the destroyer *Maddux*, an American naval vessel involved in gathering intelligence. President Johnson asked the Congress to authorize reprisal air strikes for the attacks. The Congress was not informed of the provocative nature of the American military in spying on the North Vietnamese in the Gulf of Tonkin, but they responded with the Gulf of Tonkin Resolution. The resolution granted the president their support to "take all necessary measures to repel any armed attack against forces of the United States and to prevent further aggression." This wording gave Johnson a "blank check" to wage war and was the sole premise for fighting the Vietnam War, a war in which the United States never actually declared war against any nation or nations. LBJ dramatically escalated the presence and activity of the American military in the region for the rest of his presidency.

7 WILLIAM C. WESTMORELAND

Westmoreland was a decorated veteran of both World War II and the Korean War who became the superintendent of West Point before being sent to Vietnam. Within a few months he became the commander of American forces in South Vietnam and he oversaw the increase of American troops from under twenty thousand in 1964 to almost five hundred thousand by 1968. General Westmoreland developed the "search and destroy" strategy that relied on a war of attrition dependent on a body count of the number of enemy soldiers killed as progress toward victory. After the Tet Offensive in 1968, Westmoreland's strategies fell from favor and he was replaced.

8 BODY COUNT

The key to the "search-and-destroy" strategy of fighting guerrilla forces in the Vietnam War was the belief that the United States would win if combat resulted in a death ratio of four enemy soldiers killed for every one American soldier killed. The nature of such warfare conducted in a rural country with thick jungles and the enemy's operating in tunnels made an accurate count nearly impossible, and inflation of body count estimates led to a false belief in progress. The strategy also neglected the total commitment of the Vietnamese insurgents and the North Vietnamese not only to support the existing forces but to produce more soldiers indefinitely for their nationalistic and communistic goals. The population of the enemy forces in the Vietnam War outlasted the resolve of the United States to kill them, and thus the strategy failed.

9 HO CHI MINH

Ho was a Vietnamese nationalist under French colonial rule who went to France for an education and was converted to communism. During World War II he led guerrilla attacks against Japan from just across the border with China, and when the war was over Ho sought to establish a new Vietnamese nation. When the French refused to give up their colony of French Indochina, Ho also helped lead an insurgency against them. After the departure of the French and the division of the country, Ho helped found the National Liberation Front and supplied Vietcong guerrillas from within North Vietnam along the trail through Laos that bore his name. Having firmly established the goal of spreading communism through a united Vietnam, Ho Chi Minh died in 1969 within a few years of seeing it happen.

10 OPERATION ROLLING THUNDER

Once the Gulf of Tonkin Resolution authorized retaliation, Lyndon Johnson ordered large-scale bombing of North Vietnam. The bombing campaign was named Operation Rolling Thunder and dropped over one million tons of bombs in three years. When the campaign proved ineffectual after dropping more bombs than had been dropped in all of World War II, Johnson decided to escalate the number of troops on the ground in Vietnam. After the war it was revealed that Operation Rolling Thunder had failed to force North Vietnam to negotiate a peace because the essential military assets of North Vietnam were located in underground tunnels.

11 PLEIKU

American military advisers had been located in Vietnam since before the Kennedy administration escalated their number to seventeen thousand, but at the Battle of Pleiku in 1965 an attack by the Vietcong killed eight Americans and injured 128. The Johnson administration responded with Operation Rolling Thunder but also with the placement of the first actual American ground troops into Vietnam. The large number of casualties suffered by the

Vietnamese during the Pleiku clash encouraged the development of the search and destroy missions that moved American soldiers into combat with helicopters.

12 TET OFFENSIVE

During a supposed cease-fire to allow the observance of the New Year holiday in 1968, Vietcong and North Vietnamese forces attacked all of the major cities of South Vietnam, including the capital of Saigon, as well as many small towns. Other attacks occurred at Khe Sanh and in the countryside and were all designed to demonstrate the ease with which the communist forces could coordinate widespread attacks. Although the casualties received by American forces over the weeks of fighting were the highest to that date in the Vietnam War, the casualties incurred by the attackers were considerably higher. Still, the Tet Offensive made Americans back home watching on television doubt whether the United States could win the war. General Westmoreland was denied his request to raise the number of American forces in Vietnam to over 730,000 and was eventually replaced. As a result of the Tet Offensive, stronger calls for peace back home in America revealed that although the campaign had ended in military failure, the attacks had achieved a psychological victory. The Tet Offensive and the Election of 1968 were thus major turning points in the American effort to win in Vietnam.

13 KHE SANH

When North Vietnamese soldiers began to cut off supplies and make raids around Khe Sanh village in northwest South Vietnam, General Westmoreland decided to fortify the position and supply the Marines inside the fortifications by air. Late in 1967 the North Vietnamese lay siege to the base and began attacking. By early 1968 the situation grew increasingly serious causing Westmoreland to launch Operation Niagara, the largest bombing mission in the history of aerial bombing to that point. The equivalent of five atomic bombs was dropped in an effort to eliminate the besieging enemy forces. After seventy-seven days the siege was broken, but after General Westmoreland was removed from Vietnam, the next commander abandoned the position after destroying it. The entire engagement cost over seven hundred American lives and ten thousand to fifteen thousand enemy lives, but the North Vietnamese likely staged the whole battle as a diversion to help the Tet Offensive succeed. The Battle of Khe Sanh evidenced the courage and sacrifice of American and South Vietnamese forces in the midst of strategic decisions that confused the American people.

14 MY LAI MASSACRE

In 1969, American infantrymen apparently "snapped" and murdered at least 450 unarmed South Vietnamese villagers, mostly women, children, and old men, at the village of My Lai. The shooting only stopped when an American helicopter pilot observed what was happening and landed his aircraft between the infantry patrol and the survivors telling his gunner to open fire on the Americans if they did not stop the massacre. My Lai revealed the dark side of the pressure, confusion, drug abuse, and protracted nature of the war that undermined the morale of American military personnel. The events were reported to the press and led to the court martial on charges of premeditated murder of the lieutenant in charge of the patrol.

15 THE DRAFT

The drafting of young men to fight in the Vietnam War made the war an immediate concern for millions of young men and their friends and families. In 1964, the Selective Service System began increasing the number of young men drafted to serve in the armed forces. In 1965, the monthly totals of draftees doubled. During the course of the Vietnam War, the draft brought over two million men into the armed forces; over eight million people served in the military during the years of the Vietnam War. It is likely that the possibility of being drafted led many men to volunteer for the military. Many middle-class youths often managed to get college deferments or had connections to get a stateside (in the United States) position in the National Guard or the Army Reserve. The requirements for obtaining and maintaining an educational deferment changed during the course of the war; it became increasingly difficult to obtain an educational deferment by 1968. Some men refused to comply with the draft and faced the possibility of legal consequences. Finally, as many as 100,000 draft-eligible men fled the country. The existence of the draft is cited by historians as an important reason for the growth of the antiwar movement. Since the Vietnam War, the United States has not used the draft to bring people into the armed forces.

16 VIETNAM VETERANS AGAINST THE WAR

During the Vietnam War, the antiwar movement was broad-based and included many groups, including student-based New Left groups and pacifist groups. One of the significant antiwar groups was Vietnam Veterans Against the War. Born in 1967, the organization harnessed the frustrations of returning veterans of the conflict. For many Americans, the fact that members of Vietnam Veterans Against the War had first-hand experience of the war gave the group added legitimacy. As the war progressed, many front-line soldiers grew to question the tactics, and even the purpose, of the war. In Vietnam, there were even incidents of soldiers attacking commanding officers, including "fragging"—tossing live grenades at them during action in the field. Vietnam Veterans Against the War began during the Spring Mobilization to End the War demonstration in New York City in April 1967. Several veterans gathered around a "Vietnam Veterans Against War" banner and, afterward, decided to form a group. At its height, it had around 25,000 veteran-members. In the early 1970s, the groups also addressed issues associated with the reintroduction of members of the armed forced into civilian life, including proper medical and psychological support. John Kerry, who later served as senator from Massachusetts and as secretary of state under President Barack Obama, was a prominent spokesman for the group in the early 1970s. In 1971, he testified before the Senate Fulbright Committee on the conduct of the army in the Vietnam War.

17 VIETNAMIZATION

Richard Nixon entered office with the troop level in the Vietnam War at its peak of 541,500 American military personnel. As a response to the Vietcong's use of Cambodia as a route into South Vietnam, he secretly authorized bombing of that nation in 1969. Then Nixon ordered the first troop withdrawal. As the first twenty-five thousand soldiers came home, Nixon explained on television that his goal was to gradually withdraw all American forces with a flexible schedule related to Vietnamization, the effort to support, train, and equip

South Vietnamese soldiers to defend their own country. With negotiations backed by food embargoes to the Soviet Union going on in Paris, Nixon set in motion the end of America's involvement in the Vietnam War, which came about by 1973 before he left office in disgrace. Because of Nixon's failed presidency, his successful policy of Vietnamization did not receive the necessary funding to aid South Vietnam, which fell to communism by 1975.

18 PENTAGON PAPERS

The Pentagon Papers is the popular name for a Department of Defense study outlining the events surrounding American involvement in Vietnam from 1945 to 1967. The papers included four thousand pages of government documents and three thousand pages of analysis that was considered "Top Secret-Sensitive" because they revealed, among other embarrassing facts, that President Johnson had misrepresented events and, according to the *New York Times*, lied to the American people. Daniel Ellsberg, a military analyst working as an employee at the Pentagon for the secretary of defense, released the Pentagon Papers in 1971 during the Nixon presidency, a fact that Nixon called a threat to national security. A credibility gap was thus opened in the Nixon administration that had its own problems telling the truth about its actions in prosecuting the war, and an attempt to discredit Ellsberg through divulging his mental health records, which involved a break-in similar to those that led to the Watergate Scandal. The Pentagon Papers eventually sullied the images of the Kennedy, Johnson, and Nixon administrations and opened up a possibly permanent level of distrust between the American people, specifically journalists, and the executive branch of the federal government.

19 KENT STATE SHOOTINGS

Early in 1970 the U.S. military and the South Vietnamese forces attacked across the border into Cambodia to search out and destroy communist sanctuaries from which attacks had been made into South Vietnam. Cambodia had claimed to be neutral in the Vietnam War but regularly supplied Vietcong forces within South Vietnam. The expansion of the war into a neighboring country set off large antiwar demonstrations on college campuses across the nation. Reserve Officers' Training Corps (ROTC) buildings were burned and protestors confronted police and other forces sent to contain the damage and end the riots. At Kent State in Ohio, National Guard forces fired into a crowd of protestors after being cornered against a fence, and four students were killed. Two more students were killed at Jackson State College in Mississippi ten days later. As many as one hundred thousand protestors marched on Washington, D.C., to stage a massive antiwar rally in the nation's capital.

20 WAR POWERS RESOLUTION

Congress asserted its role in the foreign policy of the United States in 1973 by issuing the War Powers Resolution. This law, in the context of the end of the Vietnam era and during the Watergate Crisis, reduced the power of the president to wage war without congressional consent. War had been declared only five times in American history, but the Korean and Vietnam Wars were presidential wars fought in often clandestine ways. A credibility gap opened between the American people and the presidents after revelations of the deception in how America entered into the war in Vietnam. The War Powers Resolution said that a president was to consult with Congress before employing military force and to notify the Congress within forty-eight hours of deployment. The law also required an end to any conflict of this nature within sixty days unless withdrawing American forces at that time would endanger them, in which case a total of ninety days were permitted before the action had to stop, unless Congress had declared war. Several subsequent presidents expressed doubts as to the constitutionality of the resolution, and some have tested the law by ignoring it.

NIXON RESIGNATION

After enjoying wide popularity and achieving a landslide victory in the election of 1972, Nixon became the first president to resign from office. He gave a short speech to the American people on television in 1974 rather than face impeachment.

THE BIG PICTURE

1. Various presidents after World War II committed the United States to policies that ultimately led to American involvement in Southeast Asia as a theater in the Cold War.

2. After some American forces were attacked by North Vietnam, the U.S. Congress granted Lyndon B. Johnson a "blank check" with which he escalated the war.

3. Confusion and disagreement about the goals and merits of the war prompted an antiwar movement that accompanied other protest movements like those for African Americans' civil rights and women's rights in a general youth revolt through the 1960s and 1970s.

4. Protests during the Vietnam era grew particularly violent as an antiauthoritarian drug culture incited riots and demonstrations in which protestors clashed with government security forces.

5. The excesses of the protracted conflict in Vietnam as well as a flawed military strategy led to the failure of the U.S. government to achieve its objectives and a revision of the abilities of American presidents to wage war by executive action alone.

Politics and Society in the 1970s

36

The erosion of our confidence in the future is threatening to destroy the social and the political fabric of America.

—Jimmy Carter, televised speech, 1979

TIMELINE	
1963	*The Feminine Mystique* sparks campaign against advertising
1970	Migration to the Sunbelt begins
1971	Twenty-sixth Amendment to the U.S. Constitution is ratified
1972	George Wallace is paralyzed in an assassination attempt; The Pill becomes available to unmarried women in all states; Phyllis Schlafly begins her campaign against the Equal Rights Amendment
1973	Stagflation begins; *Roe* v. *Wade*
1974	The Ford administration announces a campaign to "Whip Inflation Now"; The Great Recession begins
1976	The Carter campaign employs the Misery Index
1977	Jimmy Carter begins his presidency
1978	The United States, Egypt, and Israel sign the Camp David Accords
1979	Another Strategic Arms Limitation Treaty (SALT II) fails to be ratified; The core of the Three Mile Island nuclear plant suffers a meltdown
1980	Edward Kennedy challenges Jimmy Carter for the Democratic nomination; The Misery Index is used against Carter by the Reagan campaign
1981	American hostages are released after 444 days of the Iranian Hostage Crisis
1983	Astronaut Sally Ride becomes the first American woman in space

OVERVIEW

A series of events and trends in the 1970s, including economic decline and dislocation, major political scandals, a sense of moral decay, and a perception of misguided foreign policy priorities, contributed to a decline in public trust and confidence in the government.

A major source of distrust of the government was the Watergate Scandal. The scandal began in June 1972, when five men were caught breaking into the headquarters of the Democratic Party at the Watergate Hotel in Washington, D.C., and ended with the resignation of President Richard Nixon. The scandal pointed toward corruption and collusion among key members of the Nixon administration and, finally, to the president himself. Nixon resigned from the presidency in 1974.

Several additional developments led to a crisis of confidence in the 1970s. The withdrawal of the United States from Vietnam in 1973 and the defeat of the government of South Vietnam in 1975 shattered the aura of invincibility that many Americans felt in regard to the country's armed forces. Some Americans perceived that President Jimmy Carter left the United States in a weaker position in the world as well. Though Carter successfully pursued peace in the Middle East with the Camp David Accords, many Americans more vividly recall the takeover of the American embassy in Iran and the ensuing hostage crisis (1979–1981). The inability of Carter to successfully end the crisis was a bitter pill for many Americans to swallow. Carter's negotiations with Panama, resulting in the eventual transfer of the Panama Canal Zone to Panama, bolstered the notion that America's position in the world had diminished. Finally, the Arab Oil Embargo, the ensuing Energy Crisis, and the accident at the Three Mile Island nuclear facility all highlighted potential limits to economic expansion.

In many ways, the idealism and communal spirit of the 1960s gave way to different trends. On the one hand, many people began to embrace more traditional, conservative approaches to daily life. A backlash against the perceived promiscuity and permissiveness of the 1960s led to a reassertion of traditional values. The 1970s saw the rapid growth of the Christian fundamentalist movement, especially after the *Roe* v. *Wade* decision in 1973. This fundamentalist movement started in churches but soon entered the political sphere, organizing opposition to liberal and progressive social trends. This trend became more noticeable with the election of Ronald Reagan in 1980. On the other hand, many of the hippies and radicals of the 1960s began to focus more on personal improvement rather than societal change. The 1970s saw the growth of jogging and personal fitness, concerns around nutrition and diet, and interest in personal space and home improvement.

Finally, the structure of family life began to change in the 1970s. For example, from the 1970s to the present, the percentage of women engaged in the workforce has grown. Many women made the decision to focus on a career first, putting off decisions about whether to have children. Historians note a "quiet revolution" of women entering the workplace from the late 1970s through the present. The percentage of households in which women are the sole or the primary breadwinner rose from 15 percent in 1970 to over 40 percent by 2011. The divorce rate went up in the 1970s and early 1980s (although it has dropped somewhat since then) and people began marrying somewhat later in life.

1 RICHARD M. NIXON

Richard Nixon was a lawyer and World War II Navy veteran who became a congressman after the war. He was a red hunter on the House Un-American Activities Committee (HUAC) in tandem with Joseph McCarthy's investigations looking for communists in the government, and Nixon led the investigation of Alger Hiss. He went on to serve as a senator and as vice president under Dwight Eisenhower. While traveling in Latin America Nixon was attacked by mobs, and while traveling in the Soviet Union he sparred with Nikita Khrushchev in the famous Kitchen Debate about capitalism versus communism. Nixon was narrowly defeated for the presidency by John F. Kennedy in the Election of 1960 and two years later for the governorship of California, his home state. Many thought his career in politics over until he won the Election of 1968. As president, Nixon opened communist China to relations with the United States in an effort to alienate the Chinese from the Soviets. Nixon won again in 1972 but quickly became embroiled in the Watergate Scandal. After obstructing justice through passive and active resistance to investigators, Nixon faced impeachment but resigned from the presidency instead in 1974. Gerald Ford pardoned Nixon for any crimes he might have committed, and Nixon spent the rest of his life recovering his reputation by writing about foreign policy and advising subsequent presidents.

VIETNAM PULLOUT

Adding to the disillusion in the wake of the Vietnam War was the ignominious evacuation of all remaining American personnel from the embassy in Saigon just before it fell to communists from the North. President Ford could not rally support for more expenditures to help the South Vietnamese, and American prestige was dealt a severe blow by the unification of Vietnam.

2 SOUTHERN STRATEGY

Among the most curious components of the back and forth of American political values, the southern strategy led to a wholesale realignment of the former Confederate states from the Solid South of the Democratic Party to support for the Republican Party. A strategist working for the Nixon campaign popularized the idea, and Republican strategists employed it through the rest of the twentieth century. Nixon was advised to emphasize the continuing relevance of states' rights in his 1968 presidential campaign, especially while campaigning in the South. In the wake of the civil rights movement many white southerners abandoned the Democratic Party because they took Nixon's rhetoric to mean that he would not use the federal government to push for more activism on racial issues. African Americans apparently also believed that Nixon meant to stall civil rights gains or roll them back because 90 percent switched from the party of emancipation to vote for the Democratic Party. As to what Richard Nixon actually believed about civil rights, part of his enigmatic political identity was that he was a member of the National Association for the Advancement of Colored People (NAACP). Still, by Nixon's 1972 campaign he won 70 percent of the popular vote in the Deep South. Recent Republican Party candidates have repudiated the underhandedness of the southern strategy, and some have apologized for their party's use of it.

3 ENVIRONMENTAL PROTECTION AGENCY

When Congress passed the National Environmental Policy Act (NEPA), which took effect in 1970, the work of Rachel Carson and others had achieved its goal, making protection of the environment a matter of national policy. The NEPA required all federal agencies to publish an environmental impact statement regarding all their major activities, especially in matters of new pieces of legislation. The law established an advisory council to the president on environmental quality and required the president to submit to Congress an annual environmental quality report. Richard Nixon later consolidated all major programs to combat pollution and other environmental damage into the Environmental Protection Agency, or EPA, which was independent of all other existing government departments. The EPA became responsible for managing stringent controls on all federally owned public land and for enforcing laws relating to endangered species and other conservation measures. A reasonable balance was difficult to achieve between economic progress and environmental protection, and some have interpreted the activities of the EPA to be too restrictive.

> **AMERICAN INDIAN MOVEMENT**
>
> This civil rights organization was founded in 1968 but grew strong enough to hold civil disobedience campaigns through the 1970s. Some of these demonstrations involved the use of force, as when American Indian activists seized Alcatraz Island in 1970 or conducted a 71-day standoff at Wounded Knee, South Dakota, the site of the last uprising in 1890. Walks across America and several court battles were used to acquire new legal status and greater government services.

4 HENRY KISSINGER

A German immigrant, Kissinger served in the U.S. Army during World War II and returned to take a Ph.D. in government at Harvard. He was a noted scholar in the study of diplomacy, nuclear strategy, and American foreign policy and defense. He was a consultant to the National Security Council during the Berlin Crisis before becoming an actual assistant to the president for national security under Richard Nixon. Nixon then made Kissinger the secretary of state in 1973, an office Kissinger held through the Ford administration. While at the top of diplomatic circles Kissinger became famous for tremendous energy, personal and secret negotiations, and surprises like President Nixon's visit to China. Kissinger believed that the momentum of the Cold War would eventually build toward an American victory. He was the chief strategist for opening China, ending the Vietnam War, achieving détente with the Soviet Union, and supporting Israel through the Yom Kippur War. He and his Vietnamese counterpart received the Nobel Peace Prize for ending the war, and then Kissinger returned to academia.

5 DÉTENTE

Although the Cold War existed from the end of World War II to the collapse of the Soviet Union in 1991, the relationship between the Soviet Union and the United States fluctuated considerably during this time. At times the Cold War involved military confrontations, both direct and indirect, while at other times, it involved mutual coexistence or détente. Détente is the French word for loosening and refers to an easing of tensions in the Cold War and a thawing of relations between the United States and the Soviet Union. The policy is associated most strongly with President Richard Nixon. It may seem ironic that a man who made a name for himself as a strong anti-communist pursued a policy of détente. However, Nixon's strong anti-communist credentials enabled him to open relations with communist nations without being accused of being "soft on communism." In 1971, Nixon initiated an agreement with the Soviet Union whereby the Soviet Union accepted the independence of West Berlin and the United States recognized East Germany. Also, the 1972 Strategic Arms Limitation Talks (SALT) led to two arms-control agreements (see below). Tensions still existed, but détente led to discussion between the two sides, limited arms agreements, and cultural exchanges. In 1972, Nixon visited China. It was the first time an American president visited the People's Republic of China. The visit was an important step in normalizing relations with the Communist government of China.

6 STRATEGIC ARMS LIMITATION TREATIES

Under Richard Nixon and Henry Kissinger's skillful guidance of American foreign policy, negotiations opened to pursue a freeze on nuclear weapons and the systems that deployed them. Meetings in Helsinki and Vienna led to two separate agreements that were signed in Moscow. The Strategic Arms Limitation Treaty (SALT) agreements recognized that the aggressive offensive strategy of the superpowers ensured that both sides could deliver destructive blows to each other in the event of one superpower's launching of intercontinental ballistic missiles (ICBMs) and other delivery systems. Therefore, the mutual assurance of destruction deterred the outbreak of war. The SALT I agreement of 1972 permitted a limited deployment of defensive antiballistic missiles and limited the production of missiles by both superpowers. The later SALT II treaty negotiated by President Carter called for limitations on missile launchers and other delivery systems but was never ratified by the U.S. Senate. The SALT approach was later abandoned by the Reagan administration in the process of ending the Cold War and dismantling the Soviet Union.

7 WATERGATE SCANDAL

Watergate was the name of an apartment and hotel complex in Washington, D.C., that housed the Democratic National Committee offices during the campaign for the Election of 1972. Five men were caught breaking into the campaign headquarters in June 1972 and were linked to G. Gordon Liddy, an adviser to the Committee to Reelect the President (dubbed CREEP in the press). When President Nixon denied any involvement on the part of his staff and began a cover-up, reporters Bob Woodward and Carl Bernstein of the *Washington Post* began an investigation that led to Nixon's downfall. In the weeks and months that ensued, Nixon dismissed some of his staff and others resigned. Other break-ins were revealed, and when a Senate investigation opened to look into the allegations, disturbing revelations about the Nixon administration became regular fare in the press. Members of the president's staff confessed to perjury, and the existence of an "Enemies List" of politicians, journalists, scholars, and others was revealed. Those on the list were targeted for harassment by various agencies of the federal government. The existence of a group called the "Plumbers" was also revealed, their task being to stop the leaks to the press from within the administration by wiretapping, bugging, and discrediting whistleblowers. The deeper the investigations went, the less the American people felt confident in the word of their president as deception, unscrupulous campaign financing, and other nefarious practices came to light all the way back to the Johnson administration. Finally, President Nixon was accused in early impeachment proceedings of "violating the constitutional rights of citizens [and] impairing the due and proper administration of justice." Before the impeachment got underway, however, Richard Nixon announced his resignation from the presidency on television on August 8, 1974.

8 G. GORDON LIDDY

A participant in the break-in searching for Daniel Ellsberg's mental health records was former Federal Bureau of Investigation (FBI) agent G. Gordon Liddy. He went on to lead the team of "Plumbers" seeking to stop leaks to the press as an employee of the Nixon administration. In this position Liddy masterminded the break-ins of the Democratic National Headquarters in the Watergate Hotel and Office Complex during the 1972 presidential campaign. Since Liddy supervised the break-ins he was convicted of burglary, conspiracy, and other crimes. His twenty-year sentence was reduced by President Jimmy Carter to eight, and Liddy was paroled after serving over four years in federal prisons. Seven other members of the Nixon administration were indicted for crimes, and four of these also served prison time, but because Liddy refused to testify before a Senate committee he served almost as much as the other four of the president's men combined.

9 WHITE HOUSE TAPES

Central to the impeachment process that was building steam against Richard Nixon was the Senate committee's desire to know what the president knew and when he knew it. A Nixon staffer inadvertently revealed the existence of a taping system that recorded all Oval Office conversations (even those on the phone) during his testimony. The Senate committee seized on the "Nixon tapes" as a key to the investigation of the Watergate Scandal and demanded they be released. The existence of a taping system only fed the popular notion that Nixon was paranoid and devious even though the taping system had been installed by Lyndon Johnson. President Nixon instigated a series of obstructions of justice delaying the release of the tapes by claiming executive privilege. When the Supreme Court ruled that he had to release the tapes he released them slowly and with many long silences. The silences were explained by saying Nixon's secretary had accidentally erased those portions while recording the tapes. Finally, however, the tape known as the "smoking-gun tape" was released in which Nixon was recorded in 1972 instructing a staffer to contact the Central Intelligence Agency (CIA) to get the Federal Bureau of Investigation (FBI) to back down on the investigation in the interests of national security. Such a revelation caused support for Nixon to disappear and led to impeachment proceedings on the grounds that the president was guilty of obstruction of justice.

10 GERALD FORD

Gerald Ford was born Leslie King Jr., but was adopted by a stepfather and changed his name. The most athletic man to ever attain the presidency, Ford turned down a professional football career to enter a twenty-five year career as a congressman. After Spiro Agnew resigned as Nixon's first vice-president, he appointed Ford to fill his place according to the Twenty-fifth Amendment's provisions. As a universally respected and honest man, Gerald Ford set about healing the nation's wounds from Watergate and the Vietnam War, but his pardon of Nixon was so unpopular that he lost the Election of 1980 to Jimmy Carter.

11 OIL EMBARGO

In 1973, the Arab oil-producing nations—the Organization of Petroleum Exporting Countries (OPEC)—cut exports to the United States and increased the price of oil. These moves were largely in retaliation for United States support of Israel in the 1973 Yom Kippur War between Israel and its Arab neighbors. The United States had, by that time, become dependent on foreign oil. Even after the embargo was lifted, OPEC quadrupled the price of oil and set in motion the Energy Crisis of the 1970s. America had to confront a stark reality. Until the 1970s, Americans assumed petroleum was a cheap, inexhaustible commodity. Since the 1970s, Americans began to realize that there were limits to the amount of fossil fuels, particularly petroleum, available in the world, and much of it came from the volatile Middle East. Americans responded to the embargo by purchasing smaller, more fuel-efficient cars and reducing their consumption of energy. The government reduced speed limits and encouraged the development of alternative sources of energy. In more recent years, the amount of petroleum imported from the Middle East has dropped considerably. Canada now accounts for approximately 40 percent of American petroleum imports; the Persian Gulf region accounts for approximately 18 percent.

12 THE RECESSION OF THE 1970S

The economy of the United States experienced a major recession between 1973 and 1975. A major cause was the Arab Oil Embargo and the subsequent quadrupling in the price of crude oil (see above). Inflation during this period went as high as 14 percent. The scarcity of affordable fuel not only created inflation and lines of cars at gas stations, but it slowed the economy. The combined impact of inflation at a time of stagnant growth was called "stagflation" (see below). Federal monetary policies could not come up with a model to address the situation because in times of typical inflation, interest rates are typically raised; however, in times of stagnant growth, interest rates are usually lowered. The recession of 1973 to 1975 prompted Gerald Ford to resort to tax cuts to stimulate the economy. Subsequently, President Jimmy Carter reversed these tax cuts, after which President Ronald Reagan again enacted tax cuts (see page 431). By the 1980s, the economy benefitted from a steadily declining price of crude oil.

13 STAGFLATION

The condition of stagflation flummoxed Keynesian economists in the government because they were not prone to examine the role of government in hurting an economy. In the highly regulated economy that emerged from the New Deal era and the Johnson and Nixon administrations, the existence of severe inflation during a time of severe recession did not respond to either the inflationary policies under a Democrat or Republican president nor to the stimulation of their economy by deficit spending. Stagflation thus called the Keynesian economic consensus into question for the first time since the time of Franklin D. Roosevelt. Supply-side economics arose in the thinking of economists in the late 1970s as a possible solution to stagflation, and an increase in productivity coupled with tax cuts during the 1980s caused the economy to grow and conservative politicians to embrace this policy counterpoint.

14 WHIP INFLATION NOW

Gerald Ford embraced the notion that the American people could reverse stagflation themselves by reducing consumption, saving money, and feeling the solidarity of a World War II-era type of civic pride in a public drive of sacrifice for the common good. Ford was concerned about inflation and the "energy crisis" as a dual blow to the American economy. He held an economic "summit" meeting where he and his advisers debated solutions. Their idea was a voluntary anti-inflation crusade that would be led by the president who would even wear a Whip Inflation Now (WIN) button during the speech in which he launched his proposals. Ford outlined twelve steps families could take without the need for expensive government programs. Among the ways families could ". . . grow more and waste less," Ford advocated balancing family budgets, using credit wisely, economizing, recycling, and reusing. He told Americans to look for bargains while shopping and to brag about being bargain hunters. He said Americans had an "international reputation as the world's worst wasters," and said they should inventory their trash to reduce waste. Finally, Americans should all guard their health, as days lost through illness constituted terrible waste. Although these ideas all sounded rather bizarre for presidential attention, these were new ideas in the 1970s that have since become commonplace. Despite the number of supporters who wrote the White House describing their home gardens or telling what they gave up for the good of the country, the whole WIN campaign came off rather flat.

15 JIMMY CARTER

Another Navy veteran-turned-president, James (Jimmy) Carter studied nuclear physics and engineering before returning home to Georgia to take over the family business upon his father's death. Carter thus ran a business raising peanuts, ginning cotton, and warehousing. His moderate policies as a Georgia Democrat won him the governorship by 1970. He then enacted state-level reforms including an end to racial discrimination. Carter was perceived as a relaxed Washington outsider in a bid for the presidency and won over Gerald Ford in the Election of 1976, the nation's bicentennial year. Carter's open and unpretentious style won him the election but did not serve him well as president. Through the Iranian Hostage Crisis, the Soviet invasion of Afghanistan, ongoing Cold War negotiations, and the Energy Crisis he was criticized for vacillation in decision making, but his strong stance on human rights was praised by the left and influenced the United Nations. After seeming unable to solve the problem of the United States that he called "malaise," Carter lost the Election of 1980 to Ronald Reagan. After the presidency Carter and his wife, Rosalyn, devoted themselves to domestic and international humanitarian causes.

"MALAISE" SPEECH

On top of several foreign crises, President Carter gave a televised speech in 1979 in which he criticized the materialism and lack of unity in American society. Though he intended it as an FDR-style appeal to the people, the speech came across as critical and desperate and undermined the American people's faith in Carter's leadership, though not in his integrity.

16 SUN BELT

During the 1960s and 1970s over seven million Americans left the Northeast and the Midwest to move into the warmer fifteen southern states that became known as the Sun Belt. The advent of air-conditioning made the warmer climate endurable in the summers, and retired Americans preferred the warmer winters. The migration was also a result of a decline in the manufacturing industries that had been located from Pittsburgh to Cleveland, an area dubbed the Rust Belt. Heavy industries and manufacturing jobs were shifted overseas after American unions fought for higher and higher wages. Workers in Mexico would work for a week for less money than American workers were paid in an hour, and what had been a thriving iron and steel industry had by the 1980s largely disappeared. The move to the Sun Belt altered the American political equation and led to the first big boost to the economy of the South since the Civil War.

17 THREE MILE ISLAND

The 1979 failure of the cooling system of the Three Mile Island nuclear plant outside Harrisburg, Pennsylvania, raised fears of a "meltdown" of the reactor core that would lead to a catastrophic release of radiation into the atmosphere. Under the Carter administration the incident led to a shakeup of the Nuclear Regulatory Commission and a deeper focus on plant safety for the seventy-two nuclear plants in America. Although these plants produced 12 percent of the nation's electricity without any other serious incident, the 125 reactors under construction were put on hold. As of now most of those new reactors were never completed.

18 CAMP DAVID ACCORDS

President Carter's biggest foreign policy success was his participation in negotiating the Camp David Accords, an agreement between Egypt and Israel named such because the principal parties met at the American presidential retreat in Maryland. Carter met with Anwar el-Sadat of Egypt and Menachem Begin of Israel in 1978 after relations between the two had broken down. Sadat had realized after losing two wars to Israel that diplomacy was necessary, and he had become the first Arab leader to go to Israel on a visit. The two men accepted Carter's invitation and met in secret with the president for twelve days to restart negotiations. The Camp David Accords brought about an end to hostilities between the two nations by calling for a withdrawal of Israeli forces from the Sinai Peninsula they had conquered in return for free passage of Israeli ships through the Suez Canal, an end to boycotts between the nations, access for Israel to purchase Arab oil, and a proposed settlement of the problems of the Palestinian people. Sadat was assassinated by some of his own military personnel in 1981, however, and full implementation of the Camp David Accords was thwarted.

19 SOVIET INVASION OF AFGHANISTAN

Soviet intervention of Afghanistan began in 1979. Earlier, in 1978, a coup brought to power the People's Democratic Party of Afghanistan. This socialist government was unpopular with many religious-minded Afghanis, leading to a rebellion and the installing of a new anti-Soviet government. Continued instability and a hostile Afghani government led to Soviet forces intervening in late 1979 and installing a pro-Soviet government. The new government confronted a concerted rebellion led by the Afghani Mujahideen rebel group. Soviet forces remained in the country for a decade fighting against Mujahideen rebels. The Soviet invasion of Afghanistan led to President Jimmy Carter cutting off grain shipment to the Soviet Union. In addition, the United States boycotted the 1980 Summer Olympic Games, which were held in Moscow. Carter saw the presence of Soviet forces near the Middle East as a threat to American interests in the region. In response to the Soviet invasion of Afghanistan, as well as the 1979 Iranian Revolution, Carter asserted a more active role for the United States in the Middle East in 1980. The Carter Doctrine stated that the United States would repel any outside force that attempted to gain control of the Persian Gulf region. The doctrine reflects concerns about protecting United States oil interests, with an eye on halting any steps by the Soviet Union toward expanding its influence in the region. Eventually, the Soviet Union pulled out of Afghanistan (1989), but the engagement, sometimes referred to as the Soviet Union's Vietnam War, weakened the Communist government and may have contributed to the collapse of the Soviet government (1991) (see "Collapse of the Soviet Union," page 439).

After the Soviet withdrawal, disorder and civil war continued in Afghanistan, leading to the rise of the Taliban government in 1996.

20 IRANIAN HOSTAGE CRISIS

The Shah of Iran, an American-backed ally named Mohammed Reza Pahlavi, fled the country after a fundamentalist Islamic revolt established an Islamic republic under the Ayatollah Ruhollah Khomeini in 1979. When the United States allowed Pahlavi to enter America to receive medical treatment for cancer, hundreds of militant students stormed the American Embassy in Teheran and took fifty-three American personnel hostage. President Carter boycotted Iranian oil, froze Iranian assets in America, and broke off diplomatic relations with the revolutionary government of Iran. While waiting for the United Nations to intervene, Carter allowed the crisis to drag on for over a year after threatening to go to war in the Persian Gulf. United Nations efforts proved ineffectual, and Carter's one attempt at a rescue ended in disaster when two American military aircraft collided and killed eight rescuers. The constant media coverage of the crisis made it the focus of American foreign policy during the campaign for the Election of 1980, and the frustration of the American people with the insult of the hostage crisis led to victory for Ronald Reagan. After consenting to several of the Iranian demands, the Carter administration successfully negotiated the release of the hostages, but the Iranian government refused to allow the plane carrying them to leave until after Ronald Reagan finished his inaugural address.

THE BIG PICTURE

1. The Nixon administration employed a successful foreign policy but was undone by domestic issues arising from Nixon's own temperament and the atmosphere of suspicion prevalent in the Vietnam era.

2. Richard Nixon was a political moderate who began the return to law and order by expanding the power and size of the federal government.

3. As the Vietnam War wound down the Watergate Scandal erupted, and the combined impact of these events created a lasting credibility gap between the American people and their presidents.

4. The decade of the 1970s witnessed a major economic downturn, characterized by the unusual combination of high inflation and high unemployment, caused in part by the energy crisis related to the Arab oil embargo.

5. President Carter's administration faced daunting foreign issues and continuing domestic woes that together created what Carter called a crisis of confidence, a challenge he proved unequal to meet.

Mini Quiz

1. By the time of his assassination, an assessment of the Kennedy presidency might be that he

    (A) revitalized Progressive Reform through his New Frontier agenda.
    (B) finally placed African-American civil rights at the forefront of domestic politics.
    (C) was overshadowed by his ambitious vice president, Lyndon Johnson.
    (D) grew in his mastery of foreign policy but was still stalled on the domestic front.
    (E) was popular in the South and in New England, but would not likely have won reelection.

2. Lyndon Johnson's War on Poverty stressed which type of solution?

    (A) Deficit spending to provide jobs as under the New Deal
    (B) Federally funded educational and jobs-training programs
    (C) Welfare reform by reducing the time a citizen could receive government support
    (D) Tax relief for businesses hiring people who had been unemployed for at least two years
    (E) Emphasis on expanding markets through trade negotiations with other nations

3. After President Eisenhower placed Earl Warren on the Supreme Court, the highest court in the land

    (A) retreated from participating in civil rights cases.
    (B) returned to a more traditional role for the judiciary branch.
    (C) cracked down on criminals fulfilling Eisenhower's promise to restore law and order.
    (D) lost a great deal of its prestige because of impeachment proceedings against two justices.
    (E) undertook a liberal agenda unanticipated by the Eisenhower administration.

4. The Montgomery Bus Boycott in the wake of the arrest and fine of Rosa Parks

   (A) seriously lowered the bus company's revenues for over a year.
   (B) relied almost entirely on the national reputation of Martin Luther King Jr. to succeed.
   (C) had no appreciable impact as a boycott because most African Americans never rode the buses.
   (D) inspired a march on Washington, D.C., at which point the Supreme Court intervened.
   (E) ended when African Americans could no longer afford to carpool to work.

5. Which of the following was the oldest civil rights organization addressing the concerns of African Americans?

   (A) The American Civil Liberties Union
   (B) The Southern Christian Leadership Conference
   (C) The Congress of Racial Equality
   (D) The National Association for the Advancement of Colored People
   (E) The Student Non-violent Coordinating Committee

6. The Voting Rights Act of 1965 primarily addressed the continued use of

   (A) poll taxes to place economic hurdles for African-American voters in the South.
   (B) complex ballots in the North that made the voting process confusing to immigrants.
   (C) literacy tests that were interpreted by southern voting registrars to favor white voters.
   (D) labor racketeering to deliver the votes of union members to the Democratic Party.
   (E) unreasonable residency requirements before citizens could register to vote in the South.

7. The "New Look" in regard to national security policy under the Eisenhower administration sought to

   (A) achieve supremacy in satellite surveillance of the Soviet Union and its allies.
   (B) close the missile gap revealed by the launch of *Sputnik* by using the National Aeronautics and Space Administration for military purposes.
   (C) take a more aggressive stance toward communist expansion rather than merely contain it.
   (D) seek some other means of keeping the peace besides mutually assured destruction.
   (E) separate American foreign policy more and more from control of the United Nations.

8. Lyndon Johnson's approach to the Vietnam War was to

   (A) allow his generals to exercise nearly complete control over strategy and military operations.
   (B) increase the number of American military personnel even though fighting a limited war.
   (C) respond to attacks in a purely defensive war until the Congress agreed to declare war.
   (D) pressure the Chinese and Soviet governments using economic threats to end their support role.
   (E) maintain a front of restraint while sending special forces to assassinate communist leaders.

9. All of the following protest movements challenged American societal norms during the Vietnam era **EXCEPT** the

   (A) women's liberation movement.
   (B) African-American civil rights movement.
   (C) antiwar protest movement.
   (D) antinuclear energy movement.
   (E) hippie youth revolt.

10. Richard Nixon's "southern strategy" directly resulted in

   (A) many southerners switching from the Democratic to the Republican Party.
   (B) more federal dollars supporting projects in the South through "revenue sharing."
   (C) most African Americans voting for the Republican Party again.
   (D) racial riots in towns and cities through which Nixon campaigned for the presidency.
   (E) the assassination attempt on his independent opponent, the segregationist George Wallace.

11. The first Strategic Arms Limitation Treaty (SALT I) differed from the SALT II in that SALT I

   (A) limited nuclear missile manufacture, and SALT II called for destroying weapons.
   (B) limited missile delivery systems, and SALT II limited the actual missiles.
   (C) was initiated by the United States, and SALT II was initiated by the Soviet Union.
   (D) was approved by the U.S. Senate, and SALT II was not approved by the Senate.
   (E) was begun by President Nixon, and SALT II was begun by President Ford.

12. The Watergate scandal in the Nixon administration was investigated primarily by

   (A) the Federal Bureau of Investigation.
   (B) the Supreme Court.
   (C) an independent counsel assigned by the House of Representatives.
   (D) a grand jury from the District of Columbia.
   (E) a Senate committee.

13. Migration to the Sun Belt during the 1960s and 1970s occurred as a result of all of the following **EXCEPT** the

   (A) invention of reliable air-conditioning systems for homes and offices.
   (B) collapse of the heavy industries of the Rust Belt.
   (C) lowering of fares through regulation of the commercial airline industry.
   (D) increasing number of retirees seeking warmer winters.
   (E) greater influence of labor unions in the North.

14. The Camp David Accords resulted in

   (A) an increase in the territory under the control of Israel.
   (B) a settlement of the displacement problem of the Palestinian people.
   (C) a foreign policy success for President Carter with small expense to the American people.
   (D) a lessening of hostilities between Egypt and Israel.
   (E) the formation of an Islamic republic in Iran.

15. Jimmy Carter's response to the 1970s recession was most like

   (A) Franklin Roosevelt's response to the Great Depression.
   (B) Theodore Roosevelt's use of the presidency as a "bully pulpit."
   (C) Calvin Coolidge's hands-off approach to leadership.
   (D) Lyndon Johnson's launch of massive new welfare programs in his Great Society.
   (E) Gerald Ford's experimentation with voluntary compliance and tax cuts.

ANSWER EXPLANATIONS

1. **(D)** Some would suggest answer (C) as a function of an overall conspiracy theory that Lyndon B. Johnson participated in planning the assassination of John F. Kennedy (JFK), but new evidence suggests an even stronger case that Lee Harvey Oswald acted entirely alone in that he had eleven seconds to fire three shots at the president. Answers (A) and (B) are incorrect in that Kennedy's domestic agenda was mostly stalled in Congress even though his own party controlled it. Kennedy did state on national television that "race has no place in American life or law," a stance that made him decidedly unpopular in the South contrary to answer (E). His fateful trip to Dallas, Texas, was intended to shore up support in the former Confederacy. Answer (D) points to the fact that the Bay of Pigs was a foreign policy debacle, but Kennedy had reversed this initial failure by careful management of the Cuban Missile Crisis and his bold stand at the Berlin Wall.

2. **(B)** Johnson's War on Poverty included Head Start and other educational and job-training programs designed to lift people out of poverty. Answer (C) did not occur until President Bill Clinton and a Republican Congress worked out welfare reform legislation. Answers (A), (D), and (E) are more the approach of the Obama administration.

3. **(E)** Although Earl Warren had been a member of the Republican Party, when he became chief justice of the Supreme Court he led in or cooperated with liberal policies advanced not in the Congress but by judicial activism. Therefore, answer (B) is incorrect, and answers (A) and (C) are the opposite of the truth. Opponents of the Warren Court's procedures claimed they did cause the Court to lose prestige, but not for the reasons stated in answer (D), which is a fabrication.

4. **(A)** Although the segregation of buses in Montgomery was ended as a result of a ruling of the Supreme Court, the boycott did hurt the bus company economically because, contrary to answer (C), most of those riding the buses before the boycott were African Americans. Answer (D) hints at the intervention of the Supreme Court, but the march on Washington came much later in the civil rights movement. Answer (E) is incorrect in that African Americans were walking and carpooling to the end of the boycott, and answer (B) is incorrect because the boycott did not rely on a national reputation of Martin Luther King Jr., but rather gave this young, local minister his national reputation as he went on to launch the Southern Christian Leadership Conference (SCLC).

5. **(D)** The roots of the American Civil Liberties Union mentioned in answer (A) go back only to 1917, whereas the National Association for the Advancement of Colored People was founded in 1909. The other civil rights organizations were founded in the civil rights era between 1941 and 1960.

6. **(C)** As Lyndon Johnson said when he signed this legislation into law, it addresses all limitations on the right to vote, but at the time the literacy tests mentioned in answer (C) were the most egregious violation of the rights of African Americans granted by the Fifteenth Amendment to the U.S. Constitution. In 1965, seven southern states still used this practice to limit access to voting for African Americans. The other answers address problems with ballots and voting that existed before and after 1965 but were not the primary target of the Voting Rights Act.

7. **(C)** Answers (A), (B), and (D) were the initiatives of other presidential administrations throughout the Cold War, and even Eisenhower had to respond to criticisms about a "missile gap." The "New Look" referred to in the question mainly implied a departure with containment in favor of "rolling back" communism, if need be through "massive retaliation" up to and including the use of nuclear weapons. Answer (E) belies the fact that American foreign policy has never been under the control of the United Nations.

8. **(B)** Answer (B) refers to Lyndon B. Johnson's tendency to escalate the commitment of the United States without escalating the mission of the United States until almost five hundred thousand American service personnel were "in country." Answers (A) and (C) are the opposite of the truth in that Johnson micromanaged the war, and Congress never declared war. Answer (E) would be the more devious approach of Eisenhower or Nixon but was never documented, and answer (D) was Nixon's almost successful approach that accompanied his policy of Vietnamization.

9. **(D)** All of these protests occurred during the 1960s and early 1970s (and beyond) but the antinuclear movement only began in the United States at the very tail end of American involvement in Vietnam. Large-scale protests did not occur until late in the 1970s, especially after the 1979 Three Mile Island accident in Pennsylvania. American involvement in Vietnam slowed with an armistice in 1973 and ended in 1975 with the fall of Saigon to North Vietnamese and Vietcong forces.

10. **(A)** Nixon's campaign rhetoric emphasized states' rights, which southerners interpreted to mean that if he were elected president he would not continue the executive activism of the Johnson administration. For the first time since the Civil War, large numbers of southern voters voted for Nixon, the Republican candidate in 1968. This shift continued a trend begun under the administration of Franklin D. Roosevelt that for a time caused most African-American voters to support the Democratic Party. Answer (B) refers to Nixon's policy of revenue sharing, but federal funds were not distributed largely to southern states in any sort of quid pro quo arrangement. Racial riots were occurring throughout this time period and cannot be directly tied to Nixon's or any other candidate's campaign. George Wallace was a segregationist who ran on an independent ticket for the presidency against Nixon, but not until 1972 after the "southern strategy" was not needed to give Nixon a massive landslide victory that he soon squandered in the Watergate scandal.

11. **(D)** Answer (B) is the opposite of the truth of these treaties negotiated by Nixon and Carter, respectively. The one difference correctly stated is that the Senate never got around to ratifying the treaty until after American Cold War policy took a different turn under President Reagan who repudiated both SALT agreements.

12. **(E)** Although both the Federal Bureau of Investigation and the Supreme Court played a role in the investigation, and there were even independent counsels assigned (and fired) by Nixon himself, the drama unfolded in the main investigation carried out by a Senate committee.

13. **(C)** Answers (A) and (D) are obvious reasons for the migration to the Sun Belt. Answer (E) hints at the increasing demands labor unions placed on the steel industry and other heavy industries that partly led to their demise suggested in answer (B). Although the expansion of the commercial airline industry could have conceivably shrunk the time

for families seeking to visit relatives over large distances, the regulation of the industry by the federal government did not lower airfares. Deregulation put more airlines in competition and lowered fares after the Sun Belt migration was largely over.

14. **(D)** The best that can be claimed for the Camp David Accords is hinted at in answer (D), a fact reversed by the assassination of Anwar Sadat by his own people for his agreement to negotiate with the Israelis. Answer (E) hints at the revolution in Iran that deposed the Shah and installed the Ayatollah Khomeini as the Supreme Leader unrelated to the meetings between Egypt and Israel at Camp David. Answer (A) is incorrect in that Israel gave up land it had conquered on the Sinai Peninsula in return for access to the Suez Canal. Answer (B) is unfortunately still not achieved, and although the Camp David Accords were a success for President Carter as stated in answer (C), they were not cheap. The Egyptians and the Israelis agreed to Carter's terms partly because they were offered the largest single dispersal of U.S. foreign aid to two individual countries to that time in history.

15. **(B)** Franklin D. Roosevelt would have initiated massive deficit spending to start federal programs, a tactic that looked impossible and even irresponsible in the 1970s situation. Coolidge would have pushed for tax cuts, done little, and said less. Carter did not launch any massive Johnsonesque welfare spending in an era when American resources seemed tapped out, and he did not agree with Ford's experiment with small tax cuts. He raised taxes. Carter consulted with Americans of all kinds as Theodore Roosevelt (TR) did on occasion, but he limited his action to speaking to the American people as TR did in a sort of moral lecture series, the exact thing TR described as a "bully pulpit." Without any other actions to back up his words, however, Carter followed in the footsteps of neither Roosevelt and lost the Election of 1980 to Ronald Reagan.

Conservative Resurgence

37

The American spirit is still there, ready to blaze into life.

—Ronald Reagan, acceptance speech at the
Republican National Convention, 1980

TIMELINE

1953	Russel Kirk launches the conservative movement with *The Conservative Mind*
1955	William F. Buckley founds *National Review* magazine
1959	The Cold War strategic capacity rises to mutually assured destruction
1972	Venture capital meets technological innovation in "Silicon Valley"
1974	Arthur Laffer explains the Laffer Curve to advisers of Gerald Ford
1976	Bill Gates establishes Microsoft; Presidents Ford and Carter label the federal bureaucracy "Big Government"
1977	Steve Jobs establishes Apple
1979	The Contras begin opposition to Marxist Nicaraguan revolutionaries
1980	Ronald Reagan is elected to the presidency
1981	John Hinckley attempts assassination of President Reagan
1982	Nancy Reagan initiates "Just Say No" antidrug campaign
1983	U. S. Marines are killed in the Beirut bombing; U.S. forces invade Grenada to protect American lives; The Reagan administration proposes the Strategic Defense Initiative (SDI)
1984	Walter Mondale runs as the Democratic challenger to President Reagan
1986	Soviet Premiere Mikhail Gorbachev meets Reagan at Reykjavik, Iceland; Iran-Contra Scandal is exposed; The United States bombs the family compound of Muammar al Qaddafi in Libya
1987	Oliver North testifies before a joint congressional committee about Iran-Contra

OVERVIEW

The late twentieth century saw the growth of a powerful conservative movement. The movement won a stunning victory with the election of Ronald Reagan to the presidency in 1980. However, the elements of the movement had been gestating for decades.

Starting in the 1950s and 1960s, a movement of intellectual conservatives put forth a set of ideas that broke conventional wisdom and included reviving principles of governance that predated the rise of progressivism and the New Deal. The conservative movement attempted to revive traditional notions of individualism with patriotism, religion, and capitalism, all tinged with optimism. Fears about the growth of government, "creeping socialism" as President Dwight Eisenhower referred to it, united various strands of conservatism into a political agenda. Political thinkers such as Edmund Burke and John Adams and economists, such as Adam Smith, were guiding lights of this movement. The movement also gained inspiration from more contemporary thinkers such as Russell Kirk, Milton Friedman, Friedrich Hayek, and William F. Buckley. Buckley published the *National Review* magazine, which popularized conservative ideas. The movements found a staunch ally in Barry Goldwater, the 1964 Republican candidate for president. During Goldwater's campaign, Ronald Reagan emerged as an important spokesman for the campaign after a rousing speech in favor of Goldwater. The movement embraced individual freedom, free-market economics, the rule of law, respect for tradition, lower taxes, less regulation of business, equality of opportunity, a moral order, and property rights.

Even as the conservative movement united around the candidacy of Ronald Reagan in the 1980s, it was evident that different tendencies existed within the movement. To a degree, these tendencies complement one another. However, these tendencies can also be in conflict with one another. First, there were Cold War conservatives, focused on containing or rolling back communist regimes abroad. In the post-Cold War era, interventionists have argued for continued United States actions abroad, notably in the Middle East. The second tendency is the pro-business economic conservatives. These conservatives argue for lower corporate taxes, deregulation, and an economic atmosphere friendly to the priorities of big business. The third tendency within the conservative movement is the religious and cultural wing. This movement gained steam as traditional-minded people grew frustrated with what they saw as the excesses of the counterculture of the 1960s. They railed against the women's liberation movement for challenging traditional gender roles and the gay liberation movement. The public nature of drug consumption in the 1960s also angered traditional-minded people. The issue that propelled the cultural conservatives from the margins to prominence was abortion. In the wake of the *Roe* v. *Wade* decision (1973), religious conservatives found their voice. This movement was propelled forward by organizations such as the Moral Majority, founded by the Reverend Jerry Falwell in 1979.

Despite differences within the movement, it has been successful in redefining the terms of political debate in the late twentieth and early twenty-first centuries. Since the era of Ronald Reagan and George H.W. Bush (1993–2001), the ideas of the movement found voice in the "Contract with America" in the 1990s, in the election of George W. Bush in 2000, in the Tea Party Movement in the wake of the election of President Barack Obama in 2008, and in the election of Donald Trump in 2016.

1 BARRY GOLDWATER

In many ways, Republican Senator Barry Goldwater's campaign for president in 1964 represented the beginning of the ascendency of the modern conservative movement. Although President Lyndon Johnson won reelection, capturing 61 percent of the popular vote, Goldwater demonstrated to many conservatives that a principled conservative could generate grassroots enthusiasm. Younger activists, many associated with Young Americans for Freedom, were a key component of his campaign. Many had been inspired by his 1960 book, *The Conscience of a Conservative.* The movement was especially strong in the Sunbelt of the South and the West. Goldwater had inherited a department store chain from his father in Arizona and ran the business until World War II when he entered the Army Air Corps. He rose to the rank of brigadier general and after the war became a senator. As a strong anti-communist, he supported Senator Joseph McCarthy and was critical of President Harry S. Truman. Within the Republican Party, Goldwater was more conservative than President Dwight Eisenhower and most other national leaders. His voting record in the Senate showed his opposition to the Fair Deal, the New Frontier, and the Great Society. In the 1964 campaign, Johnson was able to portray Goldwater as an extremist outside of the mainstream. A famous Johnson campaign ad suggested that Goldwater's extremism could lead to nuclear war. After the election, Goldwater returned to the Senate where he advocated a more aggressive offensive war in Vietnam. He supported Nixon, but was among the Republicans who convinced Nixon into resigning for the good of the country after the Watergate Scandal (see page 413). Goldwater opposed Jimmy Carter and backed Ronald Reagan. He lived to hear President Bill Clinton pronounce "the era of big government is over" in the 1990s, after losing the Congress to the Republicans for the first time in forty years.

2 *NATIONAL REVIEW* MAGAZINE

After Russell Kirk wove the threads of conservatism into a coherent legacy with his book *The Conservative Mind*, William F. Buckley Jr. set about trying to disseminate conservative ideas by founding *National Review* magazine in 1955. Since the conservative movement lacked any driving force other than the anticommunist editorializing of several popular magazines and authors, Buckley turned his Yale-honed debating skills, acerbic wit, and infamously large vocabulary to pushing a wide range of conservative ideas. Among the magazine's subscribers was Ronald Reagan who is said to have read the biweekly periodical from cover to cover. *National Review* attacked the liberal consensus but also more extremist conservative elements like Ayn Rand, the author of *The Fountainhead* and *Atlas Shrugged*, and the John Birch Society. Buckley also shunned anti-Semitism and segregationists like George Wallace.

3 THE MORAL MAJORITY

The Reverend Jerry Falwell founded the Moral Majority political action committee (PAC) in 1979. The goals of the PAC were to promote traditional conservative values and to raise funds to help elect Ronald Reagan to the presidency. Since the Supreme Court decision in *Roe* v. *Wade* in 1973 (see page 480), opposition to abortion has been a central tenet of conservatism.

The issue of abortion convinced many evangelical Protestants to put aside their long-held suspicions of Catholicism and create a broader movement. The Moral Majority was one of several grassroots organizations in which the religious and cultural wing of the conservative movement found its voice. Another culturally conservative organization, Focus on the Family, founded in 1977 by psychologist James Dobson, promotes an abstinence-only approach to sex education, the reintroduction of prayer into the schools, and reinforcement of traditional gender roles. The organization has stood against the expansion of rights for gay, lesbian, bisexual, and transgendered people; it has been vocal in its opposition to same-sex marriage.

4 RONALD REAGAN

Reagan was an actor through the 1940s, even making training films as a soldier in World War II. As president of the Screen Actors Guild during the 1950s, he fought communism and changed from being a New Deal Democrat and fan of Franklin D. Roosevelt into being a political conservative. As his film career waned, Reagan became a spokesman for the General Electric Company and appeared regularly on television as a host of the corporation's sponsored programs. After becoming a Republican his speech in support of Barry Goldwater for president brought Reagan to national attention. As governor of California in the 1960s he cut the welfare caseload while increasing benefits, reduced the size of the state bureaucracy, and squelched student protests on university campuses. After failing twice, Reagan was elected to the presidency in 1980 and again in a landslide victory in 1984. As president, Reagan survived being shot in the chest in an assassination attempt. He also cut taxes but at the same time called for a massive buildup of military power that created huge deficits. Reagan used this military might and optimistic and moralistic rhetoric in cooperation with leaders like Margaret Thatcher of Great Britain, Pope John Paul II, and Mikhail Gorbachev of the Soviet Union to set in motion events that led to the end of the Soviet Empire. His reputation was marred by the Iran-Contra Scandal and the bankruptcy of nearly 750 savings and loans due to deregulation policies.

5 NANCY REAGAN

As a former actress, Nancy Reagan brought to the White House and the role as First Lady a touch of glamour and an interest in fashion reminiscent of the popularity of Jackie Kennedy. After having a conversation with a child about illegal drugs while on a school visit in 1982, Reagan launched a campaign to encourage all American youth to "Just Say No" to drug abuse. A result of a widespread national and international media initiative was a drug enforcement bill signed by President Reagan in 1986. After the president's near death in an assassination attempt, Nancy Reagan took a more assertive role in monitoring her husband's schedule, even to the point of consulting an astrologer for advice. Having been instrumental in converting her husband to conservative principles away from his support for the New Deal, the First Lady is said to have had unusual influence in the decision-making process of the Reagan administration. The active role Mrs. Reagan took in her husband's administration was reminiscent of Eleanor Roosevelt's and foreshadowed that of Hillary Clinton.

PROPOSITION 113

This 1978 California initiative put a cap on the state's real estate tax and forced the state government to cut social welfare services. As governor of California, Ronald Reagan leveraged the "tax revolt" for a bid at the White House.

6 LAFFER CURVE

Economist Arthur Laffer used an upside-down parabola to illustrate the notion that lowering taxes would boost the economy when he explained the idea to members of the Ford and Reagan administrations. Laffer theorized that there exists an optimal tax rate to maximize government revenue while at the same time stimulating economic growth. Building on the notions of Andrew Mellon who advised tax cuts would accomplish both goals as secretary of treasury under Calvin Coolidge, Laffer attempted to pinpoint the best level of taxation. If taxes were too low, the government would not make enough money to fulfill its obligations. If taxes were too high, as conservative economists thought they were in the 1970s, then individuals and businesses would refrain from investing in the economy because too much of their money was siphoned off by the government. If investment ceased, then the economy would sink and there would be too little tax revenue regardless of how high the tax rate was set. The Reagan administration used this theory to propound supply-side economics, the belief that job creation and economic expansion could be produced by lower taxes on the wealthiest Americans. Prosperity would then "trickle down" to the middle and lower classes. While tax cuts were enacted and the economy of the 1980s did soar, compensating cuts in spending were not enacted by Congress to balance Reagan's military spending, and deep deficits resulted.

> ### SANDRA DAY O'CONNOR
> President Reagan nominated this Arizona judge to the Supreme Court, and when she was sworn in in 1981, she was the first woman in U.S. history to become a justice on the highest court in the land. Robert Bork, however, did not fare as well when Reagan nominated him in 1987. The senate rejected Bork and ushered in a new era of more contested appointments.

7 BIG GOVERNMENT

In his inaugural address President Reagan said, "Government is not the solution to our problem; government is the problem." With these words he expressed the frustration of the majority of voting Americans with the increasing size of the federal bureaucracy. Although conservatives held that government had legitimate duties, like providing justice to all and protecting American interests at home and abroad, the so-called "Reagan Revolution" sought to roll back both the Soviet Union and the federal government's size. The Reagan administration made efforts to turn back some of the spending on domestic welfare programs that went all the way back to Lyndon Johnson's Great Society. Reagan's New Federalism sought to transfer federally funded social programs to the management of the states where more efficient and knowledgeable monitoring could reduce waste. Through the 1988 Family Welfare Reform Act the Congress performed the most important restructuring of the welfare system since the New Deal era in order to shift the emphasis to job training. Reagan attempted to place conservatives on the Supreme Court to prolong the influence of these ideas. After leaving office, however, Reagan said the one disappointment of his presidency was his failure to seriously diminish the size of government or its pervasive influence on American life.

8 PATCO STRIKE

President Ronald Reagan's approach to the economy included limiting the power of organized labor. In August 1981, the union of air traffic controllers—the Professional Air Traffic Controllers' Organization (PATCO)—declared a strike in which it sought better working conditions and pay, as well as a 32-hour work week. In addition, PATCO sought to be excluded from the civil service clauses that prohibit strikes by federal government employees. Reagan declared the PATCO strike a "peril to national safety" and ordered the workers back to work under the terms of the Taft-Hartley Act (see page 372). Only 1,300 of the nearly 13,000 controllers returned to work. Following the PATCO workers' refusal to return to work, Reagan fired over 11,000 members of the union. This action, which broke the union, was consistent with a conservative agenda that values deregulation and free-market economics. The destruction of PATCO was a major blow to organized labor in the late twentieth century. Overall, union membership dropped significantly in the second half of the twentieth century. In 1954, union membership (as a percentage of the total workforce) peaked in the United States at 35 percent; currently, it is about 12 percent. In such an environment, there has been a marked decline in the militancy of the union movement. In 1970, there were more than 380 major strikes or lockouts in the United States; by 1980, that figure dropped to under 200. In 2010, there were 11 major strikes or lockouts. The decline in union membership has also been caused by the decline of manufacturing jobs in the United States.

9 THE REAGAN DOCTRINE

The Reagan administration supported regimes that were anticommunist, regardless of their commitment to democracy. This foreign policy came to be known as the Reagan Doctrine. It resulted in a more active United States foreign policy in the developing world. The doctrine was designed to diminish the influence of the Soviet Union in Latin America, Asia, and Africa as part of an overall strategy to win the Cold War. Reagan sent troops to the island of Grenada in 1983 to topple the Marxist leaders of the country. Reagan continued to support the dictatorial regime of the Philippines led by Ferdinand Marcos despite reports of electoral fraud. The regime was finally toppled in 1986, with Corazon Aquino replacing Marcos. In Nicaragua, Reagan pursued policies to topple the Marxist-leaning Sandinista government. Earlier, in 1979, the Sandinistas had toppled a pro-American dictatorship, led by Anastasio Somoza. Reagan provided funding to the Contras, a guerrilla movement opposed to the Sandinista government. In the African nation of Angola, the Reagan administration armed rebel groups opposed to the government, who were receiving support from both the Soviet Union and Cuba. Finally, Reagan continued to support the apartheid government of South Africa, which was brutally suppressing Black protest in the 1980s, after many world leaders had distanced themselves from that government.

10 BEIRUT BOMBING

President Reagan sent U.S. Marines on a peacekeeping mission in Lebanon in 1982 as a result of the activities of the Palestinian Liberation Organization in that country. The Marines were to come between two or more sides of an internecine Islamic conflict. After Christian militia forces and even Israeli troops became involved, violence escalated, and in 1983 terrorist truck bombs destroyed both the U.S. Embassy in Beirut and the Marines' barracks killing 241 American servicemen and seventeen other Americans and wounding one hundred. Congress had authorized the participation of the Marines and naval personnel in a multinational force, but after the bombing Reagan withdrew all American military forces from Lebanon. After this first of America's lethal experiences with terrorism, President Reagan issued a new set of four parameters for American military involvement abroad. First, the cause must be "vital to our national interest." Second, the commitment must have a "clear intent and support needed to win the conflict." Third, there must be "reasonable assurance" that the cause "will have the support of the American people and Congress." Finally, military intervention must always be the last resort when no other choices remain. After his presidency, in two out of the three times American troops were deployed between 1988 and 2002 all four of these conditions were met, revealing that Reagan might have hit upon a sound policy that could avoid a quagmire.

11 GRENADA INVASION

The Soviets began to see that the Reagan administration would use the military to protect Americans and American interests around the world, a fact that hastened the end of the Cold War in the most dangerous form of brinkmanship. After a leftist government of the island nation of Grenada (just off the coast of Venezuela) slid into instability when the revolutionary leader was killed, the U.S. military invaded in 1983 to protect American citizens who were attending medical school on the island. The invasion cost nineteen American servicemen their lives, but it was largely supported by the American public. Other countries, however, claimed that the United States had violated several diplomatic agreements. Norman Schwarzkopf was second in command of the invasion and observed several weaknesses in the military preparedness of the American forces, a fact he corrected prior to the Persian Gulf War.

12 MUAMMAR AL QADDAFI

Qaddafi began his career as a dictator as a lieutenant in the Libyan military, not much higher than Corporal Hitler. Still, when he seized power in 1969 he was able to erase the constitution and impose his own will. He and his family took over the country with the backing of the military, yet curiously this dictator for a time provided his people with the highest standard of living in Africa. Qaddafi dabbled in chemical weapons and acts of terrorism, though, a fact that made him the target of a bombing raid by the U.S. military in 1986 after a bombing of a disco in Germany frequented by American service personnel. Escaping several assassination attempts by various groups, Qaddafi renounced his weapons of mass destruction after Saddam Hussein was captured, tried, and hanged. The Libyan people, however, rose against him in 2011 to end his career as a leader guilty of crimes against humanity both at home and abroad. He was deposed in a revolt by the Libyan people that was aided by NATO forces, including American military personnel, and killed while being captured.

13 CONTRAS

After sending one authoritarian dictator a message, President Reagan wanted to take a stand against communist revolutionaries in Central and South America. Reagan believed Cuba was exporting socialism to its neighbors and that Daniel Ortega, who rose to power at the head of a revolutionary group in Nicaragua called the Sandinistas, was on his way to becoming another Castro. The U.S. Congress originally backed the Reagan administration and the Central Intelligence Agency's (CIA's) desire to aid the Contras, a rebel group that opposed Ortega and the Sandinistas; however, whispers of "Vietnam quagmire" soon arose when the Contras failed to achieve victory. Aid to the Contras was cut off by the Congress by 1985 at which time

> **INTERMEDIATE-RANGE NUCLEAR FORCES TREATY**
>
> The INF Treaty of 1987 banned all intermediate-range missiles (as opposed to ICBMs) from Europe. With this achievement an end to the Cold War was in sight.

covert operations were begun to keep aiding them as an expression of containment of communism right in the Western Hemisphere. The Iran-Contra scandal was the result.

14 IRAN-CONTRA SCANDAL

After Reagan said that the United States would not negotiate with terrorists, a secret plan was revealed in 1986 that he had done just that. The Iran part of the scandal was the sale of antiaircraft missiles and other weapons to Iran in order to leverage release of American hostages being held in Lebanon. The Contra part of the scandal came in the form of funding of the Contra rebels, a group in Nicaragua fighting to overthrow the communist leader of the Sandinistas, Daniel Ortega. Because Congress would not authorize the expenditure, the secret proceeds of the arms sales to Iran were diverted for this purpose. Three hostages were released, but three more were taken. When Reagan's national security adviser, the director of the Central Intelligence Agency, and U.S. Marine Corps Lieutenant Colonel Oliver North all either resigned or were fired for their part in the scheme, Reagan appeared to have been asleep at the wheel or willfully negligent of his duty to uphold the law. Another "all-the-president's-men" Watergate-type coverup was discovered, and Reagan's ability to lead during his last two years as president was crippled.

15 OLIVER NORTH

North was a U.S. Marine Corps officer who worked in the Reagan administration for the National Security Council and ran the secret operation leading to the Iran-Contra Scandal. North took the money from weapons sales to Iran and orchestrated the supply of the Contras in Nicaragua. Before going to trial for numerous felonies, North testified to a Congressional committee about his involvement. Despite the hope of opponents of the Reagan administration that North would try to save his military career by implicating the president in the scandal, North took the blame and said Reagan knew nothing of the operation. In the subsequent trial, North was found guilty of three felonies, but the agreement for immunity from prosecution that prompted North to testify to Congress led to the dismissal of the case. Even though Oliver North's stance resembled that of G. Gordon Liddy in the Nixon administration, President Reagan could not avoid the implication that he had been asleep at the wheel and unaware of what his subordinates were doing.

16 STRATEGIC DEFENSE INITIATIVE

From the 1960s onward, after the Soviet Union and the United States both acquired nuclear arsenals that were equally capable of destroying life on the planet, the Cold War rested on the notion of Mutually Assured Destruction (MAD). This equilibrium, it was hoped, would prevent either side from launching a nuclear attack on the other. However, in 1983, President Ronald Reagan announced his intent to move away from MAD by supporting the development of a defensive system designed to eliminate or minimize the threat of incoming missiles. Technologies under development included rail guns, laser beams, and particle beams as well as antimissile missiles, all guided by supercomputers. Congress authorized as much as $30 billion toward research and development of these technologies under the broad umbrella of the Strategic Defense Initiative (SDI). Because President Reagan had referred to the Soviet Union as the "evil empire," SDI was quickly dubbed "Star Wars" in a nod to the recent epic sci-fi movies. Although the technology never reached a level of implementation, Soviet and American scientists acknowledged it was feasible. Therefore, Regan was able to use even the funding of the program as leverage in his negotiations with Soviet Premier Mikhail Gorbachev. It became apparent that the Soviet Union could not keep pace with the United States in terms of funding advances in weaponry. Russian analysts have asserted that the SDI program sped up the collapse of the Soviet Union by at least five years.

17 MIKHAIL GORBACHEV

Gorbachev was the youngest general secretary in the history of the Communist Party when he took office in 1982. He took power in the climax of the Cold War and faced huge domestic problems, and he took the unique step of criticizing the Soviet system. In an attempt to improve the standard of living in the Soviet "utopia," Gorbachev instituted a series of domestic reforms designed to increase productivity and to provide a measure of freedom. He advocated *glasnost* and *perestroika*, or openness and restructuring, respectively. Gorbachev and Reagan began a series of summit meetings through which the two men developed respect and even friendship, and after overcoming some disagreements signed the first treaty to reduce the numbers of nuclear weapons in their stockpiles. Working with the American president and advocating reforms accelerated the end of the Cold War and won Gorbachev the Nobel Peace Prize in 1990, but because his reforms did not achieve immediate success in boosting the Soviet economy he was ultimately forced to resign in 1991. By then, however, Gorbachev had dissolved the Soviet Union.

18 SILICON VALLEY

Silicon Valley is the name of an actual region in California that turned from the growing of fruit to the production of Apple computers in the 1970s. As a concept, Silicon Valley represents the history of the personal computer. Computers that used to fill entire rooms were shrunk by the invention in 1971 of the microprocessor, or the silicon microchip. Intel Corporation invented and produced the chips outside San Francisco in the Santa Clara Valley. Desktop-size personal computers were available as kits as early as 1974, and mass production was achieved for marketing by Radio Shack in 1977. Steve Jobs and Steve Wozniak founded Apple Computer, Inc., in a garage in that same year. The Apple II was the first personal computer designed for use by people other than electronics enthusiasts in the mass marketplace. IBM followed suit by 1981, and computers have continually increased in memory capacity and decreased in size ever since. Bill Gates of Microsoft Corporation introduced an operating system that put computing within the capacity of the average citizen, and devices like the computer mouse increased usability. Since the 1980s the personal computer has developed into an essential business tool and an iconic aspect of the entertainment industry. American productivity experienced a phenomenal burst as American ingenuity ushered in the Information Age.

19 BILL GATES

A modern-day wealthy industrialist and philanthropist on a level with those of the Gilded Age revolutionized the personal computer industry by founding the software company Microsoft. Just as Andrew Carnegie did of old, Gates used cutting-edge technology, sharp dealing tactics in business competition, and sophisticated marketing strategies to make himself off and on again the richest man in the world, and then he became a philanthropist. In the process he brought personal computing to the business and entertainment world and revolutionized nearly all aspects of societal interaction. Through the 1990s Gates was involved in antitrust cases in which he was accused of forcing computer manufacturers to install Windows as the operating system on their machines along with Internet Explorer, the Microsoft web browser. Gates defended his business practices in these suits saying that he was not stopping competition in the computer industry but merely trying to survive it. As a result Microsoft was not broken up by the government in the way that Bell Telephone had been.

20 STEVE JOBS

World War II had spun off the computer in the form of the giant ENIAC system. This computer was "giant" not in its computing capacity but in its sheer size. Not until 1952 did Texas Instruments develop silicon-sealed transistors that could withstand high temperatures and allow computers to decrease in size. By 1971 Intel managed to shrink computers further with their microprocessor. By 1977 Steve Jobs and Steve Wozniak founded Apple Computers, Inc. in a garage. Their company then joined the Fortune 500 in less time than any other company in American history. Apple developed a more user-friendly operating system for its Macintosh line of computers than IBM created to be used with Microsoft software. In contrasting the personas of Jobs and Gates, Bill Gates appeared to the public to be a more calculating, business-oriented intellect, whereas Steve Jobs cultivated a reputation as a mystic or guru out to change the world. Jobs died in 2011 after a long battle with pancreatic cancer.

THE BIG PICTURE

1. The pendulum of American politics swung back to the right during the 1980s after five decades of government expansion, and Ronald Reagan became the central figure in a conservative resurgence.

2. Tax cuts and increased productivity due to the development of the personal computer dramatically increased the power of the American economy, which left the 1970s recession to begin a period of phenomenal growth.

3. The optimism at home was matched by progress in the Cold War through a combination of firm rhetoric and technological breakthroughs that made the leaders of the Soviet Union realize they could not keep up the economic and ideological competition with the United States.

4. The attention of U.S. foreign policy became increasingly drawn to the Middle East as the first serious terrorist attacks on Americans further destabilized the troubled region.

5. After winning reelection in 1984 in the greatest landslide since that of Franklin D. Roosevelt in 1936, Ronald Reagan's presidency proved that despite great accomplishments all presidents are capable of serious errors in judgment that undermine their ability to govern.

Centrist Politics in an Increasingly Globalized World—1989-2001

38

*. . . I am reaching out to President Gorbachev, asking him to work with
me to bring down the last barriers to a new world of freedom. Let us
move beyond containment and once and for all end the cold war.*

—George H. W. Bush, Thanksgiving message, 1989

TIMELINE	
1988	George H. W. Bush is elected to the presidency; General Norman Schwarzkopf takes charge of U.S. Central Command; The "New Democrats" first emerge
1989	Colin Powell is named the first African-American chairman of the Joint Chiefs; The German people destroy the Berlin Wall
1990	Iraqi dictator Saddam Hussein invades Kuwait; Rush Limbaugh achieves the largest conservative radio audience
1991	Clarence Thomas is confirmed as a justice on the U.S. Supreme Court; The Soviet Union collapses; Persian Gulf War; Boris Yeltsin is the first democratically elected leader in Russian history
1992	Ross Perot makes his first bid for the presidency; William (Bill) J. Clinton is elected to the presidency; Riots occur in Los Angeles
1993	Hillary Rodham Clinton heads the task force of the Clinton health care plan; Vice President Albert Gore Jr. heads an effort to "reinvent government"
1994	Whitewater scandal breaks; Kenneth Starr is appointed independent counsel to investigate the Clintons
1995	Monica Lewinsky begins an internship at the White House
1999	President Clinton is impeached but not removed from office
2006	Saddam Hussein is hanged by an Iraqi tribunal

OVERVIEW

The last decade of the twentieth century saw two presidential administrations that would be considered more moderate in the broader context of recent American history. The administration of George H. W. Bush (1989–1993), a Republican, pursued policies that were somewhat more centrist than those pursued by his predecessor, President Ronald Reagan, and considerably more moderate than Republican political leaders who followed in his footsteps. He, for instance, approved more stringent environmental legislation and signed the Americans with Disabilities Act (ADA) (1990), prohibiting discrimination based on disability. Afterward, President Bill Clinton (1993–2001), a Democrat, broke with many of the liberal policy positions of earlier Democratic administrations and pushed the party in a centrist direction. For instance, he signed legislation "ending welfare as we know it" (1996) as well as a major crime bill that provided additional funding for law enforcement and for the building of prisons.

In regard to foreign policy, the last decade of the twentieth century was the interval between two overarching eras in American history—the Cold War and the war on terrorism. The Cold War ended with the dissolution of the Soviet Union in late 1991. The war on terrorism began with the terrorist attacks on the United States on September 11, 2001 (although smaller scale terrorist attacks occurred throughout the 1990s). The term "new world order" was often used to describe the state of global affairs in the post-Cold War era. George H.W. Bush envisioned a new era "in which the nations of the world, east and west, north and south, can prosper and live in harmony." In many ways, the Gulf War of 1991 was a test of this vision. The United States took several other foreign policy initiatives in the 1990s to shape the new global order, including interventions with NATO in Yugoslavia in both 1995 and 1999.

These foreign policy actions occurred in the context of greater globalization, a process hastened by the policies of Presidents Bush and Clinton. Globalization refers to the process of the nations of the world being increasingly linked together. There are several related elements that are often mentioned in discussions of globalization. The first element is "free trade." The major powers of the world have taken measures to reduce tariffs on imports, thus making the movement of goods and companies across the globe easier. The United States approved the North American Free Trade Agreement (NAFTA) in 1993 and joined the new World Trade Organization (WTO) in 1994 with the goal of reducing or eliminating tariffs. The second element is the perceived harm done to local cultures and customs by large corporate entities, such as McDonalds and Disney. The third element of globalization is the ease of worldwide communications brought about by the Internet. Internet use grew rapidly in the 1990s and has reshaped many aspects of daily life in the twenty-first century. Globalization is defended by many as a positive development that will create greater understanding in the world and will raise living standards in developing countries. Others, such as protestors at the 1999 meeting of the World Trade Organization in Seattle, condemn globalization as reducing environmental protections and shifting manufacturing jobs to sweatshops in poor countries.

Though the years of Presidents Bush and Clinton can be seen as a retreat from the conservative policies of the Reagan years, more staunchly conservative political leaders were not quiet during the 1990s. In Congress, conservative Republicans issued the "Contract With America" in 1994 and later spearheaded impeachment proceedings against President Clinton (1998–1999). In 2000, the inauguration of President George W. Bush, son of the first President Bush, signaled a return to a more staunchly conservative political agenda for the United States.

1 GEORGE H. W. BUSH

Son of Senator Prescott Bush, George H. W. Bush was a decorated World War II naval pilot who finished a bombing run even though his plane was hit by antiaircraft fire. After the war, Bush became wealthy as a Texas oilman. After serving as a congressman he was the ambassador to the United Nations and director of the Central Intelligence Agency among other posts. Bush was a moderate Republican who first opposed Ronald Reagan and then served as his vice president. Never truly believing in the conservative principles of his predecessor but basking in his popularity led Bush toward a collision with public opinion after winning the presidency in 1988. He was immensely popular after his handling of the first Persian Gulf War but slipped in domestic policy after agreeing to a compromise with Congress over raising taxes. Having promised to never raise taxes, the public doubted his integrity and even his ability.

2 "VOODOO ECONOMICS"

One of the more telling examples of spin, or the purposeful representation of political ideas in terms intended to alter perceptions of reality, was this phrase used by George H. W. Bush in his bid to secure the Republican nomination in 1980. Bush used the phrase to describe supply-side economics, or the reduction of income and capital gains taxes to allow the rich to keep more of their money, ostensibly to invest it in the economy to expand businesses and create more jobs. Other critics of these policies when they were advocated and implemented by Ronald Reagan termed them "Reaganomics." Reagan was the modern proponent of this approach going back at least as far as Andrew Mellon and Calvin Coolidge in the 1920s, but George H. W. Bush took a more moderate position as he did in most political questions. As the vice president under Reagan he helped unify the Republican Party but was somewhat distanced from President Reagan during Reagan's presidency. When Bush made a Reaganesque promise, "Read my lips: No new taxes," he handed his opponents an opportunity for whole new degrees of political spin when he agreed to raise taxes during his administration. President Bush was likely only following his core values that were contrary to those of his predecessor, but his one-term presidency was considered the result of having compromised his principles to accept the vice presidency and the endorsement of Reagan for the Election of 1988.

3 COLLAPSE OF THE SOVIET UNION

After Mikhail Gorbachev pulled Soviet troops out of Afghanistan, the communist superpower known as the Soviet Union began to crumble. Hungary, Poland, East Germany, Bulgaria, Czechoslovakia, and Romania all held free elections or otherwise disposed of communist rulers, and Gorbachev did nothing to stop them. President Bush continued holding summit meetings with the Soviet leader as had Reagan, and Gorbachev boldly held the first free elections in the Soviet Union since the vote in 1917 that Lenin had ignored. Gorbachev assumed he would win because of his reforms, and he won the presidency of the Soviet Union in 1990, but Boris Yeltsin won as president of the Russian Republic. Bush and Gorbachev signed the START treaty that further reduced the number of nuclear weapons and agreed to the eradication of chemical weapons. Instead of winning him support, these steps and the winning of the Nobel Prize only caused communist hardliners to attempt a coup. Gorbachev held on but his power was diminished as was that of the Communist Party. With the destruction of the Berlin Wall in 1989, the dissolution of the Warsaw Pact, and the fact that Estonia, Latvia, and Lithuania again became independent countries by 1991, Gorbachev resigned by the end of that year. The Union of Soviet Socialist Republics, or USSR, ceased to exist. A Commonwealth of Independent States retained a loose organization, and Boris Yeltsin took up the mantle of establishing a free Russia and continuing détente with the West. The Cold War was over. The United States won.

TIANANMEN SQUARE

This square in Beijing, China, was the site of a mass rally in 1989. Hundreds of thousands of protestors gathered, and when the communist government retaliated, hundreds of protestors were killed. President Bush joined the condemnation of the repression, and the bravery of China's pro-democracy voices gave hope for eventual change.

4 PERSIAN GULF WAR

After Saddam Hussein, the dictatorial leader of Iraq, invaded neighboring Kuwait in 1990, President George H.W. Bush received permission from King Fahd of Saudi Arabia to send troops to protect his country in Operation Desert Shield. This mobilization of American military power, the largest since World War II, eventually became Operation Desert Storm as the United States and twenty-seven other countries prepared to invade Kuwait in order to liberate it from Iraqi occupation. As airstrikes pummeled Iraqi military targets in both Iraq and Kuwait, Bush demanded that Hussein withdraw his forces or face more severe consequences. Hussein, the leader of the Ba'ath Party, had become the president of Iraq in 1979. His more brutal actions, including ordering the use of chemical weapons against the Kurdish population of Iraq, earned him international condemnation. Although he had the support of the United States in Iraq's war with Iran in the 1980s, Bush had come to believe that his actions in regard to Kuwait threatened the stability of the region and needed to be challenged. As the day of the ultimatum for Iraq to withdraw from Kuwait ended, the coalition force struck in Kuwait, while an even larger force swept into Iraq. Americans watched on television as coalition forces, led by General H. Norman Schwarzkopf, destroyed the most formidable force in the Middle East in one hundred hours. Kuwait was liberated, but Hussein was to stay in power, and even to suppress Shiite Muslim and Kurdish revolts. In accomplishing the original goals of the coalition, however, President George H.W. Bush was lauded as a masterful diplomatic and military leader. This assessment would come to be reevaluated in the following decade, with his son as president.

5 COLIN POWELL

Powell was a decorated Vietnam War veteran who rose in rank and influence as a military adviser to presidents of both parties from Richard Nixon and George W. Bush to Jimmy Carter and Bill Clinton. He was a national security adviser to President Reagan and became both the first African-American chairman of the Joint Chiefs of Staff under George H. W. Bush and the first African-American secretary of state under George W. Bush. He became widely known while leading in Washington during the Persian Gulf War and was instrumental in gaining support both in the United States and in the United Nations for the operations that became the Iraq War based on intelligence that Saddam Hussein was hiding a program to produce weapons of mass destruction. When no such weapons were found and the war was prolonged, Powell resigned from President Bush's cabinet after Bush won reelection in 2004.

Powell was known for most of his career as a nonpartisan adviser who was unafraid to state any disagreements over policy he held with the presidents under whom he served, and was once considered a likely candidate for the presidency himself.

6 LOS ANGELES RIOTS

Revealing that deep undercurrents of racial tension still ran through American society, riots broke out in Los Angeles in 1992 as a result of frustration over the beating of an African-American named Rodney King by Los Angeles police. After leading law enforcement personnel on a chase at over 115 mph King was apprehended, tasered, and beaten when he resisted arrest. The beatings were caught on videotape that led to a trial of four officers involved for excessive use of force. Mostly white juries acquitted the officers, and Los Angeles erupted in six days of violent rioting. Acts of arson, looting, assault, and murder occurred, many on live television. Over $1 billion in damage was done, fifty-four people killed, and two thousand injured. During the riots, King appeared on television to say, "Can we all get along?" In interviews he said he originally fled the police because he was afraid a DUI would end his parole on a robbery charge. In an odd twist on American racism, Korean and other Asian stores in the Watts neighborhoods were targeted for looting, and the owners took up assault-style semiautomatic weapons to protect them. Later trials convicted two of the officers of violating King's civil rights, and Rodney King was awarded $3.8 million in damages.

> **AMERICANS WITH DISABILITIES ACT**
>
> In keeping with his quest for a "kinder, gentler America," President Bush signed this legislation in 1990 that prohibited discrimination against those with physical or mental impairment.

7 BILL CLINTON

Bill Clinton won the presidency in 1992, moving the Democratic Party in a more centrist direction. Clinton was born and raised in Arkansas and later attended Oxford University after winning a Rhodes Scholarship. He entered national politics as a campaign worker in 1972 and attended Yale Law School where he met his wife, Hillary Rodham. He then returned to Arkansas to practice law. In 1978, he was elected to the first of four terms as governor. He led the Democratic Leadership Council in 1991 and 1992, which consisted of Democratic leaders who wanted to move the party in a more centrist direction. He ran for the presidency in 1992 with Al Gore of Tennessee. As president, Clinton enjoyed a period of economic growth during his tenure. He was able to balance the budget, and even produce a budget surplus during the last three years of his presidency, 1998–2001. Early on in his administration, he failed to implement comprehensive reform of the healthcare system. He signed legislation ending welfare as a federal program declaring "… era of big government is over." Internationally, he worked to break down trade barriers and sought to expand membership in the North Atlantic Treaty Organization. During his administration, Vice President Al Gore worked on the effort to "reinvent government" by reviewing the operations of the federal government. Gore ran unsuccessfully for the presidency in 2000 against George W. Bush. After their term in office, both Clinton and Gore have remained active. Clinton has supported the political career of his wife, Hillary Clinton, and has worked on humanitarian issues through the Clinton Foundation. Gore has been active in raising awareness of global warming and other environmental issues, most notably through the documentary film, *An Inconvenient Truth* (2006).

8 ROSS PEROT

Having been born in poverty in Texas, Perot won a nomination to the Naval Academy and served through the Korean War. After working for IBM for a time after leaving the Navy, Perot started his own business, Electronic Data Systems. Once this company became worth billions of dollars, Perot became something of a globe-trotting humanitarian crusader. He used much of his own money to run for president in 1992, splitting from the Republican Party with a third party as had Theodore Roosevelt in 1912. Perot received almost twenty million popular votes that, if they had gone to George H. W. Bush, would have given Bush a second term. He tallied over eight million votes in the much closer Election of 1996. During his 1992 campaign Perot criticized the North American Free Trade Agreement, or NAFTA, saying that the jobs departing the country for Mexico created "a giant sucking sound," and he gathered support by issuing dire warnings about the national debt on what became known as "infomericals," spots on television he paid for himself. Perot temporarily pulled out of the race only to reenter later, damaging his credibility. He remains a philanthropist, but has dropped from the public political debate.

9 NEW DEMOCRATS

Bill Clinton and his vice president, Albert Gore Jr., represented what has been called a new brand of political leadership. In the wake of the smashing victories of Ronald Reagan and the Republican takeover of Congress in 1994, New Democrats moved to the center of the political debate and announced a third way beyond the traditional liberal versus conservative mainstream values. Focusing on the economy, New Democrats advocated a combination of moderate deregulation, tax cuts for low-income families and small businesses (made up for by tax increases on the wealthiest Americans), and the international quest for free trade that resulted in the passage of the North American Free Trade Agreement (NAFTA). The movement also espoused spending restraints that helped balance budgets. Combined with the investments made during the Reagan-era tax cuts, these policies resulted in the largest peacetime expansion of the American economy in history through the 1990s.

10 WHITEWATER-GATE

The name of this scandal of the Clinton administration was so reminiscent of the Watergate Scandal of the Nixon administration that the press began attaching the "-gate" suffix to a wide range of political intrigues. The Whitewater Development Corporation was a real estate firm in which the Clintons had invested. The company failed, but not before receiving several hundred thousand dollars in federally backed loans. The Securities and Exchange Commission investigated and found several of the Clintons' associates guilty of fraud, but the Clintons escaped prosecution because of a lack of evidence linking them to any criminal behavior. Before he left office President Clinton pardoned one of the Whitewater associates who was serving time in jail for contempt of court because she refused to testify in the matter.

11 CLINTON IMPEACHMENT

The toxic nature of partisan politics came to be on full display in 1998 as Congressional Republicans voted to impeach President Bill Clinton. This was only the second time in history that a sitting president was impeached. The first president to be impeached was Andrew Johnson, in 1868. In Johnson's case (1868), impeachment was the culmination of tensions that grew between the Democratic president and Congressional Republicans over Reconstruction. In both cases, the House voted to impeach, but the Senate did not vote to remove the president from office. Clinton's impeachment originated with the accusations made that he had a sexual affair with a twenty-one-year-old intern named Monica Lewinsky. A friend of Lewinsky recorded some of their telephone conversations in which Lewinsky discussed the affair. Clinton initially publicly denied the accusations of an affair with Lewinsky. He also denied the affair before a federal grand jury. When Clinton later was forced to admit the affair, Congressional Republicans felt they had evidence of an impeachable crime—lying to a grand jury. Clinton emerged from the affair largely unscathed. Many Americans disapproved of his personal misconduct, but resented the attempt by Republicans to remove him from office. Many Americans came to see the prosecution of Clinton as more motivated by partisan divisions rather than by an impartial desire to see justice served.

12 NAFTA

In 1993, President Bill Clinton signed legislation ratifying the United States' participation in the North American Free Trade Agreement (NAFTA). The agreement had been negotiated earlier, starting in 1990, during the administration of President George H.W. Bush. The agreement eliminated all trade barriers and tariffs among the United States, Canada, and Mexico. NAFTA was the subject of much controversy when it was promoted by President Clinton. Free trade supporters promised global prosperity as more nations participate in the global economy. Opponents worried that nations would no longer be able to implement environmental regulations, ensure workers' rights, or protect fledging industries from foreign competition. Clinton's championing of NAFTA represents a conscious decision by Clinton to move the Democratic Party away from its liberal traditions and toward a more centrist approach. The move toward reducing trade barriers is often associated with economic globalization. In a more connected global economy, the major powers of the world have taken measures to reduce tariffs on imports, thus making the movement of goods and companies across the globe easier. In addition to ratifying NAFTA, the United States joined the new World Trade Organization (WTO) in 1994 with the goal of reducing or eliminating tariffs. American participation in NAFTA is still the subject of political debate in the United States. In 2016, as he was running for president, Donald Trump consistently criticized NAFTA for resulting in a loss of American manufacturing jobs, especially in the old industrial heartland of the United State—states such as Ohio, Pennsylvania, and Michigan (all of which voted for Trump in the presidential election).

13 WELFARE REFORM

As part of his repositioning of the Democratic Party toward a more centrist direction, President Bill Clinton backed the Welfare Reform Act in 1996. By signing the bill, Clinton adopted one of the planks of the Republican's "Contract With America" by ending most federal welfare entitlement programs and shifting the administration of welfare to the state level. Clinton's embrace of welfare reform shocked many liberal Democrats. The Democratic Party had pushed for federal entitlement programs since the New Deal of President Roosevelt in the 1930s. Clinton perceived that many Americans were growing weary of programs that cost taxpayers money and did not seem to lessen poverty. Some Americans argued that welfare fostered a sense of dependency among recipients and stifled individual initiative. The reform provided block grants to states. It also created the Temporary Assistance to Needy Families (TANF) program which required welfare recipients to begin work after two years—a stipulation known as "workfare." Although Clinton somewhat alienated the liberal faction of the Democratic Party, he gained a reputation for bipartisanship. Over the two decades since passage of the act, the percentage of families receiving cash welfare (as opposed to food stamps or housing vouchers) has gone down considerably—by as much as 75 percent. However, welfare reform has not lessoned the percentage of people who live in poverty.

14 CONTRACT WITH AMERICA

In 1994 the Republican Party won majorities in both houses of Congress for the first time in forty years. This victory was partly due to a series of ten proposals called the "Contract with America" that constituted the Republican agenda. After years of Big Government, the contract sought to decentralize power through deregulation, tax cuts, welfare reform, and a balanced federal budget. The House of Representatives passed nine of the measures, but the Senate passed only three. President Clinton had threatened to veto the more controversial measures if passed. Newt Gingrich, the chief architect of the contract and the congressman who became the new Speaker of the House, said the measures were intended "to restore the bonds of trust between the people and their elected representatives." One of the three points that became law required members of Congress to abide by the same workplace laws as regular Americans, especially those concerning sexual harassment. Another law reduced paperwork, and the final one banned the passage of unfunded mandates, or federal measures imposed on states with no source of funding. Laws to reform the legislative committee process and to install congressional term limits did not pass.

15 NEWT GINGRICH

This college history professor turned congressman from Georgia helped secure the first Republican majorities in both the House of Representatives and the Senate in forty years. The midterm election results in 1994 during the first term of Bill Clinton's presidency shocked political commentators and evoked more moderate positions from President Clinton who said "The era of Big Government is over." As one of the primary authors of the Contract with America and its leading advocate in the campaigns, Gingrich rose to become the Speaker of the House in 1995. With his leadership and President Clinton's move to the center, compromise legislation was enacted to balance the federal budget for the first time since 1969, to provide the largest cut in capital gains taxes in American history, and to reform the welfare system. These accomplishments and other aspects of the Contract with America were sidetracked by the impeachment process of President Clinton in which Newt Gingrich took obvious satisfaction despite the fact that he was conducting an affair with a young female staffer during the Monica Lewinsky scandal. As the figurehead of the Republican Party, Gingrich attracted criticism and resigned after Republicans lost ground in the next midterm elections. He then ran for the 2012 Republican nomination for the presidency, but lost to Mitt Romney who went on to lose to Barack Obama in the general election.

16 LINE-ITEM VETO

One of the Congressional initiatives of the new Republican majorities that President Clinton also supported and signed into law was the 1996 Line Item Veto Act. A line-item veto granted the president the power to selectively veto parts of a bill without having to veto a whole bill. The goal of such executive action was intended as a control on "pork barrel" spending, or the practice of attaching earmarks to legislation. Earmarks activate the expenditure of federal dollars for state and local projects and are attached as amendments to bills as one of the chief measures to funnel federal money into the home states of representatives and senators sponsoring the amendments. President Clinton used the line-item veto eighty-two times in signing just eleven bills before the Supreme Court struck down the measure as unconstitutional. Advocates for the establishment of a permanent line-item veto for the president say it is the most likely way to curb wasteful spending in Washington, D.C.

17 WACO STANDOFF

In 1993 agents with the federal Bureau of Alcohol, Tobacco, and Firearms surrounded a compound in Waco, Texas, occupied by a sect called the Branch Davidians that split from the Seventh-day Adventist Church. The leader of the movement, calling himself David Koresh, and others within the sect were suspected of child abuse and weapons violations. When the federal agents attempted to serve a warrant on the weapons charges, a shootout occurred in which both sides claimed the other fired first. The end result was the deaths of four agents and six Branch Davidians. A standoff then lasted fifty days until a second assault on the compound involving the Federal Bureau of Investigation employed an armored vehicle to open the wooden walls of the structure. A fire broke out that consumed the compound buildings and killed seventy-six people including twenty children. Both sides of the standoff claimed the other started the fire from which only nine Branch Davidians escaped alive.

18 OKLAHOMA CITY BOMBING

Timothy McVeigh and Terry Nichols, with the complicity of several other individuals, constructed a bomb in a rental van and detonated the device next to the Alfred P. Murrah Building in Oklahoma City in 1995. The two men were Army veterans motivated by a desire to avenge the deaths of the people who died in the tragic encounter at Waco, Texas. The Oklahoma City domestic terrorist attack was the largest in American history until the September 11 attacks, and the blast killed 168 people including children in the facility's day care. McVeigh and Nichols represented what was called "right-wing militias," or groups of conspiracy theorists who armed themselves in fear of an oppressive federal government. McVeigh was captured and executed, and Nichols was given 160 consecutive life sentences in prison without the possibility of parole. President Clinton personally helped memorialize the victims and told the nation that a restriction of civil liberties would be necessary in the wake of such an attack.

19 SOMALIA

George H. W. Bush had ordered American troops into Somalia in 1992 to help distribute food during a severe famine amid factional warfare. The United Nations declared that a state of anarchy existed and took over control of food relief. When Bill Clinton became president, he changed the mission in Somalia to one of hunting down the most violent warlords who had caused the collapse of civilization in the first place. When militants shot down a Black Hawk helicopter during a raid in 1993 in search of one of the warlords, other American troops came to the rescue. In the ensuing firefight, eighteen U.S. soldiers were killed and some of their bodies were desecrated. In a Carter-style vacillation, Clinton ordered fifteen thousand troops into Somalia but then pulled them out within five months to seek a political solution.

20 BALKAN CONFLICT

After the fall of the Soviet Union, the communist puppet-dictator of Yugoslavia was left dead in a street. The Balkans came apart. Various ethnic groups including the Croats, Serbs, Bosnians, Kosovars, and Albanians, many of whom were Muslims, all wanted autonomy in breakaway states. The North Atlantic Treaty Organization (NATO) stepped in, and President Clinton promised American support. Slobodan Milosevic, the Serbian leader, practiced ruthless displacement and genocide tactics that harkened back to those of Adolph Hitler. Three thousand Muslims were later discovered buried in a mass grave. Trying to avoid "another Vietnam," Clinton disallowed any American troops to go in on the ground. American pilots were given the mission to keep Kosovo safe for the Kosovars from no lower than 15,000 feet. Just as in Vietnam, a campaign of aerial bombardment proved ineffective against a determined enemy. Milosevic only agreed to negotiations after accomplishing what he called "ethnic cleansing" of Serbia. Another limited military engagement proved problematic because of fears that latent NATO versus Warsaw Pact tension would erupt in a larger war. The most internationally destabilizing event occurred when American aircraft accidentally bombed the Chinese embassy, straining relations with a rising superpower.

THE BIG PICTURE

1. George H. W. Bush scored giant foreign policy successes by managing the end of the Cold War after the collapse of the Soviet Union and winning the Persian Gulf War against Iraqi dictator Saddam Hussein.

2. Dissatisfaction with the Bush administration on the domestic front was manifested in a prominent third-party candidate as well as in the rise of the popularity of Bill Clinton and caused the collapse of the Reagan-era Republican Party hold on the presidency.

3. After winning the Election of 1992, Bill Clinton faced Republican control of Congress by 1994 and followed through with his previous commitments to moderate political reforms.

4. The 1990s was a decade of phenomenal economic growth combining 1980s investments, the dot-com boom on the Internet, and the Clinton administration's commitments to free trade and balanced budgets.

5. Despite the dramatically expanding economy of the Clinton years, domestic terrorism and foreign conflicts in Somalia and the Balkans undermined a feeling of prosperity.

Political Developments in the Twenty-first Century

39

If we work hard—and work together—if we rededicate ourselves to strengthening families, creating jobs, rewarding work, and reinventing government, we can lift America's fortunes once again.

—Bill Clinton, speech before Congress, 1993

TIMELINE	
1988	Osama bin Laden founds the al-Qaeda terrorist organization
1992	Balkan Conflict sparks the Bosnian War
1993	Federal law enforcement and a religious sect have a standoff in Waco, Texas
1994	U.S. forces withdraw from Somalia; Republicans launch "Contract with America" congressional campaign
1995	Newt Gingrich becomes Speaker of the House of Representatives; Oklahoma City Bombing
1996	The Taliban takes control of most of Afghanistan
1998	A line-item veto is struck down by the U.S. Supreme Court
2000	Alan Greenspan raises interest rates; Election of 2000
2001	Al-Qaeda terrorists conduct the September 11 attacks; President George W. Bush announces what becomes the Bush Doctrine; Operation Enduring Freedom begins bombing campaign in Afghanistan
2002	President Bush calls Iran, Iraq, and North Korea an "Axis of Evil"; The federal government establishes the Department of Homeland Security; Iraq ignores a UN ultimatum about weapons of mass destruction
2003	Iraq War begins
2008	Barack Obama is elected first African-American president
2011	U.S. Special Forces kill Osama bin Laden

OVERVIEW

The opening decades of the twenty-first century have seen an intensification of partisan divisions, horrific terrorist attacks, a major economic downturn, and the historic election of the nation's first African-American president. In addition, a number of social and political issues have divided Americans and led to debates around immigration policy, the status of LGBTQ people, gender roles, and family structures.

The presidency of George W. Bush (2001–2009) was dominated by the terrorist attacks of September 11, 2001, and the subsequent war on terrorism. While the terrorist attacks on the United States in 2001 were not the first terrorist incidents in the United States, the impact of the 2001 attack cannot be overstated. Following the terrorist attacks on the World Trade Center and the Pentagon, a series of foreign policy and military initiatives aimed at preventing future terrorist attacks got under way. These initiatives included prolonged and controversial military campaigns in Afghanistan and Iraq. Furthermore, Americans were forced to grapple with ethical implications of certain tactics in the war on terrorism, including "enhanced interrogation" and the indefinite detention of suspected enemy combatants. Americans continued to grapple with the issue of balancing security with civil liberties. In addition, the Bush administration took action on a number of domestic issues, from tax reform to education. His second term was dominated by a series of crises at home, including the response to the devastation caused by Hurricane Katrina and the Great Recession, which began in 2007.

The election of 2008 resulted in a profound milestone in American history—the election of the first African American to the presidency. Such an event was virtually unthinkable a generation earlier. As late as the 1960s, Jim Crow segregation was still the law of the land throughout the South and informal *de facto* segregation existed throughout the nation. The Civil Rights Movement challenged and altered many of these practices, but racist attitudes persisted among large segments of the population.

Once elected, Barack Obama only had the benefit of a Democratic Congress for the first two years of his administration. In 2010, he was able to pass the Affordable Care Act, his most significant piece of legislation. Afterward, it became increasingly difficult for him to persuade Congress to act on his legislative initiatives. The unemployment rate dropped dramatically during his time in office. It was over nine percent during his first year in office; it dropped to 4.7 percent when he left office in 2017. The recovery, however, was uneven, especially in regard to higher-paying jobs. The period of President Obama's presidency saw the emergence of a grassroots conservative movement, the Tea Party movement, which pushed the Republican Party in a rightward direction. The period also saw the emergence of the Occupy Wall Street movement, calling attention to economic inequalities and the power of corporations in shaping policies. Some of the political divisions in the United States were evident in the reaction to the candidacy and presidency of Donald Trump, who was elected in 2016. His focus on immigration and the economic impact of trade policies generated an enthusiastic grassroots movement and propelled him to the White House.

1 GEORGE W. BUSH

The Republican Party's choice for a candidate for the Election of 2000 was not clear. They looked desperately for a candidate who had strong conservative positions against gun control, abortion, and taxes. They found him in a surprising place, George H. W. Bush's family. George W. Bush graduated as a C student from Yale University and became a lieutenant in the Air National Guard where he flew F-102 fighter planes. He took his education more seriously in graduate school and became the first president to earn an MBA. After a wild youth, during which his wife told him to choose either alcohol or her (he chose her), he failed in the oil business but succeeded as the part-owner/manager of the Texas Rangers professional baseball team. After serving as governor of Texas, he campaigned for the presidency becoming the first modern candidate to specifically name Jesus Christ as the chief influence on his life. The Reagan conservative revolution seemed to have new life, and George W. Bush became the greatest political fundraiser of that time in American history, breaking the records set by Bill Clinton by a wide margin.

2 ELECTION OF 2000

George W. Bush and Albert Gore Jr. ran close campaigns that ultimately hinged on the twenty-five Electoral College votes from Florida. Disputed elections returns showed Bush winning the state with a lead of only 1,700 votes out of over six million cast. In automatic recounts the margin was dropped to around three hundred votes in an election where Gore had won over five hundred thousand more votes nationally than did Bush. All eyes were on the Electoral College, however, and on the authenticity of the Florida vote. The Florida Supreme Court said manual recounting was permissible, but not all counties completed the recounts. When the period for recounting was over, the Bush lead had actually increased to 587 votes at which point the case went to the Supreme Court. In a 7 to 2 ruling the Court said that Florida should not have authorized recounts, and in a 5 to 4 decision declared that recounting only some of the votes amounted to a violation of equal protection under the law. The Supreme Court settled the election because Albert Gore decided not to pursue further appeals and conceded the election to Bush. Later recounts completed by investigative journalists concluded that George W. Bush would have maintained a narrow victory.

3 SEPTEMBER 11 ATTACKS

The worst terrorist attacks in U.S. history occurred on September 11, 2001, when nineteen al-Qaeda operatives hijacked four jetliners and crashed them rather than merely making demands. Two planes struck the Twin Towers of the World Trade Center in New York City, and the fires ignited by the jet fuel eventually caused both towers to collapse. Another hijacked plane was flown into the Pentagon in Washington, D.C. The fourth plane was en route to the national capital and likely headed for an attack on the White House or the Capitol Building when passengers aboard the plane attacked the hijackers resulting in the plane's crashing in a field in Pennsylvania. Nearly three thousand victims, including rescue personnel, died in the crashes or as a result of the collapse of the Twin Towers. The attacks amounted to the first blow struck against the continental United States by a foreign enemy since the War of

1812. The United States retaliated by launching Operation Enduring Freedom in Afghanistan in what George W. Bush called the War on Terror. The attacks dealt a severe blow to the American economy and resulted in a streamlining of federal intelligence, national security, and law enforcement agencies into the Department of Homeland Security. Osama bin Laden and al-Qaeda claimed credit for the attacks and continued to plot other attacks on the United States, most of which have been thwarted so far.

4 OSAMA BIN LADEN AND AL-QAEDA

Soon after the September 11 terrorist attacks in 2001, it became clear that the perpetrator was the al-Qaeda network, led by Osama bin Laden. His ideology, which grew out of a militant interpretation of Islam, sanctioned terrorist acts against civilians. Bin Laden, a member of a wealthy Saudi Arabian family, funded the founding of al-Qaeda and became its leader in 1988 after fighting against Soviet forces in Afghanistan (see "Soviet Invasion of Afghanistan," page 417). Al-Qaeda broadened its goals from resisting the Soviet invasion of Afghanistan to installing a worldwide Muslim Caliphate. The organization, espousing an extremist interpretation of Islam, also sought to purge the Muslim world from what it perceived as corrupting Western influences and secularizing elements. Al-Qaeda has trained over five thousand militants and has organized assassinations, bombings, hijackings, and kidnappings including suicide attacks in the quest for martyrdom. Under bin Laden's leadership, al-Qaeda organized terrorist attacks on American embassies in Tanzania and Kenya before authorizing the September 11 attacks. After the 2001 attacks, the United States invaded Afghanistan, in part to remove the Taliban government from power (see below), and in part to find bin Laden and other leaders of al-Qaeda. Eventually, bin Laden was located living in a compound in Pakistan. U.S. Navy Seals and Central Intelligence Agency operatives stormed the compound in 2011 and killed bin Laden. His body was buried at sea. Al-Qaeda still operates, but has been greatly weakened since the death of bin Laden and other leaders.

5 DEPARTMENT OF HOMELAND SECURITY

Formed after the September 11 attacks, the Department of Homeland Security (DHS) quickly became the third largest department in the presidential cabinet. Whereas the Department of Defense oversees the projection of American military force, the DHS is responsible for the protection of the borders and domestic territory of the United States and its protectorates. The chief mission of the DHS is in preventing and responding to terrorist attacks, but it also handles immigration and, among other issues, responses to natural disaster. Similar to the reorganization and formation of federal agencies under the National Security Act in response to the new dangers during the Cold War, the formation of the DHS attempted to consolidate the efforts of the government to protect Americans and American interests in the "War on Terror." Twenty-two government agencies were placed under the department's umbrella, partly to avoid the failure to communicate across agencies that led to the success of the September 11 attacks.

6 USA PATRIOT ACT

The USA Patriot Act (Uniting and Strengthening America by Providing Appropriate Tools Required to Intercept and Obstruct Terrorism Act) passed in 2001 after the September 11 terrorist attacks and gave the government broader powers in combatting terrorism. The act gave authorities greater authority to subject political organizations to surveillance and to conduct searches of phone, Internet, medical, banking, and student records with minimal judicial oversight. It also allows authorities to investigate American citizens for "intelligence purposes," even if there is no probable cause that the individual committed a crime. Finally, the act allows for the imprisonment of noncitizens for indefinite periods with no right to counsel, habeas corpus, or opportunities to appear before public tribunals. The act generated a great deal of controversy—nearly 200 cities, towns, and three states passed resolutions stating that the Patriot Act is not enforceable within their jurisdictions claiming that among other concerns, the First, Fourth, Fifth, Sixth, Eighth, and Fourteenth Amendments were being threatened. The Patriot Act highlighted the tension that exists during times of war between national security and civil liberties. Following successful constitutional challenges to some sections of the act, the Patriot Act was renewed in 2006. In 2011, despite protests from opponents of the act, President Barack Obama signed extensions of portions of the Patriot Act.

7 AFGHANISTAN WAR

Roughly one month after the September 11, 2001, terrorist attacks, the United States and the United Kingdom invaded Afghanistan. The government of Afghanistan, the Taliban regime, sheltered and supported not only the suspects in the September 11 terrorist attacks, but Osama bin Laden himself (see above). The Taliban had come to power in 1996 and imposed an extreme version of Sharia law. The rigid and authoritarian nature of the Taliban regime generated a great deal of criticism from Afghan citizens as well as from Islamic leaders throughout the region. The American-led invasion, named Operation Enduring Freedom, targeted al-Qaeda training sites. Although Osama bin Laden was not caught, al-Qaeda forces in Afghanistan were seriously weakened. After nearly a month and a half, American-led forces, along with participants from within Afghanistan, were able to remove the Taliban from power. In December 2001, Hamid Karzai, who was fluent in English and enjoyed strong support from the West, was sworn in as interim chairman of the government in Kabul. However, instability and the resurgence of the Taliban required the continued presence of American forces. Taliban leaders have been the target of special forces operations and predator drone attacks. In 2014, President Barack Obama announced that America's major combat operations would end in December 2014. The United States has left a residual force in the country. In addition, NATO has stationed over 13,000 troops in Afghanistan to assist in maintaining security.

MCCAIN-FEINGOLD ACT

In 2001, this legislation reflected bipartisan will to reform campaign financing. While it set rules on spending for and by political candidates for federal offices, it also sought to reduce the influence of corporations and PACs spending money on behalf of a candidate. Critics suggested these later provisions limited freedom of speech, and the Supreme Court agreed.

8 BUSH DOCTRINE

In the wake of the September 11 attacks, President Bush declared that the United States would find who had orchestrated the attacks and bring them to justice. After several events targeting the United States and its interests abroad since the Persian Gulf War, Bush declared that a War on Terror had reached a turning point. In a speech before Congress he said "We will pursue nations that provide aid or safe haven to terrorism. Every nation, in every region, now has a decision to make. Either you are with us, or you are with the terrorists. From this day forward, any nation that continues to harbor or support terrorism will be regarded by the United States as a hostile regime." The Bush Doctrine was used as a justification for labeling Iran, Iraq, and North Korea examples of an "Axis of Evil" and for the invasions of Afghanistan and Iraq. In the War on Terror the emphasis shifted from retaliating for attacks to preemptively striking to prevent attacks discovered by intelligence investigations.

9 IRAQ WAR

After the Persian Gulf War the United Nations ordered Saddam Hussein to get rid of his weapons of mass destruction and not to build more, and inspectors were supposed to confirm his progress. A no-fly zone was established and enforced mostly with American and British war planes. After the September 11 attacks, the United States put increasing pressure on Hussein to comply with United Nations inspections. Because Hussein remained defiant the United Nations authorized a buildup of troops on the Iraqi border. When Hussein still refused to comply, President Bush issued an ultimatum for Saddam Hussein and his sons to leave Iraq in 2003. When they did not, Bush ordered the American invasion and bombing of Iraq that became known as the Iraq War. American and allied forces deposed Saddam Hussein, killed his sons, and captured the dictator by 2004. A new government in Iraq executed Hussein, but Iraqi insurgents and militant terrorists have kept up a steady series of attacks using improvised explosive devices (IEDs) and other means. Before leaving office, George W. Bush ordered a surge of American forces and sent an additional thirty thousand troops into Iraq in an attempt to stabilize the situation. The United States was able, under President Barack Obama, to turn over the national security of Iraq to the Iraqis and to withdraw all American forces from the country by 2012. Since that time, a new organization calling itself the Islamic State has seized territory in Syria and Iraq and used brutal tactics to destabilize the region again.

10 AXIS OF EVIL

This phrase from a 2002 State of the Union address by George W. Bush identified Iran, Iraq, and North Korea as the chief rogue nations left in the world, or at least pointed to them as prime examples of latent problems facing the United States. All three nations had a record of sponsoring terrorism and attempting to produce or secure atomic, biological, or chemical weapons of mass destruction. North Korea remains one of the most repressive communist governments in the modern world, and attempts to negotiate with North Korea to curtail its missile and nuclear weapons programs have been largely rebuffed. Recent conflicts between North and South Korea have threatened to destabilize all of East Asia including Japan. Iraq remained a fragile government as the United States withdrew its military forces from the country in the wake of the Iraq War that led to the execution of Saddam Hussein. The encouraging outcomes of the "Arab Spring" uprisings in various countries in North Africa and the Middle East have not as yet manifested successful results in Iran, which remains a revolutionary Islamic republic under the supreme leadership of Ali Khamenei despite mass demonstrations in 2009. The president of Iran, Hassan Rouhani, maintains that Iran should rise as the chief regional power and disregard the United States and Israel as checks on Iranian control of the Middle East. Despite the official position that the Holocaust never occurred during World War II and that Israel should be destroyed, Rouhani assures the world that the Iranian nuclear program is for research, domestic power generation, and other civilian purposes.

11 "ENHANCED INTERROGATION"

In the period following the September 11, 2001, terrorist attacks, there has been debate in the United States about acceptable practices in combatting terrorism. Concerns about American practices emerged following the 2004 release of photographs of U.S. Army personnel humiliating and abusing prisoners at Abu Ghraib prison in Iraq. The photos cast light on new tactics used by the United States in handling prisoners in the aftermath of the 2001 terrorist attacks. Army personnel at detention centers in Iraq, Afghanistan, and Guantanamo Bay, Cuba were given permission to use "enhanced interrogation" techniques. Critics said that these techniques, which include "waterboarding," amounted to torture. The government also began to hold suspects at these facilities indefinitely, denying them due process rights. The Supreme Court, in *Hamdan* v. *Rumsfeld* (2006), ruled that the Bush administration could not hold detainees indefinitely, without due process and without the protection of the Geneva Accords. Following continuing reports of the use of torture in the interrogation methods of the United States, Congress voted in 2006 to hold the president to the guidelines of the Geneva Convention. The bill also banned the use of evidence gathered using cruel, unusual, and inhumane treatment. Concerns about the use of torture resurfaced after the election of Donald Trump as president in 2016. Shortly after his inauguration in 2017, Trump indicated that he would entertain the use of torture in regard to terrorism suspects, even though Congress and President Obama had moved away from such tactics. President Trump said, in regard to discussions he had with members of the intelligence community, "Does it work? Does torture work? And the answer was yes. Absolutely."

12 HURRICANE KATRINA

Hurricane Katrina brought catastrophic damage to the Gulf Coast region in 2005, resulting in more than 1,000 deaths, over $100 billion in property damage, and millions of people left homeless. The heaviest damage was sustained by the city of New Orleans. The hardest hit parts of the city were predominantly African American and impoverished. Americans were shaken not simply by the magnitude of the disaster but also by how ill-prepared all levels of government were in its aftermath. Within the federal government, it appeared that the various agencies were not communicating with one another and did not grasp the seriousness of the situation. The head of the Federal Emergency Management Agency (FEMA) testified that he informed White House officials on August 29 that the levees had been breached and the city was flooding, but members of the administration of President George W. Bush stated that they did not hear of the breach until August 30. In a radio interview, Homeland Security Secretary Michael Chertoff dismissed reports of the thousands of people seeking refuge at the Convention Center. Bush's pronouncement that the head of FEMA, Michael Brown, was doing a "heck of a job" seemed to be further evidence of his inability to grasp the gravity of the situation. The mishandling of the crisis damaged President Bush's approval ratings.

13 NO CHILD LEFT BEHIND

The No Child Left Behind law, supported by President George W. Bush, attempted to reform American education by tying federal funding for schools to increased accountability through standardized testing and revised learning goals. The law extended the reach of the federal government into education, which was traditionally a state responsibility. The law required that states set learning standards that students attain "proficiency" in reading and math by 2014, and that teachers be "highly qualified" in their subject area. The law allowed students to transfer to other schools if they were attending a school that fell short of meeting these new guidelines. The law also allowed the state to take over schools and school districts that did not meet the new guidelines. The program was criticized by many states for its lack of funding to help schools reach these new goals. Also, many educators questioned the increased reliance on standardized tests in judging schools. Another element of Bush's approach to education was his embrace of school vouchers, which would allow families with children in poorly performing public schools to receive grants for children to attend private, often religious, schools. The move toward vouchers reflected the Republican Party's preference for addressing pressing social issues with private sector solutions. Advocates for public education argued that such vouchers would undermine public education by siphoning tax-payer money to private schools. Congressional Democrats ultimately rejected the call for federally-funded vouchers.

14 THE GREAT RECESSION

In 2007, the United States faced its most severe economic crisis since the Great Depression of the 1930s. The Great Recession, as the economic crisis of late 2007 to 2009 has been labeled, led to high unemployment, falling wages, and a housing crisis characterized by widespread home foreclosures. Economists point to the housing crisis of the 2000s as an important cause of the broader recession. In the 2000s, lending institutions lured first-time home buyers to take out mortgages for home purchases that were beyond their means. These risky loans, characterized by high interest rates and less than favorable terms, were referred to as "sub-prime mortgages." By 2007, the housing bubble burst as the real estate market weakened and interest rates increased. Many subprime borrowers found themselves "underwater"—that is, the market value of their home sank below the amount they owed on their mortgage. In many such situations, individuals could neither sell their homes nor afford to pay their monthly mortgage payments. Their only option was to walk away from their home and default on their loan, leading to widespread foreclosures. Since major financial institutions had invested in risky mortgages, many were damaged when foreclosure rates reached crisis proportions. By the fall of 2008, the Dow Jones Industrial Average had lost half of its value. The crisis was devastating to millions of Americans. Consumer spending was drastically reduced. Businesses laid-off 2.8 million workers in 2008.

15 BARACK H. OBAMA

President Obama followed a path to the presidency similar to that of Bill Clinton by studying and teaching constitutional law and participating in community activism and state politics. Like Ronald Reagan he achieved national political prominence by delivering a speech at his party's convention in 2004. He won a Senate seat for Illinois in that same year. In 2008, he fought off a serious challenge from Hillary Rodham Clinton for the Democratic nomination for president and beat Senator John McCain in the general election to become the first African-American president of the United States. His accomplishments to date as president include the authorization of the expenditure of nearly $800 billion in economic stimulus in an attempt to reverse a recession and passage of national health care legislation. He has placed two justices on the Supreme Court and guided the process whereby homosexuals can serve openly in the U.S. military and women can serve in combat roles. He redirected the efforts of the National Aeronautics and Space Administration from the renewal of missions to the moon to more earthbound research. President Obama ended significant American involvement in Iraq and stated his goal to withdraw all U.S. forces from Afghanistan before he left office. He authorized the missions to support the Libyan revolution that led to the capture and killing of Muammar Qaddafi and the mission that killed Osama bin Laden. Like his predecessors Reagan and Clinton, President Obama began his administration with high approval ratings that steadily dropped, but also like Reagan and Clinton he won a second term as president. Questions about the murder of four Americans, including the U.S. ambassador, in Benghazi, Libya, inappropriate use of Internal Revenue Service screening power, and the Department of Justice phone-tapping power have brought the Obama administration under new scrutiny. The 2014 mid-term elections indicated a slow economic recovery, and the growing dissatisfaction with "Obamacare" (a nickname for the national healthcare system established by the Affordable Care Act in 2010) may have led to another pendulum shift in American politics. The Republican Party won the majority in both houses of Congress and the majority of governorships.

16 AFFORDABLE CARE ACT

For decades, political leaders had discussed the importance of reforming the American healthcare system to address spiraling health-care costs and large numbers of uninsured Americans. President Bill Clinton made healthcare reform a major agenda item, but he failed to win sufficient Congressional support. In 2009, President Obama chose healthcare reform as one of his first major domestic initiatives. Many Congressional Democrats pushed for a "public option," which would have created a federal insurance program, similar to Medicare, but for people under 65 years of age. In March 2010, Democrats were able to pass a watered-down version of healthcare reform. The Patient Protection and Affordable Care Act overhauled much of the healthcare industry. Among other things, the bill allowed children to stay on their parents' health insurance plans until they were 26, prevented insurance companies from denying coverage based on an individual's "pre-existing conditions," subsidized private insurance for low- and middle-income individuals, and required all Americans to have some sort of health insurance (the "individual mandate"). Finally, the act also called for the establishment of health insurance exchanges or marketplaces in each of the fifty states. Such exchanges can be more cost efficient because individuals pool their purchasing power into larger groups. According to a March 2016 report by the Congressional Budget Office, the Affordable Care Act has provided health insurance to 24 million people. The Affordable Care Act was criticized by many Republicans. With the election of President Donald Trump in 2016, Republican leaders have promised to repeal and replace the act.

17 THE DODD-FRANK WALL STREET REFORM AND CONSUMER PROTECTION ACT

After the Great Recession of 2007 to 2009 (see above), President Barack Obama pushed for measures to add regulations to the financial industry in order to prevent some of the risky practices that led to the recession in the first place. The Dodd-Frank Wall Street Reform and Consumer Protection Act (2010) was designed to regulate financial markets and protect consumers. It constituted the most comprehensive financial reform act since the Glass-Steagall

Act of 1933, which established regulations for the banking industry. The Dodd-Frank Act established federal bodies to examine new and possibly risky practices by large corporations and to provide oversight of financial institutions to protect consumers from unsound practices. The act was designed, in part, to address the situation in which large financial firms are deemed "too big to fail." To describe certain financial institutions as "too big to fail" is to note that the size of these institutions make their failure unthinkable, because their failure would have such devastating consequences on the U.S. economy. Economists fear that if a firm is considered too big to fail, it will be more likely to engage in excessively risky behavior; such a firm realizes that a government bailout will occur if the risky behavior leads to major financial losses. This occurred, these economists argue, in the lead-up to the Great Recession. Critics argue that the Dodd-Frank Act is not strong enough to end the idea of "too big to fail."

18 DEFERRED ACTION FOR CHILDHOOD ARRIVALS (DACA)

In the late twentieth and early twenty-first centuries, debates around immigration policy have divided Americans. Some Americans insist that the government should take more stringent measures to prevent undocumented immigrants from entering the country. Others argue that steps should be taken to provide a path to citizenship for the many undocumented immigrants in the country. President Barack Obama pushed for a comprehensive reform of immigration policy that combined deportations of undocumented immigrants who were deemed dangerous with providing pathways to legal status and citizenship for most undocumented immigrants. In 2012, he enacted, through executive order, the Deferred Action for Childhood Arrivals (DACA) program, which allowed certain undocumented immigrants who entered the United States as minors to receive a renewable two-year period of deferred action from deportation. The program also contained provisions for these individuals to obtain work permits. The idea of the program was that children should not be punished for their parents' illegal action of entering the United States without documentation. In the following year, congressional leaders attempted to address the issue of immigration reform with the Border Security, Economic Opportunity, and Immigration Modernization Act. A bipartisan group of senators, labeled the "gang of eight," negotiated the bill. They hoped to solidify immigration reform in legislation, rather than allow it to be shaped on a temporary basis by executive action. The act would have provided a pathway to permanent residence status and citizenship for many undocumented immigrants as well as provisions for greater border security. The bill was approved by the Senate, but despite its bipartisan origins, was blocked by Republican opposition in the House of Representatives.

19 CITIZENS UNITED v. FEDERAL ELECTION COMMISSION

In 2010, the Supreme Court came up with a controversial ruling in *Citizens United* v. *Federal Election Commission* that changed the rules around funding political campaigns. This ruling allowed corporations and other organizations to spend unlimited amounts of money on political campaigns. Previously, the 1972 Federal Election Campaign law and the 2003 McCain-Feingold Act set limits and regulations on campaign contributions, both direct, "hard money," contributions to campaigns as well as contributions of "soft money" to political parties. In the *Citizens United* decision, the Court ruled, in a 5 to 4 decision, that the government may not restrict the spending of corporations, unions, and other groups on political campaigns. Politically-oriented nonprofits can now raise and spend unlimited amounts of money without disclosing their finances to the Federal Election Commission. The Court argued that such restrictions violated the free speech provision of the First Amendment. Later, in 2014, the Court extended the logic of the *Citizens United* decision to individual contributions. While the Court upheld the $2,700 limit on contributions to a particular candidate, it struck down limits on how much an individual could contribute to a political party or to multiple candidates. Such limits, the Court asserted, constituted unreasonable limits on free speech. The impact of the *Citizens United* decision was felt almost immediately. The decision opened the floodgates for corporate campaign contributions for the midterm election of 2010.

20 DONALD TRUMP

In 2016, Donald Trump won the presidential election and became the 45th president of the United States. Trump's background was in New York City real estate. He had become a well-known fixture in American culture through the television show, *The Apprentice*; he produced and hosted the show from 2004 to 2015. He entered a crowded field of Republican candidates for the party's nomination in 2015. The debates among the Republican candidates were freewheeling, unpredictable events, with Trump garnering a great deal of attention and air-time. By the fall of 2015, he emerged as the leading candidate for the nomination. His blunt, unpolished, and aggressive style of speaking appealed to many voters. He was perceived as "speaking his mind," unencumbered by what he called "political correctness." Many voters—Democrats and Republicans—were stunned and even disgusted by many of his comments and actions, including his questioning of the status of John McCain as a war hero. The issue of immigration was at the center of Trump's campaign for the presidency in 2016. He promised to a build a wall between the United States and Mexico to prevent people from illegally crossing the border and to temporarily block immigration from certain Muslim majority nations. In the election of 2016, he faced Hillary Clinton, who had served as First Lady (1993–2001), as senator from New York State (2001–2009), and as secretary of state under President Barack Obama (2009–2013). Clinton had faced a surprisingly strong challenge from Senator Bernie Sanders of Vermont before being chosen as the first female standard-bearer for a major party in a presidential election. In the campaign, Trump continued to stress immigration, trade deals, and security. He criticized Clinton for maintaining a private email server during her time as secretary of state, asserting that it was a sign of bad judgment. In the general election, Trump carried enough states to win 306 electoral votes and the presidency, even though he failed to win the national popular vote by nearly 2.9 million.

THE BIG PICTURE

1. After a constitutional crisis surrounding the disputed Election of 2000, George W. Bush intended to spend his presidency building on the domestic reforms presaged in the Republican Contract with America.

2. The terrorist attacks of 2001 redirected the Bush administration toward launching the war on terrorism, revamping homeland security and establishing the Bush Doctrine of preemptive war on terrorists and on nations thought to be harboring terrorists.

3. The administration of Barack Obama, the nation's first African-American president, addressed ongoing problems with the health care system in the United States and financial reform in the aftermath of the Great Recession of 2007 to 2009 despite deep political divisions in Congress and among the electorate.

4. The ongoing war on terrorism led to long-term wars in Iraq and Afghanistan, regime change and instability in both countries, the capture and trial of Iraqi leaders Saddam Hussein, debate over "enhanced interrogation" techniques and drone warfare, and the killing of Osama bin Laden by U.S. military forces.

5. Climate change, the impact of the Affordable Care Act, the rights of LGBTQ people, the status of race relations, and other issues led to bitter political divisions in the first decades of the twenty-first century and contributed to the election of President Donald Trump in 2016.

American Scientific and Technological Advances 40

Be it known that we, ORVILLE WRIGHT and WILBUR WRIGHT, citizens of the United States . . . have invented certain new and useful Improvements in Flying-Machines. . . .

—Wright Brothers' patent, 1906

TIMELINE

1744	Benjamin Franklin founds the American Philosophical Society
1749	The first Conestoga wagon is built
1780	John Adams founds the American Academy of Arts and Sciences; Scientific societies begin to flourish
1793	Samuel Slater opens the first textile factory
1794	Eli Whitney patents the cotton gin
1807	Robert Fulton builds the first commercial steamboat
1827	John James Audubon publishes *Birds of America*
1830	Steam locomotive is in operation
1834	Cyrus McCormick patents the mechanical reaper
1836	The Smithsonian Institution charitable trust is founded; Samuel Colt patents a "revolving gun"
1845	Elias Howe invents the sewing machine
1847	Samuel F. B. Morse receives a patent for the telegraph
1854	Elisha G. Otis invents the elevator brake
1857	Oliver F. Winchester organizes the New Haven Arms Company; William Kelly patents the process of making steel
1862	Richard Gatling receives a patent for his Gatling gun
1867	Typewriter is invented
1874	Joseph Glidden receives a patent for barbed wire
1876	Alexander Graham Bell receives a patent for the telephone; Thomas Edison builds the first industrial research laboratory

TIMELINE

1888	Kodak sells the first camera
1893	The first American automobile manufacturing company is founded
1897	Nikola Tesla receives first patents for the radio
1903	The Wright brothers successfully test their airplane
1916	William Coolidge invents the cathode tube improving X-ray technology
1926	The first liquid-fueled rocket is launched
1939	Television is demonstrated at the World's Fair
1940	The first mass production of a helicopter begins
1942	Scientists achieve the first sustained nuclear chain reaction
1943	Margaret Rousseau designs the first commercial penicillin plant
1947	ENIAC I becomes the first patented computer
1954	Bell Labs produces the first silicon version of a transistor
1955	Jonas Salk introduces the polio vaccine
1981	Space Shuttle takes its first orbital flight
1990	Hubble Space Telescope is placed in orbit

1 BENJAMIN FRANKLIN

Franklin was more than a statesman. His electrical experiments discovered plus and minus charges and explained lightning as an electrical phenomenon and thus put American science on the map in the respected Royal Society of London. His inventions include a musical instrument called the armonica, the Franklin stove, the lightning rod, bifocal lenses, and the rocking chair. He conceived of daylight savings time and was the first scientist to measure and map the Gulf Stream. He invented an odometer to make post offices more efficient, and he tried to better society with libraries and to protect it with fire departments.

2 SCIENTIFIC SOCIETIES

The American Academy of Arts and Sciences was founded as early as 1780 in Boston by John Adams. New Jersey founded a Society for the Promotion of Agriculture, Commerce, and Art in 1781. Other agricultural societies, chemical societies, and museums were founded by the end of the eighteenth century in an effort to elevate the useful discoveries of science and technology. Such organizations published journals that spread ideas and provided an incentive for research and development of inventions and innovations.

3 JOHN JAMES AUDUBON

Audubon was a storekeeper with drawing talent who turned his bankruptcy in the Panic of 1819 into a quest to draw and paint all of America's birds. His dramatic paintings appeared in *Birds of America* as early as 1827 but went through several reprints. His life story of roving about and adding to the advance of descriptive zoology appealed to readers during the Romantic period, and he made a living from selling his books that eventually turned to other fauna. His work bred in Americans a love of natural history, especially in the careers of zoologists like Louis Agassiz and naturalists like Henry David Thoreau, John Muir, and Theodore Roosevelt.

4 SMITHSONIAN INSTITUTION

James Smithson, an English scientist, gave his fortune upon his death to found "an establishment for the increase and diffusion of knowledge" in Washington, D.C. The Congress accepted the gift and founded the Smithsonian Institution in 1846. The Smithsonian is now the largest museum and laboratory complex in the world housing nineteen museums, the National Zoo, and nine research facilities.

5 SAMUEL SLATER

Slater has been called the father of the American Industrial Revolution. He came to the United States in 1789 as the first person who knew both how to make and to operate cloth-making machines. His first water-powered textile mill was operational by 1793 in Rhode Island. In a common system established in New England mills, Slater built three mill villages that housed his machines but also his workers, and whole families worked in the mills and shopped in the village stores. Textile manufacturing was the first large-scale process sparking industrial growth in both England and America.

6 ELI WHITNEY

Whitney solved the problem of making the production of cotton lucrative through the automation of the separation of the seeds from the fibers with his cotton gin. His original design could produce 50 pounds of cotton fibers per day, and this feat revolutionized the cultivation of cotton to become the central economic reality of many southern states. The rise of the Cotton Kingdom brought on a rise in the demand for African slaves to accomplish the other tedious tasks of growing cotton. Legal troubles hampered Whitney's production of his machines, but he grew wealthy from the manufacture of muskets for the government using interchangeable parts, a key facet of the principles of modern mass production.

7 ROBERT FULTON

Fulton was an artist born in Pennsylvania who also turned a love of mechanical things into the marriage of steam power to boats. He imported a steam engine from England and proved its feasibility aboard his first vessel, the *Clermont*, by 1807. Fulton had invented a submersible boat for naval warfare that he called a torpedo, but could not find a nation willing to purchase them. He therefore focused on a transportation business providing transit from New York City to Albany at 5 miles per hour. The use of steam-powered vessels spread across the United States and beyond as the most significant step in the transportation revolution next to the railroad.

8 CONESTOGA WAGON

This heavy-duty wagon was named for the Conestoga area of Pennsylvania where it was developed to carry goods back and forth across the Allegheny Mountains. In use as early as 1720, it remained the chief method of moving heavy goods until railroads, and a team of six horses could carry as much as 8 tons. A lighter version known as a prairie schooner became the classic means of transportation for pioneers as they traveled west. A canvas covering kept the elements out while allowing ventilation, and the boat-like shape of the wagon made it easier for horses or oxen to pull the wagon across rivers and streams. Wagon trains of travelers congregated together for safety. The invention of this device was how the West was won.

9 CYRUS MCCORMICK

The first patent for this Virginian and mechanical genius was for a hillside plow in 1831. He then developed a mechanical reaping machine that used animal power to ease the job of harvesting grain. After his iron foundry failed in the Panic of 1837, McCormick began licensing manufacturers to build and sell his improved reaper. When quality control proved inadequate with this system, McCormick opened his own factory in Chicago in 1847. Later innovations in his machinery combined the process of harvesting and threshing grain in large machines drawn by as many as forty to sixty mules.

10 SAMUEL COLT

Colt was born in Connecticut and went to sea for adventure. His love of mechanical devices, however, led to his invention of the revolver, a firearm that could be loaded with multiple shots and fired rapidly. He obtained patents and operated a factory as early as 1837, but it was not until around 1855 that the U.S. Army increased the demand for his revolvers and made his business thrive. Colt developed new machinery and the largest firearm factory in the world just in time for the Civil War. Though he died in 1862, his weapons had become famous, and the Colt .45 caliber Peacemaker was the weapon of choice for gunslingers, lawmen, and cavalry soldiers alike in settling the West.

11 STEAM LOCOMOTIVE

The greatest transportation revolution until the invention of the automobile was the development of the steam locomotive. Although the steam engine and steam-powered vehicles were invented in England, American John Stevens demonstrated a practical railroad as early as 1826, three years before a railroad was developed in Great Britain. Peter Cooper made the Tom Thumb, the first American steam locomotive in 1830. Continual improvements in locomotives led to faster speeds and heavier loads as railroads crisscrossed the East during the 1850s, and the first transcontinental railroad helped open the West by 1869. George Pullman developed a comfortable sleeping car by 1857. Railroads remain such an integral part of the American economy that many foresee the use of high-speed bullet trains as the next significant step in revolutionized transportation.

12 OLIVER F. WINCHESTER

The only weapon that could rival the Colt revolver as the most important American firearm was the lever-action rifle developed by Oliver Winchester. Winchester gathered together various inventions like a self-contained brass cartridge, a tubular magazine, and the lever-action to create the repeating rifle used in the latter part of the Civil War. Improvements in manufacturing processes maintained quality while attaining the capacity for mass production. Settlement of the West was not entirely possible due to the ferocity of the Plains Indians until soldiers and even settlers could have a repeating revolver and a repeating rifle, especially when the two fired the same type of ammunition.

13 WILLIAM KELLY

Kelly was the American ironworker who invented the process of making steel more easily by forcing air through molten iron. He made steel this way as early as 1850, but Sir Henry Bessemer patented a similar process in England and in America by 1855. By 1857 Kelly received a patent in America that supplanted Bessemer's, but the Panic of 1857 thwarted his efforts to make a successful steel plant. Kelly formed a later company bearing his name that competed with a rival plant that used the Bessemer process, but when the two combined their operations and Kelly's patent was extended in 1871, William Kelly finally achieved financial success. His career is the classic study in how trial-and-error innovation, patent law, and economic conditions can spell either success or ruin.

14 ELISHA G. OTIS

Louis Sullivan's skyscraper would hardly have been a practical invention had it not been for the elevator brake invented by Elisha Otis in 1852. Powered hoists existed previously, but Otis devised an automatic spring mechanism to catch the elevator car if the rope or cables suspending it failed. Otis demonstrated his invention at the famous Crystal Palace Exposition in 1854 after having the rope suspending his elevator cut dramatically before a rapt audience. Otis's device and the steel-framed structure developed by Sullivan transformed the look of cities across the world beginning with the ten-story Home Insurance Building built in Chicago in the 1880s.

15 SAMUEL F. B. MORSE

The other famous painter-turned-inventor besides Robert Fulton, Samuel Morse patented a device that used electricity to send messages over wires in 1840 using his code consisting of long and short electric impulses. By 1844 a telegraph line was constructed between Baltimore and Washington, D.C., over which the first message, "What hath God wrought?" was sent. By 1861 a telegraph wire stretched from ocean to ocean across America, and by 1866 a transatlantic cable connected the United States and Europe. Morse is the reason that a communications revolution accompanied the transportation revolution, both of which dramatically boosted the nineteenth-century American economy.

16 ALEXANDER GRAHAM BELL

Bell was an educator of the deaf who opened a school in Boston in 1872. Bell's method used various devices to train his students to speak. His knowledge of acoustics led him to experiment with the telegraph invented by Morse. He demonstrated the first practical telephone in 1876 and founded the Bell Telephone Company the next year. His later work paved the way for the transmission of sound by light, metal detectors, and the phonograph. Communications thus took a giant leap forward in becoming accessible to everyone just by transmitting the human voice, and Bell company laboratories became a leading research facility.

17 BARBED WIRE

The West could not have been tamed once it was won except for various patented stages in the invention of barbed wire. Joseph Glidden received the final patent in 1871. Ranchers therefore had a practical way of organizing the use of their private grasslands without the threat of free-ranging herds destroying fodder. The use of barbed wire ended the nostalgic lifestyles of cowboys herding cattle over long drives on public lands. Barbed wire also took on entirely new uses in fortifications in the trenches of World War I.

18 GATLING GUN

Richard Gatling studied the problem of battlefield injuries and deaths and came up with an interesting solution: the manufacture of the first successful machine gun. He believed his device would reduce the size of armies and therefore make war less deadly. The Gatling gun used six rotating barrels to fire ammunition at a rate of six hundred rounds per minute without overheating. His automatic weapon saw some use in the Civil War but was not adopted by the U.S. Army officially until 1866. The Gatling gun then played a role in the Great Plains warfare with American Indians and saw use around the world. Most battlefield machine guns eventually reverted to the use of a single barrel to achieve greater mobility, but Gatling's design formed the basis for several modern weapons mounted in aircraft.

19 TYPEWRITER

Before the computer the most revolutionary tool for business was the typewriter invented in 1866 by Christopher Sholes. The device was manufactured by the Remington Arms Company. As typists' speed increased, Sholes changed the keyboard to spread out letters that were used frequently and created the QWERTY keyboard in use today. Touch typing, or the ability to type using all ten fingers while looking away from the keys, was developed by a court stenographer in 1878 and dramatically increased typing speed. The telephone and the typewriter together provided the first large boost to the employment of women outside the home in positions as telephone operators who manually connected calls and as office clerks who typed business correspondence.

20 SEWING MACHINE

The invention of a practical sewing machine by Elias Howe in 1846 made possible the mass production of clothing for the first time. In 1851, Isaac Singer downsized Howe's industrial machine and added some technical innovations to produce a workable model for home use. Patent disputes between the two inventors were settled by royalty payments and then the formation of a company that combined several patents and created mass production. The first electric sewing machine was marketed in 1889 and by 1905 was in wide use across the country. The sewing machine was another labor-saving device that helped provide women with freedom from laborious hand stitching but also an employment opportunity outside the home.

21 THOMAS EDISON

Edison was homeschooled because he was considered a slow learner, but he became a telegraph operator in 1863 and pursued a passion for chemistry. By 1869 he received his first patent while working for the Western Union Telegraph Company for a device that could record votes. He invested in an electrical engineering firm that sold out and granted him a small fortune with which he started his own company. By 1876 he had founded the world's first research laboratory by hiring assistants with whom he collaborated in all his further inventions. Among these inventions were the incandescent electric lamp, an improved motion picture projector, storage battery, dictaphone, mimeograph, phonograph, and an electric locomotive. In all, Edison's laboratory received over one thousand patents, and his company was the foundation for General Electric Corporation.

22 AUTOMOBILE

No one person invented the automobile. Over one hundred thousand separate patents led to the modern car. After steam-powered automobiles and a series of attempts at using internal combustion engines, two German engineers named Daimler and Benz developed successful four-wheeled gasoline-powered automobiles. French manufacturers like Peugeot were the first to make practical gasoline automobiles for sale but their products, along with those of the first American manufacturers (Duryea and Oldsmobile), were toys for the rich. Ransome Eli Olds had begun a rudimentary assembly line in Detroit, Michigan, but the first conveyor-belt-style assembly was installed by Henry Ford by 1914. Ford had built cars for his own company since 1903, but the assembly line sped up production until a Model T Ford was completed from start to finish in ninety-three minutes. That level of production dramatically lowered the cost of automobiles and brought them within the reach of the average American. Ford's plant had made fifteen million Model Ts by 1927. The transportation revolution turned into a social revolution as widespread mobility led to hundreds of other industries to accommodate the needs of travelers.

23 CAMERA

Two Frenchmen developed a device as early as the 1830s that used light coming through an orifice to draw images on chemicals on metal plates, but the process bore the name, daguerreotype, of the one who produced more lasting images in less time. American George Eastman invented a flexible celluloid film in 1889 that when coated with emulsions produced negative images that could then be used to make photographs. Eastman invented a small box camera that he marketed as the Kodak camera for use by amateur photographers. Eastman's company developed the negatives and produced photographs, but also sold chemicals so that individuals could produce their own photos. Innovations in the camera, lenses, flash-bulbs, and film (including color by 1940) continued apace until the invention of the digital camera largely relegated Eastman's process to a hobby for purists. The widespread use of the camera was a paradigm shift in art, journalism, and history and, like the automobile, launched several spinoff industries.

24 RADIO

French and German scientists discovered electromagnetic waves, but an American named Mahlon Loomis was the first person to demonstrate their use in sending a signal in 1866. In 1896, Italian Guglielmo Marconi was the first person to use radio waves to send a message in Morse code. Marconi's "radiotelegraph" received a message across the Atlantic Ocean by 1902. American Lee Deforest invented a sensitive radio receiver that amplified signals, thus the amplitude-modulated, or AM, radio was born and could receive many signals on different frequencies. American radio patents were used by the government exclusively through World War I, but their private inventors held them again in 1919 and continued development. Radio stations capable of broadcasting voice communications and music existed in America by 1915, and American Edwin Armstrong invented frequency-modulated equipment, or FM, that could dramatically quiet static. With the invention of the transistor by Bell Laboratories in 1947, the radio, along with all other electronic equipment, could be shrunk in size. In 1965, the first FM antenna system in the world designed to allow several FM stations to broadcast simultaneously was installed atop the Empire State Building in New York City. The collected impact of all of these stages of the development of radio technology led also to microwaves, cordless devices like phones, and remote control devices for televisions and other machines.

25 AIRPLANE

Bicycle repairmen Orville and Wilbur Wright began tinkering with gliders prior to 1900 in a quest to create a flying machine. The brothers carefully modeled the curved wings of their Flyer that were able to change their shape by warping after the wings of birds. Their gliders grew in size until they launched a biplane version at Kitty Hawk, North Carolina, which they used as a testing site because of its remoteness, many sand dunes, and consistent winds. They successfully launched a manned glider in 1900. As design problems became more difficult, the Wrights invented a wind tunnel to test their designs. The first successful manned, powered flight lasted twelve seconds when they launched their Flyer off a downhill track at Kitty Hawk in 1903. The first death in a Wright Flyer occurred to one of Orville's passengers in 1908, but the American government began purchasing airplanes the next year. Airplanes were capable of being armed with machine guns by 1912 and began to make an impact on warfare in World War I. Another bicycle mechanic named Glenn Curtiss invented ailerons, a simpler method of steering airplanes than the Wright's wing-warping method. With continual innovations and the eventual manufacture using aluminum, planes developed from reconnaissance duties to serious aerial bombing. Commercial applications of air travel were not developed until after World War II.

26 X-RAY

German physicist Wilhelm Roentgen discovered what he called X-rays being generated from a cathode ray generator in 1895. He became world famous by taking the first X-ray image, an "X-ray" of his wife's hand. The revolutionary medical implications of this technology became evident when American William Coolidge invented a better cathode tube using tungsten filaments. The Coolidge tube received a patent in 1916 and created the field of radiology because it could discern tissues more clearly and help in locating tumors.

27 TELEVISION

After studying the work of European scientists who developed vacuum tubes and the cathode ray tube, American Allen B. Du Mont made the first durable and commercially practical cathode ray tube for television. Cathode ray tubes produced images on their phosphorescent surfaces by channeling beams of electrons. Du Mont developed the high-speed equipment necessary to manufacture and test his tubes by 1932. He founded a production company in 1934 and an experimental broadcasting station in New York City as early as 1938. As he predicted, his work and that of the other inventors who developed television technology brought "about a new industry, a new means of entertainment, a new marketing medium, and a new age." Developments in antennae and tuning technology increased the feasibility of television through the 1940s, and color television was available as early as 1953. By 1960 the vast majority of Americans had at least one television in their homes.

28 TRANSISTOR

The transistor has been called the most important invention of the twentieth century. John Bardeen and Walter Brattain were researchers working for Bell Laboratories when they conceived of the idea of making a three-point contact using a semiconductor. An innovation made by William Shockley made the devices easier to manufacture, and the three men received the Nobel Prize in physics in 1956. Transistors accomplished the same task as vacuum tubes but without having to warm up. They also gave off less heat and took up a fraction of the space, so solid state electronic equipment could be smaller and easier to keep cool. Accomplishments of the transistor include tremendous commercial success in the handheld transistor radio as well as national scientific success with the only successful landings of men on the moon.

29 COMPUTER

Two Harvard professors made the first modern computer for use by the U.S. Navy in 1944. The device, called the Mark I, filled a large room and weighed five tons. The Army sponsored the next generation, the ENIAC 1, which still filled a large room but was faster because it used vacuum tubes. The vacuum tubes were replaced by transistors by 1948, the transistors by the integrated circuit ("The Chip") in 1958, and the integrated circuit by the microprocessor in 1971 (the same year the "floppy" disk was introduced). Each advance in technology made computers smaller and faster. Small personal computers were first sold as kits, but Steve Wozniak and Steve Jobs began to manufacture Apple computers for the average consumer in 1976. Radio Shack and IBM marketed competitive models, and by 1981 Bill Gates offered DOS, the operating system that IBM used to allow the average person to use computers without knowing the BASIC computing language. Gates's Microsoft software company developed Windows in 1985 to compete with the user-friendly design of Macintosh computers. With computers being used to design computers, the pace of change became so fast that hardware and software suffered obsolescence every five years or less. No other technology in the history of the world has ever increased the productivity of mankind more or faster, with the possible exception of written language.

30 PENICILLIN

In 1928, Scottish scientist Alexander Fleming discovered by accident that cultures of bacteria were destroyed by a mold from which penicillin was derived. British scientists developed a technique for growing penicillin that was perfected by American scientist Andrew Moyer for production by 1943. Using a strain of the mold found in a cantaloupe in an American market, Moyer's process produced a stronger antibiotic result with much faster production, dropping the price for a dose of penicillin from $20.00 to fifty-five cents by 1946. Moyer was granted a patent for the production of penicillin in 1948, but as early as 1947 certain bacteria began mutating to acquire resistance to the drug. Hence began the war scientists wage to this day, saving millions of lives while trying to stay ahead in antibiotic research and development.

31 ATOMIC ENERGY

Once X-rays were recognized as a form of radiation, research by Pierre and Marie Curie and others uncovered the principles of radioactivity. Albert Einstein described the relationship between energy and matter theoretically by 1905. Understanding of the physics of the atom increased through the 1930s, and American scientist Enrico Fermi experimented with uranium testing the theory that nuclear fission could release tremendous energy in a sustained nuclear reaction. Einstein wrote a letter to Franklin Roosevelt stating that German scientists were working on the use of nuclear energy for military applications, and by 1942 the U.S. government devoted tremendous resources to the Manhattan Project, the attempt to construct atomic bombs before the Nazis. Enrico Fermi achieved the first controlled nuclear chain reaction in a graphite reactor at the University of Chicago before the end of 1942. While scientists worked in Oak Ridge, Tennessee, and Hanford, Washington, to produce the atomic material to fuel bombs, J. Robert Oppenheimer worked at the Los Alamos laboratory in New Mexico to design the bombs. In July of 1945 the first atomic bomb was tested at Los Alamos and was successful. The United States dropped two nuclear bombs on Japan before the Japanese government surrendered to end World War II. By 1960 nuclear reactors existed in the United States for the commercial production of electrical power that, since the tsunami-induced crisis in Japan in 2011, awaits further development as an energy solution.

32 HELICOPTER

After Russian Igor Sikorsky invented the first successful helicopter by 1940, American inventor Stanley Hiller Jr. made the first helicopter with all-metal rotor blades in 1944. Hiller's helicopter was thus much faster and more durable. Hiller proved the feasibility of helicopter flight by flying one across the United States in 1949. The Bell Aircraft company produced the first helicopter to have a bubble canopy. Bell helicopters and others revolutionized everything from law enforcement, traffic reporting, and tourism to ambulance service and the method of fighting wars. Later helicopters were tremendous antitank weapons and also crucial transport aircraft for the insertion and extraction of infantry troops in every war since the Vietnam War.

33 ROCKET

Chinese gunpowder rockets had been used in both celebrations and warfare since the thirteenth century. As early as 1898 people envisioned using rockets to reach outer space, but the first practical experiments with solid-propellant rockets were done by American Robert H. Goddard. He desired to obtain meteorological data from greater heights than possible with hot-air balloons, and his research led to a publication in 1919 explaining the math. By 1929 he developed liquid propellants to achieve higher altitudes. Goddard also developed the gyroscope to achieve better flight control, the concept of a payload space for his scientific experiments within the rockets, and the idea of parachute recovery. German scientists developed military applications for liquid-propellant rockets by the end of World War II, and American and Soviet governments attracted German scientists to their own experimental programs after the war. Intercontinental ballistic missiles were developed by both superpowers, and in 1957 the Soviets succeeded in placing an object in orbit around the earth and the arms race turned into the space race. The United States formed the National Aeronautics and Space Administration (NASA) in 1958 as a civilian agency dedicated to the peaceful exploration of space.

34 JONAS SALK

Poliomyelitis, or polio, was a dreaded childhood disease that occasionally struck adults like President Franklin D. Roosevelt. Jonas Salk was an American medical student whose research with influenza paved the way for a flu vaccine as well as the research he began in 1947 on a vaccine for polio. After eight years of painstaking research, Salk not only proved his vaccine's effectiveness in human trials but refused to patent it. His selfless labor and miraculous success endeared him to people around the world, and polio has been eradicated in countries that use his vaccine.

35 SPACE SHUTTLE

President Richard Nixon directed National Aeronautics and Space Administration (NASA) after its successful moon landing in 1969 to devote its resources to develop a new system for space transportation. NASA engineers began working on the space shuttle program the next year. The ultimate solution was to create a reusable spaceship that would be launched with two reusable solid-propellant rockets and an expendable external liquid-repellant tank. The first test model of the shuttle was affectionately named *Enterprise* after the spaceship of *Star Trek* fame, and the integrity of the aerodynamics was proven by flying it atop a 747 jumbo jet. Five free flights proved that the shuttle could glide safely to a stop on the ground. After the *Columbia* was launched into space and successfully landed in 1981, the space shuttle program conducted over one hundred safe missions and two in which the entire crew was killed. The space shuttle program ended in 2011 in favor of more robotic explorations of space.

36 HUBBLE SPACE TELESCOPE

While the space shuttle was considered the most complex technological achievement of the twentieth century, it was designed to carry payloads like the Hubble space telescope into space. The space telescope was intended to achieve clearer pictures of deep space by escaping the interference of the earth's atmosphere. Edwin Hubble was an American astronomer credited with proving the existence of other galaxies beyond the Milky Way and for observing that the universe is expanding at a constant rate; the space telescope was named in his honor. The telescope was taken into space and released in orbit by a space shuttle in 1990. A flaw of one-fiftieth of the width of a human hair caused the pictures taken by the telescope to blur, but this defect in the telescope's primary mirror was corrected in 1993 by other shuttle astronauts. Notable discoveries of the Hubble telescope shine light on the future potential of space travel by confirming the existence of new planets and new stars in over 1,500 new galaxies. Just as NASA researchers began studying the feasibility of a space shuttle years before its success, research has now begun to provide for the transplant of portions of the Earth's population to other planets.

Essential Supreme Court Cases

41

The judicial Power shall extend to all Cases, in Law and Equity, arising under this Constitution, [and] the Laws of the United States. . . .
—The United States Constitution, 1789

TIMELINE

1803	*Marbury* v. *Madison*
1810	*Fletcher* v. *Peck*
1819	*Dartmouth College* v. *Woodward*
1819	*McCulloch* v. *Maryland*
1821	*Cohens* v. *Virginia*
1824	*Gibbons* v. *Ogden*
1831–1832	Cherokee cases
1857	*Dred Scott* v. *Sandford*
1877	*Munn* v. *Illinois*
1895	*In re Debs*
1896	*Plessy* v. *Ferguson*
1901–1905	Insular cases
1904	*Northern Securities Co.* v. *United States*
1919	*Schenck* v. *United States*
1935	*Schechter Poultry Corp.* v. *United States*
1944	*Korematsu* v. *United States*
1954	*Brown* v. *Board of Education of Topeka*
1962	*Engel* v. *Vitale*
1963	*Gideon* v. *Wainwright*
1966	*Miranda* v. *Arizona*
1973	*Roe* v. *Wade*
1974	*United States* v. *Nixon*
1978	*Board of Regents* v. *Bakke*
2000	*Bush* v. *Gore*

1 MARBURY v. MADISON

As a result of the Jeffersonian Revolution in the Election of 1800, the Anti-Federalists came to power in Congress along with their chief in the executive branch. William Marbury was one of the late appointments to the federal court system by John Adams on his way out of office. Marbury was to be a justice of the peace for the District of Columbia, but the new secretary of state, James Madison, refused to give Marbury his commission, and thus Marbury sued Madison. Thomas Jefferson and other Anti-Federalists disliked President Adams's attempt to leave one branch of the central government in Federalist hands. In 1803, John Marshall, who also had been appointed to the Supreme Court by John Adams, wrote the unanimous decision that Marbury was due his commission, but Marbury's claim that the Supreme Court had jurisdiction in the case was based on the Judiciary Act of 1789, which in this case conflicted with the U.S. Constitution. Even though a decision in Marbury's favor would have helped a fellow Federalist, Marshall said the "essence of judicial duty" was to follow the Constitution when laws passed by the legislative branch and signed by the president conflicted with what the Constitution said. This case was the fundamental precedent establishing the right of the Supreme Court of judicial review that fulfilled its constitutional role to balance the power of the Congress. The case set in motion the process by which laws would be subject to constitutional examination and commanded justices to fulfill this duty. In limiting his own party's power as well as the jurisdiction of the Supreme Court, Marshall took a stance that no one could deny was impartial, yet at the same time increased the Supreme Court's and the federal government's power to protect the interests of minorities from the will of the majority. Marshall said a law that contradicted the Constitution was void.

2 FLETCHER v. PECK

This case decided in 1810 was the classic natural rights defense of contracts. Corrupt Georgia state and federal politicians had been bribed to sell thirty-five million acres of land to speculators for 1.5 cents per acre. Outraged Georgians "threw the bums out," but much of the land had already been sold before that election cleaned up the corruption. Robert Fletcher sued John Peck because he tried to withhold the title to some of the property that Fletcher had bought saying the original land deal was corrupt and the sale of it was thus void. John Marshall and the majority of the Supreme Court justices said the second land purchase by Fletcher (and other new owners) was made in good faith according to the law, and the state legislature, even though filled with new representatives, could not void a legal contract. Here was an assertion of federal judgment over states' rights and an essential precedent for sound business contracts and property rights into the future. The Supreme Court was also trying to convince Americans to elect leaders with integrity.

3 DARTMOUTH COLLEGE v. WOODWARD

This case decided in 1819 revealed that postsecondary education in America had not escaped the touch of politics. Jeffersonian-Republican leaders of New Hampshire took office and sought to dispense with the entrenched Federalists who ran the Dartmouth College by revising its charter. The Supreme Court that decided *Fletcher* v. *Peck* did not take kindly to having to teach another state about property rights and the sanctity of contracts before the law. Daniel Webster argued the case as an alumnus of Dartmouth College, and John Marshall specified in the majority ruling that the contract clause of the Constitution did apply to corporations like the one holding the original charter. The case revealed that a corporation could own property protected under the due process clause of the Bill of Rights. This determination stood even though the original charter had been granted by the king of England. The Marshall Court again limited the power of state legislatures to regulate private property and protected contracts setting a major precedent for future corporate legal interpretations.

4 MCCULLOCH v. MARYLAND

In yet another pivotal case in 1819, Marshall pronounced Alexander Hamilton's interpretation of the Constitution to be the proper one regarding the Bank of the United States (BUS). In a direct assertion of federal power over state power, the Marshall Court said that James McCulloch, the cashier of the branch of the BUS in Maryland, was correct in refusing to pay tax to the state because the bank was a federal institution. While not denying the right of Maryland to tax those under her sovereignty, Marshall said emphatically that the BUS was not under the sovereignty of any state. His famous, "The power to tax is the power to destroy" did not sit well with Thomas Jefferson, James Madison, or Andrew Jackson who all disagreed with the Marshall Court's decision, and ultimately this Second Bank of the United States was the target of Jackson's wrath in the Bank War. As long as the Marshall Court was in power, however, loose construction of the Constitution provided for a stronger central government and a curtailment of states' rights.

5 COHENS v. VIRGINIA

Since the ruling in *McCulloch* v. *Maryland* was so unpopular, Marshall took the opportunity to reiterate it in *Cohens* v. *Virginia* in 1821. The Cohens brothers had appealed their conviction for selling lottery tickets in Virginia when the state had passed a law banning the practice. The Cohens had based their sale on an act of the U.S. Congress that permitted them to hold the lottery for Washington, D.C. Lawyers representing Virginia claimed that the Supreme Court should not even be hearing the case because the Eleventh Amendment declared it outside the Court's jurisdiction. Although the Marshall Court asserted that Virginia was right to fine the Cohens brothers because the lottery law only applied locally to the District of Columbia, Marshall emphatically declared that the Supreme Court was the final arbiter of interpreting the Constitution. In other words, the Marshall Court did not permit a state to tell a branch of the federal government what it could and could not do because the Constitution was the supreme law of the land and the federal government it created was above the states.

6 GIBBONS v. OGDEN

This 1824 case was the first in the history of the Supreme Court involving the regulation of interstate trade, and the unanimous decision of the Marshall Court set a precedent for the nationalism associated with this federal power. After Robert Fulton proved the feasibility of commercial steamboat service, both Thomas Gibbons and Aaron Ogden developed steamboat lines. Gibbons took over Fulton's license from the state granting him a monopoly on the state's waterways, and Ogden had a license from the federal government allowing him a monopoly on coastal traffic between New York and New Jersey. While the New York courts upheld the monopoly granted to Gibbons, the Marshall Court said the federal permit trumped the state permit and allowed Ogden to proceed because he was involved in interstate shipping. Marshall said that states could regulate commerce within the confines of their borders, but in another assertion of centralized power over the business of the nation he set the precedent for the federal government's supremacy in regulating wider commerce. The enforcement of this decision was lax through the nineteenth century but picked up after the New Deal in the 1930s.

7 CHEROKEE CASES

The Marshall Court defined the legal status of Cherokee Indians and set precedents for future developments between the United States and other Indian tribes in two cases in 1831 and 1832. In *Cherokee Nation* v. *Georgia*, the Supreme Court denied it had jurisdiction to intervene in a dispute between the Cherokee Nation and Georgia over land rights because the Indian tribe was, according to John Marshall, a "domestic, dependent nation." This intriguing legal phrase denied the Cherokee Nation the status of a sovereign nation and declared that Indians were wards of the federal government. In *Worcester* v. *Georgia* the Marshall Court redefined its own ruling from the previous year and granted the Cherokee Nation sovereign rights to have Samuel Worcester, a Congregational minister, live on their lands as a missionary even though he did not seek a license required by state law. As Andrew Jackson's efforts to help Georgia remove the Cherokee Indians from their lands loomed, Marshall emphasized the "nation" part of "domestic, dependent nation" from the earlier case. He said the Cherokee tribe, as a nation, could make a treaty with the federal government and that a state could not interfere. Andrew Jackson illustrated the limitations on the power of the judicial branch by refusing to enforce the ruling, and the Trail of Tears commenced at the behest of Georgia and other southern states.

8 DRED SCOTT v. SANDFORD

Dred Scott was a slave whose original owner, Dr. John Emerson, had taken Scott into a free territory and a free state during his travels as an army surgeon. Scott sued for his liberty because he said that as he had spent most of the years from 1834 to 1838 on free soil he should be freed. When the case came to the Supreme Court in 1857, Scott belonged to a man named John Sanford whose name was misspelled in the court records. In its ruling, the Supreme Court under Chief Justice Roger B. Taney said that neither Scott nor any African slave or descendant of slaves was a citizen of the United States and could thus not resort to the American court system. Furthermore, the Court said that the years on free soil were no help to Scott because he sued from within the state of Missouri, which was a slave state. The implications of these decisions led the Court to state that the Missouri Compromise had been unconstitutional because citizens in territories above the 36°30' line were subject to the loss of their private property. The *Dred Scott* case proved to be one of the most divisive issues of the 1850s as the decade surged toward the Civil War. Northerners feared the ruling would allow the federal government to legalize slavery in the North and to restart the slave trade with Africa. In this regard scholars have ranked this decision to be the worst ever handed down by the Supreme Court. Just when the federal court system was needed to help stabilize the country the most, the ruling destroyed northern confidence in the legal system. The *Dred Scott* case emboldened the South and infuriated the North and was itself a cause of the war. Dred Scott, however, died in 1858 and did not live to see the ruling overturned by the Thirteenth and Fourteenth Amendments to the Constitution after the Civil War.

9 *MUNN v. ILLINOIS*

In 1877, a series of cases coming before the Supreme Court were known as the Granger Cases because they involved suits against private businesses on behalf of associations of farmers known as the Grange, or the Patrons of Husbandry. Sympathetic legislators in Illinois had passed laws setting the price grain elevator operators in Chicago could charge farmers for storage of grain. The Supreme Court under Chief Justice Morrison Waite ruled that Illinois could regulate private businesses to the extent of fixing prices, especially those in which the public had an interest. Dissenting justices said that if this interpretation was true of grain elevators it would be true of any business. By virtue of *Munn* v. *Illinois* states attempted to exert the same regulatory power over the rates charged by railroads, but lawyers for private railroads later maintained that the ruling did not apply to them because they conducted interstate business. Still, the *Munn* case is regarded as a precedent for the support of government regulation, and the federal government took over where the states' jurisdiction ceased.

10 *IN RE DEBS*

As a result of the Pullman Company's reduction in wages for its workers during the Panic of 1893, Eugene V. Debs organized a strike by the American Railway Union of which he was the president. Workers refused to handle trains with Pullman cars attached, and if any worker was fired because of the refusal, all the workers of the railroad would strike. The Pullman Strike thus immobilized the nation's railroads, and Attorney General Richard Olney sought a federal court injunction ordering the workers to get the trains moving. When violence erupted, President Grover Cleveland sent federal troops in to restore order. Eugene V. Debs was arrested for criminal conspiracy and later for contempt of court. Debs appealed his arrest and six-month jail sentence to the Supreme Court in 1895 because he had not been given a jury trial even though he was being treated as a criminal. The Supreme Court rejected Debs's plea saying the United States took the actions in question because the trains' not moving stopped mail service to the country. The Court called the Pullman Strike a public nuisance and an "unreasonable restraint of trade" as codified in the Sherman Antitrust Act. For several decades companies with labor troubles resorted to this ruling to secure court orders from compliant judges and then have the courts declare strikers in contempt of court rather than guilty of criminal offenses. Adjustments to labor laws eroded this interpretation during the New Deal of Franklin Roosevelt.

11 *PLESSY* v. *FERGUSON*

A mixed-race gentleman named Homer Plessy decided as a representative of a committee to test a Louisiana law that made African Americans ride in separate cars on railroads within the state. He boarded a train on a trip within the confines of the state and refused to sit in the segregated car. When tried in the court of a Judge Ferguson, Plessy argued that the Thirteenth and Fourteenth Amendments ended Jim Crow laws like the one in Louisiana. When he lost the case and appealed to the Supreme Court in 1896, his arguments were rejected there, too. The majority opinion stated that those amendments to the Constitution abolished practices that were inclined to restore African Americans to slavery and did not ban all distinctions based on race. The ruling stated that segregationist laws did not automatically imply that one race was inferior regardless of what people might perceive as their inherent assumption of white supremacy. The Supreme Court upheld Louisiana's law that stated, "separate but equal facilities" were constitutional, but in their arguments the justices on the majority likened transportation to education, and thus segregation in schools was tacitly sanctioned. The one dissenting justice, who interestingly was named John Marshall Harlan, said the "Constitution is colorblind, and neither knows nor tolerates classes among citizens." These words would form the basis for future arguments that overturned the ruling in the Plessy case.

12 INSULAR CASES

These fourteen cases occurred over a period from 1901 to 1905 and involved the application of the U.S. Constitution, including specifically the Bill of Rights, to territories acquired by the United States overseas (the word *insular* is a reference to islands). Echoing public opinion, the Supreme Court argued on the basis of race and background that the populations of the islands acquired during the Spanish-American War or those of Hawaii were not fit to become citizens and thus the territories were not fit to become states. Despite the jarring nature of possessing colonies in the minds of many Americans, the Court determined that the United States could possess them and could even incorporate them as territories just short of full statehood and far short of equal rights for their inhabitants. This ruling was set aside for Hawaii but not for the other islands to which the United States lays claim.

13 *NORTHERN SECURITIES CO.* v. *UNITED STATES*

After Theodore Roosevelt began to apply the Sherman Antitrust Act in the way it was intended, as a law to regulate monopolistic corporations, the Supreme Court backed him up in this case in 1903. The Northern Securities Company belonged to J. P. Morgan and associates and held controlling stock in three railroads. Lawyers for the company argued that breaking up the conglomerate would have adverse effects on the business world. Again, John Marshall Harlan rose to the occasion and said the Supreme Court could not take into account the economic consequences of following the law. The majority ruling dealt with the nebulous "unreasonable restraint of trade" clause in the antitrust legislation by saying it certainly applied to this case. Another landmark aspect of this ruling was the application of the law not just to business practices but to the ownership of stock and the power that came with it.

14 SCHENCK v. UNITED STATES

Interestingly it was not until the World War I era that the Supreme Court had to deal with the First Amendment rights regarding freedom of speech. This case in 1919 had to determine whether Charles Schenck and other socialists had violated the Espionage Act by distributing fifteen thousand leaflets that urged young men in Philadelphia to resist the draft. Schenck had mailed the papers, and several recipients complained to the Post Office that the federal mail was being used to invite citizens to join with the Socialist Party in signing a petition against "intimidation of war zealots." Schenck pled not guilty of breaking the Espionage Act but was convicted. He appealed to the Supreme Court saying his right to free speech was violated. His attorneys said his leaflet had only communicated an honest opinion and not incited anyone to do anything illegal. The case was set in the context of America's entry into the worst war the world had yet seen and the backlash in America of abuse toward German immigrants. Woodrow Wilson and leaders at all levels of government had taken the position that criticizing the war effort was unpatriotic. Justice Oliver Wendell Holmes spoke for the unanimous decision that Schenck had in fact broken the law by saying freedom of speech did not permit someone to conduct him- or herself in such a way that represented a "clear and present danger" to bring about illegal activity that, in this case, was thought to undermine national security. Charles Schenck thus had to serve out his six-month prison sentence, and the case opened the debate over what was protected and unprotected speech in American society.

15 SCHECHTER POULTRY CORP. v. UNITED STATES

This unanimous ruling by the Supreme Court in 1935 undermined the National Industrial Recovery Act, a New Deal measure under Franklin D. Roosevelt (FDR) that attempted to increase employment and stimulate business activity during the Great Depression. The law declared a national emergency and called for industries to draw up codes of fair competition that effectively raised wages but also favored big business because industry leaders themselves set the codes. In just two years 750 codes were adopted that impacted around twenty-three million people. The case hinged on the accusation that the Schechter company sold sick chickens and also violated industry codes regarding wages and hours of workers. The Supreme Court, however, determined that the chicken slaughterhouse conducted an entirely local business and was therefore not susceptible to regulation by the federal government. The Court went on to declare that a declaration of an emergency did not create or enlarge power for the executive branch, which in effect was making laws as well as enforcing them. The National Recovery Administration was determined to be unconstitutional, which caused FDR to attack the Supreme Court in his rhetoric but also through the scheme to pack the Court with supporters of the New Deal.

16 KOREMATSU v. UNITED STATES

This 1944 case focused on Fred Korematsu, whose very name revealed the circumstances that caused him to be in a predicament during World War II. Korematsu was a native-born American of Japanese descent who was rejected for military service for health reasons but still secured a job in a defense industry. As Japanese internment began, Korematsu moved away from his home (but not out of California), changed his name, and had cosmetic surgery that helped him claim to be a Mexican-American. Anti-Japanese sentiment in California had led to the internment program because the military claimed that Japanese-Americans threatened national security while living on the Pacific Coast. After refusing to comply with internment orders, Korematsu was apprehended, convicted, jailed, paroled, and then interned in a camp in Utah. The Supreme Court focused on the fact that Korematsu had remained in the restricted area rather than on the constitutionality of internment. The majority opinion said the military urgency dictated the extreme measure and said it was not racist without explaining how that could be true. Dissenting justices said the case against Korematsu was motivated by a history of anti-Japanese discrimination that had not even been extended to Germans and Italians living in America during World War II. The Congress later declared in 1983 that the decision in this case had been "overruled in the court of history" and apologized. Japanese-Americans who had been interned were given monetary compensation, and Fred Korematsu was given the Medal of Freedom by President Bill Clinton.

17 BROWN v. BOARD OF EDUCATION OF TOPEKA, KANSAS

This first major case for Chief Justice Earl Warren was the culmination of growing animosity for Jim Crow laws, the civil rights stand of President Harry S. Truman, and a protracted assault on the ruling in *Plessy* v. *Ferguson* by the National Association for the Advancement of Colored People (NAACP). Together these threads were combined by the Warren Court in what was called "a legal and social revolution in race relations and constitutionalism." The NAACP had begun in the 1930s to challenge state-imposed racial segregation in public accommodations, especially in education, and some Supreme Court cases resulted that eroded support for Jim Crow. Oliver Brown was only one of many plaintiffs encouraged by the NAACP to sue school systems to obtain access for their children to integrated schools in the early 1950s. The Warren Court argued in a unanimous decision in 1954 that separate facilities for educating different races was an inherently unequal prospect that damaged the ability of African-American children to gain a good education in an era when education in general was becoming more significant and African Americans were winning respect in various fields of life. This momentous decision that overruled the *Plessy* case and opened the door for desegregation of all public facilities had an unfortunate turn. The next unanimous decision in regard to the Brown case said that school systems should proceed with desegregation with "all deliberate speed." This phrase was notoriously used to justify the slowness of change that within ten years had only seen 2 percent of schools comply. Growing outrage over the continuing legacy of Jim Crow in the *Brown* case led to the Civil Rights Act and the Voting Rights Act of the 1960s in the context of the civil rights movement. The case also encouraged the Supreme Court to take on a greater role in societal reform and earned the Warren Court the reputation of being an activist court based more on personal convictions than on legal principle.

18 GIDEON v. WAINWRIGHT

Another unanimous decision of the Warren Court resolved the case of Clarence Earl Gideon in 1963. Gideon had been charged with breaking in and entering a billiards hall and was convicted of a felony after representing himself. He took up his own defense because he could not afford an attorney, and when he was found guilty he appealed on the grounds that he had asked the Florida court of jurisdiction to provide him with legal counsel, which the court had failed to do. Wainwright was the named representative of the Florida Department of

Corrections in the appeal. The Supreme Court did appoint a lawyer to take Gideon's case, which hinged on whether due process was given or his Fourteenth Amendment civil rights were violated by the state of Florida. With an attorney, Gideon's defense undermined the credibility of the one witness who had identified him and produced other witnesses eventually leading to Gideon's being acquitted. Previous cases had been handed down by the Supreme Court that built the very argument upon which Gideon had based his appeal, that to receive a fair trial people who could not afford an attorney should have one appointed for them. The Gideon case threatened to throw out any felony case in which the defendant did not have legal counsel, and later rulings extended the provision to misdemeanors. The office of the public defender originated in this ruling, and by 1984 a study showed that two-thirds of defendants resorted to this type of counsel. The study revealed that although private or public defense made little difference in the rate of convictions, defendants who represent themselves had a significantly lower chance of escaping conviction.

19 MIRANDA v. ARIZONA

The Warren Court's revolutionary changes to the criminal procedures in the United States climaxed with this case in 1966. The *Miranda* case proved to be one of the most controversial in the history of the Supreme Court in that some interpreted the ruling as a commitment to democratic values and fair treatment for all, whereas others attributed to the Warren Court the hamstringing of law enforcement. Ernesto Miranda was arrested and charged with a rape upon being identified by the victim. After two hours of questioning by the police, Miranda changed his denial of guilt into a written confession. Throughout the interrogation Miranda had no access to legal counsel. The majority ruling of a divided Court stated that the freedom not to incriminate oneself did not just apply to courtrooms but also during interrogation. The fact that a person was in police custody was also assumed to be a compulsion to speak. To solve the quandary of law enforcement after this ruling, the Supreme Court enunciated four provisions that all arrested people had to have read or recited to them immediately upon arrest including (1) you have the right to remain silent; (2) anything you say can and will be used against you; (3) you have the right to talk to a lawyer before being questioned and to have him present when you are being questioned; and (4) if you cannot afford a lawyer, one will be provided for you before any questioning if you so desire. Although law enforcement agencies originally decried the difficulty these steps added to their duties, most have become so accustomed to the *Miranda* warnings, as the legal notices are called, that the Warren Court's ruling has become a part of American culture. Studies have shown that arrested suspects still make confessions with some regularity.

20 ENGEL v. VITALE

While the words *wall of separation* regarding the relationship between church and state do not appear in the U.S. Constitution, they did exist in a letter by Thomas Jefferson that was quoted in Supreme Court cases considered by the Court when deciding this 1962 case. As late as 1952, the Court had refused to even hear a case that raised the constitutionality of Bible reading in public schools, but in the era of McCarthyism such a case might have led to accusations that communists had infiltrated the Supreme Court. The American Civil Liberties Union (ACLU), however, joined with ten public school students' parents in the *Engel* v. *Vitale* case to challenge a prayer authored by the state and read aloud over a school intercom system.

The parents sued the State Board of Regents of New York saying the prayer violated their religious beliefs and went against the First Amendment's ban on the establishment of religion. The majority ruling in the case did not require that all religious values be purged from public life but that schools could not sponsor them. The dissenting opinion claimed that the First Amendment merely banned the power of the government to coerce citizens in regard to religion and that the "free exercise" clause of the amendment protected the rather bland prayer.

21 REGENTS OF THE UNIVERSITY OF CALIFORNIA v. BAKKE

Allan Bakke sought enrollment in the University of California Medical School and was twice turned down. Since the medical school was actively trying to create greater racial and ethnic diversity in its student body and Bakke was white, he sued the school for reverse discrimination. The *Bakke* case was thus an opportunity for the Supreme Court to rule regarding affirmative action, the practice of favoring minorities in selection and hiring in order to compensate for past social wrongs. Bakke said he was being treated unequally while the medical school was trying to increase equality. Sixteen of the one hundred slots in each entering class were reserved for minorities, and the entrance requirements were reduced for these applicants. A sharply divided Supreme Court ruled that although schools could consider applicants' race or ethnicity in the admissions process, a specific quota such as the sixteen slots denied Bakke equal protection under the law. While Bakke was permitted to enroll in the medical school as a result, the Court did not take up the whole notion of affirmative action in other applications as had been done in previous cases regarding race relations and equality.

22 ROE v. WADE

The increased availability of contraceptives did not end the increasing number of unwanted pregnancies associated with the sexual revolution of the 1960s, and the growing feminist movement sought to secure more of what was called "reproductive rights." Although state laws had been trying to reduce the number of abortions, publicized cases of birth defects caused by botched abortions and the unsanitary and dangerous conditions in which women often had the illegal procedure done prompted some states to permit abortions in cases when the mother's life was threatened. The Supreme Court in 1973 took up the case of Jane Roe, a name used to protect the privacy of the mother in question who was later revealed to be Norma McCorvey. McCorvey first said her pregnancy was the result of a gang rape and then admitted it was the result of voluntary sexual relations with a man with whom she no longer had a relationship. The majority opinion in the case divided pregnancy into three trimesters and established that an abortion was a private decision between a woman and her doctor all through the first trimester. Any restrictions a state had on abortions at this stage were unconstitutional, and the Court permitted abortions up through the second trimester if the health of a mother was in danger. This last standard was able to be considered up into the third trimester, but the Court allowed that states had an interest in protecting the lives of fetuses during the third trimester as well and permitted stronger restrictions on such late-term abortions. Dissenting opinions said the right to abortion on demand was not found in the Constitution and that the trimester system was arbitrary. If states had an interest in protecting the life of a fetus in the third trimester, they had an interest in protecting that life all through the pregnancy. The abortion debate between advocates of a woman's right to choose abortion and the right-to-life movement's assertion that life begins at conception and should be protected from destruction continues as an undercurrent in state and federal politics.

23 UNITED STATES v. NIXON

This 1974 case was one of the most dramatic events in the saga that brought down the Nixon administration in the Watergate Scandal. When Nixon became more and more entangled in the web of deceit associated with the coverup of the Watergate break-in, his lawyers maintained that a president had nearly unlimited power, especially in matters of foreign policy and national security. The Nixon team tried to claim executive privilege and immunity from prosecution once the existence of tapes recording Oval Office conversations became known. A federal judge subpoenaed the tapes, and when the president refused to turn them over the case went to the Supreme Court. Despite the argument that the whole quandary was a dispute among the various departments within the executive branch, the Court agreed with a special prosecutor that the president had to turn over the tapes, especially because in the meantime President Nixon had released a few of the tapes. The Court did say that special deference was to be given to presidents in matters of defense and that they should not be thought of as normal citizens to be ordered about. Still, the U.S. government in two of its branches asserted that the third was not entirely immune from prosecution in criminal matters. When Nixon was forced to deliver all the tapes, the prosecution found what they called the "smoking gun," evidence that the president had conspired to obstruct justice in the prosecution of those in his administration responsible for the Watergate Scandal.

24 BUSH v. GORE

In the other great modern saga of the Supreme Court's role in monitoring the executive branch, this case saw a divided Court settle the Election of 2000 that was disputed because of voting inconsistencies in Florida. When Florida's Supreme Court ordered one county to recount nine thousand votes by hand and every county to manually verify ballots that had been marked as not voting for any presidential candidate, the Bush/Cheney campaign asked the Supreme Court of the United States to intervene. The election had been so close that the electoral votes of Florida would determine the outcome, and the electoral votes would be determined by the popular vote, the results of which were within a few hundred votes between the candidates. The Supreme Court issued a stay on the recount and eventually determined by a 7–2 vote that the Florida court's actions had undermined the equal protection under the law of all Florida voters by making special rules for some Florida voters. Furthermore, in a 5–4 split decision the Court determined that a constitutional recount could not be accomplished by the deadline set by the Florida state constitution. Thus the meager lead George W. Bush held in Florida was unaltered and the election was decided in his favor. The legacy of the settlement of the Election of 2000 this way hampered the Bush administration's ability to lead for a time, and partisan interpretations of the decision are still too fresh to make a reasoned historical view of the significance of this precedent. In an almost irrelevant conclusion to the saga, the election results in Florida were later independently verified not only to maintain George Bush's lead but to expand it.

Mini Quiz

1. An assessment of the Progressive Reform movement by a modern American politically conservative analyst might conclude that

   (A) government regulation was the key to efficient and fair economic progress.
   (B) democratic use of government power was the key to cleaning up corruption in government.
   (C) the government reforms were achieved at the expense of individual and property rights.
   (D) the federal government should become the largest employer through government contracts.
   (E) government bureaucracies were necessary to maintain order in a free society.

2. Ronald Reagan contributed to the end of the Cold War by

   (A) standing alone against communist countries' aggression in the United Nations.
   (B) negotiating new treaties calling for the reduction of intercontinental ballistic missiles (ICBMs).
   (C) restoring a fear of communism among Americans who had grown complacent to its threat.
   (D) increasing defense spending to fund technologies beyond what the Soviets could afford.
   (E) forcing Mikhail Gorbachev to pursue more openness in reforming Soviet communism.

3. The Iran-Contra scandal involved illegal, clandestine support for rebels in which country?

   (A) Iran
   (B) East Germany
   (C) Venezuela
   (D) Poland
   (E) Nicaragua

4. President George H. W. Bush and Mikhail Gorbachev signed a treaty to

(A) negotiate the transition of America's relationship to Russia as the Soviet Union collapsed.
(B) discontinue the production of chemical weapons.
(C) end Soviet involvement in Afghanistan.
(D) eliminate medium-range nuclear weapons.
(E) mutually agree to provide equal economic support to Israel.

5. The Persian Gulf War during George H. W. Bush's administration was fought to

(A) force Saddam Hussein to submit to United Nations inspections regarding his weapons programs.
(B) hunt down the terrorists responsible for the Beirut bombing that killed U.S. Marines.
(C) remove Saddam Hussein from power in Iraq as a result of his use of chemical weapons.
(D) intervene in the decade-long Iran-Iraq War to bring stability to the region.
(E) liberate Kuwait from an invasion by Iraqi forces conducted despite United Nations sanctions.

6. The unusual hurdle Clarence Thomas faced in the confirmation process for his appointment to the Supreme Court was

(A) accusations of racism against his white employees.
(B) a secondary discussion about the constitutionality of affirmative action.
(C) criticism that he would be taking the position away from an equally qualified woman.
(D) sexual harassment charges brought by a former employee.
(E) a delay in the procedure in order for the Supreme Court to decide about media access.

7. The strategy of the New Democrats of the 1990s was to

(A) repudiate Progressivism in favor of more conservative approaches to government.
(B) focus on issues relevant mostly to aging members of the baby boom generation.
(C) move to the center of the political spectrum in an era of resurgent conservatism.
(D) dismiss the use of tax cuts to boost the economy as irresponsible "voodoo economics."
(E) advance the American economy at all costs regardless of political backlash.

8. The ruling of the Supreme Court in the matters surrounding the Starr report during the Clinton administration was that

    (A)   President Clinton was guilty of perjury and obstruction of justice.

    (B)   a mistrial had occurred in the impeachment process because of procedural errors.

    (C)   the president was correct in invoking executive privilege over misdemeanor offenses.

    (D)   the trial of President Clinton in the Senate was too marred by partisanship to be conclusive.

    (E)   the president could be sued by a citizen during his term in office.

9. The main intention of giving a presidential line item veto was to

    (A)   diminish the wasteful expenditure of federal monies for "pork barrel" projects.

    (B)   accelerate the process whereby Congressional legislation could take effect in a crisis.

    (C)   fine-tune the use of American military forces in cooperation with other countries.

    (D)   advance the proposal for a new national health care system.

    (E)   restore the integrity of the legislative process and close the "credibility gap."

10. The decision by the Supreme Court in *Bush* v. *Gore* in 2000 settled the disputed election on the premise that

    (A)   the Electoral College is an outdated aspect of the presidential election process.

    (B)   the Florida state Supreme Court's decision in the matter was unfair to some voters.

    (C)   the type of ballot used by counties in Florida with disputed returns was unconstitutional.

    (D)   a state deadline for the election returns violated the nation's need to have a recount.

    (E)   once a candidate concedes the election to his or her opponent the election is decided.

11. The Smithsonian Institution was founded

    (A)   as a private research facility that was donated to the federal government in the founder's will.

    (B)   as a gift to honor the sacrifices Americans made to liberate France during World War II.

    (C)   by order of James K. Polk with taxpayer dollars at first to house discoveries in the West.

    (D)   by Congress after deliberation on how to use a private fortune donated to the United States.

    (E)   by the Royal Society of London in honor of Benjamin Franklin, its first American member.

12. The invention of barbed wire in 1871 determined that

    (A)   Americans could finally domesticate the buffalo.
    (B)   American Indians could no longer use public land to graze their cattle.
    (C)   the farmers of the Great Plains could now produce a surplus for export to Europe.
    (D)   the trench warfare begun during the Civil War would become the main strategy of other wars.
    (E)   American cowboys could no longer freely cross private lands during long drives to Chicago.

13. The two inventions below that most revolutionized the role of American women in the work force were

    (A)   the sewing machine and the camera.
    (B)   the radio and the practical elevator.
    (C)   the automobile and the airplane.
    (D)   Morse code and interchangeable parts.
    (E)   the telephone and the typewriter.

14. The major principle decided by the Supreme Court in the *Northern Securities Co.* v. *United States* case that supported Theodore Roosevelt's trust busting with the Sherman Antitrust Act was that

    (A)   there were some good trusts and some bad trusts.
    (B)   all trusts were unreasonably restraining trade and needed to be systematically broken up.
    (C)   the Court could not take into account the economic consequences of obeying the law.
    (D)   the president had the duty to take the initiative in interpreting laws pertaining to the economy.
    (E)   the president could order the prosecution of railroads because they crossed state lines.

15. The first case that came before the Supreme Court in which the Court had to decide a question about the First Amendment rights to free speech occurred in which context?

    (A)   The restoration of the two-party system after the Era of Good Feelings
    (B)   The Reconstruction era's debate about federal power in regulating states' rights
    (C)   The imperialism debate prompted by territories won in the Spanish-American War
    (D)   The wrangling over the Espionage and Sedition Acts passed during World War I
    (E)   The African-American civil rights movement in the 1950s

ANSWER EXPLANATIONS

1. **(C)** Answers (A) and (B) were foundational principles of Progressivism, a movement that modern conservatives claim to be against, although most American politicians operate entirely within a Progressive political paradigm. Answer (D) is contrary to the stated goal of conservatives to shrink Big Government, and answer (E) is another notion that arose from Progressive reforms of which conservatives typically complain while doing little to amend. Only answer (C) would be agreed upon by most conservatives in that businessmen and corporations were identified as the culprits in the nineteenth century when Progressivism arose, and whether it was the Sherman Antitrust Act assailing the property of a giant trust or the later Environmental Protection Agency regulating a small farmer's use of his or her own property conservatives would say the government had shifted from protecting liberties to reducing them.

2. **(D)** President Reagan had allies like Margaret Thatcher, Pope John Paul II, and Polish labor organizer Lech Walesa (among countless others) so he could never be said to have stood alone in the Cold War, but he did engage with Mikhail Gorbachev man to man in order to reduce intermediate-range nuclear missiles in Europe, not intercontinental ballistic missiles (ICBMs). In the surprisingly warm relationship between Reagan and Gorbachev, however, Gorbachev was not forced to pursue *glasnost* and *perestroika*; they were his own ideas. Contrary to answer (C), Reagan did not restore fear of communism through his rhetoric but openly mocked, criticized, and pronounced the coming doom of the Soviet Union on the "ash heap of history." What Reagan did almost single-handedly was change the discussion from combating the Soviet Union to ending the Soviet Union through large defense buildups, including the Strategic Defense Initiative, with which the Soviets could not keep pace. Later Russian analysts said that Reagan's stances sped up the collapse of the Soviet Union by at least five years.

3. **(E)** Oliver North's illegal and secret (he said even secret from President Reagan) operations involved using money acquired from selling weapons to Iran to support the Contra rebels fighting against Daniel Ortega's socialist regime in Nicaragua.

4. **(B)** Amid the rapidly transpiring events that led to the end of the Cold War and the nuclear arms race, almost forgotten is the agreement to end the manufacture of chemical weapons on the part of both the United States and the Soviet Union and the destruction of each nation's massive stockpiles of such weapons of mass destruction. Later START treaties hinted at in answer (D) led to the reduction of operational strengths of long-range intercontinental ballistic missiles (ICBMs) in the Cold War superpowers' arsenals. Gorbachev ended Soviet involvement in Afghanistan all on his own as he determined that the invasion of that country was the Soviet's "Vietnam." The other answers are fabrications based on peripheral issues in the Cold War.

5. **(E)** The Iran-Iraq War mentioned in answer (D) lasted ten years but was over before the Persian Gulf War began over the invasion of Kuwait by neighboring Iraq. Despite charges that the United States was mainly fighting to protect its own oil supply, the stated goal of the war was in answer (E). Although the Beirut bombing that destroyed the Marine Corps barracks occurred before the Persian Gulf War, hunting down terrorists as well as the ideas expressed in answers (A) and (C) were more associated with the presidency of the second George Bush after the September 11 attacks in 2001.

6. **(D)** Although many issues were raised in the otherwise routine grilling during a confirmation hearing for a nominee to be a justice on the Supreme Court, Clarence Thomas's particularly provocative hurdle was a sexual harassment accusation by Anita Hill, his former staffer at the Equal Employment Opportunity Commission (EEOC). The EEOC was, ironically, a government agency partly responsible for investigating such accusations, and this fact along with the fact that Clarence Thomas was only the second African-American to be nominated as a justice turned the confirmation hearings into the "media circus" mentioned in answer (E). All the other answers are fabrications based on the context of the hearings.

7. **(C)** Although Bill Clinton and Al Gore Jr., did position themselves as more moderate Democrats in the wake of the Republican takeover of the Congress, neither man nor any other New Democrats openly repudiated Progressivism as hinted in answer (A). Most politicians of the era in question had to acknowledge the influence of the baby boom generation in that they made up the bloc of voters who voted most regularly as well as a large percentage of the population, so answer (B) is nothing unique to New Democrats. Contrary to answer (D), New Democrats backed moderate tax cuts for the middle class while raising taxes for the wealthy, and these and other policies forged in compromises with Republicans helped create such a boom in the American economy that there was no political backlash as hinted in answer (E). Instead, President Clinton attained high approval ratings.

8. **(E)** Answers (B) and (C) are fabrications nearly the opposite of the truth in that President Clinton was impeached for perjury and obstruction of justice. Answer (A) is incorrect, though, because that ruling was determined by the House of Representatives, not the Supreme Court. Answer (D) hints at the partisanship in the Senate, but the result was quite conclusive; President Clinton was not removed from office. The one comfort in the entire wrenching process for most Americans was the assurance that even the president, regardless of party, was not above the law. This conclusion is the ruling the Supreme Court delivered when asked about the president's reference to executive privilege just as President Nixon had in the Watergate scandal.

9. **(A)** Despite the facts that answer (E) would possibly be an indirect result of a line-item veto as would answer (B), the main goal of political reformers in the Contract with America that led to President Clinton's being the first president to wield such a tool was to cut "pork barrel" spending attached to bills in Congress to aggrandize members and their constituents back home. Answers (C) and (D) hint at initiatives and events of the Clinton administration that were not related to the line-item veto that was eventually found to be unconstitutional by the Supreme Court.

10. **(B)** Many Americans came to the conclusion expressed in answer (A), but the Supreme Court came to the conclusion in answer (B) in that the desire to recount only some of Florida's votes violated equal protection under the law provisions of voting laws for other Florida voters. Thus the recount desired by the Gore team was denied, and a deadline for counting Florida's votes that determined the outcome of the Election of 2000 was decided to stand. The infamous "butterfly" ballots used in this election gained much national attention but were not found to be unconstitutional in their design complexities. Although Al Gore did concede the election to George Bush and then reverse his deci-

sion in order to challenge the election, such a series of actions had no legal bearing on the election's outcome.

11. **(D)** James Smithson did donate his fortune to the United States for the "diffusion of knowledge," but after much debate Congress founded the Smithsonian Institution. All of the other answers are fabrications although answer (E) correctly hints at the prestige enjoyed by Benjamin Franklin in Europe.

12. **(E)** "Range wars" were touched off by the passing of the "Wild West" and the end of long drives of cattle up out of Texas toward rail heads in Kansas to ship cattle to Chicago. The other answers should be considered plausible fabrications except for answer (A). Even "domesticated" buffalo think little of destroying barbed wire fences. American Indians did not need public land to graze their herds of cattle because they were given reservations for that purpose (albeit with inadequate pasturage to join the ranching industry). Because the herds of wild buffalo were largely eliminated by this time, farmers moving into the Trans-Mississippi West began producing surpluses right from the start. The reference to barbed wire in answer (D) as useful in war was true beginning in World War I, but it was the machine gun more than wire that made men fight in trenches.

13. **(E)** Of this list the devices that became almost exclusively the jobs of women to operate in the increasingly urbanized American society, the telephone and the typewriter established entirely new opportunities for women to work outside the home and off the farm. The sewing machine was a similar boon to women's working, but the camera less so. The other answers were more gender neutral in their economic impact on the nation.

14. **(C)** Answer (A) is the position Theodore Roosevelt (TR) took in his New Nationalism approach to the campaign for the presidency in 1912. Answer (B) is Woodrow Wilson's New Freedom stance. The Court's stance that gave TR greater leeway in enforcing the Sherman Antitrust Act was as stated in answer (C) in opposition to the defense of the Northern Securities Company that stated its dissolution would damage the American economy. Answer (E) was decided by the Supreme Court much earlier, and answer (D) is another Rooseveltian interpretation of a sort of domestic "Big Stick policy."

15. **(D)** All of these historical moments might have qualified as key opportunities to free and open debate, but that moment actually came in 1919 in the case *Schenck* v. *United States*, especially because of the anti-German sentiment of World War I evoked by the defendant's name, who was eventually found guilty of exercising his freedom of speech (and of the press) in such a way as to present a "clear and present danger" to national security.

Chapter 42
PRACTICE TESTS

ANSWER SHEET
Practice Test 1

1. Ⓐ Ⓑ Ⓒ Ⓓ Ⓔ
2. Ⓐ Ⓑ Ⓒ Ⓓ Ⓔ
3. Ⓐ Ⓑ Ⓒ Ⓓ Ⓔ
4. Ⓐ Ⓑ Ⓒ Ⓓ Ⓔ
5. Ⓐ Ⓑ Ⓒ Ⓓ Ⓔ
6. Ⓐ Ⓑ Ⓒ Ⓓ Ⓔ
7. Ⓐ Ⓑ Ⓒ Ⓓ Ⓔ
8. Ⓐ Ⓑ Ⓒ Ⓓ Ⓔ
9. Ⓐ Ⓑ Ⓒ Ⓓ Ⓔ
10. Ⓐ Ⓑ Ⓒ Ⓓ Ⓔ
11. Ⓐ Ⓑ Ⓒ Ⓓ Ⓔ
12. Ⓐ Ⓑ Ⓒ Ⓓ Ⓔ
13. Ⓐ Ⓑ Ⓒ Ⓓ Ⓔ
14. Ⓐ Ⓑ Ⓒ Ⓓ Ⓔ
15. Ⓐ Ⓑ Ⓒ Ⓓ Ⓔ
16. Ⓐ Ⓑ Ⓒ Ⓓ Ⓔ
17. Ⓐ Ⓑ Ⓒ Ⓓ Ⓔ
18. Ⓐ Ⓑ Ⓒ Ⓓ Ⓔ
19. Ⓐ Ⓑ Ⓒ Ⓓ Ⓔ
20. Ⓐ Ⓑ Ⓒ Ⓓ Ⓔ
21. Ⓐ Ⓑ Ⓒ Ⓓ Ⓔ
22. Ⓐ Ⓑ Ⓒ Ⓓ Ⓔ
23. Ⓐ Ⓑ Ⓒ Ⓓ Ⓔ
24. Ⓐ Ⓑ Ⓒ Ⓓ Ⓔ
25. Ⓐ Ⓑ Ⓒ Ⓓ Ⓔ
26. Ⓐ Ⓑ Ⓒ Ⓓ Ⓔ
27. Ⓐ Ⓑ Ⓒ Ⓓ Ⓔ
28. Ⓐ Ⓑ Ⓒ Ⓓ Ⓔ
29. Ⓐ Ⓑ Ⓒ Ⓓ Ⓔ
30. Ⓐ Ⓑ Ⓒ Ⓓ Ⓔ

31. Ⓐ Ⓑ Ⓒ Ⓓ Ⓔ
32. Ⓐ Ⓑ Ⓒ Ⓓ Ⓔ
33. Ⓐ Ⓑ Ⓒ Ⓓ Ⓔ
34. Ⓐ Ⓑ Ⓒ Ⓓ Ⓔ
35. Ⓐ Ⓑ Ⓒ Ⓓ Ⓔ
36. Ⓐ Ⓑ Ⓒ Ⓓ Ⓔ
37. Ⓐ Ⓑ Ⓒ Ⓓ Ⓔ
38. Ⓐ Ⓑ Ⓒ Ⓓ Ⓔ
39. Ⓐ Ⓑ Ⓒ Ⓓ Ⓔ
40. Ⓐ Ⓑ Ⓒ Ⓓ Ⓔ
41. Ⓐ Ⓑ Ⓒ Ⓓ Ⓔ
42. Ⓐ Ⓑ Ⓒ Ⓓ Ⓔ
43. Ⓐ Ⓑ Ⓒ Ⓓ Ⓔ
44. Ⓐ Ⓑ Ⓒ Ⓓ Ⓔ
45. Ⓐ Ⓑ Ⓒ Ⓓ Ⓔ
46. Ⓐ Ⓑ Ⓒ Ⓓ Ⓔ
47. Ⓐ Ⓑ Ⓒ Ⓓ Ⓔ
48. Ⓐ Ⓑ Ⓒ Ⓓ Ⓔ
49. Ⓐ Ⓑ Ⓒ Ⓓ Ⓔ
50. Ⓐ Ⓑ Ⓒ Ⓓ Ⓔ
51. Ⓐ Ⓑ Ⓒ Ⓓ Ⓔ
52. Ⓐ Ⓑ Ⓒ Ⓓ Ⓔ
53. Ⓐ Ⓑ Ⓒ Ⓓ Ⓔ
54. Ⓐ Ⓑ Ⓒ Ⓓ Ⓔ
55. Ⓐ Ⓑ Ⓒ Ⓓ Ⓔ
56. Ⓐ Ⓑ Ⓒ Ⓓ Ⓔ
57. Ⓐ Ⓑ Ⓒ Ⓓ Ⓔ
58. Ⓐ Ⓑ Ⓒ Ⓓ Ⓔ
59. Ⓐ Ⓑ Ⓒ Ⓓ Ⓔ
60. Ⓐ Ⓑ Ⓒ Ⓓ Ⓔ

61. Ⓐ Ⓑ Ⓒ Ⓓ Ⓔ
62. Ⓐ Ⓑ Ⓒ Ⓓ Ⓔ
63. Ⓐ Ⓑ Ⓒ Ⓓ Ⓔ
64. Ⓐ Ⓑ Ⓒ Ⓓ Ⓔ
65. Ⓐ Ⓑ Ⓒ Ⓓ Ⓔ
66. Ⓐ Ⓑ Ⓒ Ⓓ Ⓔ
67. Ⓐ Ⓑ Ⓒ Ⓓ Ⓔ
68. Ⓐ Ⓑ Ⓒ Ⓓ Ⓔ
69. Ⓐ Ⓑ Ⓒ Ⓓ Ⓔ
70. Ⓐ Ⓑ Ⓒ Ⓓ Ⓔ
71. Ⓐ Ⓑ Ⓒ Ⓓ Ⓔ
72. Ⓐ Ⓑ Ⓒ Ⓓ Ⓔ
73. Ⓐ Ⓑ Ⓒ Ⓓ Ⓔ
74. Ⓐ Ⓑ Ⓒ Ⓓ Ⓔ
75. Ⓐ Ⓑ Ⓒ Ⓓ Ⓔ
76. Ⓐ Ⓑ Ⓒ Ⓓ Ⓔ
77. Ⓐ Ⓑ Ⓒ Ⓓ Ⓔ
78. Ⓐ Ⓑ Ⓒ Ⓓ Ⓔ
79. Ⓐ Ⓑ Ⓒ Ⓓ Ⓔ
80. Ⓐ Ⓑ Ⓒ Ⓓ Ⓔ
81. Ⓐ Ⓑ Ⓒ Ⓓ Ⓔ
82. Ⓐ Ⓑ Ⓒ Ⓓ Ⓔ
83. Ⓐ Ⓑ Ⓒ Ⓓ Ⓔ
84. Ⓐ Ⓑ Ⓒ Ⓓ Ⓔ
85. Ⓐ Ⓑ Ⓒ Ⓓ Ⓔ
86. Ⓐ Ⓑ Ⓒ Ⓓ Ⓔ
87. Ⓐ Ⓑ Ⓒ Ⓓ Ⓔ
88. Ⓐ Ⓑ Ⓒ Ⓓ Ⓔ
89. Ⓐ Ⓑ Ⓒ Ⓓ Ⓔ
90. Ⓐ Ⓑ Ⓒ Ⓓ Ⓔ

Practice Test 1

TIME—60 MINUTES

Directions: Each of the questions or incomplete statements below is followed by five suggested answers or completions. Select the one that is best in each case, and then fill in the corresponding circle on the answer sheet. You can cut the answer sheet along the dotted line to make recording your answers easier. Remember to give yourself only sixty minutes to complete this test in order to prepare for the pace of the real SAT Subject Test in U.S. History.

1. What was the main contribution of Prince Henry of Portugal to European exploration?

    (A) He sought access to India via a water route around Africa.
    (B) He collected navigational instruments, which fascinated him.
    (C) He was an accomplished sea captain who launched exploration personally.
    (D) He advanced navigation science and trained skilled navigators in a school.
    (E) He raced Spain to cross the Atlantic Ocean believing the world was round.

2. The Protestant Reformation advanced the development of colonial American society by

    (A) converting Spanish and French Roman Catholics to Protestantism.
    (B) distracting English colonists from economic necessities with theological issues.
    (C) compelling dissenting groups to go to the colonies thereby increasing diversity.
    (D) increasing intolerance and persecution by enforcing strict uniformity.
    (E) questioning the authority of the Roman Catholic Church.

3. The Federalist Papers were written to

    (A) combat the growing influence of the Anti-Federalist Party.
    (B) clarify the nuances of the U.S. Constitution for political scientists.
    (C) persuade citizens of New York to support the ratification of the U.S. Constitution.
    (D) justify the need of a stronger central government in the minds of all Americans.
    (E) instruct Supreme Court justices on the interpretation of the U.S. Constitution.

4. To justify the purchase of Alaska for over $7 million, William H. Seward claimed it would

(A) end violations of the Monroe Doctrine by Russians colonizing the Northwest.
(B) tap into vast forests to combat a shortage of timber after wide deforestation.
(C) preserve native species of wild animals that were already near extinction.
(D) give a region for migration of the population in the event of climate change.
(E) secure large reserves of petroleum and gold in the Yukon Territory.

5. What caused the debate over closed shops and open shops during the rise of labor unions?

(A) Closed shops were controversial because they led to socialist subversion.
(B) As the labor movement gained political power, all factories became closed shops.
(C) Closed shops banned labor unions, whereas open shops allowed them.
(D) Management closed factories to protect private property during labor disputes.
(E) Closed shops banned non-union workers, whereas open shops allowed them.

6. During which event did Martin Luther King Jr. begin his role as a civil rights leader?

(A) The March on Washington, D. C.
(B) The Selma march
(C) The writing of the letter from the Birmingham jail
(D) The Montgomery Bus Boycott
(E) The sanitation workers' striking in Memphis

7. Which event sparked the protests at Kent State University in Ohio that led to the shooting of four students?

(A) The bombing of Khe Sanh using the conventional equivalent of five atomic bombs
(B) The bombing of North Vietnam initiated by the Nixon administration
(C) The passage of the Gulf of Tonkin Resolution by the Johnson administration
(D) The My Lai Massacre in which American troops killed innocent civilians
(E) The invasion of Cambodia to shut down Viet Cong use of the Ho Chi Minh Trail

8. What did the Congressional committee investigating the Watergate scandal seek in Richard Nixon's White House tapes?

(A) Proof of a conspiracy to use any means necessary to win the Election of 1972
(B) Who among the White House staffers would turn and help prosecute the others
(C) Proof that Nixon knew of the Watergate break-ins and that he ordered the cover-up
(D) Proof that Nixon offered money to White House staffers to buy their silence
(E) Who among the White House staffers knew that Nixon's actions were illegal

9. What impact did the Iran-Contra Scandal have on Ronald Reagan's administration?

(A) The FBI investigated a presidential administration for the first time in history.
(B) Reagan botched an attempt to rescue American hostages and lost credibility.
(C) Reagan's approval ratings plummeted but rose again by the end of his presidency.
(D) The "Teflon President" shifted the blame to his staff and thus escaped criticism.
(E) Reagan confessed to illegal activities before Congress but was later pardoned.

10. What was the result of soil depletion along the Coastal Plain of North America in the colonial period?

(A) Colonists abandoned the cultivation of cotton and other crops that depleted the soil.
(B) Colonists opened the frontier upriver from earlier settlements to find more land.
(C) Colonists solved the problem of soil depletion with fertilizers and crop rotation.
(D) Colonists made peace with American Indians to combat food shortages together.
(E) Colonists abandoned whole areas that were incapable of producing enough food.

11. What impact did the Declaratory Act have on colonial Americans after the repeal of the Stamp Act in 1766?

(A) The colonists held Parliament in greater contempt for its assertion of power over them.
(B) The colonists had to accept direct taxation without having actual representation.
(C) Such an arbitrary assertion of authority sparked immediate calls for independence.
(D) The British army had to put down violent demonstrations in New York and Boston.
(E) Patriots were unable to rally their fellow Americans to resist for almost a decade.

12. Which statement best describes the significance of the Lewis and Clark expedition?

(A) It scouted out American Indian population centers and tested their military strength.
(B) It was a race to claim territory between Spanish and British territory in the West.
(C) It explored the West to find the best route for the first transcontinental railroad.
(D) It failed to find a water route to the Pacific Ocean but sparked westward migration.
(E) It collected unique specimens and thus helped found the Smithsonian Institution.

13. "... 'Liberty first and Union afterward?'; but everywhere, spread all over in characters of living light . . . that other sentiment, dear to every true American heart—Liberty and Union, now and forever, one and inseparable!"

Which leader most likely used these words and in which debate?

(A) Henry Clay in calling for his American System, a plan for a national economy
(B) John C. Calhoun in communicating his grievances during the Nullification Crisis
(C) Henry Clay in crafting a compromise during the Nullification Crisis
(D) Andrew Jackson in defending his actions during the Bank War
(E) Daniel Webster in debating the sale of western lands

14. What action of Joseph Smith led to his arrest for treason as he led the Mormons?

    (A)   He published the Book of Mormon, a gospel account separate from the Bible.
    (B)   He established a new city for his followers in Illinois.
    (C)   He wore a military uniform and drilled militia forces.
    (D)   He instituted polygamy, the marriage of one man with multiple wives.
    (E)   He led his followers to establish a separate country in territory in the West.

15. What caused the Mexican War to break out in 1846?

    (A)   John C. Fremont's expedition in California ignited the Bear Flag Revolt.
    (B)   Zachary Taylor provoked an armed conflict at the Rio Grande River.
    (C)   Mexico rebuffed John Slidell's mission to buy land for the United States.
    (D)   James K. Polk sent the U.S. Army into Mexico to demand payment of debts.
    (E)   The U.S. Navy blockaded Mexican ports to force compliance with trade policy.

16. The Supreme Court's decision in the Dred Scott Case affected sectional tensions prior to the Civil War by

    (A)   reducing sectionalism because the balance of powers had worked at last.
    (B)   increasing southern secessionist fervor because of the overt judicial activism.
    (C)   affirming the spread of slavery was legal and thus deepening the sectional divide.
    (D)   convincing the North and the South that the government would abolish slavery.
    (E)   increasing hostility so much as to make the Civil War inevitable.

17. Which new power of the federal government resulted from the Civil War?

    (A)   The Congress was able to reverse a decision of the Supreme Court.
    (B)   The president was able to declare a national observance of a day of prayer.
    (C)   The military was able to invade a state to protect American citizens.
    (D)   The Supreme Court was able to declare a president's action unconstitutional.
    (E)   The Congress was able to draft men into military service to increase enlistment.

18. How did A. Mitchell Palmer become notorious as attorney general for the United States in the 1920s?

    (A)   Suspending civil liberties to crack down on the resurgent Ku Klux Klan
    (B)   Regulating corporations that illegally stifled business competition
    (C)   Accepting bribes from states that employed his family's road-paving company
    (D)   Looking for subversive material in surprise raids on labor union headquarters
    (E)   Investigating organized crime's ties to bootlegging alcohol during Prohibition

19. "... the general principle that the country can never again afford to let the prairies and the plantations drop lower and lower in poverty and discouragement just because its factories and brokerage houses are still flourishing may be taken as fairly established for 1934 and all future years."

The above quotation was most likely made in reference to what agency of the New Deal?

(A) The Civilian Conservation Corps
(B) The National Recovery Administration
(C) The Works Progress Administration
(D) The Agricultural Adjustment Administration
(E) The National Labor Relations Board

20. Which event was the main factor convincing leaders the Articles of Confederation had to be changed?

(A) British troops remained in forts around the Great Lakes after the Revolutionary War.
(B) The Congress failed to force states to pay taxes to fund the central government.
(C) A state had to put down Shays's Rebellion without aid from the central government.
(D) The states had intense disputes over western land claims left from colonial charters.
(E) Tecumseh resisted westward expansion with a coalition of American Indian tribes.

21. Which pairing below relates major causes of the War of 1812?

(A) Impressment of American sailors and British support for American Indian raids
(B) British encroachments on American territory and on American trade routes
(C) New British colonization in South America and Napoleon's colonial ambitions
(D) British cooperation with the French Empire and Spanish intrigues in New Orleans
(E) British destruction of American ships and siding with the French in the Quasi-War

22. All of the following were important abolitionists **EXCEPT**

(A) Lewis Tappan
(B) George Fitzhugh
(C) William Lloyd Garrison
(D) Elijah P. Lovejoy
(E) Frederick Douglass

23. In the Tenure of Office Act passed during Reconstruction, the Congress took away President Andrew Johnson's right to

(A) fire members of the executive branch without congressional approval.
(B) run for the presidency again after serving for two terms.
(C) commission general officers in the military without congressional approval.
(D) take the lead in nominating new appointments to the Cabinet.
(E) choose the leadership of federal agencies like the Freedmen's and Indian Bureaus.

24. What was the significance of the Bessemer process to the American steel industry?

   (A) Henry Bessemer's dispute with William Kelly set key precedents in patent law.
   (B) Andrew Carnegie's use of the process launched his rise in big business.
   (C) The lower expense in steel production allowed Carnegie's competition to catch up.
   (D) The process allowed the United States to exceed the British in steel production.
   (E) The process made the production of steel cheaper because it required less energy.

Courtesy of the Bancroft Library, University of California, Berkeley

25. The portrayal of Chester Arthur's circumstances in this 1881 political cartoon entitled, "The Proper Thing," suggests that the president needed to

   (A) institute stricter security procedures in the wake of the Garfield assassination.
   (B) allow citizens finally to have access to Gilded Age presidents.
   (C) support the civil service reform movement to end the graft of the spoils system.
   (D) cooperate with labor unions to end the growing gap between the rich and the poor.
   (E) come down from his imperial style of running the executive branch.

26. Which statement of belief below best expresses a principle of the Social Gospel movement?

   (A) Socialism is the political system that best follows the teachings of Jesus Christ.
   (B) Christians should emphasize preaching more than fellowship among believers.
   (C) Christians should focus more on foreign missions than on outreach at home.
   (D) Christians should address people's basic problems more than try to convert them.
   (E) The influx of such diverse immigrants should eliminate all doctrinal distinctions.

27. Booker T. Washington founded Tuskegee Institute in Alabama because he wanted to

   (A) increase the rigor of military training for blacks so they could also become officers.
   (B) teach blacks their own culture instead of preparing them to fit in with white society.
   (C) steep black students in classical literature so they could debate whites as equals.
   (D) minimize racial strife by preventing blacks from aspiring to professional careers.
   (E) improve economic potential by training blacks to be skilled craftsmen and teachers.

28. George Creel's task as the head of the Committee on Public Information during World War I was to

   (A) raise academic standards to compete with German engineering prowess.
   (B) keep journalists from releasing secret information that threatened national security.
   (C) use propaganda to increase enlistments and the purchase of war bonds.
   (D) spy on German Americans who might have connections with the Central Powers.
   (E) root out labor leaders who supported the Bolshevik Revolution in Russia.

29. Which statement below best describes the role of Eleanor Roosevelt in the Franklin Roosevelt administration?

   (A) She was a key member of her husband's Brains Trust.
   (B) She was highly skilled at entertaining and thus won her husband wider support.
   (C) She traveled across America to represent her husband and his New Deal policies.
   (D) She traveled abroad extensively and advised her husband on foreign policy.
   (E) She was her husband's main contact with his cabinet after he suffered a stroke.

30. Which statement below best expresses an issue debated at the Constitutional Convention?

   (A) Northerners accused George Washington of favoring southern opinions.
   (B) Small states and large states needed fair representation in Congress.
   (C) Delegates began to doubt the necessity of having a written constitution.
   (D) Southern delegates said they would secede if the new government abolished slavery.
   (E) All the sections of the country wanted the nation's capital to be in their own region.

31. The "Corrupt Bargain" charge from the Election of 1824 was derived from the fact that

   (A)   Andrew Jackson said after winning, "To the victor belong the spoils."
   (B)   the House of Representatives had to decide the winner.
   (C)   most Americans thought John Quincy Adams had won mainly because of his father.
   (D)   Florida, South Carolina, and Louisiana had sent in disputed election returns.
   (E)   Henry Clay became Secretary of State after supporting John Quincy Adams.

32. Which antebellum reform movement did Dorothea Dix lead?

   (A)   The abolition of slavery
   (B)   The women's suffrage movement
   (C)   The temperance crusade for the moderate use of alcohol
   (D)   The reform of treatment of the mentally ill
   (E)   The reform of prisons for juvenile delinquents

33. Why was the Filipino Insurrection more devastating than the Spanish-American War?

   (A)   Sympathy for the Filipinos made the United Kingdom an enemy of America again.
   (B)   Regional loyalties brought the Chinese in on the side of the Filipinos.
   (C)   The higher casualties and costs further split the American people over imperialism.
   (D)   Sympathy for the Filipinos led to the assassination of President William McKinley.
   (E)   Soldiers had to fight in desert conditions instead of Cuba's temperate climate.

34. Which policy did Franklin Roosevelt present as an effort to keep the United States out of World War II?

   (A)   Making America the "arsenal of democracy" with the War Production Board
   (B)   Transforming the Civilian Conservation Corps into a military training organization
   (C)   Drafting soldiers in peacetime to increase American military preparedness
   (D)   Providing the Allies in Europe money and military equipment through Lend-Lease
   (E)   Isolating aggressor nations through the policies from the Quarantine Speech

35. How did President Dwight D. Eisenhower increase Cold War tensions with the Soviet Union right before peace talks in Paris in 1960?

   (A)   By authorizing the production of the hydrogen bomb
   (B)   By authorizing another flyover of the Soviet Union by an American spy plane
   (C)   By founding NASA to get ahead in the Space Race
   (D)   By staging military maneuvers near islands claimed by China, a key Soviet ally
   (E)   By launching an insurrection in communist Cuba through the Bay of Pigs

36. Which landmark Supreme Court case did the Warren Court decide during the 1960s?

    (A) *Brown* v. *Board of Education of Topeka, Kansas*
    (B) *Engel* v. *Vitale*
    (C) *Korematsu* v. *the United States*
    (D) *Board of Regents* v. *Bakke*
    (E) *Roe* v. *Wade*

37. What role did Phyllis Schlafly play in the debate about the Equal Rights Amendment?

    (A) She helped write the amendment to gain equal rights for women in American law.
    (B) She helped found the National Organization of Women and *Ms.* Magazine.
    (C) She opposed the amendment saying it demeaned the dignity of women.
    (D) She convinced her husband, a senator, to champion the amendment in Congress.
    (E) She campaigned to stop ratification of the amendment as the governor of Indiana.

38. Why was the Battle of Saratoga significant in the American War for Independence?

    (A) The Continental Army defeated an equally matched British Army for the first time.
    (B) Soldiers from all the thirteen colonies made up the force fighting the British there.
    (C) The battle exposed the treachery of Benedict Arnold and removed him as a threat.
    (D) The American victory prevented the British capture of New York City.
    (E) The American victory convinced the French to give support to help win the war.

39. How did President John Adams respond to the XYZ Affair?

    (A) He built up the U.S. Navy while again asking France for peace.
    (B) He pushed the Federalist-dominated Congress to declare war on France.
    (C) He cut off diplomacy with the French while seeking an alliance with the British.
    (D) He ignored the problem and focused on building up America's economic strength.
    (E) He sent his son, John Quincy Adams, to clear the air with the French government.

40. How did President Thomas Jefferson respond to the outbreak of the Napoleonic Wars in Europe?

    (A) He doubled the number of frigates in the U.S. Navy.
    (B) He bought the Louisiana Purchase from France to help fund victory over the British.
    (C) He sent an invasion force into Canada on an ill-fated winter attack.
    (D) He pushed the Embargo Act through Congress to avoid being drawn into the war.
    (E) He built forts along the coastline, one of which saved Baltimore during the War of 1812.

41. What role did Stephen Austin play in the founding of Texas?

    (A) He guided the original American settlers to the northern provinces of Mexico.
    (B) He organized the resistance to Santa Anna at the Battle of the Alamo.
    (C) He rounded up volunteers from Tennessee to rescue the defenders of the Alamo.
    (D) He led the strategic retreat across Texas until beating Santa Anna at San Jacinto.
    (E) He was the president of the Lone Star Republic and then the first governor of Texas.

42. "We have no power as citizens of the free states, or in our federal capacity as members of the federal Union through the general government, to disturb slavery in the states where it exists. . . . What I insist upon is that the new territories shall be kept free from it while in the territorial condition."

Which individual most likely held the position from the quotation above in the debates about slavery prior to the Civil War?

(A) Henry Clay
(B) William H. Seward
(C) Stephen Douglas
(D) Abraham Lincoln
(E) James Buchanan

43. What practice on the part of General William Tecumseh Sherman during the Civil War made him the first modern general?

(A) He ordered his troops to dig trenches to shield them from enemy fire.
(B) He planted bombs in positions he knew his enemy would later occupy.
(C) He destroyed civilian property and confiscated scarce resources to break the enemy.
(D) He put prisoners of war in stockades without adequate food, shelter, or medical care.
(E) He used spy networks so he could anticipate what enemy generals would do next.

44. Why did Grover Cleveland succeed as the only Democrat to win the presidency during the Gilded Age?

(A) He invented the "whistle-stop" campaign, giving speeches at every railroad stop.
(B) A ghostwriter published a moving autobiography of Cleveland's soldiering days.
(C) He pledged to end Reconstruction and unite the country after the Civil War.
(D) He was the only politician from either party to support civil service reform.
(E) His opponent, James G. Blaine, made several key mistakes in a tight race.

45. How did Theodore Roosevelt reinterpret the Monroe Doctrine?

(A) He reopened the Western Hemisphere to European nations to end mutual animosity.
(B) He intervened across Latin America since the United States banned European intervention.
(C) He sought an empire for the United States since Europe's American empires were gone.
(D) He built the Panama Canal but believed European nations had the right to use it.
(E) He stopped European military inroads in Latin America with his "Big Stick" policy.

46. Early in his presidency, Franklin D. Roosevelt responded to the Great Depression by

    (A) proposing a systematic plan for the relief, recover, and reform of the economy.

    (B) waiting to see if the policies of President Hoover would help the economy.

    (C) encouraging any legislation in the Congress that might slow the economic crisis.

    (D) meeting with world leaders to solve problems causing the worldwide depression.

    (E) using propaganda in "fireside chats" on the radio while doing little of substance.

47. Why did President Harry Truman launch the Berlin Airlift during the Cold War?

    (A) Soviets in East Germany ordered the evacuation of all Germans from the city.

    (B) Soviets attacked the part of Berlin under United Nations protection.

    (C) Soviets built a wall across the city to prevent East Germans from escaping west.

    (D) Soviets cut off all road access to supply Germans on the west side of Berlin.

    (E) Soviets supplied Cuba by air and Truman wanted to retaliate in Germany.

48. What was the role of viceroys in Spain's colonial empire in the New World?

    (A) Uniting the extremely competitive conquistadors to make them work together

    (B) Ruling their portion of the empire as the legal representatives of the king

    (C) Representing the authority of the Roman Catholic Church across the hemisphere

    (D) Ruling their own private property as feudal lords and vassals to the king

    (E) Living out their lives in the New World to transplant the best of Spanish culture

49. Why did John Quincy Adams refer to the time between 1783 and 1789 as the Critical Period in American history?

    (A) The weaknesses of the Articles of Confederation threatened to ruin the country.

    (B) The continued presence of British military forces still posed a lethal threat.

    (C) The British Navy stifled the American merchant fleet's ability to help the economy.

    (D) The debate over independence had pushed the North and the South near civil war.

    (E) The weakness of the new country was obvious to united American Indian tribes.

50. What was the consequence of Thomas Jefferson's weakening of the executive branch after the Federalist presidents had strengthened it?

    (A) The three-branch government of the U.S. Constitution temporarily disappeared.

    (B) The United Kingdom moved to restore the states as colonies in the British Empire.

    (C) Americans began to value their state governments over that in Washington, D. C.

    (D) The Congress closed the Bank of the United States and repealed the Alien and Sedition Acts.

    (E) The Congress increased legislative control through its committee system.

51. What change in the election process occurred during the campaign for the presidency after Andrew Jackson's first term in office?

(A) Parties had to run candidates for president and vice president together as a "ticket."
(B) Congress placed a new hurdle, the Electoral College, to allow states to stop Jackson.
(C) Candidates pledged not to fire civil servants installed by previous administrations.
(D) Parties held national nominating conventions instead of using the old caucus system.
(E) Parties began to advertise their candidates as if they were selling a product.

52. Why did the United States acquire the southern part of the Oregon Territory rather than the United Kingdom?

(A) President James K. Polk sent a naval force that fought off the British Pacific fleet.
(B) The forts established by American mountain men discouraged British settlement.
(C) The British withdrew because American settlers vastly outnumbered them.
(D) The peaceful American Indians of the Pacific Northwest chose the United States.
(E) Missionaries from the United States convinced American Indians to reject Anglicanism.

53. How did Abraham Lincoln attempt to slow the rush toward war with Mexico?

(A) He wrote newspaper editorials criticizing pro-slavery, expansionist policies.
(B) He designed political cartoons with Thomas Nast for *Harper's Weekly* magazine.
(C) He said in Congress that he was skeptical of the claim Mexico started shooting first.
(D) He warned in speeches that if President Polk got his war, the Union would dissolve.
(E) He spoke at Cooper Union in New York City against letting slavery spread west.

54. Darwinism shaped the debate about race during the Reconstruction era by convincing the scientific community in America that

(A) natural selection would eliminate African Americans who were inferior organizers.
(B) evolution had not destined African Americans to a subordinate position in society.
(C) African Americans needed to struggle to survive so no one should help them.
(D) African Americans were the parent race since human life originated in Africa.
(E) helping African Americans worked with evolution to better the entire human race.

55. "The interpretation of constitutional principles must not be too literal. We must remember that the machinery of government would not work if it were not allowed a little play in its joints."

This 1928 quote by Justice Oliver Wendell Holmes revealed that he held which kind of views while on the Supreme Court?

(A) Progressive
(B) Loose constructionist
(C) Strict constructionist
(D) Democratic
(E) Republican

56. What was Joseph Pulitzer's editorial position for his newspaper about the possibility of war with Spain?

   (A) His correspondents should remain as objective as possible in their coverage.
   (B) He should publish daily reports of the Spanish perspective to prevent war.
   (C) President McKinley deserved criticism for his lack of foreign policy experience.
   (D) His staff should actively use propaganda to promote the oncoming war.
   (E) The conflict was insignificant and did not deserve front-page coverage.

57. Why did suburbs develop so rapidly in the United States after World War II?

   (A) The bombing of cities in Europe made Americans fear living near city centers.
   (B) Ruined farmers sought a lifestyle between country life and city life.
   (C) President Eisenhower praised the way of life of Europeans he had seen in the war.
   (D) Americans could not afford to live in cities because of a postwar economic collapse.
   (E) Builders had learned to make homes cheaply and quickly in time for the baby boom.

58. Why did England send explorers to search for a Northwest Passage in the age of European exploration of the New World?

   (A) Francis Drake said the Strait of Magellan was too dangerous for routine travel.
   (B) The English wanted access to rich fishing and whaling grounds in the Pacific Ocean.
   (C) Inuit legend said such a route existed and led to an ancient city filled with gold.
   (D) England wanted a route to Asia that would not risk attack by the Spanish Armada.
   (E) Worms attacked the hulls of wooden sailing ships in the warm South Atlantic.

59. Why did colonists at Jamestown found the Virginia House of Burgesses, the first representative assembly in the New World?

   (A) The British Crown determined the colony was too far away to answer to Parliament.
   (B) They sought a way to solve property disputes and protect their rights as Englishmen.
   (C) They sought independence and thus organized themselves into a "civil body politic."
   (D) Self-rule would prove they were better than other European colonists who lacked it.
   (E) The legislature would better organize defense against attacks by the Spanish.

60. Why did King George III's Proclamation of 1763 anger American colonists?

    (A) They wanted access to the Ohio River Valley that the king now declared off limits.
    (B) They were opposed to the expansion of the boundary of French Canada southward.
    (C) They knew the decree would incite attacks by American Indians on the frontier.
    (D) They opposed all acts of absolute monarchs after the Enlightenment in Europe.
    (E) They thought the king was punishing them for losses in the French and Indian War.

61. Why was the Gag Rule of antebellum America so detrimental to preservation of the Union?

    (A) Congress could not debate acts of secession during a national crisis.
    (B) Congress could not ask the United Kingdom to mediate the North/South divide.
    (C) Congress could not debate religious issues during the Mormon Rebellion.
    (D) Congress could seek compromise on the issue of emancipation of black slaves.
    (E) Congress could not debate immigration issues during a surge of nativism.

62. What was the response to Helen Hunt Jackson's book about the treatment of American Indians, *A Century of Dishonor*?

    (A) Americans largely ignored the book and settlement of the West continued apace.
    (B) The book sparked heated public debate but led to no action on the part of Congress.
    (C) Readers dismissed its message because she wrote with a melodramatic style.
    (D) Pioneers criticized the book because the author had no first-hand knowledge.
    (E) Congress cited the book as a turning point in relations with American Indians.

63. A corporation using vertical combination organizes its industry by

    (A) having Congress set the prices to be charged by all companies in the industry.
    (B) controlling one aspect of an industry and forcing the owners of others to comply.
    (C) owning all aspects of an industrial process and running them together efficiently.
    (D) forming associations that set industrial standards for the government to enforce.
    (E) hiring university experts to advise corporate leaders on best business practices.

64. The Pendleton Act passed in the Gilded Age intended to end political corruption by

    (A) making it illegal for business leaders to support political candidates' campaigns.
    (B) making applicants for government jobs pass tests to prove their competence.
    (C) publicizing incidents of political patronage (graft) in official reports in newspapers.
    (D) targeting Boss Tweed of Tammany Hall specifically and making an example of him.
    (E) taking the power to staff the Civil Service Reform Commission from the president.

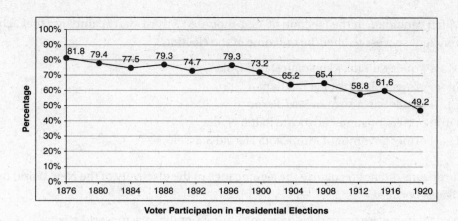

Voter Participation in Presidential Elections

65. Which conclusion can be drawn from the graph showing voting participation in presidential elections from 1876 to 1920?

(A) Wars tend to increase voting participation in U.S. history.

(B) The Civil War disillusioned Americans regarding the value of voting.

(C) The period set in motion perpetual decline in voter participation.

(D) The Election of 1912 was a major turning point in U.S. political history.

(E) Many women did not exercise their new right to vote at first.

66. Adding multiple independently targeted reentry vehicles (MIRVs) to the American nuclear arsenal was significant because

(A) having missiles with multiple warheads effectively closed the missile gap.

(B) having such a terrifying weapon made the Soviet Union give up in the Cold War.

(C) the technology was superior and allayed the fears of a first strike by the Soviets.

(D) the Chinese decided to pressure their allies to end the madness of the Cold War.

(E) all sides agreed to end the missile race in fear a terrorist would acquire a warhead.

67. "And this from a young Chicano: 'Some of us have suffered from recession all our lives.' The symptoms of this crisis of the American spirit are all around us. For the first time in the history of our country a majority of our people believe that the next 5 years will be worse than the past 5 years."

Which president most likely made the speech containing the quotation above during his presidency?

(A) John F. Kennedy

(B) Richard M. Nixon

(C) Jimmy Carter

(D) Ronald Reagan

(E) Bill Clinton

68. Which candidate in the Election of 1992 mounted a third-party campaign that achieved sufficient success to alter the outcome of the election?

    (A) Former Ku Klux Klansman David Duke
    (B) Former columnist Pat Buchanan
    (C) Former businessman Ross Perot
    (D) Former consumer advocate Ralph Nader
    (E) Former governor of Minnesota Harold Stassen

69. Europeans did not recognize the significance of the discovery of the New World by Vikings because

    (A) Vikings were barbarians with no cultural significance in world affairs.
    (B) Vikings did not even preserve a record of these accomplishments themselves.
    (C) Vikings reported that there were other humans in North America already.
    (D) Vikings did not make permanent settlements nor draw attention to them.
    (E) Europeans thought exploits like those of Leif Ericson were mythological.

70. What reform in the criminal justice system was an immediate result of the American Revolution?

    (A) The end of the practice of burning dissenters from established religions as heretics
    (B) The end of capital punishment for many crimes by imprisoning offenders instead
    (C) The end of imprisoning citizens for an inability to pay off their debts
    (D) The end of imprisoning mentally ill Americans as if they were criminals
    (E) The end of housing imprisoned juvenile delinquents with hardened adult criminals

71. Why was the two-party system of the Whigs and Democrats able to avoid civil war through compromise when that of the Republicans and Democrats could not?

    (A) The Whigs were a national party, but the Republicans had support only in the North.
    (B) The Republicans faced a Democratic Party that retained support only in the South.
    (C) Whigs did not have to contend with the threat from the Know-Nothing Party.
    (D) The Republicans lacked leaders with oratorical gifts like those of the Whigs.
    (E) The Republicans lacked the experience of being an opposition party like the Whigs.

72. The notion of Manifest Destiny led to the settlement of the West by

    (A) giving frontier towns a unifying set of values to shape into one western culture.
    (B) helping pioneer families endure isolation because they were part of a larger mission.
    (C) encouraging immigrants from Europe through this new type of American Dream.
    (D) motivating expansionist views among those who saw American society as superior.
    (E) convincing politicians to hope for reform in the pristine territories of the West.

73. Which statement below best expresses a principle behind Abraham Lincoln's plan for restoring the Union during Reconstruction?

(A) The conquered states did not need to do much because they had never actually left.

(B) He should punish the conquered states for all the bitterness they had caused.

(C) A plan that mixed benevolence with some punishment for treason was best.

(D) He should determine the relative guilt of each state and handle each separately.

(E) He should pick a governor for each state and make them adopt the 13th Amendment.

74. What did the Supreme Court decide in the "insular cases" about territories acquired in the Spanish-American War?

(A) The territories were U.S. property, but the people living there were not full citizens.

(B) The United States could not legally own territories outside its national boundaries.

(C) The islanders were not yet ready for civilization or for democracy.

(D) The United States could not hold colonies but could not let other countries have them either.

(E) The United States should develop them until they could apply for independence or statehood.

"Here's Money for Your Americans. I May Drown Some More."

75. Which statement below best conveys the message of the political cartoon above?

(A) The Kaiser viewed Woodrow Wilson as an amateur in the diplomatic arena.

(B) The reparations in the Treaty of Versailles were too high for Germany to pay.

(C) Woodrow Wilson's approach to protesting German atrocities was ineffectual.

(D) Germany did not believe that the United States would actually enter World War I.

(E) Woodrow Wilson believed that dollar diplomacy would save democracy.

76. Investors practiced margin buying prior to the Stock Market Crash in 1929 by

    (A) taking out insurance on their portfolios in case of setbacks in the market.
    (B) monitoring the profit margin on their investments to avoid excessive risk.
    (C) trusting the advice of federal regulators to avoid buying stocks at inflated prices.
    (D) purchasing small amounts of many stocks in large mutual funds to spread out risk.
    (E) buying stocks largely on credit with only a small cash down payment.

77. Stagflation was a difficult problem for the American government and economy to endure during the 1970s because

    (A) Vietnam War costs kept the government from borrowing any more to help.
    (B) government experts did not have solutions because the problems were of a new type.
    (C) the Federal Reserve had already manipulated the currency too much to help.
    (D) the main problem was the Arab Oil Embargo which was beyond American control.
    (E) President Ford's experiment with tax cuts had crippled the federal budget.

78. Which statement best describes the relative contributions of Bill Gates and Steve Jobs to the boom in the computer industry in the 1980s?

    (A) Gates had the best engineers, whereas Jobs had the best advertisers.
    (B) Gates was a pioneer in hardware, whereas Jobs was a pioneer in software.
    (C) Gates first made personal computing accessible, whereas Jobs made it user friendly.
    (D) Gates created an all-consuming monopoly, whereas Jobs set out to break it.
    (E) Gates relied on individuals' skills, whereas Jobs used a team approach to innovation.

79. President Bill Clinton was impeached because he

    (A) had inappropriate sexual relations with a junior staffer.
    (B) used federal employees to solicit women for sexual favors.
    (C) had unscrupulous real estate investments back in his home state of Arkansas.
    (D) lied under oath and obstructed justice during a federal investigation.
    (E) defied the Supreme Court by claiming executive privilege.

80. How did the French establish a presence in central North America before the British could?

    (A) French expeditions marched northward from their settlement at New Orleans.
    (B) French priests converted American Indians to Roman Catholicism to be guides.
    (C) The French went south from Canada before the British could cross the mountains.
    (D) Focusing on the fur trade made the French prone to penetrate the wilderness.
    (E) French colonists married American Indians more readily than the British did.

81. Which of the following events was most important in compelling Great Britain to end the policy of salutary neglect?

   (A) The Restoration of the British monarchy after the Puritan Revolution
   (B) The English Reformation
   (C) The Glorious Revolution
   (D) The French and Indian War
   (E) Pontiac's Rebellion

82. Which statement below best describes Alexander Hamilton's perspective on the national debt in the Early National Period?

   (A) Passing along the debts of one generation to the next was a national sin.
   (B) A national debt could be a useful unifying factor in national life.
   (C) The federal government should pay only the Continental Congress's debts.
   (D) All mature nations had debt, so the United States should be no different.
   (E) The debt was necessary, but the United States should pay it off as quickly as possible.

83. The buffalo herds in the Great Plains were a key to the settlement of the West because

   (A) destroying them allowed the United States to subdue the Plains Indians more easily.
   (B) railroads first went West in order to provide excursion trains for buffalo hunters.
   (C) American cowboys learned how to herd cattle by watching the Spanish herd them.
   (D) the sale of their hides financed the formation of most western towns.
   (E) the Texas Longhorn was a cross between buffalo and European cattle breeds.

84. Henry Cabot Lodge blocked Woodrow Wilson's efforts to bring the United States into the League of Nations after World War I because

   (A) he thought the United States entered the war just to make money for munitions companies.
   (B) he thought the president was already too popular and was growing too powerful.
   (C) he did not believe the League of Nations could accomplish its lofty goals.
   (D) he thought funding for the League of Nations would strain the federal budget.
   (E) he thought joining would remove the right of the Congress to declare war or not.

85. The outcry over the Sacco and Vanzetti case in the 1920s resulted from the

   (A) fact that the two men were proven innocent of murder after their executions.
   (B) rise of an indigenous anarchist movement that saw the men as martyrs.
   (C) general realization that nativism had gone too far in American society.
   (D) involvement of the Ku Klux Klan in the apprehension of the two defendants.
   (E) fact that evidence later proved they were guilty after they were acquitted.

86. Franklin Roosevelt's Bank Holiday impacted the nation at the outset of his presidency by

   (A)   causing many corporations to shut down in protest of his excessive use of power.
   (B)   causing more bank failures when customers later withdrew all their funds.
   (C)   proving the banking industry was guilty of causing the Great Depression.
   (D)   stopping the collapse of the banking industry because most people calmed down.
   (E)   frightening voters who made the presidential Election of 1936 the closest in history.

87. Which of the conditions described below best explains why the American military found the Vietnam War so difficult to fight and to win?

   (A)   The U.S. military had never before fought in such a tropical jungle.
   (B)   The presence of Chinese and Soviet soldiers constantly threatened a wider war.
   (C)   The supply of Soviet aircraft to the enemy prevented U.S. air superiority.
   (D)   The Vietcong were highly dedicated guerrilla fighters with foreign support.
   (E)   President Johnson's micromanagement made his strategy impossible to implement.

88. Which statement below best conveys the message of the political cartoon above?

   (A)   President Nixon's policy of Vietnamization would not end the Vietnam War.
   (B)   Asians were unable or unwilling to defend themselves against communism.
   (C)   The U.S. policy of containment of communism should not have applied to Asia.
   (D)   The conditions of fighting a war in Asia left the prospect of victory there bleak.
   (E)   The Vietnam War required that older and older men be drafted to fight in Asia.

89. The invention of the transistor radically altered the technology used in Americans' daily lives by

 (A) making electronic devices cheaper and within the means of the average consumer.
 (B) making the communications industry the focus of the twentieth-century economy.
 (C) giving a patent to a laboratory for the first time which accelerated more inventions.
 (D) replacing vacuum tubes so electronic devices could be smaller and more portable.
 (E) making communications satellites possible because transistors could work in space.

90. Muammar al Qaddafi of Libya exemplified the difficulties the United States had in combatting global terrorism because

 (A) he was a Sunni Muslim, and negotiations with him offended Shiite Muslim allies.
 (B) he still supported terrorism while giving up his weapons of mass destruction.
 (C) he violated U. N. nuclear resolutions but claimed he did so strictly for self-defense.
 (D) he sheltered Osama bin Laden while saying bin Laden did not represent all of Islam.
 (E) he led the only democratic Islamic country that belonged to the United Nations.

ANSWER KEY
Practice Test 1

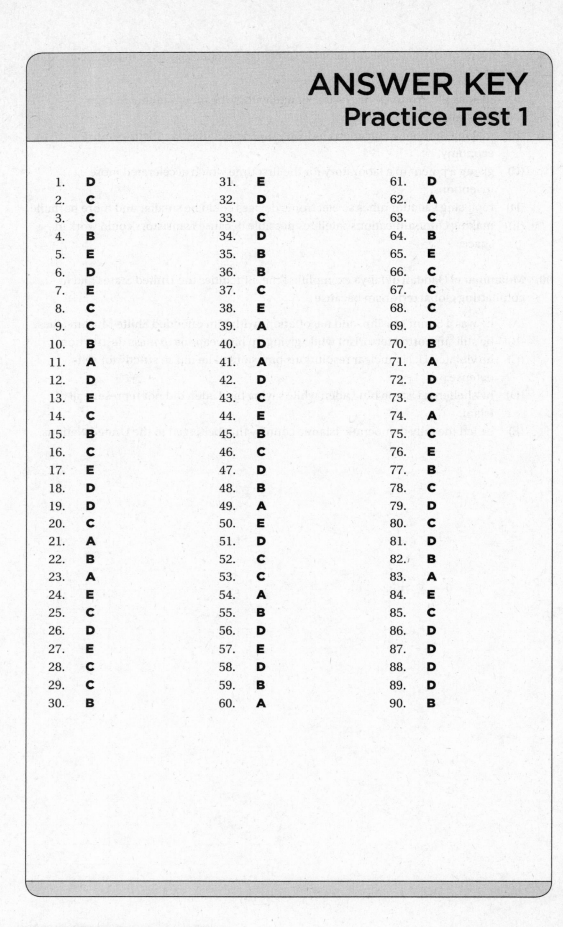

1.	D	31.	E	61.	D
2.	C	32.	D	62.	A
3.	C	33.	C	63.	C
4.	B	34.	D	64.	B
5.	E	35.	B	65.	E
6.	D	36.	B	66.	C
7.	E	37.	C	67.	C
8.	C	38.	E	68.	C
9.	C	39.	A	69.	D
10.	B	40.	D	70.	D
11.	A	41.	A	71.	A
12.	D	42.	D	72.	D
13.	E	43.	C	73.	C
14.	C	44.	E	74.	A
15.	B	45.	B	75.	C
16.	C	46.	C	76.	E
17.	E	47.	D	77.	B
18.	D	48.	B	78.	C
19.	D	49.	A	79.	D
20.	C	50.	E	80.	C
21.	A	51.	D	81.	D
22.	B	52.	C	82.	B
23.	A	53.	C	83.	A
24.	E	54.	A	84.	E
25.	C	55.	B	85.	C
26.	D	56.	D	86.	D
27.	E	57.	E	87.	D
28.	C	58.	D	88.	D
29.	C	59.	B	89.	D
30.	B	60.	A	90.	B

TEST ANALYSIS

STEP 1   Count the number of correct answers.

    Enter the total here: _____

STEP 2   Count the number of incorrect answers.

    Enter the total here: _____

STEP 3   Multiply the number of incorrect answers by .250.

    Enter the product here: _____

STEP 4   Subtract the results obtained in Step 3 from the total obtained in Step 1.

    Enter the total here: _____

STEP 5   Round the number obtained in Step 4 to the nearest whole number.

    Raw Score = _____.

Scaled Score Conversion Table

Raw Score	Scaled Score	Raw Score	Scaled Score	Raw Score	Scaled Score
90–79	800	46–45	600	8–7	400
78	790	44–43	590	6–5	390
77–76	780	42–41	580	4–3	380
75	770	40	570	2–1	370
74	760	39–38	560	0 – –1	360
73–72	750	37–36	550	–2 – –3	350
71	740	35–34	540	–4	340
70–69	730	33–32	530	–5 – –6	330
68	720	31–30	520	–7	320
67–66	710	29–28	510	–8 – –9	310
65–64	700	27	500	–10	300
63	690	26–25	490	–11 – –12	290
62–61	680	24–23	480	–13	280
60–59	670	22–21	470	–14 – –15	270
58–57	660	20–19	460	–16 – –17	260
56–55	650	18–17	450	–18 – –19	250
54–53	640	16–15	440	–20	240
52–51	630	14–13	430	–21 – –22	230
50–49	620	12–11	420		
48–47	610	10–9	410		

ANSWER EXPLANATIONS

1. **(D)** Although answers (A) and (B) are true, Prince Henry's main contribution was the school mentioned in answer (D). All European nations benefited from his school of navigation, which gave a leap forward for exploration and thus colonization. Henry was not a sea captain, nor was he really a navigator despite his moniker. He did not race Spain since the main Portuguese endeavors across the Atlantic came over fifty years after those of Spain.

2. **(C)** Answers (A) and (D) never occurred in significant enough numbers to alter all of colonial society. Answer (B) belies the fact the Protestant work ethic made colonists harder workers, not just otherworldly dreamers. Answer (E) had been going on so long in Europe that colonial America was a product of this fact, not a society developed by this fact. Answer (C) implies that both French and Spanish colonies enforced uniformity of religious belief, whereas England tried to rid itself of dissenters by granting them charters to found colonies.

3. **(C)** Although the Federalist Papers have served all of the functions alluded to in the other answers, New Yorker Alexander Hamilton (along with Madison and Jay) was trying to convince his important home state to ratify the U.S. Constitution. He published these essays as editorials in New York newspapers.

4. **(B)** Most of the other answers hint at reasons "Seward's Folly" turned out to be an excellent idea, but only answer (B) was true at the time of the Alaska Purchase. Americans found small amounts of gold, but the gold rush and oil bonanza days came later. Some propaganda and Russian bribes convinced Congress to ratify the purchase treaty, but Seward did not consider Russia a threat. The greater fear was that Russia would sell the real estate to the United Kingdom instead of to the United States.

5. **(E)** Answer (E) is the only true one because it defines what open and closed shops actually are. Answers (A) and (B) were possibilities after the rise of labor that did not actually follow the success of the movement. Answer (C) is the opposite of the truth, and answer (D) refers more to a practice of management called lockouts.

6. **(D)** All of the answers are events in which Martin Luther King Jr. took a leading role, but the Montgomery Bus Boycott was his first major step and the event that prompted him to form the Southern Christian Leadership Conference. SCLC was the organization that framed the activism in the rest of Dr. King's work.

7. **(E)** All of the answers describe controversial events associated with the Vietnam War, and protestors probably had them all in mind at times. The invasion of Cambodia, however, directly sparked the protests at Kent State when President Nixon announced it on television. Protestors said the invasion violated a pledge Nixon had made to keep the war from expanding in Southeast Asia. The students were protesting the widening credibility gap.

8. **(C)** The Congressional committee already had proof of a conspiracy, and the other answers address information they knew or wanted to know. Only answer (C) describes what the committee was really hunting for—the "smoking gun" that would prove Nixon had lied to them by denying any knowledge of the conspiracy to cover up the actions of his administration in the Watergate scandal.

9. **(C)** Answers (A) and (E) are references to the Nixon administration, although Richard Nixon never confessed to illegal activities. Answer (B) is a reference to President Carter's handling of the hostage crisis with Iran. Answer (D) is a reference to the fact that Oliver North claimed the whole Iran-Contra plan was his idea and that he acted alone, but President Reagan did not order him to say this despite being named the "Teflon President" by the press. Answer (C) describes the true impact that President Reagan's approval ratings went from over 60 percent to just over forty percent after Iran-Contra before rebounding by the end of his second term.

10. **(B)** Answer (B) is the reality that so frustrated American Indians in the path of the westward expansion that made answer (D) no longer possible. Answers (A) and (C) are much later solutions to soil depletion. In the colonial era, the solution was simply to cultivate new land. Answer (E) is incorrect because colonists put spent agricultural land to other uses.

11. **(A)** Answer (A) describes the colonists' response after their rejoicing at the repeal of the hated Stamp Act. They scorned Parliament's attempt to reassert its power over them. Answers (B) and (E) are wrong because they imply the American Revolution was a nonstarter. Still, no Americans called immediately for independence as the first recorded suggestion of this desire came over a year later, and most Americans could not seriously contemplate independence until many years later. Answer (D) alludes to later events.

12. **(D)** Answer (D) includes President Jefferson's charge to the Corps of Discovery and the result once the journey became widely known. Lewis and Clark did report about the American Indian tribes they encountered as well as their scientific discoveries, but they did not test military strength or have anything to do with founding the Smithsonian. Answers (B) and (C) are closer to the truth, but the expedition did not claim territory nor conceive of a railroad.

13. **(E)** This quote is the famous end of Daniel Webster's plea in the Webster-Hayne Debates. The quote does not refer to economics, the tariff of the Nullification Crisis, or to the Bank of the United States that Jackson hated so. John C. Calhoun stood with his fellow South Carolinian, Robert Hayne, for "Liberty first and Union afterward." The oratory nearly masks the topic of the debate, but Webster was alarmed at the sectionalism among North, South, and West evoked by the debate about the sale of western land.

14. **(C)** Answer (C), coupled with the fact that Smith announced he was running for president, made his neighbors more nervous than the institution of polygamy, the new scripture, or the new city. A mob killed Smith after he was arrested for treason. Therefore, Brigham Young led the Mormons to Utah and to their subsequent brush with the U.S. Army.

15. **(B)** All of the answers describe events related to the causes of the Mexican War except answer (D), which is false. Slidell's Mission did not directly provoke the war, and the actions of the U.S. Navy and John C. Fremont occurred after it started. The blockade, however, was not about trade policy, and Polk's interest in Mexico was more to fulfill the agenda of the southern expansionist Democrats than to collect debts. Polk sent Zachary Taylor to provoke a war, and when shooting started along the Rio Grande, Polk asked Congress to declare war, "notwithstanding all our efforts to avoid it." The prearranged Bear Flag Revolt was then free to proceed.

16. **(C)** This case gave the Supreme Court its first chance to rule on the legality of slavery, but when the balance of powers referred to in answer (A) thus finally came on line, the ruling increased sectional tensions rather than decreased them. Still, this one event did not make the Civil War inevitable. Answer (B) is truer of the North's reaction to a Supreme Court made up of appointments by a long series of expansionist, pro-slavery Democratic presidents. Answer (D) is the opposite of the truth, because the Supreme Court said the federal government did not have the constitutional right to stop the spread of slavery, let alone abolish it.

17. **(E)** Answers (B), (C), and (D) were all true of the federal government already, although the U.S. Army could not enter a state without the permission of the governor, something the seceded states would not give, of course. Answer (A) has not yet occurred in American history although many have desired to see it. Both the North and the South resorted to conscription before the Civil War ended, and the draft has been a part of American society ever since. No Congress has instituted a draft, however, since 1972.

18. **(D)** Answers (A), (C), and (E) refer erroneously to the resurgent Klan, political corruption, and the illegal sale of alcohol inherent in the Roaring Twenties. Answer (B) is incorrect because the government of the 1920s was pro-business. The infamous Palmer Raids were against labor organizations in search of subversive or Bolshevik literature. They are the classic example of a restriction on civil liberties from the First Red Scare.

19. **(D)** The reference to the prairies and the plantations indicates the agricultural bent to this quote that was stated in support of the Agricultural Adjustment Act (AAA), the goal of which was to keep farm prices at par with the high price of grain during World War I. The goal proved impossible, and the Supreme Court later found the AAA to be unconstitutional. The other agencies listed pertained to civil works projects and industrial matters unrelated to caring for farmers. The rhetoric in the quote relates to the fact that "country" folk began to experience a depressed economy ten years prior to the Stock Market Crash.

20. **(C)** Answers (A), (B), and (D) were true of the era and reveal how incredible it was that the country survived the Critical Period. The Congress under the Articles of Confederation handled the land disputes with a series of Land Ordinances. Answers (A) and (B) were pressing issues, but a rebellion in the very state where the American Revolution was born awakened leaders to the need for action. Answer (E) refers to an even greater threat to the republic but one that occurred several years after the Constitutional Convention was over.

21. **(A)** Only answer (A) contains two entirely true causes among the half dozen or more that reignited war with the Mother Country. Impressment was the forcible enlistment of men into the British Navy, and the British supported American Indian raids by supplying them liquor, guns, and other incentives. Answers (B) and (C) are false, or partly false, in that the British were making no new encroachments on American territory, nor any serious colonization attempts in South America with Napoleon organizing Europe against them. Answers (D) and (E) are false because the British did not cooperate with or side with the French at all during this era.

22. **(B)** George Fitzhugh was the leading apologist for slavery who espoused the Positive Good theory in his writings and criticized the North for imposing "wage slavery" on immigrant factory workers. All the rest were abolitionists.

23. **(A)** All of the other answers were within the right of any president in Andrew Johnson's day except the part of answer (C) that suggests the president could appoint generals and admirals (and lower officers) without congressional approval. Answer (B) was an option for presidents until 1951 when the Twenty-second Amendment limited presidents to two terms. The Tenure of Office Act was an attempt to set up President Johnson for impeachment and removal from office because he obstructed the Radical Republicans' plan for Reconstruction.

24. **(E)** Only answer (E) captures the true significance of the Bessemer process for the steel industry. Answer (A) refers to consequences more important for patent law than industry. Answer (B) neglects the fact that Carnegie was a big business industrialist before he began using the Bessemer process. That fact is why answer (C) is wrong; he was so far ahead none of his competitors caught up. The United States did become the world's leading producer of steel by 1920, but this success was due to many other factors in addition to the Bessemer process. Also, other nations used the Bessemer process of producing steel more cheaply by blowing air through molten iron.

25. **(C)** Even though Garfield had been assassinated, the business dress of those wanting access to Chester Arthur reveals they were not assassins but job seekers and grafters wanting favors. Nothing indicates that they might be labor union leaders, and Gilded Age presidents allowed all too much access to themselves through patronage. Arthur, coming out of the New York Customs House, was a considerable grafter himself, yet he did sign the Pendleton Act into law. The next day, however, he kept handing out jobs to a long line of office seekers. The cartoon portrays the crying need for civil service reform.

26. **(D)** All of the other answers twist, or as in the case of answers (B) and (C), actually state issues debated in American Christianity, and answer (A) was a criticism leveled at adherents of the Social Gospel. The chief theological shift, however, was in deemphasizing the traditional gospel message in favor of political and social activism. The Populist Revolt and Progressive Reform extend directly from this new religious worldview.

27. **(E)** Answer (A) is a reference to the famous Tuskegee Airmen recruited from Tuskegee Institute to form an all-black squadron of pilots for World War II. Booker T. Washington founded the Institute, however, as a "vocational and normal school," or one that trained the craftsmen and teachers that he saw as the essential first steps for African Americans to leave the plantations and achieve status as more dignified economic necessities to American society. Washington was accused of holding the view described in answer (D), but that was not his intention. He pursued what he considered a more practical approach for his day unlike the approaches others followed in answers (B) and (C).

28. **(C)** All the other answers allude to controversial issues arising from fighting in a war against Germany, on the side of pre-revolutionary Russia, with many German immigrants and sympathizers in the country. George Creel, however, was a successful Madison Avenue advertising executive hired by the Wilson administration to "sell" the war to the American people after Wilson had promised not to bring the country into

the Great War. Creel's efforts were successful in raising the amount of bonds sold and increasing volunteer enlistments in the military.

29. **(C)** Answer (A) is incorrect because the Brains Trust was FDR's Cabinet, of which Eleanor Roosevelt was not a member. Answer (E) alludes to a role played for Woodrow Wilson by his wife after his stroke. Answers (B) and (D) could be said of several first ladies, but the unique role Eleanor Roosevelt played was to actively represent her husband and the New Deal by traveling extensively because he was stricken with polio as an adult and largely confined to a wheelchair. Mrs. Roosevelt was the first First Lady to enter a coal mine, for example, and she even wrote a newspaper column to discuss her experiences. She thus became the most openly politically minded wife of a president to that date in history.

30. **(B)** Answers (A) and (C) are untrue because no one openly challenged George Washington's virtues or leadership until well into his presidency, and no one voiced an opinion to try to run a government without a written constitution. Answer (B) describes the issue that led to the Great Compromise that solved the problem. Answers (D) and (E) allude to issues that did arise, but only after the new government was set in motion by the U.S. Constitution.

31. **(E)** Answers (A) and (D) refer to the Elections of 1828 and 1876, respectively. The Election of 1824 did have to be determined by the House of Representatives, but constitutionally. When Henry Clay threw his support behind John Quincy Adams for the vote in the House, Andrew Jackson responded with the charge based on the result in answer (E). Answer (C) may have been true for some voters, but it implied no direct corruption.

32. **(D)** Dorothea Dix championed many of the causes listed in the other answers, but she was personally responsible for leading the cause in answer (D) to success in her lifetime.

33. **(C)** Answers (A), (B), and (D) are erroneous fabrications based on the context of the Filipino Insurrection, and the first two did not occur. President McKinley's assassin was an anarchist who did not refer to the conflict in the Philippines. Answer (E) is the opposite of the truth since the Philippines possessed jungles and a climate similar to those in Cuba, which is tropical, not temperate. Answer (C) is the only one that states the true significance of this unfortunate conflict.

34. **(D)** Answer (D) evokes FDR's call to give the Allies, ". . . all aid short of war," a measure he said would prevent the need for the United States to enter the fighting. He actually feared the United States would be drawn into the war and pursued the peacetime draft of answer (C) accordingly. Answer (E) was tantamount to a declaration of war, especially to the Japanese, but FDR did not form the War Production Board until 1942 after their attack on Pearl Harbor.

35. **(B)** Amazingly, President Eisenhower did all of these things, even setting up the invasion mentioned in answer (E) that was carried out by President Kennedy. The answer that wrecked the Paris peace summit with Nikita Khrushchev, however, was the U-2 Incident that led Eisenhower to lie to the Soviets about the flyover. Khrushchev staged a publicity coup by exposing Eisenhower's lies and destroying a chance to end the Cold War.

36. **(B)** The Supreme Court decided *Engel* v. *Vitale* in the 1960s while Earl Warren was the chief justice. Removing prayer from public schools was part of the societal flux of the

Stormy Sixties and contributed to a turning point in cultural values. All of the other cases listed were landmark cases, and knowing the decade in which each occurred can help trace changing social and political values. Answer (A) was in the 1950s. Answer (C) was in the 1940s. Answers (D) and (E) were in the 1970s.

37. **(C)** Phyllis Schlafly did not have the lofty connections implied in answers (D) and (E), but she did lead a national movement against the Equal Rights Amendment as a conservative activist. She based her opposition on the stance described in answer (C). Answer (A) implies that she supported the amendment, and answer (B) is a reference to Gloria Steinem.

38. **(E)** Answer (E) reveals that what appears to be a military history question is actually a diplomatic question. Saratoga showed France and Spain that the colonial forces had a chance of victory and caused them to supply the money, troops, and naval support crucial to an American victory. The opposing forces at Saratoga were not equally matched thanks partly to the heroic exploits of Benedict Arnold. His anger that he did not receive sufficient credit is what led him later to betray the new country. The British did capture and occupy New York City.

39. **(A)** Answer (A) is the one that correctly describes what Adams called, "my greatest contribution to peace." Like the eagle on the Great Seal of the United States, he held the arrows of the new U.S. Navy in one hand and held out the olive branch of diplomacy just long enough with the other for Napoleon to come to power and see the practical benefit of stopping the Quasi-War. Answer (B) is the opposite of the truth because the Federalists pushed Adams to make war on the French. When he would not, his own party thus abandoned him and left him a one-term president.

40. **(D)** Answers (A), (C), and (E) were the actions of other presidents in national defense, and it was Napoleon who saw the Louisiana Purchase as a source of cash. Jefferson saw only the new lands acquired for a cheap price and left Napoleon to his own devices. Jefferson's attempt to keep the United States out of war infuriated Federalists in New England, their last stronghold. His Embargo Act struck a political blow because their economy was based on the shipping of goods.

41. **(A)** Answer (B) was William Travis's doing. Answer (C) was Davy Crockett's. Answers (D) and (E) both apply to Sam Houston. Answer (A) describes Austin's contribution that led settlers to Texas after his father negotiated the migration with Santa Anna and then died.

42. **(D)** Lincoln said these words during one of the Lincoln-Douglas debates, and it was his firm stand and the position of the Republican Party until the Emancipation Proclamation paved the way for the Thirteenth Amendment to the U.S. Constitution. Stephen Douglas and President James Buchanan would not have agreed with the need to stop slavery in the territories. Douglas was for letting the people choose for themselves (popular sovereignty), and Buchanan proposed an amendment to the Constitution legalizing slavery once and for all. William H. Seward was an abolitionist senator who wound up Lincoln's secretary of state. Henry Clay was a slave owner who formed compromises that violated this premise.

43. **(C)** Answer (A) is a reference to Robert E. Lee whose troops derided him as the "King of Spades" until they realized trenches were a good idea. The other incorrect answers

refer to activities of generals from both sides of the war. The correct answer reveals that another seemingly military question is actually one foreshadowing the consequences of the wars of the twentieth century, the era that Winston Churchill called a great catastrophe. Diplomats attempted to make peace through the formation of the League of Nations and the United Nations while the specter of total war grinned in the corner. Sherman was the first general to see that modern war required the destruction of the enemy's economy and thus, his cities.

44. **(E)** Answer (A) more describes William Jennings Bryan in the Election of 1896. Answer (B) is fictitious, and answer (C) is moot because Reconstruction had already ended seven years earlier in 1877 when Cleveland won the presidency for the first time. Answer (D) is wrong because many Gilded Age presidential candidates talked about civil service reform. In a close race with almost identical platforms and persistent mudslinging, Cleveland won because James G. Blaine was gaff-prone and could not sully Cleveland's reputation enough. Cleveland had a track record as the reform governor of New York.

45. **(B)** No president would be caught dead agreeing to answer (A), and answer (C) goes beyond Theodore Roosevelt's actual stance expressed in answer (B). Answers (D) and (E) twist the truth because use of the Panama Canal was not a violation of the Monroe Doctrine and there were not significant military inroads in Latin America by European nations in Theodore Roosevelt's time.

46. **(C)** Answer (C) describes the First Hundred Days in which FDR launched the New Deal with a Rubber Stamp Congress. They wrote some bills in the morning and passed them by the afternoon! Thus, FDR did not wait on Hoover's policies but built on them with measures designed to bring relief, recovery, and reform. The New Deal was never a systematic plan, however, whether early in his administration or later. While he did publicize his actions via radio chats, the New Deal was definitely activity, not passivity. Answer (D) refers to the later economic summits of presidents like Gerald Ford.

47. **(D)** Of the other answer choices, only answer (C) is based in the truth, but the Soviets began construction of the Berlin Wall years later during John F. Kennedy's presidency. While Truman was president, Berlin was divided into four zones. The Soviets kept the east side, and the United Kingdom, the United States, and France protected the west side of the city. When the Soviet Union closed off all ground access to these three western zones, Truman responded with the remarkable Berlin Airlift until the Soviets caved under such resolve.

48. **(B)** Viceroys were courtiers sent to the New World on temporary assignments to be the legal representatives of the Spanish monarchy. They were not priests representing the church, and they were not to cultivate feudal relationships nor stay permanently. They did not lead in a military capacity as implied in answer (A).

49. **(A)** John Quincy Adams coined the term *critical period* to describe the danger the central government faced until the U.S. Constitution stabilized the country. A republic with a balanced government that recognized the sovereignty of the American people was the solution to the problems of the Articles of Confederation. The other answers all exaggerate aspects of the period, none of which amounted to a serious threat.

50. **(E)** Although answer (C) was Jefferson's intention, the Congress made sure it did not happen by creating the committee system still in place today. Answers (A) or (B) would have been disastrous if true, and curiously, Jefferson did not push for repeal of the Federalist policies in answer (D), which he hated but merely let elapse according to their original charters.

51. **(D)** The Electoral College was a part of the original design of the presidential election process, and candidates' running together as a ticket started 20 years before Jackson first ran for president in 1824. The Election of 1824 was the first in which candidates were "sold" to the American people as if they were products, and Jackson did not win his first term until 1828. Answer (C) is the opposite of Jackson's pledge to begin rotation in office for civil servants after the Era of Good Feelings. The Democrats adopted the national nominating convention idea from the short-lived Anti-Masonic Party, but democratizing the selection of the "ticket" and the platform was in keeping with Jackson's support for the Common Man.

52. **(C)** All of the answers are at least half-truths regarding the situation on the ground (or at sea) in the Oregon Territory, but answer (C) was the simple truth that foreshadowed Nathan Bedford Forrest's famous dictum on how to win, "Get there first with the most." Although Polk did dispatch the U.S. Navy to ward off British intervention in the dispute, there was never any fleet engagement between the rivals, and mountain men did not make forts in Oregon although they made the first inroads there. Missionaries did preach to American Indians of the Pacific Northwest but with deadly, not peaceful, results.

53. **(C)** All of the answers reflect circumstances of nineteenth-century political discourse, but Lincoln participated in this instance by making Spot Resolutions asking Polk to show him the spot on a map where "American blood was spilled on American soil." He doubted the president's claims and believed Polk provoked the Mexican War on purpose. He did not make the claim in answer (D) about Polk, and his Cooper Union speech came much later in his political career.

54. **(A)** Unfortunately answer (B) was not yet true because answer (A) was the application of Darwinism to the status of African Americans by leading scientists like Louis Agassiz. The obvious fact that most African Americans had been slaves for centuries apparently did not suggest an alternate hypothesis regarding their organizational skills. Answer (C) is more a reference to the attitude held by Frederick Douglass, the leading black male abolitionist, that African Americans needed nothing more from the United States government than to be left alone. Answers (D) and (E) stem from interpretations of the theory of evolution that came much later.

55. **(B)** Although Justice Oliver Wendell Holmes was a Progressive who moved the Supreme Court to the left, the stated position is not exclusively Progressive in nature. All Progressives were loose constructionists, but not all loose constructionists were Progressives. Holmes was both. Furthermore, the Progressive Reform Movement persuaded both Democrats and Republicans to adopt Alexander Hamilton's view of the U.S. Constitution, that it contained implied powers.

56. **(D)** All of the other answers are the opposite of the truth. Pulitzer published the *New York World*, the newspaper with the largest circulation in the United States, and he saw the Spanish-American War as a grand event. He plastered his front pages with his cor-

respondents' "yellow journalism" to increase circulation and to increase support for McKinley, the Republican Party, and the war. He told Frederic Remington, "You provide the pictures, and I'll provide the war."

57. **(E)** All of the other answers belie the fact that prosperity quickly returned to most people in the United States after World War II and the Great Depression both ended. President Eisenhower praised the American lifestyle over that of any he had encountered in Europe and suburban homes filled with babies typified that lifestyle. William Levitt, who had constructed housing during the war, had difficulty building his Levittowns fast enough to meet demand in suburban Pennsylvania.

58. **(D)** All of the answers refer to legitimate concerns of maritime nations of the colonial era except answer (C), which twists the legend of El Dorado, a mythic city of gold in the Spanish Empire. Copper hulls prevented the awkward situation Magellan found in having to rebuild his wooden ships completely because of damage done by worms, but the worst problem for English ships was the Spanish Armada. The Virginia Company even sent out search parties from Jamestown looking for a Northwest Passage to enable English ships to escape that gauntlet. Spain and England were at war until the defeat of the Spanish Armada in 1588.

59. **(B)** Answer (A) is incorrect because the Virginia House of Burgesses was the idea of Virginians, not the Crown. No one sought independence, however, and colonists were more concerned with attacks by American Indians than their reputation with colonists from other nations. Spain stopped attacking after the defeat of the Spanish Armada in 1588, and Virginians sought to protect their rights as Englishmen through representative government in 1619.

60. **(A)** Answer (B) is a reference to the later Quebec Act. The king was trying to avoid conflict with American Indians rather than incite attacks, which would require expensive defense he did not want to provide, so answer (C) is wrong. Answer (D) is incorrect because King George III was authoritarian, but no English monarch was an absolute ruler. He was capable of arbitrary gestures, however, or at least that is how the colonists viewed the Proclamation of 1763 rather than the reason stated in Answer (E). He ordered them to stay east of the Appalachian Mountains and denied them access to the lush Ohio River Valley, their main incentive to fighting in the French and Indian War.

61. **(D)** All of the answers evoke issues that aroused tension in antebellum America, but all are false except answer (D). The tragedy of the Gag Rule eliminated the very power Congress needed to save the Union and settle the slavery question. The British Parliament was able to stumble its way to abolition through open debate. The Civil War happened because Congress postponed indefinitely all bills regarding abolition during the last time a compromise might have been possible.

62. **(A)** Despite Ms. Jackson's best efforts, Americans largely ignored her work in her lifetime. Her book was nonfiction unlike *Uncle Tom's Cabin*, criticisms of which are the basis for answers (C) and (D). Neither the public nor Congress responded as described in answers (B) or (E).

63. **(C)** Answer (B) is actually horizontal combination, or integration, whereas the other answers describe ideas that arose after the era of the rise of big business combinations.

Andrew Carnegie took the approach described in answer (C), as did Gustavus Swift in the beef industry.

64. **(B)** Congress passed the Pendleton Act, after the assassination of President James Garfield, with the intention of ending political corruption by making civil servants pass competency tests to receive their jobs. Answer (C) was the approach of muckraking journalists, not the Congress. Boss Tweed was targeted by law enforcement, not by a law, but even his capture and imprisonment did not end the Gilded Age graft. Answers (A) and (E) might have had some impact but were never tried and are likely unconstitutional.

65. **(E)** Answer (E) is based on the fact the Election of 1920 was the first in which women could vote for a president. With the doubling of the electorate, the sudden drop to 49.2 percent participation revealed that a large number of the new voters did not exercise their new right. The 1898 Spanish-American War disproves answer (A), and there is no proof that the Great War in Europe was the reason for the 1916 uptick. Answer (B) is the opposite of the truth in that participation through the Gilded Age was much higher than it was in later presidential elections. The graph cannot support answer (C) because it does not give enough information to address the word "perpetual." Answer (D) is wrong because, even though the Election of 1912 was a major turning point, one cannot make that assertion from the low participation recorded for that election.

66. **(C)** Answer (A) is incorrect because when the United States introduced MIRVs, there was no missile gap (and there may never have been a missile gap). Answers (B), (D), and (E) would have been helpful but none of them ever occurred. Before MIRVs came on the scene with the ability to deliver up to ten warheads each, the Soviet Union believed they had a chance to knock out American missile silos because they had built much larger ICBMs than anything in the American arsenal. The chance that even a few MIRVs might get through such a "first strike" caused the Soviets to reconsider such a strategy.

67. **(C)** This quote is from Jimmy Carter and evokes the ideas about malaise and the misery index he discussed in this televised speech. Unlike his predecessors, he invited comments from average citizens and made them public. The irony of the Election of 1980, however, was that Ronald Reagan was able to use the negative rhetoric of the misery index to defeat President Carter because conditions had not improved during the Carter administration. Both Ronald Reagan and Bill Clinton led the United States with rhetoric that was more positive during times that were not as plagued by recession.

68. **(C)** Although Ralph Nader may have influenced the Election of 2000 when he took votes away from the Democrat, Al Gore, Texas business executive Ross Perot was the foil in the close Election of 1992. The other candidates listed were minor players of fringe elements with no direct impact on the elections in which they ran for president.

69. **(D)** Answer (A) belies the fact that Vikings, while barbarians, had tremendous impact on world culture. The other answers are incorrect because Vikings did report that there were other humans in North America in the tales they preserved of Leif Ericson's incredible exploits, but their discovering America first was not widely known until archaeologists discovered remnants of their settlements in the twentieth century.

70. **(B)** Only answer (B) was a direct result of the optimism created by the success of the American Revolution. Colonial Americans did not burn heretics even before the revolu-

tion, and the practices described in the other answers all went on for some time after the revolution. The reform of these other practices did not arise until after the Second Great Awakening began in the 1830s.

71. **(A)** Answer (A) reveals why Whigs like Henry Clay could engineer compromises and Republicans could not. The Republican Party began as an entirely sectional party based in the North. Answer (B) is closer to the situation in 1860 after the Democratic Party split North and South, but from their start in 1854, Republicans faced a nationally united Democratic Party. The rise of the Know-Nothings is a major cause of the breakup of the Whig Party, so answer (C) is wrong. The Whigs were able to draw on the British heritage of an opposition party as in answer (E), but so could the Republicans who attracted most northern Whigs, like Abraham Lincoln, to their party. As for oratory, Daniel Webster had been the giant of the Senate for the Whigs, but Lincoln's rhetoric revealed an original political genius that has been unparalleled since his assassination.

72. **(D)** All of the answers hint at potential consequences of the quasi-religious idea of Manifest Destiny, but only answer (D) describes its precise impact as a motivation for acquiring territory in the west beginning with the justifications for the Mexican War. Manifest Destiny implied that the United States should spread from ocean to ocean in order to liberate people from political and religious tyranny. Town leaders, pioneer families, European immigrants, and reform-minded politicians may or may not have discussed Manifest Destiny in the manner implied by the other answers, but none of their experiences or perspectives would have been possible if expansionist politicians using the rhetoric of Manifest Destiny had not acquired western territory in the first place.

73. **(C)** Answer (C) is the full truth about Lincoln's perspective behind his Ten Percent Plan. He did believe, like Andrew Johnson, the idea expressed in answer (A), but he also believed the Confederate states had committed treason and needed a certain portion of their people to acknowledge this publicly before being restored to full status as states. Answer (B) is more associated with the Radical Republicans in Congress, and answer (E) was a part of Johnson's plan for Reconstruction after Lincoln's death. Neither the presidents nor the Congress viewed any state as guiltier than the other states that seceded as suggested in answer (D), although the states were reconstructed individually.

74. **(A)** All of the answers describe opinions held by various sides of the debate over imperialism, but only answer (A) expresses the determination of the Supreme Court in these difficult cases.

75. **(C)** Answer (C) conveys the message of the cartoon about Wilson's response to the sinking of the *Lusitania* and/or other ships with Americans onboard. Eliciting pledges and demanding fines from the Germans did not deter them in the end from resorting to the unrestricted submarine warfare that brought the United States into the Great War. Answers (A), (D), and (E) may have been true but are not implied directly in the cartoon. The arrogant posture of Kaiser Wilhelm and his defiant words in the cartoon reveal that answer (B) cannot be true because they do not portray him as a defeated foe subject to the Treaty of Versailles.

76. **(E)** All of the other answers hint at practices investors use today as a result of the Stock Market Crash except answer (B), which merely describes a common practice using a different application of the word "margin." Margin buying, as described in answer (E),

was one of the chief causes of the crash because of the rampant inflation in stock prices it created and the massive risk that buyers incurred the moment the market plummeted. The rise before the fall was so profound that buyers could pay off margin debts while still making tidy profits, but in the crash, margin calls by brokers required the full value of the stocks to be paid, which almost no one could cover.

77. **(B)** Answers (A), (C), and (D) hint at difficulties that did contribute to the deep recession of the 1970s, but the deficit spending policies advised by John Maynard Keynes in the New Deal could not reverse the unprecedented stagflation (a depressed economy in a time of high inflation). With only one model to respond, Progressives were at a loss. Answer (E) actually hints at the solution attempted by President Ford and expanded by President Reagan, but the question asks about why the problem was difficult to solve, not what the solution was.

78. **(C)** The other answers are false distinctions except answer (D), which does not explain the two competitors' contributions but examines their motives. Answer (C) best sums up this odd couple's transformation of world communications and business operations. Microsoft's software made an electronic hobbyist's toy a major technological impact on people's daily lives, whereas Apple attempted to make the use of computers so simple that anyone could use them.

79. **(D)** All of the answers evoke some aspect of the investigation into President Clinton's more questionable practices, but the articles of impeachment had nothing to do with sex or real estate but rather with perjury and obstruction of justice that the House of Representatives claimed occurred while special prosecutors were looking into the other behaviors.

80. **(C)** Answer (A) is not true because the French arrived in New Orleans after traversing the Mississippi River Valley. Laying aside the cultural differences suggested in the other answers, the success of the French was mainly due to geography. Water routes made easy passage south from Canada, whereas the Appalachian Mountains proved an impenetrable barrier for the British for generations.

81. **(D)** Although the first period of salutary neglect was ended by the Restoration in 1660, another period of salutary neglect returned until the war debt from the French and Indian War compelled the British government to enforce mercantilist indirect taxes and levy direct taxes for the first time. The other events listed have no direct link to salutary neglect.

82. **(B)** Answer (A) was actually Thomas Jefferson's take on the national debt. Answer (C) is incorrect because Hamilton was for assumption, or adding the states' debt incurred during the American Revolution to the national debt. Answer (D) twists the fact that Hamilton did model the Bank of the U.S. on the Bank of England, but he did not want to fund the debt just to keep up with the nations' neighbors. Answer (E) is false because answer (B) is true.

83. **(A)** Although answer (B) describes an actual type of hunt, railroads did not go West just to provide easy access to buffalo (bison). Answer (A) is true because killing the buffalo was the key strategy to beat the Plains Indians through attrition of this "source of their

lives." Answer (D) is an exaggeration, and answers (C) and (E) are dangerously false. Do not try to lasso a buffalo, even one that is only half buffalo!

84. **(E)** Answer (A) is a reference to the erroneous conclusions of the Nye Committee that made the conclusion stated with which Senator Lodge almost surely disagreed. Lodge might very well have agreed with answers (B), (C), and (D), but his chief line of attack against joining the League is expressed in answer (E). Enough of his Irreconcilables (the Old Guard Republicans in the Senate) agreed to thwart Wilson's plans. Lodge's great fear was that the squabbling nations of Europe would drag the United States into another war against its will by removing the constitutional hurdle of having the consent of Congress to declare war.

85. **(C)** Although Sacco and Vanzetti were almost certainly guilty of murder, the majority of Americans viewed their trial as a miscarriage of justice motivated by the nativism mentioned in answer (C). They were executed and never proven innocent. The Klan had nothing to do with their capture, and if there was an anarchist movement watching the trial, it was not large enough to move the majority of the population to adopt their views.

86. **(D)** Answer (A) never happened, and answer (B) is the exact opposite of the truth. Answer (C) was an assertion made later by the Securities and Exchange Commission and never proven. The Election of 1936 was a landslide victory for FDR whose success with the Bank Holiday is described in answer (D), a result that validated his statement, "The only thing we have to fear is fear itself."

87. **(D)** Answer (A) is incorrect because the United States had fought in several tropical areas during World War II. Answers (B) and (C) would make nice excuses but were not a factor in causing the United States to lose. Answer (E) was true and troublesome, but the real difficulty lay in the dedication of the Vietcong who had been fighting foreign invaders throughout the recent history of Vietnam. A divided nation using a flawed strategy did not prevail over them any more than did the French or the Japanese.

88. **(D)** Nothing in the cartoon specifically addresses Nixon, his policy of Vietnamization, nor any failing in the Vietnamese people. Answers (A), (B), and (C) were common arguments against the Vietnam War, but the cartoon's specific message evokes the image of American soldiers wading through swamps holding their M-16 rifles up to keep them dry. This image and the terrain surrounding Uncle Sam, indicates the reality expressed in answer (D). Congress increased the age of men eligible for the draft, but no man even close to the age of the soldier portrayed in the cartoon was ever conscripted.

89. **(D)** All of the other answers evoke actual results, but they are about what people do because of the invention of the transistor. Answer (D) describes what transistors actually did to make all the other results possible.

90. **(B)** Although all of the answers allude to problems associated with what George W. Bush called the War on Terror, only answer (B) is entirely true. Answer (C) is what Qaddafi wanted the world to believe, and answers (D) and (E) are true of Turkey or Pakistan instead of Libya.

ANSWER SHEET
Practice Test 2

1. Ⓐ Ⓑ Ⓒ Ⓓ Ⓔ
2. Ⓐ Ⓑ Ⓒ Ⓓ Ⓔ
3. Ⓐ Ⓑ Ⓒ Ⓓ Ⓔ
4. Ⓐ Ⓑ Ⓒ Ⓓ Ⓔ
5. Ⓐ Ⓑ Ⓒ Ⓓ Ⓔ
6. Ⓐ Ⓑ Ⓒ Ⓓ Ⓔ
7. Ⓐ Ⓑ Ⓒ Ⓓ Ⓔ
8. Ⓐ Ⓑ Ⓒ Ⓓ Ⓔ
9. Ⓐ Ⓑ Ⓒ Ⓓ Ⓔ
10. Ⓐ Ⓑ Ⓒ Ⓓ Ⓔ
11. Ⓐ Ⓑ Ⓒ Ⓓ Ⓔ
12. Ⓐ Ⓑ Ⓒ Ⓓ Ⓔ
13. Ⓐ Ⓑ Ⓒ Ⓓ Ⓔ
14. Ⓐ Ⓑ Ⓒ Ⓓ Ⓔ
15. Ⓐ Ⓑ Ⓒ Ⓓ Ⓔ
16. Ⓐ Ⓑ Ⓒ Ⓓ Ⓔ
17. Ⓐ Ⓑ Ⓒ Ⓓ Ⓔ
18. Ⓐ Ⓑ Ⓒ Ⓓ Ⓔ
19. Ⓐ Ⓑ Ⓒ Ⓓ Ⓔ
20. Ⓐ Ⓑ Ⓒ Ⓓ Ⓔ
21. Ⓐ Ⓑ Ⓒ Ⓓ Ⓔ
22. Ⓐ Ⓑ Ⓒ Ⓓ Ⓔ
23. Ⓐ Ⓑ Ⓒ Ⓓ Ⓔ
24. Ⓐ Ⓑ Ⓒ Ⓓ Ⓔ
25. Ⓐ Ⓑ Ⓒ Ⓓ Ⓔ
26. Ⓐ Ⓑ Ⓒ Ⓓ Ⓔ
27. Ⓐ Ⓑ Ⓒ Ⓓ Ⓔ
28. Ⓐ Ⓑ Ⓒ Ⓓ Ⓔ
29. Ⓐ Ⓑ Ⓒ Ⓓ Ⓔ
30. Ⓐ Ⓑ Ⓒ Ⓓ Ⓔ

31. Ⓐ Ⓑ Ⓒ Ⓓ Ⓔ
32. Ⓐ Ⓑ Ⓒ Ⓓ Ⓔ
33. Ⓐ Ⓑ Ⓒ Ⓓ Ⓔ
34. Ⓐ Ⓑ Ⓒ Ⓓ Ⓔ
35. Ⓐ Ⓑ Ⓒ Ⓓ Ⓔ
36. Ⓐ Ⓑ Ⓒ Ⓓ Ⓔ
37. Ⓐ Ⓑ Ⓒ Ⓓ Ⓔ
38. Ⓐ Ⓑ Ⓒ Ⓓ Ⓔ
39. Ⓐ Ⓑ Ⓒ Ⓓ Ⓔ
40. Ⓐ Ⓑ Ⓒ Ⓓ Ⓔ
41. Ⓐ Ⓑ Ⓒ Ⓓ Ⓔ
42. Ⓐ Ⓑ Ⓒ Ⓓ Ⓔ
43. Ⓐ Ⓑ Ⓒ Ⓓ Ⓔ
44. Ⓐ Ⓑ Ⓒ Ⓓ Ⓔ
45. Ⓐ Ⓑ Ⓒ Ⓓ Ⓔ
46. Ⓐ Ⓑ Ⓒ Ⓓ Ⓔ
47. Ⓐ Ⓑ Ⓒ Ⓓ Ⓔ
48. Ⓐ Ⓑ Ⓒ Ⓓ Ⓔ
49. Ⓐ Ⓑ Ⓒ Ⓓ Ⓔ
50. Ⓐ Ⓑ Ⓒ Ⓓ Ⓔ
51. Ⓐ Ⓑ Ⓒ Ⓓ Ⓔ
52. Ⓐ Ⓑ Ⓒ Ⓓ Ⓔ
53. Ⓐ Ⓑ Ⓒ Ⓓ Ⓔ
54. Ⓐ Ⓑ Ⓒ Ⓓ Ⓔ
55. Ⓐ Ⓑ Ⓒ Ⓓ Ⓔ
56. Ⓐ Ⓑ Ⓒ Ⓓ Ⓔ
57. Ⓐ Ⓑ Ⓒ Ⓓ Ⓔ
58. Ⓐ Ⓑ Ⓒ Ⓓ Ⓔ
59. Ⓐ Ⓑ Ⓒ Ⓓ Ⓔ
60. Ⓐ Ⓑ Ⓒ Ⓓ Ⓔ

61. Ⓐ Ⓑ Ⓒ Ⓓ Ⓔ
62. Ⓐ Ⓑ Ⓒ Ⓓ Ⓔ
63. Ⓐ Ⓑ Ⓒ Ⓓ Ⓔ
64. Ⓐ Ⓑ Ⓒ Ⓓ Ⓔ
65. Ⓐ Ⓑ Ⓒ Ⓓ Ⓔ
66. Ⓐ Ⓑ Ⓒ Ⓓ Ⓔ
67. Ⓐ Ⓑ Ⓒ Ⓓ Ⓔ
68. Ⓐ Ⓑ Ⓒ Ⓓ Ⓔ
69. Ⓐ Ⓑ Ⓒ Ⓓ Ⓔ
70. Ⓐ Ⓑ Ⓒ Ⓓ Ⓔ
71. Ⓐ Ⓑ Ⓒ Ⓓ Ⓔ
72. Ⓐ Ⓑ Ⓒ Ⓓ Ⓔ
73. Ⓐ Ⓑ Ⓒ Ⓓ Ⓔ
74. Ⓐ Ⓑ Ⓒ Ⓓ Ⓔ
75. Ⓐ Ⓑ Ⓒ Ⓓ Ⓔ
76. Ⓐ Ⓑ Ⓒ Ⓓ Ⓔ
77. Ⓐ Ⓑ Ⓒ Ⓓ Ⓔ
78. Ⓐ Ⓑ Ⓒ Ⓓ Ⓔ
79. Ⓐ Ⓑ Ⓒ Ⓓ Ⓔ
80. Ⓐ Ⓑ Ⓒ Ⓓ Ⓔ
81. Ⓐ Ⓑ Ⓒ Ⓓ Ⓔ
82. Ⓐ Ⓑ Ⓒ Ⓓ Ⓔ
83. Ⓐ Ⓑ Ⓒ Ⓓ Ⓔ
84. Ⓐ Ⓑ Ⓒ Ⓓ Ⓔ
85. Ⓐ Ⓑ Ⓒ Ⓓ Ⓔ
86. Ⓐ Ⓑ Ⓒ Ⓓ Ⓔ
87. Ⓐ Ⓑ Ⓒ Ⓓ Ⓔ
88. Ⓐ Ⓑ Ⓒ Ⓓ Ⓔ
89. Ⓐ Ⓑ Ⓒ Ⓓ Ⓔ
90. Ⓐ Ⓑ Ⓒ Ⓓ Ⓔ

Practice Test 2

TIME—60 MINUTES

> **Directions:** Each of the questions or incomplete statements below is followed by five suggested answers or completions. Select the one that is best in each case, and then fill in the corresponding circle on the answer sheet. You can cut the answer sheet along the dotted line to make recording your answers easier. Remember to give yourself only sixty minutes to complete this test in order to prepare for the pace of the real SAT Subject Test in U.S. History.

1. The first goal for conquistadors after conquering American Indian tribes in the New World was to

   (A) distribute land evenly among their soldiers to set up feudalism.
   (B) establish missions to convert surviving American Indians to Roman Catholicism.
   (C) found universities so their descendants could rise in the Spanish aristocracy.
   (D) send gold and silver to the King of Spain to secure title to their lands.
   (E) secure enough American Indian women to begin populating a colony.

2. How did John Calvin contribute to the shaping of American society?

   (A) He wrote a creed for the Anglican Church to help secure unity in the Virginia colony.
   (B) He convinced the French king to make peace between the English and French colonies.
   (C) He shaped the worldview of Puritans and Scots-Irish Presbyterianism in English colonies.
   (D) He published the first English Bible that led to the English Reformation and colonization.
   (E) He governed Geneva, Switzerland, in ways that formed precedents for colonial America.

3. James Oglethorpe founded the colony of Georgia for all of the following reasons **EXCEPT**

(A) as a humanitarian experimental society for freed African slaves.

(B) as a penal colony for Englishmen trapped in debtor prisons.

(C) as an attempt to produce an English silk industry.

(D) as a buffer between the English colonies and the Spanish colony in Florida.

(E) as a staging area for military maneuvers against the Spanish.

4. How did American diplomats respond to French demands for tribute money during the XYZ Affair in 1798?

(A) They paid the bribe in order to gain access to Talleyrand, the French foreign minister.

(B) They sent notice to President Adams and stayed in France awaiting his instructions.

(C) They rebuffed their captors from prison until being released in a prisoner exchange.

(D) They rejected the demands so forcefully that two of them were deported.

(E) They told President Adams that he should immediately have Congress declare war.

5. Why did the United States make the Gadsden Purchase in 1853 after having already acquired the huge Mexican Cession?

(A) American prospectors crossed the border with Mexico and discovered gold there.

(B) The territory contained the best route for a southern transcontinental railroad.

(C) The government needed access to the area to capture Geronimo who used it to stage raids.

(D) Southerners saw it as the last chance to expand the Cotton Kingdom with a new state.

(E) The Mormons proved it was the best route to get to California by wagon train.

6. What about the Knights of Labor caused Samuel Gompers to leave and form the American Federation of Labor?

(A) They damaged the reputation of the labor movement by calling too many strikes.

(B) They tolerated too many socialists and communists among their leaders.

(C) They staged demonstrations to destabilize society purposefully with violence.

(D) They compromised with management too much and thus failed to bring about change.

(E) They allowed both skilled and unskilled workers to join their ranks.

7. Which statement below best explains the "Wisconsin Idea" popularized by that state's governor, Robert La Follette?

(A) Each state should decide if it should have an agrarian or an industrialized economy.

(B) Social activists should focus on one reform rather than on multiple reforms simultaneously.

(C) Charismatic political leaders should rely on experts to provide rational policy steps.

(D) The federal government should print enough paper money to pay off the national debt.

(E) Northerners and southerners needed cultural exchanges to put aside latent animosity.

8. How did Alfred Thayer Mahan's book, *The Influence of Sea Power on History*, shape American foreign or domestic policy?

(A) The United States led an international crusade for world peace through arms reductions.

(B) The United States devoted more resources to building a navy that could keep up with other nations.

(C) Congress and several presidents sought to diminish dependency on foreign trade.

(D) State governments encouraged citizens to move inland away from dangerous hurricanes.

(E) Congress passed a law to limit the Chinese immigration described in the book.

9. The Tet Offensive in 1968 weakened support for the Vietnam War by

(A) discouraging the American people because they realized the war would be a long one.

(B) giving the impression that American military commanders were losing control of the war.

(C) exposing atrocities committed by Americans against those they were supposed to protect.

(D) making Americans realize President Nixon was not up to achieving peace as he promised.

(E) shocking the United States by causing the highest number of American casualties to that point.

10. What policy proposed by Ronald Reagan during the 1980 primary season did George H. W. Bush label "voodoo economics?"

(A) Significant tax cuts would provide incentives for businesses to cause prosperity to return.

(B) Using more deficit spending than President Carter did would fix the federal budget crisis.

(C) Hiring more government workers would make the majority support tax increases.

(D) Making all economic decisions on rational, rather than ethical, grounds would end waste.

(E) Raising the salaries of elected officials would attract better minds to help end the recession.

11. Which statement best describes the significance of the Mayflower Compact?

    (A) Its publication in English newspapers attracted more colonists to New England.

    (B) It set the precedent that applied English Common Law to colonial Americans.

    (C) Its religious rhetoric ensured the establishment of the Anglican Church in New England.

    (D) It was the first written attempt to establish a government for English-speaking people.

    (E) It was modeled after a document in Virginia and made written constitutions the norm.

12. Mercantilism alienated American colonists from their mother country because they believed the English government

    (A) was giving the colonies too little economic direction through salutary neglect.

    (B) had no right to pass laws like the Navigation Acts or the Molasses Act.

    (C) was pitting the colonies against one another in unfair competition.

    (D) was stifling the agricultural basis of their economy in favor of industry.

    (E) had worked against their own economy with an unfavorable balance of trade.

13. What role did the early nineteenth-century exploits of mountain men play in the settlement of the West?

    (A) They collected specimens of new game animals for Eastern universities and museums.

    (B) They intermarried with American Indians and made peace by blending the two cultures.

    (C) They provided security at critical locations by building fortified stockades for settlers.

    (D) They helped map the West as surveyors for the U.S. Geological Survey.

    (E) They searched for furs in wilderness territories and discovered major migration routes.

14. Why do historians refer to many presidential administrations from the Gilded Age as "custodial presidencies?"

    (A) These presidents cleaned up political corruption at the highest levels of government.

    (B) These presidents merely maintained their party's image and doled out patronage.

    (C) These presidents did not need to do too much because it was an era of high prosperity.

    (D) These presidents were mostly Republicans and cleaned up the South's legacy of racism.

    (E) These presidents worked not for their own fame but for the good of the American people.

15. What assurances did Germany give in the Arabic Pledge and the Sussex Pledge prior to American involvement in World War I?

(A) They were only protecting themselves and not out to launch an empire like Napoleon.

(B) They would not use airplane technology from the United States to harm American citizens.

(C) They would limit the use of submarines against peaceful vessels in international waters.

(D) Their blockade would stop only military vessels, not merchant or passenger vessels.

(E) If the United States entered the war, no German-Americans would serve in the German army.

16. To what new goal did the legacy of the New Deal commit the United States government in managing the American economy?

(A) All laws fundamentally altering the nation's economic system must be bipartisan.

(B) Every student qualified for higher education will have free access to college.

(C) The prices and wages set by businesses should meet government standards.

(D) Every able-bodied person in the American population would have full employment.

(E) Deficit spending would only be used in the future in the case of a large war.

17. What strategy used during the Vietnam War prolonged the war and caused the United States to "fail to achieve its objectives?"

(A) Counting a battle a success if the United States killed four of the enemy for every U. S. soldier lost

(B) Accompanying U.S. missions with United Nations soldiers not authorized to fire weapons

(C) Dropping bombs on North Vietnam because it supplied the Vietcong in South Vietnam

(D) Preventing U.S. military forces from attacking unless they were attacked first

(E) Relying on inherently unstable helicopters in search-and-destroy missions

18. What impact did the launch of the Soviet satellite, *Sputnik I*, have on the Cold War policy of the United States?

(A) The United States resolved to fight only limited wars in the face of Soviet technological superiority.

(B) The United States used its position on the United Nations Security Council to veto space initiatives.

(C) The United States kept all of its atomic weapons delivery systems perpetually on high alert.

(D) The United States resolved to extend its containment policy to Africa, Asia, and Latin America.

(E) The United States increased funding for education in math, science, and foreign languages.

19. Which act of terrorism during the Reagan administration was the first significant attack against American interests by Islamists?

(A) The attack on the USS *Cole*, an American destroyer docked in Yemen
(B) The attack against the Marine Corps barracks in Beirut, Lebanon
(C) The bombing of a disco in Germany frequented by U.S. military personnel
(D) The first attack against the World Trade Center using a car bomb
(E) The destruction of the U.S. embassies in Kenya and Tanzania

20. Five-time presidential candidate Ralph Nader first gained national attention as an activist for

(A) the purity of America's water supply in an era of rampant industrial spills.
(B) individuals who expose the secrets of corporations when they are threatening the public.
(C) stopping the use of nuclear power and of nuclear weapons.
(D) consumer protection by exposing safety problems in the automobile industry.
(E) federal regulations to curtail the profit-seeking of passenger airlines.

21. How did Samuel Slater change the American economy?

(A) By using the concept of interchangeable parts to form the basis of mass production
(B) By creating the first commercially successful passenger steamboat service
(C) By developing the first successful textile mill as the basis of industrialization
(D) By inventing barbed wire that ended long drives of cattle and protected private property
(E) By developing the first celluloid film launching the era of amateur photography

22. In which of the following Supreme Court decisions did John Marshall establish the precedent of judicial review?

(A) *McCulloch* v. *Maryland*
(B) *Gibbons* v. *Ogden*
(C) *Fletcher* v. *Peck*
(D) *Marbury* v. *Madison*
(E) *Dartmouth College* v. *Woodward*

23. Where did most Irish immigrants coming to the United States after the Potato Famine reside and why?

(A) In the Midwest because they craved nothing more than owning their own farms
(B) In Appalachia, because of their cultural connections with the Scots-Irish
(C) In western cities, to put as much distance as possible between them and the British
(D) In the South, because plantations needed laborers to replace the slaves freed by war
(E) In eastern cities, because they were too poor to pursue anything except factory jobs

24. During the Nullification Crisis of the 1820s and 1830s, the Force Bill granted Andrew Jackson the power to

(A) invade a state if the state seceded from the Union.
(B) arrest the leaders of the state of South Carolina who were leading a rebellion.
(C) use the military to enforce the collection of tariffs within a state.
(D) compel southern congressmen to attend an emergency session of Congress.
(E) stop abolitionists from sending their literature to the South in the U.S. mail.

25. How did President Grover Cleveland respond to the Pullman Strike in 1894?

(A) He used the U.S. military to break the strike in order to free up the U.S. mail.
(B) He invited leaders from the Union and the company to the White House for talks.
(C) He threatened the owners he would take over the railroad in order to restart rail traffic.
(D) He ordered his attorney general to arrest the strike organizers on racketeering charges.
(E) He referred the matter to the Supreme Court, which issued an injunction to stop the strike.

26. All of the following were causes of the Great War (World War I) **EXCEPT**

(A) the assassination of the heir to the thrones of Austria-Hungary by a Serb.
(B) the sinking of the HMS *Lusitania*, a passenger ship containing American citizens.
(C) the militaristic foreign policies of all of the major European powers.
(D) the competition among the empires of the United Kingdom, France, and Germany.
(E) the unintended consequences of Bismarck's European alliance system.

27. What was the main reason the Scopes Monkey Trial attracted such national attention?

(A) The sarcastic journalism of H. L. Mencken who covered the trial for his magazine
(B) The prosecutor was frequent presidential candidate William Jennings Bryan
(C) The defense attorney was agnostic in an era of uniformity of religious belief
(D) John T. Scopes taught the principles of communism as well as the theory of evolution
(E) The Supreme Court had already made known it would hear the case if it was appealed

28. What Eisenhower administration initiative amounted to a massive public works project as large as any of the Roosevelt administration's New Deal measures?

(A) The instituting of the National Aeronautics and Space Administration
(B) The formation of the Southeast Asia Treaty Organization
(C) The passage of the National Defense Education Act
(D) The passage of the National Interstate and Defense Highways Act
(E) The instituting of the Department of Health, Education, and Welfare

29. "No, I'm not an American. I'm one of the 22 million black people who are the victims of Americanism. One of the 22 million black people who are the victims of democracy, nothing but disguised hypocrisy . . . . The 22 million victims are waking up."

Which civil rights leader most likely said these words in 1964?

(A) Martin Luther King Jr.
(B) John Lewis
(C) Malcolm X
(D) Medgar Evers
(E) Jesse Jackson

30. What change contributed the most to the large migration of the American population to the Sun Belt beginning in the 1960s?

(A) High-speed rail services allowed commuters to live in suburbs and work in southern cities.
(B) Desegregation of schools encouraged African Americans to return to the South.
(C) The Baby Boom generation desired to escape the harsh winters of the North as they aged.
(D) Urban dwellers sought refuge from the constant protests of several activist movements.
(E) Air conditioning and more affordable housing made life there more bearable.

31. Which statement best explains the role of Jesuit missionaries in establishing the culture of Spain's empire in the New World?

(A) They were an order of militant monks who fought alongside the conquistadors.
(B) As the most educated citizens, they raised the standards of church and civic institutions.
(C) They infused Roman Catholicism with insights from American Indian religions.
(D) They improved nutrition by creating new ways to raise squash, beans, and corn.
(E) As avid hunters of heretics, they preserved uniformity of belief and thus societal unity.

32. How was the economy of England's colonies in the North different from the economy of those colonies in the South?

(A) The North did not produce enough food, whereas the South exported food.
(B) The North produced cash crops, whereas the South focused on subsistence-level farming.
(C) The North could not produce cash crops, as the South could, so it turned to shipping.
(D) The North required continual financial support, whereas the South became self-sustaining.
(E) The North avoided urbanization and had to rely on cities in the South for urban services.

33. Which statement below best explains the impact of Thomas Paine's *Common Sense* on his fellow Americans during the early American Revolution?

    (A) The work had little success but was the background for the more successful *The Crisis*.

    (B) Americans rejected Paine as the mouthpiece of the Continental Congress and exiled him.

    (C) Only the most radical patriots approved of the work since it amounted to treason.

    (D) The work sold some copies, but its scholarly tone discouraged a wider audience.

    (E) The work became a turning point by convincing many bystanders to support independence.

34. What two main warnings did George Washington leave his fellow Americans in his Farewell Address?

    (A) The nation would suffer sectionalism, and foreign crises would endanger their survival.

    (B) Merchants and bankers would become a threat, and the Supreme Court would make "laws."

    (C) Slavery would one day divide the nation, and the conflict would lead to a civil war.

    (D) American Indians would mount a large attack, and the United States would need European help.

    (E) The North would eventually threaten southern rights, and the South would secede.

35. The constituents of Massachusetts Senator Daniel Webster vilified him during the debates surrounding the Compromise of 1850 because he

    (A) cooperated with slaveholders like John C. Calhoun and Henry Clay.

    (B) failed to do enough to protect their commercial interests.

    (C) sought too much attention for himself using such eloquence in his speeches.

    (D) stooped to compromise at all on slavery because they were abolitionists.

    (E) alienated his fellow Senators too much and brought the country to the brink of civil war.

36. Why did the city of Chicago develop into a major component of the late nineteenth-century American economy?

    (A) The first skyscraper constructed there became the model for all other major cities.

    (B) Railroads that converged there made it a transportation hub and a center of meat processing.

    (C) Andrew Carnegie and John D. Rockefeller found sources there for their raw materials.

    (D) Financial geniuses rebelled against Wall Street in New York City and started over there.

    (E) Millions of immigrants moved there to leave the dangers of living in eastern cities.

37. How did the design of the Brooklyn Bridge revolutionize the manufacture of steel bridges?

(A) The arches supporting the roadway were the first capable of spanning such wide spaces.

(B) Massive cranes set large, pre-assembled pieces in place that were then riveted together.

(C) Cables made of braided steel wire held up the road surface to give flexibility and strength.

(D) The foundations supporting the bridge's towers sat directly on the bed of the East River.

(E) The bridge contained a roadway, a walkway, and a railroad together for the first time.

38. The Open Door Policy initiated by Secretary of State John Hay in 1899 was a significant turning point because it revealed that the United States was

(A) a superpower able to force its will on other countries.

(B) finally ready to develop interests across the Pacific Ocean all the way to East Asia.

(C) the only disinterested power in Asia and thus a potential mediator of the conflicts of others.

(D) ready to make exclusive trade deals with China.

(E) about to take over territory on the Asian mainland to begin an empire.

39. High-level investors practiced "pumping and dumping" on the Stock Market during the 1920s by

(A) purchasing and selling stocks in day trades to produce an artificial level of market activity.

(B) selling stock among themselves to create demand and then selling out at huge profits.

(C) buying controlling shares in corporations and then merging companies into trusts.

(D) buying whole companies and selling them when their management increased the value.

(E) buying shares in many companies and then bundling them together as mutual funds.

40. The War Powers Act placed restrictions on the executive branch after the Vietnam War by making the president unable to

(A) perform surveillance on foreign countries without the prior approval of a Senate committee.

(B) use the military in countries neighboring those countries with whom the United States was at war.

(C) shape foreign policy independently with his National Security Council during times of war.

(D) conduct "shuttle diplomacy" by sending secret envoys to negotiate peace terms.

(E) send the American military into action for more than sixty days without Senate approval.

41. "There were two kinds of Spaniards, one very cruel and pitiless, whose goal was to squeeze the last drop of Indian blood in order to get rich, and one less cruel, who must have felt sorry for the Indians; but in each case they placed their own interests above the health and salvation of those poor people."

Which of the following ideas or practices associated with the Spanish Empire employed this type of rhetoric?

(A) The Columbian Exchange
(B) The Spanish Inquisition
(C) The Black Legend
(D) The annual report of viceroys
(E) The mission system

42. The Toleration Act of 1649 in colonial Maryland settled disputes between

(A) Roman Catholics and Protestants.
(B) American Indians and English colonists on the frontier.
(C) English colonists and Dutch colonists from New Amsterdam.
(D) Royal colonial governors and colonial legislatures.
(E) Colonies from the North and colonies from the South.

43. With what country or region and over what issue did Pinckney's Treaty (1796) attempt a resolution?

(A) Canada—the Maine boundary
(B) The Old Northwest—American Indian land claims in the wake of border violence
(C) Spain—access to the Mississippi River and the right of deposit in New Orleans
(D) Great Britain—debts Americans had incurred before the American Revolution
(E) France—ships captured on the high seas during the Quasi-War

44. Which political scandal in American history was associated with the Grant administration?

(A) The Teapot Dome Scandal
(B) The Burr Conspiracy
(C) The Ballinger-Pinchot Affair
(D) The Crédit-Mobilier Scandal
(E) The Indian Bureau Embezzlement Scandal

45. President Woodrow Wilson backed the creation of the Federal Reserve System because he wanted

(A) a better model of hands-on control over the economy than a National Bank could provide.

(B) to prove that the president should control the economy rather than the Congress.

(C) to better control the value of the currency by distributing Federal Reserve Banks evenly.

(D) to remove responsibility from the presidency for responding to downturns in the economy.

(E) to decentralize the banking industry while retaining a minimum level of federal oversight.

46. The United States intervened in Cuba after an insurrection there in 1898 because

(A) the United States had strongly desired to take over Cuba since before the Ostend Manifesto.

(B) Spanish forces had already attacked the U.S. naval base in the Philippine Islands.

(C) Admiral Alfred Thayer Mahan said control of Cuba would protect a future canal.

(D) Theodore Roosevelt wanted to become a war hero so he could be president one day.

(E) Cuban-Americans and the press urged support of a republic starting nearby.

47. Which principles formed the basis of Woodrow Wilson's Fourteen Points Address?

(A) Imperialism and militarism

(B) Nationalism and international law

(C) Self-determination and collective security

(D) Arbitration and reciprocal military inspections

(E) Globalism and humanitarian aid

48. Which departments in the executive branch did the National Security Act of 1947 create besides the National Security Council, the Central Intelligence Agency, and the Joint Chiefs of Staff?

(A) The Department of Energy and the Department of Defense

(B) The Department of Defense and the Department of the Air Force

(C) The Department of Veterans Affairs and the Department of the United Nations

(D) The Department of Education and the Department of Transportation

(E) The Department of Federal Security and the Department of International Trade

49. Which new reform did President Lyndon Johnson's Great Society domestic agenda champion?

    (A) Reaching out to developing nations through the Peace Corps
    (B) Caring for the old and the poor through the Social Security system
    (C) Removing all legal barriers that kept African Americans from voting
    (D) Improving education in math, science, and foreign languages to improve national security
    (E) Increasing the ability of labor unions to collectively bargain for better working conditions

50. The Supreme Court decision in *Miranda* v. *Arizona* in 1966 altered domestic law enforcement practices by banning

    (A) the practice of profiling based on race, ethnicity, sex, or age.
    (B) the interrogation of illegal immigrants without a qualified translator present.
    (C) the use during prosecution of statements made by suspects without an attorney present.
    (D) the sharing of information among the FBI, the CIA, and state or local law enforcement.
    (E) the prosecution of suspects without a defense attorney present during criminal proceedings.

51. "That loans in times of public danger, especially from foreign war, are found an indispensable resource . . . . And that in a country, which, like this, is possessed of little active wealth, or . . . little monied capital, the necessity for that resource, must, in such emergencies, be proportionally urgent."

    For which aspect of his financial program is Alexander Hamilton most likely arguing in this quotation?

    (A) The constitutionality of the Bank of the United States
    (B) The national debt as an impetus toward nationalism
    (C) The wisdom of funding bonds issued by the government at par
    (D) The need for customs duties and excise taxes to pay the national debt
    (E) The need for a Treasury Department in the new American government

52. Sacagawea contributed to the success of the Lewis and Clark Expedition mainly by

    (A) serving as a guide and translator through Shoshone tribal lands.
    (B) carrying her child on the journey which assured American Indian tribes of peaceful intent.
    (C) saving all but one member of the expedition through her knowledge of herbal remedies.
    (D) attracting her husband to the expedition who taught others necessary survival skills.
    (E) entertaining expedition members with her skills as a storyteller and dancer.

53. The main goal of the delegation sent by the Hartford Convention to the national capital during the War of 1812 was to

   (A) reform the federal government's methods of declaring war and of raising an army.
   (B) convince the federal government to adopt a new strategy to win the war.
   (C) open up negotiations with the British to end the war so trade could resume.
   (D) warn the government that New England would secede if the war continued.
   (E) initiate impeachment proceedings against President Madison who started the war.

54. Henry Clay was able to earn the title, the Great Compromiser, because he

   (A) was educated in the North but lived in the South and, thus, understood both sides.
   (B) was respected for his leadership of the War Hawks that brought on the War of 1812.
   (C) supported the Bank of the United States even though he was from the Deep South.
   (D) was a Whig but also a slave owner, so both sides of the debate in the Senate listened to him.
   (E) was respected abroad for his support as Secretary of State for Latin American revolutions.

55. President James K. Polk sent John Slidell on a secret mission to Mexico to

   (A) identify elements of Mexican society willing to revolt from Santa Anna.
   (B) negotiate the purchase of territory from Mexico that would prevent the outbreak of war.
   (C) convince the Mexican government to pay back over $3 million in defaulted loans.
   (D) find the best location for Zachary Taylor to bring his army to provoke a shooting war.
   (E) negotiate the release of American citizens arrested in Mexico on the eve of war.

56. The United States responded to the Boxer Rebellion in China by

   (A) rejecting the opium trade and insisting on the safety of Christian missionaries.
   (B) sending a military expedition to cooperate with other nations to end the fighting.
   (C) chastising other Open Door Nations for their interference in China's domestic affairs.
   (D) closing off access to selected port cities to maintain its sphere of influence.
   (E) occupying the island of Formosa militarily and letting other nations handle China.

57. Henry Ford designed the Model T automobile because he wanted to

    (A) attract a wide range of customers by making a car in many colors and configurations.
    (B) alter American society by increasing mobility through the mass production of cars.
    (C) increase the luxury of his base model car to make his company more profitable.
    (D) give the United States an economic advantage over others by producing mechanically superior cars.
    (E) encourage Americans to drive regularly to increase business for his road construction firm.

58. "... the United States may have a rapidly aging population ... [and] it may have difficulty keeping its position as a major power. Russia may have twice as many men of military age, and twice as many women to propagate the next generation. Other nations encourage reproduction ... but our country ... continues to give every advantage and preferment to the unmarried and the childless."

    In what decade of American history was the quotation above most likely written?

    (A) The 1920s
    (B) The 1930s
    (C) The 1940s
    (D) The 1950s
    (E) The 1960s

59. President Richard Nixon's political skills, values, and accomplishments can best be summarized by saying that he

    (A) was a master of domestic policy but had severe shortcomings in foreign policy.
    (B) was paranoid and alienated the nation in his first term so that he barely won reelection.
    (C) focused excessively on polling data and took positions based mostly on their popularity.
    (D) focused on restoring order in the South by using federal power to impose racial harmony.
    (E) won a landslide victory in 1972 by blending political positions but then self-destructed.

60. "They let each of us deliver a short message to our families in front of the TV cameras. I said hello to my wife and told her that I was still alive. I also let her know that I had not received any mail. The whole time I was speaking, I kept glowering at the militants lined up along the back wall."

Which event is the speaker in the quotation above most likely describing?

(A) The kidnapping of the grandchildren of William Randolph Hearst
(B) The takeover of the U.S. Embassy in Iran
(C) The capture of the Marine Corps barracks in Beirut, Lebanon
(D) The capture of American medical students in Grenada
(E) The kidnapping of American journalists by al-Qaeda in Pakistan

61. The Second Continental Congress listed all of the following grievances against King George III in the Declaration of Independence **EXCEPT**

(A) "He has refused his Assent to Laws, the most wholesome and necessary for the public good."
(B) "He has kept among us, in times of peace, Standing Armies without the consent of our legislatures."
(C) "For cutting off our Trade with all parts of the world."
(D) "For condemning the souls of men to the governance of his church, alone, for their dissent according to their own consciences."
(E) "He has plundered our seas, ravaged our Coasts, burnt our towns, and destroyed the Lives of our people."

62. All of the following geographical features were boundaries of the United States as granted under the Treaty of Paris in 1783 **EXCEPT**

(A) the shores of the Great Lakes and the St. Lawrence River.
(B) the Mississippi River.
(C) the Atlantic Ocean.
(D) the border with Spanish Florida.
(E) the midway point on Lakes Superior, Huron, Erie, and Ontario.

63. Farmers in western Pennsylvania took up arms against the United States in the 1794 Whiskey Rebellion because

(A) Congress banned the manufacture, sale, and consumption of whiskey.
(B) George Washington sent a standing army to patrol the frontier and to enforce liquor laws.
(C) they believed the federal government was ruining their livelihood through taxation.
(D) the federal government ignored American Indian attacks prompted by access to liquor.
(E) Congress refused to establish tariffs to give American distillers a fair market.

64. John Jacob Astor became one of the first rags-to-riches stories in American history because he

   (A) memorized the plans to a textile mill in England, and then he built the first one in the United States.
   (B) established the Waldorf-Astoria Hotel in New York City and then a chain of luxury hotels.
   (C) organized the first shipments of barrels of petroleum on flooded creeks in Pennsylvania.
   (D) built general stores that outfitted miners for work in the gold fields in California.
   (E) scheduled gathering times for mountain men to market their furs to the East and to Europe.

65. What did the Adams-Onis Treaty, negotiated by Secretary of State John Quincy Adams, accomplish in 1819?

   (A) It made the Mississippi and Missouri rivers the borders with Spain in the West.
   (B) It allied the United States and Spain against the threat of war with France and the United Kingdom.
   (C) It allied the United States and Spain against the Barbary Pirates in the Mediterranean Sea.
   (D) It made Spain sell Florida to the United States and clarified the borders of the Louisiana Purchase.
   (E) It gave land in Texas and California to the United States in return for help with revolts in Mexico.

66. Theodore Roosevelt's New Nationalism presidential campaign platform for the Election of 1912 differed from Woodrow Wilson's New Freedom in that

   (A) Theodore Roosevelt distrusted the idea of states' rights as dangerous, whereas Wilson supported it.
   (B) Theodore Roosevelt wanted to expand Progressivism, whereas Wilson wanted to limit government power.
   (C) Theodore Roosevelt said there were good trusts and bad trusts, whereas Wilson said all trusts were bad.
   (D) Theodore Roosevelt wanted to push for civil rights for African Americans, whereas Wilson did not.
   (E) Theodore Roosevelt wanted to isolate the United States from world affairs, whereas Wilson wanted to reach out.

Courtesy of the Library of Congress

67. Thomas Nast portrayed the Grant administration in the cartoon above in a negative light by suggesting that, during the Gilded Age, President Grant

   (A) buried his head like an ostrich to avoid dealing with the troubles created by his ineptitude.
   (B) was being swallowed up by the sheer number of scandals erupting during his presidency.
   (C) was corrupt and had lied when he said he would get to the bottom of the many scandals.
   (D) was surprised by the duplicity of his staff but did seek to prosecute every last one of them.
   (E) should resign from the presidency because there was no end to corruption otherwise.

68. The "Noble Experiment" of prohibition, begun by the Eighteenth Amendment and enforced by the Volstead Act, resulted in

   (A) the spread of "speakeasies," secret bars that actually increased alcohol consumption.
   (B) increasing numbers of young, college-educated women "turning to the bottle."
   (C) the rise of the "Flapper" culture but a considerable drop in alcohol consumption.
   (D) the ruination of thousands of grain farmers who entered the Great Depression early.
   (E) a backlash in the form of a push to make amending the Constitution more difficult.

69. Herbert Hoover responded to the Great Depression by

    (A) refusing to use the federal government's resources to provide for the welfare of the people.

    (B) building on outdated ideas that were inadequate to meet the needs of the present crisis.

    (C) displaying an inability, as a millionaire, to sympathize with the hungry and the jobless.

    (D) resisting taking action at first, but then creating a bureau to help the banking industry.

    (E) providing government funds for private organizations to advance charitable activities.

70. The invention of RADAR was critical to the success of the Allied Powers in World War II because it allowed

    (A) Allied bombers to avoid anti-aircraft fire by attacking German cities at night.

    (B) the Allied defenders of the United Kingdom to know where German bombers were coming.

    (C) the Allies to target their missiles more accurately against enemy ships, planes, and cities.

    (D) the Allies to better protect convoys at sea by revealing where enemy submarines waited.

    (E) Allied tanks to travel in complete darkness to arrange for surprise attacks at night.

71. William Pitt created a turning point in the French and Indian War and boosted colonial Americans' morale by

    (A) promising colonists land in the West if they served as soldiers.

    (B) deciding that only colonists should be fighting this colonial war.

    (C) promising land in the Ohio River Valley to any colony that would help finance the war.

    (D) giving exclusive contracts to American companies to supply the British Army.

    (E) promoting officers to the highest ranks based on merit, including George Washington.

72. "... that alien-friends are under the jurisdiction and protection of the laws of the state wherein they are; that no power over them has been delegated to the United States, nor prohibited to the individual states distinct from their power over citizens ...."

From which late eighteenth-century document is the quotation above most likely taken?

    (A) The Land Ordinances of 1785 and 1787

    (B) The Northwest Ordinances of 1787

    (C) The Federalist Papers of 1787 and 1788

    (D) The Alien and Sedition Acts of 1798

    (E) The Kentucky and Virginia Resolutions of 1798 and 1799

73. In what industry or economic activity did the 1824 landmark case regarding federal business regulations, *Gibbons* v. *Ogden,* originate?

(A) Interstate transportation
(B) Marketing of agricultural products
(C) Securing patents associated with the invention of the sewing machine
(D) Managing employees of textile mills
(E) Organizing immigrant Irish coal miners

74. What aspect of the construction of the Erie Canal set a precedent for many subsequent infrastructure improvement projects?

(A) The construction used steam power instead of animal power for the first time.
(B) The state government funded the construction as a means of boosting the economy.
(C) The construction was the first large federal expenditure for transportation.
(D) The construction used American engineers exclusively for the first time.
(E) The state sold bonds to private investors to pay for the construction.

75. Which two aspects of modern American society arose in direct connection to the construction of railroads in the nineteenth century?

(A) Steam power and the manufacture of iron bridges
(B) Business trusts and deficit spending
(C) Time zones and the amassing of capital in giant corporations
(D) The telegraph and the Bessemer process of making steel
(E) Labor unions and federal regulations about worker safety

76. All of the following were components of Henry Clay's American System for the design of a national economic plan **EXCEPT**

(A) the Second Bank of the United States.
(B) a high protective tariff.
(C) the extensive use of federal money to enhance infrastructure.
(D) the sale of western lands.
(E) a federal income tax to fund internal improvements.

77. American settlers in Texas sought independence from Mexico in 1836 because Santa Anna

(A) abolished slavery once Mexico freed itself from the Spanish Empire.
(B) committed atrocities in crushing rebellions in southern Mexico.
(C) banned further immigration by Americans and ended constitutional government.
(D) banned the sale of any Mexican land besides what was in the original Texas land grant.
(E) closed all Protestant churches and exiled all Protestant ministers from Mexico.

American Population Density, 1860

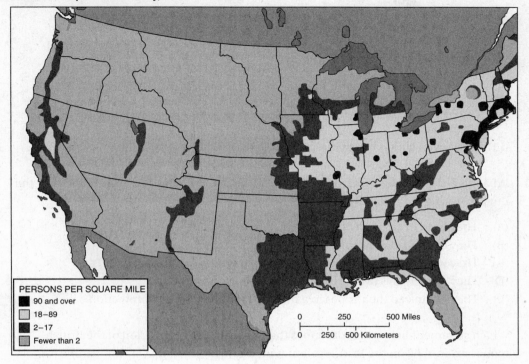

PERSONS PER SQUARE MILE
- 90 and over
- 18–89
- 2–17
- Fewer than 2

78. The above map of U.S. population density from 1860, along with societal trends of the time, supports which of the following statements?

(A) The harbor at San Francisco led to the settlement of California before much else out West.

(B) Cities became highly populated because of access to significant bodies of water.

(C) Most of the U.S. population remained east of the Appalachian Mountains.

(D) The Midwest allowed more immigrants to earn a living than could do so in the South.

(E) Many white settlers were already encroaching on territories reserved for American Indians.

79. The 1892 Homestead Strike at Andrew Carnegie's Homestead Steel Works was sparked by

(A) Carnegie's insistence that his plants would all be open shops.

(B) Carnegie's selling of the plant to Henry Clay Frick upon his retirement to Scotland.

(C) Carnegie's lowering wages because of a decline in the steel industry.

(D) a lockout by management and the lowering of wages to break a union at the plant.

(E) the discovery that Pinkerton detectives had infiltrated the union at the plant.

80. Which factor below best explains why the First Red Scare occurred in the 1920s?

(A) The new direct election of senators resulted in the election of a radical from Germany.

(B) Americans coupled growing anti-immigration sentiments with a fear of Bolshevism.

(C) Julius and Ethel Rosenberg were convicted as communist spies and executed.

(D) Seventy-five thousand Klansmen rallied in Washington, D. C. and inflamed the public.

(E) The Soviet Union began direct radio propaganda broadcasts into the country.

81. What made the Iroquois unique among the American Indian tribes encountered by the English during the colonial period?

(A) They lived in settlements that were permanent villages.

(B) They organized their tribes using matrilineal connections.

(C) They were willing to trade and to intermarry with the English colonists.

(D) They sent envoys over the ocean to visit the English court.

(E) They organized their tribes in a military confederation for protection.

82. Which statement below best describes the impact of the Restoration of the British monarchy in 1660 on the British colonies in America?

(A) The Restoration was far away and had virtually no impact on England's American colonies.

(B) The Restoration crushed the hopes of the earliest push toward independence.

(C) The Restoration ended salutary neglect and brought stringent controls for a time.

(D) The Restoration forced the Dutch to turn over New Amsterdam, which became New York.

(E) The Restoration led to strict enforcement of the existing Navigation Acts.

83. The goal of the Order of the Cincinnati in the wake of the Revolutionary War was to

(A) establish an aristocracy to rule rather than a republic.

(B) establish a republic just as the Roman war hero Cincinnatus had done for Rome.

(C) distribute land to every veteran of the war in payment for his sacrifices.

(D) establish a new country above the Ohio River between the United States and Canada.

(E) found an institution dedicated to keeping alive the patriot spirit that won the war.

84. The five promises made by James K. Polk that he subsequently kept after winning the Election of 1844 included all of the following **EXCEPT**

(A) settling the Oregon dispute with the United Kingdom.

(B) restoring the Bank of the United States that had been terminated by President Jackson.

(C) lowering the tariff.

(D) acquiring California from Mexico.

(E) leaving office after only one term as president.

85. Grover Cleveland gained enough support to win reelection as the only Democrat during the Gilded Age by

(A) supporting labor unions enough to cause workers to abandon their support for Republicans.

(B) supporting civil rights for African Americans and pushing for women to be able to vote.

(C) supporting a lower tariff and standing against state and federal political corruption.

(D) distributing a substantial federal surplus to supporters by giving them jobs and contracts.

(E) receiving financial backing of businessmen like Carnegie, Rockefeller, and J. P. Morgan.

86. The Dupuy de Lôme letter of 1897 and the Zimmermann Telegram of 1917 had much in common as causes of American wars because

(A) American intelligence operations intercepted them and leaked them to newspapers.

(B) they exposed the inner workings of the U.S. Department of State to the world.

(C) they encouraged isolationism and led to setbacks in national security.

(D) they were foreign communications that made American presidents look weak.

(E) they revealed extensive spy networks operating within the United States.

87. Which of the following incidents or policies undermined support for Franklin D. Roosevelt and for the New Deal the most?

(A) Widespread wastefulness discovered in New Deal public works projects

(B) Banning of African Americans who built the first TVA dam from living with other workers

(C) The Supreme Court's striking down policies of the Agricultural Adjustment Act and the National Rifle Association as unconstitutional

(D) Franklin D. Roosevelt's attempt to alter the Supreme Court to keep it from stopping New Deal progress

(E) John Steinbeck's exposure of a lack of help for farmers in *The Grapes of Wrath*.

Sending Forth a Dove—With Escort

88. Which World War II Allied conference is referenced in the political cartoon above?

(A) The Casablanca Conference
(B) The Atlantic Conference
(C) The Tehran Conference
(D) The Yalta Conference
(E) The Potsdam Conference

89. The Laffer Curve played a role in the Reagan administration by

(A) helping campaign directors illustrate the winning strategy for reelection in 1984.
(B) exposing the impact of stagflation and making Reagan commit to ending the recession.
(C) revealing how the Soviet Union could not keep up with the United States in military expenditures.
(D) graphing Reagan's plummeting approval rating and motivating him to rise above scandals.
(E) convincing Reagan's advisers that tax cuts were the only way to improve the economy.

90. Before the Supreme Court determined it was unconstitutional, the significance of the line-item veto for President Bill Clinton was that he could

(A) cooperate with NATO in the Balkans, despite the War Powers Act.

(B) enjoy, being from Arkansas, a power the former Confederacy gave its president.

(C) join with government reformers who wanted to end pork-barrel spending on pet projects.

(D) prove he was a New Democrat by cooperating with conservative Republicans.

(E) help the Democratic Party take control of the Congress in the mid-term elections in 1994.

ANSWER KEY
Practice Test 2

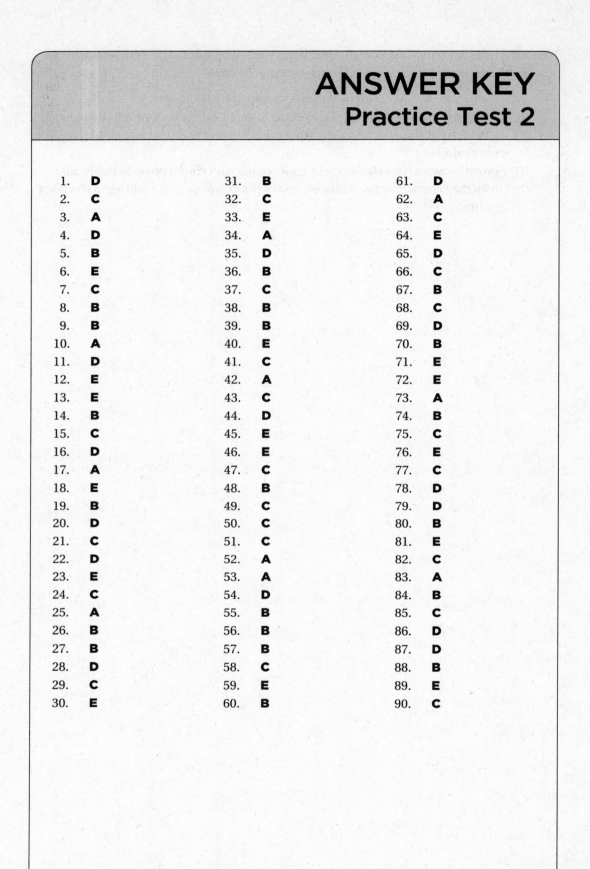

1.	**D**	31.	**B**	61.	**D**
2.	**C**	32.	**C**	62.	**A**
3.	**A**	33.	**E**	63.	**C**
4.	**D**	34.	**A**	64.	**E**
5.	**B**	35.	**D**	65.	**D**
6.	**E**	36.	**B**	66.	**C**
7.	**C**	37.	**C**	67.	**B**
8.	**B**	38.	**B**	68.	**C**
9.	**B**	39.	**B**	69.	**D**
10.	**A**	40.	**E**	70.	**B**
11.	**D**	41.	**C**	71.	**E**
12.	**E**	42.	**A**	72.	**E**
13.	**E**	43.	**C**	73.	**A**
14.	**B**	44.	**D**	74.	**B**
15.	**C**	45.	**E**	75.	**C**
16.	**D**	46.	**E**	76.	**E**
17.	**A**	47.	**C**	77.	**C**
18.	**E**	48.	**B**	78.	**D**
19.	**B**	49.	**C**	79.	**D**
20.	**D**	50.	**C**	80.	**B**
21.	**C**	51.	**C**	81.	**E**
22.	**D**	52.	**A**	82.	**C**
23.	**E**	53.	**A**	83.	**A**
24.	**C**	54.	**D**	84.	**B**
25.	**A**	55.	**B**	85.	**C**
26.	**B**	56.	**B**	86.	**D**
27.	**B**	57.	**B**	87.	**D**
28.	**D**	58.	**C**	88.	**B**
29.	**C**	59.	**E**	89.	**E**
30.	**E**	60.	**B**	90.	**C**

TEST ANALYSIS

STEP 1 **Count the number of correct answers.**

Enter the total here: _____

STEP 2 **Count the number of incorrect answers.**

Enter the total here: _____

STEP 3 **Multiply the number of incorrect answers by .250.**

Enter the product here: _____

STEP 4 **Subtract the results obtained in Step 3 from the total obtained in Step 1.**

Enter the total here: _____

STEP 5 **Round the number obtained in Step 4 to the nearest whole number.**

Raw Score = _____

Scaled Score Conversion Table

Raw Score	Scaled Score	Raw Score	Scaled Score	Raw Score	Scaled Score
90–79	800	46–45	600	8–7	400
78	790	44–43	590	6–5	390
77–76	780	42–41	580	4–3	380
75	770	40	570	2–1	370
74	760	39–38	560	0 – –1	360
73–72	750	37–36	550	–2 – –3	350
71	740	35–34	540	–4	340
70–69	730	33–32	530	–5 – –6	330
68	720	31–30	520	–7	320
67–66	710	29–28	510	–8 – –9	310
65–64	700	27	500	–10	300
63	690	26–25	490	–11 – –12	290
62–61	680	24–23	480	–13	280
60–59	670	22–21	470	–14 – –15	270
58–57	660	20–19	460	–16 – –17	260
56–55	650	18–17	450	–18 – –19	250
54–53	640	16–15	440	–20	240
52–51	630	14–13	430	–21 – –22	230
50–49	620	12–11	420		
48–47	610	10–9	410		

ANSWER EXPLANATIONS

1. **(D)** All of the answers reflect different aspects of life in the Spanish Empire, but the first priority of Pizarro and Cortés was to send as much as one-fifth of the precious metals acquired to the king of Spain. Without proper title to the lands conquered, all the rest of the operations would have been impossible or illegitimate. Conquistadors did not necessarily distribute land evenly as suggested in answer (A), nor were universities a high priority. Establishing missions to convert American Indians was a high priority, but they were more the task of the priests brought for that purpose. Answer (E) refers to intermarriage with American Indian women that occurred naturally, but the practice did require sanction of the Roman Catholic Church.

2. **(C)** The Puritans and Presbyterians took a more Calvinist position than did the creed of the Anglican Church, which John Calvin did not write. He did dedicate his *Institutes of the Christian Religion* to the French king, but the king was not a Protestant and not inclined to listen to Calvin regarding religious matters or war and peace. John Wycliffe first translated the Bible into English, although the Marian Exiles did produce the Geneva Bible while living in that Calvinist city. Geneva did set precedents for the American republic, but John Calvin never governed the city since he believed that was the duty of the civil magistrate, not church leaders. Answer (C) states the fact that most colonial American Christians saw society, politics, economics, and religion through a Calvinist lens.

3. **(A)** All of the other answers are true, and answer (A) is false because Georgia was founded without African slavery, but it was not created as a haven for freed slaves. In fact, slavery became legal there in 1751. The attempt in Georgia to produce a silk industry failed when colonists realized they had planted the wrong kind of mulberry tree all over their colony.

4. **(D)** None of the other answers are true, especially answer (A), because the demand for a bribe was the origin of the slogan, "Millions for defense but not a penny for tribute!" France deported two of the envoys because they used harsher words to rebuff the extortion. One remained in France to watch the situation, but none were imprisoned or lobbied President Adams to declare war on France.

5. **(B)** Gold was discovered in this region only after it belonged to the United States. There were Apaches and Mormons in the Southwest, and even some cotton production in New Mexico, but the stated goal of the Gadsden Purchase was to acquire the best route across the Rocky Mountains for a railroad, something the South lost access to by seceding from the Union. Thus, the United States government picked the northern transcontinental route and began construction during the Civil War.

6. **(E)** Whereas answers (B), (C), and (D) were accusations hurled at the Knights of Labor, only answer (D) had any truth to it. Gompers's main disagreement, however, was that he said skilled and unskilled laborers had different needs, grievances, and goals. He started the AFL to focus on improving the working conditions of skilled workers. Answer (A) is incorrect because the leadership of the Knights of Labor was reluctant to call strikes.

7. **(C)** Answer (C) became known as the "Wisconsin Idea" because La Follette was the first to apply it at the state level (it originated at the city level in the form of municipal commissions). This approach is the foundation of Progressive Reform and expanded to

the national level under Theodore Roosevelt. Answer (D) was the notorious "Ohio Idea" floated during the Grant administration and rejected as the sure path to hyperinflation. None of the other answers represent ideas championed by any major group or individual.

8. **(B)** Whereas some of the other answers hint at ideas held in the late nineteenth century, Mahan was an imperialist whose book launched both imperialism and militarism in the form of modern navies in the United States, the United Kingdom, and Germany (among other nations). His book had nothing to do with Chinese immigration and espoused ideas that were rather the opposite of answers (A) and (C). Answer (D) is a more current suggestion based on fears of climate change.

9. **(B)** Only answer (B) reveals the blow to morale resulting from the interpretations of the Tet Offensive by television journalists when these attacks across South Vietnam were actually the most successful series of engagements in the war for killing large numbers of Vietcong. Therefore, answer (E) is the reverse of the truth. The attacks might have contributed to Richard Nixon's election, which happened in the fall of 1968 long after the Tet Offensive was over. The My Lai massacre alluded to in answer (C) also occurred later (although it did weaken support for the war). Answer (A) is too nebulous of an idea to attach to a single series of battles in 1968. Many might already have considered four years of war since the 1964 Gulf of Tonkin Resolution a long war, and there was much more war to come.

10. **(A)** Even members of the Republican Party were so used to Nixon's assessment that "We're all Keynesians, now," that President George H. W. Bush referred to supply-side economics as "voodoo economics." Bush's action was contrary to Reagan's Eleventh Commandment, "Thou shalt not speak ill of any fellow Republican," but Reagan still chose Bush as his running mate. Answers (B), (C), and (E) were also contrary to Reagan's campaign rhetoric against Big Government. Answer (D) would also have been nonsensical to Reagan who cooperated with the Moral Majority movement to secure victory in 1984.

11. **(D)** The Mayflower Compact applied only to a tiny shipload of frightened, argumentative settlers, but its symbolic power as a precedent changed the world. The few paragraphs were the closest Englishmen had come by 1620 to designing a government on paper. The British people had called into being the monarchy, Parliament, and even Virginia's House of Burgesses without a written constitution. The Magna Carta was an attempt to limit the power of an existing government. Newspapers did not publish the Mayflower Compact in this era as an incentive for colonization. Answer (C) is wrong because the Anglican Church was the established church of Virginia, not the Puritan colonies of the North. Answer (B) is incorrect because the document that set the precedent that English Common Law applied to colonial Americans was the written constitution of the Carolina colony. John Locke wrote their Fundamental Orders much later than the Pilgrims wrote theirs, and by then written constitutions had become the norm.

12. **(E)** Mercantilism as a system resulted in the exact opposite of answer (D), but the difficulty in enforcement led to the situation in answer (A). American colonists preferred salutary neglect, however, when it came to economics. They did believe the king and his ministers had every right to pass mercantilist laws, even with indirect taxation. Instead of creating unfair competition among the colonies, mercantilism created an unfavorable

balance of trade between the colonies and England. The Mother Country wanted the colonies to remain a source of raw materials and not to advance to manufacturing that would compete with England; therefore, answer (E) is correct.

13. **(E)** Mountain men (and at least one woman) were of such independent natures that they would as a group never have consented to work for the government or a museum. Nor did they build fortifications. Their intermarriage with American Indians did little to brighten native peoples' views of white culture because mountain men were actually adopting much of American Indian culture. The Oregon Trail and other major migration routes were their main contribution since these routes started as footpaths and blazed hunting trails.

14. **(B)** All of the other answers are decidedly not true except for answer (C), which was more true of the Republican administrations from the 1920s. Patronage and an outward image of patriotic service were the main function of the presidency from after the Civil War until the beginning of the Progressive Era. Thus, Gilded Age politics are directly associated with why Mark Twain gave the era this name. This reality is why Gilded Age presidents also earned the nickname "Forgotten Presidents."

15. **(C)** Answers (A), (B), and (E) are all statements the German government did not make or would not make. Answer (D) is closer to the truth, but the official German blockade involved only their surface ships, whereas the Arabic and Sussex Pledges dealt specifically with the actions of submarines operating in international waters. Submarines did attack passenger ships, much to the horror of other nations that viewed such attacks as barbaric.

16. **(D)** Answers (A) and (B) address contemporary issues and are thus too far removed from the New Deal to have anything directly to do with its legacy. Answer (C) contains New Deal ideas associated with the National Recovery Administration, but the U.S. government has no long-term allegiance to them except in the form of a minimum wage. Answer (E) is the direct opposite of the legacy of the New Deal since Franklin Roosevelt was the first president to propose deficit spending in peacetime, and the practice continues apace. The U.S. government largely achieved the New Deal goal of full employment during World War II, and Harry Truman's Fair Deal continued the goal as a statement of government policy.

17. **(A)** Of all the difficulties encountered in fighting the Vietnam War, the most debilitating was this self-imposed and deeply flawed strategic fantasy. After the war, Vietnamese generals revealed how absurd they thought the strategy was because they were used to fighting in jungles and did not value individual citizens' lives. The United States did not take territory away from the enemy, even though it dropped bombs on North Vietnam as stated in answer (C). Answers (B) and (D) evoke struggles more recent peacekeeping forces have with rules of engagement that require them to fight limited wars. Helicopters had mechanical difficulties, but the very nature of search-and-destroy missions hampered their effectiveness more. The final death ratio was closer to 25:1, and still the United States did not keep South Vietnam from falling to communism.

18. **(E)** Although all of the answers hint at Cold War realities, the only answer directly tied to the launch of the world's first artificial satellite was the National Defense Education Act described in answer (E). The Soviets did not actually have technological superiority,

although they used the technology they had to accomplish a "first strike" in the Space Race. The United States did not veto space initiatives at the United Nations, nor did it keep its forces perpetually on high alert. Answer (D) expresses a reaction to Soviet activities on the ground rather than in orbit.

19. **(B)** Although not the very first attack, the truck bomb detonated in the Marine barracks was certainly the first significant attack (1983) and one that altered American foreign policy. Such success encouraged militants to mount more and more attacks, including all of the ones referred to in the other answers.

20. **(D)** Ralph Nader has been a busy man in that he has personally led activist initiatives in all these areas while running for president frequently. His first important public step, however, was his publication of *Unsafe at any Speed*, which targeted American cars' lack of safety features, especially in the Chevy Corvair.

21. **(C)** All of these answers were important turning points in the American economy, but Slater's contribution was his textile mill in Rhode Island. The other movers and shakers were, in order, Eli Whitney, Robert Fulton, Joseph Glidden, and George Eastman.

22. **(D)** All of these Marshall Court decisions strengthened the power of the federal government, but *Marbury* v. *Madison* specifically strengthened the Supreme Court with the precedent of judicial review, the power to determine if laws were constitutional or not. The Court would not wield this power again, however, until the *Dred Scott* decision in 1857.

23. **(E)** Answer (E) is the reason cities like New York and Boston became largely populated by immigrants. The first large migrations of the Irish occurred before the Civil War in 1845, and given total freedom of movement, it is unlikely the Catholic Irish would have wanted to seek out the Scots-Irish Protestants as neighbors. Answers (A) and (C) are untrue because most Irish immigrants of this era arrived in the United States penniless. The South found enough hands to work the cotton fields through the institution of sharecropping, which drew former slaves back to the plantations, this time to work alongside their white neighbors impoverished by the Civil War.

24. **(C)** Andrew Jackson assumed the power in answer (A) himself, and answer (E) was also in his power (and the eventual concession he made) because he controlled the postmaster general. The Force Bill specifically granted the president the power to use the military to enforce federal law; in this case, the law in question was the collection of tariffs. Answer (B) is a hint at Abraham Lincoln's later suppression of rebellion in Maryland, and answer (D) is a vague reference to Jackson's later quarrels with Congress.

25. **(A)** Answers (B), (C), (D), and (E) were all tried at one time or another by various presidents in the history of the labor movement, and even Cleveland tried to break the Pullman Strike with an injunction (from a lower federal court). When that did not work, he broke the strike with military force on the grounds that the mail must get through.

26. **(B)** All of the answers are true except for the sinking of the *Lusitania*, which happened after World War I had already begun. The killing of Americans aboard the doomed passenger liner was a cause of American involvement in the war, not of the war itself.

27. **(B)** Neither answer (D) or (E) is true. Answer (A) was a result of Bryan's being in Dayton, not the cause of the national attention. Clarence Darrow, the defense attorney, was

widely known but did not have the celebrity status of William Jennings Bryan. The merits of the case itself were a pivotal episode in the societal flux of the 1920s that undermined uniformity of belief.

28. **(D)** All of the answers express ideas that would not be foreign to the New Deal or to postwar foreign policy, but the Eisenhower highway system is the only one that meets the test of being a massive public works project. The construction of the highway system was, and remains, one of the most massive public works projects in world history. The Eisenhower administration did launch all of the initiatives in the other answers, however, in a time of great change.

29. **(C)** In 1964, the only civil rights leader with the boldness to speak in this militant manner was Malcolm X. Some or all of the other leaders may have had similar sentiments in their hearts, but they tempered their public comments to appeal to American values and mores in a manner short of the "ballot or the bullet" rhetoric of Malcolm X.

30. **(E)** All of the answers have, or will have, an impact on migration within the United States, but the invention of practical air conditioning systems and a lower cost of living made moving to the Sun Belt desirable to many classes of people, not just the elderly.

31. **(B)** American Indians came up with three-sister farming on their own. Monks accompanied conquistadors but as a rule were not warriors. Jesuits did not seek enrichment of Catholic doctrine by studying native religions. Quite the opposite was true, so much so that the Inquisition hinted at in answer (E) has some ring of truth, but Jesuits' most important role is described in answer (B). This result is why the Pope dispatched them to the New World to look for converts after Europe had lost so many souls to Protestantism.

32. **(C)** Only answer (C) is entirely true. Answer (E) is entirely false, and the other answers are false in at least one regard. The North did produce enough food, but did not have the climate or soil to produce cash crops. The South did export food, such as rice, but most cash crops were not edible, e.g., tobacco and indigo. Subsistence farming took place mostly on the frontier. Colonies became self-sustaining up and down the eastern seaboard, but that did not mean infusions of capital from England were not needed for new ventures whether in shipping, manufacturing, or agriculture.

33. **(E)** The other answers are nearly all completely false in that *Common Sense* was a bestselling pamphlet and thus influenced masses of colonial Americans, not just fringe elements. Paine specifically avoided a scholarly tone, and his work encouraged the public to push the Continental Congress toward declaring independence.

34. **(A)** Answer (A) contains the two most famous of Washington's observations that served as prophetic warnings, although he did not go so far as to predict secession and civil war. He also did not emphasize the slavery issue, although he soon after emancipated all his slaves in his will. Interestingly, Washington did predict the evolution of the Supreme Court into a legislating body, but at the time, that was not a looming danger. He did not leave specific warnings about merchants, bankers, or large-scale attacks from American Indians.

35. **(D)** All of the answers play upon aspects of Daniel Webster's character and/or experiences, but only answer (D) is entirely true. Massachusetts led in reform movements like abolition after the Second Great Awakening just as it had led in the quest for indepen-

dence after the First Great Awakening. Webster's supporters appreciated his support for commerce and admired his oratory, but they had no problem with cooperation with Clay on the tariff question even though he was a slaveholder. When it came to slavery, though, they wanted Webster to be uncompromising. He chose to attempt to keep the peace.

36. **(B)** Answer (A) is true, but it was true only because answer (B) had already occurred. Chicago was not the source of raw materials nor any safer for immigrants or financiers than eastern cities. Lake Michigan and the railroads that converged on Chicago created an unbeatable geographic advantage that made Chicago an essential transportation hub.

37. **(C)** Answer (C) is the great technological breakthrough of John and Washington Roebling, the father/son engineering team that created the Brooklyn Bridge. The other answers hint at aspects of the bridge's construction that were not unique.

38. **(B)** The Spanish-American War made the United States a world power, but not a super-power. Although answer (C) is almost true, the involvement of the United States in China was not entirely disinterested in that John Hay wanted the United States to carve out its own sphere of influence before it was too late. He suggested that Open Door nations collaborate on making trade deals, and he did not want to take over territory as Russia and Japan did.

39. **(B)** "Pumping and dumping" was a strategy aimed at boosting the price of a particular stock, like RCA, not increasing activity in the whole market. Answers (C), (D), and (E) describe legitimate business investment practices that still go on today, although pumping and dumping is now illegal. The scheme was unscrupulous even then, especially because investors bribed journalists to write positive propaganda stories to boost the price of the target company. At a given moment, those doing the pumping began dumping, and after making huge profits, they left average investors with almost worthless stock.

40. **(E)** All of the answers hint at diplomatic difficulties associated with the Vietnam War, but the War Powers Act struck at the concept behind the Gulf of Tonkin Resolution that had allowed Lyndon Johnson to escalate the war virtually single-handedly.

41. **(C)** All of these answers were issues related to the Spanish Empire in the New World, but the Black Legend originated in the writings of men like Bartolome de las Casas who wrote the lines quoted in the question. The Black Legend emphasized the brutality of the Spanish conquest of Latin America and ruthless aspects of imperial rule. The focus of such an interpretation in recent years has been none other than Christopher Columbus who some historians consider a villain.

42. **(A)** All of the other answers hint at conflicts that were present in the colonial world, but Americans resorted to violence and force in attempting to solve them. The Acts of Toleration, both in England and in colonies like Maryland, intended to spread religious toleration, especially between Roman Catholics and Protestants. However, these provisions to establish peace regarding religion sometimes wholly left out sects like Quakers and Unitarians.

43. **(C)** Pinckney's Treaty resolved the issue described in answer (C) with Spain. There was a dispute with Canada over the boundary of Maine settled by the Webster-Ashburton

Treaty of 1842. Jay's Treaty became effective in the same year as Pinckney's Treaty (1796) and settled disputes with Great Britain over British forts in the Old Northwest, raids by American Indians, and debts owed by Americans to British creditors from before the Revolutionary War. Answer (E) refers to disputes with France from the first Adams administration that were the background for the War of 1812.

44. **(D)** All of the answers refer to real political scandals. The Teapot Dome Scandal was associated with President Warren G. Harding, and the Ballinger-Pinchot Affair was associated with President William Howard Taft. The Burr Conspiracy and the embezzlement of funds within the Indian Bureau did not attach themselves to any sitting president, although Andrew Jackson had trouble explaining why, before he became a presidential contender, he had sold Aaron Burr some boats. The Crédit Mobilier scandal revealed corruption within the Grant administration as high as Vice President Schuyler Colfax who received kickbacks to ward off prosecution of the leaders of the Union Pacific Railroad.

45. **(E)** Answers (A) and (C) both imply a level of control President Wilson said he did not want in stating his position expressed in answer (E). Later presidents did use the Federal Reserve to tighten control, however. Answer (B) was a premise maintained by Theodore Roosevelt but shunned by Wilson. Answer (D) will perhaps never be possible because Americans tend to hold presidents accountable for weak economies whether the presidents' policies influence the economy or not.

46. **(E)** Most of the answers are true to a degree except for answer (C), although Admiral Mahan would not necessarily have disagreed with the premise. What made Theodore Roosevelt and other Americans listen to the pleas of Cuban-Americans and the newspapers, however, was the quest of Cubans to free themselves from Spain just as Americans had freed themselves from England. The desire for the United States to take over Cuba evidenced by the Ostend Manifesto had died out with the Civil War. Answer (B) is the opposite of the truth in that one of the opening acts of the Spanish-American War was Commodore Dewey's attack on the Spanish fleet sitting in Manila Bay in the Philippine Islands.

47. **(C)** Answer (A) is false because these were the principles Wilson spoke against, as were the darker aspects of nationalism mentioned in answer (B). Answer (C) contains the themes undergirding Wilson's call for new nations salvaged from old empires, new international commitments to disarmament and world peace, and the League of Nations. Answers (D) and (E) address issues that are more associated with the United Nations than with Wilson's platform for the League of Nations.

48. **(B)** All of the answers mention cabinet positions or proposed cabinet positions, but the two that made it into the executive branch in 1947 were those in answer (B). The Department of Defense took over the responsibilities of previous departments regarding national security, and the new significance of air power after World War II led to the creation of the Department of the Air Force. During the war, most American pilots flew for an arm of the U. S. Army called the Army Air Corps.

49. **(C)** Each of the other answers contains a Great Society program begun under previous administrations, all of which fit in with Johnson's own progressive agenda. Only answer (C) contains an initiative Johnson launched in that he prompted Congress to pass the Civil Rights Act and the Voting Rights Act, key elements of his own vision for domestic

reform. The Peace Corps was a Kennedy initiative. Franklin Roosevelt launched the Social Security system, and Eisenhower backed the National Defense Education Act referred to in answer (D). Several administrations improved the ability of labor unions to function including Woodrow Wilson and FDR.

50. **(C)** Answer C is derived from the situation that produced the new verb, *to mirandize*, that means officers have to read certain rights to those they arrest, including the right not to incriminate themselves. To avoid violating this right during interrogation, arresting officers now have to inform suspects that they can have an attorney present before they respond to any questions. Answers (A), (B), and (C) involve issues in the more recent evolution of criminal justice. Answer (E) is often associated incorrectly with the *Miranda* case, but the requirement to have an attorney present during the prosecution of a defendant stems from the earlier *Gideon* v. *Wainwright* case of 1963.

51. **(C)** All of the answers list aspects of Hamilton's financial program, but answer (C) conveys the idea behind this quote from his *First Report on the Public Credit*. He believed it was essential to fund Revolutionary War bonds at par in order to expect that the government of the United States could issue bonds in the future in case of a crisis like another war. Then Hamilton issued more bonds just to fund his launch of the Treasury Department mentioned in answer (E).

52. **(A)** All of the other answers merely hint at circumstances faced by the Corps of Discovery including illness, prolonged boredom, and possible attack from hostile American Indians, except that Sacagawea did carry her papoose. In addition, answer (D) is the opposite of the truth in that her husband brought her on the trip. Still, the remarkable exploits of this intrepid woman were instrumental in the success of the Lewis and Clark expedition mainly for the reasons stated in answer (A).

53. **(A)** Although answer (D) is a hint at the truth in that the Hartford Convention did discuss secession, that fateful doctrine was not a part of their actual proposal. Answer (A) conveys their most pressing issues because they did not support the War of 1812, which was fought against their best trade partner. Their resolutions were moot after they arrived to hear the news of the Treaty of Ghent and the heroism of Andrew Jackson's forces in defending New Orleans from the third major invasion by the British during the war.

54. **(D)** Clay was from Kentucky, not the Deep South, but he was a slave owner and a Whig. Although he did lead the War Hawks and he had been the Secretary of State under John Quincy Adams, these roles were not relevant to his success in engineering compromises prior to the Civil War. Such education as he received to launch his career as a lawyer, he received in his home state of Virginia. His pivotal role was that, as a slave owner, he could talk to John C. Calhoun, and, as a Whig, he could talk to Daniel Webster. Calhoun and Webster were on opposite poles of the debate about slavery and states' rights.

55. **(B)** All of the answers hint at issues between Mexico and the United States at the onset of the Mexican War. Slidell's mission, however, was the one effort James K. Polk made to assuage his conscience over his expansionist tendencies concerning California and Texas. He could say that he did offer Santa Anna a peaceful solution before sending Zachary Taylor to start a war.

56. **(B)** Only answer (B) states a totally accurate account of the U. S. response. The other answers hint at issues and geographic realities of the troublesome series of events associated with the fall of the Qing Dynasty in China.

57. **(B)** Answers (A) and (C) represent more the General Motors approach to the automobile industry, whereas Ford's social engineering goals for American society required a simple, affordable, and durable car to move Americans about their country in order to turn it into a nation of middle-class consumers. There were no other countries mass-producing cars, and Ford did not own a road construction firm, so answers (D) and (E) are false.

58. **(C)** This quote could only be written by an American who had gone through the Great Depression and the sacrifices of World War II prior to the baby boom, which took care of the reproduction gap.

59. **(E)** Answers (A) and (D) are nearly the exact opposite of the truth. Answer (B) is the Nixon stereotype contradicted by the landslide victory he won before he self-destructed in the Watergate scandal. Nixon was a shrewd politician as evidenced by his ability to employ liberal, conservative, and moderate agendas, but he was not known for running around and trying to get ahead of popular breezes through polls.

60. **(B)** Answer (A) refers to the kidnapping of one grandchild, Patricia Hearst, who did not have the wife referred to in the document. Militants did not capture the Marine barracks; they destroyed them with a truck bomb. No extensive televised interaction was involved with the students taken hostage in Grenada by revolutionaries, not militants. Sadly, answer (E) cannot be true because it refers to Daniel Pearl who did not survive to tell about his experiences, as did the hostages in the Iranian Hostage Crisis.

61. **(D)** Answer (D) is a fabrication. The other answers are direct quotes from the Declaration of Independence. The Declaration says nothing about the Anglican Church's being an established church in America because other churches were readily available for dissenters by the time of the American Revolution.

62. **(A)** The only shore of a Great Lake that comes close to serving as a boundary would be at the northern tip of Lake Michigan, which lies entirely within the United States. Canada and the United States share the other Great Lakes listed in answer (E).

63. **(C)** Answer (C) is a reference to Hamilton's excise tax on whiskey and the fact that it hurt frontier farmers because jugs of whiskey were much easier to transport to market than wagons filled with corn. Washington did not patrol the area with troops until after the Whiskey Rebellion started, at which point he led fifteen thousand. Hamilton would not want to initiate prohibition because Americans' thirst for whiskey promised to be an excellent source of revenue, hence the taxes.

64. **(E)** Answer (E) explains Astor's start and how he was able to found Astoria, Washington, as a trading post on the Columbia River. He later built the hotel mentioned in answer (B). Samuel Slater made the first textile mill. John D. Rockefeller flooded creeks to move oil barrels. Levi Strauss marketed the first blue jeans at his general store in California.

65. **(D)** Answer (D) reveals that John Quincy Adams had a Big-Stick policy long before Theodore Roosevelt's, and the stick was named Andrew Jackson. General Jackson led troops in the Creek War and the War of 1812, and he settled disputes with the Spanish in Florida partly by summarily hanging two British spies he captured there. Secretary

Adams used fear of what else Jackson might do to force Spain to sell Florida. The Missouri River never served as a border as the Mississippi River had, and the United States never allied with Spain. The United States took on the Barbary Pirates alone and took Texas and California from Mexico rather than bargaining with Spain for them.

66. **(C)** All of the other answers have a part that is false. Wilson was too much of a Hamiltonian to push for states' rights, and he certainly did not want to roll back Progressivism. What actions Theodore Roosevelt (TR) took for African Americans' civil rights subjected him to intense criticism, so he backed off entirely. Of all things, TR was not an isolationist. Interestingly, the idealism of Wilson's views on trusts, when met with the difficulty of enforcement, wound up operating exactly as TR's more practical approach.

67. **(B)** All of the other answers are misinterpretations of the cartoon. No one pushed Grant to resign, although he had surrounded himself with unscrupulous men whose actions, today, would have led to his forced resignation and put them in jail. Grant was surprised by the events and did pledge to get to the bottom of the scandals, but even though he did not diligently prosecute his own personnel, he was never proven to be in complicity with their crimes. Answer (B) conveys the message of Nast's image—that Grant was in over his head.

68. **(C)** Answers (A) and (B) are the myth about prohibition, whereas overall consumption of alcohol did go down. Grain farmers were ruined prior to the Great Depression because their market in Europe created by World War I had disappeared, trapping them in over-production. The failed experiment of prohibition did not lead to a desire to reform the amendment process.

69. **(D)** Answer (D) dispels another myth about the era of the Roaring Twenties and the Great Depression. Answer (A), while true at first, could not convey Hoover's complete response because his Reconstruction Finance Corporation was the foundation for Franklin Roosevelt's New Deal. Answers (B) and (C) convey the perception of Hoover, not the reality, and answer (E) is a reference to an initiative from the George W. Bush administration.

70. **(B)** Answers (A) and (E) are false because RADAR units were not yet sophisticated enough to perform these tasks in World War II. For example, airborne RADAR could help navigate bombers to their targets but not help them avoid anti-aircraft fire. Answer (B) reveals how outnumbered, brave British and American pilots had any hope of winning the Battle of Britain. The Germans, not the Allies, invented military rocket technology but did not have RADAR to guide the V-1 or V-2 missiles. RADAR could not penetrate water to search for submarines, which is why ships relied on SONAR.

71. **(E)** Early in the French and Indian War, British officers like General Braddock scorned American troops and their advice. Instead, they insisted on fighting according to European standards of military honor, which proved suicidal in Braddock's case. William Pitt wanted to win more than he wanted to honor aristocratic sensibilities, so he promoted men based on merit, including American officers like George Washington. Only then did the British succeed in conquering the French and their American Indian allies. All of the other answers are fabrications that hint at incentives often employed by armies of the era to motivate or to supply armies. None applied to the French and Indian War, however, or they did not create a significant turning point.

72. **(E)** The lines come from the Kentucky Resolutions (with comparable wording in the Virginia Resolutions) that were passed in response to the Alien and Sedition Acts. Federalists would not have used such logic that invoked states' rights, and the Land and Northwest Ordinances did not speak of states except in addressing the process by which territories could become states.

73. **(A)** *Gibbons* v. *Ogden* set precedents regarding the regulation of business. The case involved steamboat traffic between two or more states, thus interstate transportation.

74. **(B)** The concept of a state funding a canal was so novel that Dewitt Clinton was derided for proposing the idea that his "Big Ditch" could boost New York's economy and make the $7 million investment pay off. The Erie Canal transformed New York City into a major transportation hub and was just the beginning of the city's importance to American history. New equipment was invented to help speed construction, but no steam shovels were used (much to the chagrin of man and beast). States had sold bonds and used American engineers before, but never on a project of this scale. The canal's success encouraged later expenditures of federal dollars on infrastructure.

75. **(C)** Steam power was first applied to factories and steam boats, not steam trains. Deficit spending had begun in America before one could say properly that America had begun. Although telegraph wires ran right alongside railroad tracks, all the other items developed without specific relation to railroads. Railroads moved people faster than ever before, however, and the need for time zones to account for the different positions of the sun arose from a desire to avoid collisions due to scheduling errors. The immensity of the task of constructing and running railroads also necessitated the creation of the first giant corporations, and railroads thus set many important business precedents.

76. **(E)** All of the other answers were in the head of this economic visionary, but it is quite likely that Henry Clay would have fought a duel with someone over an income tax. Governments resorted to a small tax on wealth as an emergency provision during the Civil War, but not until the Sixteenth Amendment of 1913 was an income tax considered constitutional.

77. **(C)** Answers (A) and (B) are true about Santa Anna's government and were distasteful to Texans, but answer (C) cites their main grievances, the ones that drove them to seek independence. Answers (D) and (E) are plausible under the rule of a dictator, but they are false.

78. **(D)** Answer (D) is the only conclusion that is supported by both the data from the map and from a comparison of antebellum societies of the North and the South. The fertile soil and relatively flat terrain of the Midwest allowed thousands of Americans to establish thriving farms in states like Ohio, Indiana, and Illinois. The map reveals that whole areas of the South were sparsely populated, especially where there were mountainous terrain and/or less fertile soil. Answer (A) hints at San Francisco's excellent harbor but ignores the greater density farther inland due to the Gold Rush. The map apparently supports answer (B), but the statement ignores the giant impact railroads made on population density for cities like Chicago and Pittsburgh. Answer (C) belies the fact that, even though the cities on the Atlantic coast were the largest, the bulk of the population had begun to move west in what remained a largely rural society. Answer (E) is false in that the territory that would become the state of Oklahoma was the site of the Indian Territory

in question, and it was still sparsely populated. Settlers did not make substantial inroads into this region until after the Civil War.

79. **(D)** Although Carnegie preferred an open shop, he hired Pinkerton detectives only after the strike broke out. A manager at the Homestead plant, Henry Clay Frick, provoked the clash by lowering wages in order to have the justification for breaking the union. Carnegie sold his company not to Frick but to J.P. Morgan.

80. **(B)** The Bolshevik Revolution in Russia in 1917 did increase fears of especially Russian Jews as potential radicals among immigrants, and a general dislike for immigrants contributed to the Red Scare. Answers (C) and (D) were true, but, although the Klan did march in Washington, D.C., they were not communists. Julius and Ethel Rosenberg were communists, or at least spies for the Soviets, but they were executed in the Second Red Scare in the 1950s. A hint about Senator Carl Schurz as a radical is misleading because he was a liberal reformer, not a secret Bolshevik. The Soviet Union sent radical literature to American communists, but did not have the capacity to broadcast a radio signal all the way to the United States in the 1920s.

81. **(E)** All of the other answers refer to facts common to several American Indian tribes, but answer (E) was the unique quality of the Iroquois who were not a tribe but a confederation of six, then later seven, tribes all joined to face the threat of their neighbors to the west, the Huron Indians.

82. **(C)** There was no push for independence this early, and the Restoration led to the Navigation Acts rather than enforced existing acts. Charles II and his brother, who would become James II, decided they should try to run their American colonies as the Spanish ran theirs. The arbitrary nature of ending salutary neglect after almost sixty years disturbed England's American colonists, but when colonists complained, rebelled, and smuggled, the British Crown responded in the worst possible way, by ushering in more salutary neglect (until after the French and Indian War).

83. **(A)** This frightening prospect was forestalled almost single-handedly by George Washington who rejected this plan raised by his own veteran officers. The other answers hint at the geographical, social, and historical context of this bizarre episode initiated by men who had heard the Declaration of Independence read aloud to their own troops.

84. **(B)** James K. Polk desired so much to be like his hero, Andrew Jackson, that if the Bank of the United States (BUS) was restored for a third time, then Polk would have killed it as Jackson had killed the second BUS. All of the other answers are the campaign promises he fulfilled that cause historians jokingly to call the Polk administration the most successful presidency in American history. Polk's actual fifth promise was to annex Texas, which he did, thus bringing more land into the United States than any other president (Texas, Oregon, and California).

85. **(C)** Answer (A) is untrue because labor unions, insofar as they could wield political influence in the Gilded Age, already supported the Democratic Party. No candidate in the Gilded Age advocated for the changes in answer (B), and Cleveland's first opponent, James G. Blaine, was the one to receive the support mentioned in answer (E). Since answer (C) expresses Cleveland's stance, he certainly did not cooperate with the corruption in answer (D) (although there was a federal surplus in the Gilded Age).

86. **(D)** The first letter made William McKinley appear weak and compelled him to start the Spanish-American War, and the second message was made public while Woodrow Wilson seemed increasingly unable to lead the country to go to Europe to end World War I. Public opinion took over from President Wilson after the Zimmermann Telegram exposed Germany's conspiracy with Mexico and German submarines sank four unarmed American merchant vessels. Answer (A) is incorrect because British intelligence operations intercepted and then leaked the Zimmermann Telegram.

87. **(D)** The action that gained the most detractors for Franklin D. Roosevelt, even from within his own Democratic Party, was his willingness to play fast and loose with the U.S. Constitution in a way that threatened the balance of powers, as his pack-the-court scheme would likely have done. The other answers do convey events or issues that were bad press for the New Deal, but FDR, in trying to solve an economic crisis, almost created a constitutional crisis.

88. **(B)** These answer choices list the World War II conferences students should know less for their military implications and more for their geopolitical diplomatic consequences. Few will recognize the, "After the final destruction of the Nazi tyranny . . ." quote from the sixth provision of the Atlantic Charter (on the eagle's wing), but there are distinct points that should narrow the choice down to answer (B). The Atlantic Conference was the only one of those listed attended by Franklin Roosevelt and Winston Churchill alone. They met in secret on a ship off the coast of Canada and made their "peace aims," and they agreed on the steps their nations should follow to attain those aims. Visible in the cartoon is the intense nationalism evoked when news of the conference became public. Churchill had come to FDR in desperate straits, but the eagle "escort" represents the righteous anger that would translate into American military might coming to make peace.

89. **(E)** The Laffer Curve, drawn for President Reagan's advisers, could likely be the most significant drawing ever made on a napkin in a restaurant. Although Arthur Laffer said he did not originate the idea of supply-side economics, his simple illustration was instrumental in launching the Reagan Revolution. The other answers all attempt to distract by referring to actual events and circumstances within the Reagan administration.

90. **(C)** Answers (A) and (D) make reference to aspects of the Clinton administration irrelevant to the line-item veto. No recent Democratic president would rejoice to have a power just because Jefferson Davis had it as suggested in answer (B). Answer (E) is incorrect because the Republican Party took control of Congress in 1994 for the first time in forty years. Unfortunately for the hope expressed in answer (C), the line-item veto was no more a silver bullet to end pork barrel spending than the Pendleton Act had been to end Gilded Age corruption in government. Congress intended the line-item veto to be a tool to end excessive federal spending that had only local benefits instead of benefitting the whole country. President Clinton is the only president of the United States to enjoy this power because the Supreme Court quickly declared it unconstitutional.

ANSWER SHEET
Practice Test 3

1. Ⓐ Ⓑ Ⓒ Ⓓ Ⓔ
2. Ⓐ Ⓑ Ⓒ Ⓓ Ⓔ
3. Ⓐ Ⓑ Ⓒ Ⓓ Ⓔ
4. Ⓐ Ⓑ Ⓒ Ⓓ Ⓔ
5. Ⓐ Ⓑ Ⓒ Ⓓ Ⓔ
6. Ⓐ Ⓑ Ⓒ Ⓓ Ⓔ
7. Ⓐ Ⓑ Ⓒ Ⓓ Ⓔ
8. Ⓐ Ⓑ Ⓒ Ⓓ Ⓔ
9. Ⓐ Ⓑ Ⓒ Ⓓ Ⓔ
10. Ⓐ Ⓑ Ⓒ Ⓓ Ⓔ
11. Ⓐ Ⓑ Ⓒ Ⓓ Ⓔ
12. Ⓐ Ⓑ Ⓒ Ⓓ Ⓔ
13. Ⓐ Ⓑ Ⓒ Ⓓ Ⓔ
14. Ⓐ Ⓑ Ⓒ Ⓓ Ⓔ
15. Ⓐ Ⓑ Ⓒ Ⓓ Ⓔ
16. Ⓐ Ⓑ Ⓒ Ⓓ Ⓔ
17. Ⓐ Ⓑ Ⓒ Ⓓ Ⓔ
18. Ⓐ Ⓑ Ⓒ Ⓓ Ⓔ
19. Ⓐ Ⓑ Ⓒ Ⓓ Ⓔ
20. Ⓐ Ⓑ Ⓒ Ⓓ Ⓔ
21. Ⓐ Ⓑ Ⓒ Ⓓ Ⓔ
22. Ⓐ Ⓑ Ⓒ Ⓓ Ⓔ
23. Ⓐ Ⓑ Ⓒ Ⓓ Ⓔ
24. Ⓐ Ⓑ Ⓒ Ⓓ Ⓔ
25. Ⓐ Ⓑ Ⓒ Ⓓ Ⓔ
26. Ⓐ Ⓑ Ⓒ Ⓓ Ⓔ
27. Ⓐ Ⓑ Ⓒ Ⓓ Ⓔ
28. Ⓐ Ⓑ Ⓒ Ⓓ Ⓔ
29. Ⓐ Ⓑ Ⓒ Ⓓ Ⓔ
30. Ⓐ Ⓑ Ⓒ Ⓓ Ⓔ

31. Ⓐ Ⓑ Ⓒ Ⓓ Ⓔ
32. Ⓐ Ⓑ Ⓒ Ⓓ Ⓔ
33. Ⓐ Ⓑ Ⓒ Ⓓ Ⓔ
34. Ⓐ Ⓑ Ⓒ Ⓓ Ⓔ
35. Ⓐ Ⓑ Ⓒ Ⓓ Ⓔ
36. Ⓐ Ⓑ Ⓒ Ⓓ Ⓔ
37. Ⓐ Ⓑ Ⓒ Ⓓ Ⓔ
38. Ⓐ Ⓑ Ⓒ Ⓓ Ⓔ
39. Ⓐ Ⓑ Ⓒ Ⓓ Ⓔ
40. Ⓐ Ⓑ Ⓒ Ⓓ Ⓔ
41. Ⓐ Ⓑ Ⓒ Ⓓ Ⓔ
42. Ⓐ Ⓑ Ⓒ Ⓓ Ⓔ
43. Ⓐ Ⓑ Ⓒ Ⓓ Ⓔ
44. Ⓐ Ⓑ Ⓒ Ⓓ Ⓔ
45. Ⓐ Ⓑ Ⓒ Ⓓ Ⓔ
46. Ⓐ Ⓑ Ⓒ Ⓓ Ⓔ
47. Ⓐ Ⓑ Ⓒ Ⓓ Ⓔ
48. Ⓐ Ⓑ Ⓒ Ⓓ Ⓔ
49. Ⓐ Ⓑ Ⓒ Ⓓ Ⓔ
50. Ⓐ Ⓑ Ⓒ Ⓓ Ⓔ
51. Ⓐ Ⓑ Ⓒ Ⓓ Ⓔ
52. Ⓐ Ⓑ Ⓒ Ⓓ Ⓔ
53. Ⓐ Ⓑ Ⓒ Ⓓ Ⓔ
54. Ⓐ Ⓑ Ⓒ Ⓓ Ⓔ
55. Ⓐ Ⓑ Ⓒ Ⓓ Ⓔ
56. Ⓐ Ⓑ Ⓒ Ⓓ Ⓔ
57. Ⓐ Ⓑ Ⓒ Ⓓ Ⓔ
58. Ⓐ Ⓑ Ⓒ Ⓓ Ⓔ
59. Ⓐ Ⓑ Ⓒ Ⓓ Ⓔ
60. Ⓐ Ⓑ Ⓒ Ⓓ Ⓔ

61. Ⓐ Ⓑ Ⓒ Ⓓ Ⓔ
62. Ⓐ Ⓑ Ⓒ Ⓓ Ⓔ
63. Ⓐ Ⓑ Ⓒ Ⓓ Ⓔ
64. Ⓐ Ⓑ Ⓒ Ⓓ Ⓔ
65. Ⓐ Ⓑ Ⓒ Ⓓ Ⓔ
66. Ⓐ Ⓑ Ⓒ Ⓓ Ⓔ
67. Ⓐ Ⓑ Ⓒ Ⓓ Ⓔ
68. Ⓐ Ⓑ Ⓒ Ⓓ Ⓔ
69. Ⓐ Ⓑ Ⓒ Ⓓ Ⓔ
70. Ⓐ Ⓑ Ⓒ Ⓓ Ⓔ
71. Ⓐ Ⓑ Ⓒ Ⓓ Ⓔ
72. Ⓐ Ⓑ Ⓒ Ⓓ Ⓔ
73. Ⓐ Ⓑ Ⓒ Ⓓ Ⓔ
74. Ⓐ Ⓑ Ⓒ Ⓓ Ⓔ
75. Ⓐ Ⓑ Ⓒ Ⓓ Ⓔ
76. Ⓐ Ⓑ Ⓒ Ⓓ Ⓔ
77. Ⓐ Ⓑ Ⓒ Ⓓ Ⓔ
78. Ⓐ Ⓑ Ⓒ Ⓓ Ⓔ
79. Ⓐ Ⓑ Ⓒ Ⓓ Ⓔ
80. Ⓐ Ⓑ Ⓒ Ⓓ Ⓔ
81. Ⓐ Ⓑ Ⓒ Ⓓ Ⓔ
82. Ⓐ Ⓑ Ⓒ Ⓓ Ⓔ
83. Ⓐ Ⓑ Ⓒ Ⓓ Ⓔ
84. Ⓐ Ⓑ Ⓒ Ⓓ Ⓔ
85. Ⓐ Ⓑ Ⓒ Ⓓ Ⓔ
86. Ⓐ Ⓑ Ⓒ Ⓓ Ⓔ
87. Ⓐ Ⓑ Ⓒ Ⓓ Ⓔ
88. Ⓐ Ⓑ Ⓒ Ⓓ Ⓔ
89. Ⓐ Ⓑ Ⓒ Ⓓ Ⓔ
90. Ⓐ Ⓑ Ⓒ Ⓓ Ⓔ

Practice Test 3

▰▰▰▰▰▰▰▰▰▰▰▰▰▰▰▰▰▰▰▰

TIME—60 MINUTES

> **Directions:** Each of the questions or incomplete statements below is followed by five suggested answers or completions. Select the one that is best in each case, and then fill in the corresponding circle on the answer sheet. You can cut the answer sheet along the dotted line to make recording your answers easier. Remember to give yourself only sixty minutes to complete this test in order to prepare for the pace of the real SAT Subject Test in U.S. History.

1. The Treaty of Tordesillas of 1494 shaped European exploration and colonization of the New World by

    (A) revealing that Portugal and Spain would ally against the English and the French.
    (B) limiting Portugal's access to Italian navigators until Spain built more trading posts.
    (C) denying armed Spanish or Portuguese naval vessels access to the coast of the Americas.
    (D) leaving more land for Spain when dividing the New World between Spain and Portugal.
    (E) giving control of exploration and colonization by Roman Catholic nations to the Pope.

2. Maryland was unique among the thirteen colonies that eventually became the United States because this colony

    (A) passed a law allowing any Trinitarian Christian freedom of worship.
    (B) maintained the longest peaceful relations with American Indians.
    (C) began as a refuge for Roman Catholics escaping persecution in England.
    (D) was the only colony whose territory was not contiguous.
    (E) had the most aristocratic society with the most African slaves per capita.

3. The "Triangular Trade" pattern that originated in England's American colonies was

    (A) developed as a wide variety of trade routes with many Old World destinations.
    (B) established by the Board of Trade and patrolled by the British Navy.
    (C) created to be more lucrative than the annual haul of the Spanish treasure fleet.
    (D) used to transport a wide range of goods manufactured in colonial America.
    (E) operated by Scottish and Dutch middle men who exacted high fees.

4. James II of England established the Dominion of New England in 1686 because he

   (A) needed his rival, Edmund Andros, out of the way in colonial America as its governor.
   (B) wanted revenge on New England Puritans for their complicity in the execution of his father.
   (C) needed a stronger base of operations from which to stage attacks on New Amsterdam.
   (D) wanted the colonies to end their divisions and become stronger by uniting together.
   (E) wanted to run England's colonies with the same efficiency as the Spanish ran theirs.

5. Which statement best describes the values behind the post-Revolution concept of "republican motherhood"?

   (A) Mothers should rear their children to have a strong attachment to a political party.
   (B) For the first time, Americans valued women for their childbearing capacities.
   (C) Mothers should preserve the republic by teaching their children American values.
   (D) Parents should teach their daughters that motherhood was a woman's highest calling.
   (E) Schools should teach girls parenting skills to help them be better citizens and mothers.

6. "It is evident that the Yearly Meeting [of Philadelphia] does not recognize the institution of Slavery as one that can be upheld where christian [*sic*] feelings predominate; and that under this conviction its members cannot assist in carrying out such laws as may be enacted to perpetuate its existence . . . ."

   To what type of laws is the 1851 quotation above most likely referring?

   (A) Personal liberty laws
   (B) Fugitive Slave Act
   (C) Black Codes
   (D) Slave Codes
   (E) Vagrancy laws for freedmen

7. The Compromise of 1877 provided that former Confederate states

   (A) could have home rule as long as they submitted to military occupation by the Union Army.
   (B) could keep the Ku Klux Klan as a fraternal order as long as it ceased its militancy.
   (C) could rejoin the Union as long as they acknowledged freed slaves were now citizens.
   (D) could end Reconstruction as long as they agreed a Republican won the presidency in 1876.
   (E) could receive amnesty as long as 10 percent of their populations took loyalty oaths.

8. Harry S. Truman's Fair Deal campaign helped him win the presidency in his own right because he promised to

   (A) provide self-determination for nations freed from the Axis after World War II.
   (B) secure the civil rights of African Americans who had served during World War II.
   (C) provide low-cost housing for the families of servicemen who were killed in World War II.
   (D) provide a college education for any man who had served during World War II.
   (E) expand all social welfare programs and employment for Americans after World War II.

9. What did the release of the Pentagon Papers in 1971 reveal about the Vietnam War?

   (A) Strategic flaws that caused the United States to fail to achieve its objectives
   (B) Purposefully disproportionate representation of African Americans in combat roles
   (C) Consequences of a lack of coordination among the various branches of the U.S. military
   (D) Failure of the Johnson administration to portray the war and its objectives accurately
   (E) Secret peace negotiations between the Nixon administration and North Vietnam

10. Samuel de Champlain contributed to the establishment of New France by

   (A) exploring the St. Lawrence River and founding both Montreal and Quebec.
   (B) discovering the lake that bears his name and making it the boundary with New Amsterdam.
   (C) exploring the upper length of the Mississippi River and claiming the area for France.
   (D) establishing the economy of New France through the fur trade around the Great Lakes.
   (E) proving that the Mississippi River flowed to the Gulf of Mexico and founding New Orleans.

11. Where did England and France originally clash in the battles in 1754 that led to the French and Indian War?

   (A) The province of Quebec
   (B) The upper reaches of New York and Maine
   (C) The Great Lakes region
   (D) The Ohio River Valley
   (E) The Mississippi River delta

12. "There shall be neither Slavery nor involuntary Servitude in the said territory otherwise than in the punishment of crimes . . . . Provided always, That any person escaping into the same, from . . . any one of the original States . . . may be lawfully reclaimed and conveyed to the person claiming his or her labor or service aforesaid."

From which of the following documents does this quotation likely come?

(A) The Articles of Confederation
(B) The Northwest Ordinance
(C) The original U.S. Constitution
(D) The Tallmadge Amendment to the request of the Missouri Territory for statehood
(E) The Lecompton Constitution

13. The main goal of the Missouri Compromise in 1820 was to

(A) identify new territory into which Southerners could expand the institution of slavery.
(B) make Missouri a free state despite the support for slavery there.
(C) preserve the union by keeping the balance of free and slave states in the Senate.
(D) divide the Louisiana Purchase into future slave states and free states.
(E) ban the spread of slavery in newly established territories in the West.

14. McGuffey Readers were important in the common school movement because they

(A) could be accepted readily by Appalachian people because McGuffey was Scots-Irish.
(B) planted similar cultural roots in the North and the South just prior to the Civil War.
(C) perpetuated classical studies in the country founded largely by classical scholars.
(D) furthered the character-building agenda of education by teaching reading and values.
(E) elevated literary tastes because of the high quality of the writing in the reading selections.

15. The utopian experiment known as Brook Farm

(A) collapsed after the men of letters who made it famous tired of the experience and left.
(B) disappeared after one generation because the Shakers who founded it were celibate.
(C) became a famous bastion of Transcendentalism and attracted aristocrats from Europe.
(D) prospered until it was destroyed during Sherman's March to the Sea in the Civil War.
(E) moved West to escape persecution from neighbors concerned about its radical views.

16. All of the following were important aspects of "negro spirituals" during the African-American experience in slavery **EXCEPT**

   (A) the songs called back and forth among field hands to help pace their work.
   (B) the songs contained Christian messages that formed a spiritual bond between them.
   (C) the songs used rhythms that blended African and American culture.
   (D) the songs were the first attempt to teach slaves to read when they were written as hymns.
   (E) the songs were used as coded messages notifying slaves of planned escapes.

17. The Monroe Doctrine of 1823 was significant because it

   (A) affirmed the alliance between the United States and France once Napoleon Bonaparte was gone.
   (B) committed the U.S. Navy to help the British Navy end the menace of the Barbary Pirates.
   (C) ended all diplomatic conflict between the United States and the United Kingdom.
   (D) established the independence of the United States in determining its own foreign policy.
   (E) provided a way for the United Kingdom and France to pick up the pieces of Spain's crumbling empire.

18. Abraham Lincoln's actions in 1861 regarding Fort Sumter in Charleston Harbor affected the diplomatic aspects of fighting the Civil War by

   (A) allowing South Carolina to claim it fired in self-defense since Lincoln ordered an attack.
   (B) keeping the British neutral since Lincoln caught them secretly supporting the Confederacy.
   (C) allowing the North to claim the South started the war since Lincoln had only sent supplies.
   (D) making other nations fear the U.S. Navy because Lincoln used ironclads to win the battle.
   (E) cutting off supplies from European nations since Lincoln held the fort the rest of the war.

19. The Committees of Correspondence were significant during the American Revolution because they

   (A) monitored their neighbors' compliance with boycotts used to pressure Great Britain.
   (B) cataloged British actions and kept a record of grievances before the American public.
   (C) published accounts of British atrocities in newspapers in Great Britain.
   (D) appealed regularly to Spain, France, and Prussia for intervention on behalf of the United States.
   (E) spied on enemy forces in an effort to counterbalance British military superiority.

20. Alexander Hamilton defended his loose construction of the U.S. Constitution by saying

   (A) the Constitution was only a rough guideline for creative thinking about government.
   (B) the important principles of a government could never all be written down on paper.
   (C) that any excesses of interpretation would be balanced by the two-party system.
   (D) the Supreme Court would keep misinterpretations in check through judicial review.
   (E) that his steps based on the duties stated in the Constitution were necessary and proper.

21. All of the following are examples of the way President Thomas Jefferson reduced the expenditures of the federal government **EXCEPT**

   (A) by turning over the services of the post office to private companies.
   (B) by reducing the size of the navy by replacing frigates with small defensive gunboats.
   (C) by firing all the tax collectors responsible for collecting the excise tax on whiskey.
   (D) by reducing the number of ambassadors down to only those for Spain, France, and England.
   (E) by cutting the standing army down to just over three thousand professional soldiers.

22. Why did the plan of the American Colonization Society to relocate American slaves to Africa ultimately fail?

   (A) Businessmen wanted African Americans as laborers and refused to support the effort.
   (B) The government found the leader of the organization guilty of fraud and deported him.
   (C) President Lincoln said deporting slaves acknowledged the shame of American racism.
   (D) African Americans raised in the United States had little to no interest in leaving to go to Africa.
   (E) The first group of African Americans were captured upon their arrival and enslaved.

23. Sharecropping was different from slavery in that sharecroppers

   (A) cultivated corn in the South rather than cotton.
   (B) had to be male and at least fourteen years of age before working in the fields.
   (C) came from the population of poor whites as well as African Americans.
   (D) could now work for wealthy African Americans who owned plantations.
   (E) usually worked their way out of debt and eventually owned their own farms.

24. "The paupers and the physically incapacitated are an inevitable charge on society . . . . But the weak who constantly arouse the pity of humanitarians . . . are the shiftless, the imprudent, the negligent, the impractical, and the inefficient, or they are the idle, the intemperate, the extravagant, and the vicious."

The quotation above is most likely an expression of which Gilded Age perspective on wealth?

(A) The views of philanthropists like John D. Rockefeller and Andrew Mellon
(B) The policies of the Salvation Army as an expression of the Social Gospel
(C) The goals of Jane Addams's settlement house movement begun in Chicago
(D) Jacob Riis's observations about immigrants in *How the Other Half Lives*
(E) The Social Darwinism views of Herbert Spencer and William Sumner

JUSTICE IN THE WEB.

25. What accusation is symbolized in the portrayal of Jay Gould in the 1885 political cartoon above entitled "Justice in the Web" that helped make him, "The most hated man in America?"

(A) The rich are predators preying on the poor.
(B) Men as rich as Gould must become loathsome mutants of the human soul.
(C) Being rich is evil by its very nature, and those who attain riches have stolen them.
(D) Gould got rich by unfairly controlling cutting-edge communication technology.
(E) The upper class, of which Gould was a part, are justly entrapped in their own plots.

26. All of the following were Theodore Roosevelt's goals in his Square Deal **EXCEPT**

    (A) using the Sherman Antitrust Act to regulate corporations and break "bad" trusts.
    (B) establishing the Federal Reserve System to regulate the banking industry.
    (C) passing the Pure Food and Drug Act to increase the regulatory power of government.
    (D) conserving natural resources systematically in national forests and parks.
    (E) ridding the meat-packing industry of the evils exposed in Upton Sinclair's *The Jungle*.

27. Woodrow Wilson won reelection in 1916 by saying the United States should

    (A) lead in the formation of the League of Nations and end all wars.
    (B) increase patrols of the U.S. Navy with antisubmarine destroyers in the Atlantic.
    (C) avoid sending Americans to fight in World War I in Europe.
    (D) take the lead in defending freedom with military intervention in Europe.
    (E) trade with neither the United Kingdom nor Germany in order to avoid war.

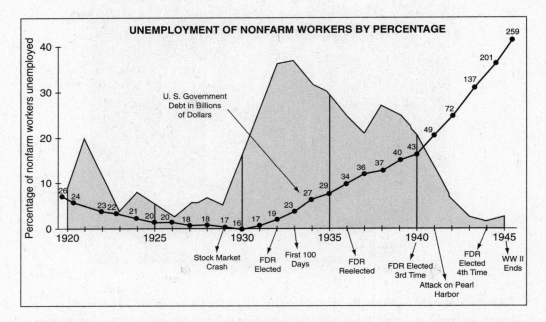

28. All of the following conclusions can be drawn from the data represented on the graph above **EXCEPT**

    (A) the economy during the 1920s helped pay down the debt from World War I.
    (B) the Stock Market Crash led to unemployment as consumption dropped.
    (C) Franklin D. Roosevelt increased New Deal deficit spending after his first reelection.
    (D) increased deficit spending for New Deal programs reduced unemployment.
    (E) the deficit spending for World War II outweighed that for New Deal programs.

29. Joseph McCarthy's professed campaign to ferret out communists from American government and society ended because

(A) blacklisted Hollywood executives produced a film lampooning McCarthyism.
(B) McCarthy's hearings became a frivolous media circus because he televised them.
(C) most people thought his charge that there were communists in the army preposterous.
(D) Arthur Miller's play, *The Crucible*, linked McCarthyism to the Salem witch trials.
(E) McCarthy's claim of communists in the State Department was unsubstantiated.

30. In what way was the 1770 Boston Massacre significantly different from how Americans portrayed it in revolutionary propaganda?

(A) The number of British soldiers involved in the incident was lower than reported.
(B) The size of the Boston mob was much larger than reported.
(C) The murder of three of the British soldiers by Americans with clubs went unreported.
(D) The drunkenness of the British officer who gave the order to fire went unreported.
(E) The provocations of the mob that caused the soldiers to fire in self-defense went unreported.

31. "Now, the fact is, we never have objected to become citizens of the United States and to conform to her laws . . . but we have required the protection and privileges of her laws to accompany that conformity on our part. We have asked this repeatedly and repeatedly has it been denied . . . ."

What type of individual from the early nineteenth century would most likely have made the plea from the quotation above?

(A) An escaped slave arguing in court to keep his or her freedom
(B) An Irish immigrant protesting abuse by the police in Boston
(C) A Chinese laborer in the California gold rush
(D) An American Indian chief protesting treatment of his tribe
(E) A female suffragist giving a speech about women's rights

32. The events known as "Bleeding Kansas" resulted from

(A) the crossing of American Indian reservations by the first transcontinental railroad.
(B) the competition between Northerners and Southerners over the spread of slavery.
(C) the migration to homesteads by African Americans trying to escape sharecropping.
(D) the range wars between farmers and cattlemen caused by the invention of barbed wire.
(E) the invasion of the free state of Kansas by Confederates during the Civil War.

33. All of the following individuals or organizations contributed to the passage of laws restricting child labor **EXCEPT**

   (A) Jane Addams and settlement houses advocating for the care of immigrant children.
   (B) muckraker Lewis Hine's photography of children working in dangerous jobs.
   (C) the American Federation of Labor which said child workers lowered the wages of adults.
   (D) the Supreme Court that declared child labor unconstitutional in a case in 1922.
   (E) the Congress that passed the Fair Labor Standards Act to help regulate child labor.

34. Which American company did Ida Tarbell attack by publishing articles from 1903 to 1904 in *McClure's Magazine*?

   (A) United States Steel
   (B) The Northern Securities Company
   (C) General Electric
   (D) Standard Oil
   (E) Western Union

35. Why did the United States government have to resort back to the Sherman Antitrust Act from 1890 even after passing the Clayton Antitrust Act in 1914?

   (A) The Supreme Court declared the Clayton Antitrust Act unconstitutional.
   (B) The Clayton Antitrust Act was unpopular because Woodrow Wilson supported it.
   (C) Corporate lawyers found loopholes around the Clayton Antitrust Act's excessive details.
   (D) President Wilson's attorney general refused to enforce the Clayton Antitrust Act.
   (E) The Clayton Antitrust Act undermined the government's support for the Allies in Europe.

36. The Dust Bowl shaped the perception of the American people regarding the New Deal by

   (A) contributing to the apparent success of the Agricultural Adjustment Act's price controls.
   (B) causing Franklin D. Roosevelt nearly to lose the Election of 1936 to Alf Landon.
   (C) shifting blame for the drought to the government's failed farm management policies.
   (D) reducing support for the New Deal among small farmers who were ruined by the drought.
   (E) increasing support for the New Deal as the Civilian Conservation Corps turned to irrigation.

37. The death of Emmett Till in Mississippi in 1955 affected the civil rights movement by

   (A) discouraging young people from taking action after seeing a photo of his dead face.
   (B) encouraging faith in the court system after his white murderers were tried and convicted.
   (C) drawing national attention to racism in the South because he was a young, northern boy.
   (D) igniting broad support since Martin Luther King Jr. and Malcolm X attended his funeral.
   (E) causing parents to forbid their children from participating in fear they would meet his fate.

38. The Bill of Rights was added to the U.S. Constitution for all of the following reasons **EXCEPT**

   (A) they attempted to prevent the abuses Americans experienced at the hands of the British.
   (B) they were concessions to states who otherwise had refused to ratify the Constitution.
   (C) they were an attempt by Anti-Federalists to counter the growing influence of Federalists.
   (D) they were the final expression of the American Revolution agreed upon by all the Founders.
   (E) they were a statement that the government was not the source but the protector of liberty.

39. "3 P.M. Attended the funeral of an Italian as far as the ferry. Hurried back to make his appearance at the funeral of a Hebrew constituent. Went conspicuously to the front both in the Catholic church and the synagogue, and later attended the Hebrew confirmation ceremonies in the synagogue."

   The quotation above is most likely taken from the account of the daily life of which type of individual prevalent during the early years of American urbanization?

   (A) A nativist politician from the Know-Nothing Party
   (B) A young college woman working in the settlement house movement in Chicago
   (C) An Irish police officer responsible for protecting immigrants in New York City
   (D) A Pinkerton detective attempting to infiltrate the socialist wing of a labor union
   (E) A Tammany Hall politician attempting to turn compassion into votes

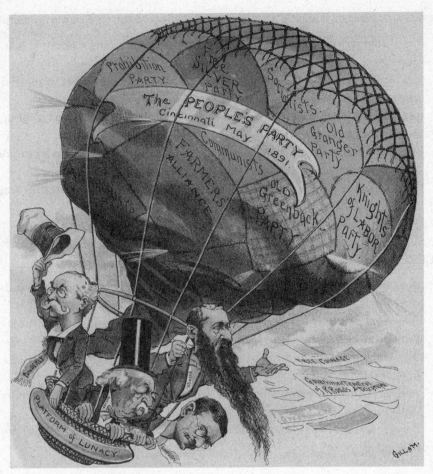

"A PARTY OF PATCHES," JUNE 6, 1891

40. The political cartoon above is suggesting that the Populist Party

   (A) could make an impact even though it was patched together from other movements.

   (B) revolved around communism regardless of the other ideas expressed by its members.

   (C) harnessed widespread discontent but was ineffectual when it came to serious reform.

   (D) was not a threat to the status quo but rather a collection of harmless propagandists.

   (E) relied too much on "hot air" and would come to nothing because of empty rhetoric.

41. Whose list of offices held includes, Governor of the Philippines, Secretary of War, Governor of Cuba, Acting Secretary of State, President of the United States, and Chief Justice of the Supreme Court?

(A) William McKinley
(B) Theodore Roosevelt
(C) William Howard Taft
(D) Woodrow Wilson
(E) Herbert Hoover

42. In the debate about American imperialism, "spheres of influence" were

(A) countries the United States believed could be turned into democratic republics.
(B) developing countries considered fruitful fields of service for American missionaries.
(C) regions where the United States sought economic privileges in exchange for aid and protection.
(D) foreign seaports considered strategic locations for future U.S. naval bases.
(E) Pacific Islands that permitted storage of coal reserves for U.S. merchant and naval vessels.

43. The U.S. government formed the Securities and Exchange Commission (SEC) during the New Deal era in order to

(A) require quarterly financial reports from companies so investors could make wise choices.
(B) end unscrupulous investment practices of banks responsible for the Stock Market Crash.
(C) avoid government regulation of Wall Street by instituting standards for self-regulation.
(D) give the sharpest stock trader, Joseph P. Kennedy, the power to reform the stock exchange.
(E) replace the Federal Reserve as the chief government agency overseeing the economy.

44. The United States Congress rejected involvement in the League of Nations but supported involvement in the United Nations because

(A) the U.N. headquarters were in New York City where the United States would have more influence.
(B) the United States was the only nation wealthy enough to fund the operations of the United Nations.
(C) the United States was assured a spot on the Security Council for its aid in ending World War II.
(D) the United States had to join in self-defense with the new threat of atomic weapons.
(E) the majority of developing nations in the United Nations agreed the United States was the key to world peace.

45. The involvement of the United States in the Korean War resulted in

    (A)   a treaty between North and South Korea dividing the peninsula at the thirty-eighth parallel.

    (B)   the defeat of South Korea by North Korea once western allies pulled out of the war.

    (C)   the defeat of North Korea by South Korea but with the Communist Party still intact.

    (D)   a United Nations resolution saying that East Asia was off limits to American intervention.

    (E)   the containment of communism with the peninsula divided as it was after World War II.

46. The 1962 Cuban Missile Crisis was resolved because

    (A)   the Soviets removed missiles from Cuba and the Americans removed missiles from Turkey.

    (B)   the United States invaded Cuba and forced Fidel Castro to turn the missiles over to U.N. inspectors.

    (C)   the U.S.S.R. removed Castro from power in Cuba and voluntarily removed the missiles.

    (D)   the U.S.S.R. relented after the United States sank a Soviet destroyer that was carrying missiles.

    (E)   the United Nations intervened and helped negotiate a peaceful solution to the crisis.

47. Which statement best describes the goals or strategies of Freedom Schools used by civil rights activists in the South during the 1960s?

    (A)   The schools trained students in the principles of the black power movement.

    (B)   Students boycotted schools that had not yet integrated as ordered by the Supreme Court.

    (C)   Children attended programs encouraging appreciation of African-American history.

    (D)   Teachers inserted civil rights issues into their lessons to inspire students to pursue freedom.

    (E)   Civil rights leaders provided workshops to train students in non-violent protest techniques.

48. Henry Kissinger's greatest contribution to keeping the peace between the communist world and the United States during the Cold War was that he

    (A)   organized NATO and SEATO as alliances to stop the spread of communism.

    (B)   helped secure the Camp David Accords in order to stop communism in the Middle East.

    (C)   negotiated an end to the Suez Crisis that threatened to ignite World War III.

    (D)   recognized the animosity between Chinese and Soviet communists and exploited it.

    (E)   developed a plan for economic aid for European nations threatened by communism.

49. Colonial American society enjoyed a greater amount of social mobility than eighteenth-century English society because

(A) American colonists experienced a longer lifespan than did their counterparts in England.
(B) the legal restraints that preserved English social classes did not exist in America.
(C) leadership in warfare was not limited to aristocrats in America as it was in England.
(D) developments in American industrial growth surpassed those of the English economy.
(E) the absence of a servant class in America gave a wider range of job opportunities.

50. The Half-way Covenant affected the society of colonial New England by

(A) boosting church membership with the first widespread revival of Protestant Christianity.
(B) eroding doctrinal purity and societal unity but making communities more democratic.
(C) creating peace with American Indians by opening church membership to them.
(D) causing more and more descendants of the Puritans to return to the Anglican Church.
(E) decreasing New Englanders' interest in religion and increasing their interest in wealth.

51. Which statement correctly explains checks and balances among the three branches of government established by the U.S. Constitution?

(A) The president can remove incompetent judges; the Congress can remove incompetent presidents; and the Supreme Court can force a gridlocked Congress to pass needed laws.
(B) The Supreme Court can settle any presidential election in which there is not a clear winner; the president can nullify judicial decisions; and the Congress can remove rogue judges.
(C) The president can veto legislation by the Congress; Congress can review the nominations of the executive branch; and the Supreme Court can declare laws to be unconstitutional.
(D) The Supreme Court can refuse to endorse a treaty; the president can refuse to enforce judicial decisions; and the Congress can vote to reverse Supreme Court decisions.
(E) The president can close a session of Congress; the Congress can declare a presidential election void; and the Supreme Court can stop enforcement of unconstitutional laws.

52. With which previous law(s) was the conflict in the Nullification Crisis in the 1830s most closely associated?

(A) The Judiciary Act of 1789
(B) The Alien and Sedition Acts of 1798
(C) The Virginia and Kentucky Resolutions of 1798-1799
(D) The Embargo Act of 1807
(E) The Non-Intercourse Act of 1809

53. The 1860 proposal known as the Crittenden Compromise attempted to prevent the Civil War by

(A) balancing the free and slave states in the Senate by purchasing land in Cuba for a new state.
(B) having the government purchase all the slaves in the South to compensate for abolition.
(C) freeing all slaves born after January 1, 1861 when each slave turned twenty-five years old.
(D) extending the Missouri Compromise line to the Pacific Ocean to balance states in the West.
(E) electing two presidents, one from the North and one from the South, to end sectionalism.

54. All of the following were foreign policy issues for the United States after the Civil War **EXCEPT**

(A) the installation of a French puppet government in Mexico despite the Monroe Doctrine.
(B) the conflict known as the Aroostook War over the border between Maine and Canada.
(C) Russian encroachment on American territory through expansion of colonies in Alaska.
(D) the United Kingdom refused to pay damages for providing the Confederacy with ships.
(E) the United Kingdom disputed a boundary with Venezuela in violation of the Monroe Doctrine.

55. The main source of capital for the companies building the first transcontinental railroad in 1862 was through

(A) selling stock to the public enthused by the idea of crossing the continent with a railroad.
(B) issuing bonds that were snatched up by foreign and domestic banks and investors.
(C) receiving an amount of money for every mile of track from the federal government.
(D) making each section of the railroad economically viable with its own resources.
(E) discovering gold and silver along the way that covered costs until passengers came onboard.

56. The Haymarket Square Riot in Chicago in 1886 affected the Knights of Labor (KOL) by

(A) attracting support to the presidential campaign of the union leader, Terence Powderly.

(B) convincing Samuel Gompers to leave the KOL to form the American Federation of Labor.

(C) creating unity between skilled and unskilled workers in the union for the first time.

(D) leading to the immediate end of the KOL to avoid tainting the overall labor movement.

(E) causing the membership of the KOL to decline and the union never to recover.

57. All of the following qualities were advantages the Progressive Reform movement had over the Populist movement **EXCEPT**

(A) support for Progressivism came from within both major political parties.

(B) Progressivism appealed to immigrants by helping them to assimilate.

(C) middle-class, well-educated citizens embraced Progressivism.

(D) Progressivism sought to address the problem of urban industrial workers.

(E) women took a leading role in Progressivism.

58. In what type of setting did the Supreme Court case *Plessy* v. *Ferguson* sanction segregation with the phrase "separate but equal?"

(A) Restaurants and other dining facilities including bars

(B) Hotels, inns, and other lodging facilities

(C) Elementary, secondary, and postsecondary educational facilities

(D) Transportation facilities including railroads and steamships

(E) Churches, synagogues, and other worship facilities

59. The United States acquired the Hawaiian Islands by

(A) taking them from Spain along with the Philippine Islands in the Spanish-American War.

(B) populating them faster than the British could causing the United Kingdom to withdraw.

(C) helping an indigenous revolution succeed and then annexing them.

(D) annexing them when Hawaiians chose the United States over the Japanese Empire.

(E) conquering them with the private armies of corporations running plantations there.

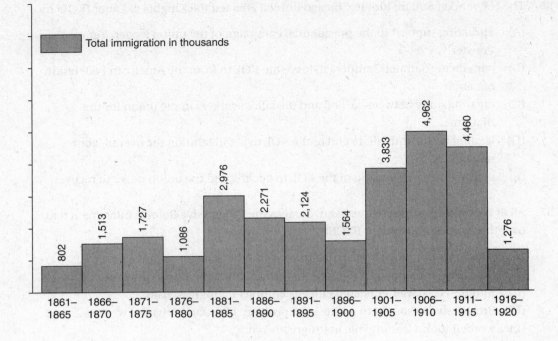

Total immigration in thousands

1861–1865	802
1866–1870	1,513
1871–1875	1,727
1876–1880	1,086
1881–1885	2,976
1886–1890	2,271
1891–1895	2,124
1896–1900	1,564
1901–1905	3,833
1906–1910	4,962
1911–1915	4,460
1916–1920	1,276

60. Which of the following conclusions about immigration to the United States from 1861 to 1920 does the data contained in the graph above support?

(A) The tensions of the Reconstruction period reduced immigration.
(B) Immigration rose dramatically during World War I as refugees fled Europe.
(C) The Gilded Age experienced a steady rate of immigration.
(D) The highest rate of immigration occurred during the New Immigration.
(E) The Quota Act and Immigration Act cut immigration rates dramatically.

61. What significant theory affecting government revenues originated with the Harding and Coolidge administrations in the 1920s?

(A) In times of prosperity, the government should issue bonds to build up emergency reserves.
(B) The government should attract foreign bond investors to fund internal improvements.
(C) The government should raise capital gains taxes when stock prices are soaring.
(D) Lower taxes would boost the economy and, in turn, raise the government's income.
(E) The government should increase taxes during economic booms to redistribute income.

VOTES FOR WOMEN A SUCCESS

NORTH AMERICA PROVES IT

62. Which statement best explains the message of the image and slogan above in which the white regions allowed women's suffrage, the black regions did not allow women's suffrage, and regions with mixed shading allowed only partial suffrage?

(A) Women's suffrage was a popular cause associated with urbanization.
(B) Canada and the United States should both be proud of their progress for women's suffrage.
(C) Areas without women's suffrage were no better than backward, repressive societies.
(D) The Populist movement undermined support for women's suffrage.
(E) Only pioneer women had shown the resolve to deserve the privilege of voting.

63. "War is no longer simply a battle between armed forces in the field. It is a struggle in which each side strives to bring to bear against the enemy the coordinated power of every individual and of every material resource at its command. The conflict extends from the soldier in the front line to the citizen in the remotest hamlet in the rear."

This 1939 assessment of the events leading up to World War II indicates that victory for either side would likely come through which of the following approaches?

(A) Performing routine strategic aerial bombing of the enemy's industrial strength
(B) Being the first power to unlock the technology behind atomic weapons
(C) Surviving the attrition of total war longer than the enemy could
(D) Arriving in the enemy's capital city first with sufficient forces to conquer it
(E) Projecting air, sea, and ground forces across more of the globe than the enemy

64. John L. Lewis contributed the most to the American labor movement by

(A) restoring belief in the solidarity of skilled and unskilled workers in given industries.

(B) being the first major labor leader to repudiate the use of strikes as tools to air grievances.

(C) ridding his national organization of socialists, communists, and other radical elements.

(D) embracing the disparate needs of both coal miners and automobile workers.

(E) being the first leader of a new cabinet position created by Theodore Roosevelt.

65. Which statement best explains how the Cold War ended?

(A) Mikhail Gorbachev destroyed communism by himself from within the Soviet Union.

(B) Communism's economic flaws undermined the ability of the Soviet Union to compete.

(C) United States military aid in Afghanistan ended Soviet imperialism.

(D) Development of "Star Wars" defensive technology caused the Soviet Union to surrender.

(E) The United Nations amassed enough support in the General Assembly to negotiate peace.

66. All of the following statements about the 1991 Persian Gulf War are true **EXCEPT**

(A) the United States acted unilaterally to liberate Kuwait after Saddam Hussein invaded.

(B) the main force attacking Iraq swept through a desert in a flanking maneuver.

(C) the United Nations supported U.S. actions in the Persian Gulf region.

(D) the United States destroyed most of the Iraqi Republican Guard forces from the air.

(E) the war was popular in the United States and boosted the president's approval rating.

67. The disputed Election of 2000 between George W. Bush and Al Gore was decided by

(A) the House of Representatives because there was no clear winner.

(B) counting ballots from military personnel and other Americans from overseas after the fact.

(C) Gore's conceding the election to avoid a delay that would go beyond constitutional limits.

(D) holding a recount in Florida where the crisis arose because of a tiny margin of victory there.

(E) the Supreme Court's declaring Bush the winner by saying recounts were unconstitutional.

68. What did Elisha G. Otis invent that made giant skyscrapers feasible?

(A) The steel I-beams that made construction of multiple stories possible
(B) Threaded steel bars used to reinforce concrete
(C) An enclosed hoist or elevator
(D) Braided steel cables of over one thousand feet in length capable of holding heavy weight
(E) An emergency brake that would activate if an elevator cable snapped

69. The Supreme Court decided during World War II in *Korematsu* v. *United States* that

(A) Japanese Americans could serve in the American military only in noncombatant roles.
(B) second-generation Japanese Americans need not be interned for national security.
(C) interning the Japanese living in the United States in camps was a reasonable precaution.
(D) the deportation of Japanese Americans was unconstitutional and should cease.
(E) interning Japanese Americans was unconstitutional, and the United States owed them compensation.

70. All of the following charges against Anne Hutchinson led to her banishment from the Massachusetts Bay Colony **EXCEPT**

(A) she was banned from teaching men about spiritual matters because she was a woman.
(B) she taught about the Bible in her home rather than in church.
(C) she taught heretical doctrines contrary to Puritan teachings.
(D) she practiced witchcraft and cursed her neighbors.
(E) she refused to submit to her earthly spiritual authorities.

71. Daniel Boone contributed to westward settlement mainly by

(A) fighting as a scout in the French and Indian War that opened the Ohio River Valley.
(B) inspiring James Fenimore Cooper's hero of the popular *Leatherstocking Tales.*
(C) blazing a trail through the Appalachian Mountains allowing easier passage.
(D) befriending American Indian tribes while hunting and trapping in the wilderness.
(E) leading Tennesseans to volunteer to hold the Alamo in the Texas War for Independence.

"Britannia: Her Colonies," John Carter Brown Library, Brown University

72. Which statement best identifies the message in the political cartoon above that Benjamin Franklin commissioned in 1767?

(A) If France won the French and Indian War, the British Empire would fall.
(B) The American colonies needed a central government to stand against American Indians.
(C) America would seek independence if Britain continued policies like the Stamp Act.
(D) British civilization had entered a period of inevitable decline as the Roman Empire did.
(E) The American colonies were the key to the continued prosperity of the British Empire.

73. All of the following were provisions of the 1774 Coercive Acts **EXCEPT**

(A) replacing Massachusetts self-government with British martial law.
(B) closing the port of Boston until damages for the Boston Tea Party were paid.
(C) allowing British military personnel to be tried in England when accused of crimes.
(D) requiring confiscation of all weapons of Americans living in Boston.
(E) permitting British military officers to take over buildings to house their troops.

74. What was the result of the 1794 Battle of Fallen Timbers?

(A) William Henry Harrison slew Tecumseh and ended his threat to westward settlement.
(B) American Indian tribes ceded their land to the United States in the Treaty of Greenville.
(C) William Henry Harrison resolved to make up for his disgrace in the War of 1812.
(D) American Indian tribes slaughtered an American militia force in coordinated attacks.
(E) American Indians decided to refuse assimilation into American society as farmers.

75. Thomas Jefferson sought the deal with the French that resulted in the Louisiana Purchase in 1803 because he

(A) hoped to secure New Orleans as an outlet for America's western yeoman farmers.
(B) sought to double the size of the country to provide enough land to avoid industrialization.
(C) wanted to make the United States stronger to prove that American values were superior.
(D) needed to secure a base on the Missouri River from which to resist Spanish encroachment.
(E) wanted to find an all-water route across North America to the Pacific Ocean.

76. In which American war did the USS *Constitution* play a decisive role?

(A) The War of 1812
(B) The Texas War for Independence
(C) The Mexican War
(D) The Civil War
(E) The Spanish-American War

77. Which statement below best describes Andrew Jackson's views about the spoils system?

(A) His own supporters should replace civil servants from previous presidential administrations.
(B) His supporters should have complete access to the White House during his presidency.
(C) Jobs in government required loyalty rather than skill, so they should go to those he trusted.
(D) Only a few bureaucrats should be replaced to reduce interruption in service in transitions.
(E) Congress should not be a part of the confirmation process for cabinet secretaries.

78. The common school movement originated in the belief that children should be

(A) compelled to attend public schools where Protestant values could be taught to all.
(B) taught to discover truth for themselves as they explored only what interested them.
(C) trained to end racism by learning to share all things in common during the school day.
(D) compelled to come to school in a republic to give the country the best chance to survive.
(E) taught to share common experiences and trained to be patriotic factory workers.

79. The invention of the cotton gin affected the institution of African slavery by

(A) limiting the influence of planter aristocrats by boosting their neighbors' production.
(B) spurring abolitionists who now believed machines could replace human laborers.
(C) decreasing the demand for slaves and allowing the African slave trade to be abolished.
(D) increasing the demand for slaves by turning cotton into a lucrative cash crop.
(E) lessening the severity of slaves' working conditions by taking over a tedious process.

80. How did the abolitionism of William Lloyd Garrison differ from that of Frederick Douglass?

(A) Garrison was mainly a writer, whereas Douglass was mainly an orator.
(B) Garrison demanded immediate emancipation, whereas Douglass wanted gradual change.
(C) Garrison's rhetoric was emotional, whereas Douglass used a more intellectual approach.
(D) Garrison refused to cooperate with women, whereas Douglass worked with them.
(E) Garrison ceased when abolition succeeded, whereas Douglass sought continual agitation.

81. The aspect of the Compromise of 1850 that contributed the most to continued sectional controversy was the

(A) North's advantage in the United States Senate once California became a free state.
(B) $10 million given to Texas for the loss of territory to the Utah and New Mexico Territories.
(C) opening of new territories in the West to slavery under the idea of popular sovereignty.
(D) banning of the slave trade in Washington, D. C.
(E) passing of a stricter Fugitive Slave Law.

82. "The Secretary of War may direct such issues of provisions, clothing, and fuel . . . for the immediate and temporary shelter and supply of destitute and suffering refugees and freedmen."

What other services did the Freedmen's Bureau provide African Americans in the South after the Civil War besides those listed in the excerpt from the congressional authorization of the agency quoted above?

(A) Passage to the North for those desiring to leave the South
(B) Monitoring of the treatment of freedmen by their new employers in the South
(C) Free college for those who had completed high school prior to the war
(D) Land confiscated from plantations of former Confederates for every family
(E) Passage back to Africa for those desiring to leave the United States

83. John D. Rockefeller had an advantage over his competitors as he entered the oil industry because he

(A) received his first oil refinery as a gift from his rich father.
(B) invented the equipment that made his refineries more technologically advanced.
(C) sold stock in Standard Oil to the public to amass enough capital to get ahead.
(D) purchased his first refinery with his own savings because he was extremely frugal.
(E) purchased his first refinery for cheap from a man who lost a fortune in a family crisis.

84. The Populist Party lost their influence in American politics as a result of the Election of 1896 because they (their)

(A) chose a candidate who turned out to be just as corrupt as any Gilded Age Republican.
(B) stood against William Jennings Bryan who exposed their flaws during the campaign.
(C) chose a woman as their candidate, and this unprecedented move eroded their support.
(D) essentially joined the Democratic Party with a one-issue campaign platform.
(E) candidate lost with an agrarian platform showing that America had urbanized.

85. Booker T. Washington's principles and activities differed from those of W. E. B. Du Bois because he

(A) focused more on economic goals, whereas Du Bois focused on political goals.
(B) focused on African Americans in the North, whereas Du Bois focused on the South.
(C) wanted his students to serve in the military, whereas Du Bois was against military service.
(D) taught his students classical literature, whereas Du Bois taught vocational skills.
(E) discounted religion in education, whereas Du Bois espoused Christian education.

NEXT!
A president who "does" things.

86. Which statement below best conveys the perspective in the cartoon above that was published during Theodore Roosevelt's presidency?

(A) The president was a meddlesome busybody who used his "bully pulpit" too much.
(B) The president was a heroic figure stamping out corruption at home and abroad.
(C) The president preferred to read about issues more than to lead reform movements.
(D) The president was more concerned with domestic reforms than with global issues.
(E) The president was a diligent, informed reformer who readily gained victories.

87. Why did Woodrow Wilson hesitate to bring the United States into World War I?

(A) The United States had grown disillusioned after its previous intervention in European conflicts.
(B) Women were now voters and did not want their sons to go to war in Europe.
(C) President Wilson did not want to be seen agreeing with Theodore Roosevelt on anything.
(D) There had been no actual threat to the United States or to American lives up until 1917.
(E) The United States needed trade with both sides to restore the economy hurt by the Panic of 1893.

88. Franklin D. Roosevelt contributed to the success of the New Deal mainly by

(A) establishing clear priorities for change from a list of reforms he had planned much earlier.
(B) garnering bipartisan support in Congress by masterfully settling party differences.
(C) communicating to Americans routinely that the New Deal would solve their problems.
(D) inspiring the richest Americans to pay more taxes because he was one of the upper class.
(E) developing a coherent strategy by picking quality advisers and bureaucrats to lead reforms.

89. Ida B. Wells contributed to civil rights for African Americans mainly by

(A) uniting abolitionists and women's suffragists to make both movements succeed faster.
(B) performing as an opera singer in auditoriums where African Americans had been banned.
(C) encouraging self-respect in African-American women by founding a cosmetics company.
(D) leading a national anti-lynching campaign that kept attention on these atrocities.
(E) leading the NAACP in Mississippi after her husband was assassinated.

90. All of the following societal factors kept the United States from slipping back into the Great Depression after World War II **EXCEPT**

(A) war profits allowed companies to invest in transitioning back to producing consumer goods.
(B) President Truman's wage and price controls in his Fair Deal that continued the New Deal.
(C) an unprecedented demand for consumer goods created by a baby boom.
(D) growth in service industries as the prosperity of the 1950s granted Americans free time.
(E) continued massive federal expenditures on national security during the Cold War.

1.	D	31.	D	61.	D
2.	C	32.	B	62.	C
3.	A	33.	D	63.	C
4.	E	34.	D	64.	A
5.	C	35.	C	65.	B
6.	B	36.	A	66.	A
7.	D	37.	C	67.	E
8.	E	38.	D	68.	E
9.	D	39.	E	69.	C
10.	A	40.	C	70.	D
11.	D	41.	C	71.	C
12.	B	42.	C	72.	E
13.	C	43.	B	73.	D
14.	D	44.	D	74.	B
15.	A	45.	E	75.	A
16.	D	46.	A	76.	A
17.	D	47.	C	77.	C
18.	C	48.	D	78.	E
19.	B	49.	B	79.	D
20.	E	50.	B	80.	E
21.	A	51.	C	81.	E
22.	D	52.	C	82.	B
23.	C	53.	D	83.	D
24.	E	54.	B	84.	D
25.	D	55.	C	85.	A
26.	B	56.	E	86.	E
27.	C	57.	E	87.	E
28.	D	58.	D	88.	C
29.	C	59.	C	89.	D
30.	E	60.	D	90.	B

TEST ANALYSIS

STEP 1 Count the number of correct answers.

Enter the total here: _____

STEP 2 Count the number of incorrect answers.

Enter the total here: _____

STEP 3 Multiply the number of incorrect answers by .250.

Enter the product here: _____

STEP 4 Subtract the results obtained in Step 3 from the total obtained in Step 1.

Enter the total here: _____

STEP 5 Round the number obtained in Step 4 to the nearest whole number.

Raw Score = _____

Scaled Score Conversion Table

Raw Score	Scaled Score	Raw Score	Scaled Score	Raw Score	Scaled Score
90–79	800	46–45	600	8–7	400
78	790	44–43	590	6–5	390
77–76	780	42–41	580	4–3	380
75	770	40	570	2–1	370
74	760	39–38	560	0 – –1	360
73–72	750	37–36	550	–2 – –3	350
71	740	35–34	540	–4	340
70–69	730	33–32	530	–5 – –6	330
68	720	31–30	520	–7	320
67–66	710	29–28	510	–8 – –9	310
65–64	700	27	500	–10	300
63	690	26–25	490	–11 – –12	290
62–61	680	24–23	480	–13	280
60–59	670	22–21	470	–14 – –15	270
58–57	660	20–19	460	–16 – –17	260
56–55	650	18–17	450	–18 – –19	250
54–53	640	16–15	440	–20	240
52–51	630	14–13	430	–21 – –22	230
50–49	620	12–11	420		
48–47	610	10–9	410		

ANSWER EXPLANATIONS

1. **(D)** Answer (A) is incorrect in that although Portugal and Spain might have allied against England and France, the Treaty of Tordesillas was to keep them from going to war against each other. That fact reveals why answer (E) is also incorrect. The Pope was trying to keep two Roman Catholic countries from fighting; there was no indication he planned to control colonization. Portugal did not need Italian navigators thanks to Prince Henry the navigator, and no treaty in the fifteenth century could have accomplished answer (C). Answer (D) reveals that although the Portuguese had exclusive access to Africa, the arc drawn by the treaty would only allow them access to Brazil. The rest of the Western Hemisphere was granted to Spain.

2. **(C)** Answer (C) is the only answer precisely true of Maryland. Answer (A) was true of Maryland but was not unique in that several colonies had similar laws. Answer (B) was true of Pennsylvania. Answer (D) was true of Massachusetts in that Maine remained a part of the colony and even the state until the Missouri Compromise in 1820. Answer (E) was true of South Carolina.

3. **(A)** Answer (A) explains the reality beyond the myth of the shape of the trade routes in the "Triangular Trade." Answer (B) is incorrect in that the Board of Trade would have frowned on those routes that bypassed the mother country just as it frowned on the export of any manufactured goods from the colonies. Answer (D) is also an anti-mercantilist premise not tolerated in Great Britain. Nothing England accomplished quite matched the lucrative nature of the annual Spanish treasure fleet from answer (C) except over the long haul when Spain's bullion ran out. Scottish and Dutch middlemen did operate in, say, the tobacco markets, but they did not control the colonial triangular trade.

4. **(E)** James II was not motivated by rivalry, revenge, or humanitarianism as hinted at in answers (A), (B), and (D), respectively. Nor did he need a base to attack the Dutch because they had already transferred their colony to England in 1664. Answer (E) indicates the British government's real intention. They wanted Andros to function as a Spanish viceroy did in the Spanish colonies in order to end salutary neglect.

5. **(C)** Answer (A) is incorrect in that political parties were not originally valued in the American republic, but answer (B) is incorrect because women had always been valued for this capacity. The additional new value placed on American women stemmed from the idea expressed in answer (C) that the republic depended on each citizen's contributions to survive. Answer (D) could be implied in the notion of "republican motherhood," but the higher calling for women was about much more than boosting population. Answer (E) is incorrect in that most American children were schooled at home by their mothers, and when schools did become more established they focused more on classical education than practical education.

6. **(B)** This answer is a close call because black codes (which included vagrancy laws) and slave codes would have been repugnant to many Christians and others in Philadelphia, but the year is the key. By 1851 all northern ire was focused on the Fugitive Slave Law associated with the Compromise of 1850, and this law was the key legal provision to perpetuate slavery's existence. Personal liberty laws mentioned in answer (A) were actually passed to protect freedmen and African Americans who were born free in an era where they could have been captured and either returned to or placed in slavery.

7. **(D)** Answer (A) is entirely a contradiction in terms; the South did not submit to military occupation, and home rule by its very definition would have meant the end of military occupation. The Klan never sought sanction, as suggested in answer (B), for its operations, fraternal or militant. Answer (C) was a tacit understanding associated with Reconstruction, not the Compromise of 1877, which was agreed upon to settle the Election of 1876 in the matter described in answer (D) for Louisiana, Florida, and South Carolina. Answer (E) evokes Lincoln's Ten Per Cent Plan that was rejected nearly immediately after his assassination.

8. **(E)** The Fair Deal took on the macro domestic problem explained in answer (E), not specifically any of the others in answers (A), (B), (C), and (D). Answer (A) was more the goal associated with the Truman Doctrine and the Marshall Plan. Answer (C) was more a function of the private sector and market forces than government action. Answer (D) is a reference to the G.I. Bill that was only indirectly a part of the Fair Deal. Truman was the first president to take formal actions to advance civil rights for African Americans, but again, the Fair Deal was focused on the bigger picture.

9. **(D)** All of the answers evoke issues associated with the Vietnam War, but even though the Pentagon Papers came out during the Nixon administration they were Daniel Ellsberg's attempt to discredit the whole war by exposing the lies of the Johnson administration. Nixon had his own struggles with telling the truth, and this bipartisan deception on the part of two presidents in a row created the "credibility gap."

10. **(A)** While Champlain did discover Lake Champlain, it did not serve as a border between New France and New Amsterdam as suggested in answer (B). Answers (C), (D), and (E) are all the accomplishments of other explorers, but Samuel de Champlain got the whole enterprise started as noted in answer (A).

11. **(D)** Answers (A), (B), and (C) all named regions fought over during the French and Indian War, but the conflict began when George Washington ran into the French in the Ohio River Valley. The Mississippi River delta was more a theater of the War of 1812 much later.

12. **(B)** Because the document bans slavery it can only be associated with the Northwest Ordinance, and the ban in question served as a major precedent evoked by Abraham Lincoln in the 1850s. All of the rest of the documents listed in one way or another supported slavery or certainly did not ban it. The Tallmadge Amendment wanted to abolish slavery from Missouri but only gradually. The Lecompton Constitution was the pro-slavery (and fraudulent) document that originally tried to organize the Kansas Territory.

13. **(C)** Answer (A) cannot be true because the main goal of the Missouri Compromise was not to please the South, or the North for that matter, as would be the case if answer (E) were true. Even the division of the Louisiana Purchase into free and slave states mentioned in answer (D) was merely the means to the end, the main goal expressed in answer (C). Answer (B) is the opposite of the truth. Henry Clay tried to keep all the competing goals from destroying the Union. The North already had an advantage in the House of Representatives by virtue of its larger population. The main goal of the compromise was to maintain the balance in the Senate where each state had equal representation regardless of population.

14. **(D)** Answer (A) is a fabrication based on a stereotype, and answer (B) does not address a significant role because common cultural roots existed long before the McGuffey Readers. Both answers (C) and (E) are opposite to the actual impact and quality of the Readers. Answer (D) relates the context of both the Readers and the common school movement in the antebellum era of reform.

15. **(A)** Answer (A) is the ironic truth of this transcendental utopia. Answer (B) was true of Oneida and other Shaker towns. Answer (C) was more the dream of Brook Farm that never came to be. Answer (D) is incorrect in that the Brook Farm was in Massachusetts, not the South. Answer (E) was truer of the utopian reforms of the Mormons, or the Church of Jesus Christ of Latter-Day Saints.

16. **(D)** All of the answers express aspects of the cultural phenomenon wrapped up in the simple elegance of "Negro spirituals" except answer (D), which was not true because these songs were not placed in hymn books or in any books until after the Freedmen's Bureau and other agencies made efforts to provide literacy to African Americans after slavery was over. Teaching slaves to read was illegal in the antebellum South, and the style in which these songs were sung was precisely the result of the illiteracy of slaves.

17. **(D)** Answer (D) is the truth amid the other answers that hint at realities of the Monroe Doctrine. There was still diplomatic conflict until the Treaty of Washington in 1871. Secretary of State John Quincy Adams and Monroe specifically said the New World empire of Spain would not be picked over by England or any other European country. Answers (A) and (B) are nearly the exact opposite of the truth. For example, the menace of the Barbary Pirates to American shipping had been ended earlier under Thomas Jefferson.

18. **(C)** Answer (C) related Lincoln's ingenious ploy. All of the other answers are fabrications in that Lincoln did not attack Ft. Sumter at all, let alone with ironclads, which did not yet exist, and Ft. Sumter fell. Answer (B) is a dim reference to the Trent Affair that occurred much later in the war.

19. **(B)** All of the other answers hint at issues surrounding the American Revolution that could have used the communication skills of Samuel Adams and others who organized the Committees of Correspondence. Only answer (A) is close to some of the operations of the Sons of Liberty and other groups searching for "enemies of the people" who cooperated with the British, but the Committees of Correspondence were specifically dedicated to the tasks mentioned in answer (B).

20. **(E)** All of the answers have been touted by some loose construction supporters at one time or another, except for answer (C), which falsely implies the Founding Fathers anticipated a two-party system in American politics, but Hamilton himself simply referred to the implied powers inherent in the elastic clause of the U.S. Constitution. Most of the other rationales exceed Hamilton's position, which actually did stem from a line in the document.

21. **(A)** Jefferson did dramatically reduce federal expenditures by taking all of these measures except for answer (A), which may eventually happen in the United States but has not yet despite the existence of many successful private shipping companies alongside a Post Office that is struggling financially.

22. **(D)** Answer (D) conveys the reality that the goal of the American Colonization Society was never popular with many of the Americans it tried to serve. Answers (A), (C), and (E) are all fabrications, especially because Abraham Lincoln actively supported colonization of South America with African Americans freed from slavery in the United States. Answer (B) relates a truth about Marcus Garvey, but he was associated with the much later Back to Africa movement of the 1920s.

23. **(C)** All of the other answers are exactly the opposite of the truth regarding sharecropping. Both white Americans and African Americans fell into sharecropping in the southern economy ruined by the Civil War. Sharecroppers regardless of race cultivated mostly cotton, and the appearance of an incentive in sharecropping led families to put all the children in the fields alongside their parents, whereas under slavery most children started working in the field at the age of eight or nine. Although some African Americans did own land and "hire" sharecroppers, some African Americans had also owned slaves in the antebellum South. The nature of sharecropping, however, created a situation where almost no sharecroppers became successful economically until after World War II began, and still the institution of tenant farming died hard.

24. **(E)** Although Jacob Riis stereotyped some of his fellow immigrants in *How the Other Half Lives*, his rhetoric never quite took on the biting edge of which the two Social Darwinists mentioned in answer (E) were capable. Rockefeller and Carnegie may have had Social Darwinian leanings but also did not go on record with such inflammatory diction. Jane Addams, the Salvation Army, and other supporters of the Social Gospel were opposed to such views on those locked in poverty.

25. **(D)** Answers (A) and (C) are too general as interpretations, whereas answer (B) is too metaphorical for the genre of this type of cartoon. Political cartoons of this nature targeted specific people with specific accusations like the one in answer (D). Answer (E) is incorrect in that Gould is portrayed as a spider on a web of telegraph wires ready to catch others, not as entrapped himself. The cartoon criticized Gould's use of the Western Union Telegraph Company he formed that by the 1880s possessed a monopoly of information by being the network to send, among other items, Associated Press stories to member newspapers around the country.

26. **(B)** Answer (B) was an initiative of Woodrow Wilson's version of Progressivism. Theodore Roosevelt took on all the others in the Square Deal.

27. **(C)** Although all of these policies were either advocated by Wilson or others in regard to the events associated with World War I, in 1916 he was elected because he promised to remain neutral when the electorate of the United States was still largely isolationist. Events after the election as well as Wilson's own change of heart led directly to American involvement by 1917.

28. **(D)** Answer (D) is the only conclusion not entirely supported by the graph in that the deficit spending of the early New Deal had a substantial impact on unemployment, but the increased deficit spending from 1937 to 1938 did not. Unemployment rose during those years until after Roosevelt's pledge to make the United States the "arsenal of democracy" led to almost full employment in World War II. Answer (A) is revealed by the low unemployment and decreasing debt levels of the 1920s (despite the fact that certain economic practices were quietly destabilizing the country). Answer (B) explains

the connection between the Stock Market Crash and the Great Depression illustrated in the graph when economic uncertainty led to decreased consumption and massive layoffs. Even though Roosevelt decreased spending late in his first term, his reelection in 1936 gave him a mandate to increase it despite growing debt, so answer (C) is true (after his reelections in 1940 and 1944, also). Answer (E) is revealed by the exponential growth in the national debt after 1941 when the United States entered the largest war in world history.

29. **(C)** Although answers (D) and (E) are true and the Second Red Scare did lead to black-listing of people in Hollywood, neither Arthur Miller's play nor any film directly discredited McCarthy like his televised investigation into the army. During the Cold War most Americans did find the hunt for communists in the army to be preposterous even though McCarthy had the temerity to discredit World War II hero George C. Marshall of Marshall Plan fame for supposedly not doing enough to keep China from becoming communist. Contrary to the media circus of many of today's televised hearings alluded to in answer (B), however, the McCarthy hearings were deadly serious affairs put on by this first American politician who understood television's political potential.

30. **(E)** Both print coverage and Paul Revere's famous engraving of the Boston Massacre downplayed the size and the ferocity of the Boston mob. The crowd was armed and attacked the British soldiers with rocks, ice chunks, and snowballs while pressing them up against a wall. Some of the mob may have had more lethal weapons, and John Adams actually defended the soldiers to prove American justice could be impartial and got them acquitted of murder on the grounds of self-defense as mentioned in answer (E). Answers (A) and (B) are the reverse of the truth and answers (C) and (D) are fabrications.

31. **(D)** Of the groups or individuals listed, only American Indians were pressured culturally, economically, and politically to become citizens of the United States and then denied the full protection of American law as in the incidents known collectively as the "Trail of Tears." Slaves, the Irish, the Chinese, and women all found themselves the victims of discrimination, but these all had to request or fight for citizenship. Thomas Jefferson and other presidents and leaders offered citizenship in the United States to American Indians, but usually the offer meant a repudiation of tribal identities and was motivated by a desire to pacify the indigenous people of North America.

32. **(B)** "Bleeding Kansas" is a reference to the antebellum events that are described in answer (B) and particularly the federal policy of popular sovereignty determining the slavery question as a result of the Kansas-Nebraska Act. Answer (A) involved bloodshed, but at the time the first transcontinental railroad was built the territory was open to use by American Indian tribes like the Cheyenne without being placed on reservations. Answer (E) is a fabrication, but answers (C) and (D) reveal that Kansas has had a vibrant history even though these events happened after the Civil War was over.

33. **(D)** All of the other answers correctly recount some of the history of the movement to end child labor. Answer (D) is correct because in the 1920s the Supreme Court viewed the first federal anti-child labor laws to be unconstitutional, not child labor itself. Answer (C) describes how labor unions opposed child labor for less than humanitarian reasons.

34. **(D)** Ida Tarbell's father had been put out of the oil-refining business by the rise of Standard Oil of Ohio, John Rockefeller's original company. Ida Tarbell wrote the serialized "history" as a muckraker bent on revenge.

35. **(C)** Answer (C) explains the reasons Wilson's New Freedom stance on trusts ultimately gave way to Theodore Roosevelt's more practical New Nationalism approach using the "watchdog" method of applying the Sherman Antitrust Act to the most serious offenders. The Supreme Court did not declare the Clayton Antitrust Act unconstitutional; it just proved to be unworkable. Woodrow Wilson was a popular Progressive with a popular agenda, so answer (B) is wrong. Answer (D) is a reference to Richard Olney, the attorney general under Grover Cleveland who refused to use even the Sherman Antitrust Act to prosecute any monopolistic trusts.

36. **(A)** Answer (A) shows how Franklin D. Roosevelt's desire to achieve parity in farm prices with the high prices experienced by American farmers during World War I was impossible to achieve by government intervention. The Dust Bowl and the Agricultural Adjustment Act combined did not achieve the goal, but because the natural disaster came during the application of the New Deal's policies they seemed more successful. Answers (B), (C), and (D) are the opposite of the truth of the situation, and answer (E) is irrelevant because the Civilian Conservation Corps (CCC) was founded earlier independently from the Dust Bowl and its effects, even though CCC workers did some of the work described.

37. **(C)** Answers (A), (B), and (E) are the exact opposite of what happened as a result of this case, which drew national attention and helped launch the civil rights movement as explained in answer (C). Answer (D) is incorrect because, even though future Supreme Court justice Thurgood Marshall was one of the lawyers helping Till's mother, neither Martin Luther King Jr. nor Malcolm X attended the trial. African Americans began to participate actively in civil rights agitation despite the dangers and the institutionalized racism revealed by this injustice.

38. **(D)** All of the other answers reflect the motives and methods of the process that gave rise to the Bill of Rights. As indicated by other amendments and even by the wrangling over what the first ten amendments actually meant as American history unfolded, there has not been and likely never will be an agreed-upon final statement about the meaning of the American Revolution.

39. **(E)** The document is actually taken from the account of a day in the life of George Washington Plunkitt, a notorious Tammany Hall grafter. The nativist politician in answer (A) would likely never be caught dead doing the things described, and although the young woman in answer (B) might do them, she would not record how she attempted to be prominent at the functions. Neither the Pinkerton detective nor the Irish police officer would record this either.

40. **(C)** This cartoon is particularly difficult to interpret without incorporating knowledge of how the Populist Party ended (by crashing and burning in the Election of 1896), and thus using information irrelevant to interpreting the message of the cartoon in real time. Still, answer (A) is belied by the fact that the hodgepodge of spokesmen and ideas is not presented as effectual but ineffectual (hence the correct answer in (C)). Answer (B) is wrong because even though the communists are labeled just beneath the party banner in the center of the balloon, the disunity on the countenances of the men in the basket

portrays a movement with no common center. Still, the very "lunacy" of the collective ideas as portrayed in the cartoon conveys the general fear all of these ideas evoked in those who benefited from the status quo, so the Populists were anything but harmless to American political traditions as suggested in answer (D). Though answer (E) is a possible interpretation of the cartoon, the "hot air" is more the joke of the cartoon than its message. The combined images and the ideas they represent reveal that the artist viewed the Populists as that "species of the genus Quack Reformers," or dreamers, who would accomplish nothing in the way of practical societal change.

41. **(C)** This incredible list of key responsibilities belongs to William Howard Taft who is largely unrecognized as a person of such influence. He was the only president to sit on the Supreme Court after his presidency, and of all these offices, chief justice was the one Taft most desired. All of the other presidents listed had colorful careers and key positions in government but none quite like Taft's that included a major office after their presidential administrations ended.

42. **(C)** Although answer (A) is more the perspective on such relationships after World War II, answer (C) conveys the best overall definition of spheres of influence. Answer (B) was certainly true for some areas and for some Americans, but answer (C) was the key in the debate. Answer (D) was true in some cases but not in all, and answer (E) is more the definition of coaling stations like Midway Island and Guam, which did not belong to any sovereign nation when American imperialism sought them out for the geographical convenience.

43. **(B)** Although answer (A) was part of the function of the Securities and Exchange Commission's (SEC's) oversight, the premise behind the agency's formation was that banks had caused the stock market crash and thus were largely responsible for the Great Depression as stated in answer (B). The SEC was created in the classic sense of a "watchdog" agency in Progressive government. Answer (C) explains part of the rationale, but the industry's establishing its own standards was more true of the movie industry than the financial industry. There is also some truth to answer (D), but it was not the premise behind the formation of the SEC but more an ironic outcome. What truth exists in answer (E) was not a forethought but more of an afterthought and thus, again, not the premise behind the formation of the SEC.

44. **(D)** All of the other answers express some of the ironies in the formation of the United Nations except (A), which was not the reason the Congress chose to involve the United States and is not necessarily true concerning the exertion of influence. Answer (B) was true, but again was not the reason to join and instead could be an argument for some against U.S. participation. Answer (C) is untrue in that the United Nations could not exist at all without the United States holding a permanent seat on the Security Council along with its major World War II allies, so joining or not was not a question at that point. Answer (E) is untrue in that more than half of the developing nations in the United Nations accept foreign aid from the United States but do not cooperate with either U.N. or U.S. goals nor recognize U.S. leadership in the world. Of these choices, only the sobering reality of answer (D) can explain the shift in American involvement from the rejection of the League of Nations to the support of U.S. leadership in the United Nations.

45. **(E)** Answer (E) is the actual outcome. All the rest are twists on the truths of the war that are not beyond imagination in the difficult negotiations of the Cold War. Answer (A) cannot be true in that no treaty was ever signed to end the Korean War. Answer (B) was not the case because South Korea remains a free and thriving economy and society in East Asia, and answer (C) is also not true in that the limited nature of the Korean War did not allow a defeat of communist forces in North Korea. Contrary to answer (D), the United Nations supported American involvement in the conflict and thus tacitly supported containment.

46. **(A)** This close call ended as described in answer (A) although the withdrawal of American missiles was not publicized and is little remembered. President Kennedy specifically disavowed any intention to perform the act described in answer (B), and answer (C) is incorrect in that Fidel Castro was never removed from power. No actual sinking of Soviet vessels occurred as suggested in answer (D) as a result of the blockade of Cuba Kennedy did establish. Answer (E) would have fulfilled the mission of the United Nations but with the Soviet Union and the United States now enemies in the Security Council any such proposals faced the veto power of either side in the Cold War.

47. **(C)** Answer (C) conveys the positive message of education and civic involvement the Freedom Schools tried to inculcate in African-American schoolchildren. The Freedom Schools were not a propaganda project for the black power movement as suggested in answer (A), nor an activist agency staging demonstrations as in answer (B). Answer (D) was perhaps a spinoff of the Freedom Schools, but not their main goal or strategy. Workshops were provided to prepare students in various locations for their encounters with the public during acts of civil disobedience, but the Freedom Schools were, again, not actively participating in activism.

48. **(D)** Answers (A) and (C) were the doings of the Eisenhower administration without the direct involvement of Kissinger, and answer (B) was accomplished by Carter himself, again without the direct participation of Kissinger. Answer (E) was more the responsibility of George C. Marshall in the Truman administration. Answer (D) reveals that if Kissinger, who worked largely in the Nixon and Ford administrations, did nothing else but recognize the Sino/Soviet dissonance he would have been instrumental in helping the free world survive the Cold War.

49. **(B)** Answer (A) was true, especially of New Englanders, but it did not necessarily alter the social class structure. Answer (B) refers to the fact that primogeniture and other laws designed to preserve the social class structure of England did not transfer to America effectively over time. Answer (C) did not transfer well either, but it did exist during colonial wars among Americans and did not play a role in social mobility. Answers (D) and (E) are false in that the colonial American economy did not experience much industrial growth, and the existence of indentured servitude prior to the American Revolution did begin a class structure in America. Part of the revolutionary nature of the American Revolution was the dissolution of a servant class, which did open up new jobs as the nineteenth century began.

50. **(B)** Answer (A) is the opposite of the impact of the Half-way Covenant and was more associated with the First Great Awakening of the 1730s and 1740s. Answer (B) explains how this compromise in membership vows undermined the whole Puritan movement

and made churches operate by congregational vote among members who were no longer believers in Puritan doctrine. Answer (C) also refers to experiences of the First Great Awakening when Jonathan Edwards and others began active mission work among American Indians after the Half-way Covenant had convinced Edwards that a revival was necessary. Answer (D) belies the trend among many breakaway groups within Christianity that even amid change they rarely go back to doctrinal roots. Answer (E) would be true except for the fact that New Englanders under Puritanism were already devoted to hard work in developing a thriving economy, just for different reasons.

51. **(C)** Although all of the other answers contain elements of checks and balances that have developed over the years and some that might be convenient even if unconstitutional, only answer (C) contains three correct statements of constitutional interactions among the three branches of government.

52. **(C)** The precedent for the concept of nullification was set in Jefferson's and Madison's reasoning in their reaction to the Alien and Sedition Acts. The resolutions passed by Virginia and Kentucky were acts of nullification, and when South Carolinians nullified what they called the "Tariff of Abominations," they were building on the notion that states should be the primary determiners of the constitutionality of federal laws. The principle of nullification was a chief cause of the threat to the Union during the antebellum period, especially because even South Carolinians viewed the tariff issue as a dry run for federal laws against slavery.

53. **(D)** Answer (D) conveys the basic ideas of Senator John Crittenden's desperate eleventh-hour attempt to stave off the war that the repeal of the Missouri Compromise for the Kansas-Nebraska Act was partly responsible for bringing on. Answer (A) is a reference to the Ostend Manifesto, which was not a compromise but a cause of the war. Answer (B) refers to Lincoln's and others' plans for compensation that were laughed to scorn in the North and the South. Answer (C) is a reference to the Tallmadge Amendment that would have only applied to Missouri if it were accepted, which it was not. Answer (E) was proposed but never seriously considered.

54. **(B)** Answer (A) refers to Maximilian who was a problem after the Civil War. So were the Russians in answer (B) until the Alaska Purchase, and the British until the Treaty of Washington produced a settlement. The Venezuela boundary dispute occurred in 1895 so it was after the Civil War, but the Aroostook War happened in the 1830s prior to the war.

55. **(C)** Answers (A) and (B) are fabrications except for the fact that the transcontinental railroad was the greatest civil engineering feat of its day. The companies only had hope of accomplishing the daunting task because the federal government wanted it done more than they did and was willing to pay for its construction and the most important internal improvement in America to that time. Answers (D) and (E) are hints about sources of capital, although answer (D) is a direct reference to James J. Hill's approach. His Great Northern railroad was the only transcontinental line built without federal assistance.

56. **(E)** Answer (E) is the only completely true answer. Answer (A) is untrue in that Powderly never ran for president of the United States. Samuel Gompers had already formed the American Federation of Labor for precisely the reason that is the reverse of answer (C), that skilled and unskilled workers united in the KOL were getting nowhere together. The

KOL did not immediately disband as suggested in answer (D) but instead died a slow death that prolonged the negative (and unfair) association resulting from the bombing at their Haymarket Square demonstration.

57. **(E)** All of the answers are true of Progressivism, but although answers (A), (B), (C), and (D) are exclusively a part of the history of this reform movement, women like Mary Lease also led the Populist revolt. Populism arose from the Patrons of Husbandry, or the Grange, which allowed women to be equal members of the organization. This fact contributed to women's receiving the right to vote in western farming states before they did in other parts of the country.

58. **(D)** Although segregation is usually thought of in legal terms in association with education, this case originated with segregated transportation facilities as in answer (D).

59. **(C)** Answer (C) conveys how private American citizens like pineapple plantation owners helped depose Queen Liliuokalani of Hawaii, and then the islands were annexed for coaling stations among other reasons. They were not a part of the Spanish Empire, although they were annexed in 1898 along with those territories and islands acquired from Spain after the Spanish-American War. Answer (B) is a reference to the process of America's acquiring the Oregon Territory, and answers (D) and (E) are fabrications. The Japanese set their sights on Hawaii but not with sufficient zeal to motivate Hawaiians until after they were already Americans. The Dole family helped fight the revolution but not as a corporation wielding private military power.

60. **(D)** Answer (D) is the only conclusion that can be completely supported by the graph in that the New Immigration occurred from 1885 to 1917, and the peak years of immigration ran from 1901 to 1915. Answer (A) is contradicted by the steady increase in immigration after the Civil War until 1875, and the Reconstruction period ending in 1877 was one of nearly constant societal tension. Answer (B) is contradicted by the steep dropoff of the rate of immigration after 1914 when World War I began through its end in 1919. Answer (C) is contradicted by the ups and downs of the rate of immigration throughout the Gilded Age that ran from 1865 to 1900. Answer (E) is contradicted by the fact that the Quota Act and the Immigration Act were both passed after 1920 and their impact on immigration is thus not displayed in the graph.

61. **(D)** Supply-side economics as described in answer (C) were not begun in the 1980s but in the 1920s by Andrew Mellon and other advisers in the Harding and Coolidge administrations. The other answers are a mixture of actual ideas that were espoused by Progressives and others along with fabricated ideas.

62. **(C)** Answer (A) is wrong because at the time when the battle for women's suffrage was reaching its climax (1890–1919), nearly all of the major U.S. cities were in regions that allowed only partial or no voting rights for women. Answer (B) ignores the mixed progress in both nations. Answer (D) is the opposite of the truth in that the Grange and the Populist movements invited the cooperation of women as full members, and the leadership of female spokespersons for both groups led western states where Populism was strong to achieve women's suffrage first. Answer (E) is associated with this connection between Populism and women's suffrage but does not go so far as to make a direct appeal for frontier women having any inherent qualities that would make them better voters. Answer (C) conveys the rhetoric of the women's suffrage movement that

women did advance civilization as the West was settled, but the ominous dark patches in the Northwest Territory and Mexico, as well as the shadow across the urban East in the United States, subtly evokes nativism and anti-Catholic sentiments. This promotional image appeals to the general view in the largely Protestant American society that any similarities with Mexico or Central America or the more Catholic regions of Canada cannot be qualities of which "the land of the free and the home of the brave" should be proud. The image captures the underlying negative stereotypes associated with the reform movements that culminated in Progressive Reform.

63. **(C)** Although answers (A), (B), and (E) became apparent strategic goals as World War II progressed, only answer (D) was thought to be important prior to the war. The document makes no reference to capital cities, however, but does refer to the terrible nature of total warfare that could only be won when the total economic might of a nation was outlasted by the total economic strength of the victor nation or nations.

64. **(A)** Answer (A) explains why John L. Lewis was venerated by coal miners and auto workers among others who joined the Congress of Industrial Organizations (CIO) that split off from the American Federation of Labor (AFL; only later to reunite as the AFL-CIO). Lewis did not repudiate strikes as did Terence Powderly of the Knights of Labor but instead routinely called them. He tolerated some level of radicalism within the umbrella of the CIO, but he was not the first secretary of labor and commerce under Roosevelt. He did embrace the needs of coal miners and auto workers that were not necessarily disparate, but his larger significance to the labor movement is conveyed in answer (A).

65. **(B)** Some claim answer (A) is true, whereas others credit Ronald Reagan, Lech Walesa, Pope John Paul II, and Margaret Thatcher, but the impact of individuals does not explain the whole truth. The United Nations proved inadequate to the task suggested in answer (E). Answer (C) describes the support that helped bog down the Soviet invasion of Afghanistan, but the stalled Soviet military all the more revealed the stalled Soviet economy. Answer (D) was also a factor, but mainly because it exposed to the Soviets and to the free world the reality expressed in answer (B). Through the Cold War the Soviet Union spent from one-quarter to one-third of its gross domestic product (GDP) on national defense, whereas the United States spent only 3 to 4 percent of its GDP to keep pace in this potentially deadliest war of attrition in human history.

66. **(A)** George W. Bush was accused of acting unilaterally (even though the United States had allies in the Iraq War). His father, George H. W. Bush, assembled a vast array of allies to drive Saddam Hussein's forces from neighboring Kuwait in the Persian Gulf War. All of the rest of the answers are true of the Persian Gulf War in contrast to some important aspects of the later war that brought Saddam Hussein to justice.

67. **(E)** All of the other answers are fabrications based on fine points of law and events surrounding this disputed election. The end result is explained in answer (E). Answer (C) is partly true in that former Vice President Al Gore did at one point concede the election, but then took back his concession and ultimately launched the suit that brought the case before the Supreme Court where only five justices made the final opinion that decided the election.

68. **(E)** Skyscrapers as designed by Louis Sullivan needed all of these inventions and innovations, but people were not inclined to get on a hoist for transportation until Elisha Otis

demonstrated his brake by personally standing in an elevator and having the rope holding himself up cut. His brake worked. One cannot conceive of skyscrapers passing much higher into the sky than the original ten-story building in Chicago without safe, working elevators in which it was at least theoretically impossible to fall. Otis is often credited with the invention of the elevator when hoists had existed for centuries. The brake made them practical for moving people.

69. **(C)** During World War II the Supreme Court upheld the federal government's internment policy. Answer (E) relates a later Supreme Court's decision in the matter and those interned were compensated slightly for their loss of private property during the war. Answer (A) belies the fact that some Japanese-Americans entered the American military and were decorated for valor in combat roles. All generations of Japanese-Americans experienced relocation and being interned.

70. **(D)** All of the other answers were enough for the Massachusetts Bay authorities to banish Anne Hutchinson from the colony even though she was never charged with practicing witchcraft. Her case and that of Roger Williams revealed that the Puritans had escaped persecution in England but did not intend to practice religious toleration in their colonies.

71. **(C)** Daniel Boone's storied career included all of the events listed in answers (A), (B), (C), and (D), but the other three events did not compare to the impact of Boone's blazing the trail through the Cumberland Gap as a long hunter in the Appalachian wilderness. The Cumberland Gap became the chief route of the opening of this area to settlement and thus impacted the whole country. Answer (E) is an accomplishment of Davy Crockett, a frontiersman often confused with Daniel Boone.

72. **(E)** Answer (A) cannot be correct since the French and Indian War was over in 1763, and answer (B) was the message of Franklin's more famous cartoon conveying the "Join, or Die" message of the Albany Plan of Union during the French and Indian War. Whereas the 1765 Stamp Act and other British policies had begun to alienate the colonies from the Mother Country, neither Franklin nor any other of the Founding Fathers had yet committed to revolution or independence (the earliest recorded statement of that goal was by Samuel Adams in 1768), so answer (C) is incorrect. While internal evidence from the cartoon would make parallels with the decline of the Roman Empire possible as in answer (D), Franklin was using that motif to strongly warn Great Britain that its mismanagement of her American colonies would ruin not only the colonies but the British Empire. His goal in 1767 was to get Britain to stop asking for too much from her colonies as evidenced by the Latin phrase "Give half to Bellisarius." Knowledge of Latin is not as important in understanding the cartoon as is knowledge of the timeline of the American Revolution.

73. **(D)** All of the other answers contributed to the Coercive Acts being called the Intolerable Acts by American colonists. The British never set out to accomplish the confiscation of all weapons suggested in answer (D), but the clash that became known as the battles of Lexington and Concord did erupt when a British military force was sent to confiscate a cache of weapons.

74. **(B)** The Treaty of Greenville came after the Battle of Fallen Timbers when several American Indian tribes ceded land to the United States. Anthony Wayne won this battle, not William Henry Harrison. Harrison won the Battle of Tippecanoe against Tecumseh,

so he was not disgraced, but Tecumseh was not killed until much later in the War of 1812. Anthony Wayne was sent to avenge a massacre of militiamen that had happened before, not during, the Battle of Fallen Timbers. Answer (E) applied later to American Indian tribes on the Great Plains, but several tribes, like the Cherokee, did come close to assimilating early in the 19th century.

75. **(A)** As much as the other answers were true all or in part regarding the Louisiana Purchase, Jefferson's first priority was to secure New Orleans once Napoleon had wrested control of it from the Spanish. Even though Jefferson was sympathetic to the principles of the French Revolution he could not afford to have a strong empire take over from a weakening empire in holding the outlet of the Mississippi River. The doubling of the country and the subsequent expeditions by Lewis and Clark and Zebulon Pike were goals established after Jefferson offered $10 million to the French for New Orleans and got the entire Louisiana Purchase for just $15 million. Answer (C) describes more the motivation of presidents from John Quincy Adams to James K. Polk in establishing policies associated with Manifest Destiny.

76. **(A)** Although Old Ironsides is still functioning in the U.S. Navy as the oldest commissioned war vessel, her practical use as a combatant ship was only during the War of 1812. The U.S. Navy played no role in the Texas War for Independence but performed admirably in all the wars in answers (C), (D), and (E). By even the Mexican War, however, naval warfare had moved beyond the technology of the USS *Constitution.*

77. **(C)** Although answer (A) conveys the commonly held misconception of Jackson's spoils system, he really once replaced about 20 percent of the civil service job holders. Answer (B) is a reference to the raucous celebration party the night of Jackson's inauguration, but the event was not a part of his routine administration. Answer (C) expresses Jackson's true position even though later presidential administrations practiced more extensive patronage. Answer (D) is the opposite of Jackson's position that the nation should avoid a parasitic civil servant class such as existed during the Era of Good Feelings. Answer (E) hints at Jackson's tendency to ignore his own cabinet in favor of his "Kitchen Cabinet" of personal advisors, but he did not question the constitutional role of Congress in confirming top-ranking members of the executive branch.

78. **(E)** The common school movement was criticized for attempting to improve society by conditioning schoolchildren to the regimented life of factory workers, but it was the first concerted effort to provide public education and answer (E) expresses these dual goals. The creation of a Catholic school system is evidence that the common schools were Protestant in tone, but answer (A) was not an official position or design of the curriculum. Answer (B) alludes to some of the later educational reform theories of John Dewey of Columbia University. Answer (C) was also not one of the original goals although Massachusetts, the state where Horace Mann launched the common school movement, was the first to provide integrated education. Answer (D) is incorrect in that the original public schools did not require compulsory attendance.

79. **(D)** Answers (A), (B), and (E) might have been true if other machines had been invented in the antebellum period that could perform all of the other laborious tasks associated with the cultivation of cotton. Because these other machines were not all invented until after World War II, slaves in the time before the Civil War were in more demand when the

most tedious task of all was made easier with the cotton gin. The cotton gin removed the seeds and other matter from the cotton fibers, and thus the plantations wanted more cotton produced with slave labor than ever before. Answer (C) is incorrect because the demand for slaves went up instead of down, but also because the African slave trade was stopped by the political will of northern congressional representatives as soon as the U.S. Constitution would allow it without regard to economic or technological breakthroughs.

80. **(E)** One half of each of the other answers is incorrect in that both men published newspapers, both men advocated immediate emancipation, both men employed emotionally moving and often inflammatory rhetoric, and both men cooperated with female abolitionists. The important contrast occurred after abolition was successful when Garrison considered his work accomplished, whereas Douglass continued to agitate for the advances of African Americans who remained, he believed, in a state of bondage.

81. **(E)** All of the answers reflect aspects of the Compromise of 1850, and some like answers (C) and (D) were controversial. The Fugitive Slave Law was a cherished victory for the South, however, that was deeply distasteful to abolitionists and others in the North who resolved to "break it at every hazard." A sort of civil disobedience resulted that involved the Underground Railroad's shepherding of escaped slaves to freedom in Canada. When the South accused the North of breaking the law, the North responded by saying an immoral law was void. The Fugitive Slave Law exposed one of the deepest irreconcilable differences that led to the outbreak of war.

82. **(B)** Answers (A), (C), and (E) are based on proposals to aid freemen that were of little practical use to them under the circumstances immediately following emancipation or were simply not desirable to freemen. Answer (D) is close to the proposal of Thaddeus Stevens for "forty acres and a mule" to be given to each African-American family, but the Freedmen's Bureau never had enough land to give or sell to a fraction of the former slaves. Land that had been confiscated from Confederates was slowly given back after pardons and other arrangements. Answer (B) was a stated goal providing a service to freedmen even though the Freedmen's Bureau's staff was challenged in meeting it.

83. **(D)** Although the other answers are plausible ways in which one might get ahead in business, Rockefeller simply followed the path of frugality in answer (D) and gained an advantage everyone else had to try to overcome by borrowing to obtain, say, the latest refining technology. Although his competitors had to then pay interest on their original capital, Rockefeller made profits from the start that he could reinvest in, among other things, the refineries of failed businessmen. Few recognize or remember that those who became vastly wealthy in the nineteenth century in America almost uniformly began as hardworking and extremely frugal young men. Among the Lions of Capitalism or Robber Barons, depending on one's view, only J. P. Morgan can be said to have inherited a fortune as a start in business.

84. **(D)** Answer (E) was true, but not the real reason the Populist Party made itself obsolete. Answer (D) explains their fatal error in being wooed into supporting the Democratic candidate who then lost the election. The other answers are plausible fabrications based on issues surrounding the Populist Party, William Jennings Bryan, and the attitude of many in the nation at the time regarding women's participation in politics.

85. **(A)** Booker T. Washington's founding of the Tuskegee Institute revealed his interest in elevating African Americans economically as his number one priority, whereas W. E. B. Du Bois demanded political equality including the vote, which had been largely taken away from African Americans by the disenfranchising practices of southern states after Reconstruction ended with the Compromise of 1877. Answer (B) is nearly the opposite of the truth, and answer (C) is a fabrication based on the existence of the famous Tuskegee Airmen in World War II. Answer (D) is also nearly the opposite of the views of the two men as is answer (E). Du Bois ultimately became a Marxist and shunned the importance of religion in changing individuals or the world.

86. **(E)** Answer (A) might be the conclusion of conservatives even within Roosevelt's own party, but the cartoonist portrays almost all of the reforms as accomplishments for good that few would argue were unnecessary or undesirable. Answer (B) is not supported by the image of Roosevelt that, though still a caricature, more closely portrays the president's actual appearance than his image in so many political cartoons of this era. The cartoon does depict Roosevelt seated and reading, but there is nothing to imply he wasn't living up to his motto, "Get action. Do things," so answer (C) is incorrect. Answer (D) is wrong because there is almost a one-to-one ratio of domestic and foreign issues addressed, best symbolized by the "War" figure with the broken sword on one side balanced on the other side by the figure representing Roosevelt's quest to preserve collegiate football by urging new rules that would take the "brutality" out of a game that led to the deaths of dozens of players each year. Answer (E) explains how Roosevelt's scholarly bent did not relegate him to inactive status as a Progressive reformer.

87. **(E)** Recent research explains Wilson's hesitancy based on depression associated with the death of his first wife, but the economic reasons expressed in answer (E) still played the most important role among these choices. Of the other choices, only answer (C) is close to the truth in that Wilson so despised Theodore Roosevelt (TR) as to be almost capable of making decisions based on choosing the opposite of whatever TR wanted, but no serious case can be made that he acted so childishly. The other answers are incorrect in that America had no tradition of foreign involvement, women did not yet have the right to vote, and German submarines had already proved to be a threat to American lives in the sinking of ships like the *Lusitania*.

88. **(C)** Answer (C) is a reference to many actions on the part of Franklin D. Roosevelt (FDR) but above all was his masterful use of the radio in his famous fireside chats. His communication skills in this regard proved the truth of his statement, "The only thing we have to fear is fear itself." All of the other answers are the exact opposite of the truth in that FDR never established clear priorities for the New Deal, he never inspired bipartisanship with his domestic agenda, he was not trusted by the members of his class, and although he chose many qualified advisers, they never developed a coherent plan for the New Deal. The power of the New Deal lay in the continual activity of the trial-and-error approach that did inspire Americans that their government was handling the situation largely because FDR told them it was. Their confidence in him was his greatest contribution because it was the key to his success.

89. **(D)** Answer (D) conveys the poignant reality of the contribution of Ida B. Wells. Answer (A) is a reference to Sojourner Truth. Answer (B) is a reference to Marian Anderson. Answer (C) is a reference to the first female African-American millionaire, Madam C.

J. Walker. Answer (E) is a reference to Myrlie Evers-Williams, the widow of assassinated National Association for the Advancement of Colored People leader Medgar Evers.

90. **(B)** The nation quickly dispensed with wage and price controls after World War II, a fact that boosted the national economy. The Fair Deal did not propose wage and price controls, and no president seriously did so again until Richard Nixon in the 1970s while facing a deep recession. The other answers relate the circumstances that contributed to a massive expansion of the American economy as opposed to a slip back to a depression. These factors, coupled with the fact that the United States was largely unscathed by World War II while the Axis countries and even the other Allied nations were severely damaged by the war, created a head start for the United States in recovering from the Great Depression and World War II over nearly every other nation on earth.

Index